Objects First with Java™
A Practical Introduction Using BlueJ

David J. Barnes and Michael Kölling

University of Kent

Sixth Edition

PEARSON

Boston Columbus Indianapolis New York San Francisco Hoboken
Amsterdam Cape Town Dubai London Madrid Milan Munich Paris Montreal Toronto
Delhi Mexico City Sao Paulo Sydney Hong Kong Seoul Singapore Taipei Tokyo

Vice President, Editorial Director, ECS: *Marcia Horton*
Executive Editor: *Tracy Johnson*
Editorial Assistant: *Kristy Alaura*
Vice President of Marketing: *Christy Lesko*
Director of Field Marketing: *Tim Galligan*
Field Marketing Manager: *Demetrius Hall*
Marketing Assistant: *Jon Bryant*
Director of Product Management: *Erin Gregg*
Team Lead, Program and Project Management: *Scott Disanno*
Program Manager: *Carole Snyder*
Project Manager: *Camille Trentacoste*
Senior Specialist, Program Planning and Support: *Maura Zaldivar-Garcia*
Cover Designer: *Marta Samsel*
Cover Art: *brm1949/Fotolia*
Inventory Manager: *Ann Lam*
Media Project Manager: *Leslie Sumrall*
Full-Service Project Management, Composition, and Art: *Chandrasekar Subramanian, SPi Global*
Printer/Bindery: *R.R. Donnelley/Crawfordsville*
Cover printer: *Phoenix Color/Hagerstown*

Copyright © 2017, 2012, 2009, 2006, 2005, 2003 by Pearson Education. All rights reserved. Manufactured in the United States of America. This publication is protected by Copyright, and permission should be obtained from the publisher prior to any prohibited reproduction, storage in a retrieval system, or transmission in any form or by any means, electronic, mechanical, photocopying, recording, or likewise. For information regarding permissions, request forms and the appropriate contacts within the Pearson Education Global Rights & Permissions department, please visit www.pearsoned.com/permissions/.

PEARSON, and ALWAYS LEARNING are exclusive trademarks in the U.S. and/or other countries owned by Pearson Education, Inc. or its affiliates.

Unless otherwise indicated herein, any third-party trademarks that may appear in this work are the property of their respective owners and any references to third-party trademarks, logos or other trade dress are for demonstrative or descriptive purposes only. Such references are not intended to imply any sponsorship, endorsement, authorization, or promotion of Pearson's products by the owners of such marks, or any relationship between the owner and Pearson Education, Inc. or its affiliates, authors, licensees or distributors.

The programs and applications presented in this book have been included for their instructional value. They have been tested with care, but are not guaranteed for any particular purpose. The publisher does not offer any warranties or representations, nor does it accept any liabilities with respect to the programs or applications.

Library of Congress Cataloging-in-Publication Data

Names: Barnes, David J. (David John), 1959 June 7- author. | Kolling,
    Michael, author.
Title: Objects first with Java : a practical introduction using BlueJ / David
    J. Barnes and Michael Kolling, University of Kent.
Description: Sixth edition. | Boston : Pearson Education Inc., [2017]
Identifiers: LCCN 2016009911| ISBN 9780134477367 | ISBN 0134477367
Subjects: LCSH: Object-oriented programming (Computer science) | Java
    (Computer program language) | Computer science—Study and teaching.
Classification: LCC QA76.34 .B385 2017 | DDC 005.1/17—dc23 LC record available at http://lccn.loc.gov/2016009911

1 16

ISBN-10:   0-13-447736-7
ISBN-13: 978-0-13-447736-7

To my wife Helen,

djb

To K.W.

mk

Contents

	Foreword	14
	Preface	15
	List of Projects Discussed in Detail in This Book	25
	Acknowledgments	28

Part 1 Foundations of Object Orientation — 29

Chapter 1 Objects and Classes — 31

1.1	Objects and classes	31
1.2	Creating objects	32
1.3	Calling methods	33
1.4	Parameters	34
1.5	Data types	35
1.6	Multiple instances	36
1.7	State	37
1.8	What is in an object?	38
1.9	Java code	39
1.10	Object interaction	40
1.11	Source code	41
1.12	Another example	43
1.13	Return values	43
1.14	Objects as parameters	44
1.15	Summary	45

Chapter 2 Understanding Class Definitions — 49

2.1	Ticket machines	49
2.2	Examining a class definition	51
2.3	The class header	53
2.4	Fields, constructors, and methods	54
2.5	Parameters: receiving data	60
2.6	Assignment	62

	2.7	Methods	63
	2.8	Accessor and mutator methods	64
	2.9	Printing from methods	67
	2.10	Method summary	70
	2.11	Summary of the naïve ticket machine	70
	2.12	Reflecting on the design of the ticket machine	71
	2.13	Making choices: the conditional statement	73
	2.14	A further conditional-statement example	75
	2.15	Scope highlighting	76
	2.16	Local variables	77
	2.17	Fields, parameters, and local variables	79
	2.18	Summary of the better ticket machine	81
	2.19	Self-review exercises	81
	2.20	Reviewing a familiar example	83
	2.21	Calling methods	85
	2.22	Experimenting with expressions: the Code Pad	87
	2.23	Summary	89

Chapter 3 Object Interaction — 95

	3.1	The clock example	95
	3.2	Abstraction and modularization	96
	3.3	Abstraction in software	97
	3.4	Modularization in the clock example	97
	3.5	Implementing the clock display	98
	3.6	Class diagrams versus object diagrams	99
	3.7	Primitive types and object types	100
	3.8	The `NumberDisplay` class	100
	3.9	The `ClockDisplay` class	108
	3.10	Objects creating objects	111
	3.11	Multiple constructors	112
	3.12	Method calls	112
	3.13	Another example of object interaction	116
	3.14	Using a debugger	120
	3.15	Method calling revisited	124
	3.16	Summary	125

Chapter 4 Grouping Objects — 129

	4.1	Building on themes from Chapter 3	129
	4.2	The collection abstraction	130

4.3	An organizer for music files	131
4.4	Using a library class	132
4.5	Object structures with collections	135
4.6	Generic classes	137
4.7	Numbering within collections	138
4.8	Playing the music files	141
4.9	Processing a whole collection	143
4.10	Indefinite iteration	148
4.11	Improving structure—the `Track` class	156
4.12	The Iterator type	159
4.13	Summary of the music-organizer project	163
4.14	Another example: an auction system	165
4.15	Summary	175

Chapter 5 Functional Processing of Collections (Advanced) 177

5.1	An alternative look at themes from Chapter 4	177
5.2	Monitoring animal populations	178
5.3	A first look at lambdas	182
5.4	The `forEach` method of collections	184
5.5	Streams	186
5.6	Summary	196

Chapter 6 More-Sophisticated Behavior 199

6.1	Documentation for library classes	200
6.2	The *TechSupport* system	201
6.3	Reading class documentation	206
6.4	Adding random behavior	211
6.5	Packages and import	217
6.6	Using maps for associations	218
6.7	Using sets	223
6.8	Dividing strings	223
6.9	Finishing the *TechSupport* system	225
6.10	Autoboxing and wrapper classes	227
6.11	Writing class documentation	229
6.12	Public versus private	232
6.13	Learning about classes from their interfaces	234
6.14	Class variables and constants	239
6.15	Class methods	242
6.16	Executing without BlueJ	244

	6.17	Further advanced material	244
	6.18	Summary	248

Chapter 7 Fixed-Size Collections—Arrays 251

	7.1	Fixed-size collections	251
	7.2	Arrays	252
	7.3	A log-file analyzer	252
	7.4	The for loop	258
	7.5	The *automaton* project	264
	7.6	Arrays of more than one dimension (advanced)	272
	7.7	Arrays and streams (advanced)	279
	7.8	Summary	280

Chapter 8 Designing Classes 283

	8.1	Introduction	284
	8.2	The *world-of-zuul* game example	285
	8.3	Introduction to coupling and cohesion	287
	8.4	Code duplication	288
	8.5	Making extensions	291
	8.6	Coupling	294
	8.7	Responsibility-driven design	298
	8.8	Localizing change	301
	8.9	Implicit coupling	302
	8.10	Thinking ahead	305
	8.11	Cohesion	306
	8.12	Refactoring	310
	8.13	Refactoring for language independence	314
	8.14	Design guidelines	319
	8.15	Summary	320

Chapter 9 Well-Behaved Objects 323

	9.1	Introduction	323
	9.2	Testing and debugging	324
	9.3	Unit testing within BlueJ	325
	9.4	Test automation	332
	9.5	Refactoring to use streams (advanced)	339
	9.6	Debugging	340
	9.7	Commenting and style	342
	9.8	Manual walkthroughs	343

	9.9	Print statements	348
	9.10	Debuggers	352
	9.11	Debugging streams (advanced)	353
	9.12	Choosing a debugging strategy	354
	9.13	Putting the techniques into practice	355
	9.14	Summary	355

Part 2   Application Structures   357

Chapter 10   Improving Structure with Inheritance   359

	10.1	The *network* example	359
	10.2	Using inheritance	371
	10.3	Inheritance hierarchies	373
	10.4	Inheritance in Java	374
	10.5	*Network*: adding other post types	377
	10.6	Advantages of inheritance (so far)	379
	10.7	Subtyping	380
	10.8	The `Object` class	386
	10.9	The collection hierarchy	387
	10.10	Summary	388

Chapter 11   More about Inheritance   391

	11.1	The problem: *network's* display method	391
	11.2	Static type and dynamic type	393
	11.3	Overriding	396
	11.4	Dynamic method lookup	398
	11.5	`super` call in methods	401
	11.6	Method polymorphism	402
	11.7	Object methods: `toString`	402
	11.8	Object equality: `equals` and `hashCode`	405
	11.9	Protected access	407
	11.10	The `instanceof` operator	409
	11.11	Another example of inheritance with overriding	410
	11.12	Summary	413

Chapter 12   Further Abstraction Techniques   417

	12.1	Simulations	417
	12.2	The foxes-and-rabbits simulation	418
	12.3	Abstract classes	433

	12.4	More abstract methods	440
	12.5	Multiple inheritance	442
	12.6	Interfaces	445
	12.7	A further example of interfaces	453
	12.8	The `Class` class	455
	12.9	Abstract class or interface?	455
	12.10	Event-driven simulations	456
	12.11	Summary of inheritance	457
	12.12	Summary	458

Chapter 13 Building Graphical User Interfaces — 461

	13.1	Introduction	461
	13.2	Components, layout, and event handling	462
	13.3	AWT and Swing	463
	13.4	The ImageViewer example	463
	13.5	ImageViewer 1.0: the first complete version	475
	13.6	ImageViewer 2.0: improving program structure	489
	13.7	ImageViewer 3.0: more interface components	495
	13.8	Inner classes	499
	13.9	Further extensions	504
	13.10	Another example: MusicPlayer	506
	13.11	Summary	509

Chapter 14 Handling Errors — 511

	14.1	The *address-book* project	512
	14.2	Defensive programming	516
	14.3	Server error reporting	519
	14.4	Exception-throwing principles	523
	14.5	Exception handling	529
	14.6	Defining new exception classes	536
	14.7	Using assertions	538
	14.8	Error recovery and avoidance	541
	14.9	File-based input/output	544
	14.10	Summary	555

Chapter 15 Designing Applications — 557

	15.1	Analysis and design	557
	15.2	Class design	564
	15.3	Documentation	566

	15.4	Cooperation	567
	15.5	Prototyping	567
	15.6	Software growth	568
	15.7	Using design patterns	570
	15.8	Summary	576

Chapter 16 A Case Study 579

	16.1	The case study	579
	16.2	Analysis and design	580
	16.3	Class design	584
	16.4	Iterative development	589
	16.5	Another example	598
	16.6	Taking things further	598

Appendix A: Working with a BlueJ Project 599

	A.1	Installing BlueJ	599
	A.2	Opening a project	599
	A.3	The BlueJ debugger	599
	A.4	Configuring BlueJ	599
	A.5	Changing the interface language	600
	A.6	Using local API documentation	600
	A.7	Changing the new class templates	600

Appendix B: Java Data Types 601

	B.1	Primitive types	601
	B.2	Casting of primitive types	602
	B.3	Object types	602
	B.4	Wrapper classes	603
	B.5	Casting of object types	603

Appendix C: Operators 605

	C.1	Arithmetic expressions	605
	C.2	Boolean expressions	606
	C.3	Short-circuit operators	607

Appendix D: Java Control Structures 609

| | D.1 | Control structures | 609 |
| | D.2 | Selection statements | 609 |

D.3	Loops	611
D.4	Exceptions	613
D.5	Assertions	615

Appendix E: Running Java without BlueJ — 617

E.1	Executing without BlueJ	617
E.2	Creating executable .jar files	619
E.3	Developing without BlueJ	619

Appendix F: Using the Debugger — 621

F.1	Breakpoints	622
F.2	The control buttons	622
F.3	The variable displays	623
F.4	The Call Sequence display	624
F.5	The Threads display	624

Appendix G: JUnit Unit-Testing Tools — 625

G.1	Enabling unit-testing functionality	625
G.2	Creating a test class	625
G.3	Creating a test method	625
G.4	Test assertions	626
G.5	Running tests	626
G.6	Fixtures	626

Appendix H: Teamwork Tools — 627

H.1	Server setup	627
H.2	Enabling teamwork functionality	627
H.3	Sharing a project	627
H.4	Using a shared project	627
H.5	Update and commit	628
H.6	More information	628

Appendix I: Javadoc — 629

I.1	Documentation comments	629
I.2	BlueJ support for javadoc	631

Appendix J: Program Style Guide — 633

J.1	Naming	633
J.2	Layout	633

	J.3	Documentation	634
	J.4	Language-use restrictions	635
	J.5	Code idioms	636

Appendix K: Important Library Classes — 637

	K.1	The `java.lang` package	637
	K.2	The `java.util` package	638
	K.3	The `java.io` and `java.nio.file` packages	639
	K.4	The `java.util.function` package	640
	K.5	The `java.net` package	640
	K.6	Other important packages	641

Appendix L: Concept Glossary — 643

Index — 649

Foreword

by James Gosling, creator of Java

Watching my daughter Kate and her middle-school classmates struggle through a Java course using a commercial IDE was a painful experience. The sophistication of the tool added significant complexity to the task of learning. I wish that I had understood earlier what was happening. As it was, I wasn't able to talk to the instructor about the problem until it was too late. This is exactly the sort of situation for which BlueJ is a perfect fit.

BlueJ is an interactive development environment with a mission: it is designed to be used by students who are learning how to program. It was designed by instructors who have been in the classroom facing this problem every day. It's been refreshing to talk to the folks who developed BlueJ: they have a very clear idea of what their target is. Discussions tended to focus more on what to leave out, than what to throw in. BlueJ is very clean and very targeting.

Nonetheless, this book isn't about BlueJ. It is about programming.

In Java.

Over the past several years Java has become widely used in the teaching of programming. This is for a number of reasons. One is that Java has many characteristics that make it easy to teach: it has a relatively clean definition; extensive static analysis by the compiler informs students of problems early on; and it has a very robust memory model that eliminates most "mysterious" errors that arise when object boundaries or the type system are compromised. Another is that Java has become commercially very important.

This book confronts head-on the hardest concept to teach: objects. It takes students from their very first steps all the way through to some very sophisticated concepts.

It manages to solve one of the stickiest questions in writing a book about programming: how to deal with the mechanics of actually typing in and running a program. Most books silently skip over the issue, or touch it lightly, leaving the instructor with the burden of figuring out how to relate the book's material to the actual steps that students have to go through to solve the exercises. Instead, this book assumes the use of BlueJ and is able to integrate the tasks of understanding the concepts with the mechanics of how students can explore them.

I wish it had been around for my daughter last year. Maybe next year . . .

Preface

New to the sixth edition

This is the sixth edition of this book, and—as always with a new edition—the content has been adapted to the latest developments in object-oriented programs.

Many of the changes this time can, on the surface, be attributed to a new version of Java: Java 8. This version was released in 2014 and is now very widely used in practice. In fact, it is the fastest adoption of any new Java version ever released; so it is time also to change the way we teach novice students.

The changes are, however, more than merely the addition of a few new language constructs. The most significant new aspects in Java 8 center around new constructs to support a (partial) functional programming style. And it is the growing popularity of functional programming that is driving this change. The difference is much deeper, and much more fundamental, than just adding new syntax. And it is the renaissance of the functional ideas in modern programming generally—not only the existence of Java 8—that makes it timely to cover these aspects in a modern edition of a programming textbook.

The ideas and techniques of functional programming, while fairly old and well known in principle, have seen a marked boost of popularity in recent years, with new languages being developed and selected functional techniques being incorporated into existing, traditionally imperative languages. One of the primary reasons for this is the change in computing hardware available, and also the changing nature of problems we wish to tackle.

Almost all programming platforms now are concurrent. Even mid-range laptops and mobile phones now have processors with multiple cores, making parallel processing a real possibility on everyday devices. But, in practice this is not happening on a large scale.

Writing applications that make optimal use of concurrent processing and multiple processors is very, very difficult. Most applications available today do not exploit current hardware to a degree approaching anything that is theoretically possible.

This is not going to change much: the opportunity (and challenge) of parallel hardware will remain, and programming these devices with traditional imperative languages will not get any easier.

This is where functional programming enters the picture.

With functional language constructs, it is possible to automate some concurrency very efficiently. Programs can potentially make use of multiple cores without much effort on the side of the programmer. Functional constructs have other advantages—more elegant expression for certain problems and often clearer readability—but it is the ability to deal with parallelism that will ensure that functional aspects of programming are going to stay with us for a long time to come.

Every teacher who wants to prepare their students for the future should give them some understanding of functional aspects as well. Without it, one will no longer be able to become a master programmer. A novice certainly does not have to master all of functional programming, but a basic understanding of what it is—and what we can achieve with it—is rapidly becoming essential.

Exactly when functional techniques should be introduced is an interesting question. We do not believe that there is a single right answer for this; various sequences are possible. Functional programming could be covered as an advanced topic at the end of the traditional corpus of this book, or it could be addressed when we first encounter the topics where it is applicable, as an alternative to the imperative techniques. It could even be covered first.

An additional question is how to treat the traditional style of programming in those areas where functional constructs are now available: should they be replaced, or do both need to be covered?

For this book, we recognize that different teachers will have different constraints and preferences. Therefore, we have designed a structure that—we hope—allows different approaches, depending on the preference of the learner or teacher.

- We have not replaced the "old-style" techniques. We cover the new, functional approach in addition to the existing material. Functional constructs in Java are most prominent when working with collections of objects, and the mastering traditional approach—using loops and explicit iteration—is still essential for any programmer. Not only are there millions of lines of code out there that are written in this style—and will be continued to be written in this style—but there are also specific cases where it is necessary to use these techniques even if one generally favors the new functional constructs. Mastering both is the goal.

- We present the new functional-construct-oriented material in the book where we discuss the problems that these constructs address. For example, we address functional collection processing as soon as we encounter collections.

- Chapters and sections covering this new material are, however, clearly marked as "advanced," and are structured in a manner that they can safely be skipped on first reading (or left out altogether).

- The previous two points enable different approaches to studying this book: if time permits, it can be read in the sequence it is presented, covering the full scope of material—including functional approaches as alternatives to imperative ones—as the problems are encountered which they address. If time is short, these advanced sections can be skipped, and emphasis can be placed on a thorough grounding in imperative, object-oriented programming. (We should emphasize that *functional* is not a contradiction to *object-oriented*: whether the functional material is included in the study, or the course emphasis is largely on imperative techniques, every reader of this book will emerge with a good understanding of object orientation!) Yet another way to approach the material is to skip the advanced sections initially, and cover them as a separate unit at a later time. They present alternative approaches to other constructs and can be covered independently.

We hope this makes clear that this book provides flexibility where readers want it, but also guidance where a reader has no clear preference: just read it in the sequence it is written.

Apart from the major changes described so far, this edition also presents numerous minor improvements. The overall structure, tone, and approach of the book is unchanged; it has worked very well in the past, and there is no reason to deviate from it. However, we continuously re-evaluate and seek to improve where we see opportunities. We now have almost 15 years of continuous experience teaching with this book, and this is reflected in the many minor improvements throughout.

This book is an introduction to object-oriented programming for beginners. The main focus of the book is general object-oriented and programming concepts from a software engineering perspective.

While the first chapters are written for students with no programming experience, later chapters are suitable for more advanced or professional programmers as well. In particular, programmers with experience in a non-object-oriented language who wish to migrate their skills into object orientation should also be able to benefit from the book.

We use two tools throughout the book to enable the concepts introduced to be put into practice: the Java programming language and the Java development environment BlueJ.

Java

Java was chosen because of both its language design and its popularity. The Java programming language itself provides a clean implementation of most of the important object-oriented concepts, and serves well as an introductory teaching language. Its popularity ensures an immense pool of support resources.

In any subject area, having a variety of sources of information available is very helpful, for teachers and students alike. For Java in particular, countless books, tutorials, exercises, compilers, environments, and quizzes already exist, in many different kinds and styles. Many of them are online and many are available free of charge. The huge amount of high quality support material makes Java an excellent choice as an introduction to object-oriented programming.

With so much Java material already available, is there still room for more to be said about it? We think there is, and the second tool we use is one of the reasons . . .

BlueJ

BlueJ deserves much comment. This book is unique in its completely integrated use of the BlueJ environment.

BlueJ is a Java development environment that is being developed and maintained by the Computing Education Research Group at the University of Kent in Canterbury, UK, explicitly as an environment for teaching introductory object-oriented programming. It is better suited to introductory teaching than other environments for a variety of reasons:

- The user interface is much simpler. Beginning students can typically use the BlueJ environment in a competent manner after 20 minutes of introduction. From then on, instruction can concentrate on the important concepts at hand—object orientation and Java—and no time needs to be wasted talking about environments, file systems, class paths, or DLL conflicts.

- The environment supports important teaching tools not available in other environments. One of them is visualization of class structure. BlueJ automatically displays a UML-like diagram representing the classes and relationships in a project. Visualizing these important concepts is a great help to both teachers and students. It is hard to grasp the concept of an object when all you ever see on the screen is lines of code! The diagram notation is a simple subset of UML, tailored to the needs of beginning students. This makes it easy to understand, but also allows migration to full UML in later courses.

- One of the most important strengths of the BlueJ environment is the user's ability to directly create objects of any class, and then to interact with their methods. This creates the opportunity for direct experimentation with objects, with little overhead in the environment. Students can almost "feel" what it means to create an object, call a method, pass a parameter, or receive a return value. They can try out a method immediately after it has been written, without the need to write test drivers. This facility is an invaluable aid in understanding the underlying concepts and language details.

- BlueJ includes numerous other tools and characteristics that are specifically designed for students of software development. Some are aimed at helping with understanding fundamental concepts (such as the scope highlighting in the editor), some are designed to introduce additional tools and techniques, such as integrated testing using JUnit, or teamwork using a version control system, such as Subversion, once the students are ready. Several of these features are unique to the BlueJ environment.

BlueJ is a full Java environment. It is not a cut-down, simplified version of Java for teaching. It runs on top of Oracle's Java Development Kit, and makes use of the standard compiler and virtual machine. This ensures that it always conforms to the official and most up-to-date Java specification.

The authors of this book have many years of teaching experience with the BlueJ environment (and many more years without it before that). We both have experienced how the use of BlueJ has increased the involvement, understanding, and activity of students in our courses. One of the authors is also the development lead of the BlueJ system.

Real objects first

One of the reasons for choosing BlueJ was that it allows an approach where teachers truly deal with the important concepts first. "Objects first" has been a battle cry for many textbook authors and teachers for some time. Unfortunately, the Java language does not make this noble goal very easy. Numerous hurdles of syntax and detail have to be overcome before the first experience with a living object arises. The minimal Java program to create and call an object typically includes

- writing a class;
- writing a main method, including concepts such as static methods, parameters, and arrays in the signature;
- a statement to create the object ("new");
- an assignment to a variable;
- the variable declaration, including variable type;
- a method call, using dot notation;
- possibly a parameter list.

As a result, most textbooks typically either

- have to work their way through this forbidding list, and only reach objects somewhere around the fourth chapter; or
- use a "Hello, world"-style program with a single static main method as the first example, thus not creating any objects at all.

With BlueJ, this is not a problem. A student can create an object and call its methods as the very first activity! Because users can create and interact with objects directly, concepts such as classes, objects, methods, and parameters can easily be discussed in a concrete manner before looking at the first line of Java syntax. Instead of explaining more about this here, we suggest that the curious reader dip into Chapter 1—things will quickly become clear then.

An iterative approach

Another important aspect of this book is that it follows an iterative style. In the computing education community, a well-known educational design pattern exists that states that important concepts should be taught early and often.[1] It is very tempting for textbook authors to try and say everything about a topic at the point where it is introduced. For example, it is common, when introducing types, to give a full list of built-in data types, or to discuss all available kinds of loop when introducing the concept of a loop.

These two approaches conflict: we cannot concentrate on discussing important concepts first, and at the same time provide complete coverage of all topics encountered. Our experience with textbooks is that much of the detail is initially distracting, and has the effect of drowning the important points, thus making them harder to grasp.

---

[1] The "Early Bird" pattern, in J. Bergin: "Fourteen Pedagogical Patterns for Teaching Computer Science," *Proceedings of the Fifth European Conference on Pattern Languages of Programs* (EuroPLop 2000), Irsee, Germany, July 2000.

In this book we touch on all of the important topics several times, both within the same chapter and across different chapters. Concepts are usually introduced at a level of detail necessary for understanding and applying to the task at hand. They are revisited later in a different context, and understanding deepens as the reader continues through the chapters. This approach also helps to deal with the frequent occurrence of mutual dependencies between concepts.

Some teachers may not be familiar with the iterative approach. Looking at the first few chapters, teachers used to a more sequential introduction will be surprised about the number of concepts touched on this early. It may seem like a steep learning curve.

It is important to understand that this is not the end of the story. Students are not expected to understand everything about these concepts immediately. Instead, these fundamental concepts will be revisited again and again throughout the book, allowing students to get a deeper understanding over time. Since their knowledge level changes as they work their way forward, revisiting important topics later allows them to gain a deeper understanding overall.

We have tried this approach with students many times. Sometimes students have fewer problems dealing with it than some long-time teachers. And remember: a steep learning curve is not a problem as long as you ensure that your students can climb it!

No complete language coverage

Related to our iterative approach is the decision not to try to provide complete coverage of the Java language within the book.

The main focus of this book is to convey object-oriented programming principles in general, not Java language details in particular. Students studying with this book may be working as software professionals for the next 30 or 40 years of their life—it is a fairly safe bet that the majority of their work will not be in Java. Every serious textbook must attempt to prepare them for something more fundamental than the language flavor of the day.

On the other hand, many Java details are essential to actually doing practical programming work. In this book we cover Java constructs in as much detail as is necessary to illustrate the concepts at hand and implement the practical work. Some constructs specific to Java have been deliberately left out of the discussion.

We are aware that some instructors will choose to cover some topics that we do not discuss in detail. However, instead of trying to cover every possible topic ourselves (and thus blowing the size of this book out to 1500 pages), we deal with it using *hooks*. Hooks are pointers, often in the form of questions that raise the topic and give references to an appendix or outside material. These hooks ensure that a relevant topic is brought up at an appropriate time, and leave it up to the reader or the teacher to decide to what level of detail that topic should be covered. Thus, hooks serve as a reminder of the existence of the topic, and as a placeholder indicating a point in the sequence where discussion can be inserted.

Individual teachers can decide to use the book as it is, following our suggested sequence, or to branch out into sidetracks suggested by the hooks in the text.

Chapters also often include several questions suggesting discussion material related to the topic, but not discussed in this book. We fully expect teachers to discuss some of these questions in class, or students to research the answers as homework exercises.

Project-driven approach

The introduction of material in the book is project driven. The book discusses numerous programming projects and provides many exercises. Instead of introducing a new construct and then providing an exercise to apply this construct to solve a task, we first provide a goal and a problem. Analyzing the problem at hand determines what kinds of solutions we need. As a consequence, language constructs are introduced as they are needed to solve the problems before us.

Early chapters provide at least two discussion examples. These are projects that are discussed in detail to illustrate the important concepts of each chapter. Using two very different examples supports the iterative approach: each concept is revisited in a different context after it is introduced.

In designing this book we have tried to use a lot of different example projects. This will hopefully serve to capture the reader's interest, and also illustrate the variety of different contexts in which the concepts can be applied. We hope that our projects serve to give teachers good starting points and many ideas for a wide variety of interesting assignments.

The implementation for all our projects is written very carefully, so that many peripheral issues may be studied by reading the projects' source code. We are strong believers in learning by reading and imitating good examples. For this to work, however, it's important that the examples are well written and worth imitating. We have tried to create great examples.

All projects are designed as open-ended problems. While one or more versions of each problem are discussed in detail in the book, the projects are designed so that further extensions and improvements can be done as student projects. Complete source code for all projects is included. A list of projects discussed in this book is provided on page xxv.

Concept sequence rather than language constructs

One other aspect that distinguishes this book from many others is that it is structured along fundamental software development tasks, not necessarily according to the particular Java language constructs. One indicator of this is the chapter headings. In this book you will not find traditional chapter titles such as "Primitive data types" or "Control structures." Structuring by fundamental development tasks allows us to present a more general introduction that is not driven by intricacies of the particular programming language utilized. We also believe that it is easier for students to follow the motivation of the introduction, and that it makes much more interesting reading.

As a result of this approach, it is less straightforward to use the book as a reference book. Introductory textbooks and reference books have different, partly competing, goals. To a certain extent a book can try to be both, but compromises have to be made at certain points. Our book is clearly designed as a textbook, and wherever a conflict occurred, the textbook style took precedence over its use as a reference book.

We have, however, provided support for use as a reference book by listing the Java constructs introduced in each chapter in the chapter introduction.

Chapter sequence

Chapter 1 deals with the most fundamental concepts of object orientation: objects, classes, and methods. It gives a solid, hands-on introduction to these concepts without going into the details of Java syntax. We briefly introduce the concept of abstraction. This will be a thread that runs through many chapters. Chapter 1 also gives a first look at some source code. We do this by using an example of graphical shapes that can be interactively drawn, and a second example of a simple laboratory class enrollment system.

Chapter 2 opens up class definitions and investigates how Java source code is written to create behavior of objects. We discuss how to define fields and implement methods, and point out the crucial role of the constructor in setting up an object's state as embodied in its fields. Here, we also introduce the first types of statement. The main example is an implementation of a ticket machine. We also investigate the laboratory class example from Chapter 1 a bit further.

Chapter 3 then enlarges the picture to discuss interaction of multiple objects. We see how objects can collaborate by invoking each other's methods to perform a common task. We also discuss how one object can create other objects. A digital alarm clock display is discussed that uses two number display objects to show hours and minutes. A version of the project that includes a GUI picks up on a running theme of the book—that we often provide additional code for the interested and able student to explore, without covering it in detail in the text. As a second major example, we examine a simulation of an email system in which messages can be sent between mail clients.

In Chapter 4 we continue by building more extensive structures of objects and pick up again on the themes of abstraction and object interaction from the preceding chapters. Most importantly, we start using collections of objects. We implement an organizer for music files and an auction system to introduce collections. At the same time, we discuss iteration over collections, and have a first look at the *for-each* and *while* loops. The first collection being used is an `ArrayList`.

Chapter 5 presents the first advanced section (a section that can be skipped if time is short): It is an introduction to functional programming constructs. The functional constructs present an alternative to the imperative collection processing discussed in Chapter 4. The same problems can be solved without these techniques, but functional constructs open some more elegant ways to achieve our goals. This chapter gives an introduction to the functional approach in general, and introduces a few of Java's language constructs.

Chapter 6 deals with libraries and interfaces. We introduce the Java library and discuss some important library classes. More importantly, we explain how to read and understand the library documentation. The importance of writing documentation in software development projects is discussed, and we end by practicing how to write suitable documentation for our own classes. `Random`, `Set`, and `Map` are examples of classes that we encounter in this chapter. We implement an *Eliza*-like dialog system and a graphical simulation of a bouncing ball to apply these classes.

Chapter 7 concentrates on one specific—but very special—type of collection: arrays. Arrays processing and the associated types of loops are discussed in detail.

In Chapter 8 we discuss more formally the issues of dividing a problem domain into classes for implementation. We introduce issues of good class design, including concepts such as responsibility-driven design, coupling, cohesion, and refactoring. An interactive, text-based adventure game (*World of Zuul*) is used for this discussion. We go through several iterations of improving the internal class structure of the game and extending its functionality, and end with a long list of proposals for extensions that may be done as student projects.

Chapter 9 deals with a whole group of issues connected to producing correct, understandable, and maintainable classes. It covers issues ranging from writing clear code (including style and commenting) to testing and debugging. Test strategies are introduced, including formalized regression testing using JUnit, and a number of debugging methods are discussed in detail. We use an example of an online shop and an implementation of an electronic calculator to discuss these topics.

Chapters 10 and 11 introduce inheritance and polymorphism, with many of the related detailed issues. We discuss a part of a social network to illustrate the concepts. Issues of code inheritance, subtyping, polymorphic method calls, and overriding are discussed in detail.

In Chapter 12 we implement a predator/prey simulation. This serves to discuss additional abstraction mechanisms based on inheritance, namely interfaces and abstract classes.

Chapter 13 develops an image viewer and a graphical user interface for the music organizer (first encountered in Chapter 4). Both examples serve to discuss how to build graphical user interfaces (GUIs).

Chapter 14 then picks up the difficult issue of how to deal with errors. Several possible problems and solutions are discussed, and Java's exception-handling mechanism is discussed in detail. We extend and improve an address book application to illustrate the concepts. Input/output is used as a case study where error-handling is an essential requirement.

Chapter 15 discusses in more detail the next level of abstraction: How to structure a vaguely described problem into classes and methods. In previous chapters we have assumed that large parts of the application structure already exist, and we have made improvements. Now it is time to discuss how we can get started from a clean slate. This involves detailed discussion of what the classes should be that implement our application, how they interact, and how responsibilities should be distributed. We use Class/Responsibilities/Collaborators (CRC) cards to approach this problem, while designing a cinema booking system.

In Chapter 16 we to bring everything together and integrate topics from the previous chapters of the book. It is a complete case study, starting with the application design, through design of the class interfaces, down to discussing many important functional and non-functional characteristics and implementation details. Concepts discussed in earlier chapters (such as reliability, data structures, class design, testing, and extendibility) are applied again in a new context.

Supplements

VideoNotes: VideoNotes are Pearson's visual tool designed to teach students key programming concepts and techniques. These short step-by-step videos demonstrate how to solve problems from design through coding. VideoNotes allow for self-paced instruction with easy navigation including the ability to select, play, rewind, fast-forward, and stop within each VideoNote exercise.

VideoNotes are located at www.pearsonhighered.com/cs-resources. Twelve months of prepaid access are included with the purchase of a new textbook. If the access code has already been revealed, it may no longer be valid. If this is the case, you can purchase a subscription by going to www.pearsonhighered.com/cs-resources and following the on-screen instructions.

Book website: All projects used as discussion examples and exercises in this book are available for download on the book's website, at http://www.bluej.org/objects-first/. The website also provides links to download BlueJ, and other resources.

Premium Website for students: The following resources are available to all readers of this book at its Premium Website, located at www.pearsonhighered.com/cs-resources:

- Program style guide for all examples in the book
- Links to further material of interest
- Complete source code for all projects

Instructor resources: The following supplements are available to qualified instructors only:

- Solutions to end-of-chapter exercises
- PowerPoint slides

Visit the Pearson Instructor Resource Center at www.pearsonhighered.com/irc to register for access or contact your local Pearson representative.

The Blueroom

Perhaps more important than the static web site resources is a very active community forum that exists for instructors who teach with BlueJ and this book. It is called the *Blueroom* and can be found at

    http://blueroom.bluej.org

The Blueroom contains a resource collection with many teaching resources shared by other teachers, as well as a discussion forum where instructors can ask questions, discuss issues, and stay up-to-date with the latest developments. Many other teachers, as well as developers of BlueJ and the authors of this book, can be contacted in the Blueroom.

List of Projects Discussed in Detail in This Book

Figures (Chapter 1)
Simple drawing with some geometrical shapes; illustrates creation of objects, method calling, and parameters.

House (Chapter 1)
An example using shape objects to draw a picture; introduces source code, Java syntax, and compilation.

Lab-classes (Chapter 1, 2, 10)
A simple example with classes of students; illustrates objects, fields, and methods. Used again in Chapter 10 to add inheritance.

Ticket-machine (Chapter 2)
A simulation of a ticket vending machine for train tickets; introduces more about fields, constructors, accessor and mutator methods, parameters, and some simple statements.

Book-exercise (Chapter 2)
Storing details of a book. Reinforcing the constructs used in the ticket-machine example.

Clock-display (Chapter 3)
An implementation of a display for a digital clock; illustrates the concepts of abstraction, modularization, and object interaction. Includes a version with an animated GUI.

Mail system (Chapter 3)
A simple simulation of an email system. Used to demonstrate object creation and interaction.

Music-organizer (Chapter 4, 11)
An implementation of an organizer for music tracks; used to introduce collections and loops. Includes the ability to play MP3 files. A GUI is added in Chapter 11.

Auction (Chapter 4)
An auction system. More about collections and loops, this time with iterators.

List of Projects Discussed in Detail in This Book

Animal-monitoring (Chapter 5, 6)
A system to monitor animal populations, e.g., in a national park. This is used to introduce functional processing of collections.

Tech-support (Chapter 6, 14)
An implementation of an *Eliza*-like dialog program used to provide "technical support" to customers; introduces use of library classes in general and some specific classes in particular; reading and writing of documentation.

Scribble (Chapter 6)
A shape-drawing program to support learning about classes from their interfaces.

Bouncing-balls (Chapter 6)
A graphical animation of bouncing balls; demonstrates interface/implementation separation and simple graphics.

Weblog-analyzer (Chapter 7, 14)
A program to analyze web access log files; introduces arrays and for loops.

Automaton (Chapter 7)
A series of examples of a cellular automaton. Used to gain practice with array programming.

Brain (Chapter 7)
A version of *Brian's Brain*, which we use to discuss two-dimensional arrays.

World-of-zuul (Chapter 8, 11, 14)
A text-based, interactive adventure game. Highly extendable, makes a great open-ended student project. Used here to discuss good class design, coupling, and cohesion. Used again in Chapter 11 as an example for use of inheritance.

Online-shop (Chapter 9)
The early stages of an implementation of a part of an online shopping website, dealing with user comments; used to discuss testing and debugging strategies.

Calculator (Chapter 9)
An implementation of a desk calculator. This example reinforces concepts introduced earlier, and is used to discuss testing and debugging.

Bricks (Chapter 9)
A simple debugging exercise; models filling pallets with bricks for simple computations.

Network (Chapter 10, 11)
Part of a social network application. This project is discussed and then extended in great detail to introduce the foundations of inheritance and polymorphism.

Foxes-and-rabbits (Chapter 12)

A classic predator–prey simulation; reinforces inheritance concepts and adds abstract classes and interfaces.

Image-viewer (Chapter 13)

A simple image-viewing and -manipulation application. We concentrate mainly on building the GUI.

Music-player (Chapter 13)

A GUI is added to the *music-organizer* project of Chapter 4 as another example of building GUIs.

Address-book (Chapter 14)

An implementation of an address book with an optional GUI interface. Lookup is flexible: entries can be searched by partial definition of name or phone number. This project makes extensive use of exceptions.

Cinema-booking-system (Chapter 15)

A system to manage advance seat bookings in a cinema. This example is used in a discussion of class discovery and application design. No code is provided, as the example represents the development of an application from a blank sheet of paper.

Taxi-company (Chapter 16)

The taxi example is a combination of a booking system, management system, and simulation. It is used as a case study to bring together many of the concepts and techniques discussed throughout the book.

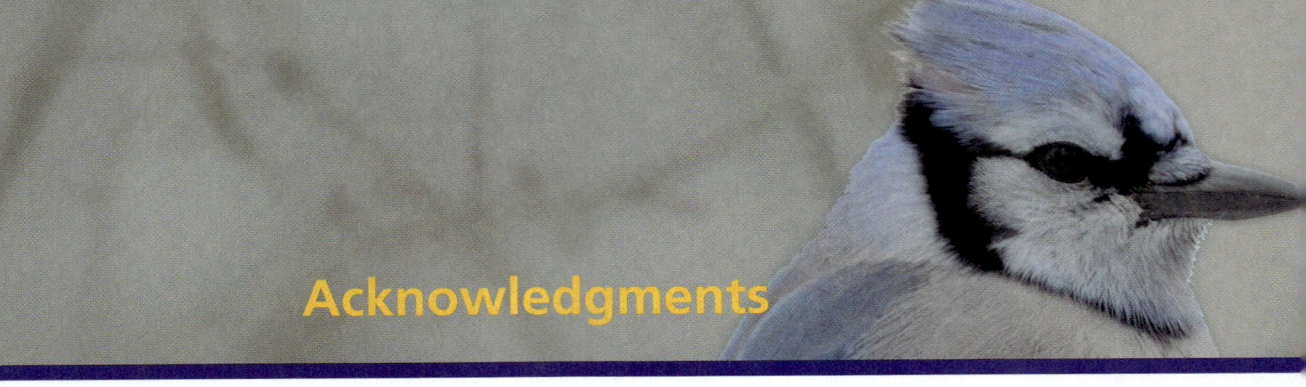

Acknowledgments

Many people have contributed in many different ways to this book and made its creation possible.

First, and most importantly, John Rosenberg must be mentioned. It is only by coincidence of circumstance that John is not one of the authors of this book. He was one of the driving forces in the development of BlueJ and the ideas and pedagogy behind it from the very beginning, and we talked about the writing of this book for several years. Much of the material in this book was developed in discussions with John. Simply the fact that there are only twenty-four hours in a day, too many of which were already taken up with too much other work, prevented him from actually writing this book. John contributed significantly to the original version of this text and helped improve it in many ways. We have appreciated his friendship and collaboration immensely.

Several other people have helped make BlueJ what it is: Bruce Quig, Davin McCall, and Andrew Patterson in Australia, and Ian Utting, Poul Henriksen, and Neil Brown in England. All have worked on BlueJ for many years, improving and extending the design and implementation in addition to their other work commitments. Without their work, BlueJ would never have reached the quality and popularity it has today, and this book might never have been written.

Another important contribution that made the creation of BlueJ and this book possible was very generous support first from Sun Microsystems and now from Oracle. Sun has very generously supported BlueJ for many years, and when Oracle acquired Sun this support has continued. We are very grateful for this crucial contribution.

The Pearson team also has done a terrific job in making this book happen, managing to bring it into the world and avert every author's worst fear—that his book might go unnoticed. Particular thanks are due to our editor, Tracy Johnson, and to Camille Trentacoste and Carole Snyder, who supported us through the writing and production process.

David would like to add his personal thanks to both staff and students of the School of Computing at the University of Kent. The students who have taken his introductory OO course have always been a privilege to teach. They also provide the essential stimulus and motivation that makes teaching so much fun. Without the valuable assistance of knowledgeable and supportive postgraduate supervisors, running classes would be impossible.

Michael would like to thank Davin and Neil who have done such excellent work in building and maintaining BlueJ and our community web sites. Without such a great team none of this could work.

Part 1 Foundations of Object Orientation

Chapter 1 Objects and Classes

Chapter 2 Understanding Class Definitions

Chapter 3 Object Interaction

Chapter 4 Grouping Objects

Chapter 5 Functional Processing of Collections (Advanced)

Chapter 6 More-Sophisticated Behavior

Chapter 7 Fixed-Size Collections—Arrays

Chapter 8 Designing Classes

Chapter 9 Well-Behaved Objects

CHAPTER 1

Objects and Classes

> **Main concepts discussed in this chapter:**
> - objects
> - methods
> - classes
> - parameters

It's time to jump in and get started with our discussion of object-oriented programming. Learning to program requires a mix of some theory and a lot of practice. In this book, we will present both, so that the two reinforce each other.

At the heart of object orientation are two concepts that we have to understand first: *objects* and *classes*. These concepts form the basis of all programming in object-oriented languages. So let us start with a brief discussion of these two foundations.

1.1 Objects and classes

Concept

Java **objects** model objects from a problem domain.

If you write a computer program in an object-oriented language, you are creating, in your computer, a model of some part of the world. The parts that the model is built up from are the *objects* that appear in the problem domain. These objects must be represented in the computer model being created. The objects from the problem domain vary with the program you are writing. They may be words and paragraphs if you are programming a word processor, users and messages if you are working on a social-network system, or monsters if you are writing a computer game.

Objects may be categorized. A class describes,—in an abstract way,—all objects of a particular kind.

We can make these abstract notions clearer by looking at an example. Assume you want to model a traffic simulation. One kind of entity you then have to deal with is cars. What is a car in our context? Is it a class or an object? A few questions may help us to make a decision.

What color is a car? How fast can it go? Where is it right now?

> **Concept**
>
> Objects are created from **classes**. The class describes the kind of object; the objects represent individual instances of the class.

You will notice that we cannot answer these questions until we talk about one specific car. The reason is that the word "car" in this context refers to the *class* car; we are talking about cars in general, not about one particular car.

If I speak of "my old car that is parked at home in my garage," we can answer the questions above. That car is red, it doesn't go very fast, and it is in my garage. Now I am talking about an object—about one particular example of a car.

We usually refer to a particular object as an *instance*. We shall use the term "instance" quite regularly from now on. "Instance" is roughly synonymous with "object"; we refer to objects as instances when we want to emphasize that they are of a particular class (such as "this object is an instance of the class car").

Before we continue this rather theoretical discussion, let us look at an example.

1.2 Creating objects

Start BlueJ and open the example named *figures*.[1] You should see a window similar to that shown in Figure 1.1.

In this window, a diagram should become visible. Every one of the colored rectangles in the diagram represents a class in our project. In this project, we have classes named `Circle`, `Square`, `Triangle`, `Person`, and `Canvas`.

Right-click on the `Circle` class and choose

```
new Circle()
```

Figure 1.1
The *figures* project in BlueJ

---

[1] We regularly expect you to undertake some activities and exercises while reading this book. At this point, we assume that you already know how to start BlueJ and open the example projects. If not, read Appendix A first.

Figure 1.2
An object on the object bench

from the pop-up menu. The system asks you for a "name of the instance"; click OK—the default name supplied is good enough for now. You will see a red rectangle toward the bottom of the screen labeled "circle1" (Figure 1.2).

> **Convention** We start names of classes with capital letters (such as `Circle`) and names of objects with lowercase letters (such as `circle1`). This helps to distinguish what we are talking about.

You have just created your first object! "Circle," the rectangular icon in Figure 1.1, represents the class `Circle`; `circle1` is an object created from this class. The area at the bottom of the screen where the object is shown is called the *object bench*.

Exercise 1.1 Create another circle. Then create a square.

1.3 Calling methods

Right-click on one of the circle objects (not the class!), and you will see a pop-up menu with several operations (Figure 1.3). Choose `makeVisible` from the menu—this will draw a representation of this circle in a separate window (Figure 1.4).

You will notice several other operations in the circle's menu. Try invoking `moveRight` and `moveDown` a few times to move the circle closer to the corner of the screen. You may also like to try `makeInvisible` and `makeVisible` to hide and show the circle.

> **Concept**
> We can communicate with objects by invoking **methods** on them. Objects usually do something if we invoke a method.

Exercise 1.2 What happens if you call `moveDown` twice? Or three times? What happens if you call `makeInvisible` twice?

The entries in the circle's menu represent operations that you can use to manipulate the circle. These are called *methods* in Java. Using common terminology, we say that these

Figure 1.3
An object's pop-up menu, listing its operations

Figure 1.4
A drawing of a circle

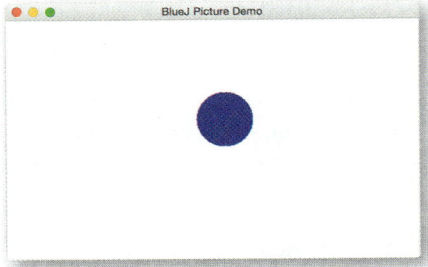

methods are *called* or *invoked*. We shall use this proper terminology from now on. We might ask you to "invoke the `moveRight` method of `circle1`."

1.4 Parameters

Now invoke the `moveHorizontal` method. You will see a dialog appear that prompts you for some input (Figure 1.5). Type in 50 and click OK. You will see the circle move 50 pixels to the right.[2]

Concept

Methods can have **parameters** to provide additional information for a task.

The `moveHorizontal` method that was just called is written in such a way that it requires some more information to execute. In this case, the information required is the distance—how far the circle should be moved. Thus, the `moveHorizontal` method is more flexible than the `moveRight` and `moveLeft` methods. The latter always move the circle a fixed distance, whereas `moveHorizontal` lets you specify how far you want to move the circle.

---

[2] A pixel is a single dot on your screen. Your screen is made up of a grid of single pixels.

Figure 1.5
A method-call dialog

Exercise 1.3 Try invoking the `moveVertical`, `slowMoveVertical`, and `changeSize` methods before you read on. Find out how you can use `moveHorizontal` to move the circle 70 pixels to the left.

Concept

The method name and the parameter types of a method are called its **signature**. They provide the information needed to invoke that method.

The additional values that some methods require are called *parameters*. A method indicates what kinds of parameters it requires. When calling, for example, the `moveHorizontal` method as shown in Figure 1.5, the dialog displays the line near the top.

```
void moveHorizontal(int distance)
```

This is called the *header* of the method. The header provides some information about the method in question. The part enclosed by parentheses (`int distance`) is the information about the required parameter. For each parameter, it defines a *type* and a *name*. The header above states that the method requires one parameter of type `int` named `distance`. The name gives a hint about the meaning of the data expected. Together, the name of a method and the parameter types found in its header are called the method's *signature*.

1.5 Data types

Concept

Parameters have **types**. The type defines what kinds of values a parameter can take.

A type specifies what kind of data can be passed to a parameter. The type `int` signifies whole numbers (also called "integer" numbers, hence the abbreviation "int").

In the example above, the signature of the `moveHorizontal` method states that, before the method can execute, we need to supply a whole number specifying the distance to move. The data entry field shown in Figure 1.5 then lets you enter that number.

In the examples so far, the only data type we have seen has been `int`. The parameters of the move methods and the `changeSize` method are all of that type.

Closer inspection of the object's pop-up menu shows that the method entries in the menu include the parameter types. If a method has no parameter, the method name is followed by an empty set of parentheses. If it has a parameter, the type and name of that parameter is displayed. In the list of methods for a circle, you will see one method with a different parameter type: the `changeColor` method has a parameter of type `String`.

The `String` type indicates that a section of text (for example, a word or a sentence) is expected. Strings are always enclosed within double quotes. For example, to enter the word *red* as a string, type

```
"red"
```

The method-call dialog also includes a section of text called a *comment* above the method header. Comments are included to provide information to the (human) reader and are described in Chapter 2. The comment of the `changeColor` method describes what color names the system knows about.

> **Exercise 1.4** Invoke the `changeColor` method on one of your circle objects and enter the string `"red"`. This should change the color of the circle. Try other colors.
>
> **Exercise 1.5** This is a very simple example, and not many colors are supported. See what happens when you specify a color that is not known.
>
> **Exercise 1.6** Invoke the `changeColor` method, and write the color into the parameter field *without* the quotes. What happens?

> **Pitfall** A common error for beginners is to forget the double quotes when typing in a data value of type `String`. If you type **green** instead of `"green"`, you will get an error message saying something like "Error: cannot find symbol - variable green."

Java supports several other data types, including decimal numbers and characters. We shall not discuss all of them right now, but rather come back to this issue later. If you want to find out about them now, see at Appendix B.

1.6 Multiple instances

Once you have a class, you can create as many objects (or instances) of that class as you like. From the class `Circle`, you can create many circles. From `Square`, you can create many squares.

> **Exercise 1.7** Create several circle objects on the object bench. You can do so by selecting **new Circle()** from the pop-up menu of the `Circle` class. Make them visible, then move them around on the screen using the "move" methods. Make one big and yellow; make another one small and green. Try the other shapes too: create a few triangles, squares, and persons. Change their positions, sizes, and colors.

Every one of those objects has its own position, color, and size. You change an attribute of an object (such as its size) by calling a method on that object. This will affect this particular object, but not others.

> **Concept**
> **Multiple instances.** Many similar objects can be created from a single class.

You may also notice an additional detail about parameters. Have a look at the `changeSize` method of the triangle. Its header is

```
void changeSize(int newHeight, int newWidth)
```

Here is an example of a method with more than one parameter. This method has two, and a comma separates them in the header. Methods can, in fact, have any number of parameters.

1.7 State

The set of values of all attributes defining an object (such as *x*-position, *y*-position, color, diameter, and visibility status for a circle) is also referred to as the object's *state*. This is another example of common terminology that we shall use from now on.

> **Concept**
> Objects have state. The **state** is represented by storing values in fields.

In BlueJ, the state of an object can be inspected by selecting the *Inspect* function from the object's pop-up menu. When an object is inspected, an *object inspector* is displayed. The object inspector is an enlarged view of the object that shows the attributes stored inside it (Figure 1.6).

Exercise 1.8 Make sure you have several objects on the object bench, and then inspect each of them in turn. Try changing the state of an object (for example, by calling the `moveLeft` method) while the object inspector is open. You should see the values in the object inspector change.

Some methods, when called, change the state of an object. For example, `moveLeft` changes the `xPosition` attribute. Java refers to these object attributes as *fields*.

Figure 1.6
An object inspector, showing details of an object

1.8 What is in an object?

On inspecting different objects, you will notice that objects of the *same* class all have the same fields. That is, the number, type, and names of the fields are the same, while the actual value of a particular field in each object may be different. In contrast, objects of a *different* class may have different fields. A circle, for example, has a "diameter" field, while a triangle has fields for "width" and "height."

The reason is that the number, types, and names of fields are defined in a class, not in an object. So the class `Circle` defines that each circle object will have five fields, named `diameter`, `xPosition`, `yPosition`, `color`, and `isVisible`. It also defines the types for these fields. That is, it specifies that the first three are of type `int`, while the color is of type `String` and the `isVisible` flag is of type `boolean`. (`boolean` is a type that can represent two values: `true` and `false`. We shall discuss it in more detail later.)

When an object of class `Circle` is created, the object will automatically have these fields. The values of the fields are stored in the object. That ensures that each circle has a color, for instance, and each can have a different color (Figure 1.7).

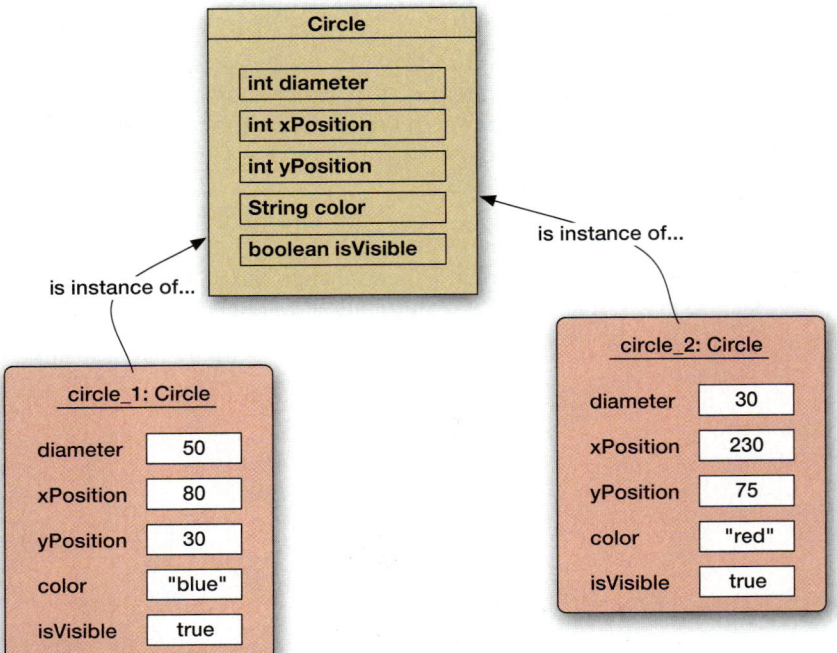

Figure 1.7
A class and its objects with fields and values

Figure 1.8
Two images created from a set of shape objects

 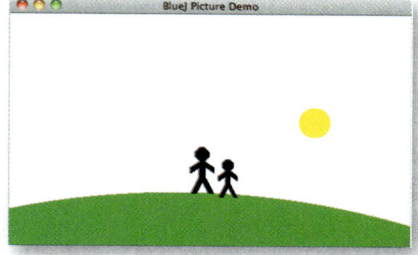

The story is similar for methods. Methods are defined in the class of the object. As a result, all objects of a given class have the same methods. However, the methods are invoked on objects. This makes it clear which object to change when, for example, a `moveRight` method is invoked.

Exercise 1.9 Figure 1.8 shows two different images. Choose one of these images and recreate it using the shapes from the *figures* project. While you are doing this, write down what you have to do to achieve this. Could it be done in different ways?

1.9 Java code

When we program in Java, we essentially write down instructions to invoke methods on objects, just as we have done with our figure objects above. However, we do not do this interactively by choosing methods from a menu with the mouse, but instead we type the commands down in textual form. We can see what those commands look like in text form by using the BlueJ Terminal.

Exercise 1.10 Select *Show Terminal* from the *View* menu. This shows another window that BlueJ uses for text output. Then select *Record method calls* from the terminal's *Options* menu. This function will cause all our method calls (in their textual form) to be written to the terminal. Now create a few objects, call some of their methods, and observe the output in the terminal window.

Using the terminal's *Record method calls* function, we can see that the sequence of creating a person object and calling its `makeVisible` and `moveRight` methods looks like this in Java text form:

```
Person person1 = new Person();
person1.makeVisible();
person1.moveRight();
```

Here, we can observe several things:

- We can see what creating an object and giving it a name looks like. Technically, what we are doing here is *storing the Person object into a variable*; we will discuss this in detail in the next chapter.
- We see that, to call a method on an object, we write the name of the object, followed by a dot, followed by the name of the method. The command ends with a parameter list—an empty pair of parentheses if there are no parameters.
- All Java statements end with a semicolon.

Instead of just looking at Java statements, we can also type them. To do this, we use the *Code Pad*. (You can switch off the *Record method calls* function now and close the terminal.)

> **Exercise 1.11** Select *Show Code Pad* from the *View* menu. This should display a new pane next to the object bench in your main BlueJ window. This pane is the *Code Pad*. You can type Java code here.

In the Code Pad, we can type Java code that does the same things we did interactively before. The Java code we need to write is exactly like that shown above.

> **Exercise 1.12** In the Code Pad, type the code shown above to create a Person object and call its `makeVisible` and `moveRight` methods. Then go on to create some other objects and call their methods.

Tip

You can recall previously used commands in the Code Pad by using the up arrow.

Typing these commands should have the same effect as invoking the same command from the object's menu. If instead you see an error message, then you have mistyped the command. Check your spelling. You will note that getting even a single character wrong will cause the command to fail.

1.10 Object interaction

For the next section, we shall work with a different example project. Close the *figures* project if you still have it open, and open the project called *house*.

> **Exercise 1.13** Open the *house* project. Create an instance of class `Picture` and invoke its `draw` method. Also, try out the `setBlackAndWhite` and `setColor` methods.

> **Exercise 1.14** How do you think the `Picture` class draws the picture?

Five of the classes in the *house* project are identical to the classes in the *figures* project. But we now have an additional class: `Picture`. This class is programmed to do exactly what we have done by hand in Exercise 1.9.

In reality, if we want a sequence of tasks done in Java, we would not normally do it by hand. Instead, we would create a class that does it for us. This is the `Picture` class.

The `Picture` class is written so that, when you create an instance, the instance creates two square objects (one for the wall, one for the window), a triangle, and a circle. Then, when you call the `draw` method, it moves them around and changes their color and size, until the canvas looks like the picture we see in Figure 1.8.

> **Concept**
>
> **Method calling.** Objects can communicate by **calling** each other's **methods**.

The important points here are that: objects can create other objects; and they can call each other's methods. In a normal Java program, you may well have hundreds or thousands of objects. The user of a program just starts the program (which typically creates a first object), and all other objects are created—directly or indirectly—by that object.

The big question now is this: How do we write the class for such an object?

1.11 Source code

Each class has some *source code* associated with it. The source code is text that defines the details of the class. In BlueJ, the source code of a class can be viewed by selecting the *Open Editor* function from the class's pop-up menu, or by double-clicking the class icon.

> **Concept**
>
> The **source code** of a class determines the structure and behavior (the fields and methods) of each of the objects of that class.

Exercise 1.15 Look at the pop-up menu of class `Picture` again. You will see an option labeled *Open Editor*. Select it. This will open a text editor displaying the source code of the class.

The source code is text written in the Java programming language. It defines what fields and methods a class has, and precisely what happens when a method is invoked. In the next chapter, we shall discuss exactly what the source code of a class contains, and how it is structured.

A large part of learning the art of programming is learning how to write these class definitions. To do this, we shall learn to use the Java language (although there are many other programming languages that could be used to write code).

When you make a change to the source code and close the editor, the icon for that class appears striped in the diagram.[3] The stripes indicate that the source has been changed. The class now needs to be compiled by clicking the *Compile* button. (You may like to read the "About compilation" note for more information on what is happening when you compile a class.) Once a class has been compiled, objects can be created again and you can try out your change.

---

[3] In BlueJ, there is no need to explicitly save the text in the editor before closing. If you close the editor, the source code will automatically be saved.

About compilation When people write computer programs, they typically use a "higher-level" programming language such as Java. A problem with that is that a computer cannot execute Java source code directly. Java was designed to be reasonably easy to read for humans, not for computers. Computers, internally, work with a binary representation of a machine code, which looks quite different from Java. The problem for us is that it looks so complex that we do not want to write it directly. We prefer to write Java. What can we do about this?

The solution is a program called the *compiler*. The compiler translates the Java code into machine code. We can write Java and run the compiler—which generates the machine code—and the computer can then read the machine code. As a result, every time we change the source code, we must first run the compiler before we can use the class again to create an object. Otherwise, the machine code version that the computer needs will not exist.

Exercise 1.16 In the source code of class **Picture**, find the part that actually draws the picture. Change it so that the sun will be blue rather than yellow.

Exercise 1.17 Add a second sun to the picture. To do this, pay attention to the field definitions close to the top of the class. You will find this code:

```
private Square wall;
private Square window;
private Triangle roof;
private Circle sun;
```

You need to add a line here for the second sun. For example:

```
private Circle sun2;
```

Then write the appropriate code in two different places for creating the second sun and making it visible when the picture is drawn.

Exercise 1.18 *Challenge exercise* (This means that this exercise might not be solved quickly. We do not expect everyone to be able to solve this at the moment. If you do, great. If you don't, then don't worry. Things will become clearer as you read on. Come back to this exercise later.) Add a sunset to the single-sun version of **Picture**. That is, make the sun go down slowly. Remember: The circle has a method **slowMoveVertical** that you can use to do this.

Exercise 1.19 *Challenge exercise* If you added your sunset to the end of the **draw** method (so that the sun goes down automatically when the picture is drawn), change this now. We now want the sunset in a separate method, so that we can call **draw** and see the picture with the sun up, and then call **sunset** (a separate method!) to make the sun go down.

Exercise 1.20 *Challenge exercise* Make a person walk up to the house after the sunset.

1.12 Another example

In this chapter, we have already discussed a large number of new concepts. To help in understanding these concepts, we shall now revisit them in a different context. For this, we use another example. Close the *house* project if you still have it open, and open the *lab-classes* project.

This project is a simplified part of a student database designed to keep track of students in laboratory classes, and to print class lists.

Exercise 1.21 Create an object of class `Student`. You will notice that this time you are prompted not only for a name of the instance, but also for some other parameters. Fill them in before clicking OK. (Remember that parameters of type `String` must be written within double quotes.)

1.13 Return values

As before, you can create multiple objects. And again, as before, the objects have methods that you can call from their pop-up menu(s).

Exercise 1.22 Create some `Student` objects. Call the `getName` method on each object. Explain what is happening.

When calling the `getName` method of the `Student` class, we notice something new: methods may return a result value. In fact, the header of each method tells us whether or not it returns a result, and what the type of the result is. The header of `getName` (as shown in the object's pop-up menu) is defined as

```
String getName()
```

The word `String` before the method name specifies the return type. In this case, it states that calling this method will return a result of type `String`. The header of `changeName` states:

```
void changeName(String replacementName)
```

The word `void` indicates that this method does not return any result.

Methods with return values enable us to get information from an object via a method call. This means that we can use methods either to change an object's state, or to find out about its state. The return type of a method is not part of its signature.

> **Concept**
>
> **Result.** Methods may return information about an object via a **return value**.

1.14 Objects as parameters

Exercise 1.23 Create an object of class **LabClass**. As the signature indicates, you need to specify the maximum number of students in that class (an integer).

Exercise 1.24 Call the **numberOfStudents** method of that class. What does it do?

Exercise 1.25 Look at the signature of the **enrollStudent** method. You will notice that the type of the expected parameter is **Student**. Make sure you have two or three students and a **LabClass** object on the object bench, then call the **enrollStudent** method of the **LabClass** object. With the input cursor in the dialog entry field, click on one of the student objects; this enters the name of the student object into the parameter field of the **enrollStudent** method (Figure 1.9). Click OK and you have added the student to the **LabClass**. Add one or more other students as well.

Exercise 1.26 Call the **printList** method of the **LabClass** object. You will see a list of all the students in that class printed to the BlueJ terminal window (Figure 1.10).

Figure 1.9
Adding a student to a **LabClass**

Figure 1.10
Output of the **LabClass** class listing

As the exercises show, objects can be passed as parameters to methods of other objects. In the case where a method expects an object as a parameter, the expected object's class name is specified as the parameter type in the method signature.

Explore this project a bit more. Try to identify the concepts discussed in the *figures* example in this context.

Exercise 1.27 Create three students with the following details:

> Snow White, student ID: A00234, credits: 24
>
> Lisa Simpson, student ID: C22044, credits: 56
>
> Charlie Brown, student ID: A12003, credits: 6

Then enter all three into a lab and print a list to the screen.

Exercise 1.28 Use the inspector on a `LabClass` object to discover what fields it has.

Exercise 1.29 Set the instructor, room, and time for a lab, and print the list to the terminal window to check that these new details appear.

1.15 Summary

In this chapter, we have explored the basics of classes and objects. We have discussed the fact that objects are specified by classes. Classes represent the general concept of things, while objects represent concrete instances of a class. We can have many objects of any class.

Objects have methods that we use to communicate with them. We can use a method to make a change to the object or to get information from the object. Methods can have parameters, and parameters have types. Methods have return types, which specify what type of data they return. If the return type is `void`, they do not return anything.

Objects store data in fields (which also have types). All the data values of an object together are referred to as the object's state.

Objects are created from class definitions that have been written in a particular programming language. Much of programming in Java is about learning to write class definitions. A large Java program will have many classes, each with many methods that call each other in many different ways.

To learn to develop Java programs, we need to learn how to write class definitions, including fields and methods, and how to put these classes together well. The rest of this book deals with these issues.

Terms introduced in this chapter:

> **object, class, instance, method, signature, parameter, type, state, source code, return value, compiler**

Exercise 1.30 In this chapter we have mentioned the data types `int` and `String`. Java has more predefined data types. Find out what they are and what they are used for. To do this, you can check Appendix B, or look it up in another Java book or in an online Java language manual. One such manual is at

`http://download.oracle.com/javase/tutorial/java/nutsandbolts/datatypes.html`

Exercise 1.31 What are the types of the following values?

```
0
"hello"
101
-1
true
"33"
3.1415
```

Exercise 1.32 What would you have to do to add a new field, for example one called name, to a circle object?

Exercise 1.33 Write the header for a method named send that has one parameter of type String, and does not return a value.

Exercise 1.34 Write the header for a method named average that has two parameters, both of type int, and returns an int value.

Exercise 1.35 Look at the book you are reading right now. Is it an object or a class? If it is a class, name some objects. If it is an object, name its class.

Exercise 1.36 Can an object have several different classes? Discuss.

CHAPTER 2

Understanding Class Definitions

Main concepts discussed in this chapter:

- fields
- constructors
- parameters
- methods (accessor, mutator)
- assignment and conditional statement

Java constructs discussed in this chapter:

field, constructor, comment, parameter, assignment (=), block, return statement, **void**, compound assignment operators (+=, −=), if-statement

---

In this chapter, we take our first proper look at the source code of a class. We will discuss the basic elements of class definitions: *fields*, *constructors*, and *methods*. Methods contain statements, and initially we look at methods containing only simple arithmetic and printing statements. Later, we introduce *conditional statements* that allow choices between different actions to be made within methods.

We shall start by examining a new project in a fair amount of detail. This project represents a naïve implementation of an automated ticket machine. As we start by introducing the most basic features of classes, we shall quickly find that this implementation is deficient in a number of ways. So we shall then proceed to describe a more sophisticated version of the ticket machine that represents a significant improvement. Finally, in order to reinforce the concepts introduced in this chapter, we take a look at the internals of the *lab-classes* example encountered in Chapter 1.

2.1 Ticket machines

Train stations often provide ticket machines that print a ticket when a customer inserts the correct money for their fare. In this chapter, we shall define a class that models something like these ticket machines. As we shall be looking inside our first Java example classes, we shall keep our simulation fairly simple to start with. That will give us the opportunity to ask some questions about how these models differ from the real-world versions, and how we might change our classes to make the objects they create more like the real thing.

Our ticket machines work by customers "inserting" money into them and then requesting a ticket to be printed. Each machine keeps a running total of the amount of money it has collected throughout its operation. In real life, it is often the case that a ticket machine offers a selection of different types of ticket, from which customers choose the one they want. Our simplified machines print tickets of only a single price. It turns out to be significantly more complicated to program a class to be able to issue tickets of different values, than it does to offer a single price. On the other hand, with object-oriented programming it is very easy to create multiple instances of the class, each with its own price setting, to fulfill a need for different types of tickets.

2.1.1 Exploring the behavior of a naïve ticket machine

> **Concept**
>
> **Object creation:** Some objects cannot be constructed unless extra information is provided.

Open the *naive-ticket-machine* project in BlueJ. This project contains only one class—`TicketMachine`—which you will be able to explore in a similar way to the examples we discussed in Chapter 1. When you create a `TicketMachine` instance, you will be asked to supply a number that corresponds to the price of tickets that will be issued by that particular machine. The price is taken to be a number of cents, so a positive whole number such as 500 would be appropriate as a value to work with.

Exercise 2.1 Create a `TicketMachine` object on the object bench and take a look at its methods. You should see the following: `getBalance`, `getPrice`, `insertMoney`, and `printTicket`. Try out the `getPrice` method. You should see a return value containing the price of the tickets that was set when this object was created. Use the `insertMoney` method to simulate inserting an amount of money into the machine. The machine stores as a balance the amount of money inserted. Use `getBalance` to check that the machine has kept an accurate record of the amount just inserted. You can insert several separate amounts of money into the machine, just like you might insert multiple coins or bills into a real machine. Try inserting the exact amount required for a ticket, and use `getBalance` to ensure that the balance is increased correctly. As this is a simple machine, a ticket will not be issued automatically, so once you have inserted enough money, call the `printTicket` method. A facsimile ticket should be printed in the BlueJ terminal window.

Exercise 2.2 What value is returned if you get the machine's balance after it has printed a ticket?

Exercise 2.3 Experiment with inserting different amounts of money before printing tickets. Do you notice anything strange about the machine's behavior? What happens if you insert too much money into the machine—do you receive any refund? What happens if you do not insert enough and then try to print a ticket?

Exercise 2.4 Try to obtain a good understanding of a ticket machine's behavior by interacting with it on the object bench before we start looking, in the next section, at how the **TicketMachine** class is implemented.

Exercise 2.5 Create another ticket machine for tickets of a different price; remember that you have to supply this value when you create the machine object. Buy a ticket from that machine. Does the printed ticket look any different from those printed by the first machine?

2.2 Examining a class definition

The exercises at the end of the previous section reveal that **TicketMachine** objects only behave in the way we expect them to if we insert the exact amount of money to match the price of a ticket. As we explore the internal details of the class in this section, we shall see why this is so.

Take a look at the source code of the **TicketMachine** class by double-clicking its icon in the class diagram within BlueJ. It should look something like Figure 2.1.

The complete text of the class is shown in Code 2.1. By looking at the text of the class definition piece by piece, we can flesh out some of the object-oriented concepts that discussed in Chapter 1. This class definition contains many of the features of Java that we will see over and over again, so it will pay greatly to study it carefully.

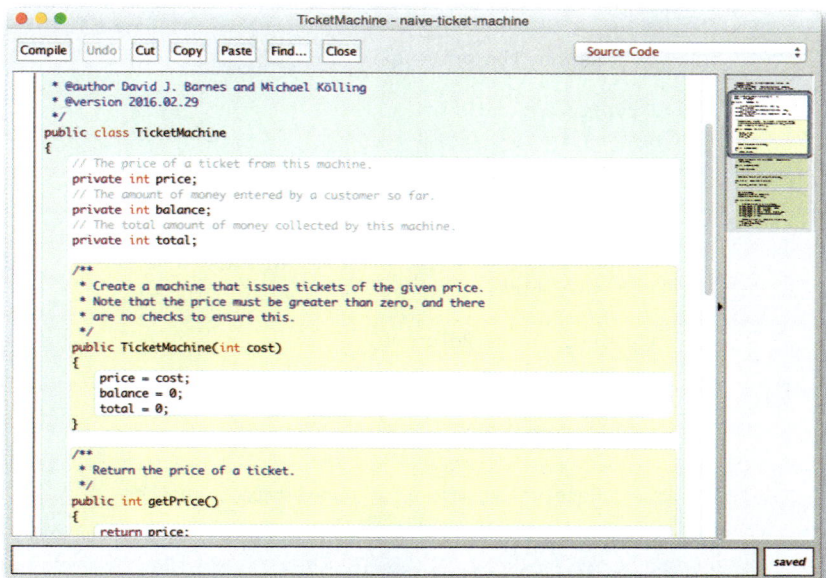

Figure 2.1
The BlueJ editor window

Code 2.1

The `TicketMachine` class

```java
/**
 * TicketMachine models a naive ticket machine that issues
 * flat-fare tickets.
 * The price of a ticket is specified via the constructor.
 * It is a naive machine in the sense that it trusts its users
 * to insert enough money before trying to print a ticket.
 * It also assumes that users enter sensible amounts.
 *
 * @author David J. Barnes and Michael Kölling
 * @version 2016.02.29
 */
public class TicketMachine
{
    // The price of a ticket from this machine.
    private int price;
    // The amount of money entered by a customer so far.
    private int balance;
    // The total amount of money collected by this machine.
    private int total;

    /**
     * Create a machine that issues tickets of the given price.
     * Note that the price must be greater than zero, and there
     * are no checks to ensure this.
     */
    public TicketMachine(int cost)
    {
        price = cost;
        balance = 0;
        total = 0;
    }

    /**
     * Return the price of a ticket.
     */
    public int getPrice()
    {
        return price;
    }

    /**
     * Return the amount of money already inserted for the
     * next ticket.
     */
    public int getBalance()
    {
        return balance;
    }

    /**
     * Receive an amount of money from a customer.
     */
```

Code 2.1 continued
The `TicketMachine` class

```java
    public void insertMoney(int amount)
    {
        balance = balance + amount;
    }

    /**
     * Print a ticket.
     * Update the total collected and
     * reduce the balance to zero.
     */
    public void printTicket()
    {
        // Simulate the printing of a ticket.
        System.out.println("##################");
        System.out.println("# The BlueJ Line");
        System.out.println("# Ticket");
        System.out.println("# " + price + " cents.");
        System.out.println("##################");
        System.out.println();

        // Update the total collected with the balance.
        total = total + balance;
        // Clear the balance.
        balance = 0;
    }
}
```

2.3 The class header

The text of a class can be broken down into two main parts: a small outer wrapping that simply names the class (appearing on a green background), and a much larger inner part that does all the work. In this case, the outer wrapping appears as follows:

```java
public class TicketMachine
{
    Inner part of the class omitted.
}
```

The outer wrappings of different classes all look much the same. The outer wrapping contains the class header, whose main purpose is to provide a name for the class. By a widely followed convention, we always start class names with an uppercase letter. As long as it is used consistently, this convention allows class names to be easily distinguished from other sorts of names, such as variable names and method names, which will be described shortly. Above the class header is a comment (shown as blue text) that tells us something about the class.

> **Exercise 2.6** Write out what you think the outer wrappers of the `Student` and `LabClass` classes might look like; do not worry about the inner part.
>
> **Exercise 2.7** Does it matter whether we write
>
>   public class TicketMachine
>
> or
>
>   class public TicketMachine
>
> in the outer wrapper of a class? Edit the source of the `TicketMachine` class to make the change, and then close the editor window. Do you notice a change in the class diagram?
>
> What error message do you get when you now press the *Compile* button? Do you think this message clearly explains what is wrong?
>
> Change the class back to how it was, and make sure that this clears the error when you compile it.
>
> **Exercise 2.8** Check whether or not it is possible to leave out the word `public` from the outer wrapper of the `TicketMachine` class.
>
> **Exercise 2.9** Put back the word `public`, and then check whether it is possible to leave out the word `class` by trying to compile again. Make sure that both words are put back as they were originally before continuing.

2.3.1 Keywords

The words "public" and "class" are part of the Java language, whereas the word "TicketMachine" is not—the person writing the class has chosen that particular name. We call words like "public" and "class" *keywords* or *reserved words* – the terms are used frequently and interchangeably. There are around 50 of these in Java, and you will soon be able to recognize most of them. A point worth remembering is that Java keywords never contain uppercase letters, whereas the words we get to choose (like "TicketMachine") are often a mix of upper- and lowercase letters.

2.4 Fields, constructors, and methods

The inner part of the class is where we define the *fields*, *constructors*, and *methods* that give the objects of that class their own particular characteristics and behavior. We can summarize the essential features of those three components of a class as follows:

- The fields store data persistently within an object.
- The constructors are responsible for ensuring that an object is set up properly when it is first created.
- The methods implement the behavior of an object; they provide its functionality.

In BlueJ, fields are shown as text on a white background, while constructors and methods are displayed as yellow boxes.

In Java, there are very few rules about the order in which you choose to define the fields, constructors, and methods within a class. In the `TicketMachine` class, we have chosen to list the fields first, the constructors second, and finally the methods (Code 2.2). This is the order that we shall follow in all of our examples. Other authors choose to adopt different styles, and this is mostly a question of preference. Our style is not necessarily better than all others. However, it is important to choose one style and then use it consistently, because then your classes will be easier to read and understand.

Code 2.2
Our ordering of fields, constructors, and methods

```
public class ClassName
{
    Fields
    Constructors
    Methods
}
```

Exercise 2.10 From your earlier experimentation with the ticket machine objects within BlueJ, you can probably remember the names of some of the methods—`printTicket`, for instance. Look at the class definition in Code 2.1 and use this knowledge, along with the additional information about ordering we have given you, to make a list of the names of the fields, constructors, and methods in the `TicketMachine` class. *Hint:* There is only one constructor in the class.

Exercise 2.11 What are the two features of the constructor that make it look significantly different from the methods of the class?

2.4.1 Fields

Concept

Fields store data for an object to use. Fields are also known as instance variables.

Fields store data persistently within an object. The `TicketMachine` class has three fields: `price`, `balance`, and `total`. Fields are also known as *instance variables*, because the word *variable* is used as a general term for things that store data in a program. We have defined the fields right at the start of the class definition (Code 2.3). All of these variables are associated with monetary items that a ticket-machine object has to deal with:

- `price` stores the fixed price of a ticket;
- `balance` stores the amount of money inserted into the machine by a user prior to asking for a ticket to be printed;
- `total` stores the total amount of money inserted into the machine by all users since the machine object was constructed (excluding any current balance). The idea is that, when a ticket is printed, any money in the balance is transferred to the total.

Code 2.3

The fields of the `TicketMachine` class

```java
public class TicketMachine
{
    private int price;
    private int balance;
    private int total;

    Constructors and methods omitted.
}
```

Fields are small amounts of space inside an object that can be used to store data persistently. Every object will have space for each field declared in its class. Figure 2.2 shows a diagrammatic representation of a ticket-machine object with its three fields. The fields have not yet been assigned any values; once they have, we can write each value into the box representing the field. The notation is similar to that used in BlueJ to show objects on the object bench, except that we show a bit more detail here. In BlueJ, for space reasons, the fields are not displayed on the object icon. We can, however, see them by opening an inspector window (Section 1.7).

Figure 2.2

An object of class `TicketMachine`

Each field has its own declaration in the source code. On the line above each in the full class definition, we have added a single line of text—a *comment*—for the benefit of human readers of the class definition:

```
// The price of a ticket from this machine.
private int price;
```

Concept

Comments are inserted into the source code of a class to provide explanations to human readers. They have no effect on the functionality of the class.

A single-line comment is introduced by the two characters "//", which are written with no spaces between them. More-detailed comments, often spanning several lines, are usually written in the form of multiline comments. These start with the character pair "/*" and end with the pair "*/". There is a good example preceding the header of the class in Code 2.1.

The definitions of the three fields are quite similar:

- All definitions indicate that they are *private* fields of the object; we shall have more to say about what this means in Chapter 6, but for the time being we will simply say that we always define fields to be private.

- All three fields are of type `int`. `int` is another keyword and represents the data type integer. This indicates that each can store a single whole-number value, which is reasonable given that we wish them to store numbers that represent amounts of money in cents.

Fields can store values that can vary over time, so they are also known as *variables*. The value stored in a field can be changed from its initial value if required. For instance, as more money is inserted into a ticket machine, we shall want to change the value stored in the `balance` field. It is common to have fields whose values change often, such as `balance` and `total`, and others that change rarely or not at all, such as `price`. The fact that the value of `price` doesn't vary once set does not alter the fact that it is still called a variable. In the following sections, we shall also meet other kinds of variables in addition to fields, but they will all share the same fundamental purpose of storing data.

The `price`, `balance`, and `total` fields are all the data items that a ticket-machine object needs to fulfill its role of receiving money from a customer, printing tickets, and keeping a running total of all the money that has been put into it. In the following sections, we shall see how the constructor and methods use those fields to implement the behavior of naïve ticket machines.

Exercise 2.12 What do you think is the *type* of each of the following fields?

```
private int count;
private Student representative;
private Server host;
```

Exercise 2.13 What are the *names* of the following fields?

```
private boolean alive;
private Person tutor;
private Game game;
```

Exercise 2.14 From what you know about the naming conventions for classes, which of the type names in Exercises 2.12 and 2.13 would you say are class names?

Exercise 2.15 In the following field declaration from the `TicketMachine` class

```
private int price;
```

does it matter which order the three words appear in? Edit the `TicketMachine` class to try different orderings. After each change, close the editor. Does the appearance of the class diagram after each change give you a clue as to whether or not other orderings are possible? Check by pressing the *Compile* button to see if there is an error message.

Make sure that you reinstate the original version after your experiments!

> **Exercise 2.16** Is it always necessary to have a semicolon at the end of a field declaration? Once again, experiment via the editor. The rule you will learn here is an important one, so be sure to remember it.
>
> **Exercise 2.17** Write in full the declaration for a field of type **int** whose name is **status**.

From the definitions of fields we have seen so far, we can begin to put a pattern together that will apply whenever we define a field variable in a class:

- They usually start with the reserved word **private**.
- They include a type name (such as **int**, **String**, **Person**, etc.).
- They include a user-chosen name for the field variable.
- They end with a semicolon.

Remembering this pattern will help you when you write your own classes.

Indeed, as we look closely at the source code of different classes, you will see patterns such as this one emerging over and over again. Part of the process of learning to program involves looking out for such patterns and then using them in your own programs. That is one reason why studying source code in detail is so useful at this stage.

2.4.2 Constructors

Concept

Constructors allow each object to be set up properly when it is first created.

Constructors have a special role to fulfill. They are responsible for ensuring that an object is set up properly when it is first created; in other words, for ensuring that an object is ready to be used immediately following its creation. This construction process is also called *initialization*.

In some respects, a constructor can be likened to a midwife: it is responsible for ensuring that the new object comes into existence properly. Once an object has been created, the constructor plays no further role in that object's life and cannot be called again. Code 2.4 shows the constructor of the **TicketMachine** class.

One of the distinguishing features of constructors is that they have the same name as the class in which they are defined—**TicketMachine** in this case. The constructor's name immediately follows the word **public**, with nothing in between.[1]

We should expect a close connection between what happens in the body of a constructor and the fields of the class. This is because one of the main roles of the constructor is to initialize the fields. It will be possible with some fields, such as **balance** and **total**, to set sensible initial values by assigning a constant number—zero in this case. With others, such as the ticket price, it is not that simple, as we do not know the price that tickets from

---

[1] While this description is a slight simplification of the full Java rule, it fits the general rule we will use in the majority of code in this book.

a particular machine will have until that machine is constructed. Recall that we might wish to create multiple machine objects to sell tickets with different prices, so no one initial price will always be right. You will know from experimenting with creating **Ticket-Machine** objects within BlueJ that you had to supply the cost of the tickets whenever you created a new ticket machine. An important point to note here is that the price of a ticket is initially determined *externally* and then has to be *passed into* the constructor. Within BlueJ, you decide the value and enter it into a dialog box. Part of the task of the constructor is to receive that value and store it in the **price** field of the newly created ticket machine, so the machine can remember what that value was without you having to keep reminding it.

Code 2.4

The constructor of the **TicketMachine** class

```
public class TicketMachine
{
    Fields omitted.

    /**
     * Create a machine that issues tickets of the given price.
     * Note that the price must be greater than zero, and there
     * are no checks to ensure this.
     */
    public TicketMachine(int cost)
    {
        price = cost;
        balance = 0;
        total = 0;
    }

    Methods omitted.
}
```

We can see from this that one of the most important roles of a field is to remember external information passed into the object, so that that information is available to an object throughout its lifetime. Fields, therefore, provide a place to store long-lasting (i.e., persistent) data.

Figure 2.3 shows a ticket-machine object after the constructor has executed. Values have now been assigned to the fields. From this diagram, we can tell that the ticket machine was created by passing in 500 as the value for the ticket price.

In the next section, we discuss how values are received by an object from outside.

Note In Java, all fields are automatically initialized to a default value if they are not explicitly initialized. For integer fields, this default value is zero. So, strictly speaking, we could have done without setting **balance** and **total** to zero, relying on the default value to give us the same result. However, we prefer to write the explicit assignments anyway. There is no disadvantage to it, and it serves well to document what is actually happening. We do not rely on a reader of the class knowing what the default value is, and we document that we really want this value to be zero and have not just forgotten to initialize it.

Figure 2.3
A `TicketMachine` object after initialization (created for 500-cent tickets)

2.5 Parameters: receiving data

Constructors and methods play quite different roles in the life of an object, but the way in which both receive values from outside is the same: via *parameters*. You may recall that we briefly encountered parameters in Chapter 1 (Section 1.4). Parameters are another sort of variable, just as fields are, so they are also used to hold data. Parameters are variables that are defined in the header of a constructor or method:

```
public TicketMachine(int cost)
```

This constructor has a single parameter, `cost`, which is of type `int`—the same type as the `price` field it will be used to set. A parameter is used as a sort of temporary messenger, carrying data originating from outside the constructor or method, and making it available inside it.

Figure 2.4 illustrates how values are passed via parameters. In this case, a BlueJ user enters the external value into the dialog box when creating a new ticket machine (shown on the left), and that value is then copied into the `cost` parameter of the new machine's constructor. This is illustrated with the arrow labeled (A). The box in the `TicketMachine` object in Figure 2.4, labeled "TicketMachine (constructor)," represents additional space for the object that is created only when the constructor executes. We shall call it the *constructor space* of the object (or *method space* when we talk about methods instead of constructors, as the situation there is the same). The constructor space is used to provide space to store the values for the constructor's parameters. In our diagrams, all variables are represented by white boxes.

We distinguish between the parameter *names* inside a constructor or method, and the parameter *values* outside, by referring to the names as *formal parameters* and the values as *actual parameters*. So `cost` is a formal parameter, and a user-supplied value such as 500 is an actual parameter.

A formal parameter is available to an object only within the body of a constructor or method that declares it. We say that the *scope* of a parameter is restricted to the body of the constructor or method in which it is declared. In contrast, the scope of a field is the whole of the class definition–it can be accessed from anywhere in the same class. This is a very important difference between these two sorts of variables.

> **Concept**
>
> The **scope** of a variable defines the section of source code from which the variable can be accessed.

2.5 Parameters: receiving data

Concept

The **lifetime** of a variable describes how long the variable continues to exist before it is destroyed.

A concept related to variable scope is variable *lifetime*. The lifetime of a parameter is limited to a single call of a constructor or method. When a constructor or method is called, the extra space for the parameter variables is created, and the external values copied into that space. Once that call has completed its task, the formal parameters disappear and the values they held are lost. In other words, when the constructor has finished executing, the whole constructor space is removed, along with the parameter variables held within it (see Figure 2.4).

In contrast, the lifetime of a field is the same as the lifetime of the object to which it belongs. When an object is created, so are the fields, and they persist for the lifetime of the object. It follows that if we want to remember the cost of tickets held in the **cost** parameter, we must store the value somewhere persistent—that is, in the **price** field.

Just as we expect to see a close link between a constructor and the fields of its class, we expect to see a close link between the constructor's parameters and the fields, because external values will often be needed to set the initial values of one or more of those fields. Where this is the case, the parameter types will closely match the types of the corresponding fields.

Figure 2.4
Parameter passing (A) and assignment (B)

Exercise 2.18 To what class does the following constructor belong?

```
public Student(String name)
```

Exercise 2.19 How many parameters does the following constructor have, and what are their types?

```
public Book(String title, double price)
```

Exercise 2.20 Can you guess what types some of the **Book** class's fields might be, from the parameters in its constructor? Can you assume anything about the names of its fields?

2.5.1 Choosing variable names

One of the things you might have noticed is that the variable names we use for fields and parameters have a close connection with the purpose of the variable. Names such as `price`, `cost`, `title`, and `alive` all tell you something useful about the information being stored in that variable. This, makes it easier to understand what is going on in the program. Given that we have a large degree of freedom in our choice of variable names, it is worth following this principle of choosing names that communicate a sense of purpose rather than arbitrary and meaningless combinations of letters and numbers.

2.6 Assignment

In the previous section, we noted the need to copy the short-lived value stored in a parameter variable into somewhere more permanent—a field variable. In order to do this, the body of the constructor contains the following *assignment statement*:

```
price = cost;
```

> **Concept**
>
> **Assignment statements** store the value represented by the right-hand side of the statement in the variable named on the left.

Assignment statements are used frequently in programming, as a means to store a value into a variable. They can be recognized by the presence of an assignment operator, such as "=" in the example above. Assignment statements work by taking the value of what appears on the right-hand side of the operator and copying that value into the variable on the left-hand side. This is illustrated in Figure 2.4 by the arrow labeled (B). The right-hand side is called an *expression*. In their most general form, expressions are things that compute values, but in this case, the expression consists of just a single variable, whose value is copied into the `price` variable. We shall see examples of more-complicated expressions later in this chapter.

One rule about assignment statements is that the type of the expression on the right-hand side must match the type of the variable to which its value is assigned. We have already met three different, commonly used types: `int`, `String`, and (very briefly) `boolean`. This rule means that we are not allowed to store an `int`-type expression in a `String`-type variable, for instance. This same rule also applies between formal parameters and actual parameters: the type of an actual-parameter expression must match the type of the formal-parameter variable. For now, we can say that the types of both must be the same, although we shall see in later chapters that this is not the whole truth.

> **Exercise 2.21** Suppose that the class **Pet** has a field called **name** that is of the type **String**. Write an assignment statement in the body of the following constructor so that the **name** field will be initialized with the value of the constructor's parameter.
>
> ```
> public Pet(String petsName)
> {
> }
> ```
>
> **Exercise 2.22** *Challenge exercise* The following object creation will result in the constructor of the **Date** class being called. Can you write the constructor's header?
>
> ```
> new Date("March", 23, 1861)
> ```
>
> Try to give meaningful names to the parameters.

2.7 Methods

The `TicketMachine` class has four methods: `getPrice`, `getBalance`, `insertMoney`, and `printTicket`. You can see them in the class's source code (Code 2.1) as yellow boxes. We shall start our look at the source code of methods by considering `getPrice` (Code 2.5).

Code 2.5
The `getPrice` method

```
public class TicketMachine
{
    Fields omitted.
    Constructor omitted.
    /**
     * Return the price of a ticket.
     */
    public int getPrice()
    {
        return price;
    }
    Remaining methods omitted.
}
```

Concept

Methods consist of two parts: a header and a body.

Methods have two parts: a *header* and a *body*. Here is the method header for `getPrice`, preceded by a descriptive comment:

```
/**
 * Return the price of a ticket.
 */
public int getPrice()
```

It is important to distinguish between method headers and field declarations, because they can look quite similar. We can tell that `getPrice` is a method and not a field because method headers always include a pair of parentheses—"(" and ")"—and no semicolon at the end of the header.

The method body is the remainder of the method after the header. It is always enclosed by a matching pair of curly brackets: "{" and "}". Method bodies contain the *declarations* and *statements* that define what an object does when that method is called. Declarations are used to create additional, temporary variable space, while statements describe the actions of the method. In `getPrice`, the method body contains a single statement, but we shall soon see examples where the method body consists of many lines of both declarations and statements.

Any set of declarations and statements between a pair of matching curly brackets is known as a *block*. So the body of the `TicketMachine` class, the bodies of the constructor, and all of the methods within the class are blocks.

There are at least two significant differences between the headers of the `TicketMachine` constructor and the `getPrice` method:

```
public TicketMachine(int cost)

public int getPrice()
```

- The method has a *return type* of `int`; the constructor has no return type. A return type is written just before the method name. This is a difference that applies in all cases.
- The constructor has a single formal parameter, `cost`, but the method has none—just a pair of empty parentheses. This is a difference that applies in this particular case.

It is an absolute rule in Java that a constructor may not have a return type. On the other hand, both constructors and methods may have any number of formal parameters, including none.

Within the body of `getPrice` there is a single statement:

```
return price;
```

This is called a *return statement*. It is responsible for returning an integer value to match the `int` return type in the method's header. Where a method contains a return statement, it is always the final statement of that method, because no further statements in the method will be executed once the return statement is executed.

Return types and return statements work together. The `int` return type of `getPrice` is a form of promise that the body of the method will do something that ultimately results in an integer value being calculated and returned as the method's result. You might like to think of a method call as being a form of question to an object, and the return value from the method being the object's answer to that question. In this case, when the `getPrice` method is called on a ticket machine, the question is, What do tickets cost? A ticket machine does not need to perform any calculations to be able to answer that, because it keeps the answer in its `price` field. So the method answers by just returning the value of that variable. As we gradually develop more-complex classes, we shall inevitably encounter more-complex questions that require more work to supply their answers.

2.8 Accessor and mutator methods

We often describe methods such as the two "get" methods of `TicketMachine` (`getPrice` and `getBalance`) as *accessor methods* (or just *accessors*). This is because they return information to the caller about the state of an object; they provide access to information about the object's state. An accessor usually contains a return statement in order to pass back that information.

There is often confusion about what "returning a value" actually means in practice. People often think it means that something is printed by the program. This is not the case at all— we shall see how printing is done when we look at the `printTicket` method. Rather, returning a value means that some information is passed internally between two different parts of the program. One part of the program has requested information from an object via a method call, and the return value is the way the object has of passing that information back to the caller.

The `get` methods of a ticket machine perform similar tasks: returning the value of one of their object's fields. The remaining methods—`insertMoney` and `printTicket`—have a

> **Concept**
>
> **Accessor methods** return information about the state of an object.

2.8 Accessor and mutator methods

Exercise 2.23 Compare the header and body of the `getBalance` method with the header and body of the `getPrice` method. What are the differences between them?

Exercise 2.24 If a call to `getPrice` can be characterized as "What do tickets cost?" how would you characterize a call to `getBalance`?

Exercise 2.25 If the name of `getBalance` is changed to `getAmount`, does the return statement in the body of the method also need to be changed for the code to compile? Try it out within BlueJ. What does this tell you about the name of an accessor method and the name of the field associated with it?

Exercise 2.26 Write an accessor method `getTotal` in the `TicketMachine` class. The new method should return the value of the `total` field.

Exercise 2.27 Try removing the return statement from the body of `getPrice`. What error message do you see now when you try compiling the class?

Exercise 2.28 Compare the method headers of `getPrice` and `printTicket` in Code 2.1. Apart from their names, what is the main difference between them?

Exercise 2.29 Do the `insertMoney` and `printTicket` methods have return statements? Why do you think this might be? Do you notice anything about their headers that might suggest why they do not require return statements?

> **Concept**
>
> **Mutator methods** change the state of an object.

much more significant role, primarily because they *change* the value of one or more fields of a ticket-machine object each time they are called. We call methods that change the state of their object *mutator methods* (or just *mutators*).

In the same way as we think of a call to an accessor as a request for information (a question), we can think of a call to a mutator as a request for an object to change its state. The most basic form of mutator is one that takes a single parameter whose value is used to directly overwrite what is stored in one of an object's fields. In a direct complement to "get" methods, these are often called "set" methods, although the `TicketMachine` does not have any of those, at this stage.

One distinguishing effect of a mutator is that an object will often exhibit slightly different behavior before and after it is called. We can illustrate this with the following exercise.

Exercise 2.30 Create a ticket machine with a ticket price of your choosing. Before doing anything else, call the `getBalance` method on it. Now call the `insertMoney` method (Code 2.6) and give a non-zero positive amount of money as the actual parameter. Now call `getBalance` again. The two calls to `getBalance` should show different outputs, because the call to `insertMoney` had the effect of changing the machine's state via its `balance` field.

The header of `insertMoney` has a `void` return type and a single formal parameter, `amount`, of type `int`. A `void` return type means that the method does not return any value to its caller. This is significantly different from all other return types. Within BlueJ, the difference is most noticeable in that no return-value dialog is shown following a call to a `void` method. Within the body of a `void` method, this difference is reflected in the fact that there is no return statement.[2]

Code 2.6

The **insert-Money** method

```java
/**
 * Receive an amount of money from a customer.
 */
public void insertMoney(int amount)
{
    balance = balance + amount;
}
```

In the body of `insertMoney`, there is a single statement that is another form of assignment statement. We always consider assignment statements by first examining the calculation on the right-hand side of the assignment symbol. Here, its effect is to calculate a value that is the sum of the number in the `amount` parameter and the number in the `balance` field. This combined value is then assigned to the `balance` field. So the effect is to increase the value in `balance` by the value in `amount`.[3]

Exercise 2.31 How can we tell from just its header that `setPrice` is a method and not a constructor?

```java
public void setPrice(int cost)
```

Exercise 2.32 Complete the body of the `setPrice` method so that it assigns the value of its parameter to the `price` field.

Exercise 2.33 Complete the body of the following method, whose purpose is to add the value of its parameter to a field named `score`.

```java
/**
 * Increase score by the given number of points.
 */
public void increase(int points)
{
    ...
}
```

---

[2] In fact, Java does allow `void` methods to contain a special form of return statement in which there is no return value. This takes the form
   `return;`
and simply causes the method to exit without executing any further code.

[3] Adding an amount to the value in a variable is so common that there is a special **compound assignment operator** to do this: +=. For instance:
   `balance += amount;`

Exercise 2.34 Is the `increase` method a mutator? If so, how could you demonstrate this?

Exercise 2.35 Complete the following method, whose purpose is to subtract the value of its parameter from a field named `price`.

```
/**
 * Reduce price by the given amount.
 */
public void discount(int amount)
{
    ...
}
```

2.9 Printing from methods

Code 2.7 shows the most complex method of the class: `printTicket`. To help your understanding of the following discussion, make sure that you have called this method on a ticket machine. You should have seen something like the following printed in the BlueJ terminal window:

```
##################
# The BlueJ Line
# Ticket
# 500 cents.
##################
```

This is the longest method we have seen so far, so we shall break it down into more manageable pieces:

- The header indicates that the method has a `void` return type, and that it takes no parameters.
- The body comprises eight statements plus associated comments.
- The first six statements are responsible for printing what you see in the BlueJ terminal window: five lines of text and a sixth blank line.
- The seventh statement adds the balance inserted by the customer (through previous calls to `insertMoney`) to the running total of all money collected so far by the machine.
- The eighth statement resets the balance to zero with a basic assignment statement, in preparation for the next customer.

Code 2.7

The `print-Ticket` method

```java
/**
 * Print a ticket.
 * Update the total collected and reduce the balance to zero.
 */
public void printTicket()
{
    // Simulate the printing of a ticket.
    System.out.println("##################");
    System.out.println("# The BlueJ Line");
    System.out.println("# Ticket");
    System.out.println("# " + price + " cents.");
    System.out.println("##################");
    System.out.println();

    // Update the total collected with the balance.
    total = total + balance;
    // Clear the balance.
    balance = 0;
}
```

Concept

The method **System.out.println** prints its parameter to the text terminal.

By comparing the output that appears with the statements that produced it, it is easy to see that a statement such as

`System.out.println("# The BlueJ Line");`

literally prints the string that appears between the matching pair of double-quote characters. The basic form of a call to `println` is

`System.out.println(something-we-want-to-print);`

where *something-we-want-to-print* can be replaced by any arbitrary string, enclosed between a pair of double-quote characters. For instance, there is nothing significant in the "#" character that is in the string—it is simply one of the characters we wish to be printed.

All of the printing statements in the `printTicket` method are calls to the `println` method of the `System.out` object that is built into the Java language, and what appears between the round brackets is the parameter to each method call, as you might expect. However, in the fourth statement, the actual parameter to `println` is a little more complicated and requires some more explanation:

`System.out.println("# " + price + " cents.");`

What it does is print out the price of the ticket, with some extra characters on either side of the amount. The two "+" operators are being used to construct a single actual parameter, in the form of a string, from three separate components:

- the string literal: `"# "` (*note the space character after the hash*);
- the value of the `price` field (note that there are no quotes around the field name because we want the field's value, not its name);
- the string literal: `" cents."` (note the space character before the word `"cents"`).

2.9 Printing from methods

When used between a string and anything else, "+" is a string-concatenation operator (i.e., it concatenates or joins strings together to create a new string) rather than an arithmetic-addition operator. So the numeric value of price is converted into a string and joined to its two surrounding strings.

Note that the final call to `println` contains no string parameter. This is allowed, and the result of calling it will be to leave a blank line between this output and any that follows after. You will easily see the blank line if you print a second ticket.

Exercise 2.36 Write down exactly what will be printed by the following statement:

```
System.out.println("My cat has green eyes.");
```

Exercise 2.37 Add a method called `prompt` to the `TicketMachine` class. This should have a `void` return type and take no parameters. The body of the method should print the following single line of output:

```
Please insert the correct amount of money.
```

Exercise 2.38 What do you think would be printed if you altered the fourth statement of `printTicket` so that `price` also has quotes around it, as follows?

```
System.out.println("# " + "price" + " cents.");
```

Exercise 2.39 What about the following version?

```
System.out.println("# price cents.");
```

Exercise 2.40 Could either of the previous two versions be used to show the price of tickets in different ticket machines? Explain your answer.

Exercise 2.41 Add a `showPrice` method to the `TicketMachine` class. This should have a `void` return type and take no parameters. The body of the method should print:

```
The price of a ticket is xyz cents.
```

where *xyz* should be replaced by the value held in the `price` field when the method is called.

Exercise 2.42 Create two ticket machines with differently priced tickets. Do calls to their `showPrice` methods show the same output, or different? How do you explain this effect?

2.10 Method summary

It is worth summarizing a few features of methods at this point, because methods are fundamental to the programs we will be writing and exploring in this book. They implement the core actions of every object.

A method with parameters will receive data passed to it from the method's caller, and will then use that data to help it perform a particular task. However, not all methods take parameters; many simply use the data stored in the object's fields to carry out their task.

If a method has a non-`void` return type, it will return some data to the place it was called from—and that data will almost certainly be used in the caller for further calculations or program manipulations. Many methods, though, have a `void` return type and return nothing, but they still perform a useful task within the context of their object.

Accessor methods have non-`void` return types and return information about the object's state. Mutator methods modify an object's state. Mutators often take parameters whose values are used in the modification, although it is still possible to write a mutating method that does not take parameters.

2.11 Summary of the naïve ticket machine

We have now examined the internal structure of the naïve `TicketMachine` class in some detail. We have seen that the class has a small outer layer that gives a name to the class, and a more substantial inner body containing fields, a constructor, and several methods. Fields are used to store data that enable objects to maintain a state that persists between method calls. Constructors are used to set up an initial state when an object is created. Having a proper initial state will enable an object to respond appropriately to method calls immediately following its creation. Methods implement the defined behavior of the class's objects. Accessor methods provide information about an object's state, and mutator methods change an object's state.

We have seen that constructors are distinguished from methods by having the same name as the class in which they are defined. Both constructors and methods may take parameters, but only methods may have a return type. Non-`void` return types allow us to pass a value out of a method to the place where the method was called from. A method with a non-`void` return type must have at least one return statement in its body; this will often be the final statement. Constructors never have a return type of any sort—not even `void`.

> Before attempting these exercises, be sure that you have a good understanding of how ticket machines behave and how that behavior is implemented through the fields, constructor, and methods of the class.
>
> **Exercise 2.43** Modify the constructor of `TicketMachine` so that it no longer has a parameter. Instead, the price of tickets should be fixed at 1,000 cents. What effect does this have when you construct ticket-machine objects within BlueJ?

Exercise 2.44 Give the class two constructors. One should take a single parameter that specifies the price, and the other should take no parameter and set the price to be a default value of your choosing. Test your implementation by creating machines via the two different constructors.

Exercise 2.45 Implement a method, `empty`, that simulates the effect of removing all money from the machine. This method should have a `void` return type, and its body should simply set the `total` field to zero. Does this method need to take any parameters? Test your method by creating a machine, inserting some money, printing some tickets, checking the total, and then emptying the machine. Is the `empty` method a mutator or an accessor?

2.12 Reflecting on the design of the ticket machine

From our study of the internals of the `TicketMachine` class, you should have come to appreciate how inadequate it would be in the real world. It is deficient in several ways:

- It contains no check that the customer has entered enough money to pay for a ticket.
- It does not refund any money if the customer pays too much for a ticket.
- It does not check to ensure that the customer inserts sensible amounts of money. Experiment with what happens if a negative amount is entered, for instance.
- It does not check that the ticket price passed to its constructor is sensible.

If we could remedy these problems, then we would have a much more functional piece of software that might serve as the basis for operating a real-world ticket machine.

In the next few sections, we shall examine the implementation of an improved ticket machine class that attempts to deal with some of the inadequacies of the naïve implementation. Open the *better-ticket-machine* project. As before, this project contains a single class: `TicketMachine`. Before looking at the internal details of the class, experiment with it by creating some instances and see whether you notice any differences in behavior between this version and the previous naïve version.

One specific difference is that the new version has an additional method, `refundBalance`. Take a look at what happens when you call it.

Code 2.8
A more sophisticated `TicketMachine`

```
/**
 * TicketMachine models a ticket machine that issues
 * flat-fare tickets.
 * The price of a ticket is specified via the constructor.
 * Instances will check to ensure that a user only enters
 * sensible amounts of money, and will only print a ticket
 * if enough money has been input.
 *
```

Code 2.8 continued

A more sophisticated `TicketMachine`

```java
 * @author David J. Barnes and Michael Kölling
 * @version 2016.02.29
 */
public class TicketMachine
{
    // The price of a ticket from this machine.
    private int price;
    // The amount of money entered by a customer so far.
    private int balance;
    // The total amount of money collected by this machine.
    private int total;

    /**
     * Create a machine that issues tickets of the given price.
     */
    public TicketMachine(int cost)
    {
        price = cost;
        balance = 0;
        total = 0;
    }

    /**
     * @Return The price of a ticket.
     */
    public int getPrice()
    {
        return price;
    }

    /**
     * Return The amount of money already inserted for the
     * next ticket.
     */
    public int getBalance()
    {
        return balance;
    }

    /**
     * Receive an amount of money from a customer.
     * Check that the amount is sensible.
     */
    public void insertMoney(int amount)
    {
        if(amount > 0) {
            balance = balance + amount;
        }
        else {
            System.out.println("Use a positive amount rather than: " +
                                amount);
        }
    }
}
```

Code 2.8 continued
A more sophisticated TicketMachine

```java
    /**
     * Print a ticket if enough money has been inserted, and
     * reduce the current balance by the ticket price. Print
     * an error message if more money is required.
     */
    public void printTicket()
    {
        if(balance >= price) {
            // Simulate the printing of a ticket.
            System.out.println("##################");
            System.out.println("# The BlueJ Line");
            System.out.println("# Ticket");
            System.out.println("# " + price + " cents.");
            System.out.println("##################");
            System.out.println();

            // Update the total collected with the price.
            total = total + price;
            // Reduce the balance by the price.
            balance = balance - price;
        }
        else {
            System.out.println("You must insert at least: " +
                              (price - balance) + " more cents.");
        }
    }

    /**
     * Return the money in the balance.
     * The balance is cleared.
     */
    public int refundBalance()
    {
        int amountToRefund;
        amountToRefund = balance;
        balance = 0;
        return amountToRefund;
    }
}
```

2.13 Making choices: the conditional statement

Code 2.8 shows the internal details of the better ticket machine's class definition. Much of this definition will already be familiar to you from our discussion of the naïve ticket machine. For instance, the outer wrapping that names the class is the same, because we have chosen to give this class the same name. In addition, it contains the same three fields to maintain object state, and these have been declared in the same way. The constructor and the two **get** methods are also the same as before.

The first significant change can be seen in the **insertMoney** method. We recognized that the main problem with the naïve ticket machine was its failure to check certain conditions. One of those missing checks was on the amount of money inserted by a customer, as it was possible for a negative amount of money to be inserted. We have remedied that failing by making use of a *conditional statement* to check that the amount inserted has a value greater than zero:

```
if(amount > 0) {
    balance = balance + amount;
}
else {
    System.out.println("Use a positive amount rather than: " +
                            amount);
}
```

> **Concept**
>
> A **conditional statement** takes one of two possible actions based upon the result of a test.

Conditional statements are also known as *if-statements*, from the keyword used in most programming languages to introduce them. A conditional statement allows us to take one of two possible actions based upon the result of a check or test. If the test is true, then we do one thing; otherwise, we do something different. This kind of either/or decision should be familiar from situations in everyday life: for instance, if I have enough money left, then I shall go out for a meal; otherwise, I shall stay home and watch a movie. A conditional statement has the general form described in the following *pseudo-code*:

```
if(perform some test that gives a true or false result) {
    Do the statements here if the test gave a true result
}
else {
    Do the statements here if the test gave a false result
}
```

Certain parts of this pseudo-code are proper bits of Java, and those will appear in almost all conditional statements–the keywords `if` and `else`, the round brackets around the test, and the curly brackets marking the two blocks–while the other three italicized parts will be fleshed out differently for each particular situation being coded.

Only one of the two blocks of statements following the test will ever be performed following the evaluation of the test. So, in the example from the `insertMoney` method, following the test of an inserted amount we shall only either add the amount to the balance or print the error message. The test uses the *greater-than operator*, ">", to compare the value in **amount** against zero. If the value is greater than zero, then it is added to the balance. If it is not greater than zero, then an error message is printed. By using a conditional statement, we have, in effect, protected the change to **balance** in the case where the parameter does not represent a valid amount. Details of other Java operators can be found in Appendix C. The obvious ones to mention at this point are "<" (less-than), "<=" (less-than or equal-to), and ">=" (greater-than or equal-to). All are used to compare two numeric values, as in the `printTicket` method.

> **Concept**
>
> **Boolean expressions** have only two possible values: true and false. They are commonly found controlling the choice between the two paths through a conditional statement.

The test used in a conditional statement is an example of a *boolean expression*. Earlier in this chapter, we introduced arithmetic expressions that produced numerical results. A boolean expression has only two possible values (**true** or **false**): the value of **amount** is either greater than zero (**true**) or it is not greater (**false**). A conditional statement makes use of those two possible values to choose between two different actions.

Exercise 2.46 Check that the behavior we have discussed here is accurate by creating a `TicketMachine` instance and calling `insertMoney` with various actual parameter values. Check the balance both before and after calling `insertMoney`. Does the balance ever change in the cases when an error message is printed? Try to predict what will happen if you enter the value zero as the parameter, and then see if you are right.

Exercise 2.47 Predict what you think will happen if you change the test in `insertMoney` to use the *greater-than or equal-to operator*:

```
if(amount >= 0)
```

Check your predictions by running some tests. What is the one situation in which it makes a difference to the behavior of the method?

Exercise 2.48 Rewrite the if-else statement so that the method still behaves correctly but the error message is printed if the boolean expression is true but the balance is increased if the expression is false. You will obviously have to rewrite the condition to make things happen this way around.

Exercise 2.49 In the *figures* project we looked at in Chapter 1 we used a `boolean` field to control a feature of the circle objects. What was that feature? Was it well suited to being controlled by a type with only two different values?

2.14 A further conditional-statement example

The `printTicket` method contains a further example of a conditional statement. Here it is in outline:

```
if(balance >= price) {
    Printing details omitted.
    // Update the total collected with the price.
    total = total + price;
    // Reduce the balance by the price.
    balance = balance - price;
}
else {
    System.out.println("You must insert at least: " +
                       (price - balance) + " more cents.");
}
```

With this if-statement, we fix the problem that the naïve version makes no check that a customer has inserted enough money for a ticket before printing. This version checks that the value in the `balance` field is at least as large as the value in the `price` field. If it is, then it is okay to print a ticket. If it is not, then we print an error message instead.

The printing of the error message follows exactly the same pattern as we saw for printing the price of tickets in the `printTicket` method; it is just a little more verbose.

```
System.out.println("You must insert at least: " +
                   (price - balance) + " more cents.");
```

The single actual parameter to the `println` method consists of a concatenation of three elements: two string literals on either side of a numeric value. In this case, the numeric value is a subtraction that has been placed in parentheses to indicate that it is the resulting value we wish to concatenate with the two strings.

> **Exercise 2.50** In this version of `printTicket`, we also do something slightly different with the `total` and `balance` fields. Compare the implementation of the method in Code 2.1 with that in Code 2.8 to see whether you can tell what those differences are. Then check your understanding by experimenting within BlueJ.
>
> **Exercise 2.51** Is it possible to remove the else part of the if-statement in the `printTicket` method (i.e., remove the word `else` and the block attached to it)? Try doing this and seeing if the code still compiles. What happens now if you try to print a ticket without inserting any money?

The `printTicket` method reduces the value of `balance` by the value of `price`. As a consequence, if a customer inserts more money than the price of the ticket, then some money will be left in the balance that could be used toward the price of a second ticket. Alternatively, the customer could ask to be refunded the remaining balance, and that is what the `refundBalance` method does, as we shall see in section 2.16.

2.15 Scope highlighting

You will have noticed by now that the BlueJ editor displays source code with some additional decoration: colored boxes around some elements, such as methods and if-statements (see, for example, Code 2.8).

These colored annotations are known as *scope highlighting*, and they help clarify logical units of your program. A *scope* (also called a *block*) is a unit of code usually indicated by a pair of curly brackets. The whole body of a class is a scope, as is the body of each method and the *if* and *else* parts of an if-statement.

As you can see, scopes are often nested: the if-statement is inside a method, which is inside a class. BlueJ helps by distinguishing different kinds of scopes with different colors.

One of the most common errors in the code of beginning programmers is getting the curly brackets wrong—either by having them in the wrong place, or by having a bracket missing altogether. Two things can greatly help in avoiding this kind of error:

- Pay attention to proper indentation of your code. Every time a new scope starts (after an open curly bracket), indent the following code one level more. Closing the scope brings the indentation back. If your indentation is completely out, use BlueJ's "Auto-layout" function (find it in the editor menu!) to fix it.

- Pay attention to the scope highlighting. You will quickly get used to the way well-structured code looks. Try removing a curly bracket in the editor or adding one at an arbitrary location, and observe how the coloring changes. Get used to recognizing when scopes look wrong.

Exercise 2.52 After a ticket has been printed, could the value in the **balance** field ever be set to a negative value by subtracting **price** from it? Justify your answer.

Exercise 2.53 So far, we have introduced you to two arithmetic operators, **+** and **-**, that can be used in arithmetic expressions in Java. Take a look at Appendix C to find out what other operators are available.

Exercise 2.54 Write an assignment statement that will store the result of multiplying two variables, **price** and **discount**, into a third variable, **saving**.

Exercise 2.55 Write an assignment statement that will divide the value in **total** by the value in **count** and store the result in **mean**.

Exercise 2.56 Write an if-statement that will compare the value in **price** against the value in **budget**. If **price** is greater than **budget**, then print the message "Too expensive"; otherwise print the message "Just right".

Exercise 2.57 Modify your answer to the previous exercise so that the message includes the value of your budget if the price is too high.

2.16 Local variables

So far, we have encountered two different sorts of variables: fields (instance variables) and parameters. We are now going to introduce a third kind. All have in common that they store data, but each sort of variable has a particular role to play.

Section 2.7 noted that a method body (or, in general, a *block*) can contain both declarations and statements. To this point, none of the methods we have looked at contain any declarations. The **refundBalance** method contains three statements and a single declaration. The declaration introduces a new kind of variable:

```
public int refundBalance()
{
    int amountToRefund;
    amountToRefund = balance;
    balance = 0;
    return amountToRefund;
}
```

What sort of variable is **amountToRefund**? We know that it is not a field, because fields are defined outside methods. It is also not a parameter, as those are always defined in the method header. The **amountToRefund** variable is what is known as a *local variable*, because it is defined *inside* a method body.

Local variable declarations look similar to field declarations, but they never have **private** or **public** as part of them. Constructors can also have local variables. Like formal parameters, local variables have a scope that is limited to the statements of the method to which they belong. Their lifetime is the time of the method execution: they are created when a method is called and destroyed when a method finishes.

> **Concept**
>
> A **local variable** is a variable declared and used within a single method. Its scope and lifetime are limited to that of the method.

You might wonder why there is a need for local variables if we have fields. Local variables are primarily used as temporary storage, to help a single method complete its task; we think of them as data storage for a single method. In contrast, fields are used to store data that persists through the life of a whole object. The data stored in fields is accessible to all of the object's methods. We try to avoid declaring as fields variables that really only have a local (method-level) usage, whose values don't have to be retained beyond a single method call. So even if two or more methods in the same class use local variables for a similar purpose, it is not appropriate to define them as fields if their values don't need to persist beyond the end of the methods.

In the **refundBalance** method, **amountToRefund** is used briefly to hold the value of the **balance** immediately prior to the latter being set to zero. The method then returns the remembered value of the balance. The following exercises will help to illustrate why a local variable is needed here, as we try to write the **refundBalance** method without one.

It is quite common to initialize local variables within their declaration. So we could abbreviate the first two statements of **refundBalance** as

```
int amountToRefund = balance;
```

but it is still important to keep in mind that there are two steps going on here: declaring the variable **amountToRefund**, and giving it an initial value.

> **Pitfall** A local variable of the same name as a field will prevent the field being accessed from within a constructor or method. See Section 3.13.2 for a way around this when necessary.

Exercise 2.58 Why does the following version of **refundBalance** not give the same results as the original?

```
public int refundBalance()
{
    balance = 0;
    return balance;
}
```

What tests can you run to demonstrate that it does not?

Exercise 2.59 What happens if you try to compile the `TicketMachine` class with the following version of `refundBalance`?

```
public int refundBalance()
{
    return balance;
    balance = 0;
}
```

What do you know about return statements that helps to explain why this version does not compile?

Exercise 2.60 What is wrong with the following version of the constructor of `TicketMachine`?

```
public TicketMachine(int cost)
{
    int price = cost;
    balance = 0;
    total = 0;
}
```

Try out this version in the *better-ticket-machine* project. Does this version compile? Create an object and then inspect its fields. Do you notice something wrong about the value of the `price` field in the inspector with this version? Can you explain why this is?

2.17 Fields, parameters, and local variables

With the introduction of `amountToRefund` in the `refundBalance` method, we have now seen three different kinds of variables: fields, formal parameters, and local variables. It is important to understand the similarities and differences between these three kinds. Here is a summary of their features:

- All three kinds of variables are able to store a value that is appropriate to their defined types. For instance, a defined type of `int` allows a variable to store an integer value.
- Fields are defined outside constructors and methods.
- Fields are used to store data that persist throughout the life of an object. As such, they maintain the current state of an object. They have a lifetime that lasts as long as their object lasts.
- Fields have class scope: they are accessible throughout the whole class, so they can be used within any of the constructors or methods of the class in which they are defined.

- As long as they are defined as `private`, fields cannot be accessed from anywhere outside their defining class.

- Formal parameters and local variables persist only for the period that a constructor or method executes. Their lifetime is only as long as a single call, so their values are lost between calls. As such, they act as temporary rather than permanent storage locations.

- Formal parameters are defined in the header of a constructor or method. They receive their values from outside, being initialized by the actual parameter values that form part of the constructor or method call.

- Formal parameters have a scope that is limited to their defining constructor or method.

- Local variables are defined inside the body of a constructor or method. They can be initialized and used only within the body of their defining constructor or method. Local variables must be initialized before they are used in an expression—they are not given a default value.

- Local variables have a scope that is limited to the block in which they are defined. They are not accessible from anywhere outside that block.

New programmers often find it difficult to work out whether a variable should be defined as a field or as a local variable. Temptation is to define all variables as fields, because they can be accessed from anywhere in the class. In fact, the opposite approach is a much better rule to adopt: define variables local to a method unless they are clearly a genuine part of an object's persistent state. Even if you anticipate using the same variable in two or more methods, define a separate version locally to each method until you are absolutely sure that persistence between method calls is justified.

Exercise 2.61 Add a new method, `emptyMachine`, that is designed to simulate emptying the machine of money. It should reset `total` to be zero, but also return the value that was stored in `total` before it was reset.

Exercise 2.62 Rewrite the `printTicket` method so that it declares a local variable, `amountLeftToPay`. This should then be initialized to contain the difference between `price` and `balance`. Rewrite the test in the conditional statement to check the value of `amountLeftToPay`. If its value is less than or equal to zero, a ticket should be printed; otherwise, an error message should be printed stating the amount left to pay. Test your version to ensure that it behaves in exactly the same way as the original version. Make sure that you call the method more than once, when the machine is in different states, so that both parts of the conditional statement will be executed on separate occasions.

Exercise 2.63 *Challenge exercise* Suppose we wished a single `TicketMachine` object to be able to issue tickets of different prices. For instance, users might press a button on the physical machine to select a discounted ticket price. What further methods and/or fields would need to be added to `TicketMachine` to allow this kind of functionality? Do you think that many of the existing methods would need to be changed as well?

Save the *better-ticket-machine* project under a new name, and implement your changes in the new project.

2.18 Summary of the better ticket machine

In developing a better version of the `TicketMachine` class, we have been able to address the major inadequacies of the naïve version. In doing so, we have introduced two new language constructs: the conditional statement and local variables.

- A conditional statement gives us a means to perform a test and then, on the basis of the result of that test, perform one or the other of two distinct actions.

- Local variables allow us to calculate and store temporary values within a constructor or method. They contribute to the behavior that their defining method implements, but their values are lost once that constructor or method finishes its execution.

You can find more details of conditional statements and the form their tests can take in Appendix D.

2.19 Self-review exercises

This chapter has covered a lot of new ground, and we have introduced a lot of new concepts. We will be building on these in future chapters, so it is important that you are comfortable with them. Try the following pencil-and-paper exercises as a way of checking that you are becoming used to the terminology that we have introduced in this chapter. Don't be put off by the fact that we suggest that you do these on paper rather than within BlueJ. It will be good practice to try things out without a compiler.

Exercise 2.64 List the name and return type of this method:

```
public String getCode()
{
    return code;
}
```

Exercise 2.65 List the name of this method and the name and type of its parameter:

```
public void setCredits(int creditValue)
{
    credits = creditValue;
}
```

Exercise 2.66 Write out the outer wrapping of a class called **Person**. Remember to include the curly brackets that mark the start and end of the class body, but otherwise leave the body empty.

Exercise 2.67 Write out definitions for the following fields:

- a field called **name** of type **String**
- a field of type **int** called **age**
- a field of type **String** called **code**
- a field called **credits** of type **int**

Exercise 2.68 Write out a constructor for a class called **Module**. The constructor should take a single parameter of type **String** called **moduleCode**. The body of the constructor should assign the value of its parameter to a field called **code**. You don't have to include the definition for **code**, just the text of the constructor.

Exercise 2.69 Write out a constructor for a class called **Person**. The constructor should take two parameters. The first is of type **String** and is called **myName**. The second is of type **int** and is called **myAge**. The first parameter should be used to set the value of a field called **name**, and the second should set a field called **age**. You don't have to include the definitions for the fields, just the text of the constructor.

Exercise 2.70 Correct the error in this method:

```
public void getAge()
{
    return age;
}
```

Exercise 2.71 Write an accessor method called **getName** that returns the value of a field called **name**, whose type is **String**.

Exercise 2.72 Write a mutator method called `setAge` that takes a single parameter of type `int` and sets the value of a field called `age`.

Exercise 2.73 Write a method called `printDetails` for a class that has a field of type `String` called `name`. The `printDetails` method should print out a string of the form "The name of this person is", followed by the value of the `name` field. For instance, if the value of the `name` field is "Helen", then `printDetails` would print:

```
The name of this person is Helen
```

If you have managed to complete most or all of these exercises, then you might like to try creating a new project in BlueJ and making up your own class definition for a **Person**. The class could have fields to record the name and age of a person, for instance. If you were unsure how to complete any of the previous exercises, look back over earlier sections in this chapter and the source code of **TicketMachine** to revise what you were unclear about. In the next section, we provide some further review material.

2.20 Reviewing a familiar example

By this point in the chapter, you have met a lot of new concepts. To help reinforce them, we shall now revisit a few in a different but familiar context. Along the way, though, watch out for one or two further new concepts that we will then cover in more detail in later chapters!

Open the *lab-classes* project that we introduced in Chapter 1, and then examine the **Student** class in the editor (Code 2.9).

Code 2.9
The **Student** class

```java
/**
 * The Student class represents a student in a student administration system.
 * It holds the student details relevant in our context.
 *
 * @author Michael Kölling and David Barnes
 * @version 2016.02.29
 */
public class Student
{
    // the student's full name
    private String name;
    // the student ID
    private String id;
    // the amount of credits for study taken so far
    private int credits;
```

Code 2.9 continued
The `Student` class

```java
/**
 * Create a new student with a given name and ID number.
 */
public Student(String fullName, String studentID)
{
    name = fullName;
    id = studentID;
    credits = 0;
}

/**
 * Return the full name of this student.
 */
public String getName()
{
    return name;
}

/**
 * Set a new name for this student.
 */
public void changeName(String replacementName)
{
    name = replacementName;
}

/**
 * Return the student ID of this student.
 */
public String getStudentID()
{
    return id;
}

/**
 * Add some credit points to the student's accumulated credits.
 */
public void addCredits(int additionalPoints)
{
    credits += additionalPoints;
}

/**
 * Return the number of credit points this student has accumulated.
 */
public int getCredits()
{
    return credits;
}

/**
 * Return the login name of this student. The login name is a combination
 * of the first four characters of the student's name and the first three
 * characters of the student's ID number.
 */
```

Code 2.9 continued
The **Student** class

```java
    public String getLoginName()
    {
        return name.substring(0,4) + id.substring(0,3);
    }

    /**
     * Print the student's name and ID number to the output terminal.
     */
    public void print()
    {
        System.out.println(name + ", student ID: " + id + ", credits: " + credits);
    }
}
```

In this small example, the pieces of information we wish to store for a student are their name, their student ID, and the number of course credits they have obtained so far. All of this information is persistent during their time as a student, even if some of it changes during that time (the number of credits). We want to store this information in fields, therefore, to represent each student's state.

The class contains three fields: **name**, **id**, and **credits**. Each of these is initialized in the single constructor. The initial values of the first two are set from parameter values passed into the constructor. Each of the fields has an associated **get** accessor method, but only **name** and **credits** have associated mutator methods. This means that the value of an **id** field remains fixed once the object has been constructed. If a field's value cannot be changed once initialized, we say that it is *immutable*. Sometimes we make the complete state of an object immutable once it has been constructed; the **String** class is an important example of this.

2.21 Calling methods

The **getLoginName** method illustrates a new feature that is worth exploring:

```java
public String getLoginName()
{
    return name.substring(0,4) +
            id.substring(0,3);
}
```

We are seeing two things in action here:

- Calling a method on another object, where the method returns a result.
- Using the value returned as a result as part of an expression.

Both **name** and **id** are **String** objects, and the **String** class has a method, **substring**, with the following header:

```java
/**
 * Return a new string containing the characters from
 * beginIndex to (endIndex-1) from this string.
 */
public String substring(int beginIndex, int endIndex)
```

An index value of zero represents the first character of a string, so **getLoginName** takes the first four characters of the **name** string and the first three characters of the **id** string, then concatenates them together to form a new string. This new string is returned as the method's result. For instance, if **name** is the string **"Leonardo da Vinci"** and **id** is the string **"468366"**, then the string **"Leon468"** would be returned by this method.

We will learn more about method calling between objects in Chapter 3.

Exercise 2.74 Draw a picture of the form shown in Figure 2.3, representing the initial state of a **Student** object following its construction, with the following actual parameter values:

```
new Student("Benjamin Jonson", "738321")
```

Exercise 2.75 What would be returned by **getLoginName** for a student with name **"Henry Moore"** and **id** **"557214"**?

Exercise 2.76 Create a **Student** with name **"djb"** and **id** **"859012"**. What happens when **getLoginName** is called on this student? Why do you think this is?

Exercise 2.77 The **String** class defines a **length** accessor method with the following header:

```
/**
 * Return the number of characters in this string.
 */
public int length()
```

so the following is an example of its use with the **String** variable **fullName**:

```
fullName.length()
```

Add conditional statements to the constructor of **Student** to print an error message if either the length of the **fullName** parameter is less than four characters, or the length of the **studentId** parameter is less than three characters. However, the constructor should still use those parameters to set the **name** and **id** fields, even if the error message is printed. *Hint:* Use if-statements of the following form (that is, having no **else** part) to print the error messages.

```
if(perform a test on one of the parameters) {
    Print an error message if the test gave a true result
}
```

See Appendix D for further details of the different types of if-statements, if necessary.

Exercise 2.78 *Challenge exercise* Modify the **getLoginName** method of **Student** so that it always generates a login name, even if either the **name** or the **id** field is not strictly long enough. For strings shorter than the required length, use the whole string.

2.22 Experimenting with expressions: the Code Pad

In the previous sections, we have seen various expressions to achieve various computations, such as the **total + price** calculation in the ticket machine and the **name.substring(0,4)** expression in the **Student** class.

In the remainder of this book, we shall encounter many more such operations, sometimes written with operator symbols (such as "+") and sometimes written as method calls (such as **substring**). When we encounter new operators and methods, it often helps to try out with different examples what they do.

The Code Pad, which we briefly used in Chapter 1, can help us experiment with Java expressions (Figure 2.5). Here, we can type in expressions, which will then be immediately evaluated and the results displayed. This is very helpful for trying out new operators and methods.

Exercise 2.79 Consider the following expressions. Try to predict their results, and then type them in the Code Pad to check your answers.

```
99 + 3
"cat" + "fish"
"cat" + 9
9 + 3 + "cat"
"cat" + 3 + 9
"catfish".substring(3,4)
"catfish".substring(3,8)
```

Did you learn anything you did not expect from the exercise? If so, what was it?

Figure 2.5
The BlueJ Code Pad

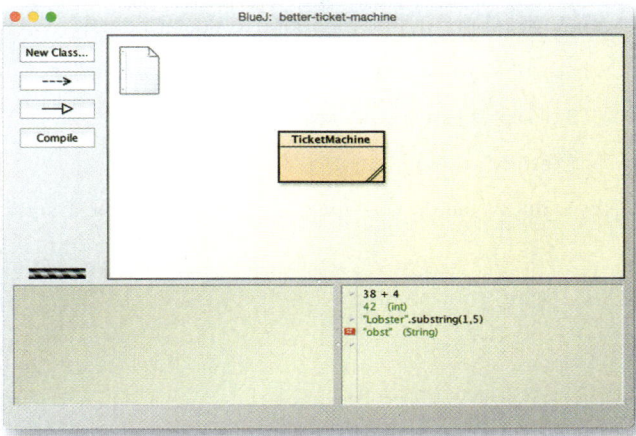

When the result of an expression in the Code Pad is an object (such as a **String**), it will be marked with a small red object symbol next to the line showing the result. You can double-click this symbol to inspect it or drag it onto the object bench for further use. You can also declare variables and write complete statements in the Code Pad.

Whenever you encounter new operators and method calls, it is a good idea to try them out here to get a feel for their behavior.

You can also explore the use of variables in the Code Pad. Try the following:

```
sum = 99 + 3;
```

You will see the following error message:

```
Error: cannot find symbol - variable sum
```

This is because Java requires that every variable (**sum**, in this case) be given a type before it can be used. Recall that every time a field, parameter, or local variable has been introduced for the first time in the source, it has had a type name in front of it, such as **int** or **String**. In light of this, now try the following in the Code Pad:

```
int sum = 0;
```

```
sum = 99 + 3;
```

This time there is no complaint, because **sum** has been introduced with a type and can be used without repeating the type thereafter. If you then type

```
sum
```

on a line by itself (with no semicolon), you will see the value it currently stores.

Now try this in the Code Pad:

```
String swimmer = "cat" + "fish";
```

```
swimmer
```

One again, we have given an appropriate type to the variable **swimmer**, allowing us to make an assignment to it and find out what it stores. This time we chose to set it to the value we wanted at the same time as declaring it.

What would you expect to see after the following?

```
String fish = swimmer;
```

```
fish
```

Try it out. What do you think has happened in the assignment?

Exercise 2.80 Open the Code Pad in the *better-ticket-machine* project. Type the following in the Code Pad:

```
TicketMachine t1 = new TicketMachine(1000);
t1.getBalance()
t1.insertMoney(500);
t1.getBalance()
```

Take care to type these lines exactly as they appear here; pay particular attention to whether or not there is a semicolon at the end of the line. Note what the calls to **getBalance** return in each case.

Exercise 2.81 Now add the following in the Code Pad:

```
TicketMachine t2 = t1;
```

What would you expect a call to **t2.getBalance()** to return? Try it out.

Exercise 2.82 Add the following:

```
t1.insertMoney(500);
```

What would you expect the following to return? Think carefully about this before you try it, and be sure to use the **t2** variable this time.

```
t2.getBalance()
```

Did you get the answer you expected? Can you find a connection between the variables **t1** and **t2** that would explain what is happening?

2.23 Summary

In this chapter, we have covered the basics of how to create a class definition. Classes contain fields, constructors, and methods that define the state and behavior of objects. Within the body of a constructor or method, a sequence of statements implements that part of its behavior. Local variables can be used as temporary data storage to assist with that. We have covered assignment statements and conditional statements, and will be adding further types of statements in later chapters.

Terms introduced in this chapter:

field, instance variable, constructor, method, method header, method body, actual parameter, formal parameter, accessor, mutator, declaration, initialization, block, statement, assignment statement, conditional statement, return statement, return type, comment, expression, operator, variable, local variable, scope, lifetime

The following exercises are designed to help you experiment with the concepts of Java that we have discussed in this chapter. You will create your own classes that contain elements such as fields, constructors, methods, assignment statements, and conditional statements.

Exercise 2.83

Below is the outline for a **Book** class, which can be found in the *book-exercise* project. The outline already defines two fields and a constructor to initialize the fields. In this and the next few exercises, you will add features to the class outline.

Add two accessor methods to the class—**getAuthor** and **getTitle**—that return the **author** and **title** fields as their respective results. Test your class by creating some instances and calling the methods.

```
/**
 * A class that maintains information on a book.
 * This might form part of a larger application such
 * as a library system, for instance.
 *
 * @author (Insert your name here.)
 * @version (Insert today's date here.)
 */
public class Book
{
    // The fields.
    private String author;
    private String title;

    /**
     * Set the author and title fields when this object
     * is constructed.
     */
    public Book(String bookAuthor, String bookTitle)
    {
        author = bookAuthor;
        title = bookTitle;
    }

    // Add the methods here...
}
```

Exercise 2.84 Add two methods, **printAuthor** and **printTitle**, to the outline **Book** class. These should print the **author** and **title** fields, respectively, to the terminal window.

Exercise 2.85 Add a field, **pages**, to the **Book** class to store the number of pages. This should be of type **int**, and its initial value should be passed to the single constructor, along with the **author** and **title** strings. Include an appropriate **getPages** accessor method for this field.

Exercise 2.86 Are the **Book** objects you have implemented immutable? Justify your answer.

Exercise 2.87 Add a method, `printDetails`, to the **Book** class. This should print details of the author, title, and pages to the terminal window. It is your choice how the details are formatted. For instance, all three items could be printed on a single line, or each could be printed on a separate line. You might also choose to include some explanatory text to help a user work out which is the author and which is the title, for example

```
Title: Robinson Crusoe, Author: Daniel Defoe, Pages: 232
```

Exercise 2.88 Add a further field, `refNumber`, to the **Book** class. This field can store a reference number for a library, for example. It should be of type **String** and initialized to the zero length string (`""`) in the constructor, as its initial value is not passed in a parameter to the constructor. Instead, define a mutator for it with the following header:

```
public void setRefNumber(String ref)
```

The body of this method should assign the value of the parameter to the `refNumber` field. Add a corresponding `getRefNumber` accessor to help you check that the mutator works correctly.

Exercise 2.89 Modify your `printDetails` method to include printing the reference number. However, the method should print the reference number only if it has been set—that is, if the `refNumber` string has a non-zero length. If it has not been set, then print the string `"ZZZ"` instead. *Hint:* Use a conditional statement whose test calls the `length` method on the `refNumber` string.

Exercise 2.90 Modify your `setRefNumber` mutator so that it sets the `refNumber` field only if the parameter is a string of at least three characters. If it is less than three, then print an error message and leave the field unchanged.

Exercise 2.91 Add a further integer field, `borrowed`, to the **Book** class. This keeps a count of the number of times a book has been borrowed. Add a mutator, `borrow`, to the class. This should update the field by 1 each time it is called. Include an accessor, `getBorrowed`, that returns the value of this new field as its result. Modify `printDetails` so that it includes the value of this field with an explanatory piece of text.

Exercise 2.92 Add a further **boolean** field, `courseText`, to the **Book** class. This records whether or not a book is being used as a text book on a course. The field should be set through a parameter to the constructor, and the field is immutable. Provide an accessor method for it called `isCourseText`.

Exercise 2.93 *Challenge exercise* Create a new project, *heater-exercise*, within BlueJ. Edit the details in the project description—the text note you see in the diagram. Create a class, **Heater**, that contains a single field, **temperature** whose type is *double-precision floating point*—see Appendix B, Section B.1, for the Java type name that corresponds to this description. Define a constructor that takes no parameters. The **temperature** field should be set to the value 15.0 in the constructor. Define the mutators **warmer** and **cooler**, whose effect is to increase or decrease the value of temperature by 5.0° respectively. Define an accessor method to return the value of **temperature**.

Exercise 2.94 *Challenge exercise* Modify your **Heater** class to define three new *double-precision floating point* fields: **min**, **max**, and **increment**. The values of **min** and **max** should be set by parameters passed to the constructor. The value of **increment** should be set to 5.0 in the constructor. Modify the definitions of **warmer** and **cooler** so that they use the value of **increment** rather than an explicit value of 5.0. Before proceeding further with this exercise, check that everything works as before.

Now modify the **warmer** method so that it will not allow the temperature to be set to a value greater than **max**. Similarly modify **cooler** so that it will not allow **temperature** to be set to a value less than **min**. Check that the class works properly. Now add a method, **setIncrement**, that takes a single parameter of the appropriate type and uses it to set the value of **increment**. Once again, test that the class works as you would expect it to by creating some **Heater** objects within BlueJ. Do things still work as expected if a negative value is passed to the **setIncrement** method? Add a check to this method to prevent a negative value from being assigned to **increment**.

CHAPTER 3
Object Interaction

Main concepts discussed in this chapter:

- abstraction
- modularization
- object creation
- object diagrams
- method calls
- debuggers

Java constructs discussed in this chapter:

class types, logic operators (**&&**, **||**), string concatenation, modulo operator (**%**), object construction (**new**), method calls (dot notation), **this**

In the previous chapters, we have examined what objects are and how they are implemented. In particular, we discussed fields, constructors, and methods when we looked at class definitions.

We shall now go one step further. To construct interesting applications, it is not enough to build individual working objects. Instead, objects must be combined so that they cooperate to perform a common task. In this chapter, we shall build a small application from three objects and arrange for methods to call other methods to achieve their goal.

3.1 The clock example

The project we shall use to discuss interaction of objects is a display for a digital clock. The display shows hours and minutes, separated by a colon (Figure 3.1). For this exercise, we shall first build a clock with a European-style 24-hour display. Thus, the display shows the time from 00:00 (midnight) to 23:59 (one minute before midnight). It turns out on closer inspection that building a 12-hour clock is slightly more difficult than a 24-hour clock; we shall leave this until the end of the chapter.

Figure 3.1
A display of a digital clock

11:03

3.2 Abstraction and modularization

A first idea might be to implement the whole clock display in a single class. That is, after all, what we have seen so far: how to build classes to do a job.

However, here we shall approach this problem slightly differently. We will see whether we can identify subcomponents in the problem that we can turn into separate classes. The reason is *complexity*. As we progress in this book, the examples we use and the programs we build will get more and more complex. Trivial tasks such as the ticket machine can be solved as a single problem. You can look at the complete task and devise a solution using a single class. For more complex problems, that, is too simplistic. As a problem grows larger, it becomes increasingly difficult to keep track of all details at the same time.

> **Concept**
>
> **Abstraction** is the ability to ignore details of parts, to focus attention on a higher level of a problem.

The solution we use to deal with the complexity problem is *abstraction*. We divide the problem into sub-problems, then again into sub-sub-problems, and so on, until the individual problems are small enough to be easy to deal with. Once we solve one of the sub-problems, we do not think about the details of that part any more, but treat the solution as a single building block for our next problem. This technique is sometimes referred to as *divide and conquer*.

Let us discuss this with an example. Imagine engineers in a car company designing a new car. They may think about the parts of the car, such as the shape of the outer body, the size and location of the engine, the number and size of the seats in the passenger area, the exact spacing of the wheels, and so on. Another engineer, on the other hand, whose job is to design the engine (team of), think of the many parts of an engine: the cylinders, the injection mechanism, the carburetor, the electronics, etc. They will think of the engine not as a single entity, but as a complex work of many parts. One of these parts may be a spark plug.

Then there is an engineer (maybe in a different company) who designs the spark plug. He will think of the spark plug as a complex artifact of many parts. He might have conducted complex studies to determine exactly what kind of metal to use for the contacts, or what kind of material and production process to use for the insulation.

The same is true for many other parts. A designer at the highest level will regard a wheel as a single part. Another engineer much further down the chain may spend her days thinking about the chemical composition necessary to produce the right materials to make the tires. For the tire engineer, the tire is a complex thing. The car company will just buy the tire from the tire company and then view it as a single entity. This is abstraction.

The engineer in the car company *abstracts from* the details of the tire manufacture to be able to concentrate on the details of the construction of, say, the wheel. The designer designing the body shape of the car abstracts from the technical details of the wheels and the engine to concentrate on the design of the body (he will just be interested in the size of the engine and the wheels).

The same is true for every other component. While someone might be concerned with designing the interior passenger space, someone else may work on developing the fabric that will eventually be used to cover the seats.

> **Concept**
>
> **Modularization** is the process of dividing a whole into well-defined parts that can be built and examined separately, and that interact in well-defined ways.

The point is, if viewed in enough detail, a car consists of so many parts that it is practically impossible for a single person to know every detail about every part at the same time. If that were necessary, no car could ever be built.

The reason why cars are successfully built is that the engineers use *modularization* and abstraction. They divide the car into independent modules (wheel, engine, gear box, seat, steering wheel, etc.) and get separate people to work on separate modules independently. When a module is built, they use abstraction. They view that module as a single component that is used to build more-complex components.

Modularization and abstraction thus complement each other. Modularization is the process of dividing large things (problems) into smaller parts, while abstraction is the process of ignoring details to focus on the bigger picture.

3.3 Abstraction in software

The same principles of modularization and abstraction discussed in the previous section are used in software development. To help us maintain an overview in complex programs, we try to identify subcomponents that we can program as independent entities. Then we try to use those subcomponents as if they were simple parts, without being concerned about their inner complexities.

In object-oriented programming, these components and subcomponents are objects. If we were trying to construct a car in software, using an object-oriented language, we would try to do what the car engineers do. Instead of implementing the car as a single, monolithic object, we would first construct separate objects for an engine, gearbox, wheel, seat, and so on, and then assemble the car object from those smaller objects.

Identifying what kinds of objects (and with these, classes) you should have in a software system for any given problem is not always easy, and we shall have a lot more to say about that later in this book. For now, we shall start with a relatively simple example. Now, back to our digital clock.

3.4 Modularization in the clock example

Let us have a closer look at the clock-display example. Using the abstraction concepts we have just described, we want to try to find the best way to view this example so that we can write some classes to implement it. One way to look at it is to consider it as consisting of a single display with four digits (two digits for the hours, two for the minutes). If we now abstract away from that very low-level view, we can see that it could also be viewed as two separate two-digit displays (one pair for the hours and one pair for the minutes). One pair starts at 0, increases by 1 each hour, and rolls back to 0 after reaching its limit of 23. The other rolls back to 0 after reaching its limit of 59. The similarity in behavior of these two displays might then lead us to abstract away even further from viewing the hours display and minutes display distinctly. Instead, we might think of them as being objects that can display values from zero up to a given limit. The value can be incremented, but, if the value reaches the limit, it rolls over to zero. Now we seem to have reached an appropriate level of abstraction that we can represent as a class: a two-digit display class.

Figure 3.2
A two-digit number display

For our clock display, we shall first program a class for a two-digit number display (Figure 3.2), then give it an accessor method to get its value, and two mutator methods to set the value and to increment it. Once we have defined this class, we can just create two objects of the class with different limits to construct the entire clock display.

3.5 Implementing the clock display

As discussed above, in order to build the clock display, we will first build a two-digit number display. This display needs to store two values. One is the limit to which it can count before rolling over to zero. The other is the current value. We shall represent both of these as integer fields in our class (Code 3.1).

Code 3.1
Class for a two-digit number display

```
public class NumberDisplay
{
    private int limit;
    private int value;

    Constructor and methods omitted.

}
```

Concept

Classes define types. A class name can be used as the type for a variable. Variables that have a class as their type can store objects of that class.

We shall look at the remaining details of this class later. First, let us assume that we can build the class `NumberDisplay`, and then let us think a bit more about the complete clock display. We would build a complete clock display by having an object that has, internally, two number displays (one for the hours, and one for the minutes). Each of the number displays would be a field in the clock display (Code 3.2). Here, we make use of a detail that we have not mentioned before: *classes define types*.

Code 3.2
The `Clock-Display` class containing two `NumberDisplay` fields

```
public class ClockDisplay
{
    private NumberDisplay hours;
    private NumberDisplay minutes;

    Constructor and methods omitted.

}
```

When we discussed fields in Chapter 2, we said that the word "private" in the field declaration is followed by a type and a name for the field. Here we use the class `NumberDisplay` as the type for the fields named `hours` and `minutes`. This shows that class names can be used as types.

The type of a field specifies what kind of values can be stored in the field. If the type is a class, the field can hold objects of that class. Declaring a field or other variable of a class type does not automatically create an object of that type; instead, the field is initially empty. We do not yet have a **NumberDisplay** object. The associated object will have to be created explicitly, and we shall see how this is done when we look at the constructor of the **ClockDisplay** class.

3.6 Class diagrams versus object diagrams

The structure described in the previous section (one **ClockDisplay** object holding two **NumberDisplay** objects) can be visualized in an *object diagram* as shown in Figure 3.3a. In this diagram, you see that we are dealing with three objects. Figure 3.3b shows the *class diagram* for the same situation.

Note that the class diagram shows only two classes, whereas the object diagram shows three objects. This has to do with the fact that we can create multiple objects from the same class. Here, we create two **NumberDisplay** objects from the **NumberDisplay** class.

These two diagrams offer different views of the same application. The class diagram shows the *static view*. It depicts what we have at the time of writing the program. We have two classes, and the arrow indicates that the class **ClockDisplay** makes use of the class **NumberDisplay** (**NumberDisplay** is mentioned in the source code of **ClockDisplay**). We also say that **ClockDisplay** *depends on* **NumberDisplay**.

To start the program, we will create an object of class **ClockDisplay**. We will program the clock display so that it automatically creates two **NumberDisplay** objects for itself. Thus, the object diagram shows the situation at *runtime* (when the application is running). This is also called the *dynamic view*.

The object diagram also shows another important detail: when a variable stores an object, the object is not stored in the variable directly, but rather an *object reference* is stored in the variable. In the diagram, the variable is shown as a white box, and the object reference is shown as an arrow. The object referred to is stored outside the referring object, and the object reference links the two.

> **Concept**
>
> The **class diagram** shows the classes of an application and the relationships between them. It gives information about the source code and presents the static view of a program.

Figure 3.3
Object diagram and class diagram for the **ClockDisplay**

> **Concept**
>
> The **object diagram** shows the objects and their relationships at one moment in time during the execution of an application. It gives information about objects at runtime and presents the dynamic view of a program.

It is very important to understand these two different diagrams and different views. BlueJ displays only the static view. You see the class diagram in its main window. In order to plan and understand Java programs, you need to be able to construct object diagrams on paper or in your head. When we think about what our program will do, we think about the object structures it creates and how these objects interact. Being able to visualize the object structures is essential.

Exercise 3.1 Think again about the *lab-classes* project that we discussed in Chapter 1 and Chapter 2. Imagine that we create a `LabClass` object and three `Student` objects. We then enroll all three students in that lab. Try to draw a class diagram and an object diagram for that situation. Identify and explain the differences between them.

Exercise 3.2 At what time(s) can a class diagram change? How is it changed?

Exercise 3.3 At what time(s) can an object diagram change? How is it changed?

Exercise 3.4 Write a definition of a field named `tutor` that can hold a reference to an object of type `Instructor`.

> **Concept**
>
> **Object references.** Variables of **object types** store references to objects.

3.7 Primitive types and object types

> **Concept**
>
> The **primitive types** in Java are the non-object types. Types such as `int`, `boolean`, `char`, `double`, and `long` are the most common primitive types. Primitive types have no methods.

Java knows two very different kinds of type: *primitive types* and *object types*. Primitive types are all predefined in the Java language. They include `int` and `boolean`. A complete list of primitive types is given in Appendix B. Object types are those defined by classes. Some classes are defined by the standard Java system (such as `String`); others are those classes we write ourselves.

Both primitive types and object types can be used as types, but there are situations in which they behave differently. One difference is how values are stored. As we could see from our diagrams, primitive values are stored directly in a variable (we have written the value directly into the variable box—for example, in Chapter 2, Figure 2.3). Objects, on the other hand, are not stored directly in the variable, but instead a reference to the object is stored (drawn as an arrow in our diagrams, as in Figure 3.3a).

We will see other differences between primitive types and object types later.

3.8 The `NumberDisplay` class

Before we start to analyze the source code of the full *clock-display* project, it will help if you gain an understanding of the `NumberDisplay` class, and how its features support the building of the `ClockDisplay` class. This can be found in the separate *number-display* project.

3.8 The NumberDisplay class

Code 3.3 shows the complete source code of the class `NumberDisplay`. Overall, this class is fairly straightforward, although it does illustrate a few new features of Java. It has the two fields discussed above (Section 3.5), one constructor, and four methods (`getValue`, `setValue`, `getDisplayValue`, and `increment`).

Code 3.3

Implementation of the **NumberDisplay** class

```java
/**
 * The NumberDisplay class represents a digital number display that can hold
 * values from zero to a given limit. The limit can be specified when creating
 * the display. The values range from zero (inclusive) to limit-1. If used,
 * for example, for the seconds on a digital clock, the limit would be 60,
 * resulting in display values from 0 to 59. When incremented, the display
 * automatically rolls over to zero when reaching the limit.
 *
 * @author Michael Kölling and David J. Barnes
 * @version 2016.02.29
 */
public class NumberDisplay
{
    private int limit;
    private int value;

    /**
     * Constructor for objects of class NumberDisplay.
     * Set the limit at which the display rolls over.
     */
    public NumberDisplay(int rollOverLimit)
    {
        limit = rollOverLimit;
        value = 0;
    }

    /**
     * Return the current value.
     */
    public int getValue()
    {
        return value;
    }

    /**
     * Return the display value (that is, the current value as a two-digit
     * String. If the value is less than ten, it will be padded with a leading
     * zero).
     */
    public String getDisplayValue()
    {
        if(value < 10) {
            return "0" + value;
        }
        else {
            return "" + value;
        }
    }
```

Code 3.3

Implementation of the **NumberDisplay** class

```java
/**
 * Set the value of the display to the new specified value. If the new
 * value is less than zero or over the limit, do nothing.
 */
public void setValue(int replacementValue)
{
    if((replacementValue >= 0) && (replacementValue < limit)) {
        value = replacementValue;
    }
}

/**
 * Increment the display value by one, rolling over to zero if the
 * limit is reached.
 */
public void increment()
{
    value = (value + 1) % limit;
}
```

Exercise 3.5 Open the *number-display* project. Select *Show Terminal* from the *View* menu and select *Record method calls*, as you did with the *figures* project in Chapter 1. This will allow you to see the result of your interactions with objects, which will be useful when we look in detail at the full *clock-display* project. Now create a **NumberDisplay** object and give it the name `hours`, rather than using the default name offered by BlueJ. Use a rollover limit of 24. Open an inspector window for this object. With the inspector open, call the object's `increment` method. Note what is shown in the Terminal window. Repeatedly call the `increment` method until the value in the inspector rolls over to zero. (If you are feeling impatient, you could always create a **NumberDisplay** object with a lower limit!)

Exercise 3.6 Create a second **NumberDisplay** object with a limit of 60, and give it the name `minutes`. Call its `increment` method and note how the method calls are represented in the Terminal window. Imagine that the `hours` and `minutes` objects on the object bench represent the two **NumberDisplay** objects managed by a **ClockDisplay** object. In effect, you are now performing the role of the **ClockDisplay** object. What should you do each time you call `increment` on `minutes` to decide whether it has rolled over and whether `increment` should therefore be called on the `hours` object?

Exercise 3.7 Select *Show Code Pad* from the *View* menu. Create a **NumberDisplay** object with limit 6 in the Code Pad by typing

```
NumberDisplay nd = new NumberDisplay(6);
```

Then call its **getValue**, **setValue**, and **increment** methods in the Code Pad (e.g., by typing **nd.getValue()**). Note that statements (mutators) need a semicolon at the end, while expressions (accessors) do not. The call to **setValue** will need to include a numerical parameter value. Use the recorded method calls in the Terminal window to help you with the correct way of writing these method calls.

Exercise 3.8 What error message do you see in the Code Pad if you type the following?

```
NumberDisplay.getValue()
```

Take a careful look at this error message and try to remember it because you will likely encounter something similar on numerous future occasions. Note that the reason for the error is that the class name, **NumberDisplay**, has been used incorrectly to try to call the **getValue** method, rather than the variable name nd.

Exercise 3.9 What error message do you see in the Code Pad if you type the following?

```
nd.setValue(int 5);
```

The error message is not actually very helpful at all. Can you work out what is incorrect about this call to **setValue**, and correct it? It would also be worth remembering this error message because it results from an easy error to make in the early stages of learning.

The constructor receives the roll-over limit as a parameter. If, for example, 24 is passed in as the roll-over limit, the display will roll over to 0 at that value. Thus, the range for the display value would be 0 to 23. This feature allows us to use this class for both hour and minute displays. For the hour display, we will create a **NumberDisplay** with limit 24; for the minute display, we will create one with limit 60. The constructor stores the roll-over limit in a field and sets the current value of the display to 0.

Next follows a simple accessor method for the current display value (**getValue**). This allows other objects to read the current value of the display.

The following sections discuss some new features that have been used in the **setValue**, **getDisplayValue** and **increment** methods.

3.8.1 The logical operators

The following mutator method `setValue` is interesting because it tries to make sure that the starting value of a `NumberDisplay` object is always valid. It reads:

```
public void setValue(int replacementValue)
{
    if((replacementValue >= 0) && (replacementValue < limit)) {
        value = replacementValue;
    }
}
```

Here, we pass the new value for the display as a parameter into the method. However, before we assign the value, we have to check whether the value is legal. The legal range for the value, as discussed above, is zero to one less than the limit. We use an if-statement to check that the value is legal before we assign it. The symbol "**&&**" is a logical "and" operator. It causes the condition in the if-statement to be true if both the conditions on either side of the "**&&**" symbol are true. See the "Logic operators" note that follows for details. Appendix C shows a complete table of logic operators in Java.

> **Logic operators** Logic operators operate on boolean values (true or false) and produce a new boolean value as a result. The three most important logical operators are **and**, **or**, and **not**. They are written in Java as:
>
>   **&&** (and)
>
>   **||** (or)
>
>   **!** (not)
>
> The expression
>
>   **a && b**
>
> is true if both **a** and **b** are true, and false in all other cases. The expression
>
>   **a || b**
>
> is true if either **a** or **b** or both are true, and false if they are both false. The expression
>
>   **!a**
>
> is true if **a** is false and false if **a** is true.

Exercise 3.10 What happens when the `setValue` method is called with an illegal value? Is this a good solution? Can you think of a better solution?

Exercise 3.11 What would happen if you replaced the "`>=`" operator in the test with "`>`" so that it reads

```
if((replacementValue > 0) && (replacementValue < limit))
```

Exercise 3.12 What would happen if you replaced the **&&** operator in the test with **||** so that it reads

```
if((replacementValue >= 0) || (replacementValue < limit))
```

Exercise 3.13 Which of the following expressions return *true*?

```
! (4 < 5)
! false
(2 > 2) || ((4 == 4) && (1 < 0))
(2 > 2) || (4 == 4) && (1 < 0)
(34 != 33) && ! false
```

After writing your answers on paper, open the Code Pad in BlueJ and try it out. Check your answers.

Exercise 3.14 Write an expression using boolean variables **a** and **b** that evaluates to *true* when **a** and **b** are either both *true* or both *false*.

Exercise 3.15 Write an expression using boolean variables **a** and **b** that evaluates to *true* when only one of **a** and **b** is *true*, and that is *false* if **a** and **b** are both *false* or both *true*. (This is also called an *exclusive or*.)

Exercise 3.16 Consider the expression (**a** && **b**). Write an equivalent expression (one that evaluates to *true* at exactly the same values for **a** and **b**) without using the **&&** operator.

3.8.2 String concatenation

The next method, **getDisplayValue**, also returns the display's value, but in a different format. The reason is that we want to display the value as a two-digit string. That is, if the current time is 3:05 a.m., we want the display to read **03:05**, and not **3:5**. To enable us to do this easily, we have implemented the **getDisplayValue** method. This method returns the current value as a string, and it adds a leading 0 if the value is less than 10. Here is the relevant section of the code:

```
if(value < 10) {
    return "0" + value;
}
else {
    return "" + value;
}
```

Note that the zero (**"0"**) is written in double quotes. Thus, we have written the *string* 0, not the *integer number* 0. Then the expression

```
"0" + value
```

"adds" a string and an integer (because the type of **value** is integer). The plus operator, therefore, represents string concatenation again, as seen in Section 2.9. Before continuing, we will now look at string concatenation a little more closely.

The plus operator (**+**) has different meanings, depending on the type of its operands. If both operands are numbers, it represents addition, as we would expect. Thus,

```
42 + 12
```

adds those two numbers, and the result is 54. However, if the operands are strings, then the meaning of the plus sign is string concatenation, and the result is a single string that consists of both operands stuck together. For example, the result of the expression

```
"Java" + "with BlueJ"
```

is the single string

```
"Javawith BlueJ"
```

Note that the system does not automatically add a space between the strings. If you want a space, you have to include it yourself within one of the strings.

If one of the operands of a plus operation is a string and the other is not, then the other operand is automatically converted to a string, and then a string concatenation is performed. Thus,

```
"answer: " + 42
```

results in the string

```
"answer: 42"
```

This works for all types. Whatever type is "added" to a string is automatically converted to a string and then concatenated.

Back to our code in the **getDisplayValue** method. If **value** contains 3, for example, then the statement

```
return "0" + value;
```

will return the string **"03"**. In the case where the value is greater than 9, we have used a little trick:

```
return "" + value;
```

Here, we concatenate **value** with an empty string. The result is that the value will be converted to a string and no other characters will be prefixed to it. We are using the plus operator for the sole purpose of forcing a conversion of the integer value to a value of type **String**.

> **Exercise 3.17** Does the **getDisplayValue** method work correctly in all circumstances? What assumptions are made within it? What happens if you create a number display with limit 800, for instance?

Exercise 3.18 Is there any difference in the result of writing

```
return value + "";
```

rather than

```
return "" + value;
```

in the `getDisplayValue` method?

Exercise 3.19 In Exercise 2.79 you were asked to investigate (among other things) the expressions

```
9 + 3 + "cat"
```

and

```
"cat" + 3 + 9
```

Predict, and then test, the result of these two expressions again. (Did they surprise you?) Explain why the results are what they are.

3.8.3 The modulo operator

The last method in the **NumberDisplay** class increments the display value by 1. It takes care that the value resets to 0 when the limit is reached:

```
public void increment()
{
    value = (value + 1) % limit;
}
```

This method uses the *modulo* operator (%). The modulo operator calculates the remainder of an integer division. For example, the result of the division

```
27 / 4
```

can be expressed in integer numbers as

```
result = 6, remainder = 3
```

The modulo operator returns just the remainder of such a division. Thus, the result of the expression **(27 % 4)** would be **3**.

Exercise 3.20 Explain the modulo operator. You may need to consult more resources (online Java language resources, other Java books, etc.) to find out the details.

Exercise 3.21 What is the result of the expression **(8 % 3)**?

Exercise 3.22 Try out the expression **(8 % 3)** in the Code Pad. Try other numbers. What happens when you use the modulo operator with negative numbers?

Exercise 3.23 What are all possible results of the expression **(n % 5)**, where n is a positive integer variable?

Exercise 3.24 What are all possible results of the expression **(n % m)**, where n and m are positive integer variables?

Exercise 3.25 Explain in detail how the increment method works.

Exercise 3.26 Rewrite the increment method without the modulo operator, using an if-statement. Which solution is better?

3.9 The `ClockDisplay` class

Now that we have seen how we can build a class that defines a two-digit number display, we shall look in more detail at the `ClockDisplay` class—the class that will create two number displays to create a full time display. Code 3.4 shows the complete source code of the `ClockDisplay` class, which can be found in the *clock-display* project.

Code 3.4
Implementation of the `ClockDisplay` class

```java
/**
 * The ClockDisplay class implements a digital clock display for a
 * European-style 24 hour clock. The clock shows hours and minutes. The
 * range of the clock is 00:00 (midnight) to 23:59 (one minute before
 * midnight).
 *
 * The clock display receives "ticks" (via the timeTick method) every minute
 * and reacts by incrementing the display. This is done in the usual clock
 * fashion: the hour increments when the minutes roll over to zero.
 *
 * @author Michael Kölling and David J. Barnes
 * @version 2016.02.29
 */
public class ClockDisplay
{
    private NumberDisplay hours;
    private NumberDisplay minutes;
    private String displayString;    // simulates the actual display

    /**
     * Constructor for ClockDisplay objects. This constructor
     * creates a new clock set at 00:00.
     */
    public ClockDisplay()
    {
        hours = new NumberDisplay(24);
        minutes = new NumberDisplay(60);
        updateDisplay();
    }
```

Code 3.4 continued

Implementation of the `ClockDisplay` class

```java
/**
 * Constructor for ClockDisplay objects. This constructor
 * creates a new clock set at the time specified by the
 * parameters.
 */
public ClockDisplay(int hour, int minute)
{
    hours = new NumberDisplay(24);
    minutes = new NumberDisplay(60);
    setTime(hour, minute);
}

/**
 * This method should get called once every minute - it makes
 * the clock display go one minute forward.
 */
public void timeTick()
{
    minutes.increment();
    if(minutes.getValue() == 0) {   // it just rolled over!
        hours.increment();
    }
    updateDisplay();
}

/**
 * Set the time of the display to the specified hour and
 * minute.
 */
public void setTime(int hour, int minute)
{
    hours.setValue(hour);
    minutes.setValue(minute);
    updateDisplay();
}

/**
 * Return the current time of this display in the format HH:MM.
 */
public String getTime()
{
    return displayString;
}

/**
 * Update the internal string that represents the display.
 */
private void updateDisplay()
{
    displayString = hours.getDisplayValue() + ":" +
                    minutes.getDisplayValue();
}
}
```

> **Exercise 3.27** Open the *clock-display* project and create a `ClockDisplay` object by selecting the following constructor:
>
>   new ClockDisplay()
>
> Call its `getTime` method to find out the initial time the clock has been set to. Can you work out why it starts at that particular time?
>
> **Exercise 3.28** Open an inspector for this object. With the inspector open, call the object's methods. Watch the `displayString` field in the inspector. Read the project comment (by double-clicking the text icon in the class diagram) for more information.
>
> **Exercise 3.29** How many times would you need to call the `timeTick` method on a newly created `ClockDisplay` object to make its time reach 01:00? How else could you make it display that time?

In this project, we use the field `displayString` to simulate the actual display device of the clock (as you could see in Exercise 3.28). Were this software to run in a real clock, we would present the output on the real clock display instead. So this string serves as our software simulation for the clock's output device.[1]

In addition to the display string, the `ClockDisplay` class has two more fields: `hours` and `minutes`. Each can hold a reference to an object of type `NumberDisplay`. The logical value of the clock's display (the current time) is stored in these `NumberDisplay` objects. Figure 3.4 shows an object diagram of this application when the current time is 15:23.

Figure 3.4
Object diagram of the clock display

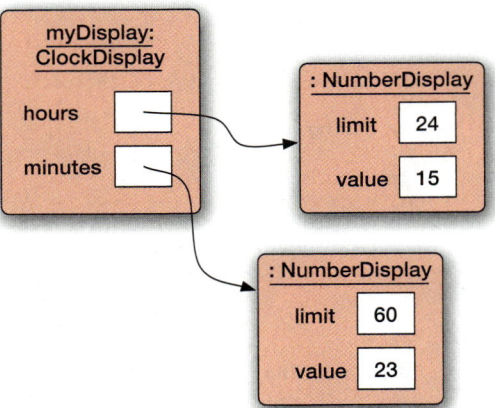

---

[1] The book projects folder also includes a version of this project with a simple graphical user interface (GUI), named *clock-display-with-GUI*. The curious reader may like to experiment with this project; however, it will not be discussed in this book.

3.10 Objects creating objects

Concept

Object creation. Objects can **create** other **objects**, using the **new** operator.

The first question we have to ask ourselves is: Where do the `NumberDisplay` objects used by the `ClockDisplay` come from? As a *user* of a clock display, when we create a `ClockDisplay` object we assume that our clock display has hours and minutes. So by simply creating a clock display, we expect that we have implicitly created two number displays for the hours and minutes.

However, as *writers* of the `ClockDisplay` class, we have to make this happen. To do this, we simply write code in the constructor of the `ClockDisplay` that creates and stores two `NumberDisplay` objects. Because the constructor is automatically executed when a `ClockDisplay` object is created, the `NumberDisplay` objects will automatically be created at the same time. Here is the code of the `ClockDisplay` constructor that makes this work:

```
public class ClockDisplay
{
    private NumberDisplay hours;
    private NumberDisplay minutes;
```

Remaining fields omitted.

```
    public ClockDisplay()
    {
        hours = new NumberDisplay(24);
        minutes = new NumberDisplay(60);
        updateDisplay();
    }
```

Methods omitted.

```
}
```

Each of the first two lines in the constructor creates a new `NumberDisplay` object and assigns it to a variable. The syntax of an operation to create a new object is

```
new ClassName (parameter-list)
```

The **new** operation does two things:

1. It creates a new object of the named class (here, `NumberDisplay`).
2. It executes the constructor of that class.

If the constructor of the class is defined to have parameters, then the actual parameters must be supplied in the new statement. For instance, the constructor of class `NumberDisplay` was defined to expect one integer parameter:

```
public NumberDisplay(int rollOverLimit)
```

Thus, the new operation for the `NumberDisplay` class, which calls this constructor, must provide one actual parameter of type `int` to match the defined constructor header:

```
new NumberDisplay(24);
```

This is the same as for methods discussed in Section 2.5. With this constructor, we have achieved what we wanted: if someone now creates a `ClockDisplay` object, the `ClockDisplay` constructor will automatically execute and create two `NumberDisplay` objects. From the point of view of a user of the `ClockDisplay` class, the creation of the `NumberDisplay` objects is implicit. However, from a writer's point of view, the creation is explicit because they have to write the code to make it happen.

The final statement in the constructor is a call to `updateDisplay` that sets up the `displayString` field. This call is explained in Section 3.12.1. Then the clock display is ready to go.

> **Exercise 3.30** Write Java statements that define a variable named `window` of type `Rectangle`, and then create a `Rectangle` object and assign it to that variable. The `Rectangle` constructor has two `int` parameters.

3.11 Multiple constructors

You might have noticed when you created a `ClockDisplay` object that the pop-up menu offered you two ways to do that:

```
new ClockDisplay()
new ClockDisplay(int hour, int minute)
```

This is because the `ClockDisplay` class contains two constructors. What they provide are alternative ways of initializing a `ClockDisplay` object. If the constructor with no parameters is used, then the starting time displayed on the clock will be 00:00. If, on the other hand, you want to have a different starting time, you can set that up by using the second constructor. It is common for class definitions to contain alternative versions of constructors or methods that provide various ways of achieving a particular task via their distinctive sets of parameters. This is known as *overloading* a constructor or method.

Concept

Overloading. A class may contain more than one constructor, or more than one method of the same name, as long as each has a distinctive set of parameter types.

> **Exercise 3.31** Look at the second constructor in `ClockDisplay`'s source code. Explain what it does and how it does it.
>
> **Exercise 3.32** Identify the similarities and differences between the two constructors. Why is there no call to `updateDisplay` in the second constructor, for instance?

3.12 Method calls

3.12.1 Internal method calls

The last line of the first `ClockDisplay` constructor consists of the statement

```
updateDisplay();
```

3.12 Method calls

Concept

Methods can call other methods of the same class as part of their implementation. This is called an **internal method call**.

This statement is a *method call*. As we have seen above, the `ClockDisplay` class has a method with the following signature:

```
private void updateDisplay()
```

The method call above invokes this method. Because this method is in the same class as the call of the method, we also call it an *internal method call*. Internal method calls have the syntax

methodName (*parameter-list*)

An internal method call does not have a variable name and a dot before the method name, which you will have observed in all of the method calls recorded in the Terminal window. A variable is not needed because, with an internal method call, an object calls the method on itself. We contrast internal and external method calls in the next section.

In our example, the method does not have any parameters, so the parameter list is empty. This is signified by the pair of parentheses with nothing between them.

When a method call is encountered, the matching method is executed, and the execution returns to the method call and continues at the next statement after the call. For a method signature to match the method call, both the name and the parameter list of the method must match. Here, both parameter lists are empty, so they match. This need to match against both method name and parameter lists is important, because there may be more than one method of the same name in a class—if that method is overloaded.

In our example, the purpose of this method call is to update the display string. After the two number displays have been created, the display string is set to show the time indicated by the number display objects. The implementation of the `updateDisplay` method will be discussed below.

3.12.2 External method calls

Now let us examine the next method: `timeTick`. The definition is:

```
public void timeTick()
{
    minutes.increment();
    if(minutes.getValue() == 0) { // it just rolled over!
        hours.increment();
    }
    updateDisplay();
}
```

Were this display connected to a real clock, this method would be called once every 60 seconds by the electronic timer of the clock. For now, we just call it ourselves to test the display.

When the `timeTick` method is called, it first executes the statement

```
minutes.increment();
```

This statement calls the `increment` method of the `minutes` object. Thus, when one of the methods of the `ClockDisplay` object is called, it in turn calls a method of another object to do part of the task. A method call to a method of another object is referred to as an *external method call*. The syntax of an external method call is

```
object . methodName ( parameter-list )
```

This syntax is known as *dot notation*. It consists of an object name, a dot, the method name, and parameters for the call. It is particularly important to note that we use the name of an *object* here and not the name of a class. We use the name `minutes` rather than `NumberDisplay`. (This essential principle was illustrated in Exercise 3.8.)

The difference between internal and external method calls is clear—the presence of an object name followed by a dot tells us that the method being called is part of another object. So in the `timeTick` method, the `ClockDisplay` object is asking the `NumberDisplay` objects to carry out part of the overall task. In other words, responsibility for the overall time-keeping task is divided up between the `ClockDisplay` class and the `NumberDisplay` class. This is a practical illustration of the *divide and conquer* principle we referred to earlier in our discussion of abstraction.

> **Concept**
>
> Methods can call methods of other objects using dot notation. This is called an **external method call**.

The `timeTick` method has an if-statement to check whether the hours should also be incremented. As part of the condition in the if-statement, it calls another method of the minutes object: `getValue`. This method returns the current value of the minutes. If that value is zero, then we know that the display just rolled over and we should increment the hours. That is exactly what the code does.

If the value of the minutes is not zero, then we're done. We do not have to change the hours in that case. Thus, the if-statement does not need an *else* part.

We should now also be able to understand the remaining three methods of the `ClockDisplay` class (see Code 3.4). The method `setTime` takes two parameters—the hour and the minute—and sets the clock to the specified time. Looking at the method body, we can see that it does so by calling the `setValue` methods of both number displays (the one for the hours and the one for the minutes). Then it calls `updateDisplay` to update the display string accordingly, just as the constructor does.

The `getTime` method is trivial—it just returns the current display string. Because we always keep the display string up to date, this is all there is to do.

Finally, the `updateDisplay` method is responsible for updating the display string so that the string correctly reflects the time as represented by the two number display objects. It is called every time the time of the clock changes. Once again, it illustrates external method calls. It works by calling the `getDisplayValue` methods of each of the `NumberDisplay` objects. These methods return the values of each separate number display. The `updateDisplay` method then uses string concatenation to join these two values, separated by a colon, into a single string.

Exercise 3.33 Given a variable

```
Printer p1;
```

which currently holds a reference to a printer object, and two methods inside the **Printer** class with the headers

```
public void print(String filename, boolean doubleSided)
public int getStatus(int delay)
```

write two possible calls to each of these methods.

Exercise 3.34 Open the *house* project from Chapter 1 and review the **Picture** class. What types of object are created by the constructor of **Picture**?

Exercise 3.35 List all of the external method calls that are made in the **draw** method of **Picture** on the **Triangle** object called **roof**.

Exercise 3.36 Does the **Picture** class contain any internal method calls?

Exercise 3.37 Remove the following two statements from the **draw** method of **Picture**:

```
window.changeColor("black");
sun.changeColor("yellow");
```

and make the color setting, instead, via a single call to an internal method called **setColor** (which you need to create).

3.12.3 Summary of the clock display

It is worth looking for a minute at the way this example uses abstraction to divide the problem into smaller parts. Looking at the source code of the class **ClockDisplay**, you will notice that we just create a **NumberDisplay** object without being particularly interested in what that object looks like internally. We can then call methods (**increment**, **getValue**) of that object to make it work for us. At this level, we simply assume that **increment** will correctly increment the display's value, without being concerned with how it does it.

In real-world projects, these different classes are often written by different people. You might already have noticed that all these two people have to agree on is what method signatures the class should have and what they should do. Then one person can concentrate on implementing the methods, while the other person can just use them.

The set of methods an object makes available to other objects is called its *interface*. We shall discuss interfaces in much more detail later in this book.

Exercise 3.38 *Challenge exercise* Change the clock from a 24-hour clock to a 12-hour clock. Be careful: This is not as easy as it might at first seem. In a 12-hour clock, the hours after midnight and after noon are not shown as 00:30, but as 12:30. Thus, the minute display shows values from 0 to 59, while the hour display shows values from 1 to 12!

Exercise 3.39 There are (at least) two ways in which you can make a 12-hour clock. One possibility is to just store hour values from 1 to 12. On the other hand, you can simply leave the clock to work internally as a 24-hour clock but change the display string of the clock display to show `4:23` or `4:23pm` when the internal value is `16:23`. Implement both versions. Which option is easier? Which is better? Why?

Exercise 3.40 Assume a class `Tree` has a field of type `Triangle` called `leaves` and a field of type `Square` called `trunk`. The constructor of `Tree` takes no parameters and its constructor creates the `Triangle` and `Square` objects for its fields. Using the *figures* project from Chapter 1, create a simple `Tree` class to fit this description. You do not need to define any methods in the class and the shapes do not have to be made visible.

Exercise 3.41 *Challenge exercise* Complete the `Tree` class described in the previous exercise, by having the constructor move the trunk square beneath the leaves triangle and then make both shapes visible. Do this by defining a method in the `Tree` class called `setup` and include a call to this method in the constructor of `Tree`. Change the size of the triangle so that it looks more like the leaves of a fir tree growing from the trunk.

3.13 Another example of object interaction

We shall now examine the same concepts with a different example, using different tools. We are still concerned with understanding how objects create other objects, and how objects call each other's methods. In the first half of this chapter, we have used the most fundamental technique to analyze a given program: code reading. The ability to read and understand source code is one of the most essential skills for a software developer, and we will need to apply it in every project we work on. However, sometimes it is beneficial to use additional tools in order to help us gain a deeper understanding about how a program executes. One tool we will now look at is a *debugger*.

> **Concept**
>
> A **debugger** is a software tool that helps in examining how an application executes. It can be used to find bugs.

A debugger is a program that lets programmers execute an application one step at a time. It typically provides functions to stop and start a program at selected points in the source code, and to examine the values of variables.

> **The name "debugger"** Errors in computer programs are commonly known as "bugs." Thus programs that help in the removal of errors are known as "debuggers."
>
> It is not entirely clear where the term "bug" comes from. There is a famous case of what is known as "the first computer bug"—a real bug (a moth, in fact)—which was found inside the Mark II computer by Grace Murray Hopper, an early computing pioneer, in 1945. A logbook still exists in the National Museum of American History of the Smithsonian Institute that shows an entry with this moth taped into the book and the remark "first actual case of bug being found." The wording, however, suggests that the term "bug" had been in use before this real one caused trouble in the Mark II.
>
> To find out more, do a web search for "first computer bug"—you will even find pictures of the moth!

Debuggers vary widely in complexity. Those for professional developers have a large number of functions for sophisticated examination of many facets of an application. BlueJ has a built-in debugger that is much simpler. We can use it to stop our program, step through it one line of code at a time, and examine the values of our variables. Despite the debugger's apparent lack of sophistication, this is enough to give us a great deal of information.

Before we start experimenting with the debugger, we will take a look at the example we will use for debugging: a simulation of an e-mail system.

3.13.1 The mail-system example

We start by investigating the functionality of the *mail-system* project. At this stage, it is not important to read the source, but mainly to execute the existing project to get an understanding of what it does.

> **Exercise 3.42** Open the *mail-system* project, which you can find in the book's support material. The idea of this project is to simulate the act of users sending mail items to each other. A user uses a mail client to send mail items to a server, for delivery to another user's mail client. First create a **MailServer** object. Now create a **MailClient** object for one of the users. When you create the client, you will need to supply a **MailServer** instance as a parameter. Use the one you just created. You also need to specify a username for the mail client. Now create a second **MailClient** in a similar way, with a different username.
>
> Experiment with the **MailClient** objects. They can be used for sending mail items from one mail client to another (using the **sendMailItem** method) and receiving messages (using the **getNextMailItem** or **printNextMailItem** methods).

Examining the mail system project, we see that:

- It has three classes: **MailServer**, **MailClient**, and **MailItem**.

- One mail-server object must be created that is used by all mail clients. It handles the exchange of messages.
- Several mail-client objects can be created. Every mail client has an associated user name.
- Mail items can be sent from one mail client to another via a method in the mail-client class.
- Mail items can be received by a mail client from the server one at a time, using a method in the mail client.
- The **MailItem** class is never explicitly instantiated by the user. It is used internally in the mail clients and server to create, store, and exchange messages.

> **Exercise 3.43** Draw an object diagram of the situation you have after creating a mail server and three mail clients. Object diagrams were discussed in Section 3.6.

The three classes have different degrees of complexity. **MailItem** is fairly trivial. We shall discuss only one small detail and leave the rest up to the reader to investigate. **MailServer** is quite complex at this stage; it makes use of concepts discussed only much later in this book. We shall not investigate that class in detail here. Instead, we just trust that it does its job—another example of the way abstraction is used to hide detail that we do not need to be aware of.

The **MailClient** class is the most interesting, and we shall examine it in some detail.

Code 3.5
Fields and constructor of the **MailItem** class

```java
public class MailItem
{
    // The sender of the item.
    private String from;
    // The intended recipient.
    private String to;
    // The text of the message.
    private String message;

    /**
     * Create a mail item from sender to the given recipient,
     * containing the given message.
     * @param from The sender of this item.
     * @param to The intended recipient of this item.
     * @param message The text of the message to be sent.
     */
    public MailItem(String from, String to, String message)
    {
        this.from = from;
        this.to = to;
        this.message = message;
    }

    Methods omitted.
}
```

3.13.2 The this keyword

The only section we will discuss from the `MailItem` class is the constructor. It uses a Java constructor that we have not encountered before. The source code is shown in Code 3.5.

The new Java feature in this code fragment is the use of the `this` keyword:

```
this.from = from;
```

The whole line is an assignment statement. It assigns the value on the right-hand side (`from`) to the variable on the left (`this.from`).

The reason for using this construct is that we have a situation known as *name overloading*—the same name being used for two different entities. The class contains three fields, named `from`, `to`, and `message`. The constructor has three parameters, also named `from`, `to`, and `message`!

So while we are executing the constructor, how many variables exist? The answer is six: three fields and three parameters. It is important to understand that the fields and the parameters are separate variables that exist independently of each other, even though they share similar names. A parameter and a field sharing a name is not really a problem in Java.

The problem we do have, though, is how to reference the six variables so as to be able to distinguish between the two sets. If we simply use the variable name "`from`" in the constructor (for example, in a statement `System.out.println(from)`), which variable will be used—the parameter or the field?

The Java specification answers this question. It specifies that the definition originating in the closest enclosing block will always be used. Because the `from` parameter is defined in the constructor, and the `from` field is defined in the class, the parameter will be used. Its definition is "closer" to the statement that uses it.

Now all we need is a mechanism to access a field when there is a more closely defined variable with the same name. That is what the `this` keyword is used for. The expression `this` refers to the current object. Writing `this.from` refers to the `from` field in the current object. Thus, this construct gives us a means to refer to the field instead of the parameter with the same name. Now we can read the assignment statement again:

```
this.from = from;
```

This statement, as we can see now, has the following effect:

field named `from` = *parameter named* `from`;

In other words, it assigns the value from the parameter to the field with the same name. This is, of course, exactly what we need to do to initialize the object properly.

One last question remains: Why are we doing this at all? The whole problem could easily be avoided just by giving the fields and the parameters different names. The reason is readability of source code.

Sometimes there is one name that perfectly describes the use of a variable—it fits so well that we do not want to invent a different name for it. We want to use it for the parameter, where it serves as a hint to the caller, indicating what needs to be passed. We also want to use it for the field, where it is useful as a reminder for the implementer of the class, indicating what the field is used for. If one name perfectly describes the use, it is reasonable to use it for both and to go through the trouble of using the **this** keyword in the assignment to resolve the name conflict.

3.14 Using a debugger

The most interesting class in the mail-system example is the mail client. We shall now investigate it in more detail by using a debugger. The mail client has three methods: **getNextMailItem**, **printNextMailItem**, and **sendMailItem**. We will first investigate the **printNextMailItem** method.

Before we start with the debugger, set up a scenario we can use to investigate (Exercise 3.44).

> **Exercise 3.44** Set up a scenario for investigation: Create a mail server, then create two mail clients for the users **"Sophie"** and "**Juan**" (you should name the instances **sophie** and **juan** as well so that you can better distinguish them on the object bench). Then use Sophie's **sendMailItem** method to send a message to Juan. Do not read the message yet.

After the setup in Exercise 3.44, we have a situation where one mail item is stored on the server for Juan, waiting to be picked up. We have seen that the **printNextMailItem** method picks up this mail item and prints it to the terminal. Now we want to investigate exactly how this works.

3.14.1 Setting breakpoints

To start our investigation, we set a breakpoint (Exercise 3.45). A breakpoint is a flag attached to a line of source code that will stop the execution of a method at that point when it is reached. It is represented in the BlueJ editor as a small stop sign (Figure 3.5).

You can set a breakpoint by opening the BlueJ editor, selecting the appropriate line (in our case, the first line of the **printNextMailItem** method) and then selecting *Set/Clear Breakpoint* from the *Tools* menu of the editor. Alternatively, you can also simply click into the area next to the line of code where the breakpoint symbol appears, to set or clear breakpoints. Note that the class has to be compiled to do this.

> **Exercise 3.45** Open the editor for the **MailClient** class and set a breakpoint at the first line of the **printNextMailItem** method, as shown in Figure 3.5.

Once you have set the breakpoint, invoke the **printNextMailItem** method on Juan's mail client. The editor window for the **MailClient** class and a debugger window will pop up (Figure 3.6).

3.14 Using a debugger   **121**

Figure 3.5
A breakpoint in the BlueJ editor

Figure 3.6
The debugger window, execution stopped at a breakpoint

Along the bottom of the debugger window are some control buttons. They can be used to continue or interrupt the execution of the program. (For a more detailed explanation of the debugger controls, see Appendix F.)

On the right-hand side of the debugger window are three areas for variable display, titled *static variables*, *instance variables*, and *local variables*. We will ignore the static-variable area for now. We will discuss static variables later, and this class does not have any.

We see that this object has two instance variables (or fields), **server** and **user**, and we can see the current values. The **user** variable stores the string **"juan"**, and the **server** variable stores a reference to another object. The object reference is what we have drawn as an arrow in the object diagrams.

Note that there is no local variable yet. This is because execution stops *before* the line with the breakpoint is executed. Because the line with the breakpoint contains the declaration of the only local variable and that line has not yet been executed, no local variable exists at the moment.

The debugger not only allows us to interrupt the execution of the program so we can inspect the variables, it also lets us step forward slowly.

3.14.2 Single stepping

When stopped at a breakpoint, clicking the *Step* button executes a single line of code and then stops again.

> **Exercise 3.46** Step one line forward in the execution of the `printNextMailItem` method by clicking the *Step* button.

The result of executing the first line of the `printNextMailItem` method is shown in Figure 3.7. We can see that execution has moved on by one line (a small black arrow next to the line of source code indicates the current position), and the local variable list in the debugger window indicates that a local variable item has been created, and an object assigned to it.

> **Exercise 3.47** Predict which line will be marked as the next line to execute after the next step. Then execute another single step and check your prediction. Were you right or wrong? Explain what happened and why.

Figure 3.7
Stopped again after a single step

We can now use the *Step* button repeatedly to step to the end of the method. This allows us to see the path the execution takes. This is especially interesting in conditional statements: we can clearly see which branch of an if-statement is executed and use this to see whether it matches our expectations.

Exercise 3.48 Call the same method (`printNextMailItem`) again. Step through the method again, as before. What do you observe? Explain why this is.

3.14.3 Stepping into methods

When stepping through the `printNextMailItem` method, we have seen two method calls to objects of our own classes. The line

```
MailItem item = server.getNextMailItem(user);
```

includes a call to the `getNextMailItem` method of the `server` object. Checking the instance variable declarations, we can see that the `server` object is declared of class `MailServer`.

The line

```
item.print();
```

calls the `print` method of the `item` object. We can see in the first line of the `printNext-MailItem` method that `item` is declared to be of class `MailItem`.

Using the *Step* command in the debugger, we have used abstraction: we have viewed the `print` method of the `item` class as a single instruction, and we could observe that its effect is to print out the details (sender, recipient, and message) of the mail item.

If we are interested in more detail, we can look further into the process and see the print method itself execute step by step. This is done by using the *Step Into* command in the debugger instead of the *Step* command. *Step Into* will step into the method being called and stop at the first line inside that method.

Exercise 3.49 Set up the same test situation as we did before. That is, send a message from Sophie to Juan. Then invoke the `printNextMailItem` message of Juan's mail client again. Step forward as before. This time, when you reach the line

```
item.print();
```

use the *Step Into* command instead of the *Step* command. Make sure you can see the text terminal window as you step forward. What do you observe? Explain what you see.

3.15 Method calling revisited

In the experiments in Section 3.14, we have seen another example of object interaction similar to one we saw before: objects calling methods of other objects. In the **printNextMailItem** method, the **MailClient** object made a call to a **MailServer** object to retrieve the next mail item. This method (**getNextMailItem**) returned a value—an object of type **MailItem**. Then there was a call to the **print** method of the mail item. Using abstraction, we can view the **print** method as a single command. Or, if we are interested in more detail, we can go to a lower level of abstraction and look inside the **print** method.

In a similar style, we can use the debugger to observe one object creating another. The **sendMessage** method in the **MailClient** class shows a good example. In this method, a **MailItem** object is created in the first line of code:

```
MailItem item = new MailItem(user, to, message);
```

The idea here is that the mail item is used to encapsulate a mail message. The mail item contains information about the sender, the recipient, and the message itself. When sending a message, a mail client creates a mail item with all this information, then stores the mail item on the mail server. There it can later be picked up by the mail client of the recipient.

In the line of code above, we see the **new** keyword being used to create the new object, and we see the parameters being passed to the constructor. (Remember: Constructing an object does two things—the object is being created, and the constructor is executed.) Calling the constructor works in a very similar fashion to calling methods. This can be observed by using the *Step Into* command at the line where the object is being constructed.

Exercise 3.50 Set a breakpoint in the first line of the **sendMailItem** method in the **MailClient** class. Then invoke this method. Use the *Step Into* function to step into the constructor of the mail item. In the debugger display for the **MailItem** object, you can see the instance variables and local variables that have the same names, as discussed in Section 3.13.2. Step further to see the instance variables get initialized.

Exercise 3.51 Use a combination of code reading, execution of methods, breakpoints, and single stepping to familiarize yourself with the **MailItem** and **MailClient** classes. Note that we have not yet discussed enough for you to understand the implementation of the **MailServer** class, so you can ignore this for now. (You can, of course, look at it if you feel adventurous, but don't be surprised if you find it slightly baffling . . .) Explain in writing how the **MailClient** and **MailItem** classes interact. Draw object diagrams as part of your explanations.

3.16 Summary

In this chapter, we have discussed how a problem can be divided into sub-problems. We can try to identify subcomponents in those objects that we want to model, and we can implement subcomponents as independent classes. Doing so helps in reducing the complexity of implementing larger applications, because it enables us to implement, test, and maintain individual classes separately.

We have seen how this approach results in structures of objects working together to solve a common task. Objects can create other objects, and they can invoke each other's methods. Understanding these object interactions is essential in planning, implementing, and debugging applications.

We can use pen-and-paper diagrams, code reading, and debuggers to investigate how an application executes or to track down bugs.

Terms introduced in this chapter

> **abstraction, modularization, divide and conquer, class diagram, object diagram, object reference, overloading, internal method call, external method call, dot notation, debugger, breakpoint**

Exercise 3.52 Use the debugger to investigate the *clock-display* project. Set breakpoints in the `ClockDisplay` constructor and each of the methods, and then single-step through them. Does it behave as you expected? Did this give you new insights? If so, what were they?

Exercise 3.53 Use the debugger to investigate the `insertMoney` method of the *better-ticket-machine* project from Chapter 2. Conduct tests that cause both branches of the if-statement to be executed.

Exercise 3.54 Add a subject line for an e-mail to mail items in the *mail-system* project. Make sure printing messages also prints the subject line. Modify the mail client accordingly.

Exercise 3.55 Given the following class (only shown in fragments here),

```
public class Screen
{
    public Screen(int xRes, int yRes)
    { ...
    }
    public int numberOfPixels()
    { ...
    }
    public void clear(boolean invert)
    { ...
    }
}
```

write some lines of Java code that create a `Screen` object. Then call its `clear` method if (and only if) its number of pixels is greater than two million. (Don't worry about things being logical here; the goal is only to write something that is syntactically correct—i.e., that would compile if we typed it in.)

Exercise 3.56 Describe the changes that would be required to the `Clock-Display` class in order to be able to display hours, minutes, and seconds. How many `NumberDisplay` objects would a `ClockDisplay` object need to use?

Exercise 3.57 Write the code for the `timeTick` method in `ClockDisplay` that displays hours, minutes, and seconds, or even implement the whole class if you wish.

Exercise 3.58 Discuss whether the current design of the `ClockDisplay` class would support the display of hours, minutes, seconds, tenths of a second, and hundredths of a second. Consider how the `timeTick` method would be coded in this case, for instance.

Exercise 3.59 *Challenge exercise* In the current design of `ClockDisplay`, a `ClockDisplay` object is responsible for detecting when a `NumberDisplay` object has rolled over to zero and then telling another `NumberDisplay` object to increment. In other words, there is no direct link between `NumberDisplay` objects. Would it be possible to have one `NumberDisplay` object tell another that it has rolled over, and that the other `NumberDisplay` object should then increment? For instance, have the minutes object tell the hour object that another hour has passed, or have the seconds object tell the minutes object that another sixty seconds have elapsed. Which of these objects would the `timeTick` method interact with? What fields would a `NumberDisplay` object have? What should the hour object do when a whole day has elapsed? Discuss the issues involved in this alternative design and, if you really feel like a challenge, try implementing it! Note that you might need to find out about the Java `null` keyword, which we don't cover until late in Chapter 4.

CHAPTER 4

Grouping Objects

Main concepts discussed in this chapter:

- collections
- loops
- iterators

Java constructs discussed in this chapter:

`ArrayList`, `Iterator`, for-each loop, while loop, `null`, anonymous objects

The main focus of this chapter is to introduce some of the ways in which objects may be grouped together into collections. In particular, we discuss the `ArrayList` class as an example of flexible-size collections. Closely associated with collections is the need to iterate over the elements they contain. For this purpose, we introduce two new control structures: the for-each loop and the while loop.

This chapter is both long and important. You may not succeed in becoming a good programmer without fully understanding the contents of this chapter. You will likely need longer to study it than was the case for previous chapters. Do not be tempted to rush through it; take your time and study it thoroughly.

4.1 Building on themes from Chapter 3

As well as introducing new material on *collections* and *iteration*, we will also be revisiting two of the key themes that were introduced in Chapter 3: *abstraction* and *object interaction*. There we saw that abstraction allows us to simplify a problem by identifying discrete components that can be viewed as a whole, rather than being concerned with their detail. We will see this principle in action when we start making use of the *library classes* that are available in Java. While these classes are not, strictly speaking, a part of the language, some of them are so closely associated with writing Java programs that they are often thought of in that way. Most people writing Java programs will constantly check the libraries to see if someone has already written a class that they can make use of. That way, they save a huge amount of effort that can be better used in working on other parts of the program. The same principle applies with most other programming languages, which also tend to have libraries of useful classes. So it pays to become familiar with the contents of the library and how to use the most common classes. The power of abstraction is that we don't usually need to know much (if anything, indeed!) about what the class looks like inside to be able to use it effectively.

If we use a library class, it follows that we will be writing code that creates instances of those classes, and then our objects will be interacting with the library objects. Therefore, object interaction will figure highly in this chapter, also.

You will find that the chapters in this book continually revisit and build on themes that have been introduced in previous chapters. We refer to this in the preface as an "iterative approach." One particular advantage of the approach is that it will help you to gradually deepen your understanding of topics as you work your way through the book.

In this chapter, we also extend our understanding of abstraction to see that it does not just mean hiding detail, but also means seeing the common features and patterns that recur again and again in programs. Recognizing these patterns means that we can often reuse part or all of a method or class we have previously written in a new situation. This particularly applies when looking at collections and iteration.

4.2 The collection abstraction

One of the abstractions we will explore in this chapter is the idea of a *collection*—the notion of grouping things so that we can refer to them and manage them all together. A collection might be large (all the students in a university), small (the courses one of the students is taking), or empty even (the paintings by Picasso that I own!).

If we own a collection of stamps, autographs, concert posters, ornaments, music, or whatever, then there are some common actions we will want to perform to the collection from time to time, regardless of what it is we collect. For instance, we will likely want to *add to* the collection, but we also might want to *reduce it*—say if we have duplicates or want to raise money for additional purchases. We also might want to *arrange it* in some way—by date of acquisition or value, perhaps. What we are describing here are typical *operations* on a collection.

In a programming context, the collection abstraction becomes a class of some sort, and the operations would be methods of that class. A particular collection (my music collection) would be an instance of the class. Furthermore, the items stored in a collection instance would, themselves, be objects.

Here are some further collection examples that are more obviously related to a programming context:

> **Concept**
>
> **Collection**
> A collection object can store an arbitrary number of other objects.

- Electronic calendars store event notes about appointments, meetings, birthdays, and so on. New notes are added as future events are arranged, and old notes are deleted as details of past events are no longer needed.

- Libraries record details about the books and journals they own. The catalog changes as new books are bought and old ones are put into storage or discarded.

- Universities maintain records of students. Each academic year adds new records to the collection, while the records of those who have left are moved to an archive collection. Listing subsets of the collection will be common: all the students taking first-year CS, or all the students due to graduate this year, for instance.

The number of items stored in a collection will vary from time to time. So far, we have not met any features of Java that would allow us to group together arbitrary numbers of items. We could, perhaps, define a class with a lot of individual fields to cover a fixed but very large number of items, but programs typically have a need for a more general solution than this provides. A proper solution would not require us either to know in advance how many items we wish to group together, or to fix an upper limit to that number.

So we will start our exploration of the Java library by looking at a class that provides the simplest possible way of grouping objects, an unsorted but ordered flexible-sized list: **ArrayList**. In the next few sections, we shall use the example of keeping track of a personal music collection to illustrate how we can group together an arbitrary number of objects in a single container object.

4.3 An organizer for music files

We are going to write a class that can help us organize our music files stored on a computer. Our class won't actually store the file details; instead, it will delegate that responsibility to the standard **ArrayList** library class, which will save us a lot of work. So, why do we need to write our own class at all? An important point to bear in mind when dealing with library classes is that they have not been written for any particular application scenario—they are general-purpose classes. One **ArrayList** might store student-record objects, while another stores event reminders. This means that it is the classes that we write for using the library classes that provide the scenario-specific operations, such as the fact that we are dealing with music files, or playing a file that is stored in the collection.

For the sake of simplicity, the first version of this project will simply work with the file names of individual music tracks. There will be no separate details of title, artist, playing time, etc. That means we will just be asking the **ArrayList** to store **String** objects representing the file names. Keeping things simple at this stage will help to avoid obscuring the key concepts we are trying to illustrate, which are the creation and usage of a collection object. Later in the chapter, we will add further sophistication to make a more viable music organizer and player.

We will assume that each music file represents a single music track. The example files we have provided with the project have both the artist's name and the track's title embedded in the file name, and we will use this feature later. For the time being, here are the basic operations we will have in the initial version of our organizer:

- It allows tracks to be added to the collection.

- It has no predetermined limit on the number of tracks it can store, aside from the memory limit of the machine on which it is run.

- It will tell us how many tracks are in the collection.

- It will list all the tracks.

We shall find that the `ArrayList` class makes it very easy to provide this functionality from our own class.

Notice that we are not being too ambitious in this first version. These features will be sufficient for illustrating the basics of creating and using the `ArrayList` class, and later versions will then build further features incrementally until we have something more sophisticated. (Most importantly, perhaps, we will later add the possibility of playing the music files. Our first version will not be able to do that.) This modest, incremental approach is much more likely to lead to success than trying to implement everything all at once.

Before we analyze the source code needed to make use of such a class, it is helpful to explore the starting behavior of the music organizer.

> **Exercise 4.1** Open the *music-organizer-v1* project in BlueJ and create a `MusicOrganizer` object. Store the names of a few audio files into it—they are simply strings. As we are not going to play the files at this stage, any file names will do, although there is a sample of audio files in the *audio* folder of the chapter that you might like to use.
>
> Check that the number of files returned by `numberOfFiles` matches the number you stored. When you use the `listFile` method, you will need to use a parameter value of **0** (zero) to print the first file, **1** (one) to print the second, and so on. We shall explain the reason for this numbering in due course.
>
> **Exercise 4.2** What happens if you create a new `MusicOrganizer` object and then call `removeFile(0)` before you have added any files to it? Do you get an error? Would you expect to get an error?
>
> **Exercise 4.3** Create a `MusicOrganizer` and add two file names to it. Call `listFile(0)` and `listFile(1)` to show the two files. Now call `removeFile(0)` and then `listFile(0)`. What happened? Is that what you expected? Can you find an explanation of what might have happened when you removed the first file name from the collection?

4.4 Using a library class

Code 4.1 shows the full definition of our `MusicOrganizer` class, which makes use of the library class `ArrayList`. Note that library classes do not appear in the BlueJ class diagram.

> **Class libraries** One of the features of object-oriented languages that makes them powerful is that they are often accompanied by *class libraries*. These libraries typically contain many hundreds or thousands of different classes that have proved useful to developers on a wide range of different projects. Java calls its libraries *packages*. Library classes are used in exactly the same way as we would use our own classes. Instances are constructed using **new**, and the classes have fields, constructors, and methods.

Code 4.1

The `MusicOrganizer` class

```java
import java.util.ArrayList;

/**
 * A class to hold details of audio files.
 *
 * @author David J. Barnes and Michael Kölling
 * @version 2016.02.29
 */
public class MusicOrganizer
{
    // An ArrayList for storing the file names of music files.
    private ArrayList<String> files;

    /**
     * Create a MusicOrganizer
     */
    public MusicOrganizer()
    {
        files = new ArrayList<>();
    }

    /**
     * Add a file to the collection.
     * @param filename The file to be added.
     */
    public void addFile(String filename)
    {
        files.add(filename);
    }

    /**
     * Return the number of files in the collection.
     * @return The number of files in the collection.
     */
    public int getNumberOfFiles()
    {
        return files.size();
    }

    /**
     * List a file from the collection.
     * @param index The index of the file to be listed.
     */
    public void listFile(int index)
    {
        if(index >= 0 && index < files.size()) {
            String filename = files.get(index);
            System.out.println(filename);
        }
    }
```

Code 4.1 continued
The `MusicOrganizer` class

```java
/**
 * Remove a file from the collection.
 * @param index The index of the file to be removed.
 */
public void removeFile(int index)
{
    if(index >= 0 && index < files.size()) {
        files.remove(index);
    }
}
}
```

4.4.1 Importing a library class

The very first line of the class file illustrates the way in which we gain access to a library class in Java, via an *import statement*:

```java
import java.util.ArrayList;
```

This makes the `ArrayList` class from the `java.util` package available to our class definition. Import statements must always be placed before class definitions in a file. Once a class name has been imported from a package in this way, we can use that class just as if it were one of our own classes. So we use `ArrayList` at the head of the `MusicOrganizer` class to define a `files` field:

```java
private ArrayList<String> files;
```

Here, we see a new construct: the mention of `String` in angle brackets: `<String>`. The need for this was alluded to in Section 4.3, where we noted that `ArrayList` is a *general-purpose* collection class—i.e., not restricted in what it can store. When we create an `ArrayList` object, however, we have to be specific about the type of objects that will be stored in that particular instance. We can store whatever type we choose, but we have to designate that type when declaring an `ArrayList` variable. Classes such as `ArrayList`, which get parameterized with a second type, are called *generic classes* (we will discuss them in more detail later).

When using collections, therefore, we always have to specify two types: the type of the collection itself (here: `ArrayList`) and the type of the elements that we plan to store in the collection (here: `String`). We can read the complete type definition `ArrayList<String>` as "*ArrayList of String*." We use this type definition as the type for our `files` variable.

As you should now have come to expect, we see a close connection between the body of the constructor and the fields of the class, because the constructor is responsible for initializing the fields of each instance. So, just as the `ClockDisplay` created `NumberDisplay` objects for its two fields, here we see the constructor of the `MusicOrganizer` creating an object of type `ArrayList` and storing it in the `files` field.

4.4.2 Diamond notation

Note that when creating the `ArrayList` instance, we have written the following statement:

```java
files = new ArrayList<>();
```

This is the so-called *diamond notation* (because the two angle brackets create a diamond shape) and it looks unusual. We have seen earlier that the **new** statement has the following form:

```
new type-name(parameters)
```

and we have also seen that the full type name for our collection is

```
ArrayList<String>
```

Therefore, with an empty parameter list, the statement to create the new collection object should look as follows:

```
files = new ArrayList<String>();
```

Indeed, writing this statement would work as well. The first version, using the diamond notation (thus leaving out the mention of the **String** type) is merely a shortcut notation for convenience. If the creation of the collection object is combined with an assignment, then the compiler can work out the type of the collection elements from the type of the variable on the left hand side of the assignment, and Java allows us to skip defining it again. The element type is automatically inferred from the variable type.

Using this form does not change the fact that the object being created will only be able to store **String** objects; it is just a convenience that saves us some typing and makes our code shorter.

4.4.3 Key methods of ArrayList

The **ArrayList** class defines quite a lot of methods, but we shall make use of only four at this stage, to support the functionality we require: **add**, **size**, **get**, and **remove**.

The first two are illustrated in the relatively straightforward **addFile** and **getNumberOfFiles** methods, respectively. The **add** method of an **ArrayList** stores an object in the list, and the **size** method tells us how many items are currently stored in it. We will look at how the **get** and **remove** methods work in Section 4.7, though you will probably get some idea beforehand simply by reading through the code of the **listFile** and **removeFile** methods.

4.5 Object structures with collections

To understand how a collection object such as an **ArrayList** operates, it is helpful to examine an object diagram. Figure 4.1 illustrates how a **MusicOrganizer** object might appear with two filename strings stored in it. Compare Figure 4.1 with Figure 4.2, where a third file name has been stored.

There are at least three important features of the **ArrayList** class that you should observe:

- It is able to increase its internal capacity as required: as more items are added, it simply makes enough room for them.
- It keeps its own private count of how many items it is currently storing. Its **size** method returns that count.
- It maintains the order of items you insert into it. The add method stores each new item at the end of the list. You can later retrieve them in the same order.

Figure 4.1

A `Music-Organizer` containing two file names

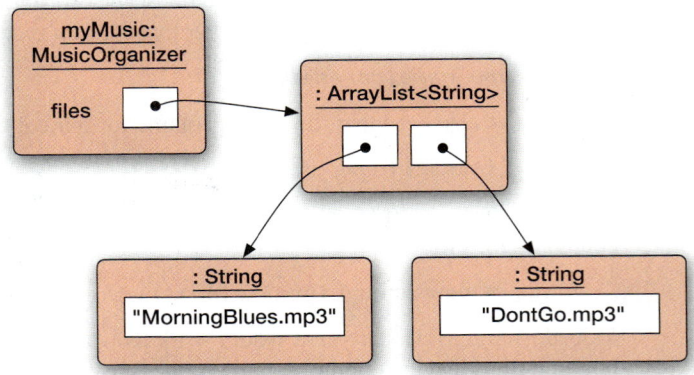

Figure 4.2

A `Music-Organizer` containing three file names

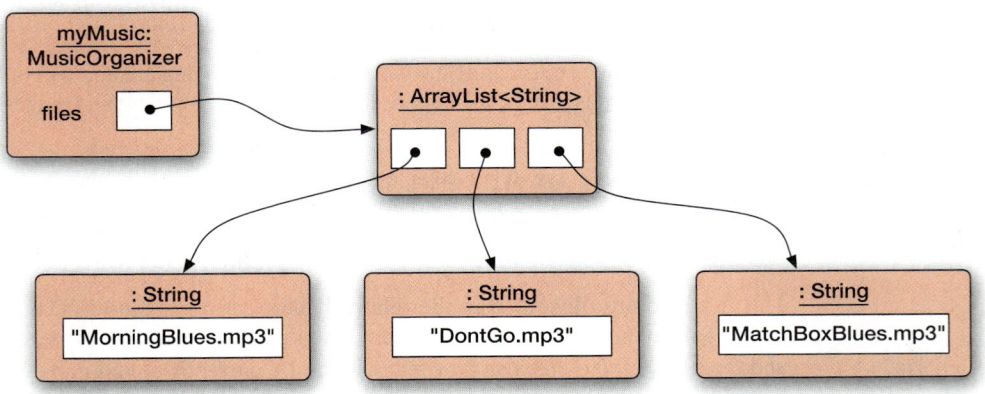

We notice that the `MusicOrganizer` object looks quite simple—it has only a single field that stores an object of type `ArrayList<String>`. All the difficult work is done in the `ArrayList` object. This is one of the great advantages of using library classes: someone has invested time and effort to implement something useful, and we are getting access to this functionality almost for free by using this class.

At this stage, we do not need to worry about *how* an `ArrayList` is able to support these features. It is sufficient to appreciate just how useful this ability is. Remember: This suppression of detail is a benefit that abstraction gives us; it means that we can utilize `ArrayList` to write any number of different classes that require storage of an arbitrary number of objects.

The second feature—the `ArrayList` object keeping its own count of inserted objects—has important consequences for the way in which we implement the `MusicOrganizer` class. Although an organizer has a `getNumberOfFiles` method, we have not actually defined a specific field for recording this information. Instead, an organizer *delegates* the responsibility for keeping track of the number of items to its `ArrayList` object.

This means that an organizer does not duplicate information that is available to it from elsewhere. If a user requests from the organizer information about the number of file names in it, the organizer will pass the question on to the `files` object, and then return whatever answer it gets from there.

Duplication of information or behavior is something we often work hard to avoid. Duplication can represent wasted effort, and can lead to inconsistencies where two things that should be identical turn out not to be, through error. We will have a lot more to say about duplication of functionality in later chapters.

4.6 Generic classes

The new notation using the angle brackets deserves a little more discussion. The type of our `files` field was declared as:

```
ArrayList<String>
```

The class we are using here is simply called `ArrayList`, but it requires a second type to be specified as a parameter when it is used to declare fields or other variables. Classes that require such a type parameter are called *generic classes*. Generic classes, in contrast to other classes we have seen so far, do not define a single type in Java, but potentially many types. The `ArrayList` class, for example, can be used to specify an *ArrayList of String*, an *ArrayList of Person*, an *ArrayList of Rectangle*, or an `ArrayList` of any other class that we have available. Each particular `ArrayList` is a separate type that can be used in declarations of fields, parameters, and return values. We could, for example, define the following two fields:

```
private ArrayList<Person> members;
private ArrayList<TicketMachine> machines;
```

These definitions state that `members` refers to an `ArrayList` that can store `Person` objects, while `machines` can refer to an `ArrayList` to store `TicketMachine` objects. Note that `ArrayList<Person>` and `ArrayList<TicketMachine>` are different types. The fields cannot be assigned to each other, even though their types were derived from the same `ArrayList` class.

Exercise 4.4 Write a declaration of a private field named `library` that can hold an `ArrayList`. The elements of the `ArrayList` are of type `Book`.

Exercise 4.5 Write a declaration of a local variable called `cs101` that can hold an `ArrayList` of `Student`.

Exercise 4.6 Write a declaration of a private field called `tracks` for storing a collection of `MusicTrack` objects.

Exercise 4.7 Write assignments to the `library`, `cs101`, and `track` variables (which you defined in the previous three exercises) to create the appropriate `ArrayList` objects. Write them once using diamond notation and once without diamond notation, specifying the full type.

Generic classes are used for a variety of purposes; we will encounter more of them later in the book. For now, collections such as `ArrayList`, and some other collections that we shall encounter shortly, are the only generic classes we need to deal with.

4.7 Numbering within collections

When exploring the *music-organizer-v1* project in the first few exercises, we noted that it was necessary to use parameter values starting at 0 to list and remove file names in the collection. The reason behind this requirement is that items stored in `ArrayList` collections have an implicit numbering, or positioning, that starts from 0. The position of an object in a collection is more commonly known as its *index*. The first item added to a collection is given index number 0, the second is given index number 1, and so on. Figure 4.3 illustrates the same situation as above, with index numbers shown in the `ArrayList` object.

This means that the last item in a collection has the index *size-1*. For example, in a list of 20 items, the last one will be at index 19.

The `listFile` and `removeFile` methods both illustrate the way in which an index number is used to gain access to an item in an `ArrayList`: one via its `get` method, and the other via its `remove` method. Note that both methods make sure that their parameter value is in the range of valid index values `[0 ... size()−1]` before passing the index on to the `ArrayList` methods. This is a good stylistic validation habit to adopt, as it prevents failure of a library-class method call when passing on parameter values that could be invalid.

> **Pitfall** If you are not careful, you may try to access a collection element that is outside the valid indices of the `ArrayList`. When you do this, you will get an error message and the program will terminate. Such an error is called an *index-out-of-bounds* error. In Java, you will see a message about an `IndexOutOfBoundsException`.

Figure 4.3
Index numbers of elements in a collection

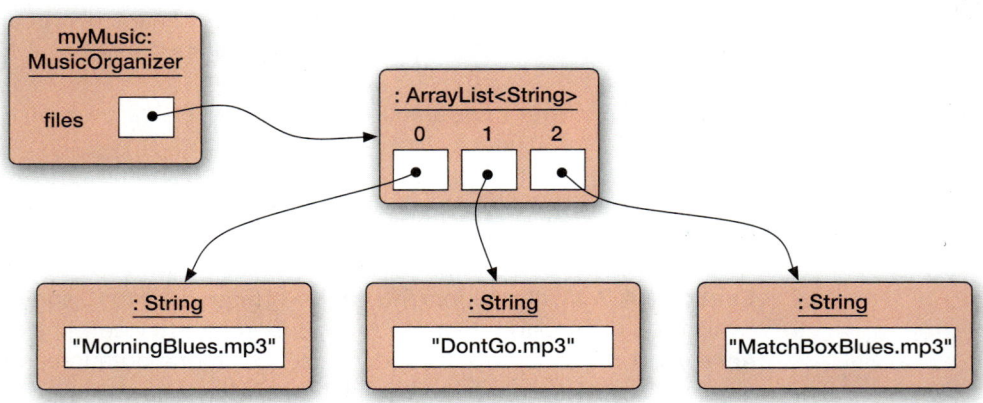

4.7 Numbering within collections

Exercise 4.8 If a collection stores 10 objects, what value would be returned from a call to its `size` method?

Exercise 4.9 Write a method call using `get` to return the fifth object stored in a collection called items.

Exercise 4.10 What is the index of the last item stored in a collection of 15 objects?

Exercise 4.11 Write a method call to add the object held in the variable `favoriteTrack` to a collection called `files`.

4.7.1 The effect of removal on numbering

As well as adding items to a collection, it is common to want to remove items, as we saw with the `removeFile` method in Code 4.1. The `ArrayList` class has a `remove` method that takes the index of the object to be removed. One detail of the removal process to be aware of is that it can change the index values at which other objects in the collection are stored. If an item with a low index number is removed, then the collection moves all subsequent items along by one position to fill in the gap. As a consequence, their index numbers will be decreased by 1.

Figure 4.4 illustrates the way in which some of the index values of items in an `ArrayList` are changed by the removal of an item from the middle of the list. Starting with the situation depicted in Figure 4.3, the object with index 1 has been removed. As a result, the object originally at index number 2 has changed to 1, whereas the object at index number 0 remains unchanged.

Furthermore, we shall see later that it is possible to insert items into an `ArrayList` at a position other than the end of it. This means that items already in the list may have their index numbers increased when a new item is added. Users need to be aware of this possible change of indices when adding or removing items.

Figure 4.4
Index number changes following removal of an item

4.7.2 The general utility of numbering with collections

The use of integer index values to access objects in a collection is something that we will see over and over again—not just with **ArrayList**s but also with several different types of collections. So it is important to understand what we have seen of this so far: that the index values start at zero; that the objects are numbered sequentially; and that there are usually no gaps in the index values of consecutive objects in the collection.

Using integer values as indices also makes it easy to express expressions in program code such as "the next item" and "the previous item" with respect to an item in the collection. If an item is at index **p**, then "the next" one will be at index **(p+1)** and "the previous" one is now at index **(p−1)**. We can also map natural-language selections such as "the first three" to program-related terminology. For example, "the items at indices **0**, **1**, and **2**" or "the last four" could be "the items at indices **(list.size()-4)** to **(list.size()-1)**".

We could even imagine working our way through the entire collection by having an integer index variable whose value is initially set to zero and is then successively increased by 1, passing its value to the **get** method to access each item in the list in order (stopping when it goes beyond the final index value of the list).

But we are getting a little ahead of ourselves. Nevertheless, in a little while we will see how all this works out in practice when we look at *loops* and *iteration*.

Exercise 4.12 Write a method call to remove the third object stored in a collection called **dates**.

Exercise 4.13 Suppose that an object is stored at index 6 in a collection. What will be its index after the objects at index 0 and index 9 are removed?

Exercise 4.14 Add a method called **checkIndex** to the **MusicOrganizer** class. It takes a single integer parameter and checks whether it is a valid index for the current state of the collection. To be valid, the parameter must lie in the range **0** to **size()−1**.

If the parameter is not valid, then it should print an error message saying what the valid range is. If the index is valid, then it prints nothing. Test your method on the object bench with both valid and invalid parameters. Does your method still work when you check an index if the collection is empty?

Exercise 4.15 Write an alternative version of **checkIndex** called **validIndex**. It takes an integer parameter and returns a boolean result. It does not print anything, but returns **true** if the parameter's value is a valid index for the current state of the collection, and **false** otherwise. Test your method on the object bench with both valid and invalid parameters. Test the empty case too.

Exercise 4.16 Rewrite both the `listFile` and `removeFile` methods in `MusicOrganizer` so that they use your `validIndex` method to check their parameter, instead of the current boolean expression. They should only call `get` or `remove` on the `ArrayList` if `validIndex` returns `true`.

4.8 Playing the music files

A nice feature of our organizer, beyond keeping a list of music files, would allow us to play them. Once again, we can use abstraction to help us here. If we have a class that has been written specifically to play audio files, then our organizer class would not need to know anything about how to do that; it could simply hand over the name of the file to the player class and leave it to do the rest.

Unfortunately, the standard Java library does not have a class that is suitable for playing mp3 files, which is the audio format we want to work with. However, many individual programmers are constantly writing their own useful classes and making them available for other people to use. These are often called "third-party libraries," and they are imported and used in the same way as are standard Java library classes.

For the next version of our project, we have made use of a set of classes from `javazoom.net` to write our own music-player class. You can find this in the version called *music-organizer-v2*. The three methods of the `MusicPlayer` class we shall be using are `playSample`, `startPlaying`, and `stop`. The first two take the name of the audio file to play. The first plays some seconds of the beginning of the file and returns when it has finished playing, while the second starts its playing in the background and then immediately returns control back to the organizer—hence the need for the `stop` method, in case you want to cancel playing. Code 4.2 shows the new elements of the `MusicOrganizer` class that access some of this playing functionality.

Code 4.2
Playing functionality of the **Music-Organizer** class

```java
import java.util.ArrayList;

/**
 * A class to hold details of audio files.
 * This version can play the files.
 *
 * @author David J. Barnes and Michael Kölling
 * @version 2016.02.29
 */
public class MusicOrganizer
{
    // An ArrayList for storing the file names of music files.
    private ArrayList<String> files;
    // A player for the music files.
    private MusicPlayer player;
```

Code 4.2 continued

Playing functionality of the **Music-Organizer** class

```java
/**
 * Create a MusicOrganizer
 */
public MusicOrganizer()
{
    files = new ArrayList<>();
    player = new MusicPlayer();
}

/**
 * Start playing a file in the collection.
 * Use stopPlaying() to stop it playing.
 * @param index The index of the file to be played.
 */
public void startPlaying(int index)
{
    String filename = files.get(index);
    player.startPlaying(filename);
}

/**
 * Stop the player.
 */
public void stopPlaying()
{
    player.stop();
}
```

Other details omitted.

```
}
```

Exercise 4.17 Create a `MusicOrganizer` object in the second version of our project. Experiment with adding some files to it and playing them.

If you want to use the files provided in the *audio* folder within the chapter, you must include the folder name in the filename parameter, as well as the file name and suffix. For example, to use the file *BlindBlake-EarlyMorningBlues.mp3* from the *audio* folder, you must pass the string `"../audio/BlindBlake-EarlyMorningBlues.mp3"` to the `addFile` method.

You can use your own mp3 files by placing them into the *audio* folder. Remember to use the folder name as part of the file name.

Also experiment with file names that do not exist. What happens when you use those?

4.8.1 Summary of the music organizer

We have made good progress with the basics of organizing our music collection. We can store the names of any number of music files and even play them. We have done this with relatively little coding effort, because we have been able to piggyback on the functionality provided by library classes: `ArrayList` from the standard Java library, and a music player that uses a third-party class library. We have also been able to do this with relatively little knowledge of the internal workings of these library classes; it was sufficient to know the names, parameter types, and return types of the key methods.

However, there is still some key functionality missing if we want a genuinely useful program—most obvious is the lack of any way to list the whole collection, for instance. This will be the topic of the next section, as we introduce the first of several Java loop-control structures.

4.9 Processing a whole collection

At the end of the last section, we said that it would be useful to have a method in the music organizer that lists all of the file names stored in the collection. Knowing that each file name in the collection has a unique index number, one way to express what we want would be to say that we wish to display the file name stored at consecutive increasing index numbers starting from zero. Before reading further, try the following exercises to see whether we can easily write such a method with the Java that we already know.

Exercise 4.18 What might the header of a `listAllFiles` method in the `MusicOrganizer` class look like? What sort of return type should it have? Does it need to take any parameters?

Exercise 4.19 We know that the first file name is stored at index zero in the `ArrayList`, and the list stores the file names as strings, so could we write the body of `listAllFiles` along the following lines?

```
System.out.println(files.get(0));
System.out.println(files.get(1));
System.out.println(files.get(2));
etc.
```

How many `println` statements would be required to complete the method?

You have probably noticed that it is not really possible to complete Exercise 4.19, because it depends on how many file names are in the list at the time they are printed. If there are three, then three `println` statements would be required; if there are four, then four statements would be needed; and so on. The `listFile` and `removeFile` methods illustrate that the range of valid index numbers at any one time is `[0 to (size()-1)]`. So a `listAllFiles` method would also have to take that dynamic size into account in order to do its job.

What we have here is the requirement to do something several times, but the number of times depends upon circumstances that may vary—in this case, the size of the collection. We shall meet this sort of requirement in nearly every program we write, and most programming languages have several ways to deal with it through the use of *loop statements*, which are also known as *iterative control structures*.

The first loop we will introduce to list the files is a special one for use with collections, which completely avoids the need to use an index variable at all: this is called a *for-each loop*.

4.9.1 The for-each loop

> **Concept**
>
> A **loop** can be used to execute a block of statements repeatedly without having to write them multiple times.

A *for-each loop* is one way to perform a set of actions repeatedly on the items in a collection, but without having to write out those actions more than once, as we saw was a problem in Exercise 4.19. We can summarize the Java syntax and actions of a for-each loop in the following pseudo-code:

```
for (ElementType element : collection) {
    loop body
}
```

The main new piece of Java is the word **for**. The Java language has two variations of the **for** loop: one is the *for-each loop*, which we are discussing here; the other one is simply called a *for loop* and will be discussed in Chapter 7.

A for-each loop has two parts: a loop header (the first line of the loop statement) and a loop body following the header. The body contains those statements that we wish to perform over and over again.

The for-each loop gets its name from the way we can read this loop: if we read the keyword **for** as "for each" and the colon in the loop header as "in," then the code structure shown above starts to make more sense, as in this pseudo-code:

```
for each element in collection do: {
    loop body
}
```

When you compare this version to the original pseudo-code in the first version, you notice that *element* was written in the form of a variable declaration as **ElementType element**. This section does indeed declare a variable that is then used for each collection element in turn. Before discussing further, let us look at an example of real Java code.

Code 4.3 shows an implementation of a **listAllFiles** method that lists all file names currently in the organizer's **ArrayList** that use such a for-each loop.

Code 4.3

Using a for-each loop to list the file names

```java
/**
 * Show a list of all the files in the collection.
 */
public void listAllFiles()
{
    for(String filename : files) {
        System.out.println(filename);
    }
}
```

In this for-each loop, the loop body—consisting of a single `System.out.println` statement—is executed repeatedly, once for each element in the `files ArrayList`. If, for example, there were four strings in the list, the `println` statement would be executed four times.

Each time before the statement is executed, the variable `filename` is set to hold one of the list elements: first the one at index **0**, then the one at index **1**, and so on. Thus, each element in the list gets printed out.

Let us dissect the loop in a little more detail. The keyword `for` introduces the loop. It is followed by a pair of parentheses, within which the loop details are defined. The first of the details is the declaration `String filename`; this declares a new local variable `filename` that will be used to hold the list elements in order. We call this variable the *loop variable*. We can choose the name of this variable just as we can that of any other variable; it does not have to be called "filename." The type of the loop variable must be the same as the declared element type of the collection we are going to use—`String` in our case.

Then follows a colon and the variable holding the collection that we wish to process. From this collection, each element will be assigned to the loop variable in turn; and for each of those assignments, the loop body is executed once. In the loop body, we then use the loop variable to refer to each element.

To test your understanding of how this loop operates, try the following exercises.

Exercise 4.20 Implement the `listAllFiles` method in your version of the music-organizer project. (A solution with this method implemented is provided in the *music-organizer-v3* version of this project, but to improve your understanding of the subject, we recommend that you write this method yourself.)

Exercise 4.21 Create a `MusicOrganizer` and store a few file names in it. Use the `listAllFiles` method to print them out; check that the method works as it should.

Exercise 4.22 Create an `ArrayList<String>` in the Code Pad by typing the following two lines:

```
import java.util.ArrayList;
new ArrayList<String>()
```

If you write the last line without a trailing semicolon, you will see the small red object icon. Drag this icon onto the object bench. Examine its methods and try calling some (such as **add**, **remove**, **size**, **isEmpty**). Also try calling the same methods from the Code Pad. You can access objects on the object bench from the Code Pad by using their names. For example, if you have an `ArrayList` named `al1` on the object bench, in the Code Pad you can type:

```
al1.size()
```

Exercise 4.23 If you wish, you could use the debugger to help you understand how the statements in the body of the loop in `listAllFiles` are repeated. Set a breakpoint just before the loop, and step through the method until the loop has processed all elements and exits.

> **Exercise 4.24** *Challenge exercise* The for-each loop does not use an explicit integer variable to access successive elements of the list. Thus, if we want to include the index of each file name in the listing, then we would have to declare our own local integer variable (**position**, say) so that we can write in the body of the loop something like:
>
> ```
> System.out.println(position + ": " + filename);
> ```
>
> See if you can complete a version of `listAllFiles` to do this. *Hint:* You will need a local variable declaration of `position` in the method, as well as a statement to update its value by one inside the for-each loop.
>
> This exercise illustrates the for-each loop really intended to be used with a separate index variable.

We have now seen how we can use a for-each loop to perform some operation (the loop body) on every element of a collection. This is a big step forward, but it does not solve all our problems. Sometimes we need a little more control, and Java provides a different loop construct to let us do more: the *while loop*.

4.9.2 Selective processing of a collection

The `listAllFiles` method illustrates the fundamental usefulness of a for-each loop: it provides access to every element of a collection, in order, via the variable declared in the loop's header. It does not provide us with the index position of an element, but we don't always need that, so that is not necessarily a problem.

Having access to every item in the collection, however, does not mean we have to do the same thing to every one; we can be more selective than that. For instance, we might want to only list the music by a particular artist, or need to find all the music with a particular phrase in the title. There is nothing to stop us doing this, because the body of a for-each loop is just an ordinary block, and we can use whatever Java statements we wish inside it. So using an if-statement in the body to select the files we want should be easy.

Code 4.4 shows a method to list only those file names in the collection that contain a particular string.

Code 4.4
Printing selected items from the collection

```java
/**
 * List the names of files matching the given search string.
 * @param searchString The string to match.
 */
public void listMatching(String searchString)
{
    for(String filename : files) {
        if(filename.contains(searchString)) {
            // A match.
            System.out.println(filename);
        }
    }
}
```

Using an if-statement and the **boolean** result of the **contains** method of the **String** class, we can "filter" which file names are to be printed and which are not. If the file name does not match, then we just ignore it—no **else** part is needed. The filtering criterion (the test in the if-statement) can be whatever we want.

Exercise 4.25 Add the **listMatching** method in Code 4.4 to your version of the project. (Use *music-organizer-v3* if you do not already have your own version.) Check that the method only lists matching files. Also try it with a search string that matches none of the file names. Is anything at all printed in this case?

Exercise 4.26 *Challenge exercise* In **listMatching**, can you find a way to print a message, once the for-each loop has finished, if no file names matched the search string? *Hint:* Use a **boolean** local variable.

Exercise 4.27 Write a method in your version of the project that plays samples of all the tracks by a particular artist, one after the other. The **listMatching** method illustrates the basic structure you need for this method. Make sure that you choose an artist with more than one file. Use the **playSample** method of the **MusicPlayer** (provided in *music-organizer-v3*). The **playSample** method plays the beginning of a track (about 15 seconds) and then returns.

Exercise 4.28 Write out the header of a for-each loop to process an **ArrayList<Track>** called **tracks**. Don't worry about the loop's body.

4.9.3 A limitation of using strings

By this point we can see that simply having file name strings containing all the details of the music track is not really satisfactory. For instance, suppose we wanted to find all tracks with the word "love" in the title. Using the unsophisticated matching technique described above, we will also find tracks by artists whose names happen to have that sequence of characters in them (e.g., Glover). While that might not seem like a particularly big problem, it does have a rather "cheap" feel about it, and it should be possible to do better with just a little more effort. What we really need is a separate class, such as **Track**, say—that stores the details of artist and title independently from the file name. Then we could more easily match titles separately from artists. The **ArrayList<String>** in the organizer would then become an **ArrayList<Track>**.

As we develop the music-organizer project in later sections, we will eventually move towards a better structure by introducing a **Track** class.

4.9.4 Summary of the for-each loop

The for-each loop is always used to iterate over a collection. It provides us with a way to access every item in the collection in sequence, one by one, and process those items in whatever way we want. We can choose to do the same thing to each item (as we did when printing the full listing) or we can be selective and filter the list (as we did when we printed only a subset of the collection). The body of the loop can be as complicated as we like.

With its essential simplicity necessarily comes some limitations. For instance, one restriction is that we cannot change what is stored in the collection while iterating over it, either by adding new items to it or removing items from it. That doesn't mean, however, that we cannot change the states of objects already within the collection.

We have also seen that the for-each loop does not provide us with an index value for the items in the collection. If we want one, then we have to declare and maintain our own local variable. The reason for this has to do with abstraction, again. When dealing with collections and iterating over them, it is worth bearing two things in mind:

- A for-each loop provides a general control structure for iterating over different types of collection.
- There are some types of collections that do not naturally associate integer indices with the items they store. We will meet some of these in Chapter 6.

So the for-each loop abstracts the task of processing a complete collection, element by element, and is able to handle different types of collection. We do not need to know the details of how it manages that.

One of the questions we have not asked is whether a for-each loop can be used if we want to stop partway through processing the collection. For instance, suppose that instead of playing every track by our chosen artist, we just wanted to find the first one and play it, without going any further. While in principle it *is* possible to do this using a for-each loop, our practice and advice is not to use a for-each loop for tasks that might not need to process the whole collection. In other words, we recommend using a for-each loop only if you *definitely* want to process *the whole collection*. Again, stated in another way, once the loop starts, you know for sure how many times the body will be executed—this will be equal to the size of the collection. This style is often called *definite iteration*. For tasks where you might want to stop partway through, there are more appropriate loops to use—for instance, the *while loop*, which we will introduce next. In these cases, the number of times the loop's body will be executed is less certain; it typically depends on what happens during the iteration. This style is often called *indefinite iteration*, and we explore it next.

4.10 Indefinite iteration

Using a for-each loop has given us our first experience with the principle of carrying out some actions repeatedly. The statements inside the loop body are repeated for each item in the associated collection, and the iteration stops when we reach the end of the collection. A for-each loop provides *definite iteration*; given the state of a particular collection, the loop body will be executed the number of times that exactly matches the size of that collection. But there are many situations where we want to repeat some actions, but we cannot predict in advance exactly how many times that might be. A for-each loop does not help us in those cases.

Imagine, for instance, that you have lost your keys and you need to find them before you can leave the house. Your search will model an indefinite iteration, because there will be many different places to look, and you cannot predict in advance how many places you will have to search before you find the keys; after all, if you could predict that, you would go straight to where they are! So you will do something like mentally composing a list of possible places they could be, and then visit each place in turn until you find them. Once found, you want to stop looking rather than complete the list (which would be pointless).

What we have here is an example of *indefinite iteration*: the (search) action will be repeated an unpredictable number of times, until the task is complete. Scenarios similar to key searching are common in programming situations. While we will not always be searching for something, situations in which we want to keep doing something until the repetition is no longer necessary are frequently encountered. Indeed, they are so common that most programming languages provide at least one—and commonly more than one—loop construct to express them. Because what we are trying to do with these loop constructs is typically more complex than just iterating over a complete collection from beginning to end, they require a little more effort to understand. But this effort will be well rewarded from the greater variety of things we can achieve with them. Our focus here will be on Java's *while loop*, which is similar to loops found in other programming languages.

4.10.1 The while loop

A *while loop* consists of a header and a body; the body is intended to be executed repeatedly. Here is the structure of a while loop where *boolean condition* and *loop body* are pseudo-code, but all the rest is the Java syntax:

```
while(boolean condition) {
    loop body
}
```

The loop is introduced with the keyword `while`, which is followed by a boolean condition. The condition is ultimately what controls how many times a particular loop will iterate. The condition is evaluated when program control first reaches the loop, and it is re-evaluated each time the loop body has been executed. This is what gives a while loop its indefinite character—the re-evaluation process. If the condition evaluates to *true*, then the body is executed; and once it evaluates to *false*, the iteration is finished. The loop's body is then skipped over and execution continues with whatever follows immediately after the loop. Note that the condition could actually evaluate to *false* on the very first time it is tested. If this happens, the body won't be executed at all. This is an important feature of the while loop: the body might be executed zero times, rather than always at least once.

Before we look at a proper Java example, let us look at a pseudo-code version of the key hunt described earlier, to try to develop a feel for how a while loop works. Here is one way to express the search:

```
while (the keys are missing) {
    look in the next place
}
```

When we arrive at the loop for the first time, the condition is evaluated: the keys are missing. That means we enter the body of the loop and look in the next place on our mental list. Having done that, we return to the condition and re-evaluate it. If we have found the keys, the loop is finished and we can skip over the loop and leave the house. If the keys are still missing, then we go back into the loop body and look in the next place. This repetitive process continues until the keys are no longer missing.[1]

Note that we could equally well express the loop's condition the other way around, as follows:

```
while (not (the keys have been found)) {
    look in the next place
}
```

The distinction is subtle—one expressed as a status to be changed, and the other as a goal that has not yet been achieved. Take some time to read the two versions carefully to be sure you understand how each works. Both are equally valid and reflect choices of expression we will have to make when writing real loops. In both cases, what we write inside the loop when the keys are finally found will mean the loop conditions "flip" from *true* to *false* the next time they are evaluated.

Exercise 4.29 Suppose we express the first version of the key search in pseudo-code as follows:

```
boolean missing = true;
while (missing) {
    if (the keys are in the next place) {
        missing = false;
    }
}
```

---

[1] At this stage, we will ignore the possibility that the keys are not found, but taking this kind of possibility into account will actually become very important when we look at real Java examples.

Try to express the second version by completing the following outline:

```
boolean found = false;
while(...) {
    if (the keys are in the next place) {
        ...
    }
}
```

4.10.2 Iterating with an index variable

For our first while loop in correct Java code, we shall write a version of the `listAllFiles` method shown in Code 4.3. This does not really illustrate the indefinite character of while loops, but it does provide a useful comparison with the equivalent, familiar for-each example. The while-loop version is shown in Code 4.5. A key feature is the way that an integer variable (`index`) is used both to access the list's elements and to control the length of the iteration.

Code 4.5

Using a while loop to list the tracks

```java
/**
 * Show a list of all the files in the collection.
 */
public void listAllFiles()
{
    int index = 0;
    while(index < files.size()) {
        String filename = files.get(index);
        System.out.println(filename);
        index++;
    }
}
```

It is immediately obvious that the while-loop version requires more effort on our part to program it. Consider:

- We have to declare a variable for the list index, and we have to initialize it ourselves to 0 for the first list element. The variable must be declared outside the loop.

- We have to work out how to express the loop's condition in order to ensure that the loop stops at the right time.

- The list elements are not automatically fetched out of the collection and assigned to a variable for us. Instead, we have to do this ourselves, using the `get` method of the `ArrayList`. The variable `filename` will be local to the body of the loop.

- We have to remember to increment the counter variable (`index`) ourselves, in order to ensure that the loop condition will eventually become *false* when we have reached the end of the list.

The final statement in the body of the while loop illustrates a special operator for incrementing a numerical variable by 1:

```
index++;
```

This is equivalent to

```
index = index + 1;
```

So far, the for-each loop is clearly nicer for our purpose. It was less trouble to write, and it is safer. The reason it is safer is that it is always guaranteed to come to an end. In our while-loop version, it is possible to make a mistake that results in an *infinite loop*. If we were to forget to increment the index variable (the last line in the loop body), the loop condition would never become *false*, and the loop would iterate indefinitely. This is a typical programming error that catches even experienced programmers from time to time. The program will then run forever. If the loop in such a situation does not contain an output statement, the program will appear to "hang": it seems to do nothing, and does not respond to any mouse clicks or key presses. In reality, the program does a lot. It executes the loop over and over, but we cannot see any effect of this, and the program seems to have died. In BlueJ, this can often be detected by the fact that the red-and-white-striped "running" indicator remains on while the program appears to be doing nothing.

So what are the benefits of a while loop over a for-each loop? They are twofold: first, the while loop does not need to be related to a collection (we can loop on any condition that we can write as a boolean expression); second, even if we are using the loop to process the collection, we do not need to process every element—instead, we could stop earlier if we wanted to by including another component in the loop's condition that expresses why we would want to stop. Of course, strictly speaking, the loop's condition actually expresses whether we want to continue, and it is the negation of this that causes the loop to stop.

A benefit of having an explicit index variable is that we can use its value both inside and outside the loop, which was not available to us in the for-each examples. So we can include the index in the listing if we wish. That will make it easier to choose a track by its position in the list. For instance:

```
int index = 0;
while(index < files.size()) {
    String filename = files.get(index);
    // Prefix the file name with the track's index.
    System.out.println(index + ": " + filename);
    index++;
}
```

Having a local index variable can be particularly important when searching a list, because it can provide a record of where the item was located, which is still available once the loop has finished. We shall see this in the next section.

4.10.3 Searching a collection

Searching is one of the most important forms of iteration you will encounter. It is vital, therefore, to have a good grasp of its essential elements. The sort of loop structures that result occur again and again in practical programming situations.

The key characteristic of a search is that it involves *indefinite iteration*; this is necessarily so, because if we knew exactly where to look, we would not need a search at all! Instead, we have to initiate a search, and it will take an unknown number of iterations before we succeed. This implies that a for-each loop is inappropriate for use when searching, because it will complete its full set of iterations.[2]

In real search situations, we have to take into account the fact that the search might fail: we might run out of places to look. That means that we typically have two finishing possibilities to consider when writing a searching loop:

- The search succeeds after an indefinite number of iterations.
- The search fails after exhausting all possibilities.

Both of these must be taken into account when writing the loop's condition. As the loop's condition should evaluate to *true* if we want to iterate one more time, each of the finishing criteria should, on their own, make the condition evaluate to *false* to stop the loop.

The fact that we end up searching the whole list when the search fails does not turn a failed search into an example of definite iteration. The key characteristic of definite iteration is that you can determine the number of iterations *when the loop starts*. This will not be the case with a search.

If we are using an index variable to work our way through successive elements of a collection, then a failed search is easy to identify: the index variable will have been incremented beyond the final item in the list. That is exactly the situation that is covered in the **listAll-Files** method in Code 4.5, where the condition is:

```
while(index < files.size())
```

The condition expresses that we want to continue as long as the index is within the valid index range of the collection; as soon as it has been incremented out of range, then we want the loop to stop. This condition works even if the list is completely empty. In this case, **index** will have been initialized to zero, and the call to the **size** method will return zero too. Because zero is not less than zero, the loop's body will not be executed at all, which is what we want.

We also need to add a second part to the condition that indicates whether we have found the search item yet and stops the search when we have. We saw in Section 4.10.1 and Exercise 4.29 that we can often express this positively or negatively, via appropriately set boolean variables:

- A variable called **searching** (or **missing**, say) initially set to *true* could keep the search going until it is set to *false* inside the loop when the item is found.
- A variable called **found**, initially set to *false* and used in the condition as **!found**, could keep the search going until set to *true* when the item is found.

Here are the two corresponding code fragments that express the full condition in both cases:

```
int index = 0;
boolean searching = true;
while(index < files.size() && searching)
```

---

[2] While there are ways to subvert this characteristic of a for-each loop, and they are used quite commonly, we consider them to be bad style and do not use them in our examples.

or

```
int index = 0;
boolean found = false;
while(index < files.size() && !found)
```

Take some time to make sure you understand these two fragments, which accomplish exactly the same loop control, but expressed in slightly different ways. Remember that the condition *as a whole* must evaluate to *true* if we want to continue looking, and *false* if we want to stop looking, for any reason. We discussed the "and" operator **&&** in Chapter 3, which only evaluates to *true* if *both* of its operands are *true*.

The full version of a method to search for the first file name matching a given search string can be seen in Code 4.6 (*music-organizer-v4*). The method returns the index of the item as its result. Note that we need to find a way to indicate to the method's caller if the search has failed. In this case, we choose to return a value that cannot possibly represent a valid location in the collection—a negative value. This is a commonly used technique in search situations: the return of an *out-of-bounds* value to indicate failure.

Code 4.6

Finding the first matching item in a list

```
/**
 * Find the index of the first file matching the given
 * search string.
 * @param searchString The string to match.
 * @return The index of the first occurrence, or -1 if
 *         no match is found.
 */
public int findFirst(String searchString)
{
    int index = 0;
    // Record that we will be searching until a match is found.
    boolean searching = true;

    while(searching && index < files.size()) {
        String filename = files.get(index);
        if(filename.contains(searchString)) {
            // A match. We can stop searching.
            searching = false;
        }
        else {
            // Move on.
            index++;
        }
    }
    if(searching) {
        // We didn't find it.
        return -1;
    }
    else {
        // Return where it was found.
        return index;
    }
}
```

It might be tempting to try to have just one condition in the loop, even though there are two distinct reasons for ending the search. A way to do this would be to artificially arrange for the value of index to be too large if we find what we are looking for. This is a practice we discourage, because it makes the termination criteria of the loop misleading, and clarity is always preferred.

4.10.4 Some non-collection examples

Loops are not only used with collections. There are many situations were we want to repeat a block of statements that does not involve a collection at all. Here is an example that prints out all even numbers from 0 up to 30:

```
int index = 0;
while(index <= 30) {
    System.out.println(index);
    index = index + 2;
}
```

In fact, this is the use of a while loop for definite iteration, because it is clear at the start how many numbers will be printed. However, we cannot use a for-each loop, because they can only be used when iterating over collections. Later we will meet a third, related loop—the *for loop*—that would be more appropriate for this particular example.

To test your own understanding of while loops aside from collections, try the following exercises.

Exercise 4.30 Write a while loop (for example, in a method called `multiplesOfFive`) that prints out all multiples of 5 between 10 and 95.

Exercise 4.31 Write a while loop to add up the values 1 to 10 and print the sum once the loop has finished.

Exercise 4.32 Write a method called `sum` with a while loop that adds up all numbers between two numbers `a` and `b`. The values for `a` and `b` can be passed to the `sum` method as parameters.

Exercise 4.33 *Challenge exercise* Write a method `isPrime(int n)` that returns *true* if the parameter `n` is a prime number, and *false* if it is not. To implement the method, you can write a while loop that divides `n` by all numbers between `2` and `(n-1)` and tests whether the division yields a whole number. You can write this test by using the modulo operator (`%`) to check whether the integer division leaves a remainder of 0 (see the discussion of the modulo operator in Section 3.8.3).

Exercise 4.34 In the `findFirst` method, the loop's condition repeatedly asks the `files` collection how many files it is storing. Does the value returned by `size` vary from one check to the next? If you think the answer is no, then rewrite the method so that the number of files is determined only once and stored in a local variable prior to execution of the loop. Then use the local variable in the loop's condition rather than the call to `size`. Check that this version gives the same results. If you have problems completing this exercise, try using the debugger to see where things are going wrong.

4.11 Improving structure—the `Track` class

We have seen in a couple of places that using strings to store all of the track details is not entirely satisfactory, and gives our music player a rather cheap feel. Any commercial player would allow us to search for tracks by artist, title, album, genre, etc., and would likely include additional details, such as track playing time and track number. One of the powers of object orientation is that it allows us to design classes that closely model the inherent structure and behaviors of the real-world entities we are often trying to represent. This is achieved through writing classes whose fields and methods match the attributes. We know enough already about how to write basic classes with fields, constructors, and accessor and mutator methods that we can easily design a `Track` class that has fields for storing separate artist and title information, for instance. In this way, we will be able to interact with the objects in the music organizer in a way that feels more natural.

So it is time to move away from storing the track details as strings, because having a separate `Track` class is the most appropriate way to represent the main data items—music tracks—that we are using in the program. However, we will not be too ambitious. One of the obvious hurdles to overcome is how to obtain the separate pieces of information we wish to store in each `Track` object. One way would be to ask the user to input the artist, title, genre, etc., each time they add a music file to the organizer. However, that would be fairly slow and laborious, so for this project, we have chosen a set of music files that have the artist and title as part of the file name. We have written a helper class for our application (called `TrackReader`) that will look for any music files in a particular folder and use their file names to fill in parts of the corresponding `Track` objects. We will not worry about the details of how this is done at this stage. (Later in this book, we will discuss the techniques and library classes used in the `TrackReader` class.) An implementation of this design is in *music-organizer-v5*.

Here are some of the key points to look for in this version:

- The main thing to review is the changes we have made to the `MusicOrganizer` class, in going from storing `String` objects in the `ArrayList` to storing `Track` objects (Code 4.7). This has affected most of the methods we developed previously.

- When listing details of the tracks in `listAllTracks`, we request the `Track` object to return a `String` containing its details. This shows that we have designed the `Track` class to be responsible for providing the details to be printed, such as artist and title. This is an example of what is called *responsibility-driven design*, which we cover in more detail in a later chapter.

- In the `playTrack` method, we now have to retrieve the file name from the selected `Track` object before passing it on to the player.

- In the music library, we have added code to automatically read from the *audio* folder and some print statements to display some information.

4.11 Improving structure—the Track class

Code 4.7
Using Track in the MusicOrganizer class

```java
import java.util.ArrayList;

/**
 * A class to hold details of audio tracks.
 * Individual tracks may be played.
 *
 * @author David J. Barnes and Michael Kölling
 * @version 2016.02.29
 */
public class MusicOrganizer
{
    // An ArrayList for storing music tracks.
    private ArrayList<Track> tracks;
    // A player for the music tracks.
    private MusicPlayer player;
    // A reader that can read music files and load them as tracks.
    private TrackReader reader;

    /**
     * Create a MusicOrganizer
     */
    public MusicOrganizer()
    {
        tracks = new ArrayList<>();
        player = new MusicPlayer();
        reader = new TrackReader();
        readLibrary("../audio");
        System.out.println("Music library loaded. " + getNumberOfTracks() +
                           " tracks.");
        System.out.println();
    }

    /**
     * Add a track to the collection.
     * @param track The track to be added.
     */
    public void addTrack(Track track)
    {
        tracks.add(track);
    }

    /**
     * Play a track in the collection.
     * @param index The index of the track to be played.
     */
    public void playTrack(int index)
    {
        if(indexValid(index)) {
            Track track = tracks.get(index);
            player.startPlaying(track.getFilename());
            System.out.println("Now playing: " + track.getArtist() +
                               " - " + track.getTitle());
        }
    }
```

Code 4.7 continued
Using `Track` in the `MusicOrganizer` class

```java
    /**
     * Show a list of all the tracks in the collection.
     */
    public void listAllTracks()
    {
        System.out.println("Track listing: ");

        for(Track track : tracks) {
            System.out.println(track.getDetails());
        }
        System.out.println();
    }

    Other methods omitted.
}
```

While we can see that introducing a `Track` class has made some of the old methods slightly more complicated, working with specialized `Track` objects ultimately results in a much better structure for the program as a whole, and allows us to develop the `Track` class to the most appropriate level of detail for representing more than just audio file names. The information is not only better structured; using a `Track` class also allows us to store richer information if we choose to, such as an image of an album cover.

With a better structuring of track information, we can now do a much better job of searching for tracks that meet particular criteria. For instance, if we want to find all tracks that contain the word "love" in their title, we can do so as follows without risking mismatches on artists' names:

```java
/**
 * List all tracks containing the given search string in their title.
 * @param searchString The search string to be found.
 */
public void findInTitle(String searchString)
{
    for(Track track : tracks) {
        String title = track.getTitle();
        if(title.contains(searchString)) {
            System.out.println(track.getDetails());
        }
    }
}
```

Exercise 4.35 Add a `playCount` field to the `Track` class. Provide methods to reset the count to zero and to increment it by one.

Exercise 4.36 Have the `MusicOrganizer` increment the play count of a track whenever it is played.

Exercise 4.37 Add a further field, of your choosing, to the **Track** class, and provide accessor and mutator methods to query and manipulate it. Find a way to use this information in your version of the project; for instance, include it in a track's details string, or allow it to be set via a method in the **MusicOrganizer** class.

Exercise 4.38 If you play two tracks without stopping the first one, both will play simultaneously. This is not very useful. Change your program so that a playing track is automatically stopped when another track is started.

4.12 The Iterator type

Iteration is a vital tool in almost every programming project, so it should come as no surprise to discover that programming languages typically provide a wide range of features that support it, each with their own particular characteristics suited for different situations.

> **Concept**
>
> An **iterator** is an object that provides functionality to iterate over all elements of a collection.

We will now discuss a third variation for how to iterate over a collection that is somewhat in the middle between the while loop and the for-each loop. It uses a while loop to perform the iteration, and an *iterator object* instead of an integer index variable to keep track of the position in the list. We have to be very careful with naming at this point, because **Iterator** (note the uppercase *I*) is a Java *class*, but we will also encounter a *method* called **iterator** (lowercase *i*), so be sure to pay close attention to these differences when reading this section and when writing your own code.

Examining every item in a collection is so common that we have already seen a special control structure—the for-each loop—that is custom made for this purpose. In addition, Java's various collection library classes provide a custom-made common type to support iteration, and **ArrayList** is typical in this respect.

The **iterator** method of **ArrayList** returns an **Iterator** object. **Iterator** is also defined in the **java.util** package, so we must add a second import statement to the class file to use it:

```
import java.util.ArrayList;
import java.util.Iterator;
```

An **Iterator** provides just four methods, and two of these are used to iterate over a collection: **hasNext** and **next**. Neither takes a parameter, but both have non-**void** return types, so they are used in expressions. The way we usually use an **Iterator** can be described in pseudo-code as follows:

```
Iterator<ElementType> it = myCollection.iterator();
while(it.hasNext()) {
    call it.next() to get the next element
    do something with that element
}
```

In this code fragment, we first use the `iterator` method of the `ArrayList` class to obtain an `Iterator` object. Note that `Iterator` is also a generic type, so we parameterize it with the type of the elements in the collection we are iterating over. Then we use that `Iterator` to repeatedly check whether there are any more elements, `it.hasNext()`, and to get the next element, `it.next()`. One important point to note is that it is the `Iterator` object that we ask to return the next item, and not the collection object. Indeed, we tend not to refer directly to the collection at all in the body of the loop; all interaction with the collection is done via the `Iterator`.

Using an `Iterator`, we can write a method to list the tracks, as shown in Code 4.8. In effect, the `Iterator` starts at the beginning of the collection and progressively works its way through, one object at a time, each time we call its `next` method.

Code 4.8
Using an **Iterator** to list the tracks

```
/**
 * List all the tracks.
 */
public void listAllTracks()
{
    Iterator<Track> it = tracks.iterator();
    while(it.hasNext()) {
        Track t = it.next();
        System.out.println(t.getDetails());
    }
}
```

Take some time to compare this version to the one using a for-each loop in Code 4.7, and the two versions of `listAllFiles` shown in Code 4.3 and Code 4.5. A particular point to note about the latest version is that we use a while loop, but we do not need to take care of the `index` variable. This is because the `Iterator` keeps track of how far it has progressed through the collection, so that it knows both whether there are any more items left (`hasNext`) and which one to return (`next`) if there is another.

One of the keys to understanding how an `Iterator` works is that the call to `next` causes the `Iterator` to return the next item in the collection *and then move past that item*. Therefore, successive calls to `next` on an `Iterator` will always return distinct items; you cannot go back to the previous item once `next` has been called. Eventually, the `Iterator` reaches the end of the collection and then returns *false* from a call to `hasNext`. Once `hasNext` has returned *false*, it would be an error to try to call `next` on that particular `Iterator` object—in effect, the `Iterator` object has been "used up" and has no further use.

On the face of it, `Iterator` seems to offer no obvious advantages over the previous ways we have seen to iterate over a collection, but the following two sections provide reasons why it is important to know how to use it.

4.12.1 Index access versus iterators

We have seen that we have at least three different ways in which we can iterate over an `ArrayList`. We can use a for-each loop (as seen in Section 4.9.1), the `get` method with an integer index variable (Section 4.10.2), or an `Iterator` object (this section).

Figure 4.5
An iterator, after one iteration, pointing to the next item to be processed

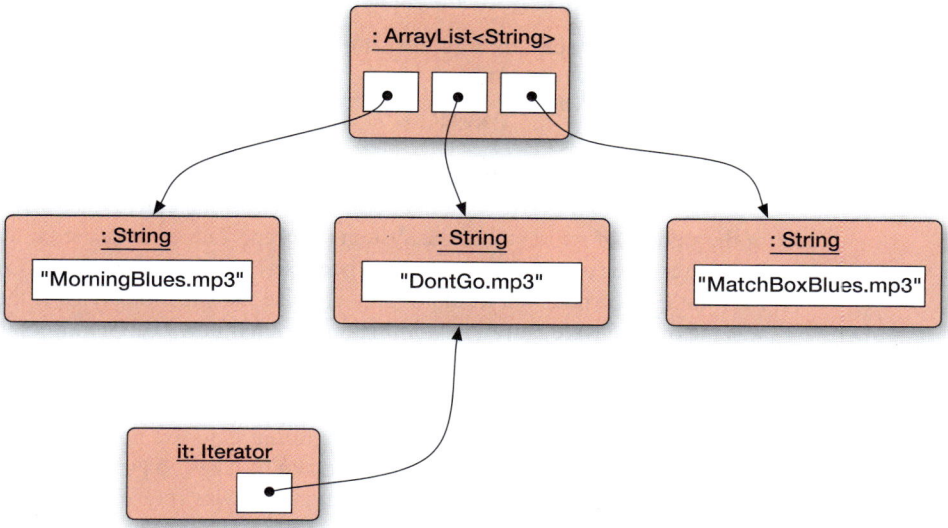

From what we know so far, all approaches seem about equal in quality. The first one was maybe slightly easier to understand, but the least flexible.

The first approach, using the for-each loop, is the standard technique used if all elements of a collection are to be processed (i.e., definite iteration), because it is the most concise for that case. The two latter versions have the benefit that iteration can more easily be stopped in the middle of processing (indefinite iteration), so they are preferable when processing only a part of the collection.

For an **ArrayList**, the two latter methods (using the while loops) are in fact equally good. This is not always the case, though. Java provides many more collection classes besides the **ArrayList**. We shall see several of them in the following chapters. For some collections, it is either impossible or very inefficient to access individual elements by providing an index. Thus, our first while loop version is a solution particular to the **ArrayList** collection and may not work for other types of collections.

The most recent solution, using an **Iterator**, is available for all collections in the Java class library and thus is an important *code pattern* that we shall use again in later projects.

4.12.2 Removing elements

Another important consideration when choosing which looping structure to use comes in when we have to remove elements from the collection while iterating. An example might be that we want to remove all tracks from our collection that are by an artist we are no longer interested in.

We can quite easily write this in pseudo-code:

```
for each track in the collection {
    if track.getArtist() is the out-of-favor artist:
        collection.remove(track)
}
```

It turns out that this perfectly reasonable operation is not possible to achieve with a for-each loop. If we try to modify the collection using one of the collection's **remove** methods while in the middle of an iteration, the system will report an error (called a **ConcurrentModificationException**). This happens because changing the collection in the middle of an iteration has the potential to thoroughly confuse the situation. What if the removed element was the one we were currently working on? If it has now been removed, how should we find the next element? There are no generally good answers to these potential problems, so using the collection's **remove** method is just not allowed during an iteration with the for-each loop.

The proper solution to removing while iterating is to use an **Iterator**. Its third method (in addition to **hasNext** and **next**) is **remove**. It takes no parameter and has a **void** return type. Calling **remove** will remove the item that was returned by the most recent call to **next**. Here is some sample code:

```
Iterator<Track> it = tracks.iterator();
while(it.hasNext()) {
    Track t = it.next();
    String artist = t.getArtist();
    if(artist.equals(artistToRemove)) {
        it.remove();
    }
}
```

Once again, note that we do not use the **tracks** collection variable in the body of the loop. While both **ArrayList** and **Iterator** have **remove** methods, we must use the **Iterator**'s **remove** method, not the **ArrayList**'s.

Using the **Iterator**'s **remove** is less flexible—we cannot remove arbitrary elements. We can remove only the last element we retrieved from the **Iterator**'s **next** method. On the other hand, using the **Iterator**'s **remove** is allowed during an iteration. Because the **Iterator** itself is informed of the removal (and does it for us), it can keep the iteration properly in sync with the collection.

Such removal is not possible with the for-each loop, because we do not have an **Iterator** there to work with. In this case, we need to use the while loop with an **Iterator**.

Technically, we can also remove elements by using the collection's **get** method with an index for the iteration. This is not recommended, however, because the element indices can change when we add or delete elements, and it is quite easy to get the iteration with indices wrong when we modify the collection during iteration. Using an **Iterator** protects us from such errors.

Exercise 4.39 Implement a method in your music organizer that lets you specify a string as a parameter, and then removes all tracks whose titles contain that string.

4.13 Summary of the music-organizer project

In the music organizer we have seen how we can use an `ArrayList` object, created from a class out of the class library, to store an arbitrary number of objects in a collection. We do not have to decide in advance how many objects we want to store, and the `ArrayList` object automatically keeps track of the number of items stored in it.

We have discussed how we can use a loop to iterate over all elements in the collection. Java has several loop constructs—the two we have used here are the *for-each loop* and the *while loop*. We typically use a for-each loop when we want to process the whole collection, and the while loop when we cannot predetermine how many iterations we need or when we need to remove elements during iteration.

With an `ArrayList`, we can access elements either by index, or we can iterate over all elements using an `Iterator` object. It will be worthwhile for you to review the different circumstances under which the different types of loop (for-each and while) are appropriate and why an `Iterator` is to be preferred over an integer index, because these sorts of decisions will have to be made over and over again. Getting them right can make it a lot easier to solve a particular problem.

Exercise 4.40 Use the *club* project to complete this and the following exercises. Your task is to complete the `Club` class, an outline of which has been provided in the project. The `Club` class is intended to store `Membership` objects in a collection.

Within `Club`, define a field for an `ArrayList`. Use an appropriate `import` statement for this field, and think carefully about the element type of the list. In the constructor, create the collection object and assign it to the field. Make sure that all the files in the project compile before moving on to the next exercise.

Exercise 4.41 Complete the `numberOfMembers` method to return the current size of the collection. Until you have a method to add objects to the collection, this will always return zero, of course, but it will be ready for further testing later.

Exercise 4.42 Membership of a club is represented by an instance of the `Membership` class. A complete version of `Membership` is already provided for you in the *club* project, and it should not need any modification. An instance contains details of a person's name and the month and year in which they joined the club. All membership details are filled out when an instance is created. A new `Membership` object is added to a `Club` object's collection via the `Club` object's `join` method, which has the following description:

```
/**
 * Add a new member to the club's collection of members.
 * @param member The member object to be added.
 */
public void join (Membership member)
```

Complete the `join` method.

When you wish to add a new **Membership** object to the **Club** object from the object bench, there are two ways you can do this. Either create a new **Membership** object on the object bench, call the **join** method on the **Club** object, and click on the **Membership** object to supply the parameter or call the **join** method on the **Club** object and type into the method's parameter dialog box:

```
new Membership ("member name ...", month, year)
```

Each time you add one, use the **numberOfMembers** method to check both that the **join** method is adding to the collection and that the **numberOfMembers** method is giving the correct result.

We shall continue to explore this project with some further exercises later in the chapter.

Exercise 4.43 *Challenge exercise* This and the following exercises present a challenge because they involve using some things that we have not covered explicitly. Nevertheless, you should be able to make a reasonable attempt at them if you have a comfortable grasp of the material covered so far. They involve adding something that most music players have: a "shuffle," or "random-play," feature.

The `java.util` package contains the **Random** class whose **nextInt** method will generate a positive random integer within a limited range. Write a method in the **MusicOrganizer** class to select a single random track from its list and play it.

Hint: You will need to import **Random** and create a **Random** object, either directly in the new method, or in the constructor and stored in a field. You will need to find the API documentation for the **Random** class and check its methods to choose the correct version of **nextInt**. Alternatively, we cover the **Random** class in Chapter 6.

Exercise 4.44 *Challenge exercise* Consider how you might play multiple tracks in a random order. Would you want to make sure that all tracks are played equally or prefer favorite tracks? How might a "play count" field in the **Track** class help with this task? Discuss the various options.

Exercise 4.45 *Challenge exercise* Write a method to play every track in the track list exactly once, in random order.

Hint: One way to do this would be to shuffle the order of the tracks in the list—or, perhaps better, a copy of the list—and then play through from start to finish. Another way would be to make a copy of the list and then repeatedly choose a random track from the list, play it, and remove it from the list until the list is empty. Try to implement one of these approaches. If you try the first, how easy is it to shuffle the list so that it is genuinely in a new random order? Are there any library methods that could help with this?

4.14 Another example: an auction system

In this section, we will follow up some of the new ideas we have introduced in this chapter by looking at them again in a different context.

The *auction* project models part of the operation of an online auction system. The idea is that an auction consists of a set of items offered for sale. These items are called "lots," and each is assigned a unique lot number by the program. A person can try to buy a lot by bidding an amount of money for it. Our auctions are slightly different from other auctions because ours offer all lots for a limited period of time.[3] At the end of that period, the auction is closed. At the close of the auction, the person who bid the highest amount for a lot is considered to have bought it. Any lots for which there are no bids remain unsold at the close. Unsold lots might be offered in a later auction, for instance.

The *auction* project contains the following classes: **Auction**, **Bid**, **Lot**, and **Person**. A close look at the class diagram for this project (Figure 4.6) reveals that the relationships between the various classes are a little more complicated than we have seen in previous projects. This will have a bearing on the way in which information is accessed during the

Figure 4.6
The class structure of the *auction* project

---

[3] For the sake of simplicity, the time-limit aspects of auctions are not implemented within the classes we are considering here.

auction activities. For instance, the diagram shows that **Auction** objects know about all the other types of objects: **Bid**, **Lot**, and **Person**. **Lot** objects know about **Bid** objects, and **Bid** objects know about **Person** objects. What the diagram cannot tell us is exactly how information stored in a **Bid** object, say, is accessed by an **Auction** object. For that, we have to look at the code of the various classes.

4.14.1 Getting started with the project

At this stage, it would be worth opening the *auction* project and exploring the source code before reading further. As well as seeing familiar use of an **ArrayList** and loops, you will likely encounter several things that you do not quite understand at first, but that is to be expected as we move on to new ideas and new ways of doing things.

An **Auction** object is the starting point for the project. People wishing to sell items enter them into the auction via the **enterLot** method, but they only supply a string description. The **Auction** object then creates a **Lot** object for each entered lot. This models the way things work in the real world: it is the auction site, rather than the sellers, for instance, that assigns lot numbers or identification codes to items. So a **Lot** object is the auction site's representation of an item for sale.

In order to bid for lots, people must register with the auction house. In our program, a potential bidder is represented by a **Person** object. These objects must be created independently on BlueJ's object bench. In our project, a **Person** object simply contains the person's name. When someone wants to bid for a lot, they call the **makeABid** method of the **Auction** object, entering the lot number they are interested in, the person object of the bidder, and how much they want to bid for it. Notice that they pass the lot number rather than the **Lot** object; **Lot** objects remain internal to the **Auction** object and are always referenced externally by their lot number.

Just as the **Auction** object creates **Lot** objects, it also transforms a monetary bid amount into a **Bid** object, which records the amount and the person who bid that amount. This is why we see a link from the **Bid** class to the **Person** class on the class diagram. However, note that there is no link from **Bid** to **Lot**; the link on the diagram is the other way around, because a **Lot** records which is currently the highest bid for that lot. This means that the **Lot** object will replace the **Bid** object it stores each time a higher bid is made.

What we have described here reveals quite a nested chain of object references. **Auction** objects store **Lot** objects; each **Lot** object can store a **Bid** object; each **Bid** object stores a **Person** object. Such chains are very common in programs, so this project offers a good opportunity to explore how they work in practice.

Exercise 4.46 Create an auction with a few lots, persons, and bids. Then use the object inspector to investigate the object structure. Start with the auction object, and continue by inspecting any further object references you encounter in the objects' fields.

4.14.2 The null keyword

From the discussion above, it should be clear that a **Bid** object is only created when someone actually makes a bid for a **Lot**. The newly created **Bid** object then stores the **Person** making the bid. This means that the **Person** field of every **Bid** object can be initialized in the **Bid** constructor, and the field will always contain a valid **Person** object.

In contrast, when a **Lot** object is created, this simply means it has been entered into the auction and it has no bidders yet. Nevertheless, it still has a **Bid** field, **highestBid**, for recording the highest bid for the lot. What value should be used to initialize this field in the **Lot** constructor?

What we need is a value for the field that makes it clear that there is currently "no object" being referred to by that variable. In some sense, the variable is "empty." To indicate this, Java provides the **null** keyword. Hence, the constructor of **Lot** has the following statement in it:

```
highestBid = null;
```

A very important principle is that, if a variable contains the **null** value, a method call should not be made on it. The reason for this should be clear: as methods belong to objects, we cannot call a method if the variable does not refer to an object. This means that we sometimes have to use an if-statement to test whether a variable contains **null** or not, before calling a method on that variable. Failure to make this test will lead to the very common runtime error called a **NullPointerException**. You will see some examples of this test in both the **Lot** and **Auction** classes.

In fact, if we fail to initialize an object-type field, it will automatically be given the value **null**. In this particular case, however, we prefer to make the assignment explicitly so that there is no doubt in the mind of the reader of the code that we expect **highestBid** to be **null** when a **Lot** object is created.

> **Concept**
>
> The Java reserved word **null** is used to mean "no object" when an object variable is not currently referring to a particular object. A field that has not explicitly been initialized will contain the value **null** by default.

Because neither the **Person** class nor the **Bid** class initiates any activity within the auction system, we shall not discuss them here in detail. Studying these classes is left as an exercise to the reader. Instead, we shall focus on the source code of the **Lot** and **Auction** classes.

4.14.3 The Lot class

The **Lot** class stores a description of the lot, a lot number, and details of the highest bid received for it so far. The most complex part of the class is the **bidFor** method (Code 4.9). This deals with what happens when a person makes a bid for the lot. When a bid is made, it is necessary to check that the new bid is higher in value than any existing bid on that lot. If it is higher, then the new bid will be stored as the current highest bid within the lot.

Here, we first check whether this bid is the highest bid. This will be the case if there has been no previous bid, or if the current bid is higher than the best bid so far. The first part of the check involves the following test:

```
highestBid == null
```

Code 4.9

Handle a bid for a lot

```java
public class Lot
{
    // The current highest bid for this lot.
    private Bid highestBid;
```

Other fields and constructor omitted.

```java
    /**
     * Attempt to bid for this lot. A successful bid
     * must have a value higher than any existing bid.
     * @param bid A new bid.
     * @return true if successful, false otherwise
     */
    public boolean bidFor(Bid bid)
    {
        if(highestBid == null) {
            // There is no previous bid.
            highestBid = bid;
            return true;
        }
        else if(bid.getValue() > highestBid.getValue()) {
            // The bid is better than the previous one.
            highestBid = bid;
            return true;
        }
        else {
            // The bid is not better.
            return false;
        }
    }
```

Other methods omitted.

```java
}
```

This is a test for whether the **highestBid** variable is currently referring to an object or not. As described in the previous section, until a bid is received for this lot, the **highestBid** field will contain the **null** value. If it is still **null**, then this is the first bid for this particular lot and it must clearly be the highest one. If it is not **null**, then we have to compare its value with the new bid. Note that the failure of the first test gives us some very useful information: we now know for sure that **highestBid** is not **null**, so we know that it is safe to call a method on it. We do not need to make a **null** test again in this second condition. Comparing the values of the two bids allows us to choose a higher new bid, or reject the new bid if it is no better.

4.14.4 The Auction class

The **Auction** class (Code 4.10) provides further illustration of the **ArrayList** and for-each loop concepts we discussed earlier in the chapter.

Code 4.10
The `Auction` class

```java
import java.util.ArrayList;

/**
 * A simple model of an auction.
 * The auction maintains a list of lots of arbitrary length.
 *
 * @author David J. Barnes and Michael Kölling.
 * @version 2016.02.29
 */
public class Auction
{
    // The list of Lots in this auction.
    private ArrayList<Lot> lots;
    // The number that will be given to the next lot entered
    // into this auction.
    private int nextLotNumber;

    /**
     * Create a new auction.
     */
    public Auction()
    {
        lots = new ArrayList<>();
        nextLotNumber = 1;
    }

    /**
     * Enter a new lot into the auction.
     * @param description A description of the lot.
     */
    public void enterLot(String description)
    {
        lots.add(new Lot(nextLotNumber, description));
        nextLotNumber++;
    }

    /**
     * Show the full list of lots in this auction.
     */
    public void showLots()
    {
        for(Lot lot : lots) {
            System.out.println(lot.toString());
        }
    }

    /**
     * Make a bid for a lot.
     * A message is printed indicating whether the bid is
     * successful or not.
     *
     * @param lotNumber The lot being bid for.
     * @param bidder The person bidding for the lot.
     * @param value  The value of the bid.
     */
```

Code 4.10 continued

The `Auction` class

```java
public void makeABid(int lotNumber, Person bidder, long value)
{
    Lot selectedLot = getLot(lotNumber);
    if(selectedLot != null) {
        Bid bid = new Bid(bidder, value);
        boolean successful = selectedLot.bidFor(bid);
        if(successful) {
            System.out.println("The bid for lot number " +
                                lotNumber + " was successful.");
        }
        else {
            // Report which bid is higher.
            Bid highestBid = selectedLot.getHighestBid();
            System.out.println("Lot number: " + lotNumber +
                                " already has a bid of: " +
                                highestBid.getValue());
        }
    }
}

/**
 * Return the lot with the given number. Return null
 * if a lot with this number does not exist.
 * @param lotNumber The number of the lot to return.
 */
public Lot getLot(int lotNumber)
{
    if((lotNumber >= 1) && (lotNumber < nextLotNumber)) {
        // The number seems to be reasonable.
        Lot selectedLot = lots.get(lotNumber - 1);
        // Include a confidence check to be sure we have the
        // right lot.
        if(selectedLot.getNumber() != lotNumber) {
            System.out.println("Internal error: Lot number " +
                                selectedLot.getNumber() +
                                " was returned instead of " +
                                lotNumber);
            // Don't return an invalid lot.
            selectedLot = null;
        }
        return selectedLot;
    }
    else {
        System.out.println("Lot number: " + lotNumber +
                            " does not exist.");
        return null;
    }
}
}
```

The `lots` field is an `ArrayList` used to hold the lots offered in this auction. Lots are entered in the auction by passing a simple description to the `enterLot` method. A new lot is created by passing the description and a unique lot number to the constructor of `Lot`. The new **Lot** object is added to the collection. The following sections discuss some additional, commonly found features illustrated in the **Auction** class.

4.14.5 Anonymous objects

The **enterLot** method in **Auction** illustrates a common idiom—anonymous objects. We see this in the following statement:

```
lots.add(new Lot(nextLotNumber, description));
```

Here, we are doing two things:

- We are creating a new **Lot** object.
- We are also passing this new object to the **ArrayList's add** method.

We could have written the same statement in two lines, to make the separate steps more explicit:

```
Lot newLot = new Lot(nextLotNumber, description);
lots.add(newLot);
```

Both versions are equivalent, but if we have no further use for the **newLot** variable, then the original version avoids defining a variable with such a limited use. In effect, we create an anonymous object—an object without a name—by passing it straight to the method that uses it.

> **Exercise 4.47** The **makeABid** method includes the following two statements:
>
> ```
> Bid bid = new Bid(bidder, value);
> boolean successful = selectedLot.bidFor(bid);
> ```
>
> The **bid** variable is only used here as a placeholder for the newly created **Bid** object before it is passed immediately to the lot's **bidFor** method. Rewrite these statements to eliminate the bid variable by using an anonymous object as seen in the **enterLot** method.

4.14.6 Chaining method calls

In our introduction to the *auction* project, we noted a chain of object references: **Auction** objects store **Lot** objects; each **Lot** object can store a **Bid** object; each **Bid** object stores a **Person** object. If the **Auction** object needs to identify who currently has the highest bid on a **Lot**, then it would need to ask the **Lot** to return the **Bid** object for that lot, then ask the **Bid** object for the **Person** who made the bid, and then ask the **Person** object for its name.

Ignoring the possibility of **null** object references, we might see something like the following sequence of statements in order to print the name of a bidder:

```
Bid bid = lot.getHighestBid();
Person bidder = bid.getBidder();
String name = bidder.getName();
System.out.println(name);
```

Because the `bid`, `bidder`, and `name` variables are being used here simply as staging posts to get to the bidder's name, it is common to see sequences like this compressed through the use of anonymous object references. For instance, we can achieve the same effect with the following:

```
System.out.println(lot.getHighestBid().getBidder().getName());
```

This looks as if methods are calling methods, but that is not how this must be read. Bearing in mind that the two sets of statements are equivalent, the chain of method calls must be read strictly from left to right:

```
lot.getHighestBid().getBidder().getName()
```

The call to `getHighestBid` returns an anonymous `Bid` object, and the `getBidder` method is then called on that object. Similarly, `getBidder` returns an anonymous `Person` object, so `getName` is called on that person.

Such chains of method calls can look complicated, but they can be unpicked if you understand the underlying rules. Even if you choose not to write your code in this more concise fashion, you should learn how to read it, because you may come across it in other programmers' code.

Exercise 4.48 Add a `close` method to the `Auction` class. This should iterate over the collection of lots and print out details of all the lots. Use a for-each loop. Any lot that has had at least one bid for it is considered to be sold, so what you are looking for is `Lot` objects whose `highestBid` field is not `null`. Use a local variable inside the loop to store the value returned from calls to the `getHighestBid` method, and then test that variable for the `null` value.

For lots with a bidder, the details should include the name of the successful bidder and the value of the winning bid. For lots with no bidder, print a message that indicates this.

Exercise 4.49 Add a `getUnsold` method to the `Auction` class with the following header:

```
public ArrayList<Lot> getUnsold()
```

This method should iterate over the `lots` field, storing unsold lots in a new `ArrayList` local variable. What you are looking for is `Lot` objects whose `highestBid` field is `null`. At the end of the method, return the list of unsold lots.

Exercise 4.50 Suppose the `Auction` class includes a method that makes it possible to remove a lot from the auction. Assuming the remaining lots do not have their `lotNumber` fields changed when a lot is removed, write down what you think the impact would be on the `getLot` method.

Exercise 4.51 Rewrite `getLot` so that it does not rely on a lot with a particular number being stored at index `(number-1)` in the collection. For instance, if lot number 2 has been removed, then lot number 3 will have been moved from index 2 to index 1, and all higher lot numbers will also have been moved by one index position. You may assume that lots are always stored in increasing order according to their lot numbers.

Exercise 4.52 Add a `removeLot` method to the `Auction` class, having the following header:

```
/**
 * Remove the lot with the given lot number.
 * @param number The number of the lot to be removed.
 * @return The Lot with the given number, or null if
 *         there is no such lot.
 */
public Lot removeLot(int number)
```

This method should not assume that a lot with a given number is stored at any particular location within the collection.

Exercise 4.53 The `ArrayList` class is found in the `java.util` package. That package also includes a class called `LinkedList`. Find out what you can about the `LinkedList` class, and compare its methods with those of `ArrayList`. Which methods do they have in common, and which are different?

4.14.7 Using collections

The `ArrayList` collection class (and others like it) is an important programming tools, because many programming problems involve working with variable-sized collections of objects. Before moving on to the next chapters, it is important that you become familiar and comfortable with how to work with them. The following exercises will help you do this.

Exercise 4.54 Continue working with the *club* project from Exercise 4.40. Define a method in the `Club` class with the following description:

```
/**
 * Determine the number of members who joined in the given
 * month.
 * @param month The month we are interested in.
 * @return The number of members who joined in that month.
 */
public int joinedInMonth(int month)
```

If the **month** parameter is outside the valid range of 1 to 12, print an error message and return zero.

Exercise 4.55 Define a method in the `Club` class with the following description:

```
/**
 * Remove from the club's collection all members who
 * joined in the given month,
 * and return them stored in a separate collection object.
 * @param month The month of the membership.
 * @param year The year of the membership.
 * @return The members who joined in the given month and year.
 */
public ArrayList<Membership> purge(int month, int year)
```

If the `month` parameter is outside the valid range of 1 to 12, print an error message and return a collection object with no objects stored in it.

Note: The `purge` method is significantly harder to write than any of the others in this class.

Exercise 4.56 Open the *products* project and complete the `StockManager` class through this and the next few exercises. `StockManager` uses an `ArrayList` to store `Product` items. Its `addProduct` method already adds a product to the collection, but the following methods need completing: `delivery`, `findProduct`, `printProductDetails`, and `numberInStock`.

Each product sold by the company is represented by an instance of the `Product` class, which records a product's ID, name, and how many of that product are currently in stock. The `Product` class defines the `increaseQuantity` method to record increases in the stock level of that product. The `sellOne` method records that one item of that product has been sold, by reducing the quantity field level by 1. `Product` has been provided for you, and you should not need to make any alterations to it.

Start by implementing the `printProductDetails` method to ensure that you are able to iterate over the collection of products. Just print out the details of each `Product` returned, by calling its `toString` method.

Exercise 4.57 Implement the `findProduct` method. This should look through the collection for a product whose `id` field matches the ID argument of this method. If a matching product is found, it should be returned as the method's result. If no matching product is found, return `null`.

This differs from the `printProductDetails` method, in that it will not necessarily have to examine every product in the collection before a match is found. For instance, if the first product in the collection matches the product ID, iteration can finish and that first `Product` object can be returned. On the other hand, it is possible that there might be no match in the collection. In that case, the whole collection will be examined without finding a product to return. In this case, the `null` value should be returned.

When looking for a match, you will need to call the `getID` method on a `Product`.

Exercise 4.58 Implement the `numberInStock` method. This should locate a product in the collection with a matching ID and return the current quantity of that product as a method result. If no product with a matching ID is found, return zero. This is relatively simple to implement once the `findProduct` method has been completed. For instance, `numberInStock` can call the `findProduct` method to do the searching and then call the `getQuantity` method on the result. Take care with products that cannot be found, though.

Exercise 4.59 Implement the `delivery` method using a similar approach to that used in `numberInStock`. It should find the product with the given ID in the list of products and then call its `increaseQuantity` method.

Exercise 4.60 *Challenge exercise* Implement a method in `StockManager` to print details of all products with stock levels below a given value (passed as a parameter to the method).

Modify the `addProduct` method so that a new product cannot be added to the product list with the same ID as an existing one.

Add to `StockManager` a method that finds a product from its name rather than its ID:

```
public Product findProduct(String name)
```

In order to do this, you need to know that two `String` objects, `s1` and `s2`, can be tested for equality with the boolean expression

```
s1.equals(s2)
```

More details about comparing `Strings` can be found in Chapter 6.

4.15 Summary

We have seen that classes such as `ArrayList` conveniently allow us to create collections containing an arbitrary number of objects. The Java library contains more collections like this, and we shall look at some of the others in Chapter 6. You will find that being able to use collections confidently is an important skill in writing interesting programs. There is hardly an application we shall see from now on that does not use collections of some form.

When using collections, the need arises to iterate over all elements in a collection to make use of the objects stored in them. For this purpose, we have seen the use of loops and iterators.

Loops are also a fundamental concept in computing that you will be using in every project from now on. Make sure you familiarize yourself sufficiently with writing loops—you will not get very far without them. When deciding on the type of loop to use in a particular situation, it is often useful to consider whether the task involves definite iteration, or indefinite iteration. Is there certainty or uncertainty about the number of iterations that will be required?

As an aside, we have mentioned the Java class library, a large collection of useful classes that we can use to make our own classes more powerful. We shall need to study the library in some more detail to see what else is in it that we should know about. This will be the topic of a future chapter.

Terms introduced in this chapter

> **collection, iterator, for-each loop, while loop, index, import statement, library, package, anonymous object, definite iteration, indefinite iteration**

Exercise 4.84 Java provides another type of loop: the *do-while loop*. Find out how this loop works and describe it. Write an example of a do-while loop that prints out the numbers from 1 to 10. To find out about this loop, find a description of the Java language (for example, at

`http://download.oracle.com/javase/tutorial/java/nutsandbolts/`

in the section "Control Flow Statements").

Exercise 4.85 Rewrite the `listAllFiles` method in the `MusicOrganizer` class from `music-organizer-v3` by using a do-while loop rather than a for-each loop. Test your solution carefully. Does it work correctly if the collection is empty?

Exercise 4.86 *Challenge exercise* Rewrite the `findFirst` method in the `MusicOrganizer` class from *music-organizer-v4* by using a do-while loop rather than a while loop. Test your solution carefully. Try searches that will succeed and others that will fail. Try searches where the file to be found is first in the list, and also where it is last in the list.

Exercise 4.87 Find out about Java's *switch-case statement*. What is its purpose? How is it used? Write an example. (This is also a *control flow statement*, so you will find information in similar locations as for the *do-while loop*.)

CHAPTER 5
Functional Processing of Collections (Advanced)

Main concepts discussed in this chapter:

- functional programming
- lambdas
- streams
- pipelines

Java constructs discussed in this chapter:

`Stream`, `lambda`, `filter`, `map`, `reduce`, `->`

This chapter introduces some advanced concepts. The advanced sections in this book (there will be some others later) can be skipped on first reading if you wish. In this chapter, we will discuss some alternative techniques to achieve the same tasks as discussed in the previous chapters. These techniques were not available in the Java language prior to version 8.

5.1 An alternative look at themes from Chapter 4

In Chapter 4, we started to look at techniques to process collections of objects. Handling collections is one of the fundamental techniques in programming; almost all computer programs process collections of some sort, and we will see much more of this throughout this book. Being able to do this well is essential.

However, learning about collections in programming has become more complicated in recent years through the introduction of new programming techniques into mainstream programming languages. These techniques can make your *program* simpler, but they make *learning* more work—there are simply more different constructs to master.

The "new" techniques are not really new—they are only new in this particular kind of language. There have always been different kinds of languages: Java, for example, is an *imperative object-oriented* language, and the style of collection processing we started to introduce in Chapter 4 is the typical imperative way to do things.

Another class of language is *functional languages*; these have been around for a long time, and they use a different style of programming. It turns out, for reasons we will discuss later, that the functional style of processing collections has advantages in some situations over the imperative style. As a result, the designers of the Java language decided at some point to add some elements of functional programming to the Java language. They did this in version 8 of the language (Java 8, released in 2014). The new techniques that were added are *streams* and *lambdas* (sometimes also called *closures*). This makes Java technically a hybrid language: a mostly imperative language with some functional elements.

For proficient programmers, this is a great thing. The new functional language constructs allow us to write more elegant and expressive programs. For learners, it creates more work: we now have to study two different ways to achieve a similar goal.

The new functional style, which we cover in this chapter, is quickly becoming popular and will likely be the dominant style of writing new code in Java within a short space of time. The imperative style covered in the previous chapter, however, is still the way most code is written today, and is still considered the "standard" Java way to do things. When you work with existing code written by other programmers (as you will most of the time), it is essential that you understand and can work with the imperative style. When you write your own code, you can choose your style: the functional and imperative styles are two different ways to solve the same problem, and one can replace the other. Going forward, we will often prefer the functional style, because it is more concise and more elegant.

In short, for a learner to become a good programmer, it is necessary to become familiar with both styles of processing collections. In this book, we present the imperative style first, and introduce the functional style in 'advanced' sections (such as this chapter).

These advanced sections can be skipped (you can now skip ahead to Chapter 6 if you want), and you will still learn how to program, and will still be able to solve the problems we present. They could also be read out of sequence (skip them now, but come back to them later) if you are short of time and want to make progress with other constructs first. For a full picture, they can be read in sequence, where they are, and you will learn the alternative constructs as you go along.

5.2 Monitoring animal populations

As before, we will use an example program to introduce and discuss the new constructs. Here, we will look at a system to monitor animal populations.

An important element of animal conservation and the protection of endangered species is the ability to monitor population numbers, and to detect when levels are healthy or in decline. Our project processes reports of sightings of different types of animal, sent back by spotters from various different places. Each sighting report consists of the name of the animal that has been seen, how many have been seen, who is sending the report (an integer ID), which area the sighting was made in (an integer), and an indication of when the sighting was made (a simple numerical value which might be the number of days since the experiment started).

The simple data requirements make it easy for spotters in remote locations to send back relatively small amounts of valuable information—perhaps in the form of a text message— to a base that is then able to aggregate the data and create reports or direct the field workers to different areas.

This approach fits well with both highly managed projects—such as might be undertaken by a National Park and involve motion triggered cameras and people evaluating the camera footage—and with loosely organized crowd-sourcing activities—such as national bird-counting days, where a large group of volunteers uses phone apps to send data.

We provide a partial implementation of such a system under the name *animal-monitoring-v1* in the book projects.

Code 5.1 shows the `Sighting` class we will be using to record details of each sighting report, from a single spotter for a particular animal, once the sighting details have been processed. In this chapter, we will not be concerning ourselves directly with format of the data sent in by the spotter. In keeping with the theme that this chapter explores, more advanced Java concepts, you are encouraged to read through the full source code of the project to find things that we have not explored in detail yet, and to use them for your own personal development. The `Sighting` class, however, is very straightforward.

Code 5.1

The `Sighting` class

```java
/**
 * Details of a sighting of a type of animal by an individual spotter.
 *
 * @author David J. Barnes and Michael Kölling
 * @version 2016.02.29
 */
public class Sighting
{
    // The animal spotted.
    private final String animal;
    // The ID of the spotter.
    private final int spotter;
    // How many were seen.
    private final int count;
    // The ID of the area in which they were seen.
    private final int area;
    // The reporting period.
    private final int period;

    /**
     * Create a record of a sighting of a particular type of animal.
     * @param animal The animal spotted.
     * @param spotter The ID of the spotter.
     * @param count How many were seen (>= 0).
     * @param area The ID of the area in which they were seen.
     * @param period The reporting period.
     */
```

Code 5.1 continued

The `Sighting` class

```java
public Sighting(String animal, int spotter, int count,
                int area, int period)
{
    this.animal = animal;
    this.spotter = spotter;
    this.count = count;
    this.area = area;
    this.period = period;
}
```

Some accessors omitted.

```java
/**
 * Return a string containing details of the animal, the number seen,
 * where they were seen, who spotted them and when.
 * @return A string giving details of the sighting.
 */
public String getDetails()
{
    return animal +
        ", count = " + count +
        ", area = " + area +
        ", spotter = " + spotter +
        ", period = " + period;
}
```

Code 5.2 shows part of the `AnimalMonitor` class that is used to aggregate the individual sightings into a list. At this point, all of the sightings from all the different spotters and areas are held together in a single collection. Among other things, the class contains methods to print the list, count the total number of sightings of a given animal, list all of the sightings by a particular spotter, remove records containing no sightings, and so on. All of these methods have been implemented using the techniques described in Chapter 4 for basic list manipulation: iteration over the full list; processing selected elements of the list based on some condition (filtering); and removal of elements. The methods implemented here are not complete for an application of this kind, but have been implemented to show examples of these different kinds of list processing.

Code 5.2

The `AnimalMonitor` class

```java
import java.util.ArrayList;
import java.util.Iterator;

/**
 * Monitor counts of different types of animal.
 * Sightings are recorded by spotters.
 *
 * @author David J. Barnes and Michael Kölling
 * @version 2016.02.29 (imperative)
 */
public class AnimalMonitor
{
    // Records of all the sightings of animals.
    private ArrayList<Sighting> sightings;
```

Code 5.2 continued

The `Animal-Monitor` class

```java
    /**
     * Create an AnimalMonitor.
     */
    public AnimalMonitor()
    {
        this.sightings = new ArrayList<>();
    }

    /**
     * Add the sightings recorded in the given filename to the current list.
     * @param filename A CSV file of Sighting records.
     */
    public void addSightings(String filename)
    {
        SightingReader reader = new SightingReader();
        sightings.addAll(reader.getSightings(filename));
    }

    /**
     * Print details of all the sightings.
     */
    public void printList()
    {
        for(Sighting record : sightings) {
            System.out.println(record.getDetails());
        }
    }

    Other methods omitted.
}
```

So far, this code, uses the imperative collection processing techniques introduced in Chapter 4. We will use this as a basis to gradually make changes to replace the list processing code with functional constructs.

Exercise 5.1 Open the *animal-monitoring-v1 project* and create an instance of the `AnimalMonitor` class. The file `sightings.csv` in the project directory contains a small sample of sighting records in *comma-separated values* (CSV) format. Pass the name of this file (*"sightings.csv"*) to the `addSightings` method of the `AnimalMonitor` object and then call `printList` to show details of the data that has been read.

Exercise 5.2 Try out the other methods of the `AnimalMonitor` object, using animal names, spotter and area IDs shown in the output from `printList`.

Exercise 5.3 Read through the full source code of the `AnimalMonitor` class to understand how the methods work. The class only uses techniques we have covered in previous chapters, so you should be able to work out the details.

Exercise 5.4 Why does the `removeZeroCounts` method use a while loop with an iterator, instead of a for-each loop as used in the other methods? Could it be written with a for-each loop? Could the other methods be written using a while loop?

5.3 A first look at lambdas

Concept

A **lambda** is a segment of code that can be stored and executed later.

Central to the new functional style of processing a collection is the concept of a *lambda*.

The basic new idea is that we can pass *a segment of code* as a parameter to a method, which can then execute this piece of code later when it needs to.

Up to now, we have seen various types of parameters—integers, strings, objects—but all these were pieces of *data*, not pieces of *code*. The ability to pass code as a parameter was new in Java 8, and it allows us to do some very useful things.

5.3.1 Processing a collection with a lambda

When we were processing our collections in Chapter 4, we wrote a loop to retrieve the collection elements one by one, and then we did something to each element. The code structure is always similar to the following pseudo-code:

```
loop (for each element in the collection):
    get one element;
    do something with the element;
end loop
```

It does not matter whether we use a for loop, a for-each loop, or a while loop, or whether we use an iterator or an index to access the elements—the principle is the same.

When using a lambda, we approach the problem differently. We pass a bit of code to the collection and say "Do this to each element in the collection." The code structure looks something like this:

Concept

In the **functional style of collection processing**, we do not retrieve each element to operate on it. Instead, we pass a code segment to the collection to be applied to each element.

```
collection.doThisForEachElement(some code);
```

We can see that the code looks much simpler. Most importantly: the loop has disappeared completely. In fact, it is not gone—it has just been moved into the *doThisForEachElement* method—but it has disappeared from our own code; we do not need to write it every time anymore.

We have made the collections more powerful: Instead of just being able to hand out their elements to us, so that we can do some work on them, the collection is now able to do work on the elements for us. This makes our life easier.

We can think about it like this: Imagine you need to give every child in a school class a haircut. In the old style, you say to the teacher: *Send me the first child.* Then you give the child a haircut. Then you say: *Send me the next child.* Another hair cutting session. And so it continues, until there are no more children left. This is the old style loop of next item/process.

In the new style, you do the following: You write down instructions for how to give a haircut, and then you give this to the teacher and say: *Do this to every child in your class.* (The teacher, here, represents the collection.) In fact, an interesting side-effect of this approach is that we don't even need to know how the teacher will complete the task. For instance, instead of cutting the hair themselves, they could decide to sub-contract the task to a separate person for each individual child, so that every child's hair is cut at the same time. The teacher would just pass on the instructions you gave them.

Your life is suddenly much easier. The teacher is doing much of the work for you. That is exactly what the new collections in Java 8 can do for you.

5.3.2 Basic syntax of a lambda

A lambda is, in some ways, similar to a method: it is a segment of code that is defined to do something, but not immediately executed. However, unlike a method, it does not belong to a class, and we will not give it a name. It is useful to compare the syntax of a lambda with that of a method performing a similar task.

A method to print out the details of a sighting might look like this:

```
public void printSighting(Sighting record)
{
    System.out.println(record.getDetails());
}
```

The equivalent lambda looks like this:

```
(Sighting record) ->
{
    System.out.println(record.getDetails());
}
```

You can now easily see the differences and the similarities. The differences are:

- There is no `public` or `private` keyword—the visibility is assumed to be `public`.
- There is no return type specified. This is because that can be worked out by the compiler from the final statement in the lambda's body. In this case, the `println` method is `void` so the lambda's return type is `void`.
- There is no name given to the lambda; it starts with the parameter list.
- An arrow (->) separates the parameter list from the lambda's body—this is the distinctive notation for a lambda.

You will find that lambdas are often used for relatively simple, one-off tasks that do not require the complexity of a full class. Some of the information about a lambda is provided by default or inferred from the context—its visibility and return type—and we have no choice over this. Furthermore, since a lambda has no associated class, there are also no instance fields and no constructor. That makes for very specialized usage of lambdas. Because of the lack of a name, lambdas are also known as *anonymous functions*.

We will encounter lambdas and function parameters several times later in this book, for example when we introduce *functional interfaces* in Chapter 12 and when we write graphical user interfaces (GUIs) in Chapter 13. For the time being, however, we will explore how to use lambdas with our collections.

5.4 The `forEach` method of collections

When introducing the idea of a lambda above, we mentioned the idea of a `doThisForEach-Element` method in the collection class. This method in Java is actually called `forEach`.

If we have a collection called `myList`, we can write

```
myList.forEach(... some code to apply to each element of list ...)
```

The parameter to this method will be a lambda—a piece of code—with the syntax as we have seen it above. The `forEach` method will then execute the lambda for each list element, passing each list element as a parameter to the lambda in turn.

Let us look at some concrete code. The `printList` method from our `AnimalMonitor` class looks like this:

```
/**
 * Print details of all the sightings.
 */
public void printList()
{
    for(Sighting record : sightings) {
        System.out.println(record.getDetails());
    }
}
```

We can now write the following lambda-based version of this method:

```
/**
 * Print details of all the sightings.
 */
public void printList()
{
    sightings.forEach(
        (Sighting record) ->
        {
            System.out.println(record.getDetails());
        }
    );
}
```

The body of this new version of `printList` consists of a single statement (even though it spans six lines), which is a call to the `forEach` method of the `sightings` list. Admittedly, this does not yet look simpler than before, but we will get there in a moment. It is important to notice that there is no explicit loop statement in this version, unlike in the previous version—the iteration is handled *implicitly* by the `forEach` method.

The parameter of the `forEach` is a lambda. The lambda itself has a parameter, named `record`. Every element of the `sightings` list will be used as a parameter to this lambda in turn, and the body of the lambda executes. This way, the details of every element will be printed.

This style of syntax is completely unlike any you will have met in previous chapters of this book, so make sure that you take some time to understand this first example of a lambda in action. Although we will shortly show some slight modifications to the syntax used here, it does illustrate a typical use of lambdas, and the fundamental ideas will be repeated in all future examples:

- A lambda starts with a list of parameters;
- An arrow symbol follows the parameters;
- Statements to be executed follow the arrow symbol.

Exercise 5.5: Open the *animal-monitoring-v1* project and rewrite the `printList` method in your version of the `AnimalMonitor` class to use a lambda, as shown above. Test that it still works and performs the same as before.

5.4.1 Variations of lambda syntax

One goal of the lambda syntax in Java is to allow us to write code clearly and concisely. The ability to omit the `public` access modifier, for example, and the return type, are a start of this. The compiler, however, allows us to go further: Several other elements can be omitted where the compiler can work them out by itself.

The first is the type of the parameter to the lambda (`record`, in our case). Since the type of the lambda parameter must always match the type of the collection elements, the compiler can work this out, and we are allowed to omit it. Our code then looks like this:

```
sightings.forEach(
    (record) ->
    {
        System.out.println(record.getDetails());
    }
);
```

The next simplification concerns parentheses and curly brackets:

- If the parameter list contains only a single parameter, then the parentheses may be omitted.
- If the body of the lambda contains only a single statement, then the curly brackets may be omitted.

Applying both of these simplifications the code now becomes short enough to fit in a single line, and we can write the `forEach` call as:

```
sightings.forEach(record -> System.out.println(record.getDetails()));
```

This is the version we shall prefer in our own code.

Once again, we encourage you to make sure you understand how this reduced syntax fits the description, as many lambdas are written in this form in practice.

The *animal-monitoring-v2* project is written using the functional style as discussed here and can be used in case you want to check your solutions to some of these exercises. However, do the exercises yourself, and use this project only if you really get stuck.

> **Benefit of lambdas** In practice, when we use lambdas, the lambda code is often short and simple, and the shortcut notation just discussed here can be used. This makes our code short and clear, and easy to write. Also, because we do not write the loop ourselves anymore, we are less likely to make errors—if we don't write the loop, it cannot be wrong.
>
> There are, however, other benefits in addition to this. One is that this allows the use of streams, discussed in the next section. Another benefit is the use of concurrency (also called parallel programming).
>
> Most computers today have multiple cores and are capable of parallel processing. However, writing code that makes good use of these multiple cores is extremely difficult. Most of our programs will just use one core most of the time, and the rest of the available processing power is wasted. Learning to write code to use all cores is a very advanced subject, and many programmers never master it.
>
> By using lambdas and moving the loop into the collection, we can now potentially use collections that handle the parallel processing for us. When we want parallelism, we just use an appropriate collection, and all the hard parallel processing code is hidden inside the collection class, written for us. Our code looks short and simple. Suddenly, using all your cores in your laptop becomes possible, with very little extra effort.
>
> We will not discuss parallel programming much in this book. However, it is interesting to know that mastering lambdas and streams prepares you well to progress to using concurrent collection classes later on.

5.5 Streams

The `forEach` method of `ArrayList` (and related collection classes) is just one particular example of a method that makes use of the *streams* feature introduced in Java 8. Streams are a little like collections, but with some important differences:

Concept

Streams unify the processing of elements of a collection and other sets of data. A stream provides useful methods to manipulate these data sets.

- Elements in a stream are not accessed via an index, but usually sequentially.
- The contents and ordering of the stream cannot be changed—changes require the creation of a new stream.
- A stream could potentially be infinite!

The stream concept is used to unify the processing of sets of data, independent of where this data set comes from. It could be the processing of elements from a collection (as we have discussed), processing messages coming in over a network, processing lines of text from a text file, or all characters from a string. It does not matter what the source of the data is—we can view any of these as a stream, then use the same techniques and methods to process the elements.

Streams add one further significant new feature over previous facilities in Java for the processing of collections: the potential for safe parallel processing. There are many situations in which the order elements in a collection are processed does not matter, or when the processing of an element in the collection is largely independent of the other elements. Where these conditions apply, parallelization of collection processing can offer significant acceleration when dealing with large amounts of data. However, we will not discuss this any further here.

An `ArrayList` is not, itself, a stream, but we can ask it to provide the source of a stream by calling its `stream` method. The stream returned will contain all the elements of the `ArrayList` in index order. If we ignore the issue of parallelization, streams do not actually enable us to do anything that we could not already program, using language features we have already met. However, streams neatly capture many of the most commonly-occurring tasks we want to perform on collections, in a form that makes them much simpler to program than we have become used to, as well as being easier to understand. In particular, we will see that operations on streams eliminate the need to write explicit loops when processing a collection—just as we see in the rewrite of the `printList` method in Exercise 5.6.

> **Exercise 5.6** Modify your own `printList` method as discussed here: try out all the syntax variations for lambdas that we have shown. Recompile and test the project with each variation to check that you have the syntax correct.

We have already seen some of that with the `forEach` method; in the remainder of this chapter we will explore the `filter`, `map`, and `reduce` methods defined on streams.

5.5.1 Filters, maps and reductions

We noted above that the contents of a stream cannot be modified, so changes require a new stream to be created. Many varied kinds of processing of streams can be achieved with only three different kinds of functions: *filter*, *map*, and *reduce*. By varying and combining these, we can do most of what we will ever need.

Before looking at the specific Java methods, we will discuss the basic idea of these functions. All of them are applied to a stream to process it in a certain way. All are very common and useful.

The filter function

> **Concept**
> We can **filter** a stream to select only specific elements.

The *filter* function takes a stream, selects some of it elements, and creates a new stream with only the selected elements (Figure 5.1). Some elements are *filtered out*. The result is a stream with fewer elements (a subset of the original).

An example from our collection of animal sightings could be to select the sightings of elephants out of all sightings recorded. We start with all sightings, apply a filter that only selects elephants, and we are left with a stream of all elephant sightings.

Figure 5.1
Applying a filter to a stream

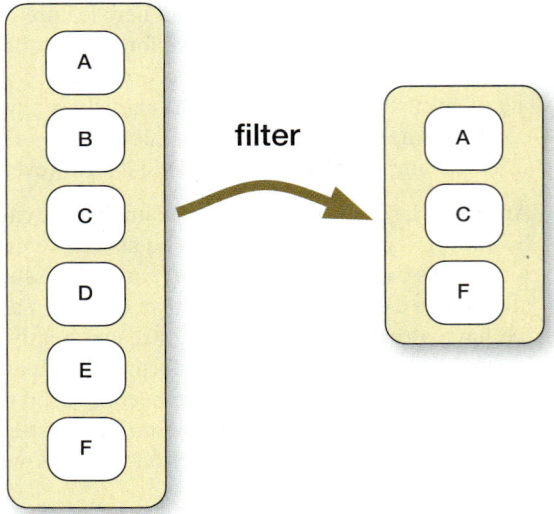

The map function

> **Concept**
>
> We can **map** a stream to a new stream, where each element of the original stream is replaced with a new element derived from the original.

The *map* function takes a stream and creates a new stream, where each element of the original stream is mapped to a new, different element in the new stream (Figure 5.2). The new stream will have the same number of elements, but the type and content of each element can be different; it is derived in some way from the original element.

In our project, an example is to replace every sighting object in the original stream with the number of animals spotted in this sighting. We start with a stream of sighting objects, and we end with a stream of integers.

Figure 5.2
Applying a map to a stream

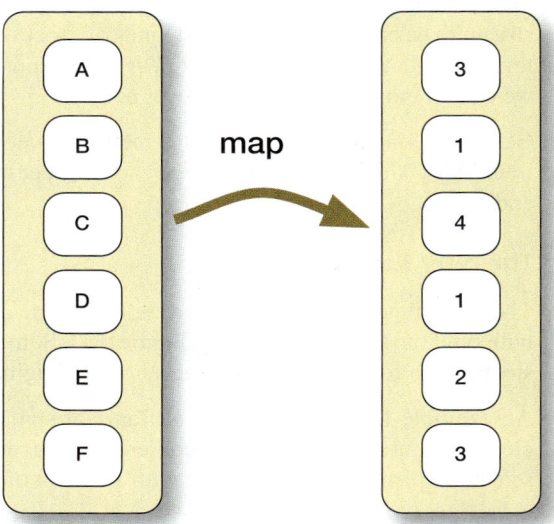

The reduce function

> **Concept**
>
> We can **reduce** a stream; reducing means to apply a function that takes a whole stream and delivers a single result.

The *reduce* function takes a stream and collapses all elements into a single result (Figure 5.3). This could be done in different ways, for example by adding all elements together, or selecting just the smallest element from the stream. We start with a stream, and we end up with a single result.

In our animal monitoring project, this would be useful for counting how many elephants we have seen: Once we have a stream of all elephant sightings, we can use *reduce* to add them all up. (Remember: each sighting instance can be of multiple animals.)

5.5.2 Pipelines

> **Concept**
>
> A **pipeline** is the combination of two or more stream functions in a chain, where each function is applied in turn.

Streams, and the stream functions, become even more useful when several functions are combined into a *pipeline*. A pipeline is the chaining of two or more of these kinds of function, so that they are applied one after the other.

Let us assume we want to find out how many elephant sightings we have recorded. We can do this by applying a filter, map, and reduce function one after the other (Figure 5.4).

In this example, we first *filter* all sightings to select only elephant sightings, then we *map* each sighting object to the number of elephants spotted in this sighting, and finally we add them all up with a *reduce* function. Notice that after the *map* function has been applied, we are no longer dealing with a stream of `Sighting` objects, but with a stream of integer values. This form of transformation between input stream and output stream is very common with the *map* function.

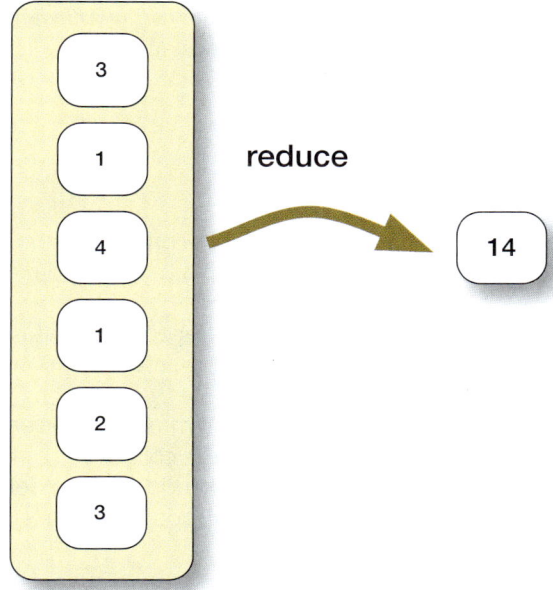

Figure 5.3
Applying a reduction to a stream

Figure 5.4

A pipeline of stream functions

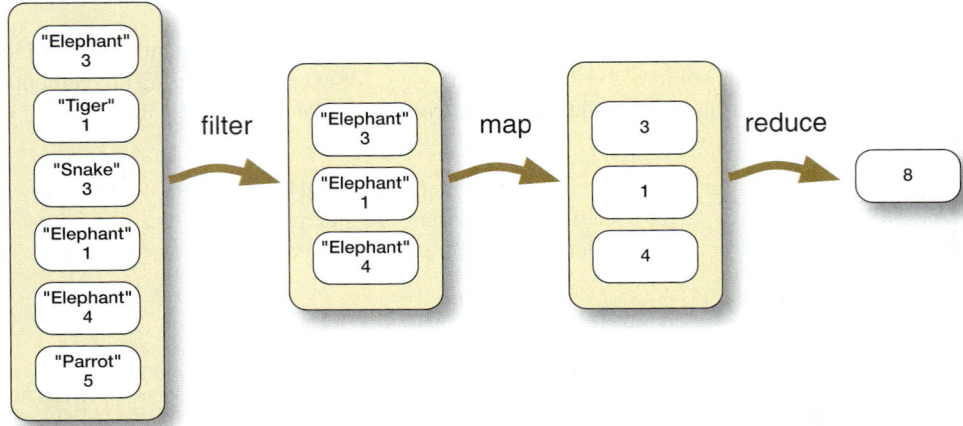

We can write this, using pseudo-code, as follows:

```
sightings.filter(name == elephant).map(count).reduce(add up);
```

This is not correct Java syntax, but you get the idea. We will look at correct Java code below.

By combining these functions in different ways, many different operations can be achieved. If we, for example, wanted to know how many reports a given spotter has made on a given day, we can do the following:

```
sightings.filter(spotter == spotterID)
        .filter(period == dayID)
        .reduce(count elements);
```

Pipelines always start with a *source* (a stream), followed by a sequence of operations. The operations are of two different kinds: *intermediate operations* and *terminal operations*. In a pipeline, the last operation must always be a terminal operation, and all others must be intermediate operations:

```
source.inter1(...).inter2(...).inter3(...).terminal(...);
```

Exercise 5.7 Write pseudo-code to determine how many elephants a particular spotter (`spotterID`) saw on a particular day (`dayID`).

Exercise 5.8 Write pseudo-code to create a stream containing only those sightings that have a count greater than 0.

Exercise 5.9 Consider the *music-organizer* project from Chapter 4 and assume that each `Track` object in the collection contains a count of how many times it has been played. Write pseudo-code to determine the total number of times tracks by the artist Big Bill Broonzy have been played.

Intermediate operations always produce a new stream to which the next operation can be applied, while terminal operations produce a result, or are void (such as `forEach` which is a terminal operation). The documentation for the stream methods always tells you whether an operation is intermediate or terminal.

We will now go on to discuss the Java syntax for the methods that implement these functions. This is where streams and lambdas meet: the parameter to each of the methods is a lambda.

5.5.3 The `filter` method

As discussed, the `filter` method creates a subset of the original stream. Typically that subset will be those elements that fulfill some condition; i.e., there is something about those particular elements that means we want to retain and act on them rather than the others. With the *music-organizer* project we might want to find all the tracks by a particular artist. With the *animal-monitoring* project we might want to find all the sightings of a given animal. Both involve iterating over their respective lists, and making a test of each element to see if it fulfills a particular requirement. If the required condition is met then we will go on to process the element in some way.

The `filter` method of a stream is an intermediate operation that passes on to its output stream only those elements from the input stream that fulfill a given condition. The method takes a lambda that receives an element and returns a `boolean` result. (A lambda that takes an element and returns *true* or *false* is called a *predicate*.) If the result is *true*, the element is included in the output stream, otherwise it is left out. For instance, we might want to select only those `Sighting` objects that relate to elephants. Here is how that might be done:

```
sightings.stream()
        .filter(s -> "Elephant".equals(s.getAnimal()))
        . . . .
```

Notice that we have to first create a stream from the sightings list, in order to be able to apply the filter function. We do not need to specify the type of the lambda's parameter, because the compiler knows that an `ArrayList<Sighting>` will deliver a stream of `Sighting` objects, so the parameter to the predicate will have the type `Sighting`.

More generally, it makes sense to make filtering part of a method that could select different types of animal, so here is how we would rewrite the `printSightingsOf` method of our original project in a stream-based version:

```
/**
 * Print details of all the sightings of the given animal.
 * @param animal The type of animal.
 */
public void printSightingsOf(String animal)
{
    sightings.stream()
            .filter(s -> animal.equals(s.getAnimal()))
            .forEach(s -> System.out.println(s.getDetails()));
}
```

It is important to know that each operation of the stream leaves its input stream unmodified. Each operation creates a fresh stream, based on its input and the operation, to pass on to the next operation in the sequence. Here the terminal operation is a `forEach` that results in the sightings that survived the previous filtering process being printed. The `forEach` method is a terminal operation because it does not return another stream as a result—it is a `void` method.

> **Exercise 5.10** Rewrite the `printSightingsOf` method in your `Animal-Monitor` class to use streams and lambdas, as shown above. Test to make sure the project still works as before.
>
> **Exercise 5.11** Write a method in the `AnimalMonitor` class to print details of all the sightings recorded on a particular `dayID`, which is passed as a parameter to the method.
>
> **Exercise 5.12** Write a method that uses two `filter` calls to print details of all the sightings of a particular animal made on a particular day—the method takes the animal name and day ID as parameters.
>
> **Exercise 5.13** Does the order of the two `filter` calls matter in your solution to the previous exercise? Justify your answer.

5.5.4 The map method

The `map` method is an intermediate operation that creates a stream with different objects, possibly of a different type, by mapping each of the original elements to a new element in the new stream.

To illustrate this, consider that when we are printing the details of a sighting, we are only actually interested in the string returned from the `getDetails` method, and not the `Sighting` object itself. An alternative to the code above (where we called `getDetails()` within the `System.out.println` call) would be to map the `Sighting` object to the details string first. The terminal operation can then just print those details:

```
/**
 * Print all the sightings by the given spotter.
 * @param spotter The ID of the spotter.
 */
public void printSightingsBy(int spotter)
{
    sightings.stream()
             .filter(sighting -> sighting.getSpotter() == spotter)
             .map(sighting -> sighting.getDetails())
             .forEach(details -> System.out.println(details));
}
```

This example is equivalent to the version we have seen before. The other example we have mentioned above—mapping to the number of animals spotted in each sighting—would look like this:

```
sightings.stream()
        .filter(sighting -> sighting.getSpotter() == spotter)
        .map(sighting -> sighting.getCount())
        . . . .
```

This code segment would result in a stream of integers, which we could then process further.

Exercise 5.14 Rewrite the `printSightingsBy` method in your project as discussed above.

Exercise 5.15 Write a method to print the counts of all sightings of a particular animal. Your method should use the `map` operation as part of the pipeline.

Exercise 5.16 If a pipeline contains a `filter` operation and a `map` operation, does the order of the operations matter to the final result? Justify your answer.

Exercise 5.17 Rewrite the `printEndangered` method in your project to use streams. Test. (To test this method, it may be easiest to write a test method that creates an `ArrayList` of animal names and calls the `printEndangered` method with it.)

Exercise 5.18 *Challenge exercise* The `printSightingsBy` method of `AnimalMonitor` contains the following terminal operation:

```
forEach(details -> System.out.println(details));
```

Replace it with the following:

```
forEach(System.out::println);
```

Take care to use the exact syntax. Does this change the operation of the method? What can you deduce from your answer to this? If you are not sure, try to find out what "::" means when using Java lambdas. We will look at this in the advanced sections of Chapter 6.

5.5.5 The reduce method

The intermediate operations we have seen so far take a stream as input and output a stream. Sometimes, however, we need an operation that will "collapse" its input stream to just a single object or value, and this is the function of the `reduce` method, which is a terminal operation.

The complete code for the example given above—selecting all animals of a given type, then mapping to the number of animals in each sighting, and finally adding all numbers—is as follows:

```
public int getCount(String animal)
{
    return sightings.stream()
        .filter(sighting -> animal.equals(sighting.getAnimal()))
        .map(sighting -> sighting.getCount())
        .reduce(0, (total, count) -> return total + count);
}
```

We can see that the parameters to the `reduce` method look a bit more elaborate than for the `filter` and `map` methods. There are two aspects here:

- The `reduce` method has two parameters. The first one in our example is 0, and the second is a lambda.
- The lambda used here itself has two parameters, called `total` and `count`.

To understand how this works, it might be useful to look at the code for adding all counts as if we were writing it in the traditional way. We would write a loop that looks like this:

```
public int getCount(String animal)
{
    int total = 0;
    for(Sighting sighting : sightings) {
        if(animal.equals(sighting.getAnimal())) {
            total = total + sighting.getCount();
        }
    }
    return total;
}
```

The process of calculating the sum involves the following steps:

- Declare a variable to hold the final value and give it an initial value of 0.
- Iterate over the list and determine which sighting records relate to the particular animal we are interested in (the filtering step).
- Obtain the count from the identified sighting (the mapping step).
- Add the count to the variable.
- Return the sum that has been accumulated in the variable over the course of the iteration.

The key point that is relevant to writing a stream-based version of this process is to recognize that the variable `total` acts as a form of "accumulator": each time a relevant count is identified, it is added into the value accumulated so far in `total` to give a new value that will be used the next time around the loop. For the process to work, `total` obviously has to be given an initial value of 0 for the first count to be added to.

The `reduce` method takes two parameters: a starting value and a lambda. Formally, the starting value is called an *identity*. It is the value to which our running total is initialized. In our code, we have passed 0 for this parameter.

The second parameter is a lambda with two parameters: one for the running total, and one for the current element of the stream. The lambda we have written in our code is:

```
(total, count) -> return total + count
```

The body of the lambda should return the result of combining the running total and the element. In our example, "combining" means just to add them. The affect of applying this `reduce` method then is to initialize a running total to zero, add each element of the stream to it, and return the total at the end.

Because there is no explicit loop in our code anymore, it might be a little tricky to understand at first, but the overall process contains all of the same elements as the version using the for-each loop.

Exercise 5.19 Rewrite your `getCount` method using streams, as shown here.

Exercise 5.20 Add a method to `AnimalMonitor` that takes three parameters: `animal`, `spotterID`, and `dayID`, and returns a count of how many sightings of the given animal were made by the spotter on a particular day.

Exercise 5.21 Add a method to `AnimalMonitor` that takes two parameters—`spotterID` and `dayID`—and returns a `String` containing the names of the animals seen by the spotter on a particular day. You should include only animals whose sighting count is greater than zero, but don't worry about excluding duplicate names if multiple non-zero sighting records were made of a particular animal. *Hint*: The principles of using `reduce` with `String` elements and a `String` result are very similar to those when using integers. Decide on the correct *identity* and formulate a two-parameter lambda that combines the running "sum" with the next element of the stream.

5.5.6 Removing from a collection

We have noted that the `filter` method does not actually change the underlying collection from which a stream was obtained. However, predicate lambdas make it relatively easy to remove all the items from a collection that match a particular condition. For instance, suppose we wish to delete from the `sightings` list all of those `Sighting` records where the count is zero. The following code makes use of the `removeIf` method of the collection:

```
/**
 * Remove from the sightings list all of those records with
 * a count of zero.
 */
public void removeZeroCounts()
{
    sightings.removeIf(sighting -> sighting.getCount() == 0);
}
```

Once again, the iteration is implicit. The `removeIf` method passes each element of the list, in turn, to the predicate lambda, then removes all those for which the lambda returns `true`. Note that this is a method of the collection (not of a stream) and it does modify the original collection.

> **Exercise 5.22** Rewrite the `removeZeroCounts` method using the `removeIf` method, as shown above.
>
> **Exercise 5.23** Write a method `removeSpotter` that removes all records reported by a given spotter.

5.5.7 Other stream methods

We have said that many common tasks can be achieved with these three kinds of operations: *filter*, *map*, and *reduce*. In practice, Java offers many more methods on streams, and we will see some of them later in this book. However, most of these are just variations of the three operations introduced here, even though they have different names.

The `Stream` class, for example, has methods called `count`, `findFirst`, and `max`—these are all variants of a reduce operation—and methods called `limit` and `skip`, which are examples of a filter.

> **Exercise 5.24** Find the API documentation for Stream in the `java.util.stream` package and read about the `count`, `findFirst`, and `max` methods. These can be called on any stream.
>
> **Exercise 5.25** Write a method in the `AnimalMonitor` class that takes a single parameter, `spotterID`, and returns a count of how many sighting records have been made by the given spotter. Use the stream's `count` method to do this.
>
> **Exercise 5.26** Write a method that takes an animal name as a parameter and returns the largest count for that animal in a single `Sighting` record.
>
> **Exercise 5.27** Write a method that takes an animal name and spotter ID and returns the first `Sighting` object stored in the `sightings` collection for that combination.
>
> **Exercise 5.28** Read about the `limit` and `skip` methods of streams and devise some methods of your own to make use of them.

5.6 Summary

In this chapter, we have introduced some new concepts that are relatively advanced for this stage of the book, but that are closely associated with the concepts covered in Chapter 4. We have looked at a *functional style* for processing streams of data. In this style, we do not write loops to process the elements in a collection. Instead, we apply a *pipeline* of operations to a stream derived from a collection, in order to transform the sequence into the form we want. Each operation in the pipeline defines what is to be done with a single element of the sequence. The most common sequence transformations are performed via the `filter`, `map`, and `reduce` methods.

Operations in a pipeline often take *lambdas* as parameters in order to specify what is to be done with each element of the sequence. A lambda is an anonymous function that takes zero or more parameters and has a block of code that performs the same role as a method body.

Looking at the *animal-monitoring-v1* project that you have been working on, you may have noticed that there are two methods left using for-each loops that we have not rewritten yet using streams. These are the methods that return new collections as method results; we have not yet discussed how to create a new collection from a stream. We will come back to this in Chapter 6, where we shall see how to create a new collection out of the transformed sequence.

Terms introduced in this chapter:

functional programming, lambda, stream, pipeline, filter, map, reduce

Exercise 5.29 Take a copy of *music-organizer-v5* from Chapter 4. Rewrite the `listAllTracks` and `listByArtist` methods of the `MusicOrganizer` class to use streams and lambdas.

CHAPTER 6

More-Sophisticated Behavior

Main concepts discussed in this chapter:

- using library classes
- writing documentation
- reading documentation

Java constructs discussed in this chapter:

`String`, `Random`, `HashMap`, `HashSet`, `Iterator`, `static`, `final`, autoboxing, wrapper classes

In Chapter 4, we introduced the class `ArrayList` from the Java class library. We discussed how this enabled us to do something that would otherwise be hard to achieve (in this case, storing an arbitrary number of objects).

This was just a single example of a useful class from the Java library. The library consists of thousands of classes, many of which are generally useful for your work, and many of which you may probably never use.

For a good Java programmer, it is essential to be able to work with the Java library and make informed choices about which classes to use. Once you have started work with the library, you will quickly see that it enables you to perform many tasks more easily than you would otherwise have been able to. Learning to work with library classes is the main topic of this chapter.

The items in the library are not just a set of unrelated, arbitrary classes that we all have to learn individually, but are often arranged in relationships, exploiting common characteristics. Here, we again encounter the concept of abstraction to help us deal with a large amount of information. Some of the most important parts of the library are the collections, of which the `ArrayList` class is one. We will discuss other sorts of collections in this chapter and see that they share many attributes among themselves, so that we can often abstract from the individual details of a specific collection and talk about collection classes in general.

New collection classes, as well as some other useful classes, will be introduced and discussed. Throughout this chapter, we will work on the construction of a single application (the *TechSupport* system), which makes use of various different library classes. A complete implementation containing all the ideas and source code discussed here, as well as several intermediate versions, is included in the book projects. While this enables you to study the complete solution, you are encouraged to follow the path through the exercises in this chapter. These will, after a brief look at the complete program, start with a very simple initial version of the project, then gradually develop and implement the complete solution.

The application makes use of several new library classes and techniques—each requiring study individually—such as hash maps, sets, string tokenization, and further use of random numbers. You should be aware that this is not a chapter to be read and understood in a single day, but that it contains several sections that deserve a few days of study each. Overall, when you finally reach the end and have managed to undertake the implementation suggested in the exercises, you will have learned about a good variety of important topics.

6.1 Documentation for library classes

The Java standard class library is extensive. It consists of thousands of classes, each of which has many methods, both with and without parameters, and with and without return types. It is impossible to memorize them all and all of the details that go with them. Instead, a good Java programmer should know:

Concept

The Java **standard class library** contains many classes that are very useful. It is important to know how to use the library.

- some of the most important classes and their methods from the library by name (`ArrayList` is one of those important ones) and
- how to find out about other classes and look up the details (such as methods and parameters).

In this chapter, we will introduce some of the important classes from the class library, and further library classes will be introduced throughout the book. More importantly, we will show you how you can explore and understand the library on your own. This will enable you to write much more interesting programs. Fortunately, the Java library is quite well documented. This documentation is available in HTML format (so that it can be read in a web browser). We shall use this to find out about the library classes.

Reading and understanding the documentation is the first part of our introduction to library classes. We will take this approach a step further, and also discuss how to prepare our own classes so that other people can use them in the same way as they would use standard library classes. This is important for real-world software development, where teams have to deal with large projects and maintenance of software over time.

One thing you may have noted about the `ArrayList` class is that we used it without ever looking at the source code. We did not check how it was implemented. That was not necessary for utilizing its functionality. All we needed to know was the name of the class, the names of the methods, the parameters and return types of those methods, and what exactly these methods do. We did not really care how the work was done. This is typical for the use of library classes.

The same is true for other classes in larger software projects. Typically, several people work together on a project by working on different parts. Each programmer should concentrate on her own area and need not understand the details of all the other parts (we discussed this in Section 3.2 where we talked about abstraction and modularization).

In effect, each programmer should be able to use the classes of other team members as if they were library classes, making informed use of them without the need to know how they work internally.

For this to work, each team member must write documentation about his class similar to the documentation for the Java standard library, which enables other people to use the class without the need to read the code. This topic will also be discussed in this chapter.

6.2 The *TechSupport* system

As always, we shall explore these issues with an example. This time, we shall use the *TechSupport* application. You can find it in the book projects under the name *tech-support1*.

TechSupport is a program intended to provide technical support for customers of the fictitious DodgySoft software company. Some time ago, DodgySoft had a technical support department with people sitting at telephones. Customers could call to get advice and help with their technical problems with the DodgySoft software products. Recently, though, business has not been going so well, and DodgySoft decided to get rid of the technical support department to save money. They now want to develop the *TechSupport* system to give the impression that support is still provided. The system is supposed to mimic the responses a technical-support person might give. Customers can communicate with the technical-support system online.

6.2.1 Exploring the *TechSupport* system

Exercise 6.1 Open and run the project *tech-support-complete*. You run it by creating an object of class **SupportSystem** and calling its **start** method. Enter some problems you might be having with your software to try out the system. See how it behaves. Type "bye" when you are done. You do not need to examine the source code at this stage. This project is the complete solution that we will have developed by the end of this chapter. The purpose of this exercise is only to give you an idea of what we plan to achieve.

> **Eliza** The idea of the *TechSupport* project is based on the ground-breaking artificial intelligence program, Eliza, developed by Joseph Weizenbaum at Massachusetts Institute of Technology in the 1960s. You can find out more about the original program by searching the web for "Eliza" and "Weizenbaum."

We will now start our more detailed exploration by using the *tech-support1* project. It is a first, rudimentary implementation of our system. We will improve it throughout the chapter. This way, we should arrive at a better understanding of the whole system than we would by just reading the complete solution.

Figure 6.1

A first *TechSupport* dialog

In Exercise 6.1, you have seen that the program essentially holds a dialog with the user. The user can type in a question, and the system responds. Try the same with our prototype version of the project, *tech-support1*.

In *TechSupport*'s complete version, the system manages to produce reasonably varied responses—sometimes they even seem to make sense! In the prototype version we are using as a starting point, the responses are much more restricted (Figure 6.1). You will notice very quickly that the response is always the same:

"That sounds interesting. Tell me more ..."

This is, in fact, not very interesting at all, and not very convincing when trying to pretend that we have a technical-support person sitting at the other end of the dialog. We will shortly try to improve this. However, before we do this, we shall explore further what we have so far.

The project diagram shows us three classes: **SupportSystem**, **InputReader**, and **Responder** (Figure 6.2). **SupportSystem** is the main class, which uses the **InputReader** to get some input from the terminal and the **Responder** to generate a response.

Examine the **InputReader** further by creating an object of this class and then looking at the object's methods. You will see that it has only a single method available, called **getInput**, which returns a string. Try it out. This method lets you type a line of input in the terminal, then returns whatever you typed as a method result. We will not examine how this works internally at this point, but just note that the **InputReader** has a **getInput** method that returns a string.

Do the same with the **Responder** class. You will find that it has a **generateResponse** method that always returns the string **"That sounds interesting. Tell me more..."**. This explains what we saw in the dialog earlier.

Now let us look at the **SupportSystem** class a bit more closely.

Figure 6.2
TechSupport class diagram

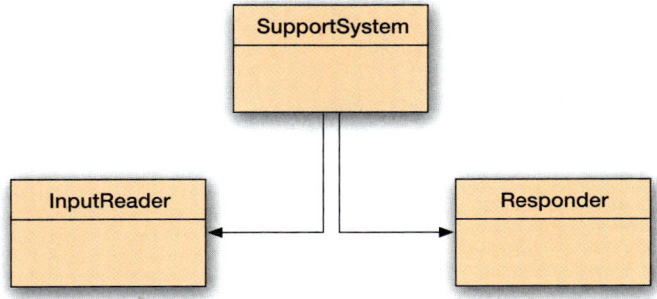

6.2.2 Reading the code

The complete source code of the **SupportSystem** class is shown in Code 6.1. Code 6.2 shows the source code of class **Responder**.

Code 6.1
The SupportSystem source code

```java
/**
 * This class implements a technical support system. It is the top level class
 * in this project. The support system communicates via text input/output
 * in the text terminal.
 *
 * This class uses an object of class InputReader to read input from the user,
 * and an object of class Responder to generate responses. It contains a loop
 * that repeatedly reads input and generates output until the users wants to
 * leave.
 *
 * @author     Michael Kölling and David J. Barnes
 * @version    0.1 (2016.02.29)
 */
public class SupportSystem
{
    private InputReader reader;
    private Responder responder;

    /**
     * Creates a technical support system.
     */
    public SupportSystem()
    {
        reader = new InputReader();
        responder = new Responder();
    }

    /**
     * Start the technical support system. This will print a welcome
     * message and enter into a dialog with the user, until the user
     * ends the dialog.
     */
```

Code 6.1 continued

The `SupportSystem` source code

```java
public void start()
{
    boolean finished = false;

    printWelcome();

    while(!finished) {
        String input = reader.getInput();

        if(input.startsWith("bye")) {
            finished = true;
        }
        else {
            String response = responder.generateResponse();
            System.out.println(response);
        }
    }

    printGoodbye();
}

/**
 * Print a welcome message to the screen.
 */
private void printWelcome()
{
    System.out.println("Welcome to the DodgySoft Technical Support System.");
    System.out.println();
    System.out.println("Please tell us about your problem.");
    System.out.println("We will assist you with any problem you might have.");
    System.out.println("Please type 'bye' to exit our system.");
}

/**
 * Print a good-bye message to the screen.
 */
private void printGoodbye()
{
    System.out.println("Nice talking to you. Bye...");
}
}
```

Looking at Code 6.2, we see that the **Responder** class is trivial. It has only one method, and that always returns the same string. This is something we shall improve later. For now, we will concentrate on the **SupportSystem** class.

SupportSystem declares two instance fields to hold an **InputReader** and a **Responder** object, and it assigns those two objects in its constructor.

At the end, it has two methods called **printWelcome** and **printGoodbye**. These simply print out some text—a welcome message and a good-bye message, respectively.

The most interesting piece of code is the method in the middle: **start**. We will discuss this method in some more detail.

Code 6.2

The `Responder` source code

```java
/**
 * The responder class represents a response generator object.
 * It is used to generate an automatic response to an input string.
 *
 * @author    Michael Kölling and David J. Barnes
 * @version   0.1 (2016.02.29)
 */
public class Responder
{
    /**
     * Construct a Responder - nothing to do
     */
    public Responder()
    {
    }

    /**
     * Generate a response.
     * @return   A string that should be displayed as the response
     */
    public String generateResponse()
    {
        return "That sounds interesting. Tell me more...";
    }
}
```

Toward the top of the method is a call to `printWelcome`, and at the end is a call to `printGoodbye`. These two calls take care of printing these sections of text at the appropriate times. The rest of this method consists of a declaration of a boolean variable and a while loop. The structure is as follows:

```
boolean finished = false;
while(!finished) {
    do something
    if(exit condition) {
        finished = true;
    }
    else {
        do something more
    }
}
```

This code pattern is a variation of the while-loop idiom discussed in Section 4.10. We use `finished` as a flag that becomes `true` when we want to end the loop (and with it, the whole program). We make sure that it is initially `false`. (Remember that the exclamation mark is a *not* operator!)

The main part of the loop—the part that is done repeatedly while we wish to continue—consists of three statements if we strip it of the check for the exit condition:

```
String input = reader.getInput();
...
String response = responder.generateResponse();
System.out.println(response);
```

Thus, the loop repeatedly

- reads some user input,
- asks the responder to generate a response, and
- prints out that response.

(You may have noticed that the response does not depend on the input at all! This is certainly something we shall have to improve later.)

The last part to examine is the check of the exit condition. The intention is that the program should end once a user types the word "bye". The relevant section of source code we find in the class reads

```
String input = reader.getInput();
if(input.startsWith("bye")) {
    finished = true;
}
```

If you understand these pieces in isolation, then it is a good idea to look again at the complete `start` method in Code 6.1 and see whether you can understand everything together.

In the last code fragment examined above, a method called `startsWith` is used. Because that method is called on the `input` variable, which holds a `String` object, it must be a method of the `String` class. But what does this method do? And how do we find out?

We might guess, simply from seeing the name of the method, that it tests whether the input string starts with the word "bye". We can verify this by experiment. Run the *TechSupport* system again and type "bye bye" or "bye everyone". You will notice that both versions cause the system to exit. Note, however, that typing "Bye" or " bye"—starting with a capital letter or with a space in front of the word—is not recognized as starting with "bye". This could be slightly annoying for a user, but it turns out that we can solve these problems if we know a bit more about the `String` class.

How do we find out more information about the `startsWith` method or other methods of the `String` class?

6.3 Reading class documentation

Concept

The Java **class library documentation** shows details about all classes in the library. Using this documentation is essential in order to make good use of library classes.

The class `String` is one of the classes of the standard Java class library. We can find out more details about it by reading the library documentation for the `String` class.

To do this, choose the *Java Class Libraries* item from the BlueJ *Help* menu. This will open a web browser displaying the main page of the Java API (Application Programming Interface) documentation.[1]

The web browser will display three frames. In the one at the top left, you see a list of packages. Below that is a list of all classes in the Java library. The large frame on the right is used to display details of a selected package or class.

---

[1] By default, this function accesses the documentation through the Internet. This will not work if your machine does not have network access. However, BlueJ can be configured to use a local copy of the Java API documentation. This is recommended, because it speeds up access and can work without an Internet connection. For details, see Appendix A.

Figure 6.3
The Java class library documentation

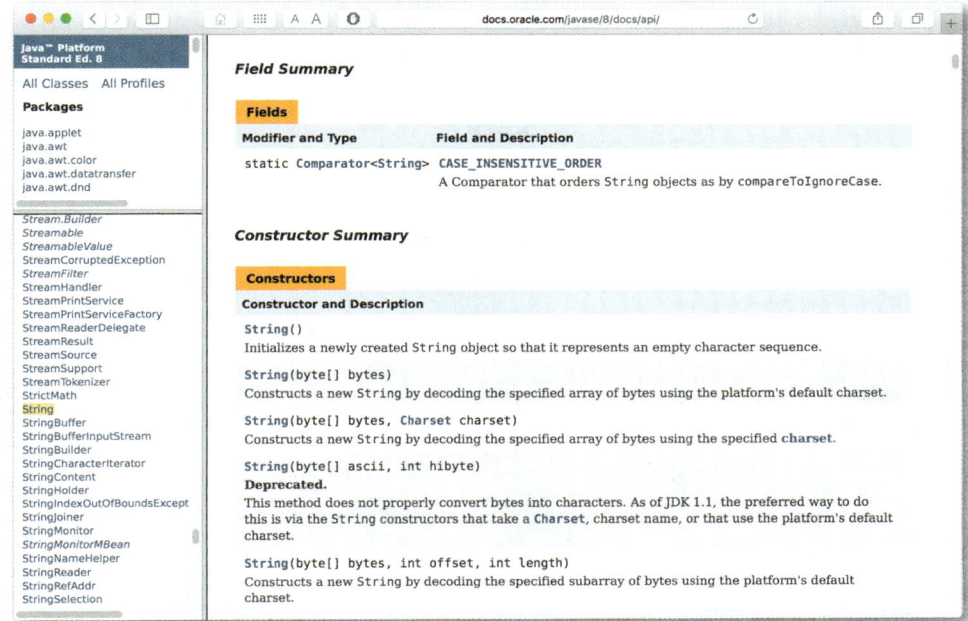

In the list of classes on the left, find and select the class **String**. The frame on the right then displays the documentation of the **String** class (Figure 6.3).

Exercise 6.2 Investigate the **String** documentation. Then look at the documentation for some other classes. What is the structure of class documentation? Which sections are common to all class descriptions? What is their purpose?

Exercise 6.3 Look up the **startsWith** method in the documentation for **String**. There are two versions. Describe in your own words what they do and the differences between them.

Exercise 6.4 Is there a method in the **String** class that tests whether a string ends with a given suffix? If so, what is it called, and what are its parameters and return type?

Exercise 6.5 Is there a method in the **String** class that returns the number of characters in the string? If so, what is it called, and what are its parameters?

Exercise 6.6 If you found methods for the two tasks above, how did you find them? Is it easy or hard to find methods you are looking for? Why?

6.3.1 Interfaces versus implementation

You will see that the documentation includes different pieces of information. They are, among other things:

- the name of the class;
- a general description of the purpose of the class;
- a list of the class's constructors and methods;
- the parameters and return types for each constructor and method;
- a description of the purpose of each constructor and method.

This information, taken together, is called the *interface* of a class. Note that the interface does *not* show the source code that implements the class. If a class is well described (that is, if its interface is well written) then a programmer does not need to see the source code to be able to use the class. Seeing the interface provides all the information needed. This is abstraction in action again.

The source code behind the scene, which makes the class work, is called the *implementation* of the class. Usually a programmer works on the implementation of one class at a time, while making use of several other classes via their interfaces.

This distinction between the interface and the implementation is a very important concept, and it will surface repeatedly in this and later chapters of this book.

> **Concept**
> The **interface** of a class describes what a class does and how it can be used without showing the implementation.

> **Concept**
> The complete source code that defines a class is called the **implementation** of that class.

> **Note** The word *interface* has several meanings in the context of programming and Java. It is used to describe the publicly visible part of a class (which is how we have just been using it here), but it also has other meanings. The user interface (often a graphical user interface) is sometimes referred to as just *the interface*, but Java also has a language construct called interface (discussed in Chapter 12) that is related but distinct from our meaning here.
>
> It is important to be able to distinguish among the different meanings of the word *interface* in a particular context.

The interface terminology is also used for individual methods. For example, the `String` documentation shows us the interface of the `length` method:

```
public int length()
```

Returns the length of this string. The length is equal to the number of Unicode code units in the string.

   Specified by:

   length in interface CharSequence

   Returns:

   the length of the sequence of characters represented by this object.

The interface of a method consists of the *header* of the method and a comment (shown here in italics). The header of a method includes (in this order):

- an access modifier (here `public`), which we shall discuss below;
- the return type of the method (here `int`);
- the method name;
- a list of parameters (which is empty in this example); the name and parameters together are also called the *signature* of the method.

The interface provides everything we need to know to make use of this method.

6.3.2 Using library-class methods

Back to our *TechSupport* system. We now want to improve the processing of input a little. We have seen in the discussion above that our system is not very tolerant: if we type "Bye" or " bye" instead of "bye", for instance, the word is not recognized. We want to change that by adjusting the text read in from a user so that these variations are all recognized as "bye".

The documentation of the `String` class tells us that it has a method called `trim` to remove spaces at the beginning and the end of the string. We can use that method to handle the second problem case.

Exercise 6.7 Find the `trim` method in the `String` class's documentation. Write down the header of that method. Write down an example call to that method on a `String` variable called `text`.

One important detail about String objects is that they are *immutable*—that is, they cannot be modified once they have been created. Note carefully that the `trim` method, for example, returns a new string; it does not modify the original string. Pay close attention to the following "Pitfall" comment.

Concept

An object is said to be **immutable** if its contents or state cannot be changed once it has been created. Strings are an example of immutable objects.

Pitfall A common error in Java is to try to modify a string—for example by writing

```
input.toUpperCase();
```

This is incorrect (strings cannot be modified), but this unfortunately does not produce an error. The statement simply has no effect, and the input string remains unchanged.

The `toUpperCase` method, as well as other string methods, does not modify the original string, but instead returns a *new* string that is similar to the original one, with some changes applied (here, with characters changed to uppercase). If we want our input variable to be changed, then we have to assign this new object back into the variable (discarding the original one), like this:

```
input = input.toUpperCase();
```

The new object could also be assigned to another variable or processed in other ways.

After studying the interface of the `trim` method, we can see that we can remove the spaces from an input string with the following line of code:

```
input = input.trim();
```

This code will request the **String** object stored in the **input** variable to create a new, similar string with the leading and trailing spaces removed. The new **String** is then stored in the **input** variable because we have no further use for the old one. Thus, after this line of code, **input** refers to a string without spaces at either end.

We can now insert this line into our source code so that it reads

```
String input = reader.getInput();
input = input.trim();
if(input.startsWith("bye")) {
    finished = true;
}
else {
    Code omitted.
}
```

The first two lines can also be merged into a single line:

```
String input = reader.getInput().trim();
```

The effect of this line of code is identical to that of the first two lines above. The right-hand side should be read as if it were parenthesized as follows:

```
(reader.getInput()).trim()
```

Which version you prefer is mainly a matter of taste. The decision should be made mainly on the basis of readability: use the version that you find easier to read and understand. Often, novice programmers will prefer the two-line version, whereas more experienced programmers get used to the one-line style.

> **Exercise 6.8** Implement this improvement in your version of the *tech-support1* project. Test it to confirm that it is tolerant of extra space around the word "bye".

Now we have solved the problem caused by spaces surrounding the input, but we have not yet solved the problem with capital letters. However, further investigation of the **String** class's documentation suggests a possible solution, because it describes a method named **toLowerCase**.

> **Exercise 6.9** Improve the code of the **SupportSystem** class in the *tech-support1* project so that case in the input is ignored. Use the **String** class's **toLowerCase** method to do this. Remember that this method will not actually change the **String** it is called on, but result in the creation of a new one being created with slightly different contents.

6.3.3 Checking string equality

An alternative solution would have been to check whether the input string *is* the string "bye" instead of whether it *starts with* the string "bye". An (incorrect!) attempt to write this code could look as follows:

```
if(input == "bye") {  // does not always work!
    ...
}
```

The problem here is that it is possible for several independent **String** objects to exist that all represent the same text. Two **String** objects, for example, could both contain the characters "bye". The equality operator (==) checks whether each side of the operator refers to *the same object*, not whether they have the same value! That is an important difference.

In our example, we are interested in the question of whether the input variable and the string constant "bye" represent the same value, not whether they refer to the same object. Thus, using the == operator is wrong. It could return false, even if the value of the input variable is "bye".[2]

The solution is to use the **equals** method, defined in the **String** class. This method correctly tests whether the contents of two **String** objects are the same. The correct code reads:

```
if(input.equals("bye")) {
    ...
}
```

This can, of course, also be combined with the **trim** and **toLowerCase** methods.

> **Pitfall** Comparing strings with the == operator can lead to unintended results. As a general rule, strings should almost always be compared with **equals**, rather than with the == operator.

Exercise 6.10 Find the **equals** method in the documentation for class **String**. What is the return type of this method?

Exercise 6.11 Change your implementation to use the **equals** method instead of **startsWith**.

6.4 Adding random behavior

So far, we have made a small improvement to the *TechSupport* project, but overall it remains very basic. One of the main problems is that it always gives the same response, regardless of the user's input. We shall now improve this by defining a set of plausible phrases with which to respond. We will then have the program randomly choose one of

---

[2] Unfortunately, Java's implementation of strings means that using == will often misleadingly give the "right" answer when comparing two different **String** objects with identical contents. However, you should *never* use == between **String** objects when you want to compare their contents.

them each time it is expected to reply. This will be an extension of the **Responder** class in our project.

To do this, we will use an `ArrayList` to store some response strings, generate a random integer number, and use the random number as an index into the response list to pick one of our phrases. In this version, the response will still not depend on the user's input (we'll do that later), but at least it will vary the response and look a lot better.

First, we have to find out how to generate a random integer number.

> **Random and pseudo-random** Generating random numbers on a computer is actually not as easy to do as one might initially think. Because computers operate in a very well-defined, deterministic way that relies on the fact that all computation is predictable and repeatable, they provide little space for real random behavior.
>
> Researchers have, over time, proposed many algorithms to produce seemingly random sequences of numbers. These numbers are typically not really random, but follow complicated rules. They are therefore referred to as *pseudo-random* numbers.
>
> In a language such as Java, the pseudo-random number generation has fortunately been implemented in a library class, so all we have to do to receive a pseudo-random number is to make some calls to the library.
>
> If you want to read more about this, do a web search for "pseudo-random numbers."

6.4.1 The **Random** class

The Java class library contains a class named **Random** that will be helpful for our project.

> **Exercise 6.12** Find the class **Random** in the Java class library documentation. Which package is it in? What does it do? How do you construct an instance? How do you generate a random number? Note that you will probably not understand everything that is stated in the documentation. Just try to find out what you need to know.
>
> **Exercise 6.13** Write a small code fragment (on paper) that generates a random integer number using this class.

To generate a random number, we have to:

- create an instance of class **Random** and
- make a call to a method of that instance to get a number.

Looking at the documentation, we see that there are various methods called *nextSomething* for generating random values of various types. The one that generates a random integer number is called `nextInt`.

6.4 Adding random behavior

The following illustrates the code needed to generate and print a random integer number:

```
Random randomGenerator;
randomGenerator = new Random();
int index = randomGenerator.nextInt();
System.out.println(index);
```

This code fragment creates a new instance of the **Random** class and stores it in the **randomGenerator** variable. It then calls the **nextInt** method to receive a random number, stores it in the index variable, and eventually prints it out.

Exercise 6.14 Write some code (in BlueJ) to test the generation of random numbers. To do this, create a new class called **RandomTester**. You can create this class in the *tech-support1* project, or you can create a new project for it. In class **RandomTester**, implement two methods: **printOneRandom** (which prints out one random number) and **printMultiRandom(int howMany)** (which has a parameter to specify how many numbers you want, and then prints out the appropriate number of random numbers).

Your class should create only a single instance of class **Random** (in its constructor) and store it in a field. Do not create a new **Random** instance every time you want a new number.

6.4.2 Random numbers with limited range

The random numbers we have seen so far were generated from the whole range of Java integers (−2147483648 to 2147483647). That is okay as an experiment, but seldom useful. More often, we want random numbers within a given limited range.

The **Random** class also offers a method to support this. It is again called **nextInt**, but it has a parameter to specify the range of numbers that we would like to use.

Exercise 6.15 Find the **nextInt** method in class **Random** that allows the target range of random numbers to be specified. What are the possible random numbers that are generated when you call this method with 100 as its parameter?

Exercise 6.16 Write a method in your **RandomTester** class called **throwDie** that returns a random number between 1 and 6 (inclusive).

Exercise 6.17 Write a method called **getResponse** that randomly returns one of the strings **"yes"**, **"no"**, or **"maybe"**.

Exercise 6.18 Extend your **getResponse** method so that it uses an **ArrayList** to store an arbitrary number of responses and randomly returns one of them.

When using a method that generates random numbers from a specified range, care must be taken to check whether the boundaries are *inclusive* or *exclusive*. The **nextInt (int n)** method in the Java library **Random** class, for example, specifies that it generates a number from **0** (inclusive) to **n** (exclusive). That means that the value **0** is included in the possible results, whereas the specified value for **n** is not. The highest number possibly returned by this call is **n–1**.

> **Exercise 6.19** Add a method to your **RandomTester** class that takes a parameter **max** and generates a random number in the range 1 to **max** (inclusive).
>
> **Exercise 6.20** Add a method to your **RandomTester** class that takes two parameters, **min** and **max**, and generates a random number in the range **min** to **max** (inclusive). Rewrite the body of the method you wrote for the previous exercise so that it now calls this new method to generate its result. Note that it should not be necessary to use a loop in this method.
>
> **Exercise 6.21** Look up the details of the **SecureRandom** class that is defined in the `java.security` package. Could this class be used instead of the **Random** class? Why are random numbers important for cryptographic security?

6.4.3 Generating random responses

Now we can look at extending the **Responder** class to select a random response from a list of predefined phrases. Code 6.2 shows the source code of class **Responder** as it is in our first version.

We shall now add code to this first version to:

- declare a field of type **Random** to hold the random number generator;
- declare a field of type **ArrayList** to hold our possible responses;
- create the **Random** and **ArrayList** objects in the **Responder** constructor;
- fill the responses list with some phrases;
- select and return a random phrase when **generateResponse** is called.

Code 6.3 shows a version of the **Responder** source code with these additions.

Code 6.3

The **Responder** source code with random responses

```java
import java.util.ArrayList;
import java.util.Random;

/**
 * The responder class represents a response generator object. It is used
 * to generate an automatic response. This is the second version of this
 * class. This time, we generate some random behavior by randomly selecting
 * a phrase from a predefined list of responses.
 *
 * @author     Michael Kölling and David J. Barnes
 * @version    0.2 (2016.02.29)
 */
```

Code 6.3 continued

The **Responder** source code with random responses

```java
public class Responder
{
    private Random randomGenerator;
    private ArrayList<String> responses;

    /**
     * Construct a Responder
     */
    public Responder()
    {
        randomGenerator = new Random();
        responses = new ArrayList<>();
        fillResponses();
    }

    /**
     * Generate a response.
     *
     * @return   A string that should be displayed as the response
     */
    public String generateResponse()
    {
        // Pick a random number for the index in the default response
        // list. The number will be between 0 (inclusive) and the size
        // of the list (exclusive).
        int index = randomGenerator.nextInt(responses.size());
        return responses.get(index);
    }

    /**
     * Build up a list of default responses from which we can pick one
     * if we don't know what else to say.
     */
    private void fillResponses()
    {
        responses.add("That sounds odd. Could you describe this in more detail?");
        responses.add("No other customer has ever complained about this \n" +
                      "before. What is your system configuration?");
        responses.add("I need a bit more information on that.");
        responses.add("Have you checked that you do not have a dll conflict?");
        responses.add("That is covered in the manual. Have you read the manual?");
        responses.add("Your description is a bit wishy-washy. Have you got \n" +
                      "an expert there with you who could describe this better?");
        responses.add("That's not a bug, it's a feature!");
        responses.add("Could you elaborate on that?");
        responses.add("Have you tried running the app on your phone?");
        responses.add("I just checked StackOverflow - they don't know either.");
    }
}
```

In this version, we have put the code that fills the response list into its own method, named **fillResponses**, which is called from the constructor. This ensures that the responses list will be filled as soon as a **Responder** object is created, but the source code for filling the list is kept separate to make the class easier to read and understand.

The most interesting code segment in this class is in the **generateResponse** method. Leaving out the comments, it reads

```
public String generateResponse()
{
    int index = randomGenerator.nextInt(responses.size());
    return responses.get(index);
}
```

The first line of code in this method does three things:

- It gets the size of the response list by calling its **size** method.
- It generates a random number between 0 (inclusive) and the size (exclusive).
- It stores that random number in the local variable **index**.

If this seems a lot of code for one line, you could also write

```
int listSize = responses.size();
int index = randomGenerator.nextInt(listSize);
```

This code is equivalent to the first line above. Which version you prefer, again, depends on which one you find easier to read.

It is important to note that this code segment will generate a random number in the range **0** to **listSize-1** (inclusive). This fits perfectly with the legal indices for an **ArrayList**. Remember that the range of indices for an **ArrayList** of size **listSize** is **0** to **listSize-1**. Thus, the computed random number gives us a perfect index to randomly access one from the complete set of the list's elements.

The last line in the method reads

```
return responses.get(index);
```

This line does two things:

- It retrieves the response at position **index** using the **get** method.
- It returns the selected string as a method result, using the **return** statement.

If you are not careful, your code may generate a random number that is outside the valid indices of the **ArrayList**. When you then try to use it as an index to access a list element, you will get an **IndexOutOfBoundsException**.

6.4.4 Reading documentation for parameterized classes

So far, we have asked you to look at the documentation for the **String** class from the **java.lang** package, and the **Random** class from the **java.util** package. You might have noticed when doing this that some class names in the documentation list look slightly different, such as **ArrayList<E>** or **HashMap<K, V>**. That is, the class name is followed by some extra information in angle brackets. Classes that look like this are called *parameterized classes* or *generic classes*. The information in the brackets tells us that when we use these classes, we must supply one or more type names in angle brackets to complete the definition. We have already seen this idea in practice in Chapter 4, where we used **ArrayList** by parameterizing it with type names such as **String**. They can also be parameterized with any other type:

```
private ArrayList<String> notes;
private ArrayList<Student> students;
```

Because we can parameterize an **ArrayList** with any other class type that we choose, this is reflected in the API documentation. So if you look at the list of methods for **ArrayList<E>**, you will see methods such as:

```
boolean add(E o)
E get(int index)
```

This tells us that the type of objects we can **add** to an **ArrayList** depends on the type used to parameterize it, and the type of the objects returned from its **get** method depends on this type in the same way. In effect, if we create an **ArrayList<String>** object and then the documentation tells us that the object has the following two methods:

```
boolean add(String o)
String get(int index)
```

whereas if we create an **ArrayList<Student>** object, then it will have these two methods:

```
boolean add(Student o)
Student get(int index)
```

We will ask you to look at the documentation for further parameterized types in later sections in this chapter.

6.5 Packages and import

There are still two lines at the top of the source file that we need to discuss:

```
import java.util.ArrayList;
import java.util.Random;
```

We encountered the import statement for the first time in Chapter 4. Now is the time to look at it a little more closely.

Java classes that are stored in the class library are not automatically available for use, like the other classes in the current project. Rather, we must state in our source code that we would like to use a class from the library. This is called *importing* the class, and is done using the **import** statement. The **import** statement has the form

> **import** *qualified-class-name*;

Because the Java library contains several thousand classes, some structure is needed in the organization of the library to make it easier to deal with the large number of classes. Java uses *packages* to arrange library classes into groups that belong together. Packages can be nested (that is, packages can contain other packages).

The classes `ArrayList` and `Random` are both in the package `java.util`. This information can be found in the class documentation. The *full name* or *qualified name* of a class is the name of its package, followed by a dot, followed by the class name. Thus, the qualified names of the two classes we used here are `java.util.ArrayList` and `java.util.Random`.

Java also allows us to import complete packages with statements of the form

```
import package-name.*;
```

So the following statement would import all class names from the `java.util` package:

```
import java.util.*;
```

Listing all used classes separately, as in our first version, is a little more work in terms of typing but serves well as a piece of documentation. It clearly indicates which classes are actually used by our class. Therefore, we shall tend to use the style of the first example, listing all imported classes separately.

There is one exception to these rules: some classes are used so frequently that almost every class would import them. These classes have been placed in the package `java.lang`, and this package is automatically imported into every class. So we do not need to write import statements for classes in `java.lang`. The class `String` is an example of such a class.

> **Exercise 6.22** Implement in your version of the *tech-support* system the random-response solution discussed here.
>
> **Exercise 6.23** What happens when you add more (or fewer) possible responses to the responses list? Will the selection of a random-response still work properly? Why or why not?

The solution discussed here is also in the book projects under the name *tech-support2*. We recommend, however, that you implement it yourself as an extension of the base version.

6.6 Using maps for associations

We now have a solution to our technical-support system that generates random responses. This is better than our first version, but is still not very convincing. In particular, the input of the user does not influence the response in any way. It is this area that we now want to improve.

The plan is that we shall have a set of words that are likely to occur in typical questions, and we will associate these words with particular responses. If the input from the user contains one of our known words, we can generate a related response. This is still a very crude method, because it does not pick up any of the meaning of the user's input, nor does it recognize a context. Still, it can be surprisingly effective, and it is a good next step.

To do this, we will use a **HashMap**. You will find the documentation for the class **HashMap** in the Java library documentation. **HashMap** is a specialization of a **Map**, which you will also find documented. You will see that you need to read the documentation of both to understand what a **HashMap** is and how it works.

Exercise 6.24 What is a **HashMap**? What is its purpose and how do you use it? Answer these questions in writing, and use the Java library documentation of **Map** and **HashMap** for your responses. Note that you will find it hard to understand everything, as the documentation for these classes is not very good. We will discuss the details later in this chapter, but see what you can find out on your own before reading on.

Exercise 6.25 **HashMap** is a parameterized class. List those of its methods that depend on the types used to parameterize it. Do you think the same type could be used for both of its parameters?

6.6.1 The concept of a map

> **Concept**
>
> A **map** is a collection that stores key/value pairs as entries. Values can be looked up by providing the key.

A map is a collection of key/value pairs of objects. As with the **ArrayList**, a map can store a flexible number of entries. One difference between the **ArrayList** and a **Map** is that with a **Map** each entry is not an object, but a *pair* of objects. This pair consists of a *key* object and a *value* object.

Instead of looking up entries in this collection using an integer index (as we did with the **ArrayList**), we use the key object to look up the value object.

An everyday example of a map is a contacts list. A contacts list contains entries, and each entry is a pair: a name and a phone number. You use a contacts list by looking up a name and getting a phone number. We do not use an index—the position of the entry in the contacts list—to find it.

A map can be organized in such a way that looking up a value for a key is easy. In the case of a contacts list, this is done using alphabetical sorting. By storing the entries in the alphabetical order of their keys, finding the key and looking up the value is easy. Reverse lookup (finding the key for a value—i.e., finding the name for a given phone number) is not so easy with a map. As with a contacts list, reverse lookup in a map is possible, but it takes a comparatively long time. Thus, maps are ideal for a one-way lookup, where we know the lookup key and need to know a value associated with this key.

6.6.2 Using a HashMap

HashMap is a particular implementation of **Map**. The most important methods of the **HashMap** class are **put** and **get**.

The **put** method inserts an entry into the map, and **get** retrieves the value for a given key. The following code fragment creates a **HashMap** and inserts three entries into it. Each entry is a key/value pair consisting of a name and a telephone number.

```
HashMap<String, String> contacts = new HashMap<>();
contacts.put("Charles Nguyen", "(531) 9392 4587");
contacts.put("Lisa Jones", "(402) 4536 4674");
contacts.put("William H. Smith", "(998) 5488 0123");
```

As we saw with **ArrayList**, when declaring a **HashMap** variable and creating a **HashMap** object, we have to say what type of objects will be stored in the map and, additionally, what type of objects will be used for the key. For the contacts list, we will use strings for both the keys and the values, but the two types will sometimes be different.

As we have seen in Section 4.4.2, when creating objects of generic classes and assigning them to a variable, we need to specify the generic types (here **<String, String>**) only once on the left hand side of the assignment, and can use the diamond operator in the object construction on the right; the generic types used for the object construction are then copied from the variable declaration.

The following code will find the phone number for Lisa Jones and print it out.

```
String number = contacts.get("Lisa Jones");
System.out.println(number);
```

Note that you pass the key (the name "Lisa Jones") to the **get** method in order to receive the value (the phone number).

Read the documentation of the **get** and **put** methods of class **HashMap** again and see whether the explanation matches your current understanding.

Exercise 6.26 How do you check how many entries are contained in a map?

Exercise 6.27 Create a class **MapTester** (either in your current project or in a new project). In it, use a **HashMap** to implement a contacts list similar to the one in the example above. (Remember that you must import `java.util.HashMap`.) In this class, implement two methods:

```
public void enterNumber(String name, String number)
```

and

```
public String lookupNumber(String name)
```

The methods should use the **put** and **get** methods of the **HashMap** class to implement their functionality.

Exercise 6.28 What happens when you add an entry to a map with a key that already exists in the map?

Exercise 6.29 What happens when you add two entries to a map with the same value and two different keys?

Exercise 6.30 How do you check whether a given key is contained in a map? (Give a Java code example.)

Exercise 6.31 What happens when you try to look up a value and the key does not exist in the map?

Exercise 6.32 How do you print out all keys currently stored in a map?

6.6.3 Using a map for the *TechSupport* system

In the *TechSupport system*, we can make good use of a map by using known words as keys and associated responses as values. Code 6.4 shows an example in which a `HashMap` named `responseMap` is created and three entries are made. For example, the word "slow" is associated with the text

> *"I think this has to do with your hardware. Upgrading your processor should solve all performance problems. Do you have a problem with our software?"*

Now, whenever somebody enters a question containing the word "slow", we can look up and print out this response. Note that the response string in the source code spans several lines but is concatenated with the `+` operator, so a single string is entered as a value into the `HashMap`.

Code 6.4

Associating selected words with possible responses

```java
private HashMap<String, String> responseMap;
...
public Responder()
{
    responseMap = new HashMap<>();
    fillResponseMap();
}

/**
 * Enter all the known keywords and their associated responses
 * into our response map.
 */
private void fillResponseMap()
{
    responseMap.put("slow",
            "I think this has to do with your hardware. Upgrading\n" +
            "your processor should solve all performance problems.\n" +
            "Have you got a problem with our software?");
    responseMap.put("bug",
            "Well, you know, all software has some bugs. But our\n" +
            "software engineers are working very hard to fix them.\n" +
            "Can you describe the problem a bit further?");
    responseMap.put("expensive",
            "The cost of our product is quite competitive. Have you\n" +
            "looked around and really compared our features?");
}
```

A first attempt at writing a method to generate the responses could now look like the **generateResponse** method below. Here, to simplify things for the moment, we assume that only a single word (for example, "slow") is entered by the user.

```
public String generateResponse(String word)
{
    String response = responseMap.get(word);
    if(response != null) {
        return response;
    }
    else {
        // If we get here, the word was not recognized. In
        // this case, we pick one of our default responses.
        return pickDefaultResponse();
    }
}
```

In this code fragment, we look up the word entered by the user in our response map. If we find an entry, we use this entry as the response. If we don't find an entry for that word, we call a method called **pickDefaultResponse**. This method can now contain the code of our previous version of **generateResponse**, which randomly picks one of the default responses (as shown in Code 6.3). The new logic, then, is that we pick an appropriate response if we recognize a word, or a random response out of our list of default responses if we don't.

> **Exercise 6.33** Implement the changes discussed here in your own version of the *TechSupport* system. Test it to get a feel for how well it works.

This approach of associating keywords with responses works quite well as long as the user does not enter complete questions, but only single words. The final improvement to complete the application is to let the user enter complete questions again, and then pick matching responses if we recognize any of the words in the questions.

This poses the problem of recognizing the keywords in the sentence that was entered by the user. In the current version, the user input is returned by the **InputReader** as a single string. We shall now change this to a new version in which the **InputReader** returns the input as a set of words. Technically, this will be a set of strings, where each string in the set represents a single word that was entered by the user.

If we can do that, then we can pass the whole set to the **Responder**, which can then check every word in the set to see whether it is known and has an associated response.

To achieve this in Java, we need to know about two things: how to cut a single string containing a whole sentence into words, and how to use sets. These issues are discussed in the next two sections.

6.7 Using sets

Concept
A **set** is a collection that stores each individual element at most once. It does not maintain any specific order.

The Java standard library includes different variations of sets implemented in different classes. The class we shall use is called `HashSet`.

Exercise 6.34 What are the similarities and differences between a `HashSet` and an `ArrayList`? Use the descriptions of `Set`, `HashSet`, `List`, and `ArrayList` in the library documentation to find out, because `HashSet` is a special case of a `Set`, and `ArrayList` is a special case of a `List`.

The two types of functionality that we need are the ability to enter elements into the set, and retrieve the elements later. Fortunately, these tasks contain hardly anything new for us. Consider the following code fragment:

```java
import java.util.HashSet;
...
HashSet<String> mySet = new HashSet<>();
mySet.add("one");
mySet.add("two");
mySet.add("three");
```

Compare this code with the statements needed to enter elements into an `ArrayList`. There is almost no difference, except that we create a `HashSet` this time instead of an `ArrayList`. Now let us look at iterating over all elements:

```java
for(String item : mySet) {
    do something with that item
}
```

Again, these statements are the same as the ones we used to iterate over an `ArrayList` in Chapter 4.

In short, using collections in Java is quite similar for different types of collections. Once you understand how to use one of them, you can use them all. The differences really lie in the behavior of each collection. A list, for example, will keep all elements entered in the desired order, provides access to elements by index, and can contain the same element multiple times. A set, on the other hand, does not maintain any specific order (the elements may be returned in a for-each loop in a different order from that in which they were entered) and ensures that each element is in the set at most once. Entering an element a second time simply has no effect.

6.8 Dividing strings

Now that we have seen how to use a set, we can investigate how we can cut the input string into separate words to be stored in a set of words. The solution is shown in a new version of the `InputReader`'s `getInput` method (Code 6.5).

Code 6.5
The `getInput` method returning a set of words

```java
/**
 * Read a line of text from standard input (the text terminal),
 * and return it as a set of words.
 *
 * @return  A set of Strings, where each String is one of the
 *          words typed by the user
 */
public HashSet<String> getInput()
{
    System.out.print("> ");                                  // print prompt
    String inputLine = reader.nextLine().trim().toLowerCase();

    String[] wordArray = inputLine.split(" ");   // split at spaces

    // add words from array into hashset
    HashSet<String> words = new HashSet<>();
    for(String word : wordArray) {
        words.add(word);
    }
    return words;
}
```

Here, in addition to using a **HashSet**, we also use the **split** method, which is a standard method of the **String** class.

The **split** method can divide a string into separate substrings and return those in an array of strings. (Arrays will be discussed in more detail in the next chapter.) The parameter to the **split** method defines at what kind of characters the original string should be split. We have defined that we want to cut our string at every space character.

The next few lines of code create a **HashSet** and copy the words from the array into the set before returning the set.[3]

Exercise 6.35 The **split** method is more powerful than it first seems from our example. How can you define exactly how a string should be split? Give some examples.

Exercise 6.36 How would you call the **split** method if you wanted to split a string at either space or tab characters? How might you break up a string in which the words are separated by colon characters (:)?

---

[3] There is a shorter, more elegant way of doing this. One could write
`HashSet<String> words = new HashSet<>(Arrays.asList(wordArray));`
to replace all four lines of code. This uses the **Arrays** class from the standard library and a *static method* (also known as *class method*) that we do not really want to discuss just yet. If you are curious, read about *class methods* in Section 6.15, and try to use this version.

Exercise 6.37 What is the difference in the result of returning the words in a `HashSet` compared with returning them in an `ArrayList`?

Exercise 6.38 What happens if there is more than one space between two words (e.g., two or three spaces)? Is there a problem?

Exercise 6.39 *Challenge exercise* Read the footnote about the `Arrays.asList` method. Find and read the sections later in this chapter about class variables and class methods. Explain in your own words how this works.

Exercise 6.40 *Challenge exercise* What are examples of other methods that the `Arrays` class provides?

Exercise 6.41 *Challenge exercise* Create a class called `SortingTest`. In it, create a method that accepts an array of `int` values as a parameter and prints the elements sorted out to the terminal (smallest element first).

6.9 Finishing the *TechSupport* system

To put everything together, we also have to adjust the `SupportSystem` and `Responder` classes to deal correctly with a set of words rather than a single string. Code 6.6 shows the new version of the `start` method from the `SupportSystem` class. It has not changed very much. The changes are:

- The `input` variable receiving the result from `reader.getInput()` is now of type `HashSet`.

- The check for ending the application is done using the `contains` method of the `HashSet` class, rather than a `String` method. (Look this method up in the documentation.)

- The `HashSet` class has to be imported using an `import` statement (not shown here).

Finally, we have to extend the `generateResponse` method in the `Responder` class to accept a set of words as a parameter. It then has to iterate over these words and check each of them with our map of known words. If any of the words is recognized, we immediately return the associated response. If we do not recognize any of the words, as before, we pick one of our default responses. Code 6.7 shows the solution.

This is the last change to the application discussed here in this chapter. The solution in the project *tech-support-complete* contains all these changes. It also contains more associations of words to responses than are shown in this chapter.

Many more improvements to this application are possible. We shall not discuss them here. Instead, we suggest some, in the form of exercises, to the reader. Some of these are quite challenging programming exercises.

Code 6.6
Final version of the start method

```java
public void start()
{
    boolean finished = false;
    
    printWelcome();
    
    while(!finished) {
        HashSet<String> input = reader.getInput();
        
        if(input.contains("bye")) {
            finished = true;
        }
        else {
            String response = responder.generateResponse(input);
            System.out.println(response);
        }
    }
    printGoodbye();
}
```

Code 6.7
Final version of the generateResponse method

```java
public String generateResponse(HashSet<String> words)
{
    for (String word : words) {
        String response = responseMap.get(word);
        if(response != null) {
            return response;
        }
    }
    
    // If we get here, none of the words from the input line was recognized.
    // In this case we pick one of our default responses (what we say when
    // we cannot think of anything else to say...)
    return pickDefaultResponse();
}
```

Exercise 6.42 Implement the final changes discussed above in your own version of the program.

Exercise 6.43 Add more word/response mappings into your application. You could copy some out of the solutions provided and add some yourself.

Exercise 6.44 Ensure that the same default response is never repeated twice in a row.

Exercise 6.45 Sometimes two words (or variations of a word) are mapped to the same response. Deal with this by mapping synonyms or related expressions to the same string, so that you do not need multiple entries in the response map for the same response.

Exercise 6.46 Identify multiple matching words in the user's input, and respond with a more appropriate answer in that case.

Exercise 6.47 When no word is recognized, use other words from the user's input to pick a well-fitting default response: for example, words such as "why", "how", and "who".

6.10 Autoboxing and wrapper classes

We have seen that, with suitable parameterization, the collection classes can store objects of any object type. There remains one problem: Java has some types that are not object types.

As we know, the simple types—such as `int`, `boolean`, and `char`—are separate from object types. Their values are not instances of classes, and it would not normally be possible to add them into a collection.

This is unfortunate. There are situations in which we might want to create a list of `int` values or a set of `char` values, for instance. What can we do?

Java's solution to this problem is *wrapper classes*. Every primitive type in Java has a corresponding wrapper class that represents the same type but is a real object type. The wrapper class for `int`, for example, is called `Integer`. A complete list of simple types and their wrapper classes is given in Appendix B.

The following statement explicitly wraps the value of the primitive `int` variable `ix` in an `Integer` object:

```
Integer iwrap = new Integer(ix);
```

And now `iwrap` could obviously easily be stored in an `ArrayList<Integer>` collection, for instance. However, storing of primitive values into an object collection is made even easier through a compiler feature known as *autoboxing*.

Whenever a value of a primitive type is used in a context that requires a wrapper type, the compiler automatically wraps the primitive-type value in an appropriate wrapper object. This means that primitive-type values can be added directly to a collection:

```
private ArrayList<Integer> markList;
...
public void storeMarkInList(int mark)
{
    markList.add(mark);
}
```

> **Concept**
>
> **Autoboxing** is performed automatically when a primitive-type value is used in a context requiring a wrapper type.

The reverse operation—*unboxing*—is also performed automatically, so retrieval from a collection might look like this:

```
int firstMark = markList.remove(0);
```

Autoboxing is also applied whenever a primitive-type value is passed as a parameter to a method that expects a wrapper type, and when a primitive-type value is stored in a wrapper-type variable. Similarly, unboxing is applied when a wrapper-type value is passed as a parameter to a method that expects a primitive-type value, and when stored in a primitive-type variable. It is worth noting that this almost makes it appear as if primitive types can be stored in collections. However, the type of the collection must still be declared using the wrapper type (e.g., `ArrayList<Integer>`, not `ArrayList<int>`).

6.10.1 Maintaining usage counts

Combining a map with autoboxing provides an easy way to maintain usage counts of objects. For instance, suppose that the company running the *TechSupport* system is receiving complaints from its customers that some of its answers bear no relation to the question being asked. The company might decide to analyze the words being used in questions and add further specific responses for those being used most frequently that it does not have ready responses for. Code 6.8 shows part of the `WordCounter` class that can be found in the *tech-support-analysis* project.

Code 6.8

The `WordCounter` class, used to count word frequencies

```java
import java.util.HashMap;
import java.util.HashSet;

/**
 * Keep a record of how many times each word was entered by users.
 *
 * @author    Michael Kölling and David J. Barnes
 * @version   1.0 (2016.02.29)
 */
public class WordCounter
{
    // Associate each word with a count.
    private HashMap<String, Integer> counts;

    /**
     * Create a WordCounter
     */
    public WordCounter()
    {
        counts = new HashMap<>();
    }

    /**
     * Update the usage count of all words in input.
     * @param input A set of words entered by the user.
     */
```

Code 6.8 continued

The `WordCounter` class, used to count word frequencies

```java
    public void addWords(HashSet<String> input)
    {
        for(String word : input) {
            int counter = counts.getOrDefault(word, 0);
            counts.put(word, counter + 1);
        }
    }
}
```

The `addWords` method receives the same set of words that are passed to the `Responder`, so that each word can be associated with a count. The counts are stored in a map of `String` to `Integer` objects.

Notice the use of the `getOrDefault` method of the `HashMap`, which takes two parameters: a key and a default value. If the key is already in use in the map then this method returns its associated value, but if the key is not in use then it will return the default value rather than `null`. This avoids having to write two different follow-up actions depending on whether the key was in use or not. Using `get`, instead, we would have had to write something like:

```java
Integer counter = counts.get(word);
if(counter == null) {
    counts.put(word, 1);
}
else {
    counts.put(word, counter + 1);
}
```

Notice how autoboxing and unboxing are used multiple times in these examples.

Exercise 6.48 What does the `putIfAbsent` method of `HashMap` do?

Exercise 6.49 Add a method to the `WordCounter` class in *tech-support-analysis* to print the usage count of each word after the "goodbye" message has been printed.

Exercise 6.50 Print counts of only those words that are not already keys in the `responseMap` in the `Responder` class. You will need to provide an accessor method for `responseMap`.

6.11 Writing class documentation

When working on your projects, it is important to write documentation for your classes as you develop the source code. It is common for programmers not to take documentation seriously enough, and this frequently creates serious problems later.

If you do not supply sufficient documentation, it may be very hard for another programmer (or yourself some time later!) to understand your classes. Typically, what you have to do in that case is to read the class's implementation and figure out what it does. This may work with a small student project, but it creates problems in real-world projects.

> **Concept**
>
> The **documentation** of a class should be detailed enough for other programmers to use the class without the need to read the implementation.

It is not uncommon for commercial applications to consist of hundreds of thousands of lines of code in several thousand classes. Imagine that you had to read all that in order to understand how an application works! You would never succeed.

When we used the Java library classes, such as **HashSet** or **Random**, we relied exclusively on the documentation to find out how to use them. We never looked at the implementation of those classes. This worked because these classes were sufficiently well documented (although even this documentation could be improved). Our task would have been much harder had we been required to read the classes' implementation before using them.

In a software development team, the implementation of classes is typically shared between multiple programmers. While you might be responsible for implementing the **SupportSystem** class from our last example, someone else might implement the **InputReader**. Thus, you might write one class while making calls to methods of other classes.

The same argument discussed for library classes holds true for classes that you write: if we can use the classes without having to read and understand the complete implementation, our task becomes easier. As with library classes, we want to see just the public interface of the class, instead of the implementation. It is therefore important to write good class documentation for our own classes as well.

Java systems include a tool called **javadoc** that can be used to generate such an interface description from source files. The standard library documentation that we have used, for example, was created from the classes' source files by **javadoc**.

6.11.1 Using javadoc in BlueJ

The BlueJ environment uses **javadoc** to let you create documentation for your class in two ways:

- You can view the documentation for a single class by switching the pop-up selector at the top right of the editor window from *Source Code* to *Documentation* (or by using *Toggle Documentation View* from the editor's *Tools* menu).

- You can use the *Project Documentation* function from the main window's *Tools* menu to generate documentation for all classes in the project.

The BlueJ tutorial provides more detail if you are interested. You can find the BlueJ tutorial in BlueJ's *Help* menu.

6.11.2 Elements of class documentation

The documentation of a class should include at least:

- the class name
- a comment describing the overall purpose and characteristics of the class
- a version number

- the author's name (or authors' names)
- documentation for each constructor and each method

The documentation for each constructor and method should include:

- the name of the method
- the return type
- the parameter names and types
- a description of the purpose and function of the method
- a description of each parameter
- a description of the value returned

In addition, each complete project should have an overall project comment, often contained in a "ReadMe" file. In BlueJ, this project comment is accessible through the text note displayed in the top left corner of the class diagram.

Exercise 6.51 Use BlueJ's *Project Documentation* function to generate documentation for your *TechSupport* project. Examine it. Is it accurate? Is it complete? Which parts are useful? Which are not? Do you find any errors in the documentation?

Some elements of the documentation, such as names and parameters of methods, can always be extracted from the source code. Other parts, such as comments describing the class, methods, and parameters, need more attention, as they can easily be forgotten, be incomplete, or be incorrect.

In Java, **javadoc** comments are written with a special comment symbol at the beginning:

```
/**
   This is a javadoc comment.
 */
```

The comment start symbol must have two asterisks to be recognized as a **javadoc** comment. Such a comment immediately preceding the class declaration is read as a class comment. If the comment is directly above a method signature, it is considered a method comment.

The exact details of how documentation is produced and formatted are different in different programming languages and environments. The content, however, should be more or less the same.

In Java, using **javadoc**, several special key symbols are available for formatting the documentation. These key symbols start with the @ symbol and include

```
@version
@author
@param
@return
```

Exercise 6.52 Find examples of `javadoc` key symbols in the source code of the *TechSupport* project. How do they influence the formatting of the documentation?

Exercise 6.53 Find out about and describe other `javadoc` key symbols. One place where you can look is the online documentation of Oracle's Java distribution. It contains a document called *javadoc—The Java API Documentation Generator* (for example, at `http://download.oracle.com/javase/8/docs/technotes/tools/windows/javadoc.html`). In this document, the key symbols are called *javadoc tags*.

Exercise 6.54 Properly document all classes in your version of the *TechSupport* project.

6.12 Public versus private

> **Concept**
>
> **Access modifiers** define the visibility of a field, constructor, or method. Public elements are accessible from inside the same class and from other classes; private elements are accessible only from within the same class.

It is time to discuss in more detail one aspect of classes that we have already encountered several times without saying much about it: *access modifiers*.

Access modifiers are the keywords **public** or **private** at the beginning of field declarations and method signatures. For example:

```
// field declaration
private int numberOfSeats;

// methods
public void setAge(int replacementAge)
{ ...
}

private int computeAverage()
{ ...
}
```

Fields, constructors, and methods can all be either public or private, although so far we have seen mostly private fields and public constructors and methods. We shall come back to this below.

Access modifiers define the visibility of a field, constructor, or method. If a method, for example, is public, it can be invoked from within the same class or from any other class. Private methods, on the other hand, can be invoked only from within the class in which they are declared. They are not visible to other classes.

Now that we have discussed the difference between the interface and the implementation of a class (Section 6.3.1), we can more easily understand the purpose of these keywords.

Remember: The interface of a class is the set of details that another programmer using the class needs to see. It provides information about how to use the class. The interface includes constructor and method signatures and comments. It is also referred to as the *public* part of a class. Its purpose is to define *what* the class does.

The implementation is the section of a class that defines precisely *how* the class works. The method bodies, containing the Java statements, and most fields are part of the implementation. The implementation is also referred to as the *private* part of a class. The user of a class does not need to know about the implementation. In fact, there are good reasons why a user *should be prevented from knowing* about the implementation (or at least from making use of this knowledge). This principle is called *information hiding*.

The `public` keyword declares an element of a class (a field or method) to be part of the interface (i.e., publicly visible); the `private` keyword declares it to be part of the implementation (i.e., hidden from outside access).

6.12.1 Information hiding

In many object-oriented programming languages, the internals of a class—its implementation—are hidden from other classes. There are two aspects to this. First, a programmer making use of a class should *not need to know* the internals; second, a user should *not be allowed to know* the internals.

> **Concept**
>
> **Information hiding** is a principle that states that internal details of a class's implementation should be hidden from other classes. It ensures better modularization of an application.

The first principle—*not need to know*—has to do with abstraction and modularization as discussed in Chapter 3. If it were necessary to know all internals of all classes we need to use, we would never finish implementing large systems.

The second principle—*not being allowed to know*—is different. It also has to do with modularization, but in a different context. The programming language does not allow access to the private section of one class by statements in another class. This ensures that one class does not depend on exactly how another class is implemented.

This is very important for maintenance work. It is a very common task for a maintenance programmer to later change or extend the implementation of a class to make improvements or fix bugs. Ideally, changing the implementation of one class should not make it necessary to change other classes as well. This issue is known as *coupling*. If changes in one part of a program do not make it necessary to also make changes in another part of the program, this is known as weak coupling or loose coupling. Loose coupling is good, because it makes a maintenance programmer's job much easier. Instead of understanding and changing many classes, she may only need to understand and change one class. For example, if a Java systems programmer makes an improvement to the implementation of the `ArrayList` class, you would hope that you would not need to change your code using this class. This will work, because you have not made any references to the implementation of `ArrayList` in your own code.

So, to be more precise, the rule that a user should not be allowed to know the internals of a class does not refer to the programmer of another class, but to the class itself. It is not usually a problem if a programmer knows the implementation details, but a class should not "know" (depend on) the internal details of another class. The programmer of both classes might even be the same person, but the classes should still be loosely coupled.

The issues of coupling and information hiding are very important, and we shall have more to say about them in later chapters.

For now, it is important to understand that the **private** keyword enforces information hiding by not allowing other classes access to this part of the class. This ensures loose coupling, and makes an application more modular and easier to maintain.

6.12.2 Private methods and public fields

Most methods we have seen so far were public. This ensures that other classes can call these methods. Sometimes, though, we have made use of private methods. In the **SupportSystem** class of the *TechSupport* system, for instance, we saw the methods **printWelcome** and **printGoodbye** declared as private methods.

The reason for having both options is that methods are actually used for different purposes. They are used to provide operations to users of a class (public methods), and they are used to break up a larger task into several smaller ones to make the large task easier to handle. In the second case, the subtasks are not intended to be invoked directly from outside the class, but are placed in separate methods purely to make the implementation of a class easier to read. In this case, such methods should be private. The **printWelcome** and **printGoodbye** methods are examples of this.

Another good reason for having a private method is for a task that is needed (as a subtask) in several of a class's methods. Instead of writing the code multiple times, we can write it once in a single private method, and then call this method from several different places. We shall see an example of this later.

In Java, fields can also be declared private or public. So far, we have not seen examples of public fields, and there is a good reason for this. Declaring fields public breaks the information-hiding principle. It makes a class that is dependent upon that information vulnerable to incorrect operation if the implementation changes. Even though the Java language allows us to declare public fields, we consider this bad style and will not make use of this option. Some other object-oriented languages do not allow public fields at all.

A further reason for keeping fields private is that it allows an object to maintain greater control over its state. If access to a private field is channeled through accessor and mutator methods, then an object has the ability to ensure that the field is never set to a value that would be inconsistent with its overall state. This level of integrity is not possible if fields are made public.

In short, fields should always be private.

Java has two more access levels. One is declared by using the **protected** keyword as access modifier; the other one is used if no access modifier at all is declared. We shall discuss these in later chapters.

6.13 Learning about classes from their interfaces

We shall briefly discuss another project to revisit and practice the concepts discussed in this chapter. The project is named *scribble*, and you can find it in the Chapter 6 folder of the book projects. This section does not introduce any new concepts, so it consists in large part of exercises, with some commentary sprinkled in.

Figure 6.4
The *scribble* project

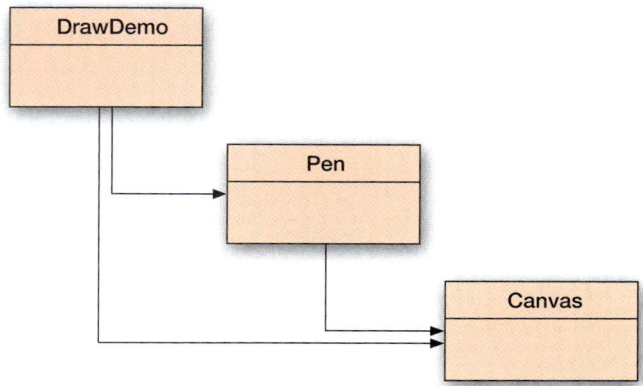

6.13.1 The *scribble* demo

The *scribble* project provides three classes: **DrawDemo**, **Pen**, and **Canvas** (Figure 6.4).

The **Canvas** class provides a window on screen that can be used to draw on. It has operations for drawing lines, shapes, and text. A canvas can be used by creating an instance interactively or from another object. The **Canvas** class should not need any modification. It is probably best to treat it as a library class: open the editor and switch to the documentation view. This displays the class's interface with the **javadoc** documentation.

The **Pen** class provides a pen object that can be used to produce drawings on the canvas by moving the pen across the screen. The pen itself is invisible, but it will draw a line when moved on the canvas.

The **DrawDemo** class provides a few small examples of how to use a pen object to produce a drawing on screen. The best starting point for understanding and experimenting with this project is the **DrawDemo** class.

Exercise 6.55 Create a **DrawDemo** object and experiment with its various methods. Read the **DrawDemo** source code and describe (in writing) how each method works.

Exercise 6.56 Create a **Pen** object interactively using its default constructor (the constructor without parameters). Experiment with its methods. While you do this, make sure to have a window open showing you the documentation of the **Pen** class (either the editor window in *Documentation* view or a web-browser window showing the project documentation). Refer to the documentation to be certain what each method does.

Exercise 6.57 Interactively create an instance of class **Canvas** and try some of its methods. Again, refer to the class's documentation while you do this.

Some of the methods in the classes **Pen** and **Canvas** refer to parameters of type **Color**. This type is defined in class **Color** in the `java.awt` package (thus, its fully qualified name is `java.awt.Color`). The **Color** class defines some color constants, which we can refer to as follows:

```
Color.RED
```

Using these constants requires the **Color** class to be imported in the using class.

> **Exercise 6.58** Find some uses of the color constants in the code of class **DrawDemo**.
>
> **Exercise 6.59** Write down four more color constants that are available in the **Color** class. Refer to the class's documentation to find out what they are.

When calling methods interactively that expect parameters of the **Color** class, we have to refer to the class slightly differently. Because the interactive dialog has no import statement (and thus the **Color** class is not automatically known), we have to write the fully qualified class name to refer to the class (Figure 6.5). This enables the Java system to find the class without using an import statement.

Now that we know how to change the color for pens and canvases, we can do some more exercises.

> **Exercise 6.60** Create a canvas. Using the canvas's methods interactively, draw a red circle near the center of the canvas. Now draw a yellow rectangle.
>
> **Exercise 6.61** How do you clear the whole canvas?

Figure 6.5
A method call with a fully qualified class name

As you have seen, we can either draw directly on to the canvas or we can use a pen object to draw. The pen provides us with an abstraction that holds a current position, rotation, and color, and this makes producing some kinds of drawings easier. Let us experiment with this a bit more, this time by writing code in a class instead of using interactive calls.

Exercise 6.62 In class **DrawDemo**, create a new method named **drawTriangle**. This method should create a pen (as in the **drawSquare** method) and then draw a green triangle.

Exercise 6.63 Write a method **drawPentagon** that draws a pentagon.

Exercise 6.64 Write a method **drawPolygon(int n)** that draws a regular polygon with **n** sides (thus, n=3 draws a triangle, n=4 draws a square, etc.).

Exercise 6.65 Write a method called **spiral** that draws a spiral (see Figure 6.6).

6.13.2 Code completion

Often, we are reasonably familiar with a library class that we are using, but we still cannot remember the exact names of all methods or the exact parameters. For this situation, development environments commonly offer some help: code completion.

Code completion is a function that is available in BlueJ's editor when the cursor is behind the dot of a method call. In this situation, typing *CTRL-space* will bring up a pop-up listing all methods in the interface of the object we are using in the call (Figure 6.7).

Figure 6.6
A spiral drawn on the canvas

Figure 6.7
Code completion

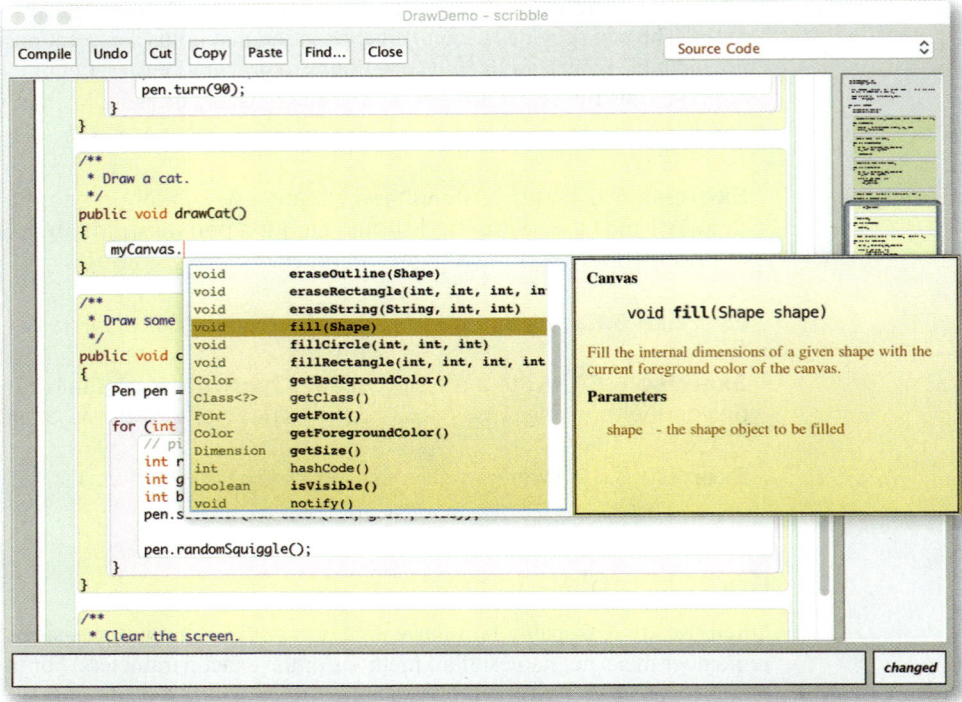

When the code completion pop-up is displayed, we can type the beginning of the method name to narrow down the method list. Hitting *Return* enters the selected method call into our source code. Code completion can also be used without a preceding object to call local methods.

Using code completion should not be a replacement for reading the documentation of a class, because it does not include all information (such as the introductory class comment). But once we are reasonably familiar with a class in general, code completion is a great aid for more easily recalling details of a method and entering the call into our source.

Exercise 6.66 In your `DrawDemo` class, type `myCanvas.er` and then press Ctrl-Space (with the cursor immediately behind the typed text) to activate code completion. How many methods are shown?

Exercise 6.67 Add a method to your `DrawDemo` class that produces a picture on the canvas directly (without using a pen object). The picture can show anything you like, but should at least include some shapes, different colors, and text. Use code completion in the process of entering your code.

6.13.3 The *bouncing-balls* demo

Open the *bouncing-balls* project and find out what it does. Create a **BallDemo** object and execute its **bounce** method.

Exercise 6.68 Change the method **bounce** in class **BallDemo** to let the user choose how many balls should be bouncing.

For this exercise, you should use a collection to store the balls. This way, the method can deal with 1, 3, or 75 balls—any number you want. The balls should initially be placed in a row along the top of the canvas.

Which type of collection should you choose? So far, we have seen an **ArrayList**, a **HashMap**, and a **HashSet**. Try the next two exercises first, before you write your implementation.

Exercise 6.69 Which type of collection (**ArrayList**, **HashMap**, or **HashSet**) is most suitable for storing the balls for the new **bounce** method? Discuss in writing, and justify your choice.

Exercise 6.70 Change the **bounce** method to place the balls randomly anywhere in the top half of the screen.

Exercise 6.71 Write a new method named **boxBounce**. This method draws a rectangle (the "box") on screen and one or more balls inside the box. For the balls, do not use **BouncingBall**, but create a new class **BoxBall** that moves around inside the box, bouncing off the walls of the box so that the ball always stays inside. The initial position and speed of the ball should be random. The **boxBounce** method should have a parameter that specifies how many balls are in the box.

Exercise 6.72 Give the balls in **boxBounce** random colors.

6.14 Class variables and constants

So far, we have not looked at the **BouncingBall** class. If you are interested in really understanding how this animation works, you may want to study this class as well. It is reasonably simple. The only method that takes some effort to understand is **move**, where the ball changes its position to the next position in its path.

We shall leave it largely to the reader to study this method, except for one detail that we want to discuss here. We start with an exercise.

> **Exercise 6.73** In class `BouncingBall`, you will find a definition of gravity (a simple integer). Increase or decrease the gravity value; compile and run the bouncing ball demo again. Do you observe a change?

The most interesting detail in this class is the line

```
private static final int GRAVITY = 3;
```

This is a construct we have not seen yet. This one line, in fact, introduces two new keywords, which are used together: **static** and **final**.

6.14.1 The static keyword

Concept

Classes can have fields. These are known as **class variables** or **static variables**. Exactly one copy exists of a class variable at all times, independent of the number of created instances.

The keyword **static** is Java's syntax to define *class variables*. Class variables are fields that are stored in a class itself, not in an object. This makes them fundamentally different from instance variables (the fields we have dealt with so far). Consider this segment of code (a part of the `BouncingBall` class):

```
public class BouncingBall
{
    // Effect of gravity.
    private static final int GRAVITY = 3;
    private int xPosition;
    private int yPosition;
```
Other fields and method omitted.
```
}
```

Now imagine that we create three `BouncingBall` instances. The resulting situation is shown in Figure 6.8.

As we can see from the diagram, the instance variables (`xPosition` and `yPosition`) are stored in each object. Because we have created three objects, we have three independent copies of these variables.

The class variable **GRAVITY**, on the other hand, is stored in the class itself. As a result, there is always exactly one copy of this variable, independent of the number of created instances.

Source code in the class can access (read and set) this kind of variable, just as it can an instance variable. The class variable can be accessed from any of the class's instances. As a result, the objects share this variable.

Class variables are frequently used if a value should always be the same for all instances of a class. Instead of storing one copy of the same value in each object, which would be a waste of space and might be hard to coordinate, a single value can be shared among all instances.

Java also supports *class methods* (also known as *static methods*), which are methods that belong to a class. We shall discuss those in a separate section later.

Figure 6.8
Instance variables and a class variable

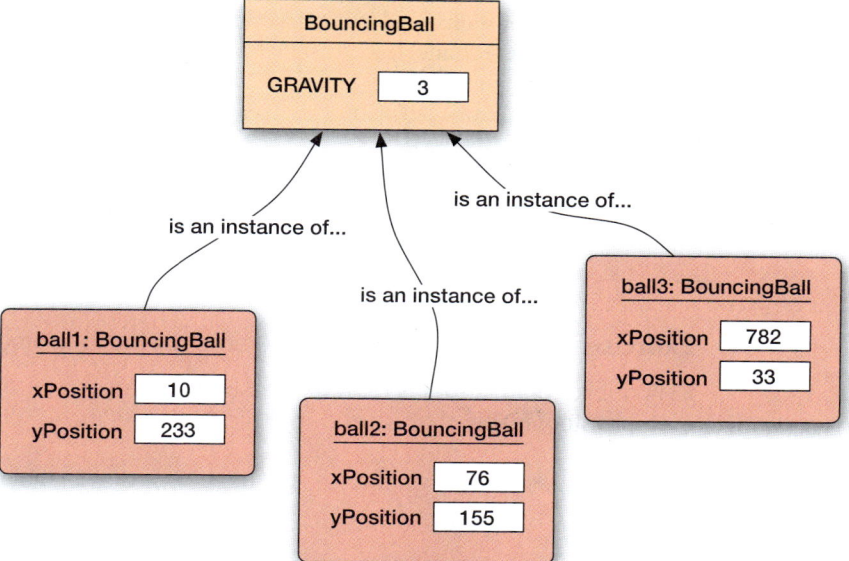

6.14.2 Constants

One frequent use for the **static** keyword is to define *constants*. Constants are similar to variables, but they cannot change their value during the execution of an application. In Java, constants are defined with the keyword **final**. For example:

```
private final int SIZE = 10;
```

Here, we define a constant named **SIZE** with the value 10. We notice that constant declarations look similar to field declarations, with two differences:

- they include the keyword **final** before the type name; and
- they must be initialized with a value at the point of declaration.

If a value is intended not to change, it is a good idea to declare it **final**. This ensures that it cannot accidentally be changed later. Any attempt to change a constant field will result in a compile-time error message. Constants are, by convention, often written in capital letters. We will follow that convention in this book.

In practice, it is frequently the case that constants apply to all instances of a class. In this situation, we declare *class constants*. Class constants are constant class fields. They are declared by using a combination of the **static** and **final** keywords. For example:

```
private static final int SIZE = 10;
```

The definition of **GRAVITY** from our bouncing-ball project is another example of such a constant. This is the style in which constants are defined most of the time. Instance-specific constants are much less frequently used.

We have encountered two more examples of constants in the *scribble* project. The first example was two constants used in the **Pen** class to define the size of the "random squiggle" (go back to the project and find them!) The second example was the use of the color constants in that project, such as **Color.RED**. In that case, we did not define the constants, but instead used constants defined in another class.

The reason we could use the constants from class **Color** is that they were declared public. As opposed to other fields (about which we commented earlier that they should never be declared public), declaring constants public is generally unproblematic and sometimes useful.

> **Exercise 6.74** Write constant declarations for the following:
> - A public variable that is used to measure tolerance, with the value 0.001.
> - A private variable that is used to indicate a pass mark, with the integer value of 40.
> - A public character variable that is used to indicate that the help command is `'h'`.
>
> **Exercise 6.75** What constant names are defined in the **java.lang.Math** class?
>
> **Exercise 6.76** In a program that uses the constant value 73.28166 in ten different places, give reasons why it makes sense to associate this value with a variable name.

6.15 Class methods

So far, all methods we have seen have been *instance methods*: they are invoked on an instance of a class. What distinguishes class methods from instance methods is that class methods can be invoked without an instance—having the class is enough.

6.15.1 Static methods

In Section 6.14, we discussed class variables. Class methods are conceptually related and use a related syntax (the keyword **static** in Java). Just as class variables belong to the class rather than to an instance, so do class methods.

A class method is defined by adding the keyword **static** in front of the type name in the method's header:

```
public static int getNumberOfDaysThisMonth()
{
    ...
}
```

Such a method can then be called by specifying the name of the class in which it is defined, before the dot in the usual dot notation. If, for instance, the above method is defined in a class called **Calendar**, the following call invokes it:

```
int days = Calendar.getNumberOfDaysThisMonth();
```

Note that the name of the class is used before the dot—no object has been created.

Exercise 6.77 Read the class documentation for class **Math** in the package **java.lang**. It contains many static methods. Find the method that computes the maximum of two integer numbers. What does its header look like?

Exercise 6.78 Why do you think the methods in the **Math** class are static? Could they be written as instance methods?

Exercise 6.79 Write a test class that has a method to test how long it takes to count from 1 to 10000 in a loop. You can use the method **currentTimeMillis** from class **System** to help with the time measurement.

Exercise 6.80 Can a static method be called from an instance method? Can an instance method be called from a static method? Can a static method be called from another static method? Answer these questions on paper, then create a test project to check your answers and try it. Explain in detail your answers and observations.

Exercise 6.81 The **Collections** class in the **java.util** packages contains a large number of static methods that can be used with collections such as **ArrayList**, **LinkedList**, **HashMap** and **HashSet**. Read the class documentation for the **min**, **max**, and **sort** methods, for instance. While you might not fully understand the explanations or the notation used, being aware that these methods exist will be useful to you.

6.15.2 Limitations of class methods

Because class methods are associated with a class rather than an instance, they have two important limitations. The first limitation is that a class method may not access any instance fields defined in the class. This is logical, because instance fields are associated with individual objects. Instead, class methods are restricted to accessing class variables from their class. The second limitation is like the first: a class method may not call an instance method from the class. A class method may only invoke other class methods defined in its class.

You will find that we write very few class methods in the examples in this book.

6.16 Executing without BlueJ

When we finish writing a program, we might want to pass it on to someone else to use. To do this, it would be nice if people could use it without the need to start BlueJ. For this to be the case, we need one more thing: a specific class method known as *the main method*.

6.16.1 The main method

If we want to start a Java application without BlueJ, we need to use a class method. In BlueJ, we typically create an object and invoke one of its methods, but without BlueJ, an application starts without any object in existence. Classes are the only things we have initially, so the first method that can be invoked must be a class method.

The Java definition for starting applications is quite simple: the user specifies the class that should be started, and the Java system will then invoke a method called `main` in that class. This method must have a specific signature:

```
public static void main(String[] args)
```

If such a method does not exist in that class, an error is reported. Appendix E describes the details of this method and the commands needed to start the Java system without BlueJ.

> **Exercise 6.82** Add a `main` method to your `SupportSystem` class in the *tech-support* project. The method should create a `SupportSystem` object and invoke the `start` method on it. Test the `main` method by invoking it from BlueJ. Class methods can be invoked from the class's pop-up menu.
>
> **Exercise 6.83** Execute the program without BlueJ.
>
> **Exercise 6.84** Can a class count how many instances have been created of that class? What is needed to do this? Write some code fragments that illustrate what needs to be done. Assume that you want a static method called `numberOfInstances` that returns the number of instances created.

6.17 Further advanced material

In the previous chapter, we introduced material that we described as "advanced" and suggested that this material could be skipped on first reading, if desired. In this section, we introduce some further advanced material and the same advice applies.

6.17.1 Polymorphic collection types (Advanced)

By now we have introduced several different collection classes from the `java.util` package, such as `ArrayList`, `HashMap` and `HashSet`. Each has a number of distinctive features that make it appropriate for particular situations. However, they also have a considerable number of similarities and methods in common. This suggests that they might be related in some way. In object-oriented programming, relationships between classes are expressed via *inheritance*. We will cover this topic in full in Chapters 10 and 11, but it may be instructive to touch briefly on it here to deepen your understanding of the different types of collection.

When trying to understand how the various collection classes are used, and the relationships between them, it helps to pay close attention to their names. From its name, it is tempting to assume that a `HashSet` must be very similar to a `HashMap`. In fact, as we have illustrated, a `HashSet` is actually much closer in usage to an `ArrayList`. Their names consist of two parts, e.g., "array" and "list." The second half tells us *what kind* of collection we are dealing with (`List`, `Map`, `Set`), and the first tells us *how it is implemented* (for instance, using an array (covered in Chapter 7) or hashing (covered in Chapter 11).

For using collections, the type of the collection (the second part) is the more important. We have discussed before that we can often abstract from the implementation; i.e., we do not need to think about it in much detail. Thus, for our purposes, a `HashSet` and a `TreeSet` are very similar. They are both sets, so they behave in the same way. The main difference is in their implementation, which is important only when we start thinking about efficiency: one implementation will perform some operations much faster than another. However, efficiency concerns come much later, and only when we have either very large collections or applications in which performance is critical.

One consequence of this similarity is that we can often ignore details of the implementation when declaring a variable that will refer to a particular collection object. In other words, we can declare the variable to be of a more abstract type, such as `List`, `Map`, or `Set`, rather than the more concrete type—`ArrayList`, `LinkedList`, `HashMap`, `TreeSet`, etc. For instance,

```
List<Track> tracks = new LinkedList<>();
```

or

```
Map<String, String> responseMap = new HashMap<>();
```

Here, the variable is declared to be of type `List`, even though the object created and stored in it is of type `LinkedList` (and the same for `Map` and `HashMap`).

Variables like `tracks` and `responseMap` in these examples are called *polymorphic variables*, because they are capable of referring to objects of different, but related, types. The variable `tracks` could refer to either an `ArrayList` or a `LinkedList`, while `responseMap` could refer to a `HashMap` or a `TreeMap`. The key point behind declaring them like this is that the way in which the variables are used in the rest of the code is independent of the exact, concrete type of the object to which they refer. A call to `add`, `clear`, `get`, `remove`, or `size` on `tracks` would all have the same syntax, and all have the same effect on the associated collection. The exact type rarely matters in any given situation. One advantage of using polymorphic variables in this way is that if we ever wished to change from one concrete type to another, the only place in the code requiring a change is the place where the object is created. Another advantage is that code that we write does not have to know the concrete type that might have been used in code written by someone else – we only need to know the abstract type: **List**, **Map**, **Set**, etc. Both of these advantages *reduce the coupling* between different parts of a program, which is a good thing and something we explore more deeply in Chapter 8.

We will explore the mechanism behind polymorphic variables in detail in Chapters 10 and 11.

6.17.2 The `collect` method of streams (Advanced)

In this section, we continue the discussion of Java 8 streams and lambdas that we started in the previous (Advanced) chapter. We explained there that it is important to know that each operation of the stream leaves its input stream unmodified. Each operation creates a fresh stream, based on its input and the operation, to pass on the next operation in the sequence. However, we will often want to use stream operations to create a fresh version of an original collection that is a modified copy—typically by filtering the original contents to either select desired objects or reject those that are not required. For this we need to use the `collect` method of a stream. The `collect` method is a *terminal operation* and so it will appear as the final operation in a pipeline of operations. It can be used to insert the elements resulting from a stream operation back into a new collection.

There are actually two versions of the `collect` method, but we will concentrate on just the simplest. Indeed, we will choose to focus on just its role in enabling us to create a new collection object as the final operation of a pipeline, and leave further exploration to the interested reader. Even the most basic usage involves multiple concepts that are already advanced for this relatively early stage of this book: streams, static methods, and polymorphism.

The `collect` method takes a `Collector` as a parameter. Essentially, this has to be something that can progressively *accumulate* the elements of its input stream in some way. There are similarities in this accumulation idea to the stream **reduce** operation we covered in the previous chapter. There we saw that a stream of numbers could be reduced to a single number; here we will reduce a stream of objects to a single object, which is another collection. Since we often won't be particularly concerned about whether the collection is an `ArrayList`, a `LinkedList`, or some other form of list type we have not met before, we can ask the `Collector` to return the collection in the form of the polymorphic type **List**.

The easiest way to obtain a `Collector` is use one of the **static** methods defined in the `Collectors` class of the `java.util.stream` package: `toList`, `toMap`, and `toSet`.

Code 6.9 shows a method from the *national-park* project we looked at in Chapter 5. This method filters the full list of `Sighting` objects to create a new **List** of only those for a specific animal. In our version in the *animal-monitoring-v1* project, this method was written in the iterative style, using a for-each loop. Here, it is rewritten in the functional style, using the `collect` method.

Code 6.9
A functional version of the `getSightingsOf` method

```java
/**
 * Return a list of all the sightings of the given animal.
 * @param animal The type of animal.
 * @return A list of all sightings of the given animal.
 */
public List<Sighting> getSightingsOf(String animal)
{
    return sightings.stream()
                    .filter(record -> animal.equals(record.getAnimal()))
                    .collect(Collectors.toList());
}
```

A subtle point to note is that the **toList** method of **Collectors** does not actually return a **List** object to be passed into the **collect** method. Rather, it returns a **Collector** that ultimately leads to the creation of a suitable concrete **List** object.

Exercise 6.85 Implement this version of the **getSightingsOf** method in your own *animal-monitoring* project.

Exercise 6.86 Rewrite the **getSightingsInArea** method from the original *animal-monitoring* project in the functional style.

6.17.3 Method references (Advanced)

Suppose that we wish to collect the objects from a filtered stream into a particular concrete type of collection, such as an **ArrayList**, rather than a polymorphic type. This requires a variation of the approach used in the previous section. We still need to pass a **Collector** to the **collect** operation, but we must obtain it in a different way. Code 6.10 shows how this might be done.

Code 6.10
Another version of the `getSightingsOf` method

```java
/**
 * Return a list of all the sightings of the given animal.
 * @param animal The type of animal.
 * @return A list of all sightings of the given animal.
 */
public List<Sighting> getSightingsOf(String animal)
{
    return sightings.stream()
                    .filter(record -> animal.equals(record.getAnimal()))
                    .collect(Collectors.toCollection(ArrayList::new));
}
```

This time we have called the static **toCollection** method of **Collectors**, which requires a single parameter whose type is **Supplier**. The parameter we have used introduces a new notation which is called a *method reference*, whose distinctive syntax is a pair of adjacent colon characters.

Method references are a convenient shorthand for some lambdas. They are often used where the compiler can easily infer the full call of a method without having to specify its details explicitly. There are four cases of method references:

a) A reference to a constructor, as we have used here:
   `ArrayList::new`
   (Note that, strictly speaking, a constructor is not actually a method.) This is a shorthand for the lambda:
   `() -> new ArrayList<>()`
b) A reference to a method call on a particular object:
   `System.out::println`
   This would be a shorthand for the lambda:
   `str -> System.out.println(str)`
   Note that `System.out` is a `public static` variable of the `System` class and the parameter `str` would be supplied by the context in which the method reference is used, for instance, as the terminal operation of a stream pipeline:
   `forEach(System.out::println)`
c) A reference to a static method:
   `Math::abs`
   This would be a shorthand for:
   `x -> Math.abs(x)`
   The parameter `x` would be supplied by the context in which the method reference is used, for instance, as part of the mapping of a stream:
   `map(Math::abs)`
d) A reference to an instance method of a particular type:
   `String::length`
   This would be shorthand for:
   `str -> str.length()`
   Once again, `str` would be supplied by context. Note that it is important to distinguish between this usage, which involves an instance method, and both usage b), which involve a specific instance, and usage c), which involves a static method.

Here we have illustrated only the simplest examples for the use of method references. More complex cases involving multiple parameters will also be encountered in the more general examples.

6.18 Summary

Dealing with class libraries and class interfaces is essential for a competent programmer. There are two aspects to this topic: reading class library descriptions (especially class interfaces) and writing them.

It is important to know about some essential classes from the standard Java class library and to be able to find out more when necessary. In this chapter, we have presented some of the most important classes, and have discussed how to browse the library documentation.

6.18 Summary

It is also important to be able to document any class that is written, in the same style as the library classes, so that other programmers can easily use the class without the need to understand the implementation. This documentation should include good comments for every project, class, and method. Using `javadoc` with Java programs will help you to do this.

Terms introduced in this chapter:

> **interface, implementation, map, set, autoboxing, wrapper classes, javadoc, access modifier, information hiding, class variable, class method, main method, static, constant, final, polymorphic variable, method reference**

Exercise 6.87 There is a rumor circulating on the Internet that George Lucas (the creator of the *Star Wars* movies) uses a formula to create the names for the characters in his stories (Jar Jar Binks, ObiWan Kenobi, etc.). The formula—allegedly—is this:

Your Star Wars *first name:*
1. Take the first three letters of your last name.
2. Add to that the first two letters of your first name.

Your Star Wars *last name:*
1. Take the first two letters of your mother's maiden name.
2. Add to this the first three letters of the name of the town or city where you were born.

And now your task: Create a new BlueJ project named *star-wars*. In it create a class named **NameGenerator**. This class should have a method named **generateStarWarsName** that generates a *Star Wars* name, following the method described above. You will need to find out about a method of the **String** class that generates a substring.

Exercise 6.88 The following code fragment attempts to print out a string in uppercase letters:

```
public void printUpper(String s)
{
    s.toUpperCase();
    System.out.println(s);
}
```

This code, however, does not work. Find out why, and explain. How should it be written properly?

Exercise 6.89 Assume that we want to swap the values of two integer variables, **a** and **b**. To do this, we write a method

```
public void swap(int i1, int i2)
{
    int tmp = i1;
    i1 = i2;
    i2 = tmp;
}
```

Then we call this method with our **a** and **b** variables:

```
swap(a, b);
```

Are **a** and **b** swapped after this call? If you test it, you will notice that they are not! Why does this not work? Explain in detail.

CHAPTER 7

Fixed-Size Collections—Arrays

> **Main concepts discussed in this chapter:**
>
> - arrays
> - for loop
>
> **Java constructs discussed in this chapter:**
>
> array, for loop, **++**, conditional operator, **?:**
>
> The main focus of this chapter is the use of array objects for fixed-size collections and the for loop.

7.1 Fixed-size collections

In Chapter 4, we looked at the way in which library classes, such as **ArrayList**, allow us to maintain collections of objects. We also looked at further collection types in Chapter 6, such as **HashSet** and **HashMap**. A significant feature of all of these collection types is that their capacity is flexible—we never have to specify how many items a particular collection will hold, and the number of items stored can be varied arbitrarily throughout the life of the collection.

This chapter is about collections that are not flexible but fixed in their capacity—at the point the collection object is created, we have to specify the maximum number of items it can store, and this cannot be changed. At first, this might seem like an unnecessary restriction, however, in some applications we know in advance exactly how many items we wish to store in a collection, and that number typically remains fixed for the life of the collection. In such circumstances, we have the option of choosing to use a specialized fixed-size collection object to store the items.

7.2 Arrays

Concept

An **array** is a special type of collection that can store a fixed number of items.

A fixed-size collection is called an *array*. Although the fixed-size nature of arrays can be a significant disadvantage in many situations, they do have at least two compensating advantages over the flexible-size collection classes:

- Access to the items held in an array is often more efficient than access to the items in a comparable flexible-size collection.

- Arrays are able to store either objects or primitive-type values. Flexible-size collections can store only objects.[1]

Another distinctive feature of arrays is that they have special syntactic support in Java; they can be accessed using a custom syntax different from the usual method calls. The reason for this is mostly historical: arrays are the oldest collection structure in programming languages, and syntax for dealing with arrays has developed over many decades. Java uses the same syntax established in other programming languages to keep things simple for programmers who are used to arrays already, even though it is not consistent with the rest of the language syntax.

In the following sections, we shall show how arrays can be used to maintain collections of fixed size. We shall also introduce a new loop structure that is often closely associated with arrays—the *for loop*. (Note that the *for loop* is different from the *for-each loop*.)

7.3 A log-file analyzer

Web servers typically maintain log files of client accesses to the web pages that they store. Given suitable tools, these logs enable web service managers to extract and analyze useful information such as:

- which are the most popular pages they provide

- which sites brought users to this one

- whether other sites appear to have broken links to this site's pages

- how much data is being delivered to clients

- the busiest periods over the course of a day, a week, or a month

Such information might help administrators to determine, for instance, whether they need to upgrade to more-powerful server machines, or when the quietest periods are in order to schedule maintenance activities.

The *weblog-analyzer* project contains an application that performs an analysis of data from such a web server. The server writes a line to a log file each time an access is made. A

---

[1] Although the autoboxing feature described in Chapter 6 provides a mechanism that also lets us store primitive values in flexible-size collections, it is nonetheless true that only arrays can directly store them.

sample log file called *weblog.txt* is provided in the project folder. Each line records the date and time of the access in the following format:

    year month day hour minute

For instance, the line below records an access at 03:45am on 7 June 2015:

    2015 06 07 03 45

The project consists of five classes: **LogAnalyzer**, **LogfileReader**, **LogEntry**, **LoglineTokenizer**, and **LogfileCreator**. We shall spend most of our time looking at the **LogAnalyzer** class, as it contains examples of both creating and using an array (Code 7.1). Later exercises will encourage you to examine and modify **LogEntry**, because it also uses an array. The **LogReader** and **LogLineTokenizer** classes use features of the Java language that we have not yet covered, so we shall not explore those in detail. The **LogfileCreator** class allows you to create your own log files containing random data.

Code 7.1
The log-file analyzer

```java
/**
 * Read web server data and analyse hourly access patterns.
 *
 * @author David J. Barnes and Michael Kölling.
 * @version    2016.02.29
 */
public class LogAnalyzer
{
    // Where to calculate the hourly access counts.
    private int[] hourCounts;
    // Use a LogfileReader to access the data.
    private LogfileReader reader;

    /**
     * Create an object to analyze hourly web accesses.
     */
    public LogAnalyzer()
    {
        // Create the array object to hold the hourly
        // access counts.
        hourCounts = new int[24];
        // Create the reader to obtain the data.
        reader = new LogfileReader();
    }

    /**
     * Analyze the hourly access data from the log file.
     */
    public void analyzeHourlyData()
    {
        while(reader.hasNext()) {
            LogEntry entry = reader.next();
            int hour = entry.getHour();
            hourCounts[hour]++;
        }
    }
}
```

Code 7.1 continued

The log-file analyzer

```java
/**
 * Print the hourly counts.
 * These should have been set with a prior
 * call to analyzeHourlyData.
 */
public void printHourlyCounts()
{
    System.out.println("Hr: Count");
    for(int hour = 0; hour < hourCounts.length; hour++) {
        System.out.println(hour + ": " + hourCounts[hour]);
    }
}

/**
 * Print the lines of data read by the LogfileReader
 */
public void printData()
{
    reader.printData();
}
}
```

The analyzer currently uses only part of the data stored in a server's log line. It provides information that would allow us to determine which hours of the day, on average, tend to be the busiest or quietest for the server. It does this by counting how many accesses were made in each one-hour period over the duration covered by the log.

> **Exercise 7.1** Explore the *weblog-analyzer* project by creating a **LogAnalyzer** object and calling its **analyzeHourlyData** method. Follow that with a call to its **printHourlyCounts** method, which will print the results of the analysis. Which are the busiest times of the day?

Over the course of the next few sections, we shall examine how this class uses an array to accomplish this task.

7.3.1 Declaring array variables

The **LogAnalyzer** class contains a field that is of an array type:

```java
private int[] hourCounts;
```

The distinctive feature of an array variable's declaration is a pair of square brackets as part of the type name: `int[]`. This indicates that the **hourCounts** variable is of type *integer array*. We say that `int` is the *base type* of this particular array, which means that the array object will store values of type `int`. It is important to distinguish between an array-variable declaration and a similar-looking simple-variable declaration:

```
int hour;       // A single int variable.
int[] hourCounts; // An int-array variable.
```

Here, the variable **hour** is able to store a single integer value, whereas **hourCounts** will be used to refer to an array object once that object has been created. An array-variable declaration does not itself create the array object. That takes place in a separate stage using the **new** operator, as with other objects.

It is worth looking at the unusual syntax again for a moment. The declaration **int[]** would in more conventional syntax appear, maybe, as **Array<int>**. That it does not has historical rather than logical reasons. You should still get used to reading it in the same way: as "array of int."

Exercise 7.2 Write a declaration for an array variable **people** that could be used to refer to an array of **Person** objects.

Exercise 7.3 Write a declaration for an array variable **vacant** that could be used to refer to an array of boolean values.

Exercise 7.4 Read through the **LogAnalyzer** class and identify all the places where the **hourCounts** variable is used. At this stage, do not worry about what all the uses mean, as they will be explained in the following sections. Note how often a pair of square brackets is used with the variable.

Exercise 7.5 What is wrong with the following array declarations? Correct them.

```
[]int counts;
boolean[5000] occupied;
```

7.3.2 Creating array objects

The next thing to look at is how an array variable is associated with an array object.

The constructor of the **LogAnalyzer** class includes a statement to create an **int** array object:

```
hourCounts = new int[24];
```

Once again, notice how different the syntax is from that of normal object creation. For instance, there are no round brackets for a constructor's parameters, because an array object does not have a constructor. This statement creates an array object that is able to store 24 separate integer values and makes the **hourCounts** array variable refer to that object. The value of 24 is the size of the array, and not a constructor parameter. Figure 7.1 illustrates the result of this assignment.

Figure 7.1
An array of 24 integers

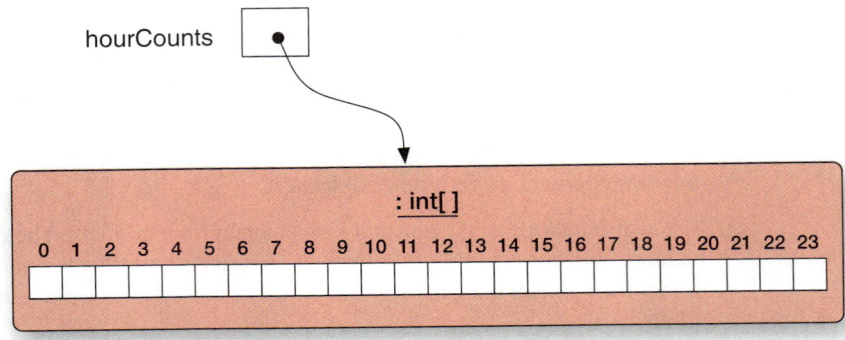

The general form of an array object's construction is

    new *type*[*integer-expression*]

The choice of *type* specifies what type of items are to be stored in the array. The *integer expression* specifies the size of the array—that is, the fixed number of items that can be stored in it.

When an array object is assigned to an array variable, the type of the array object must match the declared type of the variable. The assignment to **hourCounts** is allowed because the array object is an integer array, and **hourCounts** is an integer-array variable. The following declares a string-array variable and makes it refer to an array that has a capacity of 10 strings:

    String[] names = new String[10];

It is important to note that the creation of the array assigned to **names** does not actually create 10 strings. Rather, it creates a fixed-size collection that is able to have 10 strings stored within it. Those strings will probably be created in another part of the class to which **names** belongs. Immediately following its creation, an array object can be thought of as empty. If it is an array for objects, then the array will contain **null** values for all elements. If it is an **int** array, then all elements will be set to zero. In the next section, we shall look at the way in which items are stored into (and retrieved from) arrays.

Exercise 7.6 Given the following variable declarations,

    double[] readings;
    String[] urls;
    TicketMachine[] machines;

write assignments that accomplish the following tasks: (a) Make the **readings** variable refer to an array that is able to hold 60 **double** values; (b) Make the **urls** variable refer to an array that is able to hold 90 **String** objects; (c) Make the **machines** variable refer to an array that is able to hold 5 **TicketMachine** objects.

Exercise 7.7 How many `String` objects are created by the following declaration?

```
String[] labels = new String[20];
```

Exercise 7.8 What is wrong with the following array creation? Correct it.

```
double[] prices = new double(50);
```

7.3.3 Using array objects

The individual elements of an array are accessed by *indexing* the array. An index is an integer expression written between square brackets following the name of an array variable. For instance:

```
labels[6]
machines[0]
people[x + 10 - y]
```

The valid values for an index expression depend upon the length of the array on which they are used. As with other collections, array indices always start at zero and go up to one less than the length of the array. So, the valid indices for the **hourCounts** array are 0 to 23, inclusive.

> **Pitfall** Two very common errors are to think that the valid indices of an array start at 1, and to use the value of the length of the array as an index. Using indices outside the bounds of an array will lead to a runtime error called an `ArrayIndexOutOfBoundsException`.

Expressions that select an element from an array can be used anywhere that a variable of the base type of the array could be used. This means that we can use them on both sides of assignments, for instance. Here are some examples that use array expressions in different places:

```
labels[5] = "Quit";
double half = readings[0] / 2;
System.out.println(people[3].getName());
machines[0] = new TicketMachine(500);
```

Using an array index on the left-hand side of an assignment is the array equivalent of a mutator (or **set** method), because the contents of the array will be changed. Using one anywhere else represents the equivalent of an accessor (or **get** method).

7.3.4 Analyzing the log file

The **hourCounts** array created in the constructor of **LogAnalyzer** is used to store an analysis of the access data. The data is stored into it in the **analyzeHourlyData** method, and displayed from it in the **printHourlyCounts** method. As the task of the **analyze** method is to count how many accesses were made during each hour period, the array needs 24 locations—one for each hour period in a 24-hour day. The analyzer delegates the task of reading its log file to a **LogfileReader**.

The **LogfileReader** class is quite complex, and we suggest that you do not spend too much time investigating its implementation. Its role is to handle the task of breaking up each log line into separate data values, but we can abstract from the implementation details by considering just the headers of two of its methods:

```
public boolean hasNext()
public LogEntry next()
```

These exactly match the methods we have seen with the **Iterator** type, and a **LogfileReader** can be used in exactly the same way, except that we do not permit the **remove** method to be used. The **hasNext** method tells the analyzer whether there is at least one more entry in the log file, and the **next** method then returns a **LogEntry** object containing the values from the next log line.

From each **LogEntry**, the **analyzeHourlyData** method of the analyzer obtains the value of the hour field:

```
int hour = entry.getHour();
```

We know that the value stored in the local variable **hour** will always be in the range 0 to 23, which exactly matches the valid range of indices for the **hourCounts** array. Each location in the array is used to represent an access count for the corresponding hour. So each time an hour value is read, we wish to update the count for that hour by 1. We have written this as

```
hourCounts[hour]++;
```

Note that it is the value stored in the array element that is being incremented and not the **hour** variable. The following alternatives are both equivalent, as we can use an array element in exactly the same way as we would an ordinary variable:

```
hourCounts[hour] = hourCounts[hour] + 1;
hourCounts[hour] += 1;
```

By the end of the **analyzeHourlyData** method, we have a complete set of cumulative counts for each hour of the log period.

In the next section, we look at the **printHourlyCounts** method, as it introduces a new control structure that is well suited to iterating over an array.

7.4 The for loop

Java defines two variations of for loops, both of which are indicated by the keyword *for* in source code. In Section 4.9, we introduced the first variant, the *for-each loop*, as a convenient means to iterate over a flexible-size collection. The second variant, the *for loop*, is an alternative iterative control structure[2] that is particularly appropriate when:

---

[2] Sometimes, if people want to make clearer the distinction between the for loop and the for-each loop, they also talk about the former as the "old-style for loop," because it has been in the Java language longer than the for-each loop. The for-each loop is sometimes referred to as the "enhanced for loop."

- we wish to execute a set of statements a fixed number of times
- we need a variable inside the loop whose value changes by a fixed amount—typically increasing by 1—on each iteration

The for loop is well suited to situations requiring *definite iteration*. For instance, it is common to use a for loop when we wish to do something to every element in an array, such as printing the contents of each element. This fits the criteria, as the fixed number of times corresponds to the length of the array and the variable is needed to provide an incrementing index into the array.

A for loop has the following general form:

```
for (initialization; condition; post-body action) {
    statements to be repeated
}
```

The following concrete example is taken from the **printHourlyCounts** method of the **LogAnalyzer**:

```
for(int hour = 0; hour < hourCounts.length; hour++) {
    System.out.println(hour + ": " + hourCounts[hour]);
}
```

The result of this will be that the value of each element in the array is printed, preceded by its corresponding hour number. For instance:

```
 0: 149
 1: 149
 2: 148
  . . .
23: 166
```

When we compare this for loop to the for-each loop, we notice that the syntactic difference is in the section between the parentheses in the loop header. In this for loop, the parentheses contain three separate sections, separated by semicolons.

From a programming-language design point of view, it would have been nicer to use two different keywords for these two loops, maybe **for** and **foreach**. The reason that **for** is used for both of them is, again, a historical accident. Older versions of the Java language did not contain the for-each loop, and when it was finally introduced, Java designers did not want to introduce a new keyword at this stage, because this could cause problems with existing programs. So they decided to use the same keyword for both loops. This makes it slightly harder for us to distinguish these loops, but we will get used to recognizing the different header structures.

Even though the for loop is often used for definite iteration, the fact that it is controlled by a general boolean expression means that it is actually closer to the while loop than to the for-each loop. We can illustrate the way that a for loop executes by rewriting its general form as an equivalent while loop:

```
initialization;
while (condition) {
    statements to be repeated
    post-body action
}
```

So the alternative form for the body of `printHourlyCounts` would be

```
int hour = 0;
while(hour < hourCounts.length) {
    System.out.println(hour + ": " + hourCounts[hour]);
    hour++;
}
```

From this rewritten version, we can see that the post-body action is not actually executed until after the statements in the loop's body, despite the action's position in the for loop's header. In addition, we can see that the initialization part is executed only once—immediately before the condition is tested for the first time.

In both versions, note in particular the condition

```
hour < hourCounts.length
```

This illustrates two important points:

- All arrays contain a field **length** that contains the value of the fixed size of that array. The value of this field will always match the value of the integer expression used to create the array object. So the value of **length** here will be 24.
- The condition uses the less-than operator, **<**, to check the value of **hour** against the length of the array. So in this case, the loop will continue as long as **hour** is less than 24. In general, when we wish to access every element in an array, a for-loop header will have the following general form:

```
for(int index = 0; index < array.length; index++)
```

This is correct, because we do not wish to use an index value that is equal to the array's length; such an element will never exist.

7.4.1 Arrays and the for-each loop

Could we also rewrite the for loop shown above with a for-each loop? The answer is: almost. Here is an attempt:

```
for(int value : hourCounts) {
    System.out.println(": " + value);
}
```

This code will compile and execute. (Try it out!) From this fragment, we can see that arrays can, in fact, be used in for-each loops just like other collections. We have, however, one problem: we cannot easily print out the hour in front of the colon. This code fragment simply omits printing the hour, and just prints the colon and the value. This is because the for-each loop does not provide access to a loop-counter variable, which we need in this case to print the hour.

To fix this, we would need to define our own counter variable (similar to what we did in the while loop example). Instead of doing this, we prefer using the old-style for loop because it is more concise.

7.4.2 The for loop and iterators

In Section 4.12.2, we showed the necessity of using an `Iterator` if we wished to remove elements from a collection. There is a special use of the for loop with an `Iterator` when we want to do something like this. Suppose that we wished to remove every music track by a particular artist from our music organizer. The point here is that we need to examine every track in the collection, so a for-each loop would seem appropriate, but we know already that we cannot use it in this particular case. However, we can use a for loop as follows:

```
for(Iterator<Track> it = tracks.iterator(); it.hasNext(); ) {
    Track track = it.next();
    if(track.getArtist().equals(artist)) {
        it.remove();
    }
}
```

The important point here is that there is no post-body action in the loop's header—it is just blank. This is allowed, but we must still include the semicolon after the loop's condition. By using a for loop instead of a while loop, it is a little clearer that we intend to examine every item in the list.

Which loop should I use? We have discussed three different loops: the for-each loop, the while loop, and the for loop. As you have seen, in many situations you have a choice of using any one of these to solve your task. Usually, one loop could be rewritten using another. So how do you decide which one to use at any given point? Here are some guidelines:

- If you need to iterate over all elements in a collection, the for-each loop is almost always the most elegant loop to use. It is clear and concise (but it does not give you a loop counter).
- If you have a loop that is not related to collections (but instead performs some other action repeatedly), the for-each loop is not useful. Your choice will be between the for loop and the while loop. The for-each loop is only for collections.
- The for loop is good if you know how many iterations you need at the start of the loop (that is, how often you need to loop around). This information can be in a variable, but should not change during the loop execution. It is also very good if you need to use the loop counter explicitly.
- The while loop should be preferred if, at the start of the loop, you don't know how often you need to loop. The end of the loop can be determined on the fly by some condition (for example, repeatedly read one line from a file until we reach the end of the file).
- If you need to remove elements from the collection while looping, use a for loop with an `Iterator` if you want to examine the whole collection, or a while loop if you might want to finish before reaching the end of the collection.

Exercise 7.9 Check to see what happens if the for loop's condition is incorrectly written using the <= operator in **printHourlyCounts**:

    for(int hour = 0; hour <= hourCounts.length; hour++)

Exercise 7.10 Rewrite the body of **printHourlyCounts** so that the for loop is replaced by an equivalent while loop. Call the rewritten method to check that it prints the same results as before.

Exercise 7.11 Correct all the errors in the following method.

    /**
     * Print all the values in the marks array that are
     * greater than mean.
     * @param marks An array of mark values.
     * @param mean The mean (average) mark.
     */
    public void printGreater(double marks, double mean)
    {
        for(index = 0; index <= marks.length; index++) {
            if(marks[index] > mean) {
                System.out.println(marks[index]);
            }
        }
    }

Exercise 7.12 Modify the **LogAnalyzer** class so that it has a constructor that can take the name of the log file to be analyzed. Have this constructor pass the file name to the constructor of the **LogfileReader** class. Use the **LogfileCreator** class to create your own file of random log entries, and analyze the data.

Exercise 7.13 Complete the **numberOfAccesses** method, below, to count the total number of accesses recorded in the log file. Complete it by using a for loop to iterate over **hourCounts**:

    /**
     * Return the number of accesses recorded in the log file.
     */
    public int numberOfAccesses()
    {
        int total = 0;
        // Add the value in each element of hourCounts to
        // total.
            . . .
        return total;
    }

Exercise 7.14 Add your **numberOfAccesses** method to the **LogAnalyzer** class and check that it gives the correct result. *Hint*: You can simplify your checking by having the analyzer read log files containing just a few lines of data. That way you will find it easier to determine whether or not your method gives the correct answer. The **LogfileReader** class has a constructor with the following header, to read from a particular file:

```
/**
 * Create a LogfileReader that will supply data
 * from a particular log file.
 * @param filename The file of log data.
 */
public LogfileReader(String filename)
```

Exercise 7.15 Add a method **busiestHour** to **LogAnalyzer** that returns the busiest hour. You can do this by looking through the **hourCounts** array to find the element with the biggest count. *Hint:* Do you need to check every element to see if you have found the busiest hour? If so, use a for loop or a for-each loop. Which one is better in this case?

Exercise 7.16 Add a method **quietestHour** to **LogAnalyzer** that returns the number of the least busy hour. *Note:* This sounds almost identical to the previous exercise, but there is a small trap for the unwary. Be sure to check your method with some data in which every hour has a non-zero count.

Exercise 7.17 Which hour is returned by your **busiestHour** method if more than one hour has the biggest count?

Exercise 7.18 Add a method to **LogAnalyzer** that finds which two-hour period is the busiest. Return the value of the first hour of this period.

Exercise 7.19 *Challenge exercise* Save the *weblog-analyzer* project under a different name so that you can develop a new version that performs a more extensive analysis of the available data. For instance, it would be useful to know which days tend to be quieter than others, Are there any seven-day cyclical patterns, for instance? In order to perform analysis of daily, monthly, or yearly data, you will need to make some changes to the **LogEntry** class. This already stores all the values from a single log line, but only the hour and minute values are available via accessors. Add further methods that make the remaining fields available in a similar way. Then add a range of additional analysis methods to the analyzer.

Exercise 7.20 *Challenge exercise* If you have completed the previous exercise, you could extend the log-file format with additional numerical fields. For instance, servers commonly store a numerical code that indicates whether an access was successful or not. The value 200 stands for a successful access, 403 means that access to the document was forbidden, and 404 means that the document could not be found. Have the analyzer provide information on the number of successful and unsuccessful accesses. This exercise is likely to be very challenging, as it will require you to make changes to every class in the project.

Exercise 7.21 In the *lab-classes* project that we have discussed in previous chapters, the `LabClass` class includes a `students` field to maintain a collection of `Student` objects. Read through the `LabClass` class in order to reinforce some of the concepts we have discussed in this chapter.

Exercise 7.22 The `LabClass` class enforces a limit to the number of students who may be enrolled in a particular tutorial group. In view of this, do you think it would be more appropriate to use a fixed-size array rather than a flexible-size collection for the `students` field? Give reasons both for and against the alternatives.

Exercise 7.23 Rewrite the `listAllFiles` method in the `MusicOrganizer` class from *music-organizer-v3* by using a for loop, rather than a for-each loop.

7.5 The *automaton* project

In the following sections, we will extend our coverage of arrays to provide some further typical illustrations of their use. We will use two projects based on *cellular automata*. These are relatively simple computational structures that exhibit both interesting and intriguing patterns of "behavior." We will start with some one-dimensional examples, and then extend to two dimensions in order to explore use of two-dimensional arrays.

A cellular automaton consists of a grid of "cells" Each cell maintains a simple state consisting of a limited range of values—often just the values 0 and 1. These values might be interpreted as meaning "off" and "on," for instance, or "dead" and "alive"—although the meaning is actually arbitrary. While we could implement a cell as a class definition containing a single boolean field plus an accessor and mutator, this would likely be overkill for a basic automaton, and we prefer to represent the automaton as an array of type `int[]`. The choice of `int` over `boolean` will make it simpler to calculate the changes to state values that are required by this particular application.

At each step of the model, a new state is computed for each cell based on its previous state and the states of its neighbors. For a 1D automaton, the neighbors are the two cells to its left and right. In other words, for the cell at index `i`, the neighbors are at indices `(i - 1)` and `(i + 1)`. We will refer to the cell at index `i` as the "center" cell. What makes automata interesting is the widely differing effects that different rules to calculate new state based on those three values have on the overall behavior of the automaton over the course of multiple steps.

Code 7.2 shows a first attempt at implementing an automaton based on these principles, which can be found in the project *automaton-v1*. The rule used to calculate a cell's new state is to add the state values of a cell's two neighbors to the cell's state value and produce a result modulo 2, to force the new value to be either 0 or 1. Figure 7.2 shows the result of repeatedly applying this update rule to every cell, from a starting point at step 0 of a single cell with a value of 1, and all others with a value of 0. After the initial step, the original 1-value cell has remained with a value of 1, but its two 0-value neighbors have both become 1, while all other cells remain at 0. Subsequent steps induce further changes in the form of a symmetrical pattern.

Code 7.2

The Automaton class

```java
import java.util.Arrays;

/**
 * Model a 1D elementary cellular automaton.
 *
 * @author David J. Barnes and Michael Kölling
 * @version 2016.02.29 - version 1
 */
public class Automaton
{
    // The number of cells.
    private final int numberOfCells;
    // The state of the cells.
    private int[] state;

    /**
     * Create a 1D automaton consisting of the given number of cells.
     * @param numberOfCells The number of cells in the automaton.
     */
    public Automaton(int numberOfCells)
    {
        this.numberOfCells = numberOfCells;
        state = new int[numberOfCells];
        // Seed the automaton with a single 'on' cell in the middle.
        state[numberOfCells / 2] = 1;
    }

    /**
     * Print the current state of the automaton.
     */
    public void print()
    {
        for(int cellValue : state) {
            if(cellValue == 1) {
                System.out.print("*");
            }
            else {
                System.out.print(" ");
            }
        }
        System.out.println();
    }
```

Code 7.2 continued

The Automaton class

```java
/**
 * Update the automaton to its next state.
 */
public void update()
{
    // Build the new state in a separate array.
    int[] nextState = new int[state.length];
    // Naively update the state of each cell
    // based on the state of its two neighbors.
    for(int i = 0; i < state.length; i++) {
        int left, center, right;
        if(i == 0) {
            left = 0;
        }
        else {
            left = state[i - 1];
        }
        center = state[i];
        if(i + 1 < state.length) {
            right = state[i + 1];
        }
        else {
            right = 0;
        }
        nextState[i] = (left + center + right) % 2;
    }
    state = nextState;
}

/**
 * Reset the automaton.
 */
public void reset()
{
    Arrays.fill(state, 0);
    // Seed the automaton with a single 'on' cell.
    state[numberOfCells / 2] = 1;
}
```

Figure 7.2

The first few steps of the automaton implemented in *automaton-v1*

Step	Cell states—blank cells are in state 0.												
0							*						
1						*	*	*					
2					*		*		*				
3				*	*		*		*	*			
4			*				*				*		
5		*	*		*		*		*		*	*	
6	*		*				*				*		*
7	*	*		*		*		*		*		*	*

Exercise 7.24 Open the *automaton-v1* project and create an `AutomatonController` object. A line containing a single * should be output in the terminal window, representing the initial state of the automaton. Call the `step` method a few times to see how the state progresses. Then try the `run` method.

Exercise 7.25 After running the automaton, call the `reset` method and repeat the process in the previous exercise. Do exactly the same patterns emerge?

Exercise 7.26 How many versions of the `fill` method are there in the `java.util.Arrays` class that take a parameter of type `int[]`? What is the purpose of those methods? How is one of those methods used in the `reset` method of `Automaton`?

Exercise 7.27 Alter the constructor of `Automaton` so that more than one cell is initially in the 1-state. Do different patterns emerge this time? Are those patterns *deterministic*—i.e., does a particular starting state for the automaton always result in the same pattern?

7.5.1 The conditional operator

While the version of the automaton in *automaton-v1* works and produces interesting results, there are some improvements that we can make to its implementation. We will start by introducing a new operator that can often be used to simplify the expression of if-else statements.

You might have noticed that in Code 7.2 there are three if-else statements with a very similar structure of the following form:

```
if(condition) {
    do something;
}
else {
    do something similar;
}
```

For instance, in the `print` method we have:

```
if(cellValue == 1) {
    System.out.print("*");
}
else {
    System.out.print(" ");
}
```

and in the `update` method there is a two if-else statement assigning to the variables `left` and `right`, where the alternative actions differ only in the right-hand side expressions.

In situations such as these, we can often make use of a *conditional operator* which, in Java, consists of the two characters ? and :. This operator is called a *ternary operator* because it actually takes three operands, in contrast to the binary operators we have seen, such as +

and *, which take two. This operator is used to select one of two alternative values, based on the evaluation of a boolean expression and the general form is:

```
condition ? value1 : value2
```

If the condition is **true**, then the value of the whole expression will be *value1*, otherwise it will be *value2*. For instance, we could rewrite the body of the for-loop in the **print** method as follows:

```
String whatToPrint = cellValue == 1 ? "*" : " ";
System.out.print(whatToPrint);
```

or, more concisely:

```
System.out.print(cellValue == 1 ? "*" : " ");
```

> **Exercise 7.28** Rewrite the two if-else statements in the loop of the **update** method of the **Automaton** class of *automaton-v1* so that the assignments to **left** and **right** use conditional operators.
>
> **Exercise 7.29** Why have we created a new array, **nextState**, in the **update** method, rather than using the **state** array directly? Change the assignment to **nextState** to be an assignment to **state** in the loop body, to see if it makes any different to the automaton's behavior. If it does, can you explain why?
>
> **Exercise 7.30** Can you find a way to avoid the problems illustrated in the previous exercise without using a new array? *Hint*: how many cells' old values need to be retained on each iteration? In your opinion, which version is better: using a complete array or your solution? Justify your answer.

7.5.2 First and last iterations

The most significant improvement we can make to the **Automaton** class in Code 7.2 is the structure of the body of the for-loop in the **update** method. At the moment, the code there is very awkward because we have to take special care when dealing with the first cell (**[0]**) and the last cell (**[numberOfCells-1]**) in order to avoid trying to access non-existent elements of the array (**[-1]** to the left of the first cell and **[numberOfCells]** to the right of the last cell). For those non-existent elements, we use a state value of 0 so that we always use three values when calculating the next state of a cell.

Whenever a loop contains code to test for the special case of the first or last iteration, we should review it carefully because, those special cases can be handled differently and the checks avoided. What we really want to see in the body of a loop are statements to be executed on every iteration, and we want to avoid special cases as far as possible. It will not always be possible to eliminate exceptions, but those applying on just the first or the last iterations are those we will most likely be able to avoid.

You might also have observed about this iteration process that the "center" cell will always become the "left" neighbor the next time around; and the "right" neighbor will become the next "center" cell. This opens up the possibility of setting up the next values of **left** and **center** at the end of the loop body ready for the next iteration; i.e.:

```
nextState[i] = (left + center + right) % 2;
left = center;
center = right;
```

That only leaves **right** to be set up explicitly from the **state** array on the next iteration. Interestingly, this modification also provides a route to solving the problem of what to do about assigning to **left** on the first iteration of the loop. This change means that when the loop body is entered on all but the first iteration, **left** and **center** have already been set from the previous iteration to the values they should have for the next-state calculation. So we can simply make sure that **left** has already been set to 0, for the non-existent cell, and **center** has been set to **state[0]** immediately before the loop is entered for the first time:

```
int left = 0;
int center = state[0];
for(int i = 0; i < state.length; i++) {
    int right = i + 1 < state.length ? state[i + 1] : 0;
    nextState[i] = (left + center + right) % 2;
    left = center;
    center = right;
}
```

Notice that the variable declarations for **left** and **center** have had to be moved from inside the loop, so that their values are retained between iterations.

The next exercise asks you to implement these changes in your own version of the project. A version with all of these changes can be found in *automaton-v2* in case you have trouble or want to check your solution; make sure, however, that you make these changes yourself before looking at this.

Exercise 7.31 Rewrite the **update** method as discussed above.

Exercise 7.32 Add a method **calculateNextState** to the **Automaton** class that takes the three values, **left**, **center**, and **right**, and returns the calculation of the value of the next state. The next state of a cell was previously calculated using the following line of code:

```
nextState[i] = (left + center + right) % 2;
```

Change this line to make use of your new method instead.

> **Exercise 7.33** Experiment with different ways to calculate the next state of a cell through combining the values of **left**, **center**, and **right**, always ensuring that the result is calculated modulo 2. You don't need to include all three values in the calculation. Here are a couple of ways you might like to try:
>
> - (left + right) % 2
> - (center + right + center * right + left * center * right) % 2
>
> How many different sets of unique rules do you think there are to calculate a cell's next 0 or 1 state given the three binary values in **left**, **center**, and **right**? Is there an infinite number of possibilities?

The final improvement we would like to make to the automaton is to avoid having to keep testing for the end of the array when setting **right**. There is a commonly used solution to this—extend the array by one element! At first this sounds like cheating but, used thoughtfully and appropriately, extending an array by a single element can sometimes lead to clearer code. The idea here is that the extra element will contain the value 0 in order to serve as the right-hand neighbor of the last cell. However, that neighbor will not, itself, be included as a cell of the automaton. It will never be changed. The revised version of the body of **update** is:

```
int left = 0;
int center = state[0];
for(int i = 0; i < numberOfCells; i++) {
    int right = state[i + 1];
    nextState[i] = calculateNextState(left, center, right);
    left = center;
    center = right;
}
```

Notice very carefully that the condition of the loop has been changed, because the index variable should no longer be compared against the length of the (extended) array, but the true number of cells of the automaton. This change is essential to ensure that **[i+1]** never exceeds the bounds of the array when setting the value of **right**.

A version of the project including this code can also be found in the project *automaton-v3*.

> **Exercise 7.34** Make this improvement in your own code.

7.5.3 Lookup tables

In Chapter 6, we discussed the **HashMap** class, which allows associations to be created between objects in the form of a *(key, value) pair*. A map is a general form of a *lookup table*: the key is used to lookup an associated value in the map. Arrays are often a convenient and efficient way to implement specialised lookup tables, in applications where the key is a value from an integer range rather than an object. To fit with the way collections are indexed, the range should have 0 as its smallest value, although a range whose smallest value is non-zero can be easily converted into a 0-based range by the addition of a positive or a negative offset to all values in the range. As long as the size of the range is known, a fixed-size array can be created to hold the values of the (key, value) pair, where the key is a 0-based integer index.

We can illustrate the concept of a lookup table via the cellular automaton. If you have experimented with different formulas for the calculation of a cell's next state, then you might have noticed already that the 1D automaton we have implemented does not actually have an infinite number of ways to decide a cell's next state. The limitation is based on the following two features:

- There are only eight possible different combinations of the left, center and right values of 1 and 0: 000, 001, 010, . . . , 111

- For each of the eight combinations, the outcome can be one of only two possibilities: 0 or 1.

Taken together, these features mean that there are actually only 256 (i.e., 2^8) automata behaviors. In fact, the number of unique behaviors is considerably fewer than this—88 in total.

> **Wolfram codes** In 1983, Stephen Wolfram published a study of all possible 256 elementary cellular automata. He proposed a numerical system for defining the behavior of each type of automaton, and the code assigned to each is known as a *Wolfram code*. Given the numerical code, it is very easy to work out the applicable rule for state changes, given the values of a cell and its two neighbors, because the code itself encodes the rules. See Exercise 7.36, below, for how this works in practice, or do a web search for "elementary cellular automata".

This relatively modest number of possibilities makes it possible to implement determination of a cell's next state, via a lookup table rather than evaluation of a function. Two things are needed:

- A way to turn a (left, center, right) triplet into a number in the range 0–7. These values will be used as the index key of the lookup table.

- An 8-element integer array storing the next-state values for the eight triplet combinations. This will be the table.

The following expression illustrates how we can turn the triplet into an integer index in the range 0–7:

```
left * 4 + center * 2 + right
```

and a state table can be set up as follows:

```
int[] stateTable = new int[] {
    0, 1, 0, 0, 1, 0, 0, 1,
};
```

This illustrates the use of an *array initializer*—a list of the values to be stored in a newly-created array, enclosed in curly brackets. Notice that the size of the array being created does not need to be specified in the square brackets of `new int[]`, because the compiler is able to count how many items there are in the initializer and will make the array object exactly that size. Notice, too, the trailing comma after the final value in the initializer; the trailing comma is optional. An implementation of this version can be found in *automaton-v4*.

> **Exercise 7.35** Experiment with different initialization patterns of the lookup table in *automaton-v4*.
>
> **Exercise 7.36** *Challenge exercise* This exercise involves setting up the state table based on an additional integer parameter passed to the constructor of **Automaton**. The eight 1/0 values in the lookup table could be interpreted as eight binary digits encoding a single numerical value in the range 0–255, in much the same way as we have interpreted the triplet of cell states as representing an integer in the range 0–7. The least-significant bit would be the value in **stateTable[0]** and the most significant bit in **stateTable[7]**. So the pattern used in the initialization of **stateTable**, above, would be an encoding of the value 146 (128 + 16 + 2). In fact, that is exactly how the 256 Wolfram codes are used—a code in the range 0–255 is turned into its 8-bit binary representation and the binary digits are used as the settings of the state table. Add an integer parameter that holds a Wolfram code to the constructor of **Automaton** and use it to initialize **stateTable**. To do this you will need to find out how to extract the individual binary digits from an integer. Use the least-significant bit to set element 0 of the lookup table, the next to set element 1, and so on. *Hint*: You could either do this using integer operations such as **%** and **/**, or bit-manipulation operators such as **>>** and **&**.

7.6 Arrays of more than one dimension (advanced)

This section is an advanced section in this book. You can safely skip it at this point without missing anything you need for later chapters. We will discuss two-dimensional arrays, a specialized but useful data structure. If you were interested in the *automaton* project discussed above, you may enjoy this richer variant.

Arrays of more than one dimension are simply an extension of the one-dimensional concept. For instance, a two-dimensional array is a 1D array of 1D arrays. It is conventional to consider the first dimension of a 2D array as representing the rows of a grid, and the second dimension as representing the columns. Although we won't explore this particular feature any further, the fact that there are arrays of arrays means that two-dimensional arrays do not have to be rectangular: each row may have a different number of elements in it. In this section, we will limit our discussion of multi-dimensional arrays to two dimensions because additional dimensions simply follow the same conventions.

7.6.1 The *brain* project

There are many ways in which we could extend the sort of rules we saw with the 1D automata into two dimensions. Probably the most famous example of a 2D automaton is Conway's *Game of Life*, where the cell states are also binary (i.e., either 1 or 0). However, we will implement a slightly more sophisticated cellular automaton, which is known as *Brian's Brain* because it was devised by Brian Silverman. This time we will use a class to represent the cells because the behaviors and interactions will be significantly more complex than those of the elementary automata we looked at in the previous section.

Exercise 7.37 Open the *brain* project, create an `Environment` object and use the GUI controls to create a random initial setup for the automaton. Then either single-step it or run/pause it to obtain a feel for how it behaves (Figure 7.3).

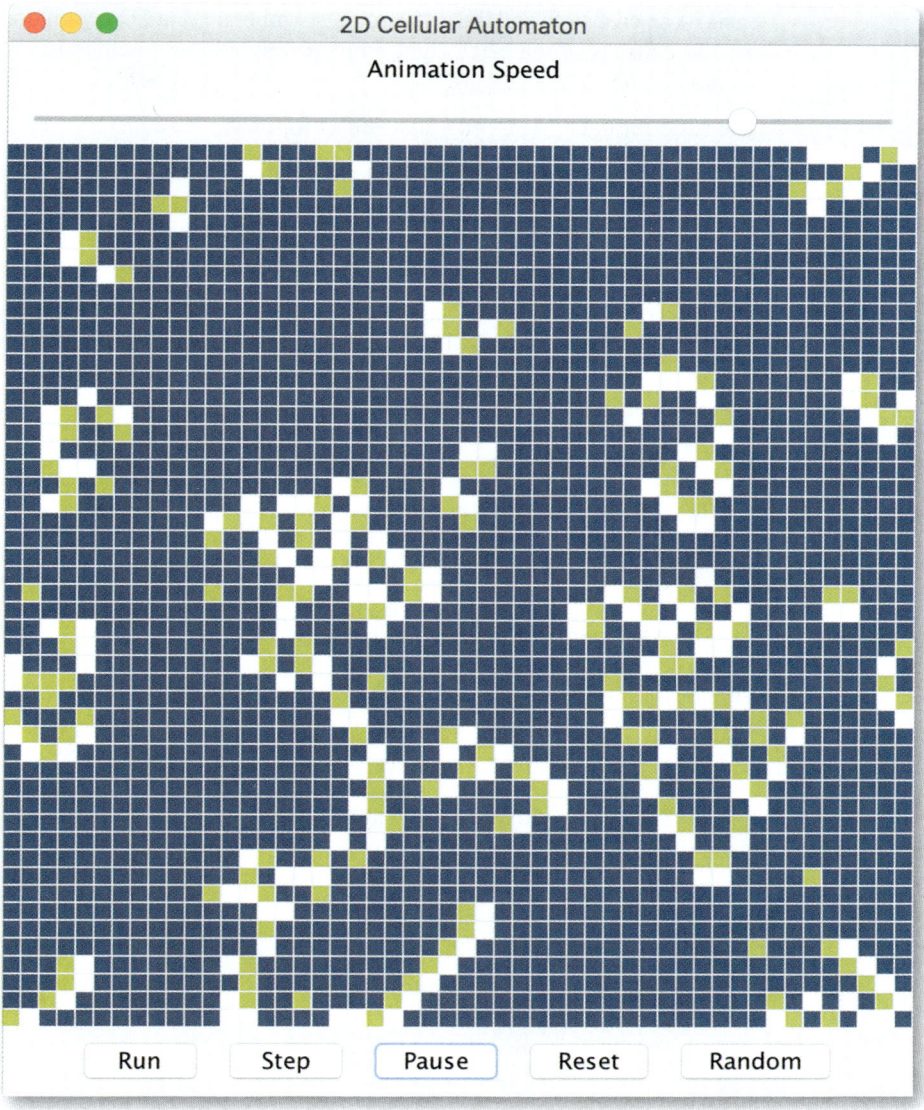

Figure 7.3
A two-dimensional automaton as shown with the *brain* project

Figure 7.4
The outer grey cells are the Moore neighborhood of the central cell

Cells in *Brian's Brain* are always in one of three possible states, which are described as *alive*, *dying* or *dead*, shown in our project using different colors. However, we should make clear that these are simply convenient labels and have no objective meaning. We will use the arbitrary values 0, 1 and 2 to represent these states although, unlike the 1D automaton, we will not compute any expressions using these values. A cell's next state is calculated on the basis of its own state and the states of its neighbors. For a 2D automaton, the neighborhood usually consists of the cell's eight, immediately-adjacent neighbors. This is known as the *Moore neighborhood* (Figure 7.4).

The rules for updating a cell's state are as follows:

- A cell that is *alive* changes its state to *dying*.

- A cell that is *dying* changes its state to *dead*.

- A cell that is *dead* changes its state to *alive* if exactly two of its neighbors are *alive*, otherwise it remains *dead*.

Code 7.3 shows the class `Cell` class that implements these concepts.

Code 7.3
A cell in a two-dimensional automaton

```java
import java.util.*;

/**
 * A cell in a 2D cellular automaton.
 * The cell has multiple possible states.
 * This is an implementation of the rules for Brian's Brain.
 * @see https://en.wikipedia.org/wiki/Brian%27s_Brain
 *
 * @author David J. Barnes and Michael Kölling
 * @version 2016.02.29
 */
public class Cell
{
    // The possible states.
    public static final int ALIVE = 0, DEAD = 1, DYING = 2;
    // The number of possible states.
    public static final int NUM_STATES = 3;

    // The cell's state.
    private int state;
    // The cell's neighbors.
    private Cell[] neighbors;

    /**
     * Set the initial state.
     * @param initialState The initial state
     */
```

Code 7.3 continued
A cell in a two-dimensional automaton

```java
    public int getNextState()
    {
        if(state == DEAD) {
            // Count the number of neighbors that are alive.
            int aliveCount = 0;
            for(Cell n : neighbors) {
                if(n.getState() == ALIVE) {
                    aliveCount++;
                }
            }
            return aliveCount == 2 ? ALIVE : DEAD;
        }
        else if(state == DYING) {
            return DEAD;
        }
        else {
            return DYING;
        }
    }

    /**
     * Receive the list of neighboring cells and take
     * a copy.
     * @param neighborList Neighboring cells.
     */
    public void setNeighbors(ArrayList<Cell> neighborList)
    {
        neighbors = new Cell[neighborList.size()];
        neighborList.toArray(neighbors);
    }

    Other methods omitted.
}
```

Each cell maintains a record of its neighbors in an array. The array is setup following a call to the **setNeighbors** method. The method receives a list of cells and copies the list into an array object via the list's **toArray** method.

7.6.2 Setting up the array

Code 7.4 shows some of those elements of the **Environment** class that set up the 2D array of **Cell** objects to model the automaton.

Code 7.4
The Environment class

```java
public class Environment
{
    // The grid of cells.
    private Cell[][] cells;
    // Visualization of the environment.
    private final EnvironmentView view;
```

Code 7.4 continued

The `Environment` class

```java
/**
 * Create an environment with the given size.
 * @param numRows The number of rows.
 * @param numCols The number of cols;
 */
public Environment(int numRows, int numCols)
{
    setup(numRows, numCols);
    randomize();
    view = new EnvironmentView(this, numRows, numCols);
    view.showCells();
}
```

Various other methods omitted.

```java
/**
 * Setup a new environment of the given size.
 * @param numRows The number of rows.
 * @param numCols The number of cols;
 */
private void setup(int numRows, int numCols)
{
    cells = new Cell[numRows][numCols];
    for(int row = 0; row < numRows; row++) {
        for (int col = 0; col < numCols; col++) {
            cells[row][col] = new Cell();
        }
    }
    setupNeighbors();
}
```

The syntax for declaring an array variable of more than one dimension is an extension of the single-dimension case—a pair of empty square brackets for each dimension:

```java
Cell[][] cells;
```

Similarly, the creation of the array object via **new** specifies the length of each dimension:

```java
cells = new Cell[numRows][numCols];
```

Remember that no `Cell` objects are actually created at this point—only the array object that will be able to store the `Cell` objects once they are created.

The `setup` method uses a typical code pattern to iterate through all elements of a two-dimensional array: a nested for loop. The pattern looks like this:

```java
for(int row = 0; row < numRows; row++) {
    for (int col = 0; col < numCols; col++) {
        . . . // do something with every element
    }
}
```

In this loop, it then sets up each cell by creating the cell object and assigning it to the current position in the array:

```
cells[row][col] = new Cell();
```

Finally, the `setup` method calls a separate `setupNeighbors` method in order to pass to each `Cell` its Moore neighborhood of adjacent cells.

You will recall from the discussion of the 1D automaton that we needed to be careful at the left- and right-hand ends of the automaton to provide a full set of neighbors for the cells at the edge. We must address the same issue with the 2D automaton. For instance, the `Cell` at location `cells[0][0]` only has three neighbors rather than eight. One approach we could have taken would have been to extend the 2D array with an extra row at the top and bottom and an extra column at the left and right—making it `(numRows+2)` by `(numCols+2)`—with a dummy *dead* cell in each of those locations. Instead, we prefer to use a "wraparound" approach to calculating the neighborhood—in other words, cells in the top row have neighbors in the bottom row and cells in the leftmost column have neighbors in the rightmost column (and vice-versa). This is also known as a *toroidal arrangement*. This way, every cell in the automaton has the full Moore neighborbood of eight cells. All that remains is to find a way to handle the cases around the edge that do not have to resort to special-case code.

If we ignore the edges for the moment, the neighbors of a cell at location `[row][col]` can be found at all the `+1` and `-1` offsets from row and col; e.g. `[row+1][col]`, `[row+1][col+1]`, `[row-1][col]`, etc. So we might write something like the following to build a list of neighbors:

```
Cell cell = cells[row][col];
for(int dr = -1; dr <= 1; dr++) {
  for(int dc = -1; dc <= 1; dc++) {
      add the neighbor at cells[row + dr][col + dc];
  }
}
```

Notice that when both `dr` and `dc` are zero, then the "neighbor" is actually `cell` and this should not be included in the neighbor list, so that is something to be addressed.

What we now need to ensure is that when `row + 1 == numRows` we obtain the value `0`, and when `row + -1 == -1` we obtain `(numRows - 1)` (similarly for `col`). The solution to the first requirement is relatively easy—the modulus operator does exactly that. But this does not cover both requirements because `(-1 % numRows)` gives −1 instead of `(numRows - 1)`. However, we can use a little trick based on the fact that `((x + numRows) % numRows) == (x % numRows)` when `x` is not negative, which means that `((row + 1 + numRows) % numRows)` gives the same result as `((row + 1) % numRows)`. But we do not see the same effect if `x` is negative, and if we add `numRows` before taking the modulus then `((-1 + numRows) % numRows)` gives `(numRows - 1)`, which is what we want. So the expression `((row + dr + numRows) % numRows)` will provide the index we need in both positive and negative cases, in order to determine the neighborhood of a cell in a wraparound grid.

Code 7.5 shows the full version of the `setupNeighbors` method of the Environment class that uses this technique. Notice that a cell is removed from its own neighborhood list before the list is passed to the cell to get around the problem when `dr` and `dc` are both zero.

Code 7.5

Setting up the neighboring cells

```java
/**
 * Give to a cell a list of its neighbors.
 */
private void setupNeighbors()
{
    int numRows = cells.length;
    int numCols = cells[0].length;
    // Allow for 8 neighbors plus the cell.
    ArrayList<Cell> neighbors = new ArrayList<>(9);
    for(int row = 0; row < numRows; row++) {
        for(int col = 0; col < numCols; col++) {
            Cell cell = cells[row][col];
            // This process will also include the cell.
            for(int dr = -1; dr <= 1; dr++) {
                for(int dc = -1; dc <= 1; dc++) {
                    int nr = (numRows + row + dr) % numRows;
                    int nc = (numCols + col + dc) % numCols;
                    neighbors.add(cells[nr][nc]);
                }
            }
            // The neighbours should not include the cell at
            // (row,col) so remove it.
            neighbors.remove(cell);
            cell.setNeighbors(neighbors);
            neighbors.clear();
        }
    }
}
```

Exercise 7.38 Conway's *Game of Life* is a much simpler automaton than *Brian's Brain*. In the *Game of Life*, a cell has only two states: alive and dead. Its next state is determined as follows:

- A count is taken of the number of its neighbors that are alive.
- If the cell is dead and has exactly three live neighbors then its next state will be alive, otherwise its next state will be dead.
- If the cell is alive then its next state also depends on the number of live neighbors. If there are fewer than two or more than three then the next state will be dead; otherwise it will be alive.

Save a copy of the *brain* project as *game-of-life* and modify the `Cell` class so that it implement's the rules for the *Game of Life*. It should not be necessary to modify any other classes.

Exercise 7.39 Modify the `Environment` class in your version of the Game of Life so that the environment is not toroidal. In other words, the next state of a cell at an outer row or column of the environment is determined by assuming that "neighbors" beyond outside the bounds of the environment are always dead. Do you observe much difference between the behavior of this version and the toroidal one?

Exercise 7.40 Use a copy of either the *brain* project or your *game-of-life* project to implement a new project in which cells can be either alive or dead. Alive cells should appear to "wander" semi-randomly through the 2D environment. Associate a movement direction with a cell. A cell that is alive should "move" in its associated direction at each step—in other words, a cell that is alive should cause one of its neighbors to be alive at the next step, and itself will become dead—this should give the appearance of movement. When an alive cell at the edge of the environment would try to "move" beyond the edge, it should instead sets its direction randomly and remain alive at the next step; i.e., it will not change the state of a neighbor.

Check your implementation of these rules by having just a single live cell in the environment at the start. When you have multiple live cells, you will need to think about what you want to happen if one cell tries to "move" into a location just vacated by another cell, or when two cells try to occupy the same neighboring cell.

7.7 Arrays and streams (advanced)

The principles of stream processing introduced in Chapter 5 apply equally well to arrays as they do to flexible collections. A stream is obtained from the contents of an array by passing the array to the static `stream` method of `java.util.Arrays`. If the array is of type `int[]` then an object of type `java.util.stream.IntStream` is returned:

```
int[] nums = { 1, 2, 3, 4, 5, };
IntStream stream = Arrays.stream(nums);
```

DoubleStream and **LongStream** types exist for equivalent stream versions of `double[]` and `long[]` arrays. Otherwise, the stream version of an array of type `T` will be of type `Stream<T>`.

The standard stream operations, such as `filter`, `limit`, `map`, `reduce`, `skip`, etc. are all available on the resulting stream, of course, so the data in a fixed-size collection can be processed in exactly the same ways as that in a flexible collection, once converted to a stream.

The static `range` method of the `IntStream` class is often used to create a stream of the integer indices of a collection; for instance:

```
IntStream indices = IntStream.range(0, nums.length);
```

The value of **nums.length** will be excluded from the stream. The following example illustrates how we might identify the indices of values in an array that are above a particular threshold. Note that it is the indices we are interested in and not the values, in this particular case:

```
int[] above = IntStream.range(0, hourCounts.length)
                       .filter(i -> hourCounts[i] > threshold)
                       .toArray();
```

The terminal **toArray** method of the stream returns an array containing the index values remaining after filtering.

7.8 Summary

In this chapter, we have discussed arrays as a means to create fixed-size collection objects. Single-dimension arrays are a collection type that is well suited for those situations in which the number of items to be stored is fixed and known in advance. They are also slightly more syntactically lightweight than flexible-sized collections, such as **ArrayList**, particularly when used to store values of the primitive types. However, aside from those specific situations, they do not offer any features that are not also readily available with collections such as lists, maps, and sets.

Terms introduced in this chapter:

array, for loop, conditional operator, lookup table

Exercise 7.41 Rewrite the following by using the static **arraycopy** method of the **System** class:

```
int[] copy = new int[original.length];
for(int i = 0; i < original.length; i++) {
    copy[i] = original[i];
}
```

Exercise 7.42 Describe what the following static methods of the **java.util.Arrays** class do: **asList**, **binarySearch**, **fill**, and **sort**? Where there are multiple versions of a method, use one that operates on an integer array as the example.

Exercise 7.43 Try to write some example code to use each of the methods mentioned in the previous exercise.

Exercise 7.44 Write statements to copy all of the elements of the 2D integer array, `original`, into a new array called `copy`. You should include the statements to create the `copy` array.

Exercise 7.45 Investigate some other 2D cellular automata and implement their rules in the *brain* project.

CHAPTER 8

Designing Classes

Main concepts discussed in this chapter:

- responsibility-driven design
- coupling
- cohesion
- refactoring

Java constructs discussed in this chapter:

enumerated types, `switch`

In this chapter, we look at some of the factors that influence the design of a class. What makes a class design either good or bad? Writing good classes can take more effort in the short term than writing bad classes, but in the long term that extra effort will almost always be justified. To help us write good classes, there are some principles that we can follow. In particular, we introduce the view that class design should be responsibility-driven, and that classes should encapsulate their data.

This chapter is, like many of the chapters before, structured around a project. It can be studied by just reading it and following our line of argument, or it can be studied in much more depth by doing the project exercises in parallel while working through the chapter.

The project work is divided into three parts. In the first part, we discuss the necessary changes to the source code and develop and show complete solutions to the exercises. The solution for this part is also available in a project accompanying this book. The second part suggests more changes and extensions, and we discuss possible solutions at a high level (the class-design level), but leave it to readers to do the lower-level work and to complete the implementation. The third part suggests even more improvements in the form of exercises. We do not give solutions—the exercises apply the material discussed throughout the chapter.

Implementing all parts makes a good programming project over several weeks. It can also be used very successfully as a group project.

8.1 Introduction

It is possible to implement an application and get it to perform its task with badly designed classes. Simply executing a finished application does not usually indicate whether it is well structured internally or not.

The problems typically surface when a maintenance programmer wants to make some changes to an existing application. If, for example, a programmer attempts to fix a bug or wants to add new functionality to an existing program, a task that might be easy and obvious with well-designed classes may well be very hard and involve a great deal of work if the classes are badly designed.

In larger applications, this effect occurs earlier on, during the initial implementation. If the implementation starts with a bad structure, then finishing it might later become overly complex, and the complete program may either not be finished contain bugs, or take a lot longer to build. In reality, companies often maintain, extend, and sell an application over many years. It is not uncommon that an implementation for software that we can buy in a software store today was started more than ten years ago. In this situation, a software company cannot afford to have badly structured code.

Because many of the effects of bad class design become most obvious when trying to adapt or extend an application, we shall do exactly that. In this chapter, we will use an example called *world-of-zuul*, which is a rudimentary implementation of a text-based adventure game. In its original state, the game is not actually very ambitious—for one thing, it is incomplete. By the end of this chapter, however, you will be in a position to exercise your imagination and design and implement your own game and make it really fun and interesting.

> **world-of-zuul** Our *world-of-zuul* game is modeled on the original *Adventure* game that was developed in the early 1970s by Will Crowther and expanded by Don Woods. The original game is also sometimes known as the *Colossal Cave Adventure*. This was a wonderfully imaginative and sophisticated game for its time, involving finding your way through a complex cave system, locating hidden treasure, using secret words, and other mysteries, all in an effort to score the maximum number of points. You can read more about it at sites such as http://jerz.setonhill.edu/if/canon/Adventure.htm and http://www.rickadams.org/adventure/, or try doing a web search for "Colossal Cave Adventure."

While we work on extending the original application, we will take the opportunity to discuss aspects of its existing class design. We will see that the implementation we start with contains examples of bad design, and we will be able to see how this impacts on our tasks and how we can fix them.

In the project examples for this book, you will find two versions of the *zuul* project: *zuul-bad* and *zuul-better*. Both implement exactly the same functionality, but some of the class structure is different, representing bad design in one project and better design in the other. The fact that we can implement the same functionality in either a good way or a bad way illustrates the fact that bad design is not usually a consequence of having a difficult problem to solve. Bad design has more to do with the decisions that we make when solving a particular problem. We cannot use the argument that there was no other way to solve the problem as an excuse for bad design.

So, we will use the project with bad design so that we can explore why it is bad, and then improve it. The better version is an implementation of the changes we discuss here.

Exercise 8.1 Open the project *zuul-bad*. (This project is called "bad" because its implementation contains some bad design decisions, and we want to leave no doubt that this should not be used as an example of good programming practice!) Execute and explore the application. The project comment gives you some information about how to run it.

While exploring the application, answer the following questions:

- What does this application do?
- What commands does the game accept?
- What does each command do?
- How many rooms are in the scenario?
- Draw a map of the existing rooms.

Exercise 8.2 After you know what the whole application does, try to find out what each individual class does. Write down for each class its purpose. You need to look at the source code to do this. Note that you might not (and need not) understand all of the source code. Often, reading through comments and looking at method headers is enough.

8.2 The *world-of-zuul* game example

From Exercise 8.1, you have seen that the *zuul* game is not yet very adventurous. It is, in fact, quite boring in its current state. But it provides a good basis for us to design and implement our own game, which will hopefully be more interesting.

We start by analyzing the classes that are already there in our first version and trying to find out what they do. The class diagram is shown in Figure 8.1.

The project shows five classes. They are **Parser**, **CommandWords**, **Command**, **Room**, and **Game**. An investigation of the source code shows, fortunately, that these classes are quite well documented, and we can get an initial overview of what they do by just reading the class comment at the top of each class. (This fact also serves to illustrate that bad design involves something deeper than simply the way a class looks or how good its documentation is.) Our understanding of the game will be assisted by having a look at the source code

Figure 8.1

Zuul class diagram

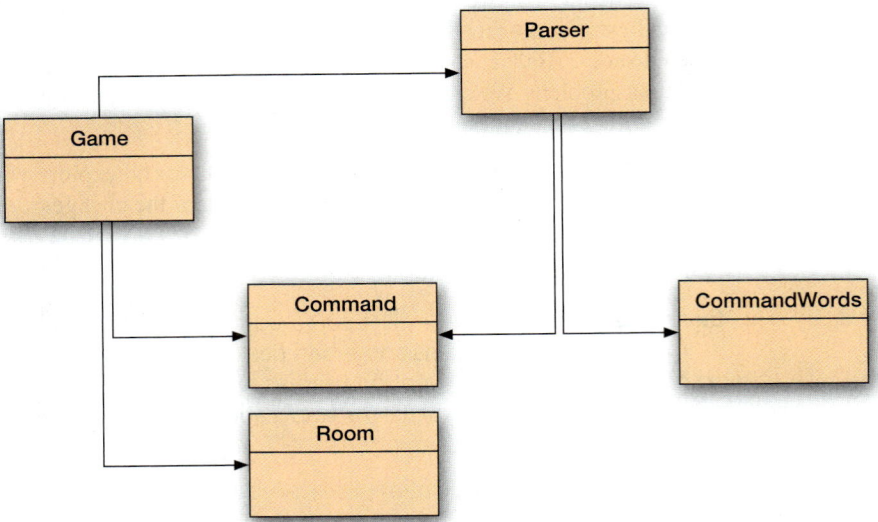

to see what methods each class has and what some of the methods appear to do. Here, we summarize the purpose of each class:

- *CommandWords* The **CommandWords** class defines all valid commands in the game. It does this by holding an array of **String** objects representing the command words.
- *Parser* The parser reads lines of input from the terminal and tries to interpret them as commands. It creates objects of class **Command** that represent the command that was entered.
- *Command* A **Command** object represents a command that was entered by the user. It has methods that make it easy for us to check whether this was a valid command and to get the first and second words of the command as separate strings.
- *Room* A **Room** object represents a location in a game. Rooms can have exits that lead to other rooms.
- *Game* The **Game** class is the main class of the game. It sets up the game and then enters a loop to read and execute commands. It also contains the code that implements each user command.

Exercise 8.3 Design your own game scenario. Do this away from the computer. Do not think about implementation, classes, or even programming in general. Just think about inventing an interesting game. This could be done with a group of people.

The game can be anything that has as its base structure a player moving through different locations. Here are some examples:

- You are a white blood cell traveling through the body in search of viruses to attack . . .
- You are lost in a shopping mall and must find the exit . . .
- You are a mole in its burrow and you cannot remember where you stored your food reserves before winter . . .
- You are an adventurer who searches through a dungeon full of monsters and other characters . . .
- You are on the bomb squad and must find and defuse a bomb before it goes off . . .

Make sure that your game has a goal (so that it has an end and the player can "win"). Try to think of many things to make the game interesting (trap doors, magic items, characters that help you only if you feed them, time limits... whatever you like). Let your imagination run wild.

At this stage, do not worry about how to implement these things.

8.3 Introduction to coupling and cohesion

If we are to justify our assertion that some designs are better than others, then we need to define some terms that will allow us to discuss the issues that we consider to be important in class design. Two terms are central when talking about the quality of a class design: *coupling* and *cohesion*.

The term *coupling* refers to the interconnectedness of classes. We have already discussed in earlier chapters that we aim to design our applications as a set of cooperating classes that communicate via well-defined interfaces. The degree of coupling indicates how tightly these classes are connected. We strive for a low degree of coupling, or *loose coupling*.

The degree of coupling determines how hard it is to make changes in an application. In a tightly coupled class structure, a change in one class can make it necessary to change several other classes as well. This is what we try to avoid, because the effect of making one small change can quickly ripple through a complete application. In addition, finding all the places where changes are necessary, and actually making the changes, can be difficult and time consuming.

In a loosely coupled system, on the other hand, we can often change one class without making any changes to other classes, and the application will still work. We shall discuss particular examples of tight and loose coupling in this chapter.

The term *cohesion* relates to the number and diversity of tasks for which a single unit of an application is responsible. Cohesion is relevant for units of a single class and an individual method.[1]

> **Concept**
>
> The term **coupling** describes the interconnectedness of classes. We strive for loose coupling in a system—that is, a system where each class is largely independent and communicates with other classes via a small, well-defined interface.

---

[1] We sometimes also use the term *module* (or *package* in Java) to refer to a multi-class unit. *Cohesion* is relevant at this level too.

> **Concept**
>
> The term **cohesion** describes how well a unit of code maps to a logical task or entity. In a highly cohesive system, each unit of code (method, class, or module) is responsible for a well-defined task or entity. Good class design exhibits a high degree of cohesion.

Ideally, one unit of code should be responsible for one cohesive task (that is, one task that can be seen as a logical unit). A method should implement one logical operation, and a class should represent one type of entity. The main reason behind the principle of cohesion is reuse: if a method or a class is responsible for only one well-defined thing, then it is much more likely it can be used again in a different context. A complementary advantage of following this principle is that, when change *is* required to some aspect of an application, we are likely to find all the relevant pieces located in the same unit.

We shall discuss with examples below how cohesion influences the quality of class design.

Exercise 8.4 Draw (on paper) a map for the game you invented in Exercise 8.3. Open the *zuul-bad* project and save it under a different name (e.g., *zuul*). This is the project you will use for making improvements and modifications throughout this chapter. You can leave off the *-bad* suffix, because it will (hopefully) soon not be that bad anymore.

As a first step, change the **createRooms** method in the **Game** class to create the rooms and exits you invented for your game.

8.4 Code duplication

Code duplication is an indicator of bad design. The **Game** class shown in Code 8.1 contains a case of code duplication. The problem with code duplication is that any change to one version must also be made to another if we are to avoid inconsistency. This increases the amount of work a maintenance programmer has to do, and it introduces the danger of bugs. It very easily happens that a maintenance programmer finds one copy of the code and, having changed it, assumes that the job is done. There is nothing indicating that a second copy of the code exists, and it might incorrectly remain unchanged.

Code 8.1
Selected sections of the (badly designed) **Game** class

```java
public class Game
{
    Some code omitted.
    private void createRooms()
    {
        Room outside, theater, pub, lab, office;

        // create the rooms
        outside = new Room("outside the main entrance of the university");
        theater = new Room("in a lecture theater");
        pub = new Room("in the campus pub");
        lab = new Room("in a computing lab");
        office = new Room("in the computing admin office");
```

8.4 Code duplication

Code 8.1 continued
Selected sections of the (badly designed) Game class

Concept
Code duplication (having the same segment of code in an application more than once) is a sign of bad design. It should be avoided.

```java
        // initialize room exits
        outside.setExits(null, theater, lab, pub);
        theater.setExits(null, null, null, outside);
        pub.setExits(null, outside, null, null);
        lab.setExits(outside, office, null, null);
        office.setExits(null, null, null, lab);

        currentRoom = outside;  // start game outside
    }
```

Some code omitted.

```java
    /**
     * Print out the opening message for the player.
     */
    private void printWelcome()
    {
        System.out.println();
        System.out.println("Welcome to the World of Zuul!");
        System.out.println("Zuul is a new incredibly boring adventure game.");
        System.out.println("Type 'help' if you need help.");
        System.out.println();
        System.out.println("You are " + currentRoom.getDescription());
        System.out.print("Exits: ");
        if(currentRoom.northExit != null) {
            System.out.print("north ");
        }
        if(currentRoom.eastExit != null) {
            System.out.print("east ");
        }
        if(currentRoom.southExit != null) {
            System.out.print("south ");
        }
        if(currentRoom.westExit != null) {
            System.out.print("west ");
        }
        System.out.println();
    }
```

Some code omitted.

```java
    /**
     * Try to go in one direction. If there is an exit, enter
     * the new room, otherwise print an error message.
     */
    private void goRoom(Command command)
    {
        if(!command.hasSecondWord()) {
            // if there is no second word, we don't know where to go...
            System.out.println("Go where?");
            return;
        }
```

Code 8.1 continued

Selected sections of the (badly designed) **Game** class

```java
        String direction = command.getSecondWord();

        // Try to leave current room.
        Room nextRoom = null;
        if(direction.equals("north")) {
            nextRoom = currentRoom.northExit;
        }
        if(direction.equals("east")) {
            nextRoom = currentRoom.eastExit;
        }
        if(direction.equals("south")) {
            nextRoom = currentRoom.southExit;
        }
        if(direction.equals("west")) {
            nextRoom = currentRoom.westExit;
        }

        if (nextRoom == null) {
            System.out.println("There is no door!");
        }
        else {
            currentRoom = nextRoom;
            System.out.println("You are " + currentRoom.getDescription());
            System.out.print("Exits: ");
            if(currentRoom.northExit != null) {
                System.out.print("north ");
            }
            if(currentRoom.eastExit != null) {
                System.out.print("east ");
            }
            if(currentRoom.southExit != null) {
                System.out.print("south ");
            }
            if(currentRoom.westExit != null) {
                System.out.print("west ");
            }
            System.out.println();
        }
    }
}
```

Some code omitted.

Both the `printWelcome` and `goRoom` methods contain the following lines of code:

```java
System.out.println("You are" + currentRoom.getDescription());
System.out.print("Exits:");
if(currentRoom.northExit != null) {
    System.out.print("north");
}
if(currentRoom.eastExit != null) {
    System.out.print("east");
}
```

```
        if(currentRoom.southExit != null) {
            System.out.print("south");
        }
        if(currentRoom.westExit != null) {
            System.out.print("west");
        }
        System.out.println();
```

Code duplication is usually a symptom of poor cohesion. The problem here has its roots in the fact that both methods in question do two things: `printWelcome` prints the welcome message and prints the information about the current location, while `goRoom` changes the current location then prints information about the (new) current location.

Both methods print information about the current location, but neither can call the other, because they also do other things. This is bad design.

A better design would use a separate, more cohesive method whose sole task is to print the current location information (Code 8.2). Both the `printWelcome` and `goRoom` methods can then make calls to this method when they need to print this information. This way, writing the code twice is avoided, and when we need to change it, we need to change it only once.

Code 8.2

printLocationInfo as a separate method

```
private void printLocationInfo()
{
    System.out.println("You are " + currentRoom.getDescription());
    System.out.print("Exits: ");
    if(currentRoom.northExit != null) {
        System.out.print("north ");
    }
    if(currentRoom.eastExit != null) {
        System.out.print("east ");
    }
    if(currentRoom.southExit != null) {
        System.out.print("south ");
    }
    if(currentRoom.westExit != null) {
        System.out.print("west ");
    }
    System.out.println();
}
```

Exercise 8.5 Implement and use a separate `printLocationInfo` method in your project, as discussed in this section. Test your changes.

8.5 Making extensions

The *zuul-bad* project does work. We can execute it, and it correctly does everything that it was intended to do. However, it is in some respects quite badly designed. A well-designed alternative would perform in the same way; we would not notice any difference just by executing the program.

Once we try to make modifications to the project, however, we will notice significant differences in the amount of work involved in changing badly designed code, compared with changes to a well-designed application. We will investigate this by making some changes to the project. While we are doing this, we will discuss examples of bad design when we see them in the existing source, and we will improve the class design before we implement our extensions.

8.5.1 The task

The first task we will attempt is to add a new direction of movement. Currently, a player can move in four directions: *north*, *east*, *south*, and *west*. We want to allow for multilevel buildings (or cellars, or dungeons, or whatever you later want to add to your game) and add *up* and *down* as possible directions. A player can then type **"go down"** to move, say, down into a cellar.

8.5.2 Finding the relevant source code

Inspection of the given classes shows us that at least two classes are involved in this change: **Room** and **Game**.

Room is the class that stores (among other things) the exits of each room. As we saw in Code 8.1, in the **Game** class the exit information from the current room is used to print out information about exits and to move from one room to another.

The **Room** class is fairly short. Its source code is shown in Code 8.3. Reading the source, we can see that the exits are mentioned in two different places: they are listed as fields at the top of the class, and they get assigned in the **setExits** method. To add two new directions, we would need to add two new exits (**upExit** and **downExit**) in these two places.

Code 8.3

Source code of the (badly designed) Room class

```java
public class Room
{
    public String description;
    public Room northExit;
    public Room southExit;
    public Room eastExit;
    public Room westExit;

    /**
     * Create a room described "description."  Initially, it has
     * no exits. "description" is something like "a kitchen" or
     * "an open court yard."
     * @param description The room's description.
     */
    public Room(String description)
    {
        this.description = description;
    }
```

Code 8.3 continued

Source code of the (badly designed) Room class

```java
    /**
     * Define the exits of this room.  Every direction either leads
     * to another room or is null (no exit there).
     * @param north The north exit.
     * @param east The east east.
     * @param south The south exit.
     * @param west The west exit.
     */
    public void setExits(Room north, Room east, Room south, Room west)
    {
        if(north != null) {
            northExit = north;
        }
        if(east != null) {
            eastExit = east;
        }
        if(south != null) {
            southExit = south;
        }
        if(west != null) {
            westExit = west;
        }
    }

    /**
     * @return The description of the room.
     */
    public String getDescription()
    {
        return description;
    }
}
```

It is a bit more work to find all relevant places in the **Game** class. The source code is somewhat longer (it is not fully shown here), and finding all the relevant places takes some patience and care.

Reading the code shown in Code 8.1, we can see that the **Game** class makes heavy use of the exit information of a room. The **Game** object holds a reference to one room in the **currentRoom** variable, and frequently accesses this room's exit information.

- In the **createRoom** method, the exits are defined.
- In the **printWelcome** method, the current room's exits are printed out so that the player knows where to go when the game starts.
- In the **goRoom** method, the exits are used to find the next room. They are then used again to print out the exits of the next room we have just entered.

If we now want to add two new exit directions, we will have to add the *up* and *down* options in all these places. However, read the following section before you do this.

8.6 Coupling

The fact that there are so many places where all exits are enumerated is symptomatic of poor class design. When declaring the exit variables in the **Room** class, we need to list one variable per exit; in the `setExits` method, there is one if statement per exit; in the `goRoom` method, there is one if statement per exit; in the `printLocationInfo` method, there is one if statement per exit; and so on. This design decision now creates work for us: when adding new exits, we need to find all these places and add two new cases. Imagine the effect if we decided to use directions such as northwest, southeast, etc.!

To improve the situation, we decide to use a `HashMap` to store the exits, rather than separate variables. Doing this, we should be able to write code that can cope with any number of exits and does not need so many modifications. The `HashMap` will contain a mapping from a named direction (e.g., `"north"`) to the room that lies in that direction (a **Room** object). Thus, each entry has a `String` as the key and a **Room** object as the value.

This is a change in the way a room stores information internally about neighboring rooms. Theoretically, this is a change that should affect only the *implementation* of the **Room** class (*how* the exit information is stored), not the *interface* (*what* the room stores).

Ideally, when only the implementation of a class changes, other classes should not be affected. This would be a case of *loose* coupling.

In our example, this does not work. If we remove the exit variables in the **Room** class and replace them with a `HashMap`, the **Game** class will not compile any more. It makes numerous references to the room's exit variables, which all would cause errors.

We see that we have a case here of *tight* coupling. In order to clean this up, we will decouple these classes before we introduce the `HashMap`.

8.6.1 Using encapsulation to reduce coupling

> **Concept**
>
> Proper **encapsulation** in classes reduces coupling and thus leads to a better design.

One of the main problems in this example is the use of public fields. The exit fields in the **Room** class have all been declared `public`. Clearly, the programmer of this class did not follow the guidelines we have set out earlier in this book ("Never make fields public!"). We shall now see the result. The **Game** class in this example can make direct accesses to these fields (and it makes extensive use of this fact). By making the fields public, the **Room** class has exposed in its interface not only the fact that it has exits, but also exactly how the exit information is stored. This breaks one of the fundamental principles of good class design: *encapsulation*.

The encapsulation guideline (hiding implementation information from view) suggests that only information about *what* a class can do should be visible to the outside, not about *how* it does it. This has a great advantage: if no other class knows how our information is stored, then we can easily change how it is stored without breaking other classes.

We can enforce this separation of *what* and *how* by making the fields private, and using an accessor method to access them. The first stage of our modified **Room** class is shown in Code 8.4.

Code 8.4

Using an accessor method to decrease coupling

```java
public class Room
{
    private String description;
    private Room northExit;
    private Room southExit;
    private Room eastExit;
    private Room westExit;

    Existing methods unchanged.

    public Room getExit(String direction)
    {
        if(direction.equals("north")) {
            return northExit;
        }
        if(direction.equals("east")) {
            return eastExit;
        }
        if(direction.equals("south")) {
            return southExit;
        }
        if(direction.equals("west")) {
            return westExit;
        }
        return null;
    }
}
```

Having made this change to the **Room** class, we need to change the **Game** class as well. Wherever an exit variable was accessed, we now use the accessor method. For example, instead of writing

```java
nextRoom = currentRoom.eastExit;
```

we now write

```java
nextRoom = currentRoom.getExit("east");
```

This makes coding one section in the **Game** class much easier as well. In the **goRoom** method, the replacement suggested here will result in the following code segment:

```java
Room nextRoom = null;
if(direction.equals("north")) {
    nextRoom = currentRoom.getExit("north");
}
if(direction.equals("east")) {
    nextRoom = currentRoom.getExit("east");
}
if(direction.equals("south")) {
    nextRoom = currentRoom.getExit("south");
}
```

```
if(direction.equals("west")) {
    nextRoom = currentRoom.getExit("west");
}
```

Instead, this whole code segment can now be replaced with:

```
Room nextRoom = currentRoom.getExit(direction);
```

Exercise 8.6 Make the changes we have described to the **Room** and **Game** classes.

Exercise 8.7 Make a similar change to the `printLocationInfo` method of **Game** so that details of the exits are now prepared by the **Room** rather than the **Game**. Define a method in **Room** with the following header:

```
/**
 * Return a description of the room's exits,
 * for example, "Exits: north west".
 * @return A description of the available exits.
 */
public String getExitString()
```

So far, we have not changed the representation of the exits in the **Room** class. We have only cleaned up the interface. The *change* in the **Game** class is minimal—instead of an access of a public field, we use a method call—but the *gain* is dramatic. We can now make a change to the way exits are stored in the room, without any need to worry about breaking anything in the **Game** class. The internal representation in **Room** has been completely decoupled from the interface. Now that the design is the way it should have been in the first place, exchanging the separate exit fields for a **HashMap** is easy. The changed code is shown in Code 8.5.

Code 8.5
Source code of the **Room** class

```
import java.util.HashMap;
```
Class comment omitted.

```java
public class Room
{
    private String description;
    private HashMap<String, Room> exits;        // stores exits of this room.

    /**
     * Create a room described "description." Initially, it has no exits.
     * "description" is something like "a kitchen" or "an open court yard."
     * @param description The room's description.
     */
    public Room(String description)
    {
        this.description = description;
        exits = new HashMap<>();
    }
}
```

Code 8.5 continued

Source code of the Room class

```java
    /**
     * Define an exit from this room.
     * @param direction The direction of the exit.
     * @param neighbor  The room to which the exit leads.
     */
    public void setExit(Room north, Room east, Room south, Room west)
    {
        if(north != null) {
            exits.put("north", north);
        }
        if(east != null) {
            exits.put("east", east);
        }
        if(south != null) {
            exits.put("south", south);
        }
        if(west != null) {
            exits.put("west", west);
        }
    }

    /**
     * Return the room that is reached if we go from this room in direction
     * "direction."  If there is no room in that direction, return null.
     * @param direction The exit's direction.
     * @return The room in the given direction.
     */
    public Room getExit(String direction)
    {
        return exits.get(direction);
    }

    /**
     * @return The description of the room
     * (the one that was defined in the constructor).
     */
    public String getDescription()
    {
        return description;
    }
}
```

It is worth emphasizing again that we can make this change now without even checking whether anything will break elsewhere. Because we have changed only private aspects of the **Room** class, which, by definition, cannot be used in other classes, this change does not impact on other classes. The interface remains unchanged.

A by-product of this change is that our **Room** class is now even shorter. Instead of listing four separate variables, we have only one. In addition, the **getExit** method is considerably simplified.

Recall that the original aim that set off this series of changes was to make it easier to add the two new possible exits in the *up* and *down* direction. This has already become much easier. Because we now use a **HashMap** to store exits, storing these two additional directions will work without any change. We can also obtain the exit information via the **getExit** method without any problem.

The only place where knowledge about the four existing exits (*north*, *east*, *south*, *west*) is still coded into the source is in the `setExits` method. This is the last part that needs improvement. At the moment, the method's header is

```
public void setExits(Room north, Room east, Room south, Room west)
```

This method is part of the interface of the **Room** class, so any change we make to it will inevitably affect some other classes by virtue of coupling. We can never completely decouple the classes in an application; otherwise objects of different classes would not be able to interact with one another. Rather, we try to keep the degree of coupling as low as possible. If we have to make a change to `setExits` anyway, to accommodate additional directions, then our preferred solution is to replace it entirely with this method:

```
/**
 * Define an exit from this room.
 * @param direction The direction of the exit.
 * @param neighbor The room in the given direction.
 */
public void setExit(String direction, Room neighbor)
{
    exits.put(direction, neighbor);
}
```

Now, the exits of this room can be set one exit at a time, and any direction can be used for an exit. In the **Game** class, the change that results from modifying the interface of **Room** is as follows. Instead of writing

```
lab.setExits(outside, office, null, null);
```

we now write

```
lab.setExit("north", outside);
lab.setExit("east", office);
```

We have now completely removed the restriction from **Room** that it can store only four exits. The **Room** class is now ready to store *up* and *down* exits, as well as any other direction you might think of (northwest, southeast, etc.).

Exercise 8.8 Implement the changes described in this section in your own *zuul* project.

8.7 Responsibility-driven design

We have seen in the previous section that making use of proper encapsulation reduces coupling and can significantly reduce the amount of work needed to make changes to an application. Encapsulation, however, is not the only factor that influences the degree of coupling. Another aspect is known by the term *responsibility-driven design*.

Responsibility-driven design expresses the idea that each class should be responsible for handling its own data. Often, when we need to add some new functionality to an application, we need to ask ourselves in which class we should add a method to implement this new function. Which class should be responsible for the task? The answer is that the class that is responsible for storing some data should also be responsible for manipulating it.

How well responsibility-driven design is used influences the degree of coupling and, therefore, again, the ease with which an application can be modified or extended. As usual, we will discuss this in more detail with our example.

8.7.1 Responsibilities and coupling

The changes to the **Room** class that we discussed in Section 8.6.1 make it quite easy now to add the new directions for up and down movement in the **Game** class. We investigate this with an example. Assume that we want to add a new room (the cellar) under the office. All we have to do to achieve this is to make some small changes to **Game**'s `createRooms` method to create the room and to make two calls to set the exits:

> **Concept**
>
> **Responsibility-driven design** is the process of designing classes by assigning well-defined responsibilities to each class. This process can be used to determine which class should implement which part of an application function.

```
private void createRooms()
{
    Room outside, theater, pub, lab, office, cellar;
    ...
    cellar = new Room("in the cellar");
    ...
    office.setExit("down", cellar);
    cellar.setExit("up", office);
}
```

Because of the new interface of the **Room** class, this will work without problems. The change is now very easy and confirms that the design is getting better.

Further evidence of this can be seen if we compare the original version of the `printLocationInfo` method shown in Code 8.2 with the `getExitString` method shown in Code 8.6 that represents a solution to Exercise 8.7.

Because information about its exits is now stored only in the room itself, it is the room that is responsible for providing that information. The room can do this much better than any other object, because it has all the knowledge about the internal storage structure of the exit data. Now, inside the **Room** class, we can make use of the knowledge that exits are stored in a **HashMap**, and we can iterate over that map to describe the exits.

Consequently, we replace the version of `getExitString` shown in Code 8.6 with the version shown in Code 8.7. This method finds all the names for exits in the **HashMap** (the keys in the **HashMap** are the names of the exits) and concatenates them to a single **String**, which is then returned. (We need to import **Set** from `java.util` for this to work.)

Exercise 8.9 Look up the `keySet` method in the documentation of **HashMap**. What does it do?

Exercise 8.10 Explain, in detail and in writing, how the `getExitString` method shown in Code 8.7 works.

Code 8.6

The `getExitString` method of `Room`

```java
/**
 * Return a description of the room's exits,
 * for example, "Exits: north west."
 * @return A description of the available exits.
 */
public String getExitString()
{
    String exitString = "Exits: ";
    if(northExit != null) {
        exitString += "north ";
    }
    if(eastExit != null) {
        exitString += "east ";
    }
    if(southExit != null) {
        exitString += "south ";
    }
    if(westExit != null) {
        exitString += "west ";
    }
    return exitString;
}
```

Code 8.7

A revised version of `getExitString`

```java
/**
 * Return a description of the room's exits,
 * for example "Exits: north west."
 * @return A description of the available exits.
 */
public String getExitString()
{
    String returnString = "Exits:";
    Set<String> keys = exits.keySet();
    for(String exit : keys) {
        returnString += " " + exit;
    }
    return returnString;
}
```

Our goal to reduce coupling demands that, as far as possible, changes to the **Room** class do not require changes to the **Game** class. We can still improve this.

Currently, we have still encoded in the **Game** class the knowledge that the information we want from a room consists of a description string and the exit string:

```
System.out.println("You are " + currentRoom.getDescription());
System.out.println(currentRoom.getExitString());
```

What if we add items to rooms in our game? Or monsters? Or other players?

When we describe what we see, the list of items, monsters, and other players should be included in the description of the room. We would need not only to make changes to the **Room** class to add these things, but also to change the code segment above where the description is printed out.

This is again a breach of the responsibility-driven design rule. Because the **Room** class holds information about a room, it should also produce a description for a room. We can improve this by adding to the **Room** class the following method:

```
/**
 * Return a long description of this room, of the form:
 *     You are in the kitchen.
 *     Exits: north west
 * @return A description of the room, including exits.
 */
public String getLongDescription()
{
    return "You are " + description + ".\n" + getExitString();
}
```

In the **Game** class, we then write

```
System.out.println(currentRoom.getLongDescription());
```

The "long description" of a room now includes the description string and information about the exits, and may in the future include anything else there is to say about a room. When we make these future extensions, we will have to make changes to only the **Room** class.

> **Concept**
>
> One of the main goals of a good class design is that of **localizing change**: making changes to one class should have minimal effects on other classes.

Exercise 8.11 Implement the changes described in this section in your own *zuul* project.

Exercise 8.12 Draw an object diagram with all objects in your game, the way they are just after starting the game.

Exercise 8.13 How does the object diagram change when you execute a *go* command?

8.8 Localizing change

Another aspect of the decoupling and responsibility principles is that of *localizing change*. We aim to create a class design that makes later changes easy by localizing the effects of a change.

Ideally, only a single class needs to be changed to make a modification. Sometimes several classes need change, but we then aim at this being as few classes as possible. In addition, the changes needed in other classes should be obvious, easy to detect, and easy to carry out.

To a large extent, we can achieve this by following good design rules such as using responsibility-driven design and aiming for loose coupling and high cohesion. In addition, however, we should have modification and extension in mind when we create our applications. It is important to anticipate that an aspect of our program might change, in order to make any changes easy.

8.9 Implicit coupling

We have seen that the use of public fields is one practice that is likely to create an unnecessarily tight form of coupling between classes. With this tight coupling, it may be necessary to make changes to more than one class for what should have been a simple modification. Therefore, public fields should be avoided. However, there is an even worse form of coupling: *implicit coupling*.

Implicit coupling is a situation where one class depends on the internal information of another, but this dependence is not immediately obvious. The tight coupling in the case of the public fields was not good, but at least it was obvious. If we change the public fields in one class and forget about the other, the application will not compile any longer, and the compiler will point out the problem. In cases of implicit coupling, omitting a necessary change can go undetected.

We can see the problem arising if we try to add further command words to the game.

Suppose that we want to add the command *look* to the set of legal commands. The purpose of *look* is merely to print out the description of the room and the exits again (we "look around the room"). This could be helpful if we have entered a sequence of commands in a room so that the description has scrolled out of view and we cannot remember where the exits of the current room are.

We can introduce a new command word simply by adding it to the array of known words in the `validCommands` array in the `CommandWords` class:

```
// a constant array that holds all valid command words
private static final String validCommands[] = {
    "go", "quit", "help", "look"
};
```

This shows an example of good cohesion: instead of defining the command words in the parser, which would have been one obvious possibility, the author created a separate class just to define the command words. This makes it very easy for us to now find the place where command words are defined, and it is easy to add one. The author was obviously thinking ahead, assuming that more commands might be added later, and created a structure that makes this very easy.

We can test this already. When we make this change and then execute the game and type the command *look*, nothing happens. This contrasts with the behavior of an unknown command word; if we type any unknown word, we see the reply

```
I don't know what you mean...
```

Thus, the fact that we do not see this reply indicates that the word was recognized, but nothing happens because we have not yet implemented an action for this command.

We can fix this by adding a method for the *look* command to the **Game** class:

```
private void look()
{
    System.out.println(currentRoom.getLongDescription());
}
```

You should, of course, also add a comment for this method. After this, we only need to add a case for the *look* command in the **processCommand** method, which will invoke the `look` method when the *look* command is recognized:

```
if(commandWord.equals("help")) {
    printHelp();
}
else if(commandWord.equals("go")) {
    goRoom(command);
}
else if(commandWord.equals("look")) {
    look();
}
else if(commandWord.equals("quit")) {
    wantToQuit = quit(command);
}
```

Try this out, and you will see that it works.

Exercise 8.14 Add the *look* command to your version of the zuul game.

Exercise 8.15 Add another command to your game. For a start, you could choose something simple, such as a command *eat* that, when executed, just prints out "You have eaten now and you are not hungry any more." Later, we can improve this so that you really get hungry over time and you need to find food.

Coupling between the **Game**, **Parser**, and **CommandWords** classes so far seems to have been very good—it was easy to make this extension, and we got it to work quickly.

The problem that was mentioned before—implicit coupling—becomes apparent when we now issue a help command. The output is

```
You are lost. You are alone. You wander
around at the university.
Your command words are:
go quit help
```

Now we notice a small problem. The help text is incomplete: the new command, *look*, is not listed.

This seems easy to fix: we can just edit the help text string in the **Game's printHelp** method. This is quickly done and does not seem a great problem. But suppose we had not noticed this error now. Did you think of this problem before you just read about it here?

This is a fundamental problem, because every time a command is added, the help text needs to be changed, and it is very easy to forget to make this change. The program compiles and runs, and everything seems fine. A maintenance programmer may well believe that the job is finished and release a program that now contains a bug.

This is an example of implicit coupling. When commands change, the help text must be modified (coupling), but nothing in the program source clearly points out this dependence (thus implicit).

A well-designed class will avoid this form of coupling by following the rule of responsibility-driven design. Because the **CommandWords** class is responsible for command words, it should also be responsible for printing command words. Thus, we add the following method to the **CommandWords** class:

```
/**
 * Print all valid commands to System.out.
 */
public void showAll()
{
    for(String command : validCommands) {
        System.out.print(command + " ");
    }
    System.out.println();
}
```

The idea here is that the **printHelp** method in **Game**, instead of printing a fixed text with the command words, invokes a method that asks the **CommandWords** class to print all its command words. Doing this ensures that the correct command words will always be printed, and adding a new command will also add it to the help text without further change.

The only remaining problem is that the **Game** object does not have a reference to the **CommandWords** object. You can see in the class diagram (Figure 8.1) that there is no arrow from **Game** to **CommandWords**. This indicates that the **Game** class does not even know of the existence of the **CommandWords** class. Instead, the game just has a parser, and the parser has command words.

We could now add a method to the parser that hands the **CommandWords** object to the **Game** object so that they could communicate. This would, however, increase the degree of coupling in our application. **Game** would then depend on **CommandWords**, which it currently does not. Also, we would see this effect in the class diagram: **Game** would then have an arrow to **CommandWords**.

The arrows in the diagram are, in fact, a good first indication of how tightly coupled a program is—the more arrows, the more coupling. As an approximation of good class design, we can aim at creating diagrams with few arrows.

Thus, the fact that **Game** did not have a reference to **CommandWords** is a good thing! We should not change this. From **Game's** viewpoint, the fact that the **CommandWords** class exists is an implementation detail of the parser. The parser returns commands, and whether it uses a **CommandWords** object to achieve this or something else is entirely up to the parser's implementation.

A better design just lets the **Game** talk to the **Parser**, which in turn may talk to **CommandWords**. We can implement this by adding the following code to the **printHelp** method in **Game**:

```
System.out.println("Your command words are:");
parser.showCommands();
```

All that is missing, then, is the **showCommands** method in the **Parser**, which delegates this task to the **CommandWords** class. Here is the complete method (in class **Parser**):

```
/**
 * Print out a list of valid command words.
 */
public void showCommands()
{
    commands.showAll();
}
```

Exercise 8.16 Implement the improved version of printing out the command words, as described in this section.

Exercise 8.17 If you now add another new command, do you still need to change the **Game** class? Why?

The full implementation of all changes discussed in this chapter so far is available in your code examples in a project named *zuul-better*. If you have done the exercises so far, you can ignore this project and continue to use your own. If you have not done the exercises but want to do the following exercises in this chapter as a programming project, you can use the *zuul-better* project as your starting point.

8.10 Thinking ahead

The design we have now is an important improvement to the original version. It is, however, possible to improve it even more.

One characteristic of a good software designer is the ability to think ahead. What might change? What can we safely assume will stay unchanged for the life of the program?

One assumption that we have hard-coded into most of our classes is that this game will run as a text-based game with terminal input and output. But will it always be like this?

It might be an interesting extension later to add a graphical user interface with menus, buttons, and images. In that case, we would not want to print the information to the text terminal anymore. We might still have command words, and we might still want to show them when a player enters a help command. But we might then show them in a text field in a window, rather than using `System.out.println`.

It is good design to try to encapsulate all information about the user interface in a single class or a clearly defined set of classes. Our solution from Section 8.9, for example—the `showAll` method in the `CommandWords` class—does not follow this design rule. It would be nice to define that `CommandWords` is responsible for *producing* (but not *printing*!) the list of command words, but that the `Game` class should decide how it is presented to the user.

We can easily achieve this by changing the `showAll` method so that it returns a string containing all command words instead of printing them out directly. (We should probably rename it `getCommandList` when we make this change.) This string can then be printed in the `printHelp` method in `Game`.

Note that this does not gain us anything right now, but we might profit from the improved design in the future.

> **Exercise 8.18** Implement the suggested change. Make sure that your program still works as before.
>
> **Exercise 8.19** Find out what the *model-view-controller* pattern is. You can do a web search to get information, or you can use any other sources you find. How is it related to the topic discussed here? What does it suggest? How could it be applied to this project? (Only *discuss* its application to this project, as an actual implementation would be an advanced challenge exercise.)

8.11 Cohesion

We introduced the idea of cohesion in Section 8.3: a unit of code should always be responsible for one, and only one, task. We shall now investigate the cohesion principle in more depth and analyze some examples.

The principle of cohesion can be applied to classes and methods: classes should display a high degree of cohesion, and so should methods.

8.11.1 Cohesion of methods

When we talk about cohesion of methods, we seek to express the ideal that any one method should be responsible for one, and only one, well-defined task.

We can see an example of a cohesive method in the `Game` class. This class has a private method named `printWelcome` to show the opening text, and this method is called when the game starts in the `play` method (Code 8.8).

Code 8.8

Two methods with a good degree of cohesion

```java
/**
 *  Main play routine. Loops until end of play.
 */
public void play()
{
    printWelcome();

    // Enter the main command loop. Here we repeatedly read commands and
    // execute them until the game is over.

    boolean finished = false;
    while (! finished) {
        Command command = parser.getCommand();
        finished = processCommand(command);
    }
    System.out.println("Thank you for playing.  Good bye.");
}

/**
 * Print out the opening message for the player.
 */
private void printWelcome()
{
    System.out.println();
    System.out.println("Welcome to the World of Zuul!");
    System.out.println("Zuul is a new, boring adventure game.");
    System.out.println("Type 'help' if you need help.");
    System.out.println();
    System.out.println(currentRoom.getLongDescription());
}
```

Concept

Method cohesion A cohesive method is responsible for one, and only one, well-defined task.

From a functional point of view, we could have just entered the statements from the `printWelcome` method directly into the `play` method and achieved the same result without defining an extra method and making a method call. The same can, by the way, be said for the `processCommand` method that is also invoked in the `play` method: this code, too, could have been written directly into the `play` method.

It is, however, much easier to understand what a segment of code does and to make modifications if short, cohesive methods are used. In the chosen method structure, all methods are reasonably short and easy to understand, and their names indicate their purposes quite clearly. These characteristics represent valuable help for a maintenance programmer.

8.11.2 Cohesion of classes

The rule of cohesion of classes states that each class should represent one single, well-defined entity in the problem domain.

> **Concept**
>
> **Class cohesion** A cohesive class represents one well-defined entity.

As an example of class cohesion, we now discuss another extension to the *zuul* project. We now want to add *items* to the game. Each room may hold an item, and each item has a description and a weight. An item's weight can be used later to determine whether it can be picked up or not.

A naïve approach would be to add two fields to the **Room** class: **itemDescription** and **itemWeight**. We could now specify the item details for each room, and we could print out the details whenever we enter a room.

This approach, however, does not display a good degree of cohesion: the **Room** class now describes both a room and an item. It also suggests that an item is bound to a particular room, which we might not wish to be the case.

A better design would create a separate class for items, probably called **Item**. This class would have fields for a description and weight, and a room would simply hold a reference to an item object.

> **Exercise 8.20** Extend either your adventure project or the *zuul-better* project so that a room can contain a single item. Items have a description and a weight. When creating rooms and setting their exits, items for this game should also be created. When a player enters a room, information about an item in this room should be displayed.
>
> **Exercise 8.21** How should the information be produced about an item present in a room? Which class should produce the string describing the item? Which class should print it? Why? Explain in writing. If answering this exercise makes you feel you should change your implementation, go ahead and make the changes.

The real benefits of separating rooms and items in the design can be seen if we change the specification a little. In a further variation of our game, we want to allow not only a single item in each room, but an unlimited number of items. In the design using a separate **Item** class, this is easy. We can create multiple **Item** objects and store them in a collection of items in the room.

With the first, naïve approach, this change would be almost impossible to implement.

> **Exercise 8.22** Modify the project so that a room can hold any number of items. Use a collection to do this. Make sure the room has an **addItem** method that places an item into the room. Make sure all items get shown when a player enters a room.

8.11.3 Cohesion for readability

There are several ways in which high cohesion benefits a design. The two most important ones are *readability* and *reuse*.

The example discussed in Section 8.11.1, cohesion of the `printWelcome` method, is clearly an example in which increasing cohesion makes a class more readable and thus easier to understand and maintain.

The class-cohesion example in Section 8.11.2 also has an element of readability. If a separate `Item` class exists, a maintenance programmer will easily recognize where to start reading code if a change to the characteristics of an item is needed. Cohesion of classes also increases readability of a program.

8.11.4 Cohesion for reuse

The second great advantage of cohesion is a higher potential for reuse.

The class-cohesion example in Section 8.11.2 shows an example of this: by creating a separate `Item` class, we can create multiple items and thus use the same code for more than a single item.

Reuse is also an important aspect of method cohesion. Consider a method in the `Room` class with the following header:

```
public Room leaveRoom(String direction)
```

This method could return the room in the given direction (so that it can be used as the new `currentRoom`) and also print out the description of the new room that we just entered.

This seems like a possible design, and it can indeed be made to work. In our version, however, we have separated this task into two methods:

```
public Room getExit(String direction)
public String getLongDescription()
```

The first is responsible for returning the next room, whereas the second produces the room's description.

The advantage of this design is that the separate tasks can be reused more easily. The `getLongDescription` method, for example, is now used not only in the `goRoom` method, but also in `printWelcome` and the implementation of the *look* command. This is only possible because it displays a high degree of cohesion. Reusing it would not be possible in the version with the `leaveRoom` method.

> **Exercise 8.23** Implement a *back* command. This command does not have a second word. Entering the *back* command takes the player into the previous room he/she was in.

Exercise 8.24 Test your new command. Does it work as expected? Also, test cases where the command is used incorrectly. For example, what does your program do if a player types a second word after the *back* command? Does it behave sensibly?

Exercise 8.25 What does your program do if you type "back" twice? Is this behavior sensible?

Exercise 8.26 *Challenge exercise* Implement the *back* command so that using it repeatedly takes you back several rooms, all the way to the beginning of the game if used often enough. Use a `Stack` to do this. (You may need to find out about stacks. Look at the Java library documentation.)

8.12 Refactoring

When designing applications, we should attempt to think ahead, anticipate possible changes in the future, and create highly cohesive, loosely coupled classes and methods that make modifications easy. This is a noble goal, but we cannot always anticipate all future adaptations, and it is not feasible to prepare for all possible extensions we can think of.

This is why *refactoring* is important.

Concept

Refactoring is the activity of restructuring an existing design to maintain a good class design when the application is modified or extended.

Refactoring is the activity of restructuring existing classes and methods to adapt them to changed functionality and requirements. Often in the lifetime of an application, functionality is gradually added. One common consequence is that, as a side-effect of this, methods and classes slowly grow in length.

It is tempting for a maintenance programmer to add some extra code to existing classes or methods. Doing this for some time, however, decreases the degree of cohesion. When more and more code is added to a method or a class, it is likely that at some stage it will represent more than one clearly defined task or entity.

Refactoring is the rethinking and redesigning of class and method structures. Most commonly, the effect is that classes are split in two or that methods are divided into two or more methods. Refactoring can also include the joining of multiple classes or methods into one, but that is less common than splitting.

8.12.1 Refactoring and testing

Before we provide an example of refactoring, we need to reflect on the fact that, when we refactor a program, we are usually proposing to make some potentially large changes to something that already works. When something is changed, there is a likelihood that errors will be introduced. Therefore, it is important to proceed cautiously; and, prior to refactoring, we should establish that a set of tests exists for the current version of the program. If tests do not exist, then we should first decide how we can reasonably test the functionality of the program and record those tests (for instance, by writing them down) so that we can repeat the same tests later. We will discuss testing more formally in the next chapter. If you are already familiar with automated testing, use automated tests. Otherwise, manual (but systematic) testing is sufficient for now.

Once a set of tests has been decided, the refactoring can start. Ideally, the refactoring should then follow in two steps:

- The first step is to refactor in order to improve the internal structure of the code, but without making any changes to the functionality of the application. In other words, the program should, when executed, behave exactly as it did before. Once this stage is completed, the previously established tests should be repeated to ensure that we have not introduced unintended errors.

- The second step is taken only once we have reestablished the baseline functionality in the refactored version. Then we are in a safe position to enhance the program. Once that has been done, of course, testing will need to be conducted on the new version.

Making several changes at the same time (refactoring and adding new features) makes it harder to locate the source of problems when they occur.

Exercise 8.27 What sort of baseline functionality tests might we wish to establish in the current version of the game?

8.12.2 An example of refactoring

As an example, we shall continue with the extension of adding items to the game. In Section 8.11.2, we started adding items, suggesting a structure in which rooms can contain any number of items. A logical extension to this arrangement is that a player should be able to pick up items and carry them around. Here is an informal specification of our next goal:

- The player can pick up items from the current room.
- The player can carry any number of items, but only up to a maximum weight.
- Some items cannot be picked up.
- The player can drop items in the current room.

To achieve these goals, we can do the following:

- If not already done, we add a class **Item** to the project. An item has, as discussed above, a description (a string) and a weight (an integer).

- We should also add a field **name** to the **Item** class. This will allow us to refer to the item with a name shorter than that of the description. If, for instance, there is a book in the current room, the field values of this item might be:

    name: **book**
    description: **an old, dusty book bound in gray leather**
    weight: **1200**

If we enter a room, we can print out the item's description to tell the player what is there. But for commands, the name will be easier to use. For instance, the player might then type *take book* to pick up the book.

- We can ensure that some items cannot be picked up, by just making them very heavy (more than a player can carry). Or should we have another `boolean` field `canBePickedUp`? Which do you think is the better design? Does it matter? Try answering this by thinking about what future changes might be made to the game.

- We add commands *take* and *drop* to pick up and drop items. Both commands have an item name as a second word.

- Somewhere we have to add a field (holding some form of collection) to store the items currently carried by the player. We also have to add a field with the maximum weight the player can carry, so that we can check it each time we try to pick up something. Where should these go? Once again, think about future extensions to help you make the decision.

This last task is what we will discuss in more detail now, in order to illustrate the process of refactoring.

The first question to ask ourselves when thinking about how to enable players to carry items is: Where should we add the fields for the currently carried items and the maximum weight? A quick look over the existing classes shows that the `Game` class is really the only place where it can be fit in. It cannot be stored in `Room`, `Item`, or `Command`, because there are many different instances of these classes over time, which are not all always accessible. It does not make sense in `Parser` or `CommandWords` either.

Reinforcing the decision to place these changes in the `Game` class is the fact that it already stores the current room (information about where the player is right now), so adding the current items (information about what the player has) seems to fit with this quite well.

This approach could be made to work. It is, however, not a solution that is well designed. The `Game` class is fairly big already, and there is a good argument that it contains too much as it is. Adding even more does not make this better.

We should ask ourselves again which class or object this information should belong to. Thinking carefully about the type of information we are adding here (carried items, maximum weight), we realize that this is information about a *player*! The logical thing to do (following responsibility-driven design guidelines) is to create a `Player` class. We can then add these fields to the `Player` class, and create a `Player` object at the start of the game, to store the data.

The existing field `currentRoom` also stores information about the player: the player's current location. Consequently, we should now also move this field into the `Player` class.

Analyzing it now, it is obvious that this design better fits the principle of responsibility-driven design. Who should be responsible for storing information about the player? The `Player` class, of course.

In the original version, we had only a single piece of information for the player: the current room. Whether we should have had a `Player` class even back then is up for discussion.

There are arguments both ways. It would have been nice design, so, yes, maybe we should. But having a class with only a single field and no methods that do anything of significance might have been regarded as overkill.

Sometimes there are gray areas such as this one, where either decision is defensible. But after adding our new fields, the situation is quite clear. There is now a strong argument for a **Player** class. It would store the fields and have methods such as **dropItem** and **pickUpItem** (which can include the weight check and might return false if we cannot carry it).

What we did when we introduced the **Player** class and moved the **currentRoom** field from **Game** into **Player** was refactoring. We have restructured the way we represent our data, to achieve a better design under changed requirements.

Programmers not as well trained as us (or just being lazy) might have left the **currentRoom** field where it was, seeing that the program worked as it was and there did not seem to be a great need to make this change. They would end up with a messy class design.

The effect of making the change can be seen if we think one step further ahead. Assume that we now want to extend the game to allow for multiple players. With our nice new design, this is suddenly very easy. We already have a **Player** class (the **Game** holds a **Player** object), and it is easy to create several **Player** objects and store in **Game** a collection of players instead of a single player. Each player object would hold its own current room, items, and maximum weight. Different players could even have different maximum weights, opening up the even wider concept of having players with quite different capabilities—their carrying capability being just one of many.

The lazy programmer who left **currentRoom** in the **Game** class, however, has a serious problem now. Because the entire game has only a single current room, current locations of multiple players cannot easily be stored. Bad design usually bites back to create more work for us in the end.

Doing good refactoring is as much about thinking in a certain mindset as it is about technical skills. While we make changes and extensions to applications, we should regularly question whether an original class design still represents the best solution. As the functionality changes, arguments for or against certain designs change. What was a good design for a simple application might not be good any more when some extensions are added.

Recognizing these changes and actually making the refactoring modifications to the source code usually saves a lot of time and effort in the end. The earlier we clean up our design, the more work we usually save.

We should be prepared to *factor out* methods (turn a sequence of statements from the body of an existing method into a new, independent method) and classes (take parts of a class and create a new class from it). Considering refactoring regularly keeps our class design clean and saves work in the end. Of course, one of the things that will actually mean that refactoring makes life harder in the long run is if we fail to adequately test the refactored version against the original. Whenever we embark on a major refactoring task, it is essential to ensure that we test well, before and after the change. Doing these tests manually (by creating and testing objects interactively) will get tedious very quickly. We shall investigate how we can improve our testing—by automating it—in the next chapter.

Exercise 8.28 Refactor your project to introduce a separate **Player** class. A **Player** object should store at least the current room of the player, but you may also like to store the player's name or other information.

Exercise 8.29 Implement an extension that allows a player to pick up one single item. This includes implementing two new commands: *take* and *drop*.

Exercise 8.30 Extend your implementation to allow the player to carry any number of items.

Exercise 8.31 Add a restriction that allows the player to carry items only up to a specified maximum weight. The maximum weight a player can carry is an attribute of the player.

Exercise 8.32 Implement an *items* command that prints out all items currently carried and their total weight.

Exercise 8.33 Add a *magic cookie* item to a room. Add an *eat cookie* command. If a player finds and eats the magic cookie, it increases the weight that the player can carry. (You might like to modify this slightly to better fit into your own game scenario.)

8.13 Refactoring for language independence

One feature of the *zuul* game that we have not commented on yet is that the user interface is closely tied to commands written in English. This assumption is embedded in both the **CommandWords** class, where the list of valid commands is stored, and the **Game** class, where the **processCommand** method explicitly compares each command word against a set of English words. If we wish to change the interface to allow users to use a different language, then we would have to find all the places in the source code where command words are used and change them. This is a further example of a form of implicit coupling, which we discussed in Section 8.9.

If we want to have language independence in the program, then ideally we should have just one place in the source code where the actual text of command words is stored and have everywhere else refer to commands in a language-independent way. A programming language feature that makes this possible is *enumerated types*, or *enums*. We will explore this feature of Java via the *zuul-with-enums* projects.

8.13.1 Enumerated types

Code 8.9 shows a Java enumerated type definition called **CommandWord**.

8.13 Refactoring for language independence

Code 8.9

An enumerated type for command words

```
/**
 * Representations for all the valid command words for the game.
 *
 * @author  Michael Kölling and David J. Barnes
 * @version 2016.02.29
 */
public enum CommandWord
{
    // A value for each command word, plus one for unrecognized commands.
    GO, QUIT, HELP, UNKNOWN
}
```

In its simplest form, an enumerated type definition consists of an outer wrapper that uses the word **enum** rather than **class**, and a body that is simply a list of variable names denoting the set of values that belong to this type. By convention, these variable names are fully capitalized. We never create objects of an enumerated type. In effect, each name within the type definition represents a unique instance of the type that has already been created for us to use. We refer to these instances as **CommandWord.GO**, **CommandWord.QUIT**, etc. Although the syntax for using them is similar, it is important to avoid thinking of these values as being like the numeric class constants we discussed in Section 6.14. Despite the simplicity of their definition, enumerated type values are proper objects, and are not the same as integers.

How can we use the **CommandWord** type to make a step toward decoupling the game logic of *zuul* from a particular natural language? One of the first improvements we can make is to the following series of tests in the **processCommand** method of **Game**:

```
if(command.isUnknown()) {
    System.out.println("I don't know what you mean...");
    return false;
}
String commandWord = command.getCommandWord();
if(commandWord.equals("help")) {
    printHelp();
}
else if(commandWord.equals("go")) {
    goRoom(command);
}
else if(commandWord.equals("quit")) {
    wantToQuit = quit(command);
}
```

If **commandWord** is made to be of type **CommandWord** rather than **String**, then this can be rewritten as:

```
if(commandWord == CommandWord.UNKNOWN) {
    System.out.println("I don't know what you mean...");
}
else if(commandWord == CommandWord.HELP) {
    printHelp();
}
```

```
        else if(commandWord == CommandWord.GO) {
            goRoom(command);
        }
        else if(commandWord == CommandWord.QUIT) {
            wantToQuit = quit(command);
        }
```

In fact, now that we changed the type to **CommandWord**, we could also use a *switch statement* instead of the series of if statements. This expresses the intent of this code segment a little more clearly.[2]

```
switch (commandWord) {
    case UNKNOWN:
        System.out.println("I don't know what you mean...");
        break;
    case HELP:
        printHelp();
        break;
    case GO:
        goRoom(command);
        break;
    case QUIT:
        wantToQuit = quit(command);
        break;
}
```

> **Concept**
>
> A **switch statement** selects a sequence of statements for execution from multiple different options.

The switch statement takes the variable in the parentheses following the `switch` keyword (**commandWord** in our case) and compares it to each of the values listed after the `case` keywords. When a case matches, the code following it is executed. The `break` statement causes the switch statement to abort at that point, and execution continues after the switch statement. For a fuller description of the switch statement, see Appendix D.

Now we just have to arrange for the user's typed commands to be mapped to the corresponding **CommandWord** values. Open the *zuul-with-enums-v1* project to see how we have done this. The most significant change can be found in the **CommandWords** class. Instead of using an array of strings to define the valid commands, we now use a map between strings and **CommandWord** objects:

```
public CommandWords()
{
    validCommands = new HashMap<>();
    validCommands.put("go", CommandWord.GO);
    validCommands.put("help", CommandWord.HELP);
    validCommands.put("quit", CommandWord.QUIT);
}
```

---

[2] In fact, string literals can also be used as case values in switch statements, in order to avoid a long sequence of if-else-if comparisons.

The command typed by a user can now easily be converted to its corresponding enumerated type value.

Exercise 8.34 Review the source code of the *zuul-with-enums-v1* project to see how it uses the **CommandWord** type. The classes **Command**, **CommandWords**, **Game**, and **Parser** have all been adapted from the *zuul-better* version to accommodate this change. Check that the program still works as you would expect.

Exercise 8.35 Add a *look* command to the game, along the lines described in Section 8.9.

Exercise 8.36 "Translate" the game to use different command words for the **GO** and **QUIT** commands. These could be from a real language or just made-up words. Do you only have to edit the **CommandWords** class to make this change work? What is the significance of this?

Exercise 8.37 Change the word associated with the HELP command and check that it works correctly. After you have made your changes, what do you notice about the welcome message that is printed when the game starts?

Exercise 8.38 In a new project, define your own enumerated type called **Direction** with values **NORTH**, **SOUTH**, **EAST**, and **WEST**.

8.13.2 Further decoupling of the command interface

The enumerated **CommandWord** type has allowed us to make a significant decoupling of the user interface language from the game logic, and it is almost completely possible to translate the commands into another language just by editing the **CommandWords** class. (At some stage, we should also translate the room descriptions and other output strings, probably by reading them from a file, but we shall leave this until later.) There is one further piece of decoupling of the command words that we would like to perform. Currently, whenever a new command is introduced into the game, we must add a new value to the **CommandWord**, and an association between that value and the user's text in the **CommandWords** classes. It would be helpful if we could make the **CommandWord** type self-contained—in effect, move the text–value association from **CommandWords** to **CommandWord**.

Java allows enumerated type definitions to contain much more than a list of the type's values. We will not explore this feature in much detail, but just give you a flavor of what is possible. Code 8.10 shows an enhanced **CommandWord** type that looks quite similar to an ordinary class definition. This can be found in the *zuul-with-enums-v2* project.

Code 8.10

Associating command strings with enumerated type values

```java
/**
 * Representations for all the valid command words for the game
 * along with a string in a particular language.
 * 
 * @author  Michael Kölling and David J. Barnes
 * @version 2016.02.29
 */
public enum CommandWord
{
    // A value for each command word along with its
    // corresponding user interface string.
    GO("go"), QUIT("quit"), HELP("help"), UNKNOWN("?");

    // The command string.
    private String commandString;

    /**
     * Initialize with the corresponding command string.
     * @param commandString The command string.
     */
    CommandWord(String commandString)
    {
        this.commandString = commandString;
    }

    /**
     * @return The command word as a string.
     */
    public String toString()
    {
        return commandString;
    }
}
```

The main points to note about this new version of **CommandWord** are that:

- Each type value is followed by a parameter value—in this case, the text of the command associated with that value.

- Unlike the version in Code 8.9, a semicolon is required at the end of the list of type values.

- The type definition includes a constructor. This does not have the word **public** in its header. Enumerated type constructors are never public, because we do not create the instances. The parameter associated with each type value is passed to this constructor.

- The type definition includes a field, **commandString**. The constructor stores the command string in this field.

- A **toString** method has been used to return the text associated with a particular type value.

With the text of the commands stored in the **CommandWord** type, the **CommandWords** class in *zuul-with-enums-v2* uses a different way to create its map between text and enumerated values:

```
validCommands = new HashMap<String, CommandWord>();
for(CommandWord command : CommandWord.values()) {
    if(command != CommandWord.UNKNOWN) {
        validCommands.put(command.toString(), command);
    }
}
```

Every enumerated type defines a **values** method that returns an array filled with the value objects from the type. The code above iterates over the array and calls the **toString** method to obtain the command **String** associated with each value.

Exercise 8.39 Add your own *look* command to *zuul-with-enums-v2*. Do you only need to change the **CommandWord** type?

Exercise 8.40 Change the word associated with the *help* command in **CommandWord**. Is this change automatically reflected in the welcome text when you start the game? Take a look at the **printWelcome** method in the **Game** class to see how this has been achieved.

8.14 Design guidelines

An often-heard piece of advice to beginners about writing good object-oriented programs is, "Don't put too much into a single method" or "Don't put everything into one class." Both suggestions have merit, but frequently lead to the counter-questions, "How long should a method be?" or "How long should a class be?"

After the discussion in this chapter, these questions can now be answered in terms of cohesion and coupling. A method is too long if it does more than one logical task. A class is too complex if it represents more than one logical entity.

You will notice that these answers do not give clear-cut rules that specify exactly what to do. Terms such as *one logical task* are still open to interpretation, and different programmers will decide differently in many situations.

These are *guidelines*—not cast-in-stone rules. Keeping these in mind, though, will significantly improve your class design and enable you to master more complex problems and write better and more interesting programs.

> It is important to understand the following exercises as suggestions, not as fixed specifications. This game has many possible ways in which it can be extended, and you are encouraged to invent your own extensions. You do not need to do all the exercises here to create an interesting game; you may want to do more,

or you may want to do different ones. Here are some suggestions to get you started.

Exercise 8.41 Add some form of time limit to your game. If a certain task is not completed in a specified time, the player loses. A time limit can easily be implemented by counting the number of moves or the number of entered commands. You do not need to use real time.

Exercise 8.42 Implement a trapdoor somewhere (or some other form of door that you can only cross one way).

Exercise 8.43 Add a *beamer* to the game. A beamer is a device that can be *charged* and *fired*. When you charge the beamer, it memorizes the current room. When you fire the beamer, it transports you immediately back to the room it was charged in. The beamer could either be standard equipment or an item that the player can find. Of course, you need commands to charge and fire the beamer.

Exercise 8.44 Add locked doors to your game. The player needs to find (or otherwise obtain) a key to open a door.

Exercise 8.45 Add a transporter room. Whenever the player enters this room, he/she is randomly transported into one of the other rooms. Note: Coming up with a good design for this task is not trivial. It might be interesting to discuss design alternatives for this with other students. (We discuss design alternatives for this task at the end of Chapter 11. The adventurous or advanced reader may want to skip ahead and have a look.)

8.15 Summary

In this chapter, we have discussed what are often called the *nonfunctional aspects* of an application. Here, the issue is not so much to get a program to perform a certain task, but to do this with well-designed classes.

Good class design can make a huge difference when an application needs to be corrected, modified, or extended. It also allows us to reuse parts of the application in other contexts (for example, for other projects) and thus creates benefits later.

There are two key concepts under which class design can be evaluated: coupling and cohesion. Coupling refers to the interconnectedness of classes, cohesion to modularization into appropriate units. Good design exhibits loose coupling and high cohesion.

One way to achieve a good structure is to follow a process of responsibility-driven design. Whenever we add a function to the application, we try to identify which class should be responsible for which part of the task.

When extending a program, we use regular refactoring to adapt the design to changing requirements and to ensure that classes and methods remain cohesive and loosely coupled.

Terms introduced in this chapter:

code duplication, coupling, cohesion, encapsulation, responsibility-driven design, implicit coupling, refactoring

Exercise 8.46 *Challenge exercise* In the **processCommand** method in **Game**, there is a switch statement (or a sequence of if statements) to dispatch commands when a command word is recognized. This is not a very good design, because every time we add a command, we have to add a case here. Can you improve this design? Design the classes so that handling of commands is more modular and new commands can be added more easily. Implement it. Test it.

Exercise 8.47 Add characters to the game. Characters are similar to items, but they can talk. They speak some text when you first meet them, and they may give you some help if you give them the right item.

Exercise 8.48 Add moving characters. These are like other characters, but every time the player types a command, these characters can move into an adjoining room.

Exercise 8.49 Add a class called `GameMain` to your project. Define just a `main` method within it and have them method create a `Game` object and call its `play` method.

CHAPTER 9

Well-Behaved Objects

Main concepts discussed in this chapter:

- testing
- debugging
- unit testing
- test automation

Java constructs introduced in this chapter:

(No new Java constructs are introduced in this chapter.)

9.1 Introduction

If you have followed the previous chapters in this book, and if you have implemented the exercises we have suggested, then you have written a good number of classes by now. One observation that you will likely have made is that a class you write is rarely perfect after the first attempt to write its source code. Usually, it does not work correctly at first, and more work is needed to complete it.

The problems you are dealing with will shift over time. Beginners typically struggle with Java *syntax errors*. Syntax errors are errors in the structure of the source code itself. They are easy to spot, because the compiler will highlight them and display some sort of error message.

More experienced programmers who tackle more complicated problems usually have less difficulty with the language syntax. They are more concerned with *logical errors* instead.

A logical error is a problem where the program compiles and executes without an obvious error, but delivers the wrong result. Logical problems are much more severe and harder to find than syntax errors. In fact, it is sometimes not easy to detect that there is an error in the first place.

Writing syntactically correct programs is relatively easy to learn, and good tools (such as compilers) exist to detect syntax errors and point them out. Writing logically correct programs, on the other hand, is very difficult for any nontrivial problem, and proof that a

> **Concept**
>
> **Testing** is the activity of finding out whether a piece of code (a method, class, or program) produces the intended behavior.

program is correct cannot, in general, be automated. It is so hard, in fact, that most software that is commercially sold is known to contain a significant number of bugs.

Thus, it is essential for a competent software engineer to learn how to deal with correctness, and how to reduce the number of errors in a class.

In this chapter, we shall discuss a variety of activities that are related to improving the correctness of a program. These include testing, debugging, and writing for maintainability.

Testing is an activity that is concerned with finding out whether a segment of code contains any errors. Testing well is not easy, and there is much to think about when testing a program.

Debugging comes after testing. If tests have shown that an error is present, we use debugging techniques to find out exactly where the error is and how to fix it. There can be a significant amount of work between knowing that an error exists, finding the cause, and fixing it.

> **Concept**
>
> **Debugging** is the attempt to pinpoint and fix the source of an error.

Writing for maintainability is maybe the most fundamental topic. It is about trying to write code in such a way that errors are avoided in the first place and, if they still slip in, that they can be found as easily as possible. Code style and commenting are part of it, as are the code quality principles that we have discussed in the previous chapter. Ideally, code should be easy to understand so that the original programmer avoids introducing errors and a maintenance programmer can easily find possible errors.

In practice, this is not always simple. But there are big differences between few and many errors, and also between the effort it takes to debug well-written code and not-so-well-written code.

9.2 Testing and debugging

Testing and debugging are crucial skills in software development. You will often need to check your programs for errors, then locate the source of those errors when they occur. In addition, you might also be responsible for testing other people's programs or modifying them. In the latter case, the debugging task is closely related to the process of understanding someone else's code, and there is a lot of overlap in the techniques you might use to do both. In the sections that follow, we shall investigate the following testing and debugging techniques:

- manual unit testing within BlueJ
- test automation
- manual walkthroughs
- print statements
- debuggers

We shall look at the first two testing techniques in the context of some classes that you might have written for yourself, and the remaining debugging techniques in the context of understanding someone else's source code.

9.3 Unit testing within BlueJ

Concept

unit testing refers to tests of the individual parts of an application, such as methods and classes.

The term *unit testing* refers to a test of the individual parts of an application, as opposed to *application testing*, which is testing of the complete application. The units being tested can be of various sizes. They may be a group of classes, a single class, or even a single method. It is worth observing that unit testing can be done long before an application is complete. Any single method, once written and compiled, can (and should) be tested.

Because BlueJ allows us to interact directly with individual objects, it offers unique ways to conduct testing on classes and methods. One of the points we want to stress in this section is that it is never too early to start testing. There are several benefits in early experimentation and testing. First, they give us valuable experience with a system; this can make it possible to spot problems early enough to fix them at a much lower cost than if they had not been uncovered until much later in the development. Second, we can start building up a series of test cases and results that can be used over and over again as the system grows. Each time we make a change to the system, these test cases allow us to check that we have not inadvertently introduced errors into the rest of the system as a result of the changes.

In order to illustrate this form of testing within BlueJ, we shall use the *online-shop* project, which represents an early stage in the development of software for an online sales shop (such as Amazon.com). Our project contains only a very small part of this application, namely the part that deals with customer comments for sales items.

Open the *online-shop* project. Currently, it contains only two classes: **SalesItem** and **Comment**. The intended functionality of this part of the application—concentrating solely on handling customer comments—is as follows:

- Sales items can be created with a description and price.
- Customer comments can be added to and removed from sales items.
- Comments include a comment text, an author's name, and a rating. The rating is in the range of 1 to 5 (inclusive).
- Each person may leave only one comment. Subsequent attempts to leave a comment by the same author are rejected.
- The user interface (not implemented in this project yet) will include a question asking, "Was this comment helpful to you?" with Yes and No buttons. A user clicking Yes or No is known as *upvoting* or *downvoting* the comment. The balance of up and down votes is kept for comments, so that the most useful comments (the ones with the highest vote balance) can be displayed at the top.

The **Comment** class in our project stores information about a single comment. For our testing, we shall concentrate on the **SalesItem** class, shown in Code 9.1. Objects of this class represent a single sales item, including all comments left for this item.

As part of our testing, we should check several parts of the intended functionality, including:

- Can comments be added and removed from a sales item?
- Does the **showInfo** method correctly show all the information stored about a sales item?

- Are the constraints (ratings must be 1 to 5, only one comment per person) enforced correctly?
- Can we correctly find the most helpful comment (the one with the most votes)?

We shall find that all of these can be tested conveniently using the object bench within BlueJ. In addition, we shall see that the interactive nature of BlueJ makes it possible to simplify some of the testing by making controlled alterations to a class under test.

Code 9.1

The `SalesItem` class

```java
import java.util.ArrayList;
import java.util.Iterator;

/**
 * The class represents sales items on an online e-commerce site (such as
 * Amazon.com). SalesItem objects store all information relevant to this item,
 * including description, price, customer comments, etc.
 *
 * NOTE: The current version is incomplete! Currently, only code dealing with
 * customer comments is here.
 *
 * @author Michael Kölling and David J. Barnes
 * @version 0.1 (2016.02.29)
 */
public class SalesItem
{
    private String name;
    private int price;   // in cents
    private ArrayList<Comment> comments;

    /**
     * Create a new sales item.
     */
    public SalesItem(String name, int price)
    {
        this.name = name;
        this.price = price;
        comments = new ArrayList<>();
    }

    /**
     * Return the name of this item.
     */
    public String getName()
    {
        return name;
    }

    /**
     * Return the price of this item.
     */
    public int getPrice()
    {
        return price;
    }
```

Code 9.1 continued

The `SalesItem` class

```java
/**
 * Return the number of customer comments for this item.
 */
public int getNumberOfComments()
{
    return comments.size();
}

/**
 * Add a comment to the comment list of this sales item. Return true if
 * successful; false if the comment was rejected.
 *
 * The comment will be rejected if the same author has already left a
 * comment, or if the rating is invalid. Valid ratings are numbers between
 * 1 and 5 (inclusive).
 */
public boolean addComment(String author, String text, int rating)
{
    if(ratingInvalid(rating)) {   // reject invalid ratings
        return false;
    }

    if(findCommentByAuthor(author) != null) {
        // reject mutiple comments by same author
        return false;
    }

    comments.add(new Comment(author, text, rating));
    return true;
}

/**
 * Remove the comment stored at the index given. If the index is invalid,
 * do nothing.
 */
public void removeComment(int index)
{
    if(index >=0 && index < comments.size()) {  // if index is valid
        comments.remove(index);
    }
}

/**
 * Upvote the comment at "index." That is: count this comment as more
 * helpful. If the index is invalid, do nothing.
 */
public void upvoteComment(int index)
{
    if(index >=0 && index < comments.size()) {  // if index is valid
        comments.get(index).upvote();
    }
}
```

Code 9.1 continued

The `SalesItem` class

```java
/**
 * Downvote the comment at "index." That is: count this comment as less
 * helpful. If the index is invalid, do nothing.
 */
public void downvoteComment(int index)
{
    if(index >=0 && index < comments.size()) { // if index is valid
        comments.get(index).downvote();
    }
}

/**
 * Show all comments on screen. (Currently, for testing purposes: print
 * to the terminal. Modify later for web display.)
 */
public void showInfo()
{
    System.out.println("*** " + name + " ***");
    System.out.println("Price: " + priceString(price));
    System.out.println();
    System.out.println("Customer comments:");
    for(Comment comment : comments) {
        System.out.println("-----------------------------------------");
        System.out.println(comment.getFullDetails());
    }
    System.out.println();
    System.out.println("=========================================");
}

/**
 * Return the most helpful comment. The most useful comment is the one
 * with the highest vote balance. If there are multiple comments with
 * equal highest balance, return any one of them.
 */
public Comment findMostHelpfulComment()
{
    Iterator<Comment> it = comments.iterator();
    Comment best = it.next();
    while(it.hasNext()) {
        Comment current = it.next();
        if(current.getVoteCount() > best.getVoteCount() {
            best = current;
        }
    }
    return best;
}

/**
 * Check whether the given rating is invalid. Return true if it is
 * invalid. Valid ratings are in the range [1..5].
 */
private boolean ratingInvalid(int rating)
{
    return rating < 0 || rating > 5;
}
```

Code 9.1 continued

The `SalesItem` class

```java
/**
 * Find the comment by the author with the given name.
 *
 * @return The comment if it exists; null if it doesn't.
 */
private Comment findCommentByAuthor(String author)
{
    for(Comment comment : comments) {
        if(comment.getAuthor().equals(author)) {
            return comment;
        }
    }
    return null;
}

/**
 * For a price given as an int, return a readable String representing the
 * same price. The price is given in whole cents. For example for
 * price==12345, the following String is returned: $123.45
 */
private String priceString(int price)
{
    int dollars = price / 100;
    int cents = price - (dollars*100);
    if(cents <= 9) {
        return "$" + dollars + ".0" + cents;   // zero padding
    }
    else {
        return "$" + dollars + "." + cents;
    }
}
```

9.3.1 Using inspectors

When testing interactively, using object inspectors is often very helpful. In preparation for our testing, create a `SalesItem` object on the object bench and open its inspector by selecting the *Inspect* function from the object's menu. Select the **comments** field and open its inspector as well (Figure 9.1). Check that the list has been created (is not null) and is initially of size 0. Check also that the size grows as you add comments. Leave the comment-list inspector open to assist with subsequent tests.

An essential component of testing classes that use data structures is checking that they behave properly both when the data structures are empty and—if appropriate—when they are full. Testing for full data structures only applies to those that have a fixed limit, such as arrays. In our case, where we use an `ArrayList`, testing for the list being full does not apply, because the list expands as needed. However, making tests with an empty list is important, as this is a special case that needs special treatment.

A first test that can be performed on `SalesItem` is to call its `showInfo` method before any comments have been added. This should correctly show the item's description and price, and no comments.

Figure 9.1
Inspector for the **comments** list

A key feature of good testing is to ensure that *boundaries* are checked, because these are often the points at which things go wrong. The boundaries associated with the **SalesItem** class are, for example, the empty comment list. Boundaries set for the **Comment** class include the restriction of the rating to the range 1 to 5. Ratings at the top and bottom of this range are boundary cases. It will be important to check not only ratings in the middle of this range, but also the maximum and minimum possible rating.

In order to conduct tests along these lines, create a **SalesItem** object on the object bench and try the following as initial tests of the comment functionality. If you perform these tests carefully, they should uncover two errors in our code.

Exercise 9.1 Add several comments to the sales item while keeping an eye on the inspector for the comments list. Make sure the list behaves as expected (that is, its size should increase). You may also like to inspect the *elementData* field of the ArrayList object.

Exercise 9.2 Check that the **showInfo** method correctly prints the item information, including the comments. Try this both for items with and without comments.

Exercise 9.3 Check that the **getNumberOfComments** method works as expected.

Exercise 9.4 Now check that duplicate authors are correctly handled—i.e., that further comments by the same author are rejected. When trying to add a comment with an author name for whom a comment already exists, the **addComment** method should return **false**. Check also that the comment was not added to the list.

Exercise 9.5 Perform boundary checking on the rating value. That is, create comments not only with medium ratings, but also with top and bottom ratings. Does this work correctly?

Exercise 9.6 Good boundary testing also involves testing values that lie just beyond the valid range of data. Test 0 and 6 as rating values. In both cases, the comment should be rejected (`addComment` should return `false`, and the comment should not be added to the comment list).

Exercise 9.7 Test the `upvoteComment` and `downvoteComment` methods. Make sure that the vote balance is correctly counted.

Exercise 9.8 Use the `upvoteComment` and `downvoteComment` methods to mark some comments as more or less helpful. Then test the `findMostHelpfulComment` method. This method should return the comment that was voted most helpful. You will notice that the method returns an object reference. You can use the *Inspect* function in the method result dialog to check whether the correct comment was returned. Of course, you will need to know which is the correct comment in order to check whether you get the right result.

Exercise 9.9 Do boundary testing of the `findMostHelpfulComment` method. That is, call this method when the comments list is empty (no comments have been added). Does this work as expected?

Exercise 9.10 The tests in the exercises above should have uncovered two bugs in our code. Fix them. After fixing these errors, is it safe to assume that all previous tests will still work as before? Section 9.4 will discuss some of the testing issues that arise when software is corrected or enhanced.

From these exercises, it is easy to see how valuable interactive method invocations and inspectors are in giving immediate feedback on the state of an object, often avoiding the need to add print statements to a class when testing or debugging it.

9.3.2 Positive versus negative testing

> **Concept**
>
> **Positive testing** is the testing of cases that are expected to succeed.

When deciding about what to test, we generally distinguish *positive* and *negative* test cases. Positive testing is the testing of functionality that we expect to work. For example, adding a comment by a new author with a valid rating is a positive test. When testing positive test cases, we have to convince ourselves that the code did indeed work as expected.

Negative testing is the test of cases that we expect to fail. Using an invalid rating, or attempting to store a second comment from the same author, are both negative tests. When testing negative cases, we expect the program to handle this error in some specified, controlled way.

> **Pitfall** It is a very common error for inexperienced testers to conduct only positive tests. Negative tests—testing that what should go wrong indeed does go wrong, and does so in a well-defined manner—are crucial for a good test procedure.

> **Concept**
> **Negative testing** is the testing of cases that are expected to fail.

Exercise 9.11 Which of the test cases mentioned in the previous exercises are positive tests and which are negative? Make a table of each category. Can you think of further positive tests? Can you think of further negative ones?

9.4 Test automation

> **Concept**
> **test automation** simplifies the process of regression testing.

One reason why thorough testing is often neglected is that it is both a time-consuming and a relatively boring activity, if done manually. You will have noticed, if you did all exercises in the previous section, that testing thoroughly can become tedious very quickly. This particularly becomes an issue when tests have to be run not just once but possibly hundreds or thousands of times. Fortunately, there are techniques available that allow us to automate repetitive testing, and so remove much of the drudgery associated with it. The next section looks at test automation in the context of *regression testing*.

9.4.1 Regression testing

It would be nice if we could assume that correcting errors only ever improves the quality of a program. Sadly, experience shows that it is all too easy to introduce further errors when modifying software. Thus, fixing an error at one spot may introduce another error at the same time.

As a consequence, it is desirable to run *regression tests* whenever a change is made to software. Regression testing involves rerunning tests that have previously passed, to ensure that the new version still passes them. It is much more likely to be performed if it can be automated. One of the easiest ways to automate regression tests is to write a program that acts as a *test rig*, or *test harness*.

9.4.2 Automated testing using JUnit

Support for regression testing is integrated in BlueJ (and many other development environments) using a testing system called JUnit. JUnit is a testing framework devised by Erich Gamma and Kent Beck for the Java language, and similar systems are now available for many other programming languages.

> **JUnit** JUnit is a popular testing framework to support organized unit testing and regression testing in Java. It is available independent of specific development environments, as well as integrated in many environments. JUnit was developed by Erich Gamma and Kent Beck. You can find the software and a lot of information about it at `http://www.junit.org`.

Figure 9.2
A project with a test class

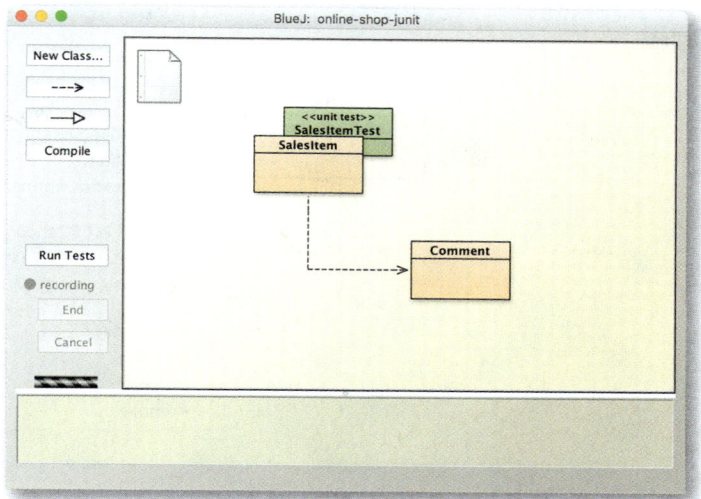

To start investigating regression testing with our example, open the *online-shop-junit* project. This project contains the same classes as the previous one, plus an additional class, `SalesItemTest`.

`SalesItemTest` is a test class. The first thing to note is that its appearance is different from what we have seen previously (Figure 9.2). It is annotated as a `<<unit test>>`, its color is different from that of the ordinary classes in the diagram, and it is attached to the `SalesItem` class (it will be moved with this class if `SalesItem` is moved in the diagram).

You will note that Figure 9.2 also shows some additional controls in the main window, below the *Compile* button. These allow you to use the built-in regression testing tools. If you have not used JUnit in BlueJ before, the testing tools are switched off, and the buttons will not yet be visible on your system. You should switch on these testing tools now. To do this, open the *Interface* tab in your *Preferences* dialog, and ensure that the *Show unit testing tools* option is selected.

A further difference is apparent in the menu that appears when we right-click the test class (Figure 9.3). There are three new sections in the menu instead of a list of constructors.

Using test classes, we can automate regression testing. The test class contains code to perform a number of prepared tests and check their results. This makes repeating the same tests much easier.

A test class is usually associated with an ordinary project class. In this case, `SalesItemTest` is associated with the `SalesItem` class, and we say that `SalesItem` is the *reference class* for `SalesItemTest`.

In our project, the test class has already been created, and it already contains some tests. We can now execute these tests by clicking the *Run Tests* button.

Figure 9.3

The pop-up menu for a test class

> **Exercise 9.12** Run the tests in your project, using the *Run Tests* button. You should see a window similar to Figure 9.4, summarizing the results of the tests.

Figure 9.4 shows the result of running three tests named **testAddComment**, **testInit**, and **testIllegalRating**, which are defined in the test class. The ticks immediately to the left of the test names indicate that the tests succeeded. You can achieve the same result by selecting the *Test All* option from the pop-up menu associated with the test class, or running the tests individually by selecting them from the same menu.

Figure 9.4

The Test Results window

Test classes are clearly different in some way from ordinary classes, and if you open the source code of **SalesItemTest**, you will notice that it has some new features. At this stage of the book, we are not going to discuss in detail how test classes work internally, but it is worth noting that although the source code of **SalesItemTest** could have been written by a person, it was, in fact, *automatically generated* by BlueJ. Some of the comments were then added afterwards to document the purpose of the tests.

Each test class typically contains tests for the functionality of its reference class. It is created by using the right mouse button over a potential reference class and selecting *Create Test Class* from the pop-up menu. Note that **SalesItem** already has a test class, so this additional menu item does not appear in its class menu, but the one for **Comment** does have this option, as it currently has no associated test class.

The test class contains source code both to run tests on a reference class and to check whether the tests were successful or not. For instance, here is one of the statements from **testInit** that checks that the price of the item is 1000 at that point:

```
assertEquals(1000, salesIte1.getPrice());
```

When such tests are run, BlueJ is able to display the results in the window shown in Figure 9.4.

In the next section, we shall discuss how BlueJ supports creation of tests so that you can create your own automated tests.

Exercise 9.13 Create a test class for the **Comment** class in the *online-shop-junit* project.

Exercise 9.14 What methods are created automatically when a new test class is created?

9.4.3 Recording a test

As we discussed at the beginning of Section 9.4, test automation is desirable because manually running and re-running tests is a time-consuming process. BlueJ makes it possible to combine the effectiveness of manual unit testing with the power of test automation, by enabling us to record manual tests, then replay them later for the purposes of regression testing. The **SalesItemTest** class was created via this process.

Suppose that we wanted to thoroughly test the **addComment** method of the **SalesItem** class. This method, as we have seen, adds customer comments if they are valid. There are several tests we would like to make, such as:

- adding a first comment to an empty comment list (positive)
- adding further comments when other comments already exist (positive)
- attempting to add a comment with an author who has already submitted a comment (negative)
- attempting to add a comment with an invalid rating (negative)

The first of these already exists in the `SalesItemTest` class. We will now describe how to create the next one using the *online-shop-junit* project.

A test is recorded by telling BlueJ to start recording, performing the test manually, and then signaling the end of the test. The first step is done via the menu attached to a test class. This tells BlueJ which class you wish the new test to be stored in. Select *Create Test Method . . .* from the `SalesItemTest` class's pop-up menu. You will be prompted for a name for the test method. By convention, we start the name with the prefix "test." For example, to create a method that tests adding two comments, we might call that method `testTwoComments`.[1]

> **Concept**
>
> An **assertion** is an expression that states a condition that we expect to be true. If the condition is false, we say that the assertion fails. This indicates an error in our program.

Once you have entered a name and clicked *OK,* a red recording indicator appears to the left of the class diagram, and the *End* and *Cancel* buttons become available. *End* is used to indicate the end of the test-creation process and *Cancel* to abandon it.

Once recording is started, we just carry out the actions that we would with a normal manual test:

- Create a `SalesItem` object.
- Add a comment to the sales item.

Once `addComment` has been called, a new dialog window will appear (Figure 9.5). This is an extended version of the normal method result window, and it is a crucial part of the automated testing process. Its purpose is to allow you to specify what the result of the method call *should be.* This is called an *assertion*.

Figure 9.5
The Method Result dialog with assertion facility

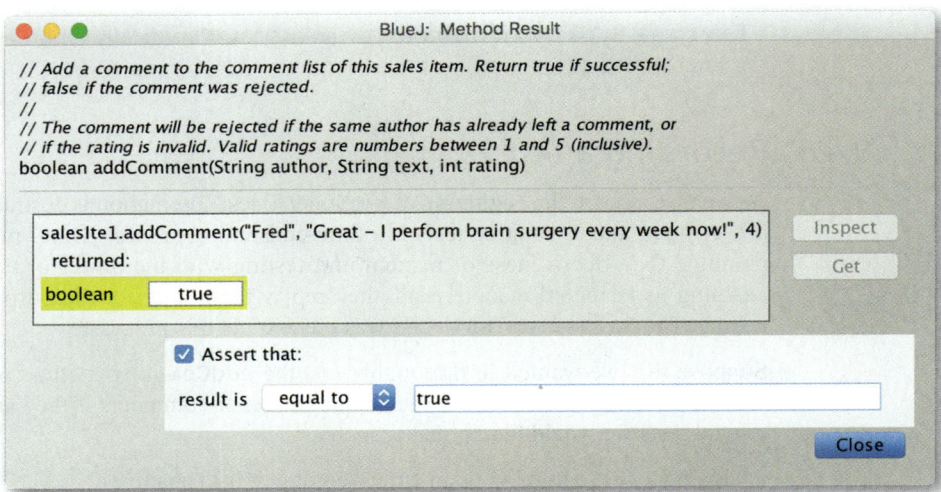

---

[1] Earlier versions of JUnit, up to version 3, required the method names to start with the prefix "test." This is not a requirement anymore in current versions.

In this case, we expect the method return value to be *true*, and we want to include a check in our test to make sure that this is really the case. We can now make sure that the *Assert that* checkbox is checked, enter *true* in the dialog, and select the *Close* button.

- Add a second comment to your sales item. Make sure the comments are valid (they have unique authors and the rating is valid). Assert that the result is true for the second comment addition as well.

- We now expect two comments to exist. To test that this is indeed the case, call the `getNumberOfComments` method and assert that the result is 2.

This is the final stage of the test. We then press the *End* button to stop the recording. At that point, BlueJ adds source code to the `SalesItemTest` class for our new method, `testTwoComments`, then compiles the class and clears the object bench. The resulting generated method is shown in Code 9.2.

Code 9.2
An automatically generated test method

```java
@Test
public void testTwoComments()
{
    SalesItem salesIte1 = new SalesItem("Java book", 12345);
    assertEquals(true, salesIte1.addComment("James Duckling",
                                            "Great book!", 4));
    assertEquals(true, salesIte1.addComment("Fred", "Like it", 3));
    assertEquals(2, salesIte1.getNumberOfComments());
}
```

As can be seen, the method contains statements that reproduce the actions made when recording it: a `SalesItem` object is created, and the `addComment` and `getNumberOfComments` methods are called. The call to `assertEquals` checks that the result returned by these methods matches the expected value. You can also see a new construct, `@Test`, before the method. This is an *annotation* that identifies this method as a test method.

The exercises below are provided so that you can try this process for yourself. They include an example to show what happens if the actual value does not match the expected value.

Exercise 9.15 Create a test to check that `addComment` returns `false` when a comment from the same author already exists.

Exercise 9.16 Create a test that performs negative testing on the boundaries of the rating range. That is, test the values 0 and 6 as a rating (the values just outside the legal range). We expect these to return `false`, so assert `false` in the result dialog. You will notice that one of these actually (incorrectly) returns `true`. This is the bug we uncovered earlier in manual testing. Make sure that you assert `false` anyway. The assertion states the *expected* result, not the *actual* result.

Exercise 9.17 Run all tests again. Explore how the *Test Result* dialog displays the failed test. Select the failed test in the list. What options do you have available to explore the details of the failed test?

Exercise 9.18 Create a test class that has **Comment** as its reference class. Create a test that checks whether the author and rating details are stored correctly after creation. Record separate tests that check whether the **upvote** and **downvote** methods work as expected.

Exercise 9.19 Create tests for **SalesItem** that test whether the **findMostHelpfulComment** method works as expected. Note that this method returns a **Comment** object. During your testing, you can use the *Get* button in the method result dialog to get the result object onto the object bench, which then allows you to make further method calls and add assertions for this object. This allows you to identify the comment object returned (e.g., by checking its author). You can also assert that the result is *null* or *not null*, depending on what you expect.

9.4.4 Fixtures

> **Concept**
>
> A **fixture** is a set of objects in a defined state that serves as a basis for unit tests.

As a set of test methods is built up, it is common to find yourself creating similar objects for each one. For instance, every test of the **SalesItem** class will involve creating at least one **SalesItem** and initializing it, often by adding one or more comments. An object or a group of objects that is used in more than one test is known as a *fixture*. Two menu items associated with a test class enable us to work with fixtures in BlueJ: *Object Bench to Test Fixture* and *Test Fixture to Object Bench*. In your project, create two **SalesItem** objects on the object bench. Leave one without any comments, and add two comments to the other. Now select *Object Bench to Test Fixture* from **SalesItemTest**. The objects will disappear from the object bench, and if you examine the source code of **SalesItemTest**, you will see that its **setUp** method looks something like Code 9.3, where **salesItem1** and **salesItem2** have been defined as fields.

Code 9.3
Creating a fixture

```java
/**
 * Sets up the test fixture.
 *
 * Called before every test case method.
 */
@Before
public void setUp()
{
    salesItem1 = new SalesItem("Java book", 12345);
    salesItem2 = new SalesItem("Harry Potter", 1250);
    salesItem2.addComment("Fred", "Best book ever", 5);
}
```

The significance of the `setUp` method is that it is automatically called immediately before every test method is called. (The `@Before` annotation above the method header ensures this.) This means that the individual test methods no longer need to create their own versions of the fixture objects.

Once we have a fixture associated with a test class, recording tests becomes significantly simpler. Whenever we create a new test method, the objects from the fixture will automatically appear on the object bench—there is no longer a need to create new test objects manually each time.

Should we wish to add further objects to the fixture at any time, one of the easiest ways is to select *Test Fixture to Object Bench*, add further objects to the object bench in the usual way, then select *Object Bench to Test Fixture*. We could also edit the `setUp` method in the editor and add further fields directly to the test class.

Test automation is a powerful concept because it makes it more likely that tests will be written in the first place, and more likely that they will be run and rerun as a program develops. You should try to get into the habit of starting to write unit tests early in the development of a project, and of keeping them up to date as the project progresses. In Chapter 14, we shall return to the subject of assertions in the context of error handling.

Exercise 9.20 Add further automated tests to your project until you reach a point where you are reasonably confident of the correct operation of the classes. Use both positive and negative tests. If you discover any errors, be sure to record tests that guard against recurrence of these errors in later versions.

In Section 9.6, we look at debugging—the activity that starts when we have noticed the existence of an error and we need to find and fix it.

9.5 Refactoring to use streams (advanced)

In previous advanced sections of this book, we have introduced streams as an alternative to loops when processing collections. The *online-shop* project provides an opportunity for another exercise in rewriting traditional loops using streams. If you have worked through the previous advanced exercises, you may also like to do this one.

Exercise 9.21 Rewrite all loops in the `SalesItem` class using streams. When you are finished, this class should not contain any explicit loop anymore. Once you are finished, rerun your tests to convince yourself that your rewriting of the code has not broken any of the intended functionality.

9.6 Debugging

Testing is important, and testing well helps uncover the existence of errors. However, testing alone is not enough. After detecting the existence of an error, we also have to find its cause and fix it. That's where debugging comes in.

To discuss various approaches to debugging, we use a hypothetical scenario. Imagine that you have been asked to join an existing project team that is working on an implementation of a software calculator (Figure 9.6). You have been drafted in because a key member of the programming team, Hacker T. Largebrain, has just been promoted to a management position on another project. Before leaving, Hacker assured the team you are joining that his implementation of the part of the calculator he was responsible for was finished and fully tested. He had even written some test software to verify that this was the case. You have been asked to take over the class and ensure that it is properly commented prior to integration with the classes being written by other members of the team.

The software for the calculator has been carefully designed to separate the user interface from the calculator logic, so that the calculator might be used in different contexts later on. The first version, which we are looking at here, will run with a graphical user interface, as shown in Figure 9.6. However, in later extensions to the project, it is intended that the same calculator implementation should be able to run in a web browser or on a mobile device. In preparation for this, the application has been split into separate classes, most importantly `UserInterface`, to implement the graphical user interface, and `CalcEngine`, to implement the calculation logic. It is the latter class for which Hacker was responsible. This class should remain unchanged when the calculator runs with a different user interface.

To investigate how the `CalcEngine` class is used by other classes, it is useful to look at its *interface*. Confusingly, we are now not talking about the *user interface*, but about the *class interface*. This double meaning of the term *interface* is unfortunate, but it is important to understand both meanings.

Figure 9.6
The user interface of a software calculator

The class interface is the summary of the public-method headers that other classes can use. It is what other classes can see and how they can interact with our class. The interface is shown in the `javadoc` documentation of a class and in the *Documentation* view in the editor. Code 9.4 shows the interface of the `CalcEngine` class.

Code 9.4
The interface of the arithmetic logic unit

```java
/**
 * @return The value currently displayed on the calculator.
 */
public int getDisplayValue();

/**
 * A number button was pressed.
 * @param number The single digit.
 */
public void numberPressed(int number);

/**
 * The '+' button was pressed.
 */
public void plus();

/**
 * The '-' button was pressed.
 */
public void minus();

/**
 * The '=' button was pressed.
 */
public void equals();

/**
 * The 'C' (clear) button was pressed.
 */
public void clear();
```

Such an interface can be written before the full classes are implemented. It represents a simple form of contract between the `CalcEngine` class and other parts of the program that wish to use it. The `CalcEngine` class provides the implementation of this interface. The interface describes a minimum set of methods that will be implemented in the logic component, and for each method the return type and parameters are fully defined. Note that the interface gives no details of exactly what its implementing class will do internally when notified that a plus operator has been pressed; that is left to its implementers. In addition, the implementing class might well have additional methods not listed here.

In the sections that follow, we shall look at Hacker's attempt to implement this interface. In this case, we decide that the best way to understand Hacker's software prior to documenting it is to explore its source and the behavior of its objects.

9.7 Commenting and style

Open the *calculator-engine* project to view the classes. This is Hacker's own version of the project, containing only the calculator engine and a test class, but not the user interface class. The `CalcEngineTester` class takes the place of the user interface at this stage of development. This illustrates another positive feature of defining interfaces between classes: it becomes easier to develop mock-ups of the other classes for the purpose of testing.

If you take a look at the `CalcEngine` class, you will find that its author has paid attention to some important areas of good style:

- The class has been given a multiline comment at the top, indicating the purpose of the class. Also included are annotations indicating author and version number.
- Each method of the interface has a comment indicating its purpose, parameters, and return type. This will certainly make it easier to generate project documentation for the interface, as discussed in Chapter 6.
- The layout of the class is consistent, with appropriate amounts of white-space indentation used to indicate the distinct levels of nested blocks and control structures.
- Expressive variable names and method names have been chosen.

Although these conventions may seem time-consuming during implementation, they can be of enormous benefit in helping someone else to understand your code (as we have to in this scenario), or in helping you to remember what a class does if you have taken a break from working on it.

We also note another detail that looks less promising: Hacker has not used a specialized unit test class to capture his tests, but has written his own test class. As we know about unit test support in BlueJ, we wonder why.

This does not necessarily have to be bad. Handwritten test classes may be just as good, but it makes us a little suspicious. Did Hacker really know what he was doing? We shall come back to this point a bit later.

So, maybe Hacker's abilities are as great as he thinks they are, and in that case you will not have much to do to make the class ready for integration with the others! Try the following exercises to see if this is the case.

> **Exercise 9.22** Make sure the classes in the project are compiled, and then create a `CalcEngineTester` object within BlueJ. Call the `testAll` method. What is printed in the terminal window? Do you believe the final line of what it says?
>
> **Exercise 9.23** Using the object you created in the previous exercise, call the `testPlus` method. What result does it give? Is that the same result as was printed by the call to `testAll`? Call `testPlus` one more time. What result does it give now? Should it always give the same answer? If so, what should that answer be? Take a look at the source of the `testPlus` method to check.

Exercise 9.24 Repeat the previous exercise with the `testMinus` method. Does it always give the same result?

The experiments above should have alerted you to the fact that not all seems to be right with the `CalcEngine` class. It looks like it contains some errors. But what are they, and how can we find them? In the sections that follow, we shall consider a number of different ways in which we can try to locate where errors are occurring in a class.

9.8 Manual walkthroughs

Manual walkthroughs are a relatively underused technique, perhaps because they are a particularly "low-tech" debugging and testing technique. However, do not let this fool you into thinking that they are not useful. A manual walkthrough involves printing copies of the classes you are trying to understand or debug, then getting away from your computer! It is all too easy to spend a lot of time sitting in front of a computer screen not making much progress in trying to deal with a programming problem. Relocating and refocusing your efforts can often free your mind to attack a problem from a completely different direction. We have often found that going off to lunch or cycling home from the office brings enlightenment that has otherwise eluded us through hours of slogging away at the keyboard.

> **Concept**
>
> A **walkthrough** is an activity of working through a segment of code line by line while observing changes of state and other behavior of the application.

A walkthrough involves both reading classes and tracing the flow of control between classes and objects. This helps us understand both how objects interact with one another and how they behave internally. In effect, a walkthrough is a pencil-and-paper simulation of what happens inside the computer when you run a program. In practice, it is best to focus on a narrow portion of an application, such as a single logical grouping of actions or even a single method call.

9.8.1 A high-level walkthrough

We shall illustrate the walkthrough technique with the *calculator-engine* project. You might find it useful to print out copies of the `CalcEngine` and `CalcEngineTester` classes in order to follow through the steps of this technique.

We shall start by examining the `testPlus` method of the `CalcEngineTester` class, as it contains a single logical grouping of actions that should help us gain an understanding of how several methods of the `CalcEngine` class work together to fulfill the computation role of a calculator. As we work our way through it, we shall often make penciled notes of questions that arise in our minds.

1. For this first stage, we do not want to delve into too much detail. We simply want to look at how the `testPlus` method uses an engine object, without exploring the internal details of the engine. From earlier experimentation, it would appear that there are some errors to be found, but we do not know whether the errors are in the tester or the engine. So the first step is to check that the tester appears to be using the engine appropriately.

2. We note that the first statement of **testPlus** assumes that the **engine** field already refers to a valid object:

    ```
    engine.clear();
    ```

    We can verify that this is the case by checking the tester's constructor. It is a common error for an object's fields not to have been initialized properly, either in their declarations or in a constructor. If we attempt to use a field with no associated object, then a **NullPointerException** is a likely runtime error.

3. The first statement's call to **clear** appears to be an attempt to put the calculator engine into a valid starting state, ready to receive instructions to perform a calculation. This looks like a reasonable thing to do, equivalent to pressing a "reset" or "clear" key on a real calculator. At this stage, we do not look at the engine class to check exactly what the **clear** method does. That can wait until we have achieved a level of confidence that the tester's actions are reasonable. Instead, we simply make a penciled note to check that **clear** puts the engine into a valid starting state as expected.

4. The next statement in **testPlus** is the entry of a digit via the **numberPressed** method:

    ```
    engine.numberPressed(3);
    ```

    This is reasonable, as the first step in making a calculation is to enter the first operand. Once again, we do not look to see what the engine does with the number. We simply assume that it stores it somewhere for later use in the calculation.

5. The next statement calls **plus**, so we now know that the full value of the left operand is 3. We make a penciled note of this fact on the printout, or make a tick against this assertion in one of the comments of **testPlus**. Similarly, we should note or confirm that the operation being executed is addition. This seems like a trivial thing to do, but it is very easy for a class's comments to get out of step with the code they are supposed to document. So checking the comments at the same time as we read the code can help us avoid being misled by them later.

6. Next, another single digit is entered as the right operand by a further call to **numberPressed**.

7. Completion of the addition is requested by a call to the **equals** method. We make a penciled note that, from the way it has been used in **testPlus**, the **equals** method appears not to return the expected result of the calculation. This is something else that we can check when we look at **CalcEngine**.

8. The final statement of **testPlus** obtains the value that should appear in the calculator's display:

    ```
    return engine.getDisplayValue();
    ```

    Presumably, this is the result of the addition, but we cannot know that for sure without looking in detail at **CalcEngine**. Once again, we make a note to check that this is indeed the case.

With our examination of **testPlus** completed, we have gained a reasonable degree of confidence that it uses the engine appropriately: that is, simulating a recognizable sequence of key presses to complete a simple calculation. We might remark that the method is not particularly ambitious—both operands are single-digit numbers, and only a single operator is used. However, that is not unusual in test methods, because it is important to test for the most basic functionality before testing more complex combinations. Nevertheless, some more complex tests should be added to the tester at some stage.

> **Exercise 9.25** Perform a similar walkthrough of your own with the **testMinus** method. Does that raise any further questions in your mind about things you might like to check when looking at **CalcEngine** in detail?

Before looking at the **CalcEngine** class, it is worth walking through the **testAll** method to see how it uses the **testPlus** and **testMinus** methods we have been looking at. From this, we observe the following:

1 The **testAll** method is a straight-line sequence of print statements.

2 It contains one call to each of **testPlus** and **testMinus**, and the values they return are printed out for the user to see. We might note that there is nothing to tell the user what the results should be. This makes it hard for the user to confirm that the results are correct.

3 The final statement boldly states:

> **All tests passed.**

but the method contains no tests to establish the truth of this assertion! There should be a proper means of establishing both what the result values should be, and whether they have been calculated correctly or not. This is something we should remedy as soon as we have the chance to get back to the source of this class.

At this stage, we should not be distracted by the final point into making changes that do not directly address the errors we are looking for. If we make those sorts of changes, we could easily end up masking the errors. One of the crucial requirements for successful debugging is to be able to trigger the error you are looking for easily and reproducibly. When that is the case, it is much easier to assess the effect of an attempted correction.

Having checked over the test class, we are in a position to examine the source of the **CalcEngine** class. We can do so armed with a reasonable sequence of method calls to explore from the walkthrough of the **testPlus** method, as well as with a set of questions thrown up by it.

9.8.2 Checking state with a walkthrough

A `CalcEngine` object is quite different in style from its tester. This is because the engine is a completely passive object. It initiates no activity of its own, but simply responds to external method calls. This is typical of the server style of behavior. Server objects often rely heavily on their state to determine how they should respond to method calls. This is particularly true of the calculator engine. So an important part of conducting the walkthrough is to be sure that we always have an accurate representation of its state. One way to do this on paper is by making up a table of an object's fields and their values (Figure 9.7). A new line can be entered to keep a running log of the values following each method call.

This technique makes it quite easy to check back if something appears to go wrong. It is also possible to compare the states after two calls to the same method.

1 As we start the walkthrough of `CalcEngine`, we document the initial state of the engine, as in the first row of values in Figure 9.7. All of its fields are initialized in the constructor. As we observed when walking through the tester, object initialization is important, and we make a note here to check that the default initialization is sufficient—particularly as the default value of `previousOperator` would appear not to represent a meaningful operator. Furthermore, this makes us think about whether it really is meaningful to have a *previous* operator before the first real operator in a calculation. In noting these questions, we do not necessarily have to try to discover the answers right away, but they provide prompts as we discover more about the class.

2 The next step is to see how a call to `clear` changes the engine's state. As shown in the second data row of Figure 9.7, the state remains unchanged at this point because `displayValue` is already set to 0. But we note another question here: Why is the value of only one of the fields set by this method? If this method is supposed to implement a form of reset, why not clear all of the fields?

3 Next, a call to `numberPressed` with an actual parameter of 3 is investigated. The method multiplies an existing value of `displayValue` by 10 and then adds in the new digit. This correctly models the effect of appending a new digit onto the right-hand end of an existing number. It relies on `displayValue` having a sensible initial value of 0 when the first digit of a new number is entered, and our investigation of the `clear` method gives us confidence that this will be the case. So this method looks all right.

4 Continuing to follow the order of calls in the `testPlus` method, we next look at `plus`. Its first statement calls the `applyPreviousOperator` method. Here we have to decide whether to continue ignoring nested method calls or whether to break off and see what it does. Taking a quick look at the `applyPreviousOperator` method, we can see that

Figure 9.7
Informal tabulation of an object's state

Method called	displayValue	leftOperand	previousOperator
initial state	0	0	' '
clear	0	0	' '
numberPressed(3)	3	0	' '

9.8 Manual walkthroughs

it is fairly short. Furthermore, it is clearly going to alter the state of the engine, and we shall not be able to continue documenting the state changes unless we follow it up. So we would certainly decide to follow the nested call. It is important to remember where we came from, so we mark the listing just inside the **plus** method before following through the **applyPreviousOperator** method. If following a nested method call is likely to lead to further nested calls, we need to use something more than a simple mark to help us find our way back to the caller. In that case, it is better to mark the call points with ascending numerical values, reusing previous values as calls return.

5 The **applyPreviousOperator** method gives us some insights into how the **previousOperator** field is used. It also appears to answer one of our earlier questions: whether having a space as the initial value for the previous operator was satisfactory. The method explicitly checks to see whether **previousOperator** contains either a + or a − before applying it. So another value will not result in an incorrect operation being applied. By the end of this method, the value of **leftOperand** will have been changed, so we note its new value in the state table.

6 Returning to the **plus** method, the remaining two fields have their values set, so the next row of the state table contains the following values:

        plus   0   3   '+'

The walkthrough of the engine can be continued in a similar fashion, by documenting the state changes, gaining insights into its behavior, and raising questions along the way. The following exercises should help you complete the walkthrough.

Exercise 9.26 Complete the state table based on the following subsequent calls found in the **testPlus** method:

```
numberPressed(4);
equals();
getDisplayValue();
```

Exercise 9.27 When walking through the **equals** method, did you feel the same reassurances that we felt in **applyPreviousOperator** about the default value of **previousOperator**?

Exercise 9.28 Walkthrough a call to **clear** immediately following the call to **getDisplayValue** at the end of your state table, and record the new state. Is the engine in the same state as it was at the previous call to **clear**? If not, what impact do you think this could have on any subsequent calculations?

Exercise 9.29 In the light of your walkthrough, what changes do you think should be made to the **CalcEngine** class? Make those changes to a paper version of the class, and then try the walkthrough all over again. You should not need to walk through the **CalcEngineTester** class, just repeat the actions of its **testAll** method.

> **Exercise 9.30** Try a walkthrough of the following sequence of calls on your corrected version of the engine:
>
> ```
> clear();
> numberPressed(9);
> plus();
> numberPressed(1);
> minus();
> numberPressed(4);
> equals();
> ```
>
> What should the result be? Does the engine appear to behave correctly and leave the correct answer in `displayValue`?

9.8.3 Verbal walkthroughs

Another way in which the walkthrough technique can be used to find errors in a program is to try explaining to another person what a class or method does. This works in two completely different ways:

- The person you explain the code to might spot the error for you.
- You will often find that the simple act of trying to put into words what a piece of code should do is enough to trigger in your own mind an understanding of why it does not.

This latter effect is so common that it can often be worth explaining a piece of code to someone who is completely unfamiliar with it—not in anticipation that *they* will find the error, but that *you* will!

9.9 Print statements

Probably the most common technique used to understand and debug programs—even amongst experienced programmers—is to annotate methods temporarily with print statements. Print statements are popular because they exist in most languages, they are available to everyone, and they are very easy to add with any editor. No additional software or language features are required to make use of them. As a program runs, these additional print statements will typically provide a user with information such as:

- which methods have been called
- the values of parameters
- the order in which methods have been called
- the values of local variables and fields at strategic points

Code 9.5 shows an example of how the `numberPressed` method might look with print statements added. Such information is particularly helpful in providing a picture of the way in which the state of an object changes as mutators are called. To help support this, it is often worth including a debugging method that prints out the current values of all the fields of an object. Code 9.6 shows such a `reportState` method for the `CalcEngine` class.

Code 9.5
A method with debugging print statements added

```java
/**
 * A number button was pressed.
 * @param number The single digit.
 */
public void numberPressed(int number)
{
    System.out.println("numberPressed called with: " + number);

    displayValue = displayValue * 10 + number;

    System.out.println("displayValue is: " + displayValue +
                        "at end of numberPressed");
}
```

Code 9.6
A state-reporting method

```java
/**
 * Print the values of this object's fields.
 * @param where Where this state occurs.
 */
public void reportState(String where)
{
    System.out.println("displayValue: " + displayValue +
                    " leftOperand: " + leftOperand +
                    " previousOperator: " + previousOperator +
                    " at " + where);
}
```

If each method of `CalcEngine` contained a print statement at its entry point and a call to `reportState` at its end, Figure 9.8 shows the output that might result from a call to the tester's `testPlus` method. (This was generated from a version of the calculator engine that can be found in the *calculator-engine-print* project.) Such output allows us to build up a picture of how control flows between different methods. For instance, we can see from the order in which the state values are reported that a call to `plus` contains a nested call to `applyPreviousOperator`.

Print statements can be very effective in helping us understand programs or locate errors, but there are a number of disadvantages:

- It is not usually practical to add print statements to every method in a class. So they are only fully effective if the right methods have been annotated.

- Adding too many print statements can lead to information overload. A large amount of output can make it difficult to identify what you need to see. Print statements inside loops are a particular source of this problem.

- Once their purpose has been served, it can be tedious to remove them.

- There is also the chance that, having removed them, they will be needed again later. It can be very frustrating to have to put them back in again!

Figure 9.8

Debugging output from a call to `testPlus`

```
clear called
displayValue: 0 leftOperand: 0 previousOperator:   at end of clear
numberPressed called with: 3
displayValue: 3 leftOperand: 0 previousOperator:   at end of number...
plus called
applyPreviousOperator called
displayValue: 3 leftOperand: 3 previousOperator:   at end of apply...
displayValue: 0 leftOperand: 3 previousOperator: + at end of plus
numberPressed called with: 4
displayValue: 4 leftOperand: 3 previousOperator: + at end of number...
equals called
displayValue: 7 leftOperand: 0 previousOperator: + at end of equals
```

Exercise 9.31 Open the *calculator-engine-print* project and complete the addition of print statements to each method and the constructor.

Exercise 9.32 Create a `CalcEngineTester` in the project and run the `testAll` method. Does the output that results help you identify where the problem lies?

Exercise 9.33 Do you feel that the amount of output produced by the fully annotated `CalcEngine` class is too little, too much, or about right? If you feel that it is too little or too much, either add further print statements or remove some until you feel that you have the right level of detail.

Exercise 9.34 What are the respective advantages and disadvantages of using manual walkthroughs or print statements for debugging? Discuss.

9.9.1 Turning debugging information on or off

If a class is still under development when print statements are added, we often do not want to see the output every time the class is used. It is best if we can find a way to turn the printing on or off as required. The most common way to achieve this is to add an extra **boolean** debugging field to the class, then make printing dependent upon the value of the field. Code 9.7 illustrates this idea.

Code 9.7

Controlling whether debugging information is printed or not

```java
/**
 * A number button was pressed.
 * @param number The single digit.
 */
public void numberPressed(int number)
{
    if(debugging) {
        System.out.println("numberPressed called with: " + number);
    }
}
```

Code 9.7 continued
Controlling whether debugging information is printed or not

```
        displayValue = displayValue * 10 + number;

        if(debugging) {
            reportState();
        }
    }
```

A more economical variation on this theme is to replace the direct calls to print statements with calls to a specialized printing method added to the class.[2] The printing method would print only if the **debugging** field is **true**. Therefore, calls to the printing method would not need to be guarded by an if statement. Code 9.8 illustrates this approach. Note that this version assumes that **reportState** either tests the **debugging** field itself or calls the new **printDebugging** method.

Code 9.8
A method for selectively printing debugging information

```
    /**
     * A number button was pressed.
     * @param number The single digit.
     */
    public void numberPressed(int number)
    {
        printDebugging("numberPressed called with: " + number);

        displayValue = displayValue * 10 + number;
        reportState();
    }

    /**
     * Only print the debugging information if debugging is true.
     * @param info The debugging information.
     */
    public void printDebugging(String info)
    {
        if(debugging) {
            System.out.println(info);
        }
    }
```

As you can see from these experiments, it takes some practice to find the best level of detail to print out to be useful. In practice, print statements are often added to one or a small number of methods at a time, when we have a rough idea in what area of our program an error might be hiding.

---

[2] In fact, we could move this method to a specialized debugging class, but we shall keep things simple in this discussion.

9.10 Debuggers

In Chapter 3, we introduced the use of a debugger to understand how an existing application operates and how its objects interact. In a very similar manner, we can use the debugger to track down errors.

The debugger is essentially a software tool that provides support for performing a walk-through on a segment of code. We typically set a breakpoint at the statement where we want to start our walkthrough and then use the *Step* or *Step Into* functions to do the actual walking.

One advantage is that the debugger automatically takes care of keeping track of every object's state, and, thus, doing this is quicker and less error prone than doing the same manually. A disadvantage is that debuggers typically do not keep a permanent record of state changes, so it is harder to go back and check the state as it was a few statements earlier.

A debugger typically also gives you information about the *call sequence* (or *stack*) at each point in time. The call sequence shows the name of the method containing the current statement, the name of the method that the current method was called from, and the name of the method that *that* method was called from, and so on. Thus, the call sequence contains a record of all currently active, unfinished methods—similar to what we have done manually during our walkthrough by writing marks next to method-call statements.

In BlueJ, the call sequence is displayed on the left-hand side of the debugger window (Figure 9.9). Every method name in that sequence can be selected to inspect the current values of that method's local variables.

Figure 9.9

The BlueJ debugger window, with execution stopped at a breakpoint

Exercise 9.35 Using the *calculator-engine* project, set a breakpoint in the first line of the `testPlus` method in the `CalcEngineTester` class. Execute this method. When the debugger appears, walk through the code step by step. Experiment with both the *Step* and *Step Into* buttons.

Exercise 9.36 *Challenge exercise* In practice, you will probably find that Hacker T. Largebrain's attempt to program the `CalcEngine` class is too full of errors to be worth trying to fix. Instead, write your own version of the class from scratch. The *calculator-gui* project contains classes that provide the GUI shown in Figure 9.6. You can use this project as the basis for your own implementation of the `CalcEngine` class. Be sure to document your class thoroughly and to create a thorough set of tests for your implementation so that your experience with Hacker's code will not have to be repeated by your successor! Make sure to use a dedicated unit test class for your testing, instead of writing tests into a standard class; as you have seen, this makes asserting the correct results much easier.

9.11 Debugging streams (advanced)

All of the debugging techniques we have described in this chapter apply equally well when writing code that uses streams. The only nuance is the complexity of a typical statement that involves the use of streams. It would not be uncommon for a single statement to contain three or more operations as part of a pipeline, and the ordering and logical flow between those operations will be critical to the correct outcome of the statement. So, it will often be useful to inspect the state of the stream at intermediate points of the pipeline.

The **peek** method is a stream operation that provides the equivalent of using print statements, as a way to examine the state of a pipeline at various points. It is an intermediate operation that can be inserted at any point within a pipeline. It takes a consumer lambda expression as a parameter, but also passes the elements of its input stream unmodified through to its output stream.

For instance, suppose that you are reviewing some reasonably complex code—written by somebody else—in the *animal-monitoring* project. The code is meant to create a list of sightings specific to a particular animal, area, and spotter. They might have written this in a single statement as follows:

```
List<Sighting> result =
    sightings.stream()
            .filter(record -> animal == record.getAnimal() &&
                              area == record.getArea() &&
                              spotter == record.getSpotter())
            .collect(Collectors.toList());
```

Imagine that the list produced by this code is always empty, even though you are using test data with sighting records that should definitely match. Clearly there must be something wrong with the `filter` operation, but you cannot immediately spot the problem. One of the easiest ways to get to the bottom of this would be to split the single filter operation into three separate filters, and to print out fields of the remaining elements after each filtration step. The following version does this:

```
List<Sighting> result =
   sightings.stream()
            .filter(record -> animal == record.getAnimal())
            .peek(r -> System.out.println(r.getAnimal()))
            .filter(record -> area == record.getArea()
            .peek(r -> System.out.println(r.getArea()))
            .filter(record -> spotter == record.getSpotter())
            .peek(r -> System.out.println(r.getDetails()))
            .collect(Collectors.toList());
```

From this version you would be quite likely to find that the first filter operation is not passing on any records to the next, because the test for string equality has not been made using the `equals` method. Once that has been corrected, the tests could be rerun and eventually the `peek` operations removed.

A `peek` operation can also be a convenient way to create a position in the middle of a pipeline sequence for setting a breakpoint for a debugger. In this case, you would be more likely to be interested in the states of the objects rather than having something printed, so a consumer lambda that does nothing would be used as the parameter to `peek`, for instance:

```
peek(r -> { })
```

9.12 Choosing a debugging strategy

We have seen that several different debugging and testing strategies exist: written and verbal walkthroughs, use of print statements (either temporary or permanent, with enabling switches), interactive testing using the object bench, writing your own test class, and using a dedicated unit test class.

In practice, we would use different strategies at different times. Walkthroughs, print statements, and interactive testing are useful techniques for initial testing of newly written code, to investigate how a program segment works, or for debugging. Their advantage is that they are quick and easy to use, they work in any programming language, and they are (except for the interactive testing) independent of the environment. Their main disadvantage is that the activities are not easily repeatable. This is okay for debugging, but for testing we need something better: we need a mechanism that allows easy repetition for regression testing. Using unit test classes has the advantage that—once they have been set up—tests can be replayed any number of times.

So Hacker's way of testing—writing his own test class—was one step in the right direction, but was, flawed. We know now that his problem was that although his class contained reasonable method calls for testing, it did not include any assertions on the method results, and thus did not detect test failure. Using a dedicated unit test class can solve these problems.

Exercise 9.37 Open your project again and add better testing by replacing Hacker's test class with a unit test class attached to the `CalcEngine`. Add similar tests to those Hacker used (and any others you find useful), and include correct assertions.

9.13 Putting the techniques into practice

This chapter has described several techniques that can be used either to understand a new program or to test for errors in a program. The *bricks* project provides a chance for you to try out those techniques with a new scenario. The project contains part of an application for a company producing bricks. Bricks are delivered to customers on pallets (stacks of bricks). The `Pallet` class provides methods telling the height and weight of an individual pallet, according to the number of bricks on it.

Exercise 9.38 Open the *bricks* project. Test it. There are at least four errors in this project. See if you can find them and fix them. What techniques did you use to find the errors? Which technique was most useful?

9.14 Summary

When writing software, we should anticipate that it will contain logical errors. Therefore, it is essential to consider both testing and debugging to be normal activities within the overall development process. BlueJ is particularly good at supporting interactive unit testing of both methods and classes. We have also looked at some basic techniques for automating the testing process and performing simple debugging.

Writing good JUnit tests for our classes ensures that errors are detected early, and they give a good indication which part of the system an error originates in, making the resulting debugging task much easier.

Terms introduced in this chapter:

syntax error, logical error, testing, debugging, unit testing, JUnit, positive testing, negative testing, regression testing, manual walkthrough, call sequence

Part 2: Application Structures

Chapter 10	Improving Structure with Inheritance
Chapter 11	More about Inheritance
Chapter 12	Further Abstraction Techniques
Chapter 13	Building Graphical User Interfaces
Chapter 14	Handling Errors
Chapter 15	Designing Applications
Chapter 16	A Case Study

CHAPTER 10
Improving Structure with Inheritance

Main concepts discussed in this chapter:

- inheritance
- subtyping
- substitution
- polymorphic variables

Java constructs discussed in this chapter:

`extends`, `super` (in constructor), cast, `Object`

In this chapter, we introduce some additional object-oriented constructs to improve the general structure of our applications. The main concepts we shall use to design better program structures are *inheritance* and *polymorphism*.

Both of these concepts are central to the idea of object orientation, and you will discover later how they appear in various forms in everything we discuss from now on. However, it is not only the following chapters that rely heavily on these concepts. Many of the constructs and techniques discussed in earlier chapters are influenced by aspects of inheritance and polymorphism, and we shall revisit some issues introduced earlier and gain a fuller understanding of the interconnections between different parts of the Java language.

Inheritance is a powerful construct that can be used to create solutions to a variety of different problems. As always, we will discuss the important aspects using an example. In this example, we will first introduce only some of the problems that are addressed by using inheritance structures, and discuss further uses and advantages of inheritance and polymorphism as we progress through this chapter.

The example we discuss to introduce these new structures is called *network*.

10.1 The *network* example

The *network* project implements a prototype of a small part of a social-network application. The part we are concentrating on is the *news feed*—the list of messages that should appear on screen when a user opens the network's main page.

Here, we will start small and simple, with a view to extending and growing the application later. Initially, we have only two types of posts appearing in our news feed: text posts (which we call *messages*), and photo posts consisting of a photo and a caption.

The part of the application that we are prototyping here is the engine that stores and displays these posts. The functionality that we want to provide with this prototype should include at least the following:

- It should allow us to create text and photo posts.
- Text posts consist of a message of arbitrary length, possibly spanning multiple lines. Photo posts consist of an image and a caption. Some additional details are stored with each post.
- It should store this information permanently so that it can be used later.
- It should provide a search function that allows us to find, for example, all posts by a certain user, or all photos within a given date range.
- It should allow us to display lists of posts, such as a list of the most recent posts, or a list of all posts by a given user.
- It should allow us to remove information.

The details we want to store for each message post are:

- the username of the author
- the text of the message
- a time stamp (time of posting)
- how many people like this post
- a list of comments on this post by other users

The details we want to store for each photo post are:

- the username of the author
- the filename of the image to display
- the caption for the photo (one line of text)
- a time stamp (time of posting)
- how many people like this post
- a list of comments on this post by other users

10.1.1 The *network* project: classes and objects

To implement the application, we first have to decide what classes to use to model this problem. In this case, some of the classes are easy to identify. It is quite straightforward to decide that we should have a class **MessagePost** to represent message posts, and a class **PhotoPost** to represent photo posts.

Figure 10.1
Fields in **Message-Post** and **Photo-Post** objects

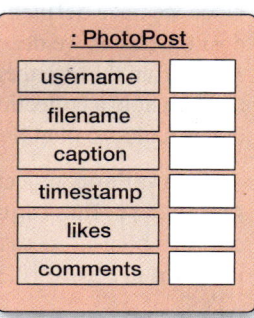

Figure 10.2
Details of the **MessagePost** and **PhotoPost** classes

Objects of these classes should then encapsulate all the data we want to store about these objects (Figure 10.1).

Some of these data items should probably also have accessor and mutator methods (Figure 10.2).[1] For our purpose, it is not important to decide on the exact details of all the methods right now, but just to get a first impression of the design of this application. In this figure, we have defined accessor and mutator methods for those fields that may change over time ("liking" or "unliking" a post and adding a comment) and assume for now that the other fields are set in the constructor. We have also added a method called **display** that will show details of a **MessagePost** or **PhotoPost** object.

---

[1] The notation style for class diagrams that is used in this book and in BlueJ is a subset of a widely used notation called UML. Although we do not use everything from UML (by far), we attempt to use UML notation for those things that we show. The UML style defines how fields and methods are shown in a class diagram. The class is divided into three parts that show (in this order from the top) the class name, the fields, and the methods.

Once we have defined the **MessagePost** and **PhotoPost** classes, we can create as many post objects as we need—one object per message post or photo post that we want to store. Apart from this, we then need another object: an object representing the complete news feed that can hold a collection of message posts and a collection of photo posts. For this, we shall create a class called **NewsFeed**.

The **NewsFeed** object could itself hold two collection objects (for example, of types **ArrayList<MessagePost>** and **ArrayList<PhotoPost>**). One of these collections can then hold all message posts, the other all photo posts. An object diagram for this model is shown in Figure 10.3.

Figure 10.3
Objects in the *network* application

The corresponding class diagram, as BlueJ displays it, is shown in Figure 10.4. Note that BlueJ shows a slightly simplified diagram: classes from the standard Java library (**ArrayList** in this case) are not shown. Instead, the diagram focuses on user-defined classes. Also, BlueJ does not show field and method names in the diagram.

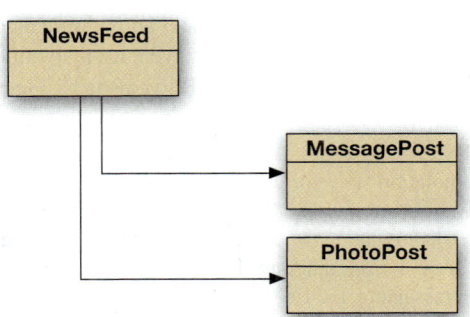

Figure 10.4
BlueJ class diagram of *network*

In practice, to implement the full *network* application, we would have more classes to handle things such as saving the data to a database and providing a user interface, most likely through a web browser. These are not very relevant to the present discussion, so we shall skip describing those for now, and concentrate on a more detailed discussion of the core classes mentioned here.

10.1.2 *Network* source code

So far, the design of the three current classes (**MessagePost**, **PhotoPost**, and **News-Feed**) has been very straightforward. Translating these ideas into Java code is equally easy. Code 10.1 shows the source code of the **MessagePost** class. It defines the appropriate fields, sets in its constructor all the data items that are not expected to change over time, and provides accessor and mutator methods where appropriate. It also implements a first, simple version of the `display` method to show the post in the text terminal.

Code 10.1
Source code of the **MessagePost** class

```java
import java.util.ArrayList;

/**
 * This class stores information about a post in a social network.
 * The main part of the post consists of a (possibly multi-line)
 * text message. Other data, such as author and time, are also stored.
 *
 * @author Michael Kölling and David J. Barnes
 * @version 0.1
 */
public class MessagePost
{
    private String username;    // username of the post's author
    private String message;     // an arbitrarily long, multi-line message
    private long timestamp;
    private int likes;
    private ArrayList<String> comments;

    /**
     * Constructor for objects of class MessagePost.
     *
     * @param author   The username of the author of this post.
     * @param text     The text of this post.
     */
    public MessagePost(String author, String text)
    {
        username = author;
        message = text;
        timestamp = System.currentTimeMillis();
        likes = 0;
        comments = new ArrayList<>();
    }

    /**
     * Record one more "Like" indication from a user.
     */
    public void like()
    {
        likes++;
    }
```

Code 10.1 continued

Source code of the **MessagePost** class

```java
/**
 * Record that a user has withdrawn his/her "Like" vote.
 */
public void unlike()
{
    if (likes > 0) {
        likes--;
    }
}

/**
 * Add a comment to this post.
 *
 * @param text  The new comment to add.
 */
public void addComment(String text)
{
    comments.add(text);
}

/**
 * Return the text of this post.
 *
 * @return The post's text.
 */
public String getText()
{
    return message;
}

/**
 * Return the time of creation of this post.
 *
 * @return The post's creation time, as a system time value.
 */
public long getTimeStamp()
{
    return timestamp;
}

/**
 * Display the details of this post.
 *
 * (Currently: Print to the text terminal. This is simulating display
 * in a web browser for now.)
 */
public void display()
{
    System.out.println(username);
    System.out.println(message);
    System.out.print(timeString(timestamp));

    if(likes > 0) {
        System.out.println("  -  " + likes + " people like this.");
    }
    else {
        System.out.println();
    }
```

Code 10.1 continued
Source code of the `MessagePost` class

```java
        if(comments.isEmpty()) {
            System.out.println("   No comments.");
        }
        else {
            System.out.println("   " + comments.size() +
                             " comment(s). Click here to view.");
        }
    }

    /**
     * Create a string describing a time point in the past in terms
     * relative to current time, such as "30 seconds ago" or "7 minutes ago".
     * Currently, only seconds and minutes are used for the string.
     *
     * @param time  The time value to convert (in system milliseconds)
     * @return      A relative time string for the given time
     */
    private String timeString(long time)
    {
        long current = System.currentTimeMillis();
        long pastMillis = current - time;      // time passed in milliseconds
        long seconds = pastMillis/1000;
        long minutes = seconds/60;
        if(minutes > 0) {
            return minutes + " minutes ago";
        }
        else {
            return seconds + " seconds ago";
        }
    }
}
```

Some details are worth mentioning:

- Some simplifications have been made. For example, comments for a post are stored as strings. In a more complete version, we would probably use a custom class for comments, as comments also have additional detail such as an author and a time. The "like" count is stored as a simple integer. We are currently not recording which user liked a post. While these simplifications make our prototype incomplete, they are not relevant for our main discussion here, and we shall leave them as they are for now.

- The time stamp is stored as a single number, of type `long`. This reflects common practice. We can easily get the system time from the Java system, as a `long` value in milliseconds. We have also written a short method, called `timeString`, to convert this number into a relative time string, such as "5 minutes ago." In our final application, the system would have to use real time rather than system time, but again, system time is good enough for our prototype for now.

Note that we do not intend right now to make the implementation complete in any sense. It serves to provide a feel for what a class such as this might look like. We will use this as the basis for our following discussion of inheritance.

Now let us compare the `MessagePost` source code with the source code of class `PhotoPost`, shown in Code 10.2. Looking at both classes, we quickly notice that they are very similar. This is not surprising, because their purpose is similar: both are used to store information about news-feed posts, and the different types of post have a lot in common. They differ only in their details, such as some of their fields and corresponding accessors and the bodies of the `display` method.

Code 10.2

Source code of the **PhotoPost** class

```java
import java.util.ArrayList;

/**
 * This class stores information about a post in a social network.
 * The main part of the post consists of a photo and a caption.
 * Other data, such as author and time, are also stored.
 *
 * @author Michael Kölling and David J. Barnes
 * @version 0.1
 */
public class PhotoPost
{
    private String username;    // username of the post's author
    private String filename;    // the name of the image file
    private String caption;     // a one line image caption
    private long timestamp;
    private int likes;
    private ArrayList<String> comments;

    /**
     * Constructor for objects of class PhotoPost.
     *
     * @param author    The username of the author of this post.
     * @param filename  The filename of the image in this post.
     * @param caption   A caption for the image.
     */
    public PhotoPost(String author, String filename, String caption)
    {
        username = author;
        this.filename = filename;
        this.caption = caption;
        timestamp = System.currentTimeMillis();
        likes = 0;
        comments = new ArrayList<>();
    }

    /**
     * Record one more "Like" indication from a user.
     */
    public void like()
    {
        likes++;
    }

    /**
     * Record that a user has withdrawn his/her "Like" vote.
     */
```

Code 10.2 continued
Source code of the **PhotoPost** class

```java
    public void unlike()
    {
        if (likes > 0) {
            likes--;
        }
    }

    /**
     * Add a comment to this post.
     *
     * @param text  The new comment to add.
     */
    public void addComment(String text)
    {
        comments.add(text);
    }

    /**
     * Return the file name of the image in this post.
     *
     * @return The post's image file name.
     */
    public String getImageFile()
    {
        return filename;
    }

    /**
     * Return the caption of the image of this post.
     *
     * @return The image's caption.
     */
    public String getCaption()
    {
        return caption;
    }

    /**
     * Return the time of creation of this post.
     *
     * @return The post's creation time, as a system time value.
     */
    public long getTimeStamp()
    {
        return timestamp;
    }

    /**
     * Display the details of this post.
     *
     * (Currently: Print to the text terminal. This is simulating display
     * in a web browser for now.)
     */
```

Code 10.2 continued

Source code of the **PhotoPost** class

```java
    public void display()
    {
        System.out.println(username);
        System.out.println("   [" + filename + "]");
        System.out.println("    " + caption);
        System.out.print(timeString(timestamp));

        if(likes > 0) {
            System.out.println("  -  " + likes + " people like this.");
        }
        else {
            System.out.println();
        }

        if(comments.isEmpty()) {
            System.out.println("    No comments.");
        }
        else {
            System.out.println("    " + comments.size() +
                               " comment(s). Click here to view.");
        }
    }

    /**
     * Create a string describing a time point in the past in terms
     * relative to current time, such as "30 seconds ago" or "7 minutes ago".
     * Currently, only seconds and minutes are used for the string.
     *
     * @param time  The time value to convert (in system milliseconds)
     * @return      A relative time string for the given time
     */
    private String timeString(long time)
    {
        long current = System.currentTimeMillis();
        long pastMillis = current - time;        // time passed in milliseconds
        long seconds = pastMillis/1000;
        long minutes = seconds/60;
        if(minutes > 0) {
            return minutes + " minutes ago";
        }
        else {
            return seconds + " seconds ago";
        }
    }
}
```

Next, let us examine the source code of the **NewsFeed** class (Code 10.3). It, too, is quite simple. It defines two lists (each based on class **ArrayList**) to hold the collection of message posts and the collection of photo posts. The empty lists are created in the constructor. It then provides two methods for adding items: one for adding message posts, one for adding photo posts. The last method, named **show**, prints a list of all message and photo posts to the text terminal.

Code 10.3
Source code of the **NewsFeed** class

```java
import java.util.ArrayList;

/**
 * The NewsFeed class stores news posts for the news feed in a social network
 * application.
 *
 * Display of the posts is currently simulated by printing the details to the
 * terminal. (Later, this should display in a browser.)
 *
 * This version does not save the data to disk, and it does not provide any
 * search or ordering functions.
 *
 * @author Michael Kölling and David J. Barnes
 * @version 0.1
 */
public class NewsFeed
{
    private ArrayList<MessagePost> messages;
    private ArrayList<PhotoPost> photos;

    /**
     * Construct an empty news feed.
     */
    public NewsFeed()
    {
        messages = new ArrayList<>();
        photos = new ArrayList<>();
    }

    /**
     * Add a text post to the news feed.
     *
     * @param text  The text post to be added.
     */
    public void addMessagePost(MessagePost message)
    {
        messages.add(message);
    }

    /**
     * Add a photo post to the news feed.
     *
     * @param photo  The photo post to be added.
     */
    public void addPhotoPost(PhotoPost photo)
    {
        photos.add(photo);
    }

    /**
     * Show the news feed. Currently: print the news feed details to the
     * terminal. (To do: replace this later with display in web browser.)
     */
```

Code 10.3 continued

Source code of the **NewsFeed** class

```java
    public void show()
    {
        // display all text posts
        for(MessagePost message : messages) {
            message.display();
            System.out.println();   // empty line between posts
        }

        // display all photos
        for(PhotoPost photo : photos) {
            photo.display();
            System.out.println();   // empty line between posts
        }
    }
}
```

This is by no means a complete application. It has no user interface yet (so it will not be usable outside BlueJ), and the data entered is not stored to the file system or in a database. This means that all data entered will be lost each time the application ends. There are no functions to sort the displayed list of posts—for example, by date and time or by relevance. Currently, we will always get messages first, in the order in which they were entered, followed by the photos. Also, the functions for entering and editing data, as well as searching for data and displaying it, are not flexible enough for what we would want from a real program.

However, this does not matter in our context. We can work on improving the application later. The basic structure is there, and it works. This is enough for us to discuss design problems and possible improvements.

> **Exercise 10.1** Open the project *network-v1*. It contains the classes exactly as we have discussed them here. Create some **MessagePost** objects and some **PhotoPost** objects. Create a **NewsFeed** object. Enter the posts into the news feed, and then display the feed's contents.
>
> **Exercise 10.2** Try the following. Create a **MessagePost** object. Enter it into the news feed. Display the news feed. You will see that the post has no associated comments. Add a comment to the **MessagePost** object on the object bench (the one you entered into the news feed). When you now list the news feed again, will the post listed there have a comment attached? Try it. Explain the behavior you observe.

10.1.3 Discussion of the *network* application

Even though our application is not yet complete, we have done the most important part. We have defined the core of the application—the data structure that stores the essential information.

This was fairly straightforward so far, and we could now go ahead and design the rest that is still missing. Before doing that, though, we will discuss the quality of the solution so far.

There are several fundamental problems with our current solution. The most obvious one is *code duplication*.

We have noticed above that the `MessagePost` and `PhotoPost` classes are very similar. In fact, the majority of the classes' source code is identical, with only a few differences. We have already discussed the problems associated with code duplication in Chapter 8. Apart from the annoying fact that we have to write everything twice (or copy and paste, then go through and fix all the differences), there are often problems associated with maintaining duplicated code. Many possible changes would have to be done twice. If, for example, the type of the comment list is changed from `ArrayList<String>` to `ArrayList<Comment>` (so that more details can be stored), this change has to be made once in the `MessagePost` class and again in the `PhotoPost` class. In addition, associated with maintenance of code duplication is always the danger of introducing errors, because the maintenance programmer might not realize that an identical change is needed at a second (or third) location.

There is another spot where we have code duplication: in the `NewsFeed` class. We can see that everything in that class is done twice—once for message posts, and once for photo posts. The class defines two list variables, then creates two list objects, defines two `add` methods, and has two almost-identical blocks of code in the `show` method to print out the lists.

The problems with this duplication become clear when we analyze what we would have to do to add another type of post to this program. Imagine that we want to store not only text messages and photo posts, but also activity posts. Activity posts can be automatically generated and inform us about an activity of one of our contacts, such as "Fred has changed his profile picture" or "Jacob is now friends with Feena." Activity posts seem similar enough that it should be easy to modify our application to do this. We would introduce another class, `ActivityPost`, and essentially write a third version of the source code that we already have in the `MessagePost` and `PhotoPost` classes. Then we have to work through the `NewsFeed` class and add another list variable, another list object, another `add` method, and another loop in the `show` method.

We would have to do the same for a fourth type of post. The more we do this, the more the code-duplication problem increases, and the harder it becomes to make changes later. When we feel uncomfortable about a situation such as this one, it is often a good indicator that there may be a better alternative approach. For this particular case, the solution is found in object-oriented languages. They provide a distinctive feature that has a big impact on programs involving sets of similar classes. In the following sections, we will introduce this feature, which is called *inheritance*.

10.2 Using inheritance

Concept

Inheritance allows us to define one class as an extension of another.

Inheritance is a mechanism that provides us with a solution to our problem of duplication. The idea is simple: instead of defining the `MessagePost` and `PhotoPost` classes completely independently, we first define a class that contains everything these two have in common. We shall call this class `Post`. Then we can declare that a `MessagePost` is a `Post` and a `PhotoPost` is a `Post`. Finally, we add those extra details needed for a message post to the `MessagePost` class, and those for a photo post to the `PhotoPost` class. The essential feature of this technique is that we need to describe the common features only once.

Figure 10.5 shows a class diagram for this new structure. At the top, it shows the class **Post**, which defines all fields and methods that are common to all posts (messages and photos). Below the **Post** class, it shows the **MessagePost** and **PhotoPost** classes, which hold only those fields and methods that are unique to each particular class.

This new feature of object-oriented programming requires some new terminology. In a situation such as this one, we say that the class **MessagePost** *inherits from* class **Post**. Class **PhotoPost** also inherits from **Post**. In the vernacular of Java programs, the expression "class **MessagePost** *extends* class **Post**" could be used, because Java uses an **extends** keyword to define the inheritance relationship (as we shall see shortly). The arrows in the class diagram (usually drawn with hollow arrow heads) represent the inheritance relationship.

> **Concept**
>
> A **superclass** is a class that is extended by another class.

Class **Post** (the class that the others inherit from) is called the *parent class* or *superclass*. The inheriting classes (**MessagePost** and **PhotoPost** in this example) are referred to as *child classes* or *subclasses*. In this book, we will use the terms "superclass" and "subclass" to refer to the classes in an inheritance relationship.

> **Concept**
>
> A **subclass** is a class that extends (inherits from) another class. It inherits all fields and methods from its superclass.

Inheritance is sometimes also called an *is-a* relationship. The reason is that a subclass is a specialization of a superclass. We can say that "a message post *is a* post" and "a photo post *is a* post."

The purpose of using inheritance is now fairly obvious. Instances of class **MessagePost** will have all fields defined in class **MessagePost** *and* in class **Post**. (**MessagePost** inherits the fields from **Post**.) Instances of **PhotoPost** will have all fields defined in **PhotoPost** and in **Post**. Thus, we achieve the same as before, but we need to define the fields **username**, **timestamp**, **likes**, and **comments** only once, while being able to use them in two different places.

Figure 10.5
MessagePost and **PhotoPost** inheriting from **Post**

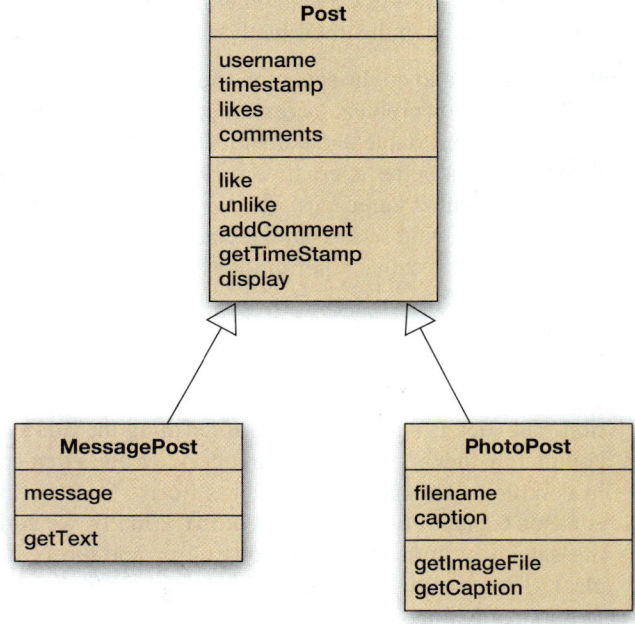

The same holds true for methods: instances of subclasses have all methods defined in both the superclass and the subclass. In general, we can say: because a message post is a post, a message-post object has everything that a post has, and more. And because a photo post is also a post, it has everything that a post has, and more.

Thus, inheritance allows us to create two classes that are quite similar, while avoiding the need to write the identical part twice. Inheritance has a number of other advantages, which we discuss below. First, however, we will take another, more general look at inheritance hierarchies.

10.3 Inheritance hierarchies

Inheritance can be used much more generally than shown in the example above. More than two subclasses can inherit from the same superclass, and a subclass can, in turn, be a superclass to other subclasses. The classes then form an *inheritance hierarchy*.

The best-known example of an inheritance hierarchy is probably the classification of species used by biologists. A small part is shown in Figure 10.6. We can see that a poodle is a dog, which is a mammal, which is an animal.

We know some things about poodles—for example, that they are alive, they can bark, they eat meat, and they give birth to live young. On closer inspection, we see that we know some of these things not because they are poodles, but because they are dogs, mammals, or animals. An instance of class **Poodle** (an actual poodle) has all the characteristics of a poodle, a dog, a mammal, and an animal, because a poodle is a dog, which is a mammal, and so on.

The principle is simple: inheritance is an abstraction technique that lets us categorize classes of objects under certain criteria and helps us specify the characteristics of these classes.

> **Concept**
>
> Classes that are linked through inheritance relationships form an **inheritance hierarchy**.

Exercise 10.3 Draw an inheritance hierarchy for the people in your place of study or work. For example, if you are a university student, then your university probably has students (first-year students, second-year students, . . .), professors, tutors, office personnel, etc.

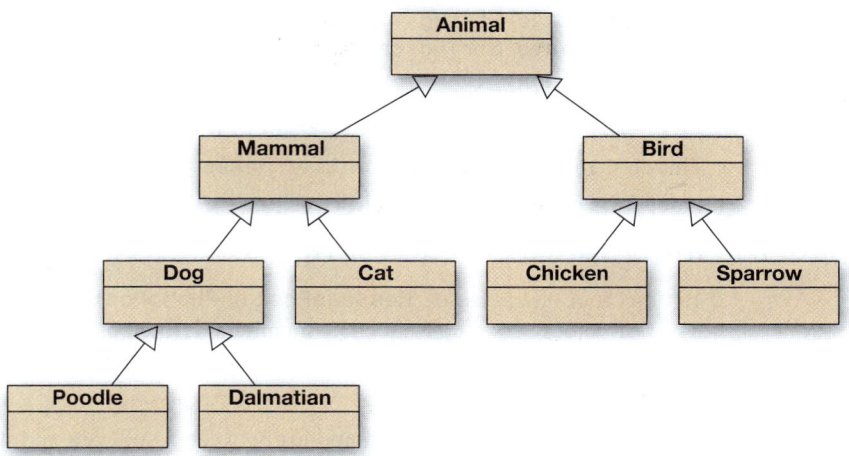

Figure 10.6
An example of an inheritance hierarchy

10.4 Inheritance in Java

Before discussing more details of inheritance, we will have a look at how inheritance is expressed in the Java language. Here is a segment of the source code of the **Post** class:

```java
public class Post
{
    private String username; // username of the post's author
    private long timestamp;
    private int likes;
    private ArrayList<String> comments;

    // Constructors and methods omitted.
}
```

There is nothing special about this class so far. It starts with a normal class definition and defines **Post**'s fields in the usual way. Next, we examine the source code of the **MessagePost** class:

```java
public class MessagePost extends Post
{
    private String message;

    // Constructors and methods omitted.
}
```

There are two things worth noting here. First, the keyword **extends** defines the inheritance relationship. The phrase "**extends Post**" specifies that this class is a subclass of the **Post** class. Second, the **MessagePost** class defines only those fields that are unique to **MessagePost** objects (only **message** in this case). The fields from **Post** are inherited and do not need to be listed here. Objects of class **MessagePost** will nonetheless have fields for **username**, **timestamp**, and so on.

Next, let us have a look at the source code of class **PhotoPost**:

```java
public class PhotoPost extends Post
{
    private String filename;
    private String caption;

    // Constructors and methods omitted.
}
```

This class follows the same pattern as the **MessagePost** class. It uses the **extends** keyword to define itself as a subclass of **Post** and defines its own additional fields.

10.4.1 Inheritance and access rights

To objects of other classes, **MessagePost** or **PhotoPost** objects appear just like all other types of objects. As a consequence, members defined as **public** in either the superclass or subclass portions will be accessible to objects of other classes, but members defined as **private** will be inaccessible.

In fact, the rule on privacy also applies between a subclass and its superclass: a subclass cannot access private members of its superclass. It follows that if a subclass method needed to access or change private fields in its superclass, then the superclass would need to provide appropriate accessor and/or mutator methods. However, an object of a subclass may call any public methods defined in its superclass as if they were defined locally in the subclass—no variable is needed, because the methods are all part of the same object.

This issue of access rights between super- and subclasses is one we will discuss further in Chapter 11, when we introduce the **protected** modifier.

> **Exercise 10.4** Open the project *network-v2*. This project contains a version of the *network* application, rewritten to use inheritance, as described above. Note that the class diagram displays the inheritance relationship. Open the source code of the **MessagePost** class and remove the "**extends Post**" phrase. Close the editor. What changes do you observe in the class diagram? Add the "**extends Post**" phrase again.
>
> **Exercise 10.5** Create a **MessagePost** object. Call some of its methods. Can you call the inherited methods (for example, **addComment**)? What do you observe about the inherited methods?
>
> **Exercise 10.6** In order to illustrate that a subclass can access non-private elements of its superclass without any special syntax, try the following slightly artificial modification to the **MessagePost** and **Post** classes. Create a method called **printShortSummary** in the **MessagePost** class. Its task is to print just the phrase "Message post from *NAME*", where *NAME* should show the name of the author. However, because the **username** field is private in the **Post** class, it will be necessary to add a public **getUserName** method to **Post**. Call this method from **printShortSummary** to access the name for printing. Remember that no special syntax is required when a subclass calls a superclass method. Try out your solution by creating a **MessagePost** object. Implement a similar method in the **PhotoPost** class.

10.4.2 Inheritance and initialization

When we create an object, the constructor of that object takes care of initializing all object fields to some reasonable state. We have to look more closely at how this is done in classes that inherit from other classes.

When we create a **MessagePost** object, we pass two parameters to the message post's constructor: the name of the author and the message text. One of these contains a value for a field defined in class **Post**, and the other a value for a field defined in class **MessagePost**. All of these fields must be correctly initialized, and Code 10.4 shows the code segments that are used to achieve this in Java.

Several observations can be made here. First, the class **Post** has a constructor, even though we do not intend to create an instance of class **Post** directly.[2] This constructor receives the

---

[2] Currently, there is nothing actually preventing us from creating a **Post** object, although that was not our intention when we designed these classes. In Chapter 12, we shall see some techniques that allow us to make sure that **Post** objects cannot be created directly, but only **MessagePost** or **PhotoPost** objects.

Code 10.4

Initialization of subclass and superclass fields

```java
public class Post
{
    private String username;    // username of the post's author
    private long timestamp;
    private int likes;
    private ArrayList<String> comments;

    /**
     * Constructor for objects of class Post.
     *
     * @param author    The username of the author of this post.
     */
    public Post(String author)
    {
        username = author;
        timestamp = System.currentTimeMillis();
        likes = 0;
        comments = new ArrayList<>();
    }

    Methods omitted.
}

public class MessagePost extends Post
{
    private String message;    // an arbitrarily long, multi-line message

    /**
     * Constructor for objects of class MessagePost.
     *
     * @param author    The username of the author of this post.
     * @param text      The text of this post.
     */
    public MessagePost(String author, String text)
    {
        super(author);
        message = text;
    }

    Methods omitted.
}
```

parameters needed to initialize the **Post** fields, and it contains the code to do this initialization. Second, the **MessagePost** constructor receives parameters needed to initialize both **Post** and **MessagePost** fields. It then contains the following line of code:

```java
super(author);
```

The keyword **super** is a call from the subclass constructor to the constructor of the superclass. Its effect is that the **Post** constructor is executed as part of the **MessagePost** constructor's execution. When we create a message post, the **MessagePost** constructor is called, which, in turn, as its first statement, calls the **Post** constructor. The **Post** constructor initializes the post's fields, and then returns to the **MessagePost** constructor, which initializes the remaining field defined in the **MessagePost** class. For this to work, those parameters needed for the initialization of the post fields are passed on to the superclass constructor as parameters to the **super** call.

In Java, a subclass constructor must always call the *superclass constructor* as its first statement. If you do not write a call to a superclass constructor, the Java compiler will insert a superclass call automatically, to ensure that the superclass fields are properly initialized. The inserted call is equivalent to writing

```
super();
```

Inserting this call automatically works only if the superclass has a constructor without parameters (because the compiler cannot guess what parameter values should be passed). Otherwise, an error will be reported.

In general, it is a good idea to always include explicit superclass calls in your constructors, even if it is one that the compiler could generate automatically. We consider this good style, because it avoids the possibility of misinterpretation and confusion in case a reader is not aware of the automatic code generation.

> **Concept**
>
> **Superclass constructor** The constructor of a subclass must always invoke the constructor of its superclass as its first statement. If the source code does not include such a call, Java will attempt to insert a call automatically.

Exercise 10.7 Set a breakpoint in the first line of the **MessagePost** class's constructor. Then create a **MessagePost** object. When the debugger window pops up, use *Step Into* to step through the code. Observe the instance fields and their initialization. Describe your observations.

10.5 *Network*: adding other post types

Now that we have our inheritance hierarchy set up for the *network* project so that the common elements of the items are in the **Post** class, it becomes a lot easier to add other types of posts. For instance, we might want to add event posts, which consist of a description of a standard event (e.g., "Fred has joined the 'Neal Stephenson fans' group."). Standard events might be a user joining a group, a user becoming friends with another, or a user changing their profile picture. To achieve this, we can now define a new subclass of **Post** named **EventPost** (Figure 10.7). Because **EventPost** is a subclass of **Post**, it automatically inherits all fields and methods that we have already defined in **Post**. Thus, **EventPost** objects already have a username, a time stamp, a likes counter, and comments. We can then concentrate on adding attributes that are specific to event posts, such as the event type. The event type might be stored as an enumeration constant (see Chapter 8) or as a string describing the event.

This is an example of how inheritance enables us to *reuse* existing work. We can reuse the code that we have written for photo posts and message posts (in the **Post** class) so that it

Figure 10.7

Network items with an **EventPost** class

> **Concept**
>
> Inheritance allows us to **reuse** previously written classes in a new context.

also works for the **EventPost** class. The ability to reuse existing software components is one of the great benefits that we get from the inheritance facility. We will discuss this in more detail later.

This reuse has the effect that a lot less new code is needed when we now introduce additional post types. Because new post types can be defined as subclasses of **Post**, only the code that is actually different from **Post** has to be added.

Now imagine that we change the requirements a bit: event posts in our *network* application will not have a "Like" button or comments attached. They are for information only. How do we achieve this? Currently, because **EventPost** is a subclass of **Post**, it automatically inherits the **likes** and **comments** fields. Is this a problem?

We could leave everything as it is and decide to never display the likes count or comments for event posts—just ignore the fields. This does not feel right. Having the fields present but unused invites problems. Someday, a maintenance programmer will come along who does not realize that these fields should not be used and try to process them.

Or we could write **EventPost** without inheriting from **Post**. But then we are back to code duplication for the **username** and **timestamp** fields and their methods.

The solution is to refactor the class hierarchy. We can introduce a new superclass for all posts that have comments attached (named **CommentedPost**), which is a subclass of **Post** (Figure 10.8). We then shift the **likes** and **comments** fields from the **Post** class to this new class. **MessagePost** and **PhotoPost** are now subclasses of our new **CommentedPost** class, while **EventPost** inherits from **Posts** directly. **MessagePost** objects inherit everything from both superclasses and have the same fields and methods as before. Objects of class **EventPost** will inherit the **username** and **timestamp**, but not the comments.

This is a very common situation in designing class hierarchies. When the hierarchy does not seem to fit properly, we have to refactor the hierarchy.

Figure 10.8
Adding more post types to *network*

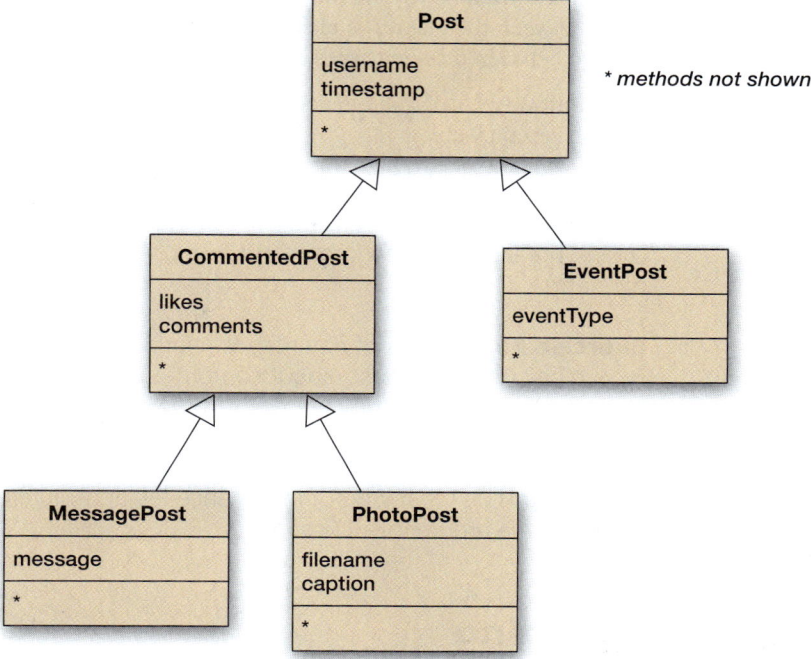

Classes that are not intended to be used to create instances, but whose purpose is exclusively to serve as superclasses for other classes (such as **Post** and **CommentedPost**), are called *abstract classes*. We shall investigate this in more detail in Chapter 12.

Exercise 10.8 Open the *network-v2* project. Add a class for event posts to the project. Create some event-post objects and test that all methods work as expected.

10.6 Advantages of inheritance (so far)

We have seen several advantages of using inheritance for the *network* application. Before we explore other aspects of inheritance, we shall summarize the general advantages we have encountered so far:

- **Avoiding code duplication** The use of inheritance avoids the need to write identical or very similar copies of code twice (or even more often).
- **Code reuse** Existing code can be reused. If a class similar to the one we need already exists, we can sometimes subclass the existing class and reuse some of the existing code, rather than having to implement everything again.

- **Easier maintenance** Maintaining the application becomes easier, because the relationship between the classes is clearly expressed. A change to a field or a method that is shared between different types of subclasses needs to be made only once.
- **Extendibility** Using inheritance, it becomes much easier to extend an existing application in certain ways.

> **Exercise 10.9** Order these items into an inheritance hierarchy: apple, ice cream, bread, fruit, food item, cereal, orange, dessert, chocolate mousse, baguette.
>
> **Exercise 10.10** In what inheritance relationship might a *touch pad* and a *mouse* be? (We are talking about computer input devices here, not a small furry mammal.)
>
> **Exercise 10.11** Sometimes things are more difficult than they first seem. Consider this: In what kind of inheritance relationship are *Rectangle* and *Square*? What are the arguments? Discuss.

10.7 Subtyping

The one thing we have not yet investigated is how the code in the **NewsFeed** class was changed when we modified our project to use inheritance. Code 10.5 shows the full source code of class **NewsFeed**. We can compare this with the original source shown in Code 10.3.

Code 10.5
Source code of the **NewsFeed** class (second version)

```java
import java.util.ArrayList;

/**
 * The NewsFeed class stores news posts for the news feed in a
 * social network application.
 *
 * Display of the posts is currently simulated by printing the
 * details to the terminal. (Later, this should display in a browser.)
 *
 * This version does not save the data to disk, and it does not
 * provide any search or ordering functions.
 *
 * @author Michael Kölling and David J. Barnes
 * @version 0.2
 */
public class NewsFeed
{
    private ArrayList<Post> posts;

    /**
     * Construct an empty news feed.
     */
```

Code 10.5

Source code of the **NewsFeed** class (second version)

```java
    public NewsFeed()
    {
        posts = new ArrayList<>();
    }

    /**
     * Add a post to the news feed.
     *
     * @param post  The post to be added.
     */
    public void addPost(Post post)
    {
        posts.add(post);
    }

    /**
     * Show the news feed. Currently: print the news feed details
     * to the terminal. (To do: replace this later with display
     * in web browser.)
     */
    public void show()
    {
        // display all posts
        for(Post post : posts) {
            post.display();
            System.out.println();   // empty line between posts
        }
    }
}
```

Concept
Subtype As an analog to the class hierarchy, types form a type hierarchy. The type defined by a subclass definition is a subtype of the type of its superclass.

As we can see, the code has become significantly shorter and simpler since our change to use inheritance. Where in the first version (Code 10.3) everything had to be done twice, it now exists only once. We have only one collection, only one method to add posts, and one loop in the **show** method.

The reason why we could shorten the source code is that, in the new version, we can use the type **Post** where we previously used **MessagePost** and **PhotoPost**. We investigate this first by examining the **addPost** method.

In our first version, we had two methods to add posts to the news feed. They had the following headers:

```java
public void addMessagePost(MessagePost message)
public void addPhotoPost(PhotoPost photo)
```

In our new version, we have a single method to serve the same purpose:

```java
public void addPost(Post post)
```

The parameters in the original version are defined with the types **MessagePost** and **PhotoPost**, ensuring that we pass **MessagePost** and **PhotoPost** objects to these methods, because actual parameter types must match the formal parameter types. So far, we have interpreted the requirement that parameter types must match as meaning "must be of the same type"—for instance, that the type name of an actual parameter must be the same as the type name of the corresponding formal parameter. This is only part of the truth, in fact, because an object of a subclass can be used wherever its superclass type is required.

10.7.1 Subclasses and subtypes

We have discussed earlier that classes define types. The type of an object that was created from class `MessagePost` is `MessagePost`. We also just discussed that classes may have subclasses. Thus, the types defined by the classes can have subtypes. In our example, the type `MessagePost` is a subtype of type `Post`.

10.7.2 Subtyping and assignment

When we want to assign an object to a variable, the type of the object must match the type of the variable. For example,

```
Car myCar = new Car();
```

is a valid assignment, because an object of type `Car` is assigned to a variable declared to hold objects of type `Car`. Now that we know about inheritance, we must state the typing rule more completely: a variable can hold objects of its declared type, or of any subtype of its declared type.

> **Concept**
>
> **Variables and subtypes** Variables may hold objects of their declared type or of any subtype of their declared type.

Imagine that we have a class `Vehicle` with two subclasses, `Car` and `Bicycle` (Figure 10.9). In this case, the typing rule allows all the following assignments:

```
Vehicle v1 = new Vehicle();
Vehicle v2 = new Car();
Vehicle v3 = new Bicycle();
```

The type of a variable declares what it can store. Declaring a variable of type `Vehicle` states that this variable can hold vehicles. But because a car is a vehicle, it is perfectly legal to store a car in a variable that is intended for vehicles. (Think of the variable as a garage: if someone tells you that you may park a vehicle in a garage, you would think that parking either a car or a bicycle in the garage would be okay.)

This principle is known as *substitution*. In object-oriented languages, we can substitute a subclass object where a superclass object is expected, because the subclass object is a special case of the superclass. If, for example, someone asks us to give them a pen, we can

Figure 10.9
An inheritance hierarchy

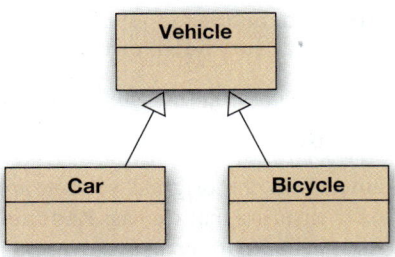

10.7 Subtyping

> **Concept**
>
> **Substitution**
> Subtype objects may be used wherever objects of a supertype are expected. This is known as substitution.

fulfill the request perfectly well by giving them a fountain pen or a ballpoint pen. Both fountain pen and ballpoint pen are subclasses of pen, so supplying either where an object of class **Pen** was expected is fine.

However, doing it the other way is not allowed:

    Car c1 = new Vehicle(); // this is an error!

This statement attempts to store a **Vehicle** object in a **Car** variable. Java will not allow this, and an error will be reported if you try to compile this statement. The variable is declared to be able to store cars. A vehicle, on the other hand, may or may not be a car—we do not know. Thus, the statement may be wrong, and therefore not allowed.

Similarly:

    Car c2 = new Bicycle(); // this is an error!

This is also an illegal statement. A bicycle is not a car (or, more formally, the type **Bicycle** is not a subtype of **Car**), and thus the assignment is not allowed.

Exercise 10.12 Assume that we have four classes: **Person**, **Teacher**, **Student**, and **PhDStudent**. **Teacher** and **Student** are both subclasses of **Person**. **PhDStudent** is a subclass of **Student**.

a. Which of the following assignments are legal, and why or why not?

    Person p1 = new Student();
    Person p2 = new PhDStudent();
    PhDStudent phd1 = new Student();
    Teacher t1 = new Person();
    Student s1 = new PhDStudent();

b. Suppose that we have the following legal declarations and assignments:

    Person p1 = new Person();
    Person p2 = new Person();
    PhDStudent phd1 = new PhDStudent();
    Teacher t1 = new Teacher();
    Student s1 = new Student();

Based on those just mentioned, which of the following assignments are legal, and why or why not?

    s1 = p1
    s1 = p2
    p1 = s1;
    t1 = s1;
    s1 = phd1;
    phd1 = s1;

Exercise 10.13 Test your answers to the previous question by creating barebones versions of the classes mentioned in that exercise and trying it out in BlueJ.

10.7.3 Subtyping and parameter passing

Passing a parameter (that is, assigning an actual parameter to a formal parameter variable) behaves in exactly the same way as an assignment to a variable. This is why we can pass an object of type **MessagePost** to a method that has a parameter of type **Post**. We have the following definition of the **addPost** method in class **NewsFeed**:

```
public void addPost(Post post)
{
   . . .
}
```

We can now use this method to add message posts and photo posts to the feed:

```
NewsFeed feed = new NewsFeed();
MessagePost message = new MessagePost(. . .);
PhotoPost photo = new PhotoPost(. . .);
feed.addPost(message);
feed.addPost(photo);
```

Because of subtyping rules, we need only one method (with a parameter of type **Post**) to add both **MessagePost** and **PhotoPost** objects.

We will discuss subtyping in more detail in the next chapter.

10.7.4 Polymorphic variables

Variables holding object types in Java are *polymorphic* variables. The term "polymorphic" (literally, *many shapes*) refers to the fact that a variable can hold objects of different types (namely, the declared type or any subtype of the declared type). Polymorphism appears in object-oriented languages in several contexts—polymorphic variables are just the first example. We will discuss other incarnations of polymorphism in more detail in the next chapter.

For now, we just observe how the use of a polymorphic variable helps us simplify our **show** method. The body of this method is

```
for(Post post : posts) {
    post.display();
    System.out.println(); // empty line between posts
}
```

Here, we iterate through the list of posts (held in an **ArrayList** in the **posts** variable). We get out each post and then invoke its **display** method. Note that the actual posts that we get out of the list are of type **MessagePost** or **PhotoPost**, not of type **Post**. We can, however, use a loop variable of type **Post**, because variables are polymorphic.

The **post** variable is able to hold **MessagePost** and **PhotoPost** objects, because these are subtypes of **Post**.

Thus, the use of inheritance in this example has removed the need for two separate loops in the **show** method. Inheritance avoids code duplication not only in the server classes, but also in clients of those classes.

> **Note** When doing the exercises, you may have noticed that the **show** method has a problem: not all details are printed out. Solving this problem requires some more explanation. We will provide this in the next chapter.

Exercise 10.14 What has to change in the **NewsFeed** class when another **Post** subclass (for example, a class **EventPost**) is added? Why?

10.7.5 Casting

Sometimes the rule that we cannot assign from a supertype to a subtype is more restrictive than necessary. If we know that the supertype variable holds a subtype object, the assignment could actually be allowed. For example:

```
Vehicle v;
Car c = new Car();
v = c;  // correct
c = v;  // error
```

The above statements would not compile: we get a compiler error in the last line, because assigning a **Vehicle** variable to a **Car** variable (supertype to subtype) is not allowed. However, if we execute these statements in sequence, we know that we could actually allow this assignment. We can see that the variable **v** actually contains an object of type **Car**, so the assignment to **c** would be okay. The compiler is not that smart. It translates the code line by line, so it looks at the last line in isolation without knowing what is currently stored in variable **v**. This is called *type loss*. The type of the object in **v** is actually **Car**, but the compiler does not know this.

We can get around this problem by explicitly telling the type system that the variable **v** holds a **Car** object. We do this using a *cast operator*:

```
c = (Car) v;  // okay
```

The cast operator consists of the name of a type (here, **Car**) written in parentheses in front of a variable or an expression. Doing this will cause the compiler to believe that the object is a **Car**, and it will not report an error. At runtime, however, the Java system will check that it really is a **Car**. If we were careful, and it is truly is a **Car**, everything is fine. If the object in **v** is of another type, the runtime system will indicate an error (called a **ClassCast-Exception**), and the program will stop.[3]

---
[3] Exceptions are discussed in detail in Chapter 14.

Now consider this code fragment, in which **Bicycle** is also a subclass of **Vehicle**:

```
Vehicle v;
Car c;
Bicycle b;
c = new Car();
v = c; // okay
b = (Bicycle) c; // compile time error!
b = (Bicycle) v; // runtime error!
```

The last two assignments will both fail. The attempt to assign **c** to **b** (even with the cast) will be a compile-time error. The compiler notices that **Car** and **Bicycle** do not form a subtype/supertype relationship, so **c** can never hold a **Bicycle** object—the assignment could never work.

The attempt to assign **v** to **b** (with the cast) will be accepted at compile time, but will fail at runtime. **Vehicle** is a superclass of **Bicycle**, and thus **v** can potentially hold a **Bicycle** object. At runtime, however, it turns out that the object in **v** is not a **Bicycle** but a **Car**, and the program will terminate prematurely.

Casting should be avoided wherever possible, because it can lead to runtime errors, and that is clearly something we do not want. The compiler cannot help us to ensure correctness in this case.

In practice, casting is very rarely needed in a well-structured, object-oriented program. In almost all cases, when you use a cast in your code, you could restructure your code to avoid this cast and end up with a better-designed program. This usually involves replacing the cast with a polymorphic method call (more about this will be covered in the next chapter).

10.8 The `Object` class

Concept

All classes with no explicit superclass have **Object** as their superclass.

All classes have a superclass. So far, it has appeared as if most classes we have seen do not have a superclass. In fact, while we can declare an explicit superclass for a class, all classes that have no superclass declaration implicitly inherit from a class called **Object**.

Object is a class from the Java standard library that serves as a superclass for all objects. Writing a class declaration such as

```
public class Person
{
    . . .
}
```

is equivalent to writing

```
public class Person extends Object
{
    . . .
}
```

Figure 10.10
All classes inherit from `Object`

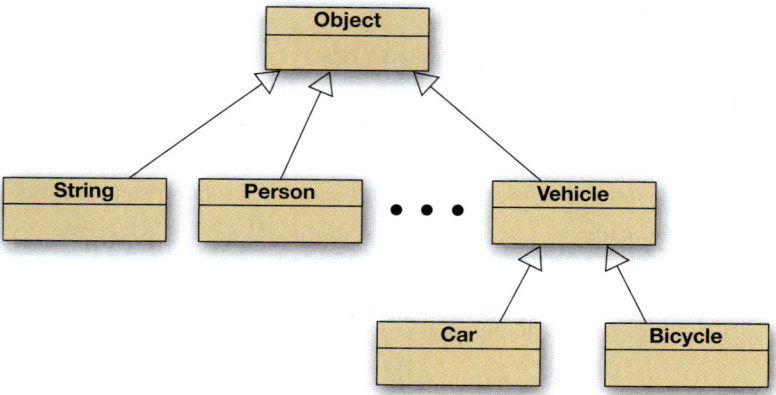

The Java compiler automatically inserts the `Object` superclass for all classes without an explicit `extends` declaration, so it is never necessary to do this for yourself. Every single class (with the sole exception of the `Object` class itself) inherits from `Object`, either directly or indirectly. Figure 10.10 shows some randomly chosen classes to illustrate this.

Having a common superclass for all objects serves two purposes: First, we can declare polymorphic variables of type `Object` to hold any object. Having variables that can hold any object type is not often useful, but there are some situations where this can help. Second, the `Object` class can define some methods that are then automatically available for every existing object. Of particular importance are the methods `toString`, `equals`, and `hashCode` which `Object` defines. This second point becomes interesting a bit later, and we shall discuss this in more detail in the next chapter.

10.9 The collection hierarchy

The Java library uses inheritance extensively in the definition of the collections classes. Class `ArrayList`, for example, inherits from a class called `AbstractList`, which, in turn, inherits from `AbstractCollection`. We shall not discuss this hierarchy here, because it is described in detail at various easily accessible places. One good description is at Oracle's web site at `http://download.oracle.com/javase/tutorial/collections/index.html`.

Note that some details of this hierarchy require an understanding of Java *interfaces*. We discuss those in Chapter 12.

Exercise 10.15 Use the documentation of the Java standard class libraries to find out about the inheritance hierarchy of the collection classes. Draw a diagram showing the hierarchy.

10.10 Summary

This chapter has presented a first view of inheritance. All classes in Java are arranged in an inheritance hierarchy. Each class may have an explicitly declared superclass, or it inherits implicitly from the class `Object`.

Subclasses usually represent specializations of superclasses. Because of this, the inheritance relationship is also referred to as an is-a relationship (a car *is-a* vehicle).

Subclasses inherit all fields and methods of a superclass. Objects of subclasses have all fields and methods declared in their own classes, as well as those from all superclasses. Inheritance relationships can be used to avoid code duplication, to reuse existing code, and to make an application more maintainable and extendable.

Subclasses also form subtypes, which leads to polymorphic variables. Subtype objects may be substituted for supertype objects, and variables are allowed to hold objects that are instances of subtypes of their declared type.

Inheritance allows the design of class structures that are easier to maintain and more flexible. This chapter contains only an introduction to the use of inheritance for the purpose of improving program structures. More uses of inheritance and their benefits will be discussed in the following chapters.

Terms introduced in this chapter:

inheritance, superclass (parent), subclass (child), *is-a*, **inheritance hierarchy, abstract class, subtype substitution, polymorphic variable, type loss, cast**

Exercise 10.16 Go back to the *lab-classes* project from Chapter 1. Add instructors to the project (every lab class can have many students and a single instructor). Use inheritance to avoid code duplication between students and instructors (both have a name, contact details, etc.).

Exercise 10.17 Draw an inheritance hierarchy representing parts of a computer system (processor, memory, disk drive, DVD drive, printer, scanner, keyboard, mouse, etc.).

Exercise 10.18 Look at the code below. You have four classes (O, X, T, and M) and a variable of each of these.

```
O o;
X x;
T t;
M m;
```

The following assignments are all legal (assume that they all compile):

```
m = t;
m = x;
o = t;
```

The following assignments are all illegal (they cause compiler errors):

```
o = m;
o = x;
x = o;
```

What can you say about the relationships of these classes? Draw a class diagram.

Exercise 10.19 Draw an inheritance hierarchy of `AbstractList` and all its (direct and indirect) subclasses as they are defined in the Java standard library.

CHAPTER 11

More about Inheritance

Main concepts discussed in this chapter:

- method polymorphism
- overriding
- static and dynamic type
- dynamic method lookup

Java constructs discussed in this chapter:

`super` (in method), `toString`, `protected`, `instanceof`

The last chapter introduced the main concepts of inheritance by discussing the *network* example. While we have seen the foundations of inheritance, there are still numerous important details that we have not yet investigated. Inheritance is central to understanding and using object-oriented languages, and understanding it in detail is necessary to progress from here.

In this chapter, we shall continue to use the *network* example to explore the most important of the remaining issues surrounding inheritance and polymorphism.

11.1 The problem: *network's* display method

When you experimented with the *network* examples in Chapter 10, you probably noticed that the second version—the one using inheritance—has a problem: the `display` method does not show all of a post's data.

Let us look at an example. Assume that we create a `MessagePost` and a `PhotoPost` object with the following data:

The message post:

> Leonardo da Vinci
>
> Had a great idea this morning.
> But now I forgot what it was. Something to do with flying . . .
>
> 40 seconds ago. 2 people like this.
>
> No comments.

The photo post:

Alexander Graham Bell
[experiment.jpg]   I think I might call this thing 'telephone'.
12 minutes ago. 4 people like this.
No comments.

If we enter these objects into the news feed[1] and then invoke the first version of the news feed's **show** method (the one without inheritance), it prints

Leonardo da Vinci
Had a great idea this morning.
But now I forgot what it was. Something to do with flying . . .
40 seconds ago - 2 people like this.
   No comments.

Alexander Graham Bell
[experiment.jpg]
I think I might call this thing 'telephone'.
12 minutes ago - 4 people like this.
   No comments.

While the formatting isn't pretty (because, in the text terminal, we don't have formatting options available), all the information is there, and we can imagine how the **show** method might be adapted later to show the data in a nicer formatting in a different user interface.

Compare this with the second *network* version (with inheritance), which prints only

Leonardo da Vinci
40 seconds ago - 2 people like this.
   No comments.

Alexander Graham Bell
12 minutes ago - 4 people like this.
   No comments.

We note that the message post's text, as well as the photo post's image filename and caption, are missing. The reason for this is simple. The **display** method in this version is implemented in the **Post** class, not in **MessagePost** and **PhotoPost** (Figure 11.1). In the methods of **Post**, only the fields declared in **Post** are available. If we tried to access the **MessagePost**'s **message** field from **Post**'s **display** method, an error would be reported. This illustrates the important principle that inheritance is a one-way street: **MessagePost** inherits the fields of **Post**, but **Post** still does not know anything about fields in its subclasses.

---

[1] The text for the message post is a two-line string. You can enter a multiline text into a string by using "\n" in the string for the line break.

Figure 11.1
Display, version 1:
`display` method in superclass

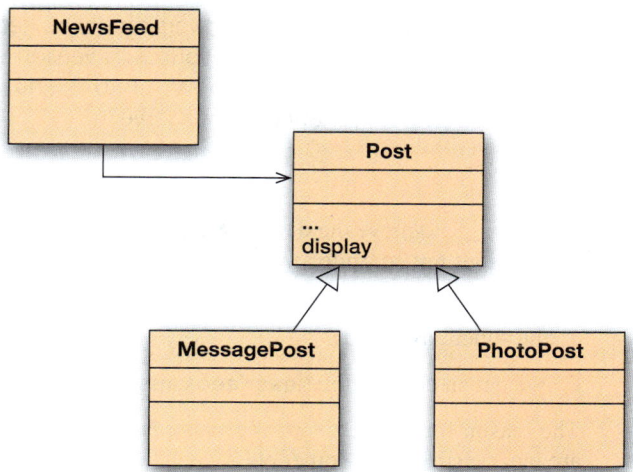

11.2 Static type and dynamic type

Trying to solve the problem of developing a complete polymorphic `display` method leads us into a discussion of *static* and *dynamic types* and *method lookup*. But let us start at the beginning.

A first attempt to solve the display problem might be to move the `display` method to the subclasses (Figure 11.2). That way, because the method would now belong to the **MessagePost** and **PhotoPost** classes, it could access the specific fields of **MessagePost** and **PhotoPost**. It could also access the inherited fields by calling accessor methods defined in the **Post** class. That should enable it to display a complete set of information again. Try out this approach by completing Exercise 11.1.

Figure 11.2
Display, version 2:
`display` method in subclasses

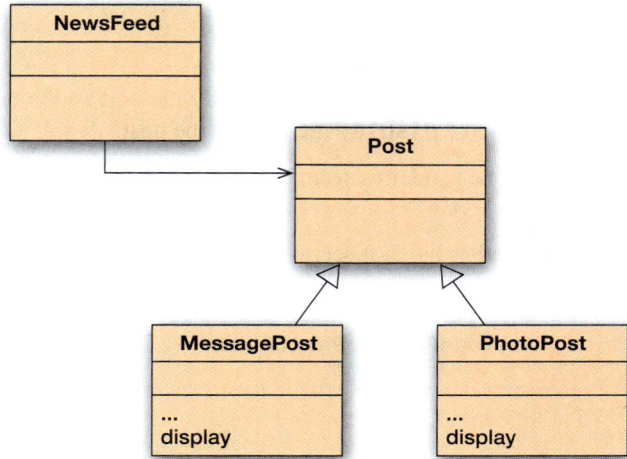

> **Exercise 11.1** Open your last version of the *network* project. (You can use *network-v2* if you do not have your own version yet.) Remove the `display` method from class **Post** and move it into the **MessagePost** and **PhotoPost** classes. Compile. What do you observe?

When we try to move the `display` method from **Post** to the subclasses, we notice that the project does not compile any more. There are two fundamental issues:

- We get errors in the **MessagePost** and **PhotoPost** classes, because we cannot access the superclass fields.

- We get an error in the **NewsFeed** class, because it cannot find the `display` method.

The reason for the first sort of error is that the fields in **Post** have private access, and so are inaccessible to any other class—including subclasses. Because we do not wish to break encapsulation and make these fields public, as was suggested above, the easiest way to solve this is to define public accessor methods for them. However, in Section 11.9, we shall introduce a further type of access designed specifically to support the superclass–subclass relationship.

The reason for the second sort of error requires a more detailed explanation, and this is explored in the next section.

11.2.1 Calling `display` from NewsFeed

First, we investigate the problem of calling the `display` method from **NewsFeed**. The relevant lines of code in the **NewsFeed** class are:

```
for(Post post : posts) {
    post.display();
    System.out.println();
}
```

The for-each statement retrieves each post from the collection; the first statement inside its body tries to invoke the `display` method on the post. The compiler informs us that it cannot find a `display` method for the post.

On the one hand, this seems logical; **Post** does not have a `display` method any more (see Figure 11.2).

On the other hand, it seems illogical and is annoying. We know that every **Post** object in the collection is in fact a **MessagePost** or a **PhotoPost** object, and both have `display` methods. This should mean that `post.display()` ought to work, because, whatever it is—**MessagePost** or **PhotoPost**—we know that it does have a `display` method.

To understand in detail why it does not work, we need to look more closely at types. Consider the following statement:

```
Car c1 = new Car();
```

We say that the type of `c1` is `Car`. Before we encountered inheritance, there was no need to distinguish whether by "type of `c1`" we meant "the type of the variable `c1`" or "the type of the object stored in `c1`." It did not matter, because the type of the variable and the type of the object were always the same.

Now that we know about subtyping, we need to be more precise. Consider the following statement:

```
Vehicle v1 = new Car();
```

> **Concept**
>
> The **static type** of a variable **v** is the type as declared in the source code in the variable declaration statement.

What is the type of `v1`? That depends on what precisely we mean by "type of `v1`." The type of the variable `v1` is `Vehicle`; the type of the object stored in `v1` is `Car`. Through subtyping and substitution rules, we now have situations where the type of the variable and the type of the object stored in it are not exactly the same.

Let us introduce some terminology to make it easier to talk about this issue:

- We call the declared type of the variable the *static type,* because it is declared in the source code—the static representation of the program.

- We call the type of the object stored in a variable the *dynamic type,* because it depends on assignments at runtime—the dynamic behavior of the program.

> **Concept**
>
> The **dynamic type** of a variable **v** is the type of the object that is currently stored in **v**.

Thus, looking at the explanations above, we can be more precise: the static type of `v1` is `Vehicle`, the dynamic type of `v1` is `Car`. We can now also rephrase our discussion about the call to the post's `display` method in the `NewsFeed` class. At the time of the call

```
post.display();
```

the static type of `post` is `Post`, while the dynamic type is either `MessagePost` or `PhotoPost` (Figure 11.3). We do not know which one of these it is, assuming that we have entered both `MessagePost` and `PhotoPost` objects into the feed.

Figure 11.3
Variable of type `Post` containing an object of type `PhotoPost`

The compiler reports an error because, for type checking, the static type is used. The dynamic type is often only known at runtime, so the compiler has no other choice but to use the static type if it wants to do any checks at compile time. The static type of `post` is `Post`, and `Post` does not have a `display` method. It makes no difference that all known subtypes of `Post` do have a `display` method. The behavior of the compiler is reasonable in this respect, because it has no guarantee that *all* subclasses of `Post` will, indeed, define a `display` method, and this is impossible to check in practice.

In other words, to make this call work, class `Post` must have a `display` method, so we appear to be back to our original problem without having made any progress.

Exercise 11.2 In your *network* project, add a `display` method in class **Post** again. For now, write the method body with a single statement that prints out only the username. Then modify the `display` methods in **MessagePost** and **PhotoPost** so that the **MessagePost** version prints out only the message and the **PhotoPost** version prints only the caption. This removes the other errors encountered above (we shall come back to those below).

You should now have a situation corresponding to Figure 11.4, with `display` methods in three classes. Compile your project. (If there are errors, remove them. This design should work.)

Before executing, predict which of the `display` methods will get called if you execute the news feed's `show` method.

Try it out. Enter a message post and a photo post into the news feed and call the news feed's `show` method. Which `display` methods were executed? Was your prediction correct? Try to explain your observations.

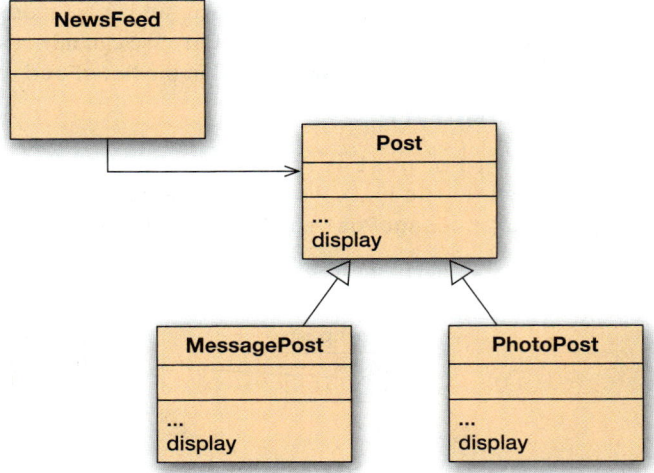

Figure 11.4
Display, version 3: `display` method in subclasses and superclass

11.3 Overriding

The next design we shall discuss is one where both the superclass and the subclasses have a `display` method (Figure 11.4). The header of all the `display` methods is exactly the same.

Code 11.1 shows the relevant details of the source code of all three classes. Class **Post** has a `display` method that prints out all the fields that are declared in **Post** (those common to message posts and photo posts), and the subclasses **MessagePost** and **PhotoPost** print out the fields specific to **MessagePost** and **PhotoPost** objects, respectively.

Code 11.1

Source code of the `display` methods in all three classes

```java
public class Post
{
    ...
    public void display()
    {
        System.out.println(username);
        System.out.print(timeString(timestamp));
        
        if(likes > 0) {
            System.out.println("  -  " + likes + " people like this.");
        }
        else {
            System.out.println();
        }
        
        if(comments.isEmpty()) {
            System.out.println("   No comments.");
        }
        else {
            System.out.println("   " + comments.size() +
                               " comment(s). Click here to view.");
        }
    }
}

public class MessagePost extends Post
{
    ...
    public void display()
    {
        System.out.println(message);
    }
}

public class PhotoPost extends Post
{
    ...
    public void display()
    {
        System.out.println("   [" + filename + "]");
        System.out.println("   " + caption);
    }
}
```

Concept

Overriding
A subclass can override a method implementation. To do this, the subclass declares a method with the same signature as the superclass, but with a different method body. The overriding method takes precedence for method calls on subclass objects.

This design works a bit better. It compiles, and it can be executed, even though it is not perfect yet. An implementation of this design is provided in the project *network-v3*. (If you have done Exercise 11.2, you already have a similar implementation of this design in your own version.)

The technique we are using here is called *overriding* (sometimes it is also referred to as *redefinition*). Overriding is a situation where a method is defined in a superclass (method `display` in class `Post` in this example), and a method with exactly the same signature is defined in the subclass. The annotation `@Override` may be added before the version in the subclass to make it clear that a new version of an inherited method is being defined.

In this situation, objects of the subclass have two methods with the same name and header: one inherited from the superclass and one from the subclass. Which one will be executed when we call this method?

11.4 Dynamic method lookup

One surprising detail is what exactly is printed once we execute the news feed's `show` method. If we again create and enter the objects described in Section 11.1, the output of the `show` method in our new version of the program is

```
Had a great idea this morning.
But now I forgot what it was. Something to do with flying . . .

[experiment.jpg]
I think I might call this thing 'telephone'.
```

We can see from this output that the `display` methods in `MessagePost` and in `PhotoPost` were executed, but not the one in `Post`.

This may seem strange at first. Our investigation in Section 11.2 has shown that the compiler insisted on a `display` method in class `Post`—methods in the subclasses were not enough. This experiment now shows that the method in class `Post` is then not executed at all, but the subclass methods are. In short:

- Type checking uses the static type, but at runtime, the methods from the dynamic type are executed.

This is a fairly important statement. To understand it better, we look in more detail at how methods are invoked. This procedure is known as *method lookup*, *method binding*, or *method dispatch*. We will use the term "*method lookup*" in this book.

We start with a simple method-lookup scenario. Assume that we have an object of a class `PhotoPost` stored in a variable `v1` declared of type `PhotoPost` (Figure 11.5).

Figure 11.5
Method lookup with a simple object

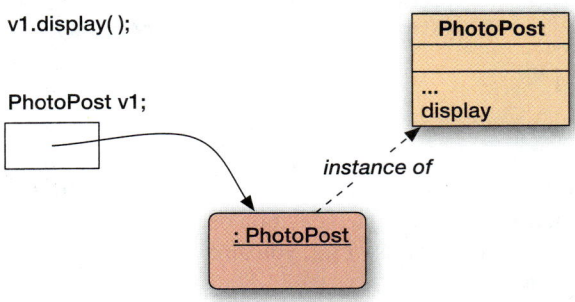

The **PhotoPost** class has a **display** method and no declared superclass. This is a very simple situation—there is no inheritance or polymorphism involved here. We then execute the statement

```
v1.display();
```

When this statement executes, the **display** method is invoked in the following steps:

1. The variable **v1** is accessed.
2. The object stored in that variable is found (following the reference).
3. The class of the object is found (following the "instance of" reference).
4. The implementation of the **display** method is found in the class and executed.

This is all very straightforward and not surprising.

Next, we look at method lookup with inheritance. This scenario is similar, but this time the **PhotoPost** class has a superclass **Post**, and the **display** method is defined only in the superclass (Figure 11.6).

We execute the same statement. The method invocation then starts in a similar way: steps 1 through 3 from the previous scenario are executed again, but then it continues differently:

4. No **display** method is found in class **PhotoPost**.
5. Because no matching method was found, the superclass is searched for a matching method. If no method is found in the superclass, the next superclass (if it exists) is searched. This continues all the way up the inheritance hierarchy to the **Object** class, until a method is found. Note that at runtime, a matching method should definitely be found, or else the class would not have compiled.
6. In our example, the **display** method is found in class **Post**, and will be executed.

Figure 11.6
Method lookup with inheritance

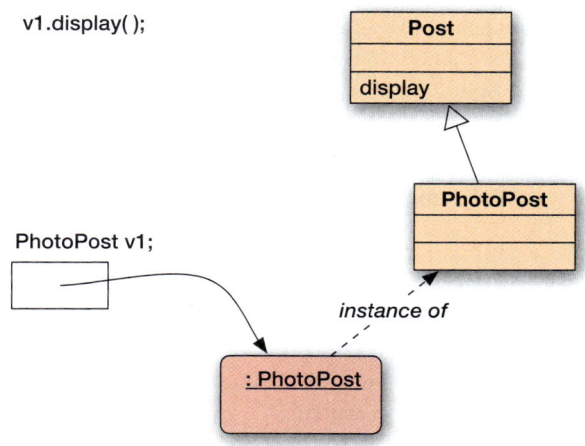

Figure 11.7
Method lookup with polymorphism and overriding

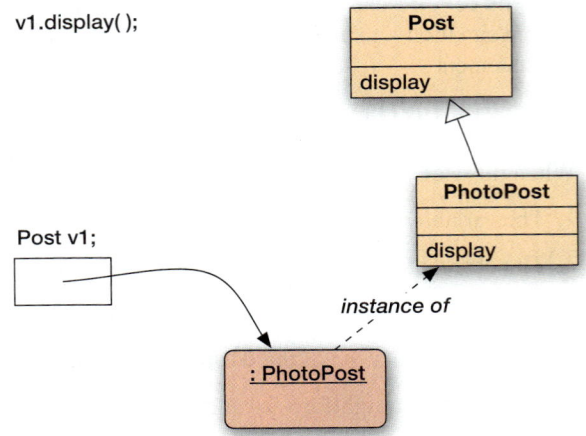

This scenario illustrates how objects inherit methods. Any method found in a superclass can be invoked on a subclass object and will correctly be found and executed.

Next, we come to the most interesting scenario: method lookup with a polymorphic variable and method overriding (Figure 11.7). The scenario is again similar to the one before, but there are two changes:

- The declared type of the variable **v1** is now **Post**, not **PhotoPost**.
- The **display** method is defined in class **Post** and then redefined (overridden) in class **PhotoPost**.

This scenario is the most important one for understanding the behavior of our *network* application, and in finding a solution to our **display** method problem.

The steps in which method execution takes place are exactly the same as steps 1 through 4 from scenario 1. Read them again.

Some observations are worth noting:

- No special lookup rules are used for method lookup in cases where the dynamic type is not equal to the static type. The behavior we observe is a result of the general rules.
- Which method is found first and executed is determined by the dynamic type, not the static type. In other words, the fact that the declared type of the variable **v1** is now **Post** does not have any effect. The instance we are dealing with is of class **PhotoPost**—that is all that matters.
- Overriding methods in subclasses take precedence over superclass methods. Because method lookup starts in the dynamic class of the instance (at the bottom of the inheritance hierarchy), the last redefinition of a method is found first, and this is the one that is executed.
- When a method is overridden, only the last version (the one lowest in the inheritance hierarchy) is executed. Versions of the same method in any superclasses are also not automatically executed.

This explains the behavior that we observe in our *network* project. Only the `display` methods in the subclasses (`MessagePost` and `PhotoPost`) are executed when posts are printed out, leading to incomplete listings. In the next section, we discuss how to fix this.

11.5 super call in methods

Now that we know in detail how overridden methods are executed, we can understand the solution to the problem. It is easy to see that what we would want to achieve is for every call to a `display` method of, say, a `PhotoPost` object, to result in both the `display` method of the `Post` class and that of the `PhotoPost` class being executed for the same object. Then all the details would be printed out. (A different solution will be discussed later in this chapter.)

This is, in fact, quite easy to achieve. We can simply use the `super` construct, which we have already encountered in the context of constructors in Chapter 10. Code 11.2 illustrates this idea with the `display` method of the `PhotoPost` class.

Code 11.2
Redefining method with a `super` call

```
public void display()
{
    super.display();
    System.out.println("   [" + filename + "]");
    System.out.println("   " + caption);
}
```

When `display` is now called on a `PhotoPost` object, initially the `display` method in the `PhotoPost` class will be invoked. As its first statement, this method will in turn invoke the `display` method of the superclass, which prints out the general post information. When control returns from the superclass method, the remaining statements of the subclass method print the distinctive fields of the `PhotoPost` class.

There are three details worth noting:

- Contrary to the case of `super` calls in constructors, the method name of the superclass method is explicitly stated. A `super` call in a method always has the form

    `super.method-name( parameters )`

- The parameter list can, of course, be empty.

- Again, contrary to the rule for `super` calls in constructors, the `super` call in methods may occur anywhere within that method. It does not have to be the first statement.

- And contrary to the case of `super` calls in constructors, no automatic `super` call is generated and no `super` call is required; it is entirely optional. So the default behavior gives the effect of a subclass method completely hiding (i.e., overriding) the superclass version of the same method.

Exercise 11.3 Modify your latest version of the *network* project to include the `super` call in the `display` method. Test it. Does it behave as expected? Do you see any problems with this solution?

It is worth reiterating what was illustrated in Exercise 10.6: that in the absence of method overriding, the non-private methods of a superclass are directly accessible from its subclasses without any special syntax. A **super** call only has to be made when it is necessary to access the superclass version of an *overridden* method.

If you completed Exercise 11.3, you will have noticed that this solution works, but is not perfect yet. It prints out all details, but in a different order from what we wanted. We will fix this last problem later in the chapter.

11.6 Method polymorphism

Concept

Method polymorphism. Method calls in Java are polymorphic. The same method call may at different times invoke different methods, depending on the dynamic type of the variable used to make that call.

What we have just discussed in the previous sections (Sections 11.2–11.5) is yet another form of polymorphism. It is what is known as *polymorphic method dispatch* (or *method polymorphism* for short).

Remember that a polymorphic variable is one that can store objects of varying types (every object variable in Java is potentially polymorphic). In a similar manner, Java method calls are polymorphic, because they may invoke different methods at different times. For instance, the statement

```
post.display();
```

could invoke the **MessagePost**'s **display** method at one time and the **PhotoPost**'s **display** method at another, depending on the dynamic type of the **post** variable.

11.7 Object methods: `toString`

Concept

Every object in Java has a **toString** method that can be used to return a string representation of itself. Typically, to make it useful, an object should override this method.

In Chapter 10, we mentioned that the universal superclass, **Object**, implements some methods that are then part of all objects. The most interesting of these methods is **toString**, which we introduce here (if you are interested in more detail, you can look up the interface for **Object** in the standard library documentation).

> **Exercise 11.4** Look up **toString** in the library documentation. What are its parameters? What is its return type?

The purpose of the **toString** method is to create a string representation of an object. This is useful for any objects that are ever to be textually represented in the user interface, but also helps for all other objects; they can then easily be printed out for debugging purposes, for instance.

The default implementation of **toString** in class **Object** cannot supply a great amount of detail. If, for example, we call **toString** on a **PhotoPost** object, we receive a string similar to this:

```
PhotoPost@65c221c0
```

The return value simply shows the object's class name and a magic number.[2]

> **Exercise 11.5** You can easily try this out. Create an object of class **PhotoPost** in your project, and then invoke the **toString** method from the **Object** sub-menu in the object's pop-up menu.

To make this method more useful, we would typically override it in our own classes. We can, for example, define the **Post's display** method in terms of a call to its **toString** method. In this case, the **toString** method would not print out the details, but just create a string with the text. Code 11.3 shows the changed source code.

Code 11.3 toString method for Post and MessagePost

```java
public class Post
{
    ...
    public String toString()
    {
        String text = username + "\n" + timeString(timestamp);
        if(likes > 0) {
            text += "  -  " + likes + " people like this.\n";
        }
        else {
            text += "\n";
        }

        if(comments.isEmpty()) {
            return text + "   No comments.\n";
        }
        else {
            return text + "   " + comments.size() +
                   " comment(s). Click here to view.\n";
        }
    }

    public void display()
    {
        System.out.println(toString());
    }
}
```

---

[2] The magic number is in fact the memory address where the object is stored. It is not very useful except to establish identity. If this number is the same in two calls, we are looking at the same object. If it is different, we have two distinct objects.

Code 11.3 continued
toString method for **Post** and **MessagePost**

```java
public class MessagePost extends Post
{
    ...
    public String toString()
    {
        return super.toString() + message + "\n";
    }

    public void display()
    {
        System.out.println(toString());
    }
}
```

Ultimately, we would plan on removing the **display** methods completely from these classes. A great benefit of defining just a **toString** method is that we do not mandate in the **Post** classes what exactly is done with the description text. The original version always printed the text to the output terminal. Now, any client (e.g., the **NewsFeed** class) is free to do whatever it chooses with this text. It might show the text in a text area in a graphical user interface; save it to a file; send it over a network; show it in a web browser; or, as before, print it to the terminal.

The statement used in the client to print the post could now look as follows:

```
System.out.println(post.toString());
```

In fact, the **System.out.print** and **System.out.println** methods are special in this respect: if the parameter to one of the methods is not a **String** object, then the method automatically invokes the object's **toString** method. Thus we do not need to write the call explicitly and could instead write

```
System.out.println(post);
```

Now consider the modified version of the **show** method of class **NewsFeed** shown in Code 11.4. In this version, we have removed the **toString** call. Would it compile and run correctly?

Code 11.4
New version of **NewsFeed show** method

```java
public class NewsFeed
{
    Fields, constructors, and other methods omitted.

    /**
     * Show the news feed. Currently: print the news feed details to the
     * terminal. (To do: replace this later with display in web browser.)
     */
    public void show()
    {
        for(Post post : posts) {
            System.out.println(post);
        }
    }
}
```

In fact, the method *does* work as expected. If you can explain this example in detail, then you probably already have a good understanding of most of the concepts that we have introduced in this and the previous chapter! Here is a detailed explanation of the single `println` statement inside the loop.

- The for-each loop iterates through all posts and places them in a variable with the static type **Post**. The dynamic type is either **MessagePost** or **PhotoPost**.

- Because this object is being printed to **System.out** and it is not a **String**, its **toString** method is automatically invoked.

- Invoking this method is valid only because the class **Post** (the static type!) has a **toString** method. (Remember: Type checking is done with the static type. This call would not be allowed if class **Post** had no **toString** method. However, the **toString** method in class **Object** guarantees that this method is always available for any class.)

- The output appears properly with all details, because each possible dynamic type (**MessagePost** and **PhotoPost**) overrides the **toString** method and the dynamic method lookup ensures that the redefined method is executed.

The **toString** method is generally useful for debugging purposes. Often, it is very convenient if objects can easily be printed out in a sensible format. Most of the Java library classes override **toString** (all collections, for instance, can be printed out like this), and often it is a good idea to override this method for our classes as well.

11.8 Object equality: equals and hashCode

It is often necessary to determine whether two objects are "the same." The **Object** class defines two methods, **equals** and **hashCode**, that have a close link with determining similarity. We actually have to be careful when using phrases such as "the same"; this is because it can mean two quite different things when talking about objects. Sometimes we wish to know whether two different variables are referring to the same object. This is exactly what happens when an object variable is passed as a parameter to a method: there is only one object, but both the original variable and the parameter variable refer to it. The same thing happens when any object variable is assigned to another. These situations produce what is called *reference equality*. Reference equality is tested for using the **==** operator. So the following test will return **true** if both **var1** and **var2** are referring to the same object (or are both **null**), and **false** if they are referring to anything else:

```
var1 == var2
```

Reference equality takes no account at all of the *contents* of the objects referred to, just whether there is one object referred to by two different variables or two distinct objects. That is why we also define *content equality*, as distinct from reference equality. A test for content equality asks whether two objects are the same internally—that is, whether the internal states of two objects are the same. This is why we rejected using reference equality for making string comparisons in Chapter 6.

What content equality between two particular objects means is something that is defined by the objects' class. This is where we make use of the **equals** method that every class inherits from the **Object** superclass. If we need to define what it means for two objects to be equal according to their internal states, then we must override the **equals** method, which then allows us to write tests such as

```
var1.equals(var2)
```

This is because the **equals** method inherited from the **Object** class actually makes a test for reference equality. It looks something like this:

```
public boolean equals(Object obj)
{
    return this == obj;
}
```

Because the **Object** class has no fields, there is no state to compare, and this method obviously cannot anticipate fields that might be present in subclasses.

The way to test for content equality between two objects is to test whether the values of their two sets of fields are equal. Notice, however, that the parameter of the **equals** method is of type **Object**, so a test of the fields will make sense only if we are comparing fields of the same type. This means that we first have to establish that the type of the object passed as a parameter is the same as that of the object it is being compared with. Here is how we might think of writing the method in the **Student** class of the *lab-classes* project from Chapter 1:

```
public boolean equals(Object obj)
{
    if(this == obj) {
        return true; // Reference equality.
    }
    if(!(obj instanceof Student)) {
        return false; // Not the same type.
    }
    // Gain access to the other student's fields.
    Student other = (Student) obj;
    return name.equals(other.name) &&
            id.equals(other.id) &&
            credits == other.credits;
}
```

The first test is just an efficiency improvement; if the object has been passed a reference to itself to compare against, then we know that content equality must be true. The second test makes sure that we are comparing two students. If not, then we decide that the two objects cannot be equal. Having established that we have another student, we use a cast and another variable of the right type so that we can access its details properly. Finally, we make use of the fact that the private elements of an object are directly accessible to an instance of the same class; this is essential in situations such as this one, because there will not necessarily be accessor methods defined for every private field in a class. Notice that we have consistently used content-equality tests rather than reference-equality tests on the object fields **name** and **id**.

It will not always be necessary to compare every field in two objects in order to establish that they are equal. For instance, if we know for certain that every **Student** is assigned a unique **id**, then we need not test the **name** and **credits** fields as well. It would then be possible to reduce the final statement above to

```
return id.equals(other.id);
```

Whenever the **equals** method is overridden, the **hashCode** method should also be overridden. The **hashCode** method is used by data structures such as **HashMap** and **HashSet** to provide efficient placement and lookup of objects in these collections. Essentially, the **hashCode** method returns an integer value that represents an object. From the default implementation in **Object**, distinct objects have distinct **hashCode** values.

There is an important link between the **equals** and **hashCode** methods in that two objects that are the same as determined by a call to **equals** must return identical values from **hashCode**. This stipulation, or contract, can be found in the description of **hashCode** in the API documentation of the **Object** class.[3] It is beyond the scope of this book to describe in detail a suitable technique for calculating hash codes, but we recommend that the interested reader see Joshua Bloch's *Effective Java*, whose technique we use here.[4] Essentially, an integer value should be computed making use of the values of the fields that are compared by the overridden **equals** method. Here is a hypothetical **hashCode** method that uses the values of an integer field called **count** and a **String** field called **name** to calculate the code:

```
public int hashCode()
{
    int result = 17; // An arbitrary starting value.
    // Make the computed value depend on the order in which
    // the fields are processed.
    result = 37 * result + count;
    result = 37 * result + name.hashCode();
    return result;
}
```

11.9 Protected access

In Chapter 10, we noted that the rules on public and private visibility of class members apply between a subclass and its superclass, as well as between classes in different inheritance hierarchies. This can be somewhat restrictive, because the relationship between a superclass and its subclasses is clearly closer than it is with other classes. For this reason, object-oriented languages often define a level of access that lies between the complete restriction of private access and the full availability of public access. In Java, this is called *protected access* and is provided by the **protected** keyword as an alternative to **public** and **private**. Code 11.5 shows an example of a protected accessor method, which we could add to class **Post**.

---

[3] Note that it is not essential that unequal objects always return distinct hash codes.

[4] Joshua Bloch: *Effective Java*, 2nd edition. Addison-Wesley. ISBN: 0-321-35668-3.

Code 11.5
An example of a protected method

```
protected long getTimeStamp()
{
    return timestamp;
}
```

Concepts

Declaring a field or a method **protected** allows direct access to it from (direct or indirect) subclasses.

Protected access allows access to the fields or methods within a class itself and from all its subclasses, but not from other classes.[5] The `getTimeStamp` method shown in Code 11.5 can be called from class **Post** or any subclasses, but not from other classes. Figure 11.8 illustrates this. The oval areas in the diagram show the group of classes that are able to access members in class **SomeClass**.

While protected access can be applied to any member of a class, it is usually reserved for methods and constructors. It is not usually applied to fields, because that would be a weakening of encapsulation. Wherever possible, mutable fields in superclasses should remain private. There are, however, occasional valid cases where direct access by subclasses is desirable. Inheritance represents a much closer form of coupling than does a normal client relationship.

Inheritance binds the classes closer together, and changing the superclass can more easily break the subclass. This should be taken into consideration when designing classes and their relationships.

Figure 11.8
Access levels: private, protected, and public

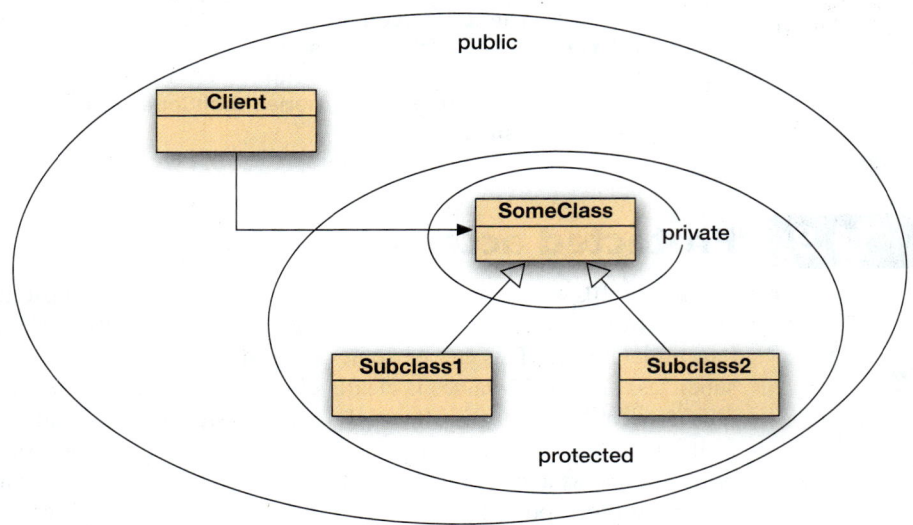

---

[5] In Java, this rule is not as clear-cut as described here, because Java includes an additional level of visibility, called *package level*, but with no associated keyword. We will not discuss this further, and it is more general to consider protected access as intended for the special relationship between superclass and subclass.

Exercise 11.6 The version of `display` shown in Code 11.2 produces the output shown in Figure 11.9. Reorder the statements in the method in your version of the *network* project so that it prints the details as shown in Figure 11.10.

Figure 11.9
Possible output from `display`: superclass call at the beginning of `display` (shaded areas printed by superclass method).

```
Leonardo da Vinci
40 seconds ago - 2 people like this.
   No comments.
Had a great idea this morning.
But now I forgot what it was. Something to do with flying...
```

Figure 11.10
Alternative output from `display` (shaded areas printed by super-class method)

```
Had a great idea this morning.
But now I forgot what it was. Something to do with flying...
Leonardo da Vinci
40 seconds ago - 2 people like this.
   No comments.
```

Exercise 11.7 Having to use a superclass call in `display` is somewhat restrictive in the ways in which we can format the output, because it is dependent on the way the superclass formats its fields. Make any necessary changes to the **Post** class and to the `display` method of **MessagePost** so that it produces the output shown in Figure 11.11. Any changes you make to the **Post** class should be visible only to its subclasses. *Hint:* You could add protected accessors to do this.

Figure 11.11
Output from `display` mixing subclass and superclass details (shaded areas represent superclass details)

```
Leonardo da Vinci
Had a great idea this morning.
But now I forgot what it was. Something to do with flying...
40 seconds ago - 2 people like this.
   No comments.
```

11.10 The `instanceof` operator

One of the consequences of the introduction of inheritance into the *network* project has been that the **NewsFeed** class knows only about **Post** objects and cannot distinguish between message posts and photo posts. This has allowed all types of posts to be stored in a single list.

However, suppose that we wish to retrieve just the message posts or just the photo posts from the list; how would we do that? Or perhaps we wish to look for a message by a particular author? That is not a problem if the **Post** class defines a **getAuthor** method, but this will find both message and photo posts. Will it matter which type is returned?

There are occasions when we need to rediscover the distinctive dynamic type of an object rather than dealing with a shared supertype. For this, Java provides the **instanceof** operator. The **instanceof** operator tests whether a given object is, directly or indirectly, an instance of a given class. The test

```
obj instanceof MyClass
```

returns **true** if the dynamic type of **obj** is **MyClass** or any subclass of **MyClass**. The left operand is always an object reference, and the right operand is always the name of a class. So

```
post instanceof MessagePost
```

returns **true** only if **post** is a **MessagePost**, as opposed to a **PhotoPost**, for instance.

Use of the **instanceof** operator is often followed immediately by a cast of the object reference to the identified type. For instance, here is some code to identify all of the message posts in a list of posts and to store them in a separate list.

```java
ArrayList<MessagePost> messages = new ArrayList<>();
for(Post post : posts) {
    if(post instanceof MessagePost) {
        messages.add((MessagePost) post);
    }
}
```

It should be clear that the cast here does not alter the post object in any way, because we have just established that it already is a **MessagePost** object.

11.11 Another example of inheritance with overriding

To discuss another example of a similar use of inheritance, we go back to a project from Chapter 8: the *zuul* project. In the *world-of-zuul* game, we used a set of **Room** objects to create a scene for a simple game. Exercise 8.45 suggested that you implement a transporter room (a room that beams you to a random location in the game if you try to enter or leave it). We revisit this exercise here, because its solution can greatly benefit from inheritance. If you don't remember this project well, have a quick read through Chapter 8 again, or look at your own *zuul* project.

There is no single solution to this task. Many different solutions are possible and can be made to work. Some are better than others—more elegant, easier to read, and easier to maintain and to extend.

Assume that we want to implement this task so that the player is automatically transported to a random room when she tries to leave the magic transporter room. The most straightforward solution that comes to mind first for many people is to deal with this in the **Game** class, which implements the player's commands. One of the commands is *go*, which is implemented in the **goRoom** method. In this method, we used the following statement as the central section of code:

```
nextRoom = currentRoom.getExit(direction);
```

This statement retrieves from the current room the neighboring room in the direction we want to go. To add our magic transportation, we could modify this in a form similar to the following:

```
if(currentRoom.getName().equals("Transporter room")) {
    nextRoom = getRandomRoom();
}
else {
    nextRoom = currentRoom.getExit(direction);
}
```

The idea here is simple: we just check whether we are in the transporter room. If we are, then we find the next room by getting a random room (of course, we have to implement the **getRandomRoom** method somehow); otherwise, we just do the same as before.

While this solution works, it has several drawbacks. The first is that it is a bad idea to use text strings, such as the room's name, to identify the room. Imagine that someone wanted to translate your game into another language—say, to German. They might change the names of the rooms—"Transporter room" becomes "Transporterraum"—and suddenly the game does not work any more! This is a clear case of a maintainability problem.

The second solution, which is slightly better, would be to use an instance variable instead of the room's name to identify the transporter room. Similar to this:

```
if(currentRoom == transporterRoom) {
    nextRoom = getRandomRoom();
}
else {
    nextRoom = currentRoom.getExit(direction);
}
```

This time, we assume that we have an instance variable **transporterRoom** of class **Room**, where we store the reference to our transporter room.[6] Now the check is independent of the room's name. That is a bit better.

There is still a case for further improvement, though. We can understand the shortcomings of this solution when we think about another maintenance change. Imagine that we want to add two more transporter rooms, so that our game has three different transporter locations.

A very nice aspect of our existing design was that we could set up the floor plan in a single spot, and the rest of the game was completely independent of it. We could easily change the layout of the rooms, and everything would still work—high score for maintainability! With our current solution, though, this is broken. If we add two new transporter rooms, we have to add two more instance variables or an array (to store references to those rooms), and we have to modify our **goRoom** method to add a check for those rooms. In terms of easy changeability, we have gone backwards.

---

[6] Make sure that you understand why a test for reference equality is the most appropriate here.

The question, therefore, is: Can we find a solution that does not require a change to the command implementation each time we add a new transporter room? Following is our next idea.

We can add a method **isTransporterRoom** in the **Room** class. This way, the **Game** object does not need to remember all the transporter rooms—the rooms themselves do. When rooms are created, they could receive a boolean flag indicating whether a given room is a transporter room. The **goRoom** method could then use the following code segment:

```
if(currentRoom.isTransporterRoom()) {
    nextRoom = getRandomRoom();
}
else {
    nextRoom = currentRoom.getExit(direction);
}
```

Now we can add as many transporter rooms as we like; there is no need for any more changes to the **Game** class. However, the **Room** class has an extra field whose value is really needed only because of the nature of one or two of the instances. Special-case code such as this is a typical indicator of a weakness in class design. This approach also does not scale well should we decide to introduce further sorts of special rooms, each requiring its own flag field and accessor method.[7]

With inheritance, we can do better and implement a solution that is even more flexible than this one. We can implement a class **TransporterRoom** as a subclass of class **Room**. In this new class, we override the **getExit** method and change its implementation so that it returns a random room:

```
public class TransporterRoom extends Room
{
    /**
     * Return a random room, independent of the direction
     * parameter.
     * @param direction Ignored.
     * @return A random room.
     */
    public Room getExit(String direction)
    {
        return findRandomRoom();
    }

    /*
     * Choose a random room.
     * @return A random room.
     */
    private Room findRandomRoom()
    {
        ... // implementation omitted
    }
}
```

---

[7] We might also think of using **instanceof**, but the point here is that none of these ideas is the best.

The elegance of this solution lies in the fact that no change at all is needed in either the original **Game** or **Room** classes! We can simply add this class to the existing game, and the **goRoom** method will continue to work as it is. Adding the creation of a **TransporterRoom** to the setup of the floor plan is (almost) enough to make it work. Note, too, that the new class does not need a flag to indicate its special nature—its very type and distinctive behavior supply that information.

Because **TransporterRoom** is a subclass of **Room**, it can be used everywhere a **Room** object is expected. Thus, it can be used as a neighboring room for another room or be held in the **Game** object as the current room.

What we have left out, of course, is the implementation of the **findRandomRoom** method. In reality, this is probably better done in a separate class (say **RoomRandomizer**) than in the **TransporterRoom** class itself. We leave this as an exercise for the reader.

Exercise 11.8 Implement a transporter room with inheritance in your version of the *zuul* project.

Exercise 11.9 Discuss how inheritance could be used in the *zuul* project to implement a player and a monster class.

Exercise 11.10 Could (or should) inheritance be used to create an inheritance relationship (super-, sub-, or sibling class) between a character in the game and an item?

11.12 Summary

When we deal with classes with subclasses and polymorphic variables, we have to distinguish between the static and dynamic type of a variable. The static type is the declared type, while the dynamic type is the type of the object currently stored in the variable.

Type checking is done by the compiler using the static type, whereas at runtime method lookup uses the dynamic type. This enables us to create very flexible structures by overriding methods. Even when using a supertype variable to make a method call, overriding enables us to ensure that specialized methods are invoked for every particular subtype. This ensures that objects of different classes can react distinctly to the same method call.

When implementing overriding methods, the **super** keyword can be used to invoke the superclass version of the method. If fields or methods are declared with the **protected** access modifier, subclasses are allowed to access them, but other classes are not.

Terms introduced in this chapter:

> **static type, dynamic type, overriding, redefinition, method lookup, method dispatch, method polymorphism, protected**

Exercise 11.11 Assume that you see the following lines of code:

```
Device dev = new Printer();
dev.getName();
```

`Printer` is a subclass of `Device`. Which of these classes must have a definition of method `getName` for this code to compile?

Exercise 11.12 In the same situation as in the previous exercise, if both classes have an implementation of `getName`, which one will be executed?

Exercise 11.13 Assume that you write a class `Student` that does not have a declared superclass. You do not write a `toString` method. Consider the following lines of code:

```
Student st = new Student();
String s = st.toString();
```

Will these lines compile? If so, what exactly will happen when you try to execute?

Exercise 11.14 In the same situation as before (class `Student`, no `toString` method), will the following lines compile? Why?

```
Student st = new Student();
System.out.println(st);
```

Exercise 11.15 Assume that your class **Student** overrides **toString** so that it returns the student's name. You now have a list of students. Will the following code compile? If not, why not? If yes, what will it print? Explain in detail what happens.

```
for(Object st : myList) {
    System.out.println(st);
}
```

Exercise 11.16 Write a few lines of code that result in a situation where a variable **x** has the static type **T** and the dynamic type **D**.

CHAPTER 12

Further Abstraction Techniques

Main concepts discussed in this chapter:

- abstract classes
- interfaces
- multiple inheritance

Java constructs discussed in this chapter:

`abstract`, `implements`, `interface`

In this chapter, we examine further inheritance-related techniques that can be used to enhance class structures and improve maintainability and extensibility. These techniques introduce an improved method of representation of abstractions in object-oriented programs.

The previous two chapters have discussed the most important aspects of inheritance in application design, but several more advanced uses and problems have been ignored so far. We will now complete the picture with a more advanced example.

The project we use for this chapter is a simulation. We use it to discuss inheritance again and see that we run into some new problems. Abstract classes and interfaces are then introduced to deal with these problems.

12.1 Simulations

Computers are frequently used to simulate real systems. These include systems that model traffic flows in a city, forecast weather, simulate the spread of infection, analyze the stock market, do environmental simulations, and much more. In fact, many of the most powerful computers in the world are used for running some sort of simulation.

When creating a computer simulation, we try to model the behavior of a subset of the real world in a software model. Every simulation is necessarily a simplification of the real thing. Deciding which details to leave out and which to include is often a challenging task. The more detailed a simulation is, the more accurate it may be in forecasting the behavior of the real system. But more detail increases the complexity of the model and the requirements for both more computing power and more programmer time. A well-known example is weather forecasting: climate models in weather simulations have been improved by adding more and more detail over the last few decades. As a result, weather forecasts have improved significantly in accuracy (but are far from perfect, as we all have experienced at some time). Much of this improvement has been made possible through advances in computer technology.

The benefit of simulations is that we can undertake experiments that we could not do with the real system, either because we have no control over the real thing (for instance, the weather) or because it is too costly, too dangerous, or irreversible in case of disaster. We can use the simulation to investigate the behavior of the system under certain circumstances or to investigate "what if" questions.

An example of the use of environmental simulations is to try to predict the effects of human activity on natural habitats. Consider the case of a national park containing endangered species and a proposal to build a freeway through the middle of it, completely separating the two halves. The supporters of the freeway proposal claim that splitting the park in half will lead to little actual land loss and make no difference to the animals in it, but environmentalists claim otherwise. How can we tell what the effect is likely to be without building the freeway? Simulation is one option. An essential question in all cases of this kind will be, of course, "How good is the simulation?" One can "prove" just about anything with an ill-designed simulation. Gaining trust in it through controlled experiments will be essential.

The issue in this particular case boils down to whether it is significant for the survival of a species to have a single, connected habitat area, or whether two disjoint areas (with the same total size as the other) are just as good. Rather than building the freeway first and then observing what happens, we will try to simulate the effect in order to make a well-informed decision.[1]

Our simulation will necessarily be simpler than the scenario we have described, because we are using it mainly to illustrate new features of object-oriented design and implementation. Therefore, it will not have the potential to simulate accurately many aspects of nature, but some of the simulation's characteristics are nonetheless interesting. In particular, it will demonstrate the structure of typical simulations. In addition, its accuracy may surprise you; it would be a mistake to equate greater complexity with greater accuracy. It is often the case that a simplified model of something can provide greater insight and understanding than a more complex one, from which it is often difficult to isolate the underlying mechanisms—or even be sure that the model is valid.

12.2 The foxes-and-rabbits simulation

The simulation scenario we have chosen to work with in this chapter uses the freeway example from above as its basis. It involves tracking populations of foxes and rabbits within an enclosed area. This is just one particular example of what are known as *predator–prey*

---

[1] In this particular case, by the way, size does matter: the size of a natural park has a significant impact on its usefulness as a habitat for animals.

simulations. Such simulations are often used to model the variation in population sizes that result from a predator species feeding on a prey species. A delicate balance exists between such species. A large population of prey will potentially provide plenty of food for a small population of predators. However, too many predators could kill off all the prey and leave the hunters with nothing to eat. Population sizes could also be affected by the size and nature of the environment. For instance, a small, enclosed environment could lead to overcrowding and make it easy for the predators to locate their prey, or a polluted environment could reduce the stock of prey and prevent even a modest population of predators from surviving. Because predators in one context are often prey for other species (think of cats, birds, and worms, for instance), loss of one part of the food chain can have dramatic effects on the survival of other parts.

As we have done in previous chapters, we will start with a version of an application that works perfectly well from a user's point of view, but whose internal view is not so good when judged by the principles of good object-oriented design and implementation. We will use this base version to develop several improved versions that progressively introduce new abstraction techniques.

One particular problem that we wish to address in the base version is that it does not make good use of the inheritance techniques that were introduced in Chapter 10. However, we will start by examining the mechanism of the simulation, without being too critical of its implementation. Once we understand how it works, we shall be in a good position to make some improvements.

> **Predator–prey modeling** There is a long history of trying to model predator–prey relationships mathematically before the invention of the computer, because they have economic, as well as environmental, importance. For instance, mathematical models were used in the early twentieth century to explain variations in the level of fish stocks in the Adriatic Sea as a side effect of World War I. To find out more about the background of this topic, and perhaps gain an understanding of population dynamics, do a web search for the Lotka-Volterra model.

12.2.1 The *foxes-and-rabbits* project

Open the *foxes-and-rabbits-v1* project. The class diagram is shown in Figure 12.1.

The main classes we will focus on in our discussion are **Simulator**, **Fox**, and **Rabbit**. The **Fox** and **Rabbit** classes provide simple models of the behavior of a predator and prey, respectively. In this particular implementation, we have not tried to provide an accurate biological model of real foxes and rabbits; rather, we are simply trying to illustrate the principles of typical predator–prey simulations. Our main concerns will be on the aspects that most affect population size: birth, death, and food supply.

The **Simulator** class is responsible for creating the initial state of the simulation, then controlling and executing it. The basic idea is simple: the simulator holds collections of foxes and rabbits, and it repeatedly gives those animals an opportunity to live through one

Figure 12.1

Class diagram of the *foxes-and-rabbits* project

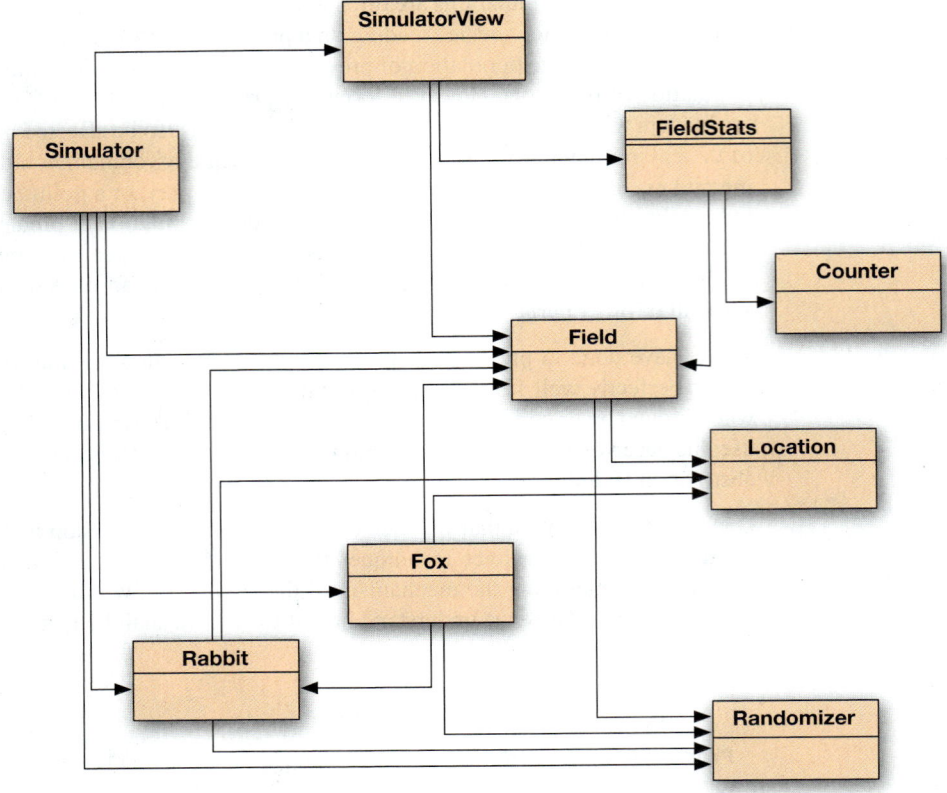

step[2] of their life cycle. At each step, each fox and each rabbit is allowed to carry out the actions that characterize their behaviors. After each step (when all the animals have had the chance to act), the new current state of the field is displayed on screen.

We can summarize the purpose of the remaining classes as follows:

- **Field** represents a two-dimensional enclosed field. The field is composed of a fixed number of locations, which are arranged in rows and columns. At most, one animal may occupy a single location within the field. Each field location can hold an animal, or it can be empty.

- **Location** represents a two-dimensional position within the field, specified by a row and a column value.

- These five classes together (**Simulator**, **Fox**, **Rabbit**, **Field**, and **Location**) provide the model for the simulation. They completely determine the simulation behavior.

---

[2] We won't define how much time a "step" actually represents. In practice, this has to be decided by a combination of such things as what we are trying to discover, what events we are simulating, and how much real time is available to run the simulation.

- The **Randomizer** class provides us with a degree of control over random aspects of the simulation, such as when new animals are born.

- The classes **SimulatorView**, **FieldStats**, and **Counter** provide a graphical display of the simulation. The display shows an image of the field and counters for each species (the current number of rabbits and foxes).

- **SimulatorView** provides a visualization of the state of the field. An example can be seen in Figure 12.2.

- **FieldStats** provides to the visualization counts of the numbers of foxes and rabbits in the field.

- A **Counter** stores a current count for one type of animal to assist with the counting.

Try the following exercises to gain an understanding of how the simulation operates before reading about its implementation.

Exercise 12.1 Create a **Simulator** object, using the constructor without parameters, and you should see an initial state of the simulation similar to that in Figure 12.2. The more numerous rectangles represent the rabbits. Does the number of foxes change if you call the **simulateOneStep** method just once?

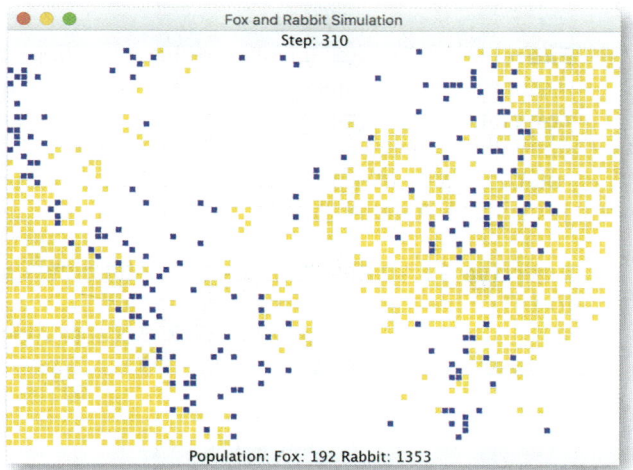

Figure 12.2
The graphical display of the *foxes-and-rabbits* simulation

Exercise 12.2 Does the number of foxes change on every step? What natural processes do you think we are modeling that cause the number of foxes to increase or decrease?

Exercise 12.3 Call the **simulate** method with a parameter to run the simulation continuously for a significant number of steps, such as 50 or 100. Do the numbers of foxes and rabbits increase or decrease at similar rates?

Exercise 12.4 What changes do you notice if you run the simulation for a much longer time, say for 4,000 steps? You can use the `runLongSimulation` method to do this.

Exercise 12.5 Use the `reset` method to create a new starting state for the simulation, and then run it again. Is an identical simulation run this time? If not, do you see broadly similar patterns emerging anyway?

Exercise 12.6 If you run a simulation for long enough, do all of the foxes or all of the rabbits ever die off completely? If so, can you pinpoint any reasons why that might be occurring?

Exercise 12.7 In the source code of the `Simulator` class, find the `simulate` method. In its body, you will see a call to a `delay` method that is commented out. Uncomment this call and run the simulation. Experiment with different delays so you can observe the simulation behavior more clearly. At the end, leave it in a state that makes the simulation look useful on your computer.

Exercise 12.8 Make a note of the numbers of foxes and rabbits at each of the first few steps, and at the end of a long run. It will be useful to have a record of these when we come to make changes later on and perform regression testing.

Exercise 12.9 After having run the simulation for a while, call the static `reset` method of the `Randomizer` class, and then the `reset` method of the `Simulator` object. Now run the first few steps again, and you should see the original simulation repeated. Take a look at the code of the `Randomizer` class to see if you can work out why this might be. You might need to look at the API for the `java.util.Random` class to help you with this.

Exercise 12.10 Check to see that setting the `useShared` field in `Randomizer` to `false` breaks the repeatability of the simulations seen in Exercise 12.9. Be sure to restore it to `true` afterwards, because repeatability will be an important element in later testing.

Now that we have a broad, external understanding of what this project does, we will look in detail at the implementation of the `Rabbit`, `Fox`, and `Simulator` classes.

12.2.2 The `Rabbit` class

The source code of the `Rabbit` class is shown in Code 12.1.

The `Rabbit` class contains a number of class variables that define configuration settings that are common to all rabbits. These include values for the maximum age to which a rabbit can live (defined as a number of simulation steps) and the maximum number of offspring

Code 12.1
The `Rabbit` class

Import statement and class comment omitted.

```java
public class Rabbit
{
    // Characteristics shared by all rabbits (class variables).

    // The age at which a rabbit can start to breed.
    private static final int BREEDING_AGE = 5;
    // The age to which a rabbit can live.
    private static final int MAX_AGE = 40;
    // The likelihood of a rabbit breeding.
    private static final double BREEDING_PROBABILITY = 0.12;
    // The maximum number of births.
    private static final int MAX_LITTER_SIZE = 4;
    // A shared random number generator to control breeding.
    private static final Random rand = Randomizer.getRandom();

    // Individual characteristics (instance fields).

    // The rabbit's age.
    private int age;
    // Whether the rabbit is alive or not.
    private boolean alive;
    // The rabbit's position.
    private Location location;
    // The field occupied.
    private Field field;

    /**
     * Create a new rabbit. A rabbit may be created with age
     * zero (a new born) or with a random age.
     *
     * @param randomAge If true, the rabbit will have a random age.
     * @param field The field currently occupied.
     * @param location The location within the field.
     */
    public Rabbit(boolean randomAge, Field field, Location location)
    {
        Body of constructor omitted.
    }

    /**
     * This is what the rabbit does most of the time - it runs
     * around. Sometimes it will breed or die of old age.
     * @param newRabbits A list to return newly born rabbits.
     */
    public void run(List<Rabbit> newRabbits)
    {
        incrementAge();
        if(alive) {
            giveBirth(newRabbits);
            // Try to move into a free location.
            Location newLocation = field.freeAdjacentLocation(location);
            if(newLocation != null) {
                setLocation(newLocation);
            }
```

Code 12.1 continued
The **Rabbit** class

```java
        else {
            // Overcrowding.
            setDead();
        }
    }
}

/**
 * Indicate that the rabbit is no longer alive.
 * It is removed from the field.
 */
public void setDead()
{
    alive = false;
    if(location != null) {
        field.clear(location);
        location = null;
        field = null;
    }
}

/**
 * Increase the age.
 * This could result in the rabbit's death.
 */
private void incrementAge()
{
    age++;
    if(age > MAX_AGE) {
        setDead();
    }
}

/**
 * Check whether or not this rabbit is to give birth at this step.
 * New births will be made into free adjacent locations.
 * @param newRabbits A list to return newly born rabbits.
 */
private void giveBirth(List<Rabbit> newRabbits)
{
    // New rabbits are born into adjacent locations.
    // Get a list of adjacent free locations.
    List<Location> free = field.getFreeAdjacentLocations(location);
    int births = breed();
    for(int b = 0; b < births && free.size() > 0; b++) {
        Location loc = free.remove(0);
        Rabbit young = new Rabbit(false, field, loc);
        newRabbits.add(young);
    }
}

/**
 * Generate a number representing the number of births,
 * if it can breed.
 * @return The number of births (may be zero).
 */
```

Code 12.1 continued

The **Rabbit** class

```
    private int breed()
    {
        int births = 0;
        if(canBreed() && rand.nextDouble() <= BREEDING_PROBABILITY) {
            births = rand.nextInt(MAX_LITTER_SIZE) + 1;
        }
        return births;
    }
```

Other methods omitted.

it can produce at any one step. Centralized control of random aspects of the simulation is provided through a single, shared **Random** object supplied by the **Randomizer** class. This is what makes possible the repeatability seen in Exercise 12.9. In addition, each individual rabbit has four instance variables that describe its state: its age as a number of steps, whether it is still alive, and its location in a particular field.

Exercise 12.11 Do you feel that omitting gender as an attribute in the **Rabbit** class is likely to lead to an inaccurate simulation? Write down the arguments for and against including it.

Exercise 12.12 Are there other simplifications that you feel are present in our implementation of the **Rabbit** class, compared with real life? Discuss whether these could have a significant impact on the accuracy of the simulation.

Exercise 12.13 Experiment with the effects of altering some or all of the values of the class variables in the **Rabbit** class. For instance, what effect does it have on the populations if the breeding probability of rabbits is much higher or much lower than it currently is?

A rabbit's behavior is defined in its **run** method, which in turn uses the **giveBirth** and **incrementAge** methods and implements the rabbit's movement. At each simulation step, the **run** method will be called and a rabbit will increase its age; if old enough, it might also breed, and it will then try to move. Both the movement and the breeding behaviors have random components. The direction in which the rabbit moves is randomly chosen, and breeding occurs randomly, controlled by the class variable **BREEDING_PROBABILITY**.

You can already see some of the simplifications that we have made in our model of rabbits: there is no attempt to distinguish males from females, for instance, and a rabbit could potentially give birth to a new litter at every simulation step once it is old enough.

12.2.3 The Fox class

There is a lot of similarity between the **Fox** and the **Rabbit** classes, so only the distinctive elements of **Fox** are shown in Code 12.2.

Code 12.2
The **Fox** class

Import statements and class comment omitted.

```java
public class Fox
{
    // Characteristics shared by all foxes (class variables).

    // The food value of a single rabbit. In effect, this is the
    // number of steps a fox can go before it has to eat again.
    private static final int RABBIT_FOOD_VALUE = 9;
```

Other static fields omitted.

```java
    // Individual characteristics (instance fields).

    // The fox's age.
    private int age;
    // Whether the fox is alive or not.
    private boolean alive;
    // The fox's position.
    private Location location;
    // The field occupied.
    private Field field;
    // The fox's food level, which is increased by eating rabbits.
    private int foodLevel;

    /**
     * Create a fox. A fox can be created as a new born (age zero
     * and not hungry) or with a random age and food level.
     *
     * @param randomAge If true the fox will have random age and hunger level.
     * @param field The field currently occupied.
     * @param location The location within the field.
     */
    public Fox(boolean randomAge, Field field, Location location)
    {
```

Body of constructor omitted.

```java
    }

    /**
     * This is what the fox does most of the time: it hunts for
     * rabbits. In the process, it might breed, die of hunger,
     * or die of old age.
     * @param field The field currently occupied.
     * @param newFoxes A list to return newly born foxes.
     */
    public void hunt(List<Fox> newFoxes)
    {
        incrementAge();
        incrementHunger();
```

Code 12.2 continued

The **Fox** class

```java
            if(alive) {
                giveBirth(newFoxes);
                // Move towards a source of food if found.
                Location newLocation = findFood();
                if(newLocation == null) {
                    // No food found - try to move to a free location.
                    newLocation = field.freeAdjacentLocation(location);
                }
                // See if it was possible to move.
                if(newLocation != null) {
                    setLocation(newLocation);
                }
                else {
                    // Overcrowding.
                    setDead();
                }
            }
        }

        /**
         * Look for rabbits adjacent to the current location.
         * Only the first live rabbit is eaten.
         * @return Where food was found, or null if it wasn't.
         */
        private Location findFood()
        {
            List<Location> adjacent = field.adjacentLocations(location);
            Iterator<Location> it = adjacent.iterator();
            while(it.hasNext()) {
                Location where = it.next();
                Object animal = field.getObjectAt(where);
                if(animal instanceof Rabbit) {
                    Rabbit rabbit = (Rabbit) animal;
                    if(rabbit.isAlive()) {
                        rabbit.setDead();
                        foodLevel = RABBIT_FOOD_VALUE;
                        return where;
                    }
                }
            }
            return null;
        }

        Other methods omitted.

}
```

For foxes, the **hunt** method is invoked at each step and defines their behavior. In addition to aging and possibly breeding at each step, a fox searches for food (using **findFood**). If it is able to find a rabbit in an adjacent location, then the rabbit is killed and the fox's food level is increased. As with rabbits, a fox that is unable to move is considered dead through overcrowding.

Exercise 12.14 As you did for rabbits, assess the degree to which we have simplified the model of foxes and evaluate whether you feel the simplifications are likely to lead to an inaccurate simulation.

Exercise 12.15 Does increasing the maximum age for foxes lead to a significantly higher numbers of foxes throughout a simulation, or is the rabbit population more likely to be reduced to zero as a result?

Exercise 12.16 Experiment with different combinations of settings (breeding age, maximum age, breeding probability, litter size, etc.) for foxes and rabbits. Do species always disappear completely in some configurations? Are there configurations that are stable—i.e., that produce a balance of numbers for a significant length of time?

Exercise 12.17 Experiment with different sizes of fields. (You can do this by using the second constructor of `Simulator`.) Does the size of the field affect the likelihood of species surviving?

Exercise 12.18 Compare the results of running a simulation with a single large field, and two simulations with fields that each have half the area of the single field. This models something close to splitting an area in half with a freeway. Do you notice any significant differences in the population dynamics between the two scenarios?

Exercise 12.19 Repeat the investigations of the previous exercise, but vary the proportions of the two smaller fields. For instance, try three-quarters and one quarter, or two-thirds and one-third. Does it matter at all how the single field is split?

Exercise 12.20 Currently, a fox will eat at most one rabbit at each step. Modify the `findFood` method so that rabbits in all adjacent locations are eaten at a single step. Assess the impact of this change on the results of the simulation. Note that the `findFood` method currently returns the location of the single rabbit that is eaten, so you will need to return the location of one of the eaten rabbits in your version. However, don't forget to return `null` if there are no rabbits to eat.

Exercise 12.21 Following from the previous exercise, if a fox eats multiple rabbits at a single step, there are several different possibilities as to how we can model its food level. If we add all the rabbit's food values, the fox will have a very high food level, making it unlikely to die of hunger for a very long time. Alternatively, we could impose a ceiling on the fox's food level. This models the effect of a predator that kills prey regardless of whether it is hungry or not. Assess the impacts on the resulting simulation of implementing this choice.

Exercise 12.22 *Challenge exercise* Given the random elements in the simulation, argue why the population numbers in an apparently stable simulation could ultimately collapse.

12.2.4 The `Simulator` class: setup

The `Simulator` class is the central part of the application that coordinates all the other pieces. Code 12.3 illustrates some of its main features.

Code 12.3
Part of the
`Simulator` class

Import statements and class comment omitted.

```java
public class Simulator
{
    Static variables omitted.
    // Lists of animals in the field.
    private List<Rabbit> rabbits;
    private List<Fox> foxes;
    // The current state of the field.
    private Field field;
    // The current step of the simulation.
    private int step;
    // A graphical view of the simulation.
    private SimulatorView view;

    /**
     * Create a simulation field with the given size.
     * @param depth Depth of the field. Must be greater than zero.
     * @param width Width of the field. Must be greater than zero.
     */
    public Simulator(int depth, int width)
    {
        if(width <= 0 || depth <= 0) {
            System.out.println("The dimensions must be >= zero.");
            System.out.println("Using default values.");
            depth = DEFAULT_DEPTH;
            width = DEFAULT_WIDTH;
        }

        rabbits = new ArrayList<>();
        foxes = new ArrayList<>();
        field = new Field(depth, width);

        // Create a view of the state of each location in the field.
        view = new SimulatorView(depth, width);
        view.setColor(Rabbit.class, Color.ORANGE);
        view.setColor(Fox.class, Color.BLUE);

        // Setup a valid starting point.
        reset();
    }
```

Code 12.3 continued
Part of the **Simulator** class

```java
/**
 * Run the simulation for the given number of steps.
 * Stop before the given number of steps if it ceases to be viable.
 * @param numSteps The number of steps to run for.
 */
public void simulate(int numSteps)
{
    for(int step=1; step <= numSteps && view.isViable(field); step++) {
        simulateOneStep();
        // delay(60);    // uncomment this to run more slowly
    }
}

/**
 * Run the simulation from its current state for a single step. Iterate
 * over the whole field updating the state of each fox and rabbit.
 */
public void simulateOneStep()
{
    Method body omitted.
}

/**
 * Reset the simulation to a starting position.
 */
public void reset()
{
    step = 0;
    rabbits.clear();
    foxes.clear();
    populate();

    // Show the starting state in the view.
    view.showStatus(step, field);
}

/**
 * Randomly populate the field with foxes and rabbits.
 */
private void populate()
{
    Random rand = Randomizer.getRandom();
    field.clear();
    for(int row = 0; row < field.getDepth(); row++) {
        for(int col = 0; col < field.getWidth(); col++) {
            if(rand.nextDouble() <= FOX_CREATION_PROBABILITY) {
                Location location = new Location(row, col);
                Fox fox = new Fox(true, field, location);
                foxes.add(fox);
            }
            else if(rand.nextDouble() <= RABBIT_CREATION_PROBABILITY) {
                Location location = new Location(row, col);
                Rabbit rabbit = new Rabbit(true, field, location);
                rabbits.add(rabbit);
            }
```

Code 12.3 continued
Part of the **Simulator** class

```
                    // else leave the location empty.
            }
        }
    }
}

Other methods omitted.

}
```

The **Simulator** has three important parts: its constructor, the **populate** method, and the **simulateOneStep** method. (The body of **simulateOneStep** is shown in Code 12.4.)

When a **Simulator** object is created, all other parts of the simulation are constructed by it (the field, the lists to hold the different types of animals, and the graphical interface). Once all these have been set up, the simulator's **populate** method is called (indirectly, via the **reset** method) to create the initial populations. Different probabilities are used to decide whether a particular location will contain one of these animals. Note that animals created at the start of the simulation are given a random initial age. This serves two purposes:

1. It represents more accurately a mixed-age population that should be the normal state of the simulation.

2. If all animals were to start with an age of zero, no new animals would be created until the initial population had reached their respective breeding ages. With foxes eating rabbits regardless of the fox's age, there is a risk that either the rabbit population will be killed off before it has a chance to reproduce, or that the fox population will die of hunger.

Exercise 12.23 Modify the **populate** method of **Simulator** to determine whether setting an initial age of zero for foxes and rabbits is always catastrophic. Make sure that you run it a sufficient number of times—with different initial states, of course!

Exercise 12.24 If an initial random age is set for rabbits but not foxes, the rabbit population will tend to grow large while the fox population remains very small. Once the foxes do become old enough to breed, does the simulation tend to behave again like the original version? What does this suggest about the relative sizes of the initial populations and their impact on the outcome of the simulation?

12.2.5 The **Simulator** class: a simulation step

The central part of the **Simulator** class is the **simulateOneStep** method shown in Code 12.4. It uses separate loops to let each type of animal move (and possibly breed or do whatever it is programmed to do). Because each animal can give birth to new animals, lists for these to be stored in are passed as parameters to the **hunt** and **run** methods of **Fox** and **Rabbit**. The newly born animals are then added to the master lists at the end of the step. Running longer simulations is trivial. To do this, the **simulateOneStep** method is called repeatedly in a simple loop.

Code 12.4

Inside the `Simulator` class: simulating one step

```java
public void simulateOneStep()
{
    step++;

    // Provide space for newborn rabbits.
    List<Rabbit> newRabbits = new ArrayList<>();
    // Let all rabbits act.
    for(Iterator<Rabbit> it = rabbits.iterator(); it.hasNext(); ) {
        Rabbit rabbit = it.next();
        rabbit.run(newRabbits);
        if(! rabbit.isAlive()) {
            it.remove();
        }
    }

    // Provide space for newborn foxes.
    List<Fox> newFoxes = new ArrayList<>();
    // Let all foxes act.
    for(Iterator<Fox> it = foxes.iterator(); it.hasNext(); ) {
        Fox fox = it.next();
        fox.hunt(newFoxes);
        if(! fox.isAlive()) {
            it.remove();
        }
    }

    // Add the newly born foxes and rabbits to the main lists.
    rabbits.addAll(newRabbits);
    foxes.addAll(newFoxes);

    view.showStatus(step, field);
}
```

In order to let each animal act, the simulator holds separate lists of the different types of animals. Here, we make no use of inheritance, and the situation is reminiscent of the first version of the *network* project introduced in Chapter 10.

Exercise 12.25 Each animal is always held in two different data structures: the `Field` and the `Simulator`'s `rabbits` and `foxes` lists. There is a risk that they could be inconsistent with each other. Check that you thoroughly understand how the `Field` and the animal lists are kept consistent between the `simulateOneStep` method in `Simulator`, `hunt` in `Fox`, and `run` in `Rabbit`.

Exercise 12.26 Do you think it would be better for `Simulator` not to keep separate lists of foxes and rabbits, but to generate these lists again from the contents of the field at the beginning of each simulation step? Discuss this.

Exercise 12.27 Write a test to ensure that, at the end of a simulation step, there is no animal (dead or alive) in the field that is not in one of the lists and vice versa. Should there be any dead animals in any of those places at that stage?

12.2.6 Taking steps to improve the simulation

Now that we have examined how the simulation operates, we are in a position to make improvements to its internal design and implementation. Making progressive improvements through the introduction of new programming features will be the focus of subsequent sections. There are several points at which we could start, but one of the most obvious weaknesses is that no attempt has been made to exploit the advantages of inheritance in the implementation of the **Fox** and **Rabbit** classes, which share a lot of common elements. In order to do this, we shall introduce the concept of an *abstract class*.

Exercise 12.28 Identify the similarities and differences between the **Fox** and **Rabbit** classes. Make separate lists of the fields, methods, and constructors, and distinguish between the class variables (static fields) and instance variables.

Exercise 12.29 Candidate methods for placement in a superclass are those that are identical in all subclasses. Which methods are truly identical in the **Fox** and **Rabbit** classes? In reaching a conclusion, you might like to consider the effect of substituting the values of class variables into the bodies of the methods that use them.

Exercise 12.30 In the current version of the simulation, the values of all similarly named class variables are different. If the two values of a particular class variable (**BREEDING_AGE**, say) were identical, would it make any difference to your assessment of which methods are truly identical?

12.3 Abstract classes

Chapter 10 introduced concepts such as inheritance and polymorphism that we ought to be able to exploit in the simulation application. For instance, the **Fox** and **Rabbit** classes share many similar characteristics that suggest they should be subclasses of a common superclass, such as **Animal**. In this section, we will start to make such changes in order to improve the design and implementation of the simulation as a whole. As with the project in Chapter 10, using a common superclass should avoid code duplication in the subclasses and simplify the code in the client class (here, **Simulator**). It is important to note that we are undertaking a process of refactoring and that these changes should not change the essential characteristics of the simulation as seen from a user's viewpoint.

12.3.1 The **Animal** superclass

For the first set of changes, we will move the identical elements of **Fox** and **Rabbit** to an **Animal** superclass. The project *foxes-and-rabbits-v1* provides a copy of the base version of the simulation for you to follow through the changes we make.

- Both **Fox** and **Rabbit** define **age**, **alive**, **field**, and **location** attributes. However, at this point we will only move **alive**, **location**, and **field** to the **Animal** superclass, and come back to discuss the **age** field later. As is our normal practice with instance fields, we will keep all of these private in the superclass. The initial values are set in the constructor of **Animal**, with **alive** set to **true**, and **field** and **location** passed via **super** calls from the constructors of **Fox** and **Rabbit**.

- These fields will need accessors and mutators, so we can move the existing **getLocation**, **setLocation**, **isAlive**, and **setDead** from **Fox** and **Rabbit**. We will also need to add a **getField** method in **Animal** so that direct access to **field** from the subclass methods **run**, **hunt**, **giveBirth**, and **findFood** can be replaced.

- In moving these methods, we have to think about the most appropriate visibility for them. For instance, **setLocation** is private in both **Fox** and **Rabbit**, but cannot be kept private in **Animal** because **Fox** and **Rabbit** would not be able to call it. So we should raise it to **protected** visibility, to indicate that it is for subclasses to call.

- In a similar vein, notice that **setDead** was public in **Rabbit**, but private in **Fox**. Should it therefore be public in **Animal**? It was public in **Rabbit** because a fox needs to be able to call a rabbit's **setDead** method when it eats its prey. Now that they are sibling classes of a shared superclass, a more appropriate visibility is **protected**, again indicating that this is a method that is not a part of an animal's general interface—at least at this stage of the project's development.

Making these changes is a first step toward eliminating code duplication through the use of inheritance, in much the same way as we did in Chapter 10.

Exercise 12.31 What sort of regression-testing strategy could you establish before undertaking the process of refactoring on the simulation? Is this something you could conveniently automate?

Exercise 12.32 The **Randomizer** class provides us with a way to control whether the "random" elements of the simulation are repeatable or not. If its **useShared** field is set to **true**, then a single **Random** object is shared between all of the simulation objects. In addition, its **reset** method resets the starting point for the shared **Random** object. Use these features as you work on the following exercise, to check that you do not change anything fundamental about the overall simulation as you introduce an **Animal** class.

Create the **Animal** superclass in your version of the project. Make the changes discussed above. Ensure that the simulation works in a similar manner as before. You should be able to check this by having the old and new versions of the project open side by side, for instance, and making identical calls on **Simulator** objects in both, expecting identical outcomes.

Exercise 12.33 How has using inheritance improved the project so far? Discuss this.

12.3.2 Abstract methods

So far, use of the **Animal** superclass has helped to avoid a lot of the code duplication in the **Rabbit** and **Fox** classes, and has potentially made it easier to add new animal types in the future. However, as we saw in Chapter 10, intelligent use of inheritance should also simplify the client class—in this case, **Simulator**. We shall investigate this now.

In the **Simulator** class, we have used separate typed lists of foxes and rabbits and per-list iteration code to implement each simulation step. The relevant code is shown in Code 12.4. Now that we have the **Animal** class, we can improve this. Because all objects in our animal collections are a subtype of **Animal**, we can merge them into a single collection and hence iterate just once using the **Animal** type. However, one problem with this is evident from the single-list solution in Code 12.5. Although we know that each item in the list is an **Animal**, we still have to work out which type of animal it is in order to call the correct action method for its type—**run** or **hunt**. We determine the type using the **instanceof** operator.

Code 12.5
An unsatisfactory single-list solution to making animals act

```java
for(Iterator<Animal> it = animals.iterator(); it.hasNext(); ) {
    Animal animal = it.next();
    if(animal instanceof Rabbit) {
        Rabbit rabbit = (Rabbit) animal;
        rabbit.run(newAnimals);
    }
    else if(animal instanceof Fox) {
        Fox fox = (Fox) animal;
        fox.hunt(newAnimals);
    }
    else {
        System.out.println("found unknown animal");
    }
    // Remove dead animals from the simulation.
    if(! animal.isAlive()) {
        it.remove();
    }
}
```

The fact that in Code 12.5 each type of animal must be tested for and cast separately, and that special code exists for each animal class, is a good sign that we have not taken full advantage of what inheritance has to offer. A better solution is placing a method in the superclass (**Animal**), letting an animal act, and then overriding it in each subclass so that we have a polymorphic method call to let each animal act appropriately, without the need to test for the specific animal types. This is a standard refactoring technique in situations like this, where we have subtype-specific behavior invoked from a context that only deals with the supertype.

Let us assume that we create such a method, called **act**, and investigate the resulting source code. Code 12.6 shows the code implementing this solution.

Code 12.6

The fully improved solution to animal action

```
// Let all animals act.
for(Iterator<Animal> it = animals.iterator(); it.hasNext(); ) {
    Animal animal = it.next();
    animal.act(newAnimals);
    // Remove dead animals from the simulation.
    if(! animal.isAlive()) {
        it.remove();
    }
}
```

Several observations are important at this point:

- The variable we are using for each collection element (**animal**) is of type **Animal**. This is legal, because all objects in the collection are foxes or rabbits and are all subtypes of **Animal**.

- We assume that the specific action methods (**run** for **Rabbit**, **hunt** for **Fox**) have been renamed **act**. Instead of telling each animal exactly what to do, we are just telling it to "act," and we leave it up to the animal itself to decide what exactly it wants to do. This reduces coupling between **Simulator** and the individual animal subclasses.

- Because the dynamic type of the variable determines which method is actually executed (as discussed in Chapter 11), the fox's action method will be executed for foxes, and the rabbit's method for rabbits.

- Because type checking is done using the static type, this code will compile only if class **Animal** has an **act** method with the right header.

The last of these points is the only remaining problem. Because we are using the statement

```
animal.act(newAnimals);
```

and the variable **animal** is of type **Animal**, this will compile only if **Animal** defines an **act** method—as we saw in Chapter 11. However, the situation here is rather different from the situation we encountered with the **display** method in Chapter 11. There, the superclass version of **display** had a useful job to do: print the fields defined in the superclass. Here, although each particular animal has a specific set of actions to perform, we cannot describe in any detail the actions for animals in general. The particular actions depend on the specific subtype.

Our problem is to decide how we should define **Animal**'s **act** method.

The problem is a reflection of the fact that no instance of class **Animal** will ever exist. There is no object in our simulation (or in nature) that is just an animal and not also an instance of a more specific subclass. These kinds of classes, which are not intended for creating objects but serve only as superclasses, are known as *abstract classes*. For animals, for example, we can

> **Concept**
>
> An **abstract method** definition consists of a method header without a method body. It is marked with the keyword `abstract`.

say that each animal can act, but we cannot describe exactly how it acts without referring to a more specific subclass. This is typical for abstract classes, and it is reflected in Java constructs.

For the `Animal` class, we wish to state that each animal has an `act` method, but we cannot give a reasonable implementation in class `Animal`. The solution in Java is to declare the method *abstract*. Here is an example of an abstract `act` method:

```java
abstract public void act(List<Animal> newAnimals);
```

An abstract method is characterized by two details:

1. It is prefixed with the keyword `abstract`.
2. It does not have a method body. Instead, its header is terminated with a semicolon.

Because the method has no body, it can never be executed. But we have already established that we do not want to execute an `Animal`'s `act` method, so that is not a problem.

Before we investigate in detail the effects of using an abstract method, we shall introduce more formally the concept of an abstract class.

12.3.3 Abstract classes

It is not only methods that can be declared abstract; classes can be declared abstract as well. Code 12.7 shows an example of class `Animal` as an abstract class. Classes are declared abstract by inserting the keyword `abstract` into the class header.

Code 12.7
`Animal` as an abstract class

```java
public abstract class Animal
{
    Fields omitted.

    /**
     * Make this animal act - that is: make it do whatever it wants/needs
     * to do.
     *
     * @param newAnimals A list to receive newly born animals.
     */
    abstract public void act(List<Animal> newAnimals);

    Other methods omitted.
}
```

> **Concept**
>
> An **abstract class** is a class that is not intended for creating instances. Its purpose is to serve as a superclass for other classes. Abstract classes may contain abstract methods.

Classes that are not abstract (all classes we have seen previously) are called *concrete classes*.

Declaring a class abstract serves several purposes:

- No instances can be created of abstract classes. Trying to use the **new** keyword with an abstract class is an error and will not be permitted by the compiler. This is mirrored in BlueJ: right-clicking on an abstract class in the class diagram will not list any constructors in the pop-up menu. This serves our intention discussed above: we stated that we did not want instances of class **Animal** created directly—this class serves only as a superclass. Declaring the class abstract enforces this restriction.

- Only abstract classes can have abstract methods. This ensures that all methods in concrete classes can always be executed. If we allowed an abstract method in a concrete class, we would be able to create an instance of a class that lacked an implementation for a method.

- Abstract classes with abstract methods force subclasses to override and implement those methods declared abstract. If a subclass does not provide an implementation for an inherited abstract method, it is itself abstract, and no instances may be created. For a subclass to be concrete, it must provide implementations for *all* inherited abstract methods.

> **Concept**
>
> **Abstract subclass.** For a subclass of an abstract class to become concrete, it must provide implementations for all inherited abstract methods. Otherwise, the subclass will itself be abstract.

Now we can start to see the purpose of abstract methods. Although they do not provide an implementation, they nonetheless ensure that all concrete subclasses have an implementation of this method. In other words, even though class **Animal** does not implement the **act** method, it ensures that all existing animals have an implemented **act** method. This is done by ensuring that

- no instance of class **Animal** can be created directly, and
- all concrete subclasses must implement the **act** method.

Although we cannot create an instance of an abstract class directly, we can otherwise use an abstract class as a type in the usual ways. For instance, the normal rules of polymorphism allow us to handle foxes and rabbits as instances of the **Animal** type. So those parts of the simulation that do not need to know whether they are dealing with a specific subclass can use the superclass type instead.

Exercise 12.34 Although the body of the loop in Code 12.6 no longer deals with the **Fox** and **Rabbit** types, it still deals with the **Animal** type. Why is it not possible for it to treat each object in the collection simply using the **Object** type?

Exercise 12.35 Is it necessary for a class with one or more abstract methods to be defined as abstract? If you are not sure, experiment with the source of the **Animal** class in the *foxes-and-rabbits-v2* project.

Exercise 12.36 Is it possible for a class that has no abstract methods to be defined as abstract? If you are not sure, change **act** to be a concrete method in the **Animal** class by giving it a method body with no statements.

Exercise 12.37 Could it ever make sense to define a class as abstract if it has no abstract methods? Discuss this.

Exercise 12.38 Which classes in the `java.util` package are abstract? Some of them have **Abstract** in the class name, but is there any other way to tell from the documentation? Which concrete classes extend them?

Exercise 12.39 Can you tell from the API documentation for an abstract class which (if any) of its methods are abstract? Do you *need* to know which methods are abstract?

Exercise 12.40 Review the overriding rules for methods and fields discussed in Chapter 11. Why are they particularly significant in our attempts to introduce inheritance into this application?

Exercise 12.41 The changes made in this section have removed the dependencies (couplings) of the `simulateOneStep` method on the **Fox** and **Rabbit** classes. The **Simulator** class, however, is still coupled to **Fox** and **Rabbit**, because these classes are referenced in the `populate` method. There is no way to avoid this; when we create animal instances, we have to specify exactly what kind of animal to create.

This could be improved by splitting the **Simulator** into two classes: one class, **Simulator**, that runs the simulation and is completely decoupled from the concrete animal classes, and another class, **PopulationGenerator** (created and called by the simulator), that creates the population. Only this class is coupled to the concrete animal classes, making it easier for a maintenance programmer to find places where change is necessary when the application is extended. Try implementing this refactoring step. The **PopulationGenerator** class should also define the colors for each type of animal.

The project *foxes-and-rabbits-v2* provides an implementation of our simulation with the improvements discussed here. It is important to note that the change in **Simulator** to processing all the animals in a single list, rather than in separate lists, means that the simulation results in version 2 will not be identical to those in version 1.

In the book projects, you will find a third version of this project: *foxes-and-rabbits-graph*. This project is identical to *foxes-and-rabbits-v2* in its model (i.e., the animal/fox/rabbit/simulator implementations), but it adds a second view to the project: a graph showing population numbers over time. We will discuss some aspects of its implementation a little later in this chapter; for now, just experiment with this project.

Exercise 12.42 Open and run the *foxes-and-rabbits-graph* project. Pay attention to the *Graph View* output. Explain, in writing, the meaning of the graph you see, and try to explain why it looks the way it looks. Is there a relationship between the two curves?

Exercise 12.43 Repeat some of your experiments with different sizes of fields (especially smaller fields). Does the *Graph View* give you any new insights or help you understand or explain what you see?

If you have done all the exercises in this chapter so far, then your version of the project will be the same as *foxes-and-rabbits-v2* and similar to *foxes-and-rabbits-graph*, except for the graph display. You can continue the exercises from here on with either version of these projects.

12.4 More abstract methods

When we created the `Animal` superclass in Section 12.3.1, we did this by identifying common elements of the subclasses, but we chose not to move the **age** field and the methods associated with it. This might be overly conservative. We could have easily moved the **age** field to `Animal` and provided for it there an accessor and a mutator that were called by subclass methods, such as `incrementAge`. Why didn't we move `incrementAge` and `canBreed` into `Animal`, then? The reason for not moving these is that, although several of the remaining method bodies in `Fox` and `Rabbit` contain textually identical statements, their use of class variables with different values means that they cannot be moved directly to the superclass. In the case of `canBreed`, the problem is the **BREEDING_AGE** variable, while **breed** depends on **BREEDING_PROBABILITY** and **MAX_LITTER_SIZE**. If `canBreed` is moved to `Animal`, for instance, then the compiler will need to have access to a value for the subtype-specific breeding age in class `Animal`. It is tempting to define a **BREEDING_AGE** field in the `Animal` class and assume that its value will be overridden by similarly named fields in the subclasses. However, fields are handled differently from methods in Java: they cannot be overridden by subclass versions.[3] This means that a `canBreed` method in `Animal` would use a meaningless value defined in that class, rather than one that is specific to a particular subclass.

The fact that the field's value would be meaningless gives us a clue as to how we can get around this problem and, as a result, move more of the similar methods from the subclasses to the superclass.

Remember that we defined **act** as abstract in `Animal` because having a body for the method would be meaningless. If we access the breeding age with a method rather than a field, we can get around the problems associated with the age-dependent properties. This approach is shown in Code 12.8.

Code 12.8

The `canBreed` method of `Animal`

```java
/**
 * An animal can breed if it has reached the breeding age.
 * @return true if the animal can breed
 */
public boolean canBreed()
{
    return age >= getBreedingAge();
}

/**
 * Return the breeding age of this animal.
 * @return The breeding age of this animal.
 */
abstract protected int getBreedingAge();
```

---

[3] This rule applies regardless of whether a field is static or not.

The `canBreed` method has been moved to `Animal` and rewritten to use the value returned from a method call rather than the value of a class variable. For this to work, a method `getBreedingAge` must be defined in class `Animal`. Because we cannot specify a breeding age for animals in general, we can again use an `abstract` method in the `Animal` class and concrete redefinitions in the subclasses. Both `Fox` and `Rabbit` will define their own versions of `getBreedingAge` to return their particular values of `BREEDING_AGE`:

```
/**
 * @return The age at which a rabbit starts to breed.
 */
public int getBreedingAge()
{
    return BREEDING_AGE;
}
```

> **Concept**
>
> **Superclass method calls.** Calls to non-private instance methods from within a superclass are always evaluated in the wider context of the object's dynamic type.

So even though the call to `getBreedingAge` originates in the code of the superclass, the method called is defined in the subclass. This may seem mysterious at first but it is based on the same principles we described in Chapter 11 in using the dynamic type of an object to determine which version of a method is called at runtime. The technique illustrated here makes it possible for each instance to use the value appropriate to its subclass type. Using the same approach, we can move the remaining methods, `incrementAge` and `breed`, to the superclass.

Exercise 12.44 Using your latest version of the project (or the *foxes-and-rabbits-v2* project in case you have not done all the exercises), record the number of foxes and rabbits over a small number of steps, to prepare for regression testing of the changes to follow.

Exercise 12.45 Move the `age` field from `Fox` and `Rabbit` to `Animal`. Initialize it to zero in the constructor. Provide accessor and mutator methods for it and use these in `Fox` and `Rabbit` rather than in direct accesses to the field. Make sure the program compiles and runs as before.

Exercise 12.46 Move the `canBreed` method from `Fox` and `Rabbit` to `Animal`, and rewrite it as shown in Code 12.8. Provide appropriate versions of `getBreedingAge` in `Fox` and `Rabbit` that return the distinctive breeding age values.

Exercise 12.47 Move the `incrementAge` method from `Fox` and `Rabbit` to `Animal` by providing an abstract `getMaxAge` method in `Animal` and concrete versions in `Fox` and `Rabbit`.

Exercise 12.48 Can the `breed` method be moved to `Animal`? If so, make this change.

Exercise 12.49 In light of all the changes you have made to these three classes, reconsider the visibility of each method and make any changes you feel are appropriate.

Exercise 12.50 Was it possible to make these changes without having any impact on any other classes in the project? If so, what does this suggest about the degrees of encapsulation and coupling that were present in the original version?

Exercise 12.51 *Challenge exercise* Define a completely new type of animal for the simulation, as a subclass of `Animal`. You will need to decide what sort of impact its existence will have on the existing animal types. For instance, your animal might compete with foxes as a predator on the rabbit population, or your animal might prey on foxes but not on rabbits. You will probably find that you need to experiment quite a lot with the configuration settings you use for it. You will need to modify the `populate` method to have some of your animals created at the start of a simulation.

You should also define a new color for your new animal class. You can find a list of predefined color names on the API page documenting the `Color` class in the `java.awt` package.

Exercise 12.52 *Challenge exercise* The text of the `giveBirth` methods in `Fox` and `Rabbit` is very similar. The only difference is that one creates new `Fox` objects and the other creates new `Rabbit` objects. Is it possible to use the technique illustrated with `canBreed` to move the common code into a shared `giveBirth` method in `Animal`? If you think it is, try it out. *Hint*: The rules on polymorphic substitution apply to values returned from methods as well as in assignment and parameter passing.

12.5 Multiple inheritance

12.5.1 An `Actor` class

In this section, we discuss some possible future extensions and some programming constructs to support these.

The first obvious extension for our simulation is the addition of new animals. If you have attempted Exercise 12.51 then you will have touched on this already. We should, however, generalize this a bit: maybe not all participants in the simulation will be animals. Our current structure assumes that all acting participants in the simulation are animals and that they inherit from the `Animal` superclass. One enhancement that we might like to make is the introduction of human predators to the simulation, as either hunters or trappers. They do not neatly fit the existing assumption of purely animal-based actors. We might also extend the simulation to include plants eaten by the rabbits, or even some aspects of the weather. The plants as food would influence the population of rabbits (in effect, rabbits become predators of the plants), and the growth of the plants might be influenced by the weather. All these new components would act in the simulation, but they are clearly not animals, so it would be inappropriate to have them as subclasses of `Animal`.

12.5 Multiple inheritance

As we consider the potential for introducing further actors into the simulation, it is worth revealing why we chose to store details of the animals in both a **Field** object and an **Animal** list. Visiting each animal in the list is what constitutes a single simulation step. Placing all participants in a single list keeps the basic simulation step simple. However, this clearly duplicates information, which risks creating inconsistency. One reason for this design decision is that it allows us to consider participants in the simulation that are not actually within the field—a representation for the weather might be one example of this.

To deal with more general actors, it seems like a good idea to introduce an **Actor** superclass. The **Actor** class would serve as a superclass to all kinds of simulation participants, independent of what they are. Figure 12.3 shows a class diagram for this part of the simulation. The **Actor** and **Animal** classes are abstract, while **Rabbit**, **Fox**, and **Hunter** are concrete classes.

The **Actor** class would include the common part of all actors. One thing all possible actors have in common is that they perform some kind of action. We will also need to know whether an actor is still active or not. So the only definitions in class **Actor** are those of abstract **act** and **isActive** methods:

```
// all comments omitted
public abstract class Actor
{
    abstract public void act(List<Actor> newActors);
    abstract public boolean isActive();
}
```

This should be enough to rewrite the actor loop in the **Simulator** (Code 12.6), using class **Actor** instead of class **Animal**. (Either the **isAlive** method could be renamed to **isActive**, or a separate **isActive** method in **Animal** could simply call the existing **isAlive** method.)

Figure 12.3
Simulation structure with **Actor**

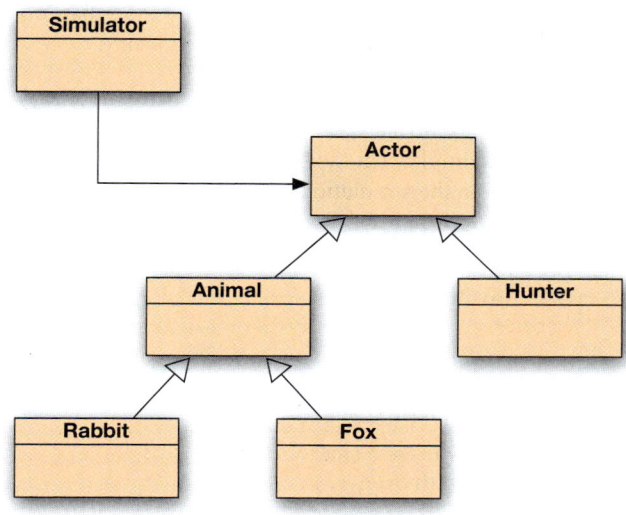

> **Exercise 12.53** Introduce the `Actor` class into your simulation. Rewrite the `simulateOneStep` method in `Simulator` to use `Actor` instead of `Animal`. You can do this even if you have not introduced any new participant types. Does the `Simulator` class compile? Or is there something else that is needed in the `Actor` class?

This new structure is more flexible because it allows easier addition of non-animal actors. In fact, we could even rewrite the statistics-gathering class, `FieldStats`, as an `Actor`—it too acts once every step. Its action would be to update its current count of animals.

12.5.2 Flexibility through abstraction

By moving towards the notion of the simulation being responsible for managing actor objects, we have succeeded in abstracting quite a long way away from our original very specific scenario of foxes and rabbits in a rectangular field. This process of abstraction has brought with it an increased flexibility that may allow us to widen even further the scope of what we might do with a general simulation framework. If we think through the requirements of other similar simulation scenarios, then we might come up with ideas for additional features that we could introduce.

For instance, it might be useful to simulate other predator–prey scenarios such as a marine simulation involving fish and sharks, or fish and fishing fleets. If the marine simulation were to involve modeling food supplies for the fish, then we would probably not want to visualize plankton populations—either because the numbers are too vast, or because their size is too small. Environmental simulations might involve modeling the weather, which, while it is clearly an actor, also might not require visualization in the field cells.

In the next section, we shall investigate the separation of visualization from acting, as a further extension to our simulation framework.

12.5.3 Selective drawing

One way to implement the separation of visualization from acting is to change the way it is performed in the simulation. Instead of iterating over the whole field every time and drawing actors in every position, we could iterate over a separate collection of drawable actors. The code in the simulator class would look similar to this:

```
// Let all actors act.
for(Actor actor : actors) {
    actor.act(...);
}
// Draw all drawables.
for(Drawable item : drawables) {
    item.draw(...);
}
```

Figure 12.4
Actor hierarchy with **Drawable** class

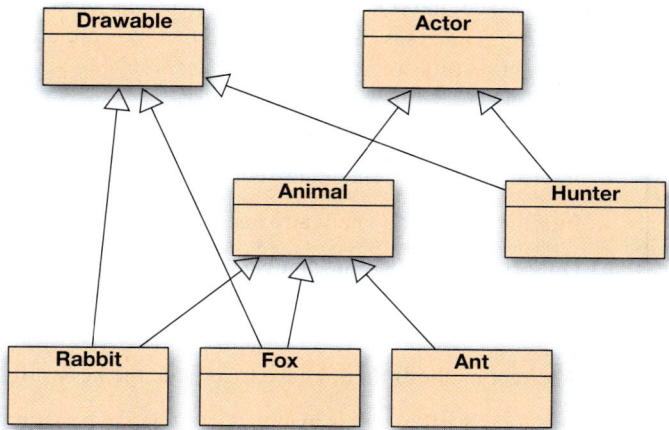

All of the actors would be in the **actors** collection, and those actors we want to show on screen would also be in the **drawables** collection. For this to work, we need another superclass called **Drawable**, which declares an abstract **draw** method. Drawable actors must then inherit from both **Actor** and **Drawable**. (Figure 12.4 shows an example where we assume that we have ants, which act but are too numerous to visualize.)

12.5.4 Drawable actors: multiple inheritance

Concept

Multiple inheritance. A situation in which a class inherits from more than one superclass is called multiple inheritance

The scenario presented here uses a structure known as *multiple inheritance*. Multiple inheritance exists in cases where one class has more than one immediate superclass.[4] The subclass then has all the features of both superclasses and those defined in the subclass itself.

Multiple inheritance is quite easy to understand in principle but can lead to significant complications in the implementation of a programming language. Different object-oriented languages vary in their treatment of multiple inheritance: some languages allow the inheritance of multiple superclasses; others do not. Java lies somewhere in the middle. It does not allow multiple inheritance of classes, but provides another construct, called an "interface," that allows a limited form of multiple inheritance. Interfaces are discussed in the next section.

12.6 Interfaces

Up to this point in the book, we have used the term "interface" in an informal sense, to represent that part of a class that couples it to other classes. Java captures this concept more formally by allowing *interface types* to be defined.

---

[4] Don't confuse this case with the regular situation where a single class might have several superclasses in its inheritance hierarchy, such as **Fox**, **Animal**, **Actor**, and **Object**. This is not what is meant by multiple inheritance.

> **Concept**
>
> A Java **interface** is a specification of a type (in the form of a type name and a set of methods). It often does not provide an implementation for most of its methods.

At first glance, interfaces are similar to classes. In their most common form they are closest to abstract classes in which all the methods are abstract. We can summarize the most significant features of interfaces as follows:

- The keyword `interface` is used instead of `class` in the header of the declaration.
- Interfaces do not contain any constructors.
- Interfaces do not contain any instance fields.
- Only fields that are constant class fields (`static` and `final`) with public visibility are allowed in an interface. The `public`, `static`, and `final` keywords may be omitted, therefore; they are assumed automatically.
- Abstract methods do not have to include the keyword `abstract` in their header.

Prior to Java 8, all methods in an interface had to be abstract, but the following non-abstract method types are also now available in interfaces:

- Methods marked with the `default` keyword have a method body.
- Methods marked with the `static` keyword have a method body.

All methods in an interface—whether abstract, concrete or static—have public visibility, so the `public` keyword may be omitted in their definition.

12.6.1 An *Actor* interface

Code 12.9 shows **Actor** defined as an interface type.

Code 12.9 The **Actor** interface

```java
/**
 * The interface to be extended by any class wishing
 * to participate in the simulation.
 */
public interface Actor
{
    /**
     * Perform the actor's regular behavior.
     * @param newActors A list for receiving newly created actors.
     */
    void act(List<Actor> newActors);

    /**
     * Is the actor still active?
     * @return true if still active, false if not.
     */
    boolean isActive();
}
```

A class can inherit from an interface in a similar way to that for inheriting from a class. However, Java uses a different keyword—`implements`—for inheriting interfaces.

12.6 Interfaces

A class is said to *implement* an interface if it includes an *implements clause* in its class header. For instance:

```
public class Fox extends Animal implements Drawable
{
    Body of class omitted.
}
```

As in this case, if a class both extends a class and implements an interface, then the extends clause must be written first in the class header.

Two of our abstract classes in the example above, **Actor** and **Drawable**, are good candidates for being written as interfaces. Both of them contain only the definition of methods, without method implementations. Thus, they already fit the most abstract definition of an interface perfectly: they contain no instance fields, no constructors, and no method bodies.

The class **Animal** is a different case. It is a real abstract class that provides a partial implementation with instance fields, a constructor and many methods with bodies. It has only a single abstract method in its original version. Given all of these characteristics, it must remain as a class rather than becoming an interface.

Exercise 12.54 Redefine as an interface the abstract class **Actor** in your project. Does the simulation still compile? Does it run? Make any changes necessary to make it runnable again.

Exercise 12.55 Are the fields in the following interface class fields or instance fields?

```
public interface Quiz
{
    int CORRECT = 1;
    int INCORRECT = 0;
    ...
}
```

What visibility do they have?

Exercise 12.56 What are the errors in the following interface?

```
public interface Monitor
{
    private static final int THRESHOLD = 50;
    private int value;
    public Monitor (int initial);
    void update(int reading);
    int getThreshold()
    {
        return THRESHOLD;
    }
    ...
}
```

12.6.2 Default methods in interfaces

A method marked as `default` in an interface will have a method body, which is inherited by all implementing classes. The addition of default methods to interfaces in Java 8 muddied the waters in the distinction between abstract classes and interfaces, since it is no longer true that interfaces never contain method bodies. However, it is important to exercise caution when considering defining a default method in an interface. It should be borne in mind that default methods were added to the language primarily to support the addition of new methods to interfaces in the API that existed before Java 8. Default methods made it possible to change existing interfaces without breaking the many classes that already implemented the older versions of those interfaces.

From the other limitations of interfaces—no constructors and no instance fields—it should be clear that the functionality possible in a default method is strictly limited, since there is no state that can be examined or manipulated directly by them. In general, therefore, when writing our own interfaces we will tend to limit ourselves to purely abstract methods. Furthermore, when discussing features of interfaces in this chapter we will often ignore the case of non-abstract methods for the sake of simplicity.

12.6.3 Multiple inheritance of interfaces

As mentioned above, Java allows any class to extend at most one other class. However, it allows a class to implement any number of interfaces (in addition to possibly extending one class). Thus, if we define both `Actor` and `Drawable` as interfaces instead of abstract classes, we can define class `Hunter` (Figure 12.4) to implement both of them:

```
public class Hunter implements Actor, Drawable
{
    // Body of class omitted.
}
```

The class `Hunter` inherits the methods of all interfaces (`act` and `draw`, in this case) as abstract methods. It must, then, provide method definitions for both of them by overriding the methods, or the class itself must be declared abstract.

The `Animal` class shows an example where a class does not implement an inherited interface method. `Animal`, in our new structure in Figure 12.4, inherits the abstract method `act` from `Actor`. It does not provide a method body for this method, which makes `Animal` itself abstract (it must include the `abstract` keyword in the class header). The `Animal` subclasses then implement the `act` method and become concrete classes.

The presence of default methods in interfaces can lead to complications in the implementation of multiple interfaces by a class. Where a class implements multiple interfaces and two or more of the interfaces have a default method with the same signature then the implementing class *must* override that method—even if the alternative versions of the method are identical. The reason for this is that, in the general case, it needs to be clear exactly which of the alternative implementations should be inherited by the class. The class may override either by calling the preferred version in the overriding method, or by defining a completely different implementation. The header of the overriding method will not contain the `default` keyword, since that is only used in interfaces.

There is a new syntax involving the keyword **super** for calling a default method from one of the interfaces in an overriding method. For instance, suppose the **Actor** and **Drawable** interfaces both define a default method called, **reset**, that has a **void** return type and takes no parameters. If a class implementing both interfaces overrides this method by calling both default versions then the overriding method might be defined as follows:

```
public void reset()
{
    Actor.super.reset();
    Drawable.super.reset();
}
```

In other words, an implementing class that overrides an inherited default method can call that default method using the syntax:

InterFaceName.super.*methodName*(. . .)

Exercise 12.57 *Challenge exercise* Add a non-animal actor to the simulation. For instance, you could introduce a **Hunter** class with the following properties. Hunters have no maximum age and neither feed nor breed. At each step of the simulation, a hunter moves to a random location anywhere in the field and fires a fixed number of shots into random target locations around the field. Any animal in one of the target locations is killed.

Place just a small number of hunters in the field at the start of the simulation. Do the hunters remain in the simulation throughout, or do they ever disappear? If they do disappear, why might that be, and does that represent realistic behavior?

What other classes required changing as a result of introducing hunters? Is there a need to introduce further decoupling to the classes?

12.6.4 Interfaces as types

When a class implements an interface, it often does not inherit any implementation from it. The question, then, is: What do we actually gain by implementing interfaces?

When we introduced inheritance in Chapter 10, we emphasized two great benefits of inheritance:

1. The subclass inherits the code (method implementations and fields) from the superclass. This allows reuse of existing code and avoids code duplication.

2. The subclass becomes a subtype of the superclass. This allows polymorphic variables and method calls. In other words, it allows different special cases of objects (instances of subclasses) to be treated uniformly (as instances of the supertype).

Interfaces are not primarily used for the first benefit but for the second. An interface defines a type just as a class does. This means that variables can be declared to be of interface types, even though no objects of that type can exist (only subtypes).

In our example, even though **Actor** is now an interface, we can still declare an **Actor** variable in the **Simulator** class. The simulation loop still works unchanged.

Interfaces can have no direct instances, but they serve as supertypes for instances of other classes.

12.6.5 Interfaces as specifications

In this chapter, we have introduced interfaces as a means to implement multiple inheritance in Java. This is one important use of interfaces, but there are others.

The most important characteristic of interfaces is that they almost completely separate the definition of the functionality (the class's "interface" in the wider sense of the word) from its implementation. A good example of how this can be used in practice can be found in the Java collection hierarchy.

The collection hierarchy defines (among other types) the interface **List** and the classes **ArrayList** and **LinkedList** (Figure 12.5). The **List** interface specifies the full functionality of a list, without constraining its underlying structural implementation. The subclasses (**LinkedList** and **ArrayList**) provide two completely different structural implementations of the same interface. This is interesting, because the two implementations differ greatly in the efficiency of some of their functions. Random access to elements in the middle of the list, for example, is much faster with the **ArrayList**. Inserting or deleting elements, however, can be much faster in the **LinkedList**.

Which implementation is better in any given application can be hard to judge in advance. It depends a lot on the relative frequency with which certain operations are performed and on some other factors. In practice, the best way to find out is often to try it out: implement the application with both alternatives and measure the performance.

The existence of the **List** interface makes it very easy to do this. If, instead of using **ArrayList** or **LinkedList** as variable and parameter types, we always use **List**, our application will work independently of the specific type of list we are currently using. Only when we create a new list do we really have to use the name of the specific implementation. We would, for instance, write

```
List<Type> myList = new ArrayList<>();
```

Figure 12.5
The **List** interface and its subclasses

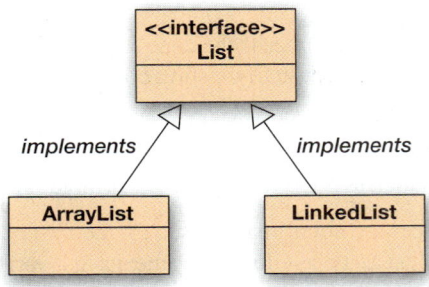

Note that the polymorphic variable's type is just **List** of **Type**. This way, we can change the whole application to use a linked list by just changing **ArrayList** to **LinkedList** in a single location when the list is being created.

12.6.6 Library support through abstract classes and interfaces

In Chapter 6, we pointed out the importance of paying attention to the names of the collection classes: **ArrayList**, **LinkedList**, **HashSet**, **TreeSet**, etc. Now that we have been introduced to abstract classes and interfaces, we can see why these particular names have been chosen. The **java.util** package defines several important collection abstractions in the form of interfaces, such as **List**, **Map**, and **Set**. The concrete class names have been chosen to communicate information about both what kind of interface they conform to and some of the underlying implementation detail. This information is very useful when it comes to making informed decisions about the right concrete class to use in a particular setting. However, by using the highest-level abstract type (be it abstract class or interface) for our variables, wherever possible, our code will remain flexible in light of future library changes—such as the addition of a new **Map** or **Set** implementation, for instance.

In Chapter 13, where we introduce the Java GUI libraries, we will be making enormous use of abstract classes and interfaces as we see how to create quite sophisticated functionality with very little additional code.

Exercise 12.58 Which methods do **ArrayList** and **LinkedList** have that are not defined in the **List** interface? Why do you think that these methods are not included in **List**?

Exercise 12.59 Write a class that can make comparisons between the efficiency of the common methods from the **List** interface in the **ArrayList** and **LinkedList** classes such as **add**, **get**, and **remove**. Use the polymorphic-variable technique described above to write the class so that it only knows it is performing its tests on objects of the interface type **List** rather than on the concrete types **ArrayList** and **LinkedList**. Use large lists of objects for the tests, to make the results significant. You can use the **currentTimeMillis** method of the **System** class for getting hold of the start and finish time of your test methods.

Exercise 12.60 Read the API description for the **sort** methods of the **Collections** class in the **java.util** package. Which interfaces are mentioned in the descriptions? Which methods in the **java.util.List** interface have **default** implementations?

Exercise 12.61 *Challenge exercise* Investigate the **Comparable** interface. This is a *parameterized* interface. Define a simple class that implements **Comparable**. Create a collection containing objects of this class and sort the collection. *Hint*: The **LogEntry** class of the *weblog-analyzer* project in Chapter 7 implements this interface.

12.6.7 Functional interfaces and lambdas (advanced)

Java 8 introduced a special classification for interfaces that contain just a single abstract method (regardless of the number of default and/or static methods they contain). Such an interface is called a *functional interface*. The annotation `@FunctionalInterface` may be included with the declaration to allow the compiler to check that the interface conforms to the rules for functional interfaces.

There is a special relationship between functional interfaces and lambda expressions. Anywhere that an object of a functional interface type is required, a lambda expression may be used instead. In the following chapter, we shall see extensive use of this feature when implementing graphical user interfaces.

This link between lambdas and functional interfaces is important. In particular, it gives us a convenient means to associate a lambda expression with a type, for example to declare a variable that can hold a lambda. The `java.util.function` package defines a large number of interfaces that provide convenience names for the most commonly occurring types of lambda expression. In general, the interface names indicate the return type and the parameter types of their single method, and hence a lambda of that type. For example:

- `Consumer` interfaces relate to lambdas with a `void` return type. For instance, `DoubleConsumer` takes a single `double` parameter and returns no result.
- `BinaryOperator` interfaces take two parameters and return a result of the same type. For instance, `IntBinaryOperator` takes two `int` parameters and returns an `int` result.
- `Supplier` interfaces return a result of the indicated type. For instance, `LongSupplier`.
- `Predicate` interfaces return a `boolean` result. For instance, `IntPredicate`.

All of these interfaces extend the `Function` interface, whose single abstract method is called `apply`. One potentially useful functional interface type, defined in the `java.lang` package, is `Runnable`. This fills a gap in the list of `Consumer` interfaces in that it takes no parameters and has a `void` return type. However, its single abstract method is called `run`.

Functional interface types allow lambdas to be assigned to variables or passed as actual parameters. For example, suppose we have pairs of *name* and *alias* strings that we wish to format in a particular way, such as `"Michelangelo Merisi (AKA Caravaggio)"`. A lambda taking two `String` parameters and returning a `String` result is compatible with the `BinaryOperator` interface, and we might give a type and name to a lambda as follows:

```
BinaryOperator<String> aka =
    (name, alias) -> return name + " (AKA " + alias + ")";
```

This lambda would be used by calling its `apply` method with appropriate parameters, for instance:

```
System.out.println(aka.apply("Michelangelo Merisi",
                             "Caravaggio"));
```

12.7 A further example of interfaces

In the previous section, we have discussed how interfaces can be used to separate the specification of a component from its implementation so that different implementations can be "plugged in," thus making it easy to replace components of a system. This is often done to separate parts of a system that are logically only loosely coupled.

We have seen an example of this (without discussing it explicitly) at the end of Section 12.3. There, we investigated the *foxes-and-rabbits-graph* project, which added another view of the populations in the form of a line graph. Looking at the class diagram for this project, we can see that the addition also makes use of a Java interface (Fig 12.6).

The previous versions of the *foxes-and-rabbits* project contained only one `SimulatorView` class. This was a concrete class, and it provided the implementation of a grid-based view of the field. As we have seen, the visualization is quite separate from the simulation logic (the field and the actors), and different visualization views are possible.

For this project, `SimulatorView` was changed from a class to an interface, and the implementation of this view was moved into a class named `GridView`.

`GridView` is identical to the previous `SimulatorView` class. The new `SimulatorView` interface was constructed by searching through the `Simulator` class to find all methods that are actually called from outside, then defining an interface that specifies exactly those methods. They are:

```
view.setColor(classObject, color);
view.isViable(field);
view.showStatus(step, field);
view.reset();
```

We can now easily define the complete `SimulatorView` interface:

```java
import java.awt.Color;
public interface SimulatorView
{
    void setColor(Class<?> animalClass, Color color);
    boolean isViable(Field field);
    void showStatus(int step, Field field);
    void reset();
}
```

Figure 12.6
The `SimulatorView` interface and implementing classes

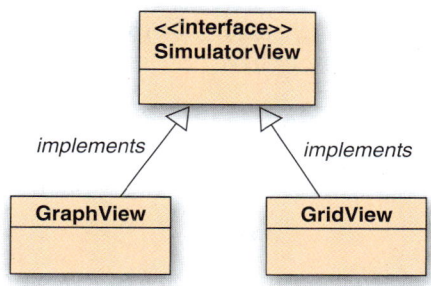

The one slightly tricky detail in the definition above is the use of the type `Class<?>` as the first parameter of the `setColor` method. We will explain that in the next section.

The previous `SimulatorView` class, now called `GridView`, is specified to implement the new `SimulatorView` interface:

```
public class GridView extends JFrame implements SimulatorView
{
    ...
}
```

It does not require any additional code, because it already implements the interface's methods. However, after making these changes, it becomes fairly easy to "plug in" other views for the simulation by providing further implementations of the `SimulatorView` interface. The new class `GraphView`, which produces the line graph, is an example of this.

Once we have more than one view implementation, we can easily replace the current view with another or, as we have in our example, even display two views at the same time. In the `Simulator` class, the concrete subclasses `GridView` and `GraphView` are only mentioned once when each view was constructed. Thereafter, they are stored in a collection holding elements of the `SimulatorView` supertype, and only the interface type is used to communicate with them.

The implementations of the `GridView` and `GraphView` classes are fairly complex, and we do not expect you to fully understand them at this stage. The pattern of providing two implementations for a single interface, however, is important here, and you should make sure that you understand this aspect.

Exercise 12.62 Review the source code of the `Simulator` class. Find all occurrences of the view classes and interfaces, and trace all variables declared using any of these types. Explain exactly how the views are used in the `Simulator` class.

Exercise 12.63 Implement a new class `TextView` that implements `SimulatorView`. `TextView` provides a textual view of the simulation. After every simulation step, it prints out one line in the form

    Foxes: 121 Rabbits: 266

Use `TextView` instead of `GridView` for some tests. (Do not delete the `GridView` class. We want to have the ability to change between different views!)

Exercise 12.64 Can you manage to have all three views active at the same time?

12.8 The `Class` class

In Chapter 10, we described the paradoxically named `Object` class. It shouldn't surprise you, therefore, that there is also a `Class` class! This is where talking about classes and objects can become very confusing.

We used the `Class` type in defining the `SimulatorView` interface in the previous section. The `Class` class has nothing specifically to do with interfaces; it is a general feature of Java, but we just happen to be meeting it for the first time here. The idea is that each type has a `Class` object associated with it.

The `Object` class defines the method `getClass` to return the `Class` associated with an object. Another way to get the `Class` object for a type is to write "`.class`" after the type name: for instance, `Fox.class` or `int.class`—notice that even the primitive types have `Class` objects associated with them.

The `Class` class is a generic class—it has a type parameter specifying the specific class subtype we are referencing. For example, the type of `String.class` is `Class<String>`. We can use a question mark in place of the type parameter—`Class<?>`—if we want to declare a variable that can hold all class objects of all types.

`Class` objects are particularly useful if we want to know whether the type of two objects is the same. We use this feature in the original `SimulatorView` class to associate each animal type with a color in the field. `SimulatorView` has the following field to map one to the other:

```
private Map<Class<?>, Color> colors;
```

When the view is set up, the constructor of `Simulator` has the following calls to its `setColor` method:

```
view.setColor(Rabbit.class, Color.ORANGE);
view.setColor(Fox.class, Color.BLUE);
```

We won't go into any further detail about `Class<?>`, but this description should be sufficient to enable you to understand the code shown in the previous section.

12.9 Abstract class or interface?

In some situations, a choice has to be made between whether to use an abstract class or an interface, while in other cases, either abstract classes or interfaces can do the job. Prior to the introduction of default methods in Java 8, the issue appeared to be clearer: if a type needed elements of concrete implementation—such as instance fields, constructors, or method bodies—then an abstract class would have to be used. However, the present availability of default methods in interfaces should not really change the answer to this question in most cases. In general, it is preferable to avoid defining default methods in interfaces except for the purpose of adapting legacy code.

If we have a choice, interfaces are usually preferable. Interfaces are relatively lightweight types that minimize constraints on implementing classes. Furthermore, if we provide a type as an abstract class, then subclasses cannot extend any other classes. Because interfaces allow multiple inheritance, the use of an interface does not create such a restriction. Interfaces cleanly separate the type specification from the implementation, and this creates less coupling. Therefore, using interfaces leads to a more flexible and more extensible structure.

12.10 Event-driven simulations

The style of simulation we have used in this chapter has the characteristic of time passing in discrete, equal-length steps. At each time step, each actor in the simulation was asked to act—i.e., take the actions appropriate to its current state. This style of simulation is sometimes called *time-based*, or *synchronous*, simulation. In this particular simulation, most of the actors will have had something to do at each time step: move, breed, and eat. In many simulation scenarios, however, actors spend large numbers of time steps doing nothing—typically, waiting for something to happen that requires some action on their part. Consider the case of a newly born rabbit in our simulation, for instance. It is repeatedly asked whether it is going to breed, even though it takes several time steps before this is possible. Isn't there a way to avoid asking this unnecessary question until the rabbit is actually ready?

There is also the question of the most appropriate size of the time step. We deliberately left vague the issue of how much real time a time step represents, and the various actions actually require significantly different amounts of time (eating and movement should occur much more frequently than giving birth, for instance). Is there a way to decide on a time-step size that is not so small that most of the time nothing will be happening, or too long that different types of actions are not distinguished clearly enough between time steps?

An alternative approach is to use an *event-based*, or *asynchronous*, simulation style. In this style, the simulation is driven by maintaining a schedule of future events. The most obvious difference between the two styles is that, in an event-based simulation, time passes in uneven amounts. For instance, one event might occur at time t and the next two events occur at times $t + 2$ and time $t + 8$, while the following three events might all occur at time $t + 9$.

For a fox-and-rabbits simulation, the sort of events we are talking about would be birth, movement, hunting, and death from natural causes. What typically happens is that, as each event occurs, a fresh event is scheduled for some point in the future. For instance, when a birth event occurs, the event marking that animal's death from old age will be scheduled. All future events are stored in an ordered queue, where the next event to take place is held at the head of the queue. It is important to appreciate that newly scheduled events will not always be placed at the end of the current queue; they will often have to be inserted somewhere before the end, in order to keep the queue in time order. In addition, some future events will be rendered obsolete by events that occur before them—an obvious example is that the natural-death event for a rabbit will not take place if the rabbit is eaten beforehand!

Event-driven simulations lend themselves particularly well to the techniques we have described in this chapter. For instance, the concept of an event is likely to be implemented as an **Event** abstract class containing concrete details of when the event will occur, but only abstract details of what the event involves. Concrete subclasses of **Event** will then supply the specific details for the different event types. Typically, the main simulation loop will not need to be concerned with the concrete event types, but will be able to use polymorphic method calls when an event occurs.

Event-based simulations are often more efficient and are preferable where large systems and large amounts of data are involved, while synchronous simulations are better for producing time-based visualizations (such as animations of the actors) because time flows more evenly.

Exercise 12.65 Find out some more about how event-driven simulations differ from time-based simulations.

Exercise 12.66 Look at the `java.util` package to see if there are any classes that might be well suited to storing an event queue in an event-based simulation.

Exercise 12.67 *Challenge exercise* Rewrite the foxes-and-rabbits simulation in the event-based style.

12.11 Summary of inheritance

In Chapters 10 through 12, we have discussed many different aspects of inheritance techniques. These include code inheritance and subtyping as well as inheriting from interfaces, abstract classes, and concrete classes.

In general, we can distinguish two main purposes of using inheritance: we can use it to inherit code (code inheritance), and we can use it to inherit the type (subtyping). The first is useful for code reuse, the second for polymorphism and specialization.

When we inherit from ("extend") concrete classes, we do both: we inherit the implementation and the type. When we inherit from ("implement") interfaces, we separate the two: we inherit a type but (usually) no implementation. For cases where parts of both are useful, we can inherit from abstract classes; here, we inherit the type and a partial implementation.

When inheriting a complete implementation, we can choose to add or override methods. When no or only partial implementation of a type is inherited, the subclass must provide the implementation before it can be instantiated.

Some other object-oriented languages also provide mechanisms to inherit code without inheriting the type. Java does not provide such a construct.

12.12 Summary

In this chapter, we have discussed the fundamental structure of computer simulations. We have then used this example to introduce abstract classes and interfaces as constructs that allow us to create further abstractions and develop more-flexible applications.

Abstract classes are classes that are not intended to have any instances. Their purpose is to serve as superclasses to other classes. Abstract classes may have both abstract methods—methods that have a header but no body—and full method implementations. Concrete subclasses of abstract classes must override abstract methods to provide the missing method implementations.

Another construct for defining types in Java is the interface. Java interfaces are similar to completely abstract classes: they define method headers, but generally provide no implementation. Interfaces define types that can be used for variables.

Interfaces can be used to provide a specification for a class (or part of an application) without stating anything about the concrete implementation.

Java allows multiple inheritance of interfaces (which it calls "implements" relationships) but only single inheritance for classes ("extends" relationships). Multiple inheritance is made more complicated by the presence of conflicting default methods.

Terms introduced in this chapter:

abstract method, abstract class, concrete class, abstract subclass, multiple inheritance, interface (Java construct), implements

12.12 Summary

Exercise 12.68 Can an abstract class have concrete (non-abstract) methods? Can a concrete class have abstract methods? Can you have an abstract class without abstract methods? Justify your answers.

Exercise 12.69 Look at the code below. You have five types—classes or interfaces—(U, G, B, Z, and X) and a variable of each of these types.

```
U u;
G g;
B b;
Z z;
X x;
```

The following assignments are all legal (assume that they all compile).

```
u = z;
x = b;
g = u;
x = u;
```

The following assignments are all illegal (they cause compiler errors).

```
u = b;
x = g;
b = u;
z = u;
g = x;
```

What can you say about the types and their relationships? (What relationship are they to each other?)

Exercise 12.70 Assume that you want to model people in a university to implement a course management system. There are different people involved: staff members, students, teaching staff, support staff, tutors, technical-support staff, and student technicians. Tutors and student technicians are interesting: tutors are students who have been hired to do some teaching, and student technicians are students who have been hired to help with the technical support.

Draw a type hierarchy (classes and interfaces) to represent this situation. Indicate which types are concrete classes, abstract classes, and interfaces.

Exercise 12.71 *Challenge exercise* Sometimes class/interface pairs exist in the *Java standard library* that define exactly the same methods. Often, the interface name ends with *Listener* and the class name with *Adapter*. An example is **PrintJobListener** and **PrintJobAdapter**. The interface defines some method headers, and the adapter class defines the same methods, each with an empty method body. What might the reason be for having them both?

Exercise 12.72 The collection library has a class named `TreeSet`, which is an example of a sorted set. Elements in this set are kept in order. Carefully read the description of this class, and then write a class `Person` that can be inserted into a `TreeSet`, which will then sort the `Person` objects by age.

Exercise 12.73 Use the API documentation for the `AbstractList` class to write a concrete class that maintains an unmodifiable list.

CHAPTER 13
Building Graphical User Interfaces

Main concepts discussed in this chapter:

- constructing GUIs
- interface components
- GUI layout
- event handling

Java constructs discussed in this chapter:

`JFrame`, `JLabel`, `JButton`, `JMenuBar`, `JMenu`, `JMenuItem`, `ActionEvent`, `Color`, `FlowLayout`, `BorderLayout`, `GridLayout`, `BoxLayout`, `Box`, `JOptionPane`, `EtchedBorder`, `EmptyBorder`, anonymous inner classes

13.1 Introduction

So far in this book, we have concentrated on writing applications with text-based interfaces. The reason is not that text-based interfaces have any great advantage in principle; they just have the one advantage that they are easier to create.

We did not want to distract too much attention from the important software-development issues in the early stages of learning about object-oriented programming. These were issues such as object structure and interaction, class design, and code quality.

Graphical user interfaces (GUIs) are also constructed from interacting objects, but they have a very specialized structure, and we avoided introducing them before discussing object structures in more general terms. Now, however, we are ready to have a look at the construction of GUIs.

Some of the material in this chapter makes extensive use of the *lambda expression* feature that was introduced in Java 8. That feature was covered in detail in Chapter 5 of this book—a chapter that we designated as "Advanced" for that particular point in the book. If you have not yet read that chapter, we recommend that you now do so in order to familiarise yourself with the syntax and usage of lambda expressions. In addition, it would be worth reviewing the advanced material in Chapter 12, as significant use is made of abstract classes and interface types in the Java GUI libraries.

GUIs give our applications an interface consisting of windows, menus, buttons, and other graphical components. They make applications look much more like the "typical" applications people are used to.

Note that we are stumbling about the double meaning of the word *interface* again here. The interfaces we are talking about now are neither interfaces of classes nor the Java interface construct. We are now talking about *user interfaces*—the part of an application that is visible on screen for the user to interact with.

Once we know how to create GUIs with Java, we can develop much-better-looking programs.

13.2 Components, layout, and event handling

The details involved in creating GUIs are extensive. In this book, we will not be able to cover all details of all of the possible things you can do with them, but we shall discuss the general principles and a good number of examples.

All GUI programming in Java is done through the use of dedicated standard class libraries. Once we understand the principles, we can find out all the necessary details by working with the standard library documentation.

The principles we need to understand can be divided into three topic areas:

- What kinds of elements can we show on screen?
- How do we arrange those elements?
- How do we react to user input?

We shall discuss these questions under the keywords *components*, *layout*, and *event handling*.

Components are the individual parts that a GUI is built from. They are things such as buttons, menus, menu items, checkboxes, sliders, text fields, and so on. The Java library contains a good number of ready-made components, and we can also write our own. We shall have to learn what the important components are, how to create them, and how to make them look the way we want them to look.

> **Concept**
> A GUI is built by arranging **components** on screen. Components are represented by objects.

Layout deals with the issue of how to arrange the components on screen. Older, more primitive GUI systems handled this with two-dimensional coordinates: the programmer specified *x*- and *y*-coordinates (in pixels) for the position and the size of each component. In more modern GUI systems, this is too simplistic. We have to take into account different screen resolutions, different fonts, users resizing windows, and many other aspects that make layout more difficult. The solution will be a scheme where we can specify the layout in more general terms. We can, for example, specify that a particular component should be below this other one, or that this component should be stretched if the window gets resized but this other should always have a constant size. We shall see that this is done using *layout managers*.

> **Concept**
> Arranging the **layout** of components is achieved by using layout managers.

Event handling refers to the technique we shall use to deal with user input. Once we have created our components and positioned them on screen, we also have to make sure that

Concept

The term **event handling** refers to the task of reacting to user events, such as mouse-button clicks or keyboard input.

something happens when a user clicks a button. The model used by the Java library for this is event-based: if a user activates a component (e.g., clicks a button or selects a menu item) the system will generate an event. Our application can then receive a notification of the event (by having one of its methods invoked), and we can take appropriate action.

We shall discuss each of these areas in much more detail later in this chapter. First, however, we shall briefly introduce a bit more background and terminology.

13.3 AWT and Swing

Java has three GUI libraries. The oldest is called *AWT* (Abstract Window Toolkit) and was introduced as part of the original Java API. Later, a much-improved GUI library, called *Swing,* was added to Java. More recently, the *JavaFX* library has been added. In this chapter we shall concentrate on using Swing, but many of the principles we cover will apply equally well to GUI libraries in general.

Swing makes use of some of the AWT classes, replaces some AWT classes with its own versions, and adds many new classes (Figure 13.1). This means that we shall use some AWT classes that are still used with Swing programs, but use the Swing versions of all classes that exist in both libraries.

Wherever there are equivalent classes in AWT and Swing, the Swing versions have been identified by adding the letter *J* to the start of the class name. You will, for example, see classes named `Button` and `JButton`, `Frame` and `JFrame`, `Menu` and `JMenu`, and so on. The classes starting with a *J* are the Swing versions; these are the ones we shall use, and the two should not be mixed in an application.

That is enough background for a start. Let us look at some code.

13.4 The ImageViewer example

As always, we shall discuss the new concepts by using an example. The application we shall build in this chapter is an image viewer (Figure 13.2). This is a program that can open and display image files in JPEG and PNG formats, perform some image transformations, and save the images back to disk.

Figure 13.1
AWT and Swing

Figure 13.2
A simple image-viewer application

Concept

Image format
Images can be stored in different formats. The differences primarily affect file size and the quality of the image.

As part of this, we shall use our own image class to represent an image while it is in memory, implement various filters to change the image's appearance, and use Swing components to build a user interface. While doing this, we shall concentrate our discussion on the GUI aspects of the program.

If you are curious to see what we will build, you can open and try out the *imageviewer1-0* project—that is the version displayed in Figure 13.2; just create an **ImageViewer** object. There are some sample images in the *images* folder inside the *chapter13* folder (one level up from the project folder). You can, of course, also open your own images. Here, we start slowly, initially with something much simpler, and we work our way to the complete application step by step.

13.4.1 First experiments: creating a frame

Almost everything you see in a GUI is contained in a top-level window. A top-level window is one that is under the control of the operating system's window management and which typically can be moved, resized, minimized, and maximized independently.

Java calls these top-level windows *frames*. In Swing, they are represented by a class called **JFrame**.

Code 13.1

A first version of an **ImageViewer** class

```java
import java.awt.*;
import java.awt.event.*;
import javax.swing.*;

/**
 * ImageViewer is the main class of the image viewer application. It builds
 * and displays the application GUI and initialises all other components.
 *
 * To start the application, create an object of this class.
 *
 * @author Michael Kölling and David J. Barnes.
 * @version 0.1
 */
public class ImageViewer
{
    private JFrame frame;

    /**
     * Create an ImageViewer show it on screen.
     */
    public ImageViewer()
    {
        makeFrame();
    }

    // ---- swing stuff to build the frame and all its components ----

    /**
     * Create the Swing frame and its content.
     */
    private void makeFrame()
    {
        frame = new JFrame("ImageViewer");
        Container contentPane = frame.getContentPane();

        JLabel label = new JLabel("I am a label. I can display some text.");
        contentPane.add(label);

        frame.pack();
        frame.setVisible(true);
    }
}
```

To get a GUI on screen, the first thing we have to do is create and display a frame. Code 13.1 shows a complete class (already named **ImageViewer** in preparation for things to come) that shows a frame on screen. This class is available in the book projects as *imageviewer0-1* (the number stands for version 0.1).

Exercise 13.1 Open the *imageviewer0-1* project. (This will become the basis of your own image viewer.) Create an instance of class **ImageViewer**. Resize the resulting frame (make it larger). What do you observe about the placement of the text in the frame?

We shall now discuss the `ImageViewer` class shown in Code 13.1 in some detail.

The first three lines in that class are import statements of all classes in the packages `java.awt`, `java.awt.event`, and `javax.swing`.[1] We need many of the classes in these packages for all Swing applications we create, so we shall always import the three packages completely in our GUI programs.

Looking at the rest of the class shows very quickly that all the interesting stuff is in the `makeFrame` method. This method takes care of constructing the GUI. The class's constructor contains only a call to this method. We have done this so that all the GUI construction code is at a well-defined place and is easy to find later (cohesion!). We shall do this in all our GUI examples.

The class has one instance variable of type `JFrame`. This is used to hold the frame that the image viewer wants to show on screen. Let us now take a closer look at the `makeFrame` method.

The first line in this method is

```
frame = new JFrame("ImageViewer");
```

This statement creates a new frame and stores it in our instance variable for later use.

As a general principle, you should, in parallel with studying the examples in this book, look at the class documentation for all classes we encounter. This applies to all the classes we use; we shall not point this out every time from now on, but just expect you to do it.

Exercise 13.2 Find the documentation for class `JFrame`. What is the purpose of the `ImageViewer` parameter that we used in the constructor call above?

> **Concept**
>
> Components are placed in a frame by adding them to the frame's **menu bar** or **content pane**.

A frame consists of three parts: the *title bar*, an optional *menu bar*, and the *content pane* (Figure 13.3). The exact appearance of the title bar depends on the underlying operating system. It usually contains the window title and a few window controls.

The menu bar and the content pane are under the control of the application. To both, we can add some components to create a GUI. We shall concentrate on the content pane first.

13.4.2 Adding simple components

Immediately following creation of the `JFrame`, the frame will be invisible and its content pane will be empty. We continue by adding a label to the content pane:

```
Container contentPane = frame.getContentPane();
JLabel label = new JLabel("I am a label.");
contentPane.add(label);
```

The first line gets the content pane from the frame. We always have to do this; GUI components are added to a frame by adding them to the frame's content pane.[2]

---

[1] The `swing` package is really in a package called `javax` (ending with an *x*), not `java`. The reason for this is largely historic—there does not seem to be a logical explanation for it.

[2] Java also has an **add** method for adding components directly in the `JFrame` class, which will also add the component to the content pane. However, we need access to the content pane for other reasons later anyway, so we do the adding of components to the content pane at this point as well.

Figure 13.3
Different parts of a frame

The content pane itself is of type **Container**. A container is a Swing component that can hold arbitrary groups of other components—rather like an **ArrayList** can hold an arbitrary collection of objects. We shall discuss containers in more detail later.

We then create a label component (type **JLabel**) and add it to the content pane. A label is a component that can display text and/or an image.

Finally, we have the two lines

```
frame.pack();
frame.setVisible(true);
```

The first line causes the frame to arrange the components inside it properly, and to size itself appropriately. We always have to call the **pack** method on the frame after we have added or resized components.

The last line finally makes the frame visible on screen. We always start out with the frame being invisible so that we can arrange all the components inside the frame without the construction process being visible on screen. Then, when the frame is built, we can show it in a completed state.

Exercise 13.3 Another often-used Swing component is a button (type **JButton**). Replace the label in the example above with a button.

Exercise 13.4 What happens when you add two labels (or two buttons) to the content pane? Can you explain what you observe? Experiment with resizing the frame.

13.4.3 An alternative structure

We have chosen to develop our application by creating a **JFrame** object as an attribute of the **ImageViewer** and populating it with further GUI components that are created outside the frame object. An alternative structure for this top level would be to define **ImageViewer** as a subclass of **JFrame** and populate it internally. This style is also commonly seen. Code 13.2 shows the equivalent of Code 13.1 in this style. This version is available as the project *imageviewer0-1a*. While it is worth being familiar with both styles, neither is obviously superior to the other. We will continue with our original version in the rest of this chapter.

Code 13.2
An alternative structure for the **ImageViewer** class

```java
import java.awt.*;
import java.awt.event.*;
import javax.swing.*;

/**
 * ImageViewer is the main class of the image viewer application. It builds
 * and displays the application GUI and initialises all other components.
 *
 * To start the application, create an object of this class.
 *
 * @author Michael Kölling and David J. Barnes.
 * @version 0.1a
 */
public class ImageViewer extends JFrame
{
    /**
     * Create an ImageViewer and show it on screen.
     */
    public ImageViewer()
    {
        super("ImageViewer");
        makeFrame();
    }

    // ---- swing stuff to build the frame and all its components ----

    /**
     * Create the Swing frame and its content.
     */
    private void makeFrame()
    {
        Container contentPane = getContentPane();

        JLabel label = new JLabel("I am a label. I can display some text.");
        contentPane.add(label);

        pack();
        setVisible(true);
    }
}
```

13.4.4 Adding menus

Our next step toward building a GUI is to add menus and menu items. This is conceptually easy but contains one tricky detail: How do we arrange to react to user actions, such as the selection of a menu item? We discuss this below.

First, we create the menus. Three classes are involved:

- **JMenuBar**—An object of this class represents a menu bar that can be displayed below the title bar at the top of a window (see Figure 13.3). Every window has at most one **JMenuBar**.[3]

- **JMenu**—Objects of this class represent a single menu (such as the common *File, Edit, or Help* menus). Menus are often held in a menu bar. They could also appear as pop-up menus, but we shall not do that now.

- **JMenuItem**—Objects of this class represent a single menu item inside a menu (such as *Open* or *Save*).

For our image viewer, we shall create one menu bar, and several menus and menu items.

The class **JFrame** has a method called **setJMenuBar**. We can create a menu bar and use this method to attach our menu bar to the frame:

```
JMenuBar menubar = new JMenuBar();
frame.setJMenuBar(menubar);
```

Now we are ready to create a menu and add it to the menu bar:

```
JMenu fileMenu = new JMenu("File");
menubar.add(fileMenu);
```

These two lines create a menu labeled *File* and insert it into our menu bar. Finally, we can add menu items to the menu. The following lines add two items, labeled *Open* and *Quit*, to the *File* menu:

```
JMenuItem openItem = new JMenuItem("Open");
fileMenu.add(openItem);
JMenuItem quitItem = new JMenuItem("Quit");
fileMenu.add(quitItem);
```

Exercise 13.5 Add the menu and menu items discussed here to your image-viewer project. What happens when you select a menu item?

Exercise 13.6 Add another menu called *Help* that contains a menu item named *About ImageViewer*. (Note: To increase readability and cohesion, it may be a good idea to move the creation of the menus into a separate method, perhaps named **makeMenuBar**, which is called from our **makeFrame** method.)

---

[3] In Mac OS, the native display is different: the menu bar is at the top of the screen, not the top of each window. In Java applications, the default behavior is to attach the menu bar to the window. It can be placed at the top of the screen with Java applications by using a Mac OS–specific property.

So far, we have achieved half of our task; we can create and display menus. But the second half is missing—nothing happens yet when a user selects a menu. We now have to add code to react to menu selections. This is discussed in the next section.

13.4.5 Event handling

> **Concept**
>
> An object can listen to component events by implementing an **event-listener** interface.

Swing uses a very flexible model to deal with GUI input: an *event-handling* model with *event listeners*.

The Swing framework itself and some of its components raise events when something happens that other objects may be interested in. There are different types of events caused by different types of actions. When a button is clicked or a menu item is selected, the component raises an `ActionEvent`. When a mouse is clicked or moved, a `MouseEvent` is raised. When a frame is closed or iconified, a `WindowEvent` is generated. There are many other types of events.

Any of our objects can become an event listener for any of these events. When it is a listener, it will get notified about any of the events it listens to. An object becomes an event listener by implementing one of several existing listener interfaces. If it implements the right interface, it can register itself with a component it wants to listen to.

Let us look at an example. A menu item (class `JMenuItem`) raises an `ActionEvent` when it is activated by a user. Objects that want to listen to these events must implement the `ActionListener` interface from the `java.awt.event` package.

There are two alternative styles for implementing event listeners: either a single object listens for events from many different event sources, or each distinct event source is assigned its own unique listener. We shall discuss both styles in the next two sections.

13.4.6 Centralized receipt of events

In order to make our `ImageViewer` object the single listener to all events from the menu, we have to do three things:

1. We must declare in the class header that it implements the `ActionListener` interface.

2. We have to implement a method with the signature

    ```
    public void actionPerformed(ActionEvent e)
    ```

    This is the only method declared in the `ActionListener` interface.

3. We must call the `addActionListener` method of the menu item to register the `ImageViewer` object as a listener.

Numbers 1 and 2—implementing the interface and defining its method—ensure that our object is a subtype of `ActionListener`. Number 3 then registers our own object as a listener for the menu items. Code 13.3 shows the source code for this in context.

Note especially the lines

```
JMenuItem openItem = new JMenuItem("Open");
openItem.addActionListener(this);
```

Code 13.3

Adding an action listener to a menu item

```java
public class ImageViewer
    implements ActionListener
{

    Fields and constructor omitted.

    /**
     * Receive notification of an action.
     * @param event Details of the action.
     */
    public void actionPerformed(ActionEvent event)
    {
        System.out.println("Menu item: " + event.getActionCommand());
    }

    /**
     * Create the Swing frame and its content.
     */
    private void makeFrame()
    {
        frame = new JFrame("ImageViewer");
        makeMenuBar(frame);

        Other GUI building code omitted.
    }

    /**
     * Create the main frame's menu bar.
     * @param frame   The frame that the menu bar should be added to.
     */
    private void makeMenuBar(JFrame frame)
    {
        JMenuBar menubar = new JMenuBar();
        frame.setJMenuBar(menubar);

        // create the File menu
        JMenu fileMenu = new JMenu("File");
        menubar.add(fileMenu);

        JMenuItem openItem = new JMenuItem("Open");
        openItem.addActionListener(this);
        fileMenu.add(openItem);

        JMenuItem quitItem = new JMenuItem("Quit");
        quitItem.addActionListener(this);
        fileMenu.add(quitItem);
    }
}
```

in the code example. Here, a menu item is created, and the current object (the **ImageViewer** object itself) is registered as an action listener by passing **this** as a parameter to the **addActionListener** method.

The effect of registering our object as a listener with the menu item is that our own **actionPerformed** method will be called by the menu item each time the item is activated. When our method is called, the menu item will pass along a parameter of type **ActionEvent** that provides some details about the event that has occurred. These details include the exact time of the event, the state of the modifier keys (the shift, control, and meta keys), a "command string," and more.

The command string is a string that somehow identifies the component that caused the event. For menu items, this is by default the label text of the item.

In our example in Code 13.3, we register the same listener object for both menu items. This means that both menu items will invoke the same **actionPerformed** method when they are activated.

In the **actionPerformed** method, we simply print out the command string of the item to demonstrate that this scheme works. Here, we could now add code to properly handle the menu invocation.

This code example, as discussed this far, is available in the book projects as project *imageviewer0-2*.

Exercise 13.7 Implement the menu-handling code, discussed above, in your own imageviewer project. Alternatively, open the *imageviewer0-2* project and carefully examine the source code. Describe in writing and in detail the sequence of events that results from activating the *Quit* menu item.

Exercise 13.8 Add another menu item called *Save*.

Exercise 13.9 Add three private methods to your class, named **openFile**, **saveFile**, and **quit**. Change the **actionPerformed** method so that it calls the corresponding method when a menu item is activated.

Exercise 13.10 If you have done Exercise 13.6 (adding a *Help* menu), make sure that its menu item also gets handled appropriately.

We note that this approach works. We can now implement methods to handle menu items to do our various program tasks. There is, however, one other aspect we should investigate: the current solution is not very nice in terms of maintainability and extendibility.

Examine the code that you had to write in the **actionPerformed** method for Exercise 13.9. There are several problems. They are:

- You probably used an if-statement and the **getActionCommand** method to find out which item was activated. For example, you could write:

```
if(event.getActionCommand().equals("Open")) ...
```

Depending on the item label string for performing the function is not a good idea. What if you now translated the interface into another language? Just changing the text on the menu item would have the effect that the program does not work anymore. (Or you would have to find all places in the code where this string was used and change them all—a tedious and error-prone procedure.)

- Having a central dispatch method (such as our **actionPerformed**) is not a nice structure at all. We essentially make every separate item call a single method, only to write tedious code in that method to call separate methods for every item from there. This is annoying in maintenance terms (for every additional menu item we have to add a new if-statement in **actionPerformed**); it also seems a waste of effort. It would be much nicer if we could make every menu item call a separate method directly.

In the next section, we show how Java 8's lambda expressions can significantly simplify the code for event handling.

13.4.7 Lambda expressions as event handlers

The material in this section makes extensive use of the *lambda expression* feature that was introduced in Java 8, and which was covered in detail in Chapter 5 of this book.

The **ActionListener** interface contains a single abstract method, which means that it fits the definition of a *functional interface*, as discussed in Chapter 12. There we noted that a lambda expression may be used wherever an object of a functional interface type is required. So when calling the **addActionListener** method of a **JMenuItem**, we can use a lambda expression to specify the actions to be taken when the associated **ActionEvent** occurs. The following code shows the full syntax for a lambda expression used as the event handler for the *Open* menu item:

```
openItem.addActionListener(
    (ActionEvent e) -> { openFile(); }
);
```

When a menu item is selected, the associated listener lambda expression will receive an **ActionEvent** object—with which it does nothing—and the body of the listener calls the **openFile** method defined in the enclosing **ImageViewer** class. The body of a lambda expression is able to access any of the members of the enclosing class, including those that are private.

> **Exercise 13.11** Implement menu-item handling with lambda expressions, as discussed here, in your own version of the image viewer.

We can use the simplified syntax for lambda expressions that allows us to leave out the parameter type for lambdas with a single parameter and the curly brackets for a single statement body. The code to add the listener then looks as follows:

```
openItem.addActionListener(e -> openFile());
```

Version 0-3 of the *imageviewer* project implements its listeners in this way.

> **Exercise 13.12** Open the *imageviewer0-3* project and examine it; that is, test it and read its source code. Don't worry about understanding everything, because some new features are the subject of this section.
>
> **Exercise 13.13** You will notice that activating the *Quit* menu item now quits the program. Examine how this is done. Look up the library documentation for any classes and methods involved.

Many of the listener interfaces associated with GUIs are functional interfaces and it will be appropriate to implement listeners using the lambda syntax. We will follow this convention in future versions of the *imageviewer* project. For non-functional interfaces—i.e., those containing more than one abstract method—a different syntax is required, and we cover this in Section 13.8, Inner classes.

Note also that `ImageViewer` does not implement `ActionListener` anymore (we removed its `actionPerformed` method), but the lambda expressions do. (Lambda expressions implement interfaces just by virtue of providing an implementation that matches the signature of the method in the functional interface.) This now allows us to use lambda expressions as action listeners for the menu items.

In summary, instead of having the image-viewer object listen to all action events, we create separate listeners for each possible event—defined by a lambda—where each listener listens to one single event type. As every listener has its own implementation of the `actionPerformed` method, we can now write specific handling code in these methods. Also, because the lambdas are in the scope of the enclosing class, they can make full use of the enclosing class in the implementation of their body, because they can access the enclosing class's private fields and methods.

This structure is cohesive and extendable. If we need an additional menu item, we just add code to create the item and the lambda that handles its function. No listing in a central method is required.

However, using lambdas can make code quite hard to read if the lambda expression is long. It is strongly recommended to use them only for very short handler functionality and for well-established code idioms. For more complex code, it may be best for the lambda to call a separate method defined in the enclosing class—as we have done here—or to consider the use of an *inner class*. Inner classes are discussed in Section 13.8.

13.4.8 Summary of key GUI elements

At the beginning of this chapter, we listed the three areas of GUI construction: components, layout, and event handling. So far, we have concentrated on two of these areas. We have encountered a small number of components (labels, buttons, menus, menu items), and we have discussed the handling of action events in quite some detail.

Getting to the current state (showing a frame with a label and a few menus) was hard work, and we had to discuss a lot of background concepts. It gets easier from now on—really! Understanding the event handling for menu items was probably the most difficult detail we had to master for our example.

Adding more menus and other components to the frame will now be quite easy—just more of the same. The one entirely new area we shall have to look at is *layout*: how to arrange the components in the frame.

13.5 ImageViewer 1.0: the first complete version

We shall now work on creating the first complete version—one that can really accomplish the main task: display some images.

13.5.1 Image-processing classes

On the way to the solution, we shall investigate one more interim version: *imageviewer0-4*. Its class structure is shown in Figure 13.4.

As you can see, we have added three new classes: **OFImage**, **ImagePanel**, and **ImageFileManager**. **OFImage** is a class to represent an image that we want to display and manipulate. **ImageFileManager** is a helper class that provides static methods to read an image file (in JPEG or PNG format) from disk and return it in **OFImage** format, then save the **OFImage** back to disk. **ImagePanel** is a custom Swing component to show the image in our GUI.

We shall briefly discuss the most important aspects of each of these classes in some more detail. We shall not, however, explain them completely—that is left as an investigation for the curious reader.

The **OFImage** class is our own custom format for representing an image in memory. You can think of an **OFImage** as a two-dimensional array of pixels. Each of the pixels can

Figure 13.4
The class structure of the image viewer application

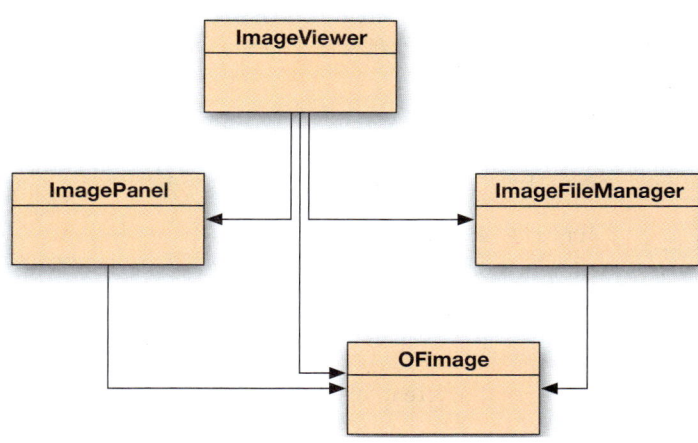

have a color. We use the standard class **Color** (from package **java.awt**) to represent each pixel's color. (Have a look at the documentation of class **Color** as well; we shall need it later.)

OFImage is implemented as a subclass of the Java standard class **BufferedImage** (from package **java.awt.image**). **BufferedImage** gives us most of the functionality we want (it also represents an image as a two-dimensional array), but it does not have methods to set or get a pixel using a **Color** object (it uses different formats for this, which we do not want to use). So we made our own subclass that adds these two methods.

For this project, we can treat **OFImage** like a library class; you will not need to modify this class.

The most important methods from **OFImage** for us are:

- **getPixel** and **setPixel** to read and modify single pixels
- **getHeight** and **getWidth** to find out about the image's size.

The **ImageFileManager** class offers three methods: one to read a named image file from disk and return it as an **OFImage**, one to write an **OFImage** file to disk, and one to open a file-chooser dialog to let a user select an image to open. The methods can read files in the standard JPEG and PNG formats, and the **save** method will write files in JPEG format. This is done using the standard Java image I/O methods from the **ImageIO** class (package **javax.imageio**).

The **ImagePanel** class implements a custom-made Swing component to display our image. Custom-made Swing components can easily be created by writing a subclass of an existing component. As such, they can be inserted into a Swing container and displayed in our GUI like any other Swing component. **ImagePanel** is a subclass of **JComponent**. The other important point to note here is that **ImagePanel** has a **setImage** method that takes an **OFImage** as a parameter to display any given **OFImage**.

13.5.2 Adding the image

Now that we have prepared the classes for dealing with images, adding the image to the user interface is easy. Code 13.4 shows the important differences from previous versions.

Code 13.4
ImageViewer class with **ImagePanel**

```
public class ImageViewer
{
    private JFrame frame;
    private ImagePanel imagePanel;

    Constructor and quit method omitted.

    /**
     * Open function: open a file chooser to select a new image file.
     */
```

Code 13.4 continued
ImageViewer class with **ImagePanel**

```java
    private void openFile()
    {
        OFImage image = ImageFileManager.getImage();
        imagePanel.setImage(image);
        frame.pack();
    }

    /**
     * Create the Swing frame and its content.
     */
    private void makeFrame()
    {
        frame = new JFrame("ImageViewer");
        makeMenuBar(frame);

        Container contentPane = frame.getContentPane();

        imagePanel = new ImagePanel();
        contentPane.add(imagePanel);

        // building is done - arrange the components and show
        frame.pack();
        frame.setVisible(true);
    }

    makeMenuBar method omitted.
}
```

When comparing this code with the previous version, we note that there are only two small changes:

- In method **makeFrame**, we now create and add an **ImagePanel** component instead of a **JLabel**. Doing this is no more complicated than adding the label. The **ImagePanel** object is stored in an instance field so that we can access it again later.

- Our **openFile** method has now been changed to actually open and display an image file. Using our image-processing classes, this also is easy now. The **ImageFileManager** class has a method to select and open an image, and the **ImagePanel** object has a method to display that image. One thing to note is that we need to call `frame.pack()` at the end of the **openFile** method, as the size of our image component has changed. The **pack** method will recalculate the frame layout and redraw the frame so that the size change is properly handled.

Exercise 13.14 Open and test the *imageviewer0-4* project. The folder for this chapter's projects also includes a folder called *images*. Here, you can find some test images you can use. Of course, you can also use your own images.

> **Exercise 13.15** What happens when you open an image and then resize the frame? What if you first resize the frame and then open an image?

With this version, we have solved the central task; we can now open an image file from disk and display it on screen. Before we call our project "version 1.0," however, and thus declare it finished for the first time, we want to add a few more improvements (see Figure 13.2).

- We want to add two labels: one to display the image filename at the top and a status text at the bottom.
- We want to add a *Filter* menu that contains some filters that change the image's appearance.
- We want to add a *Help* menu that contains an *About ImageViewer* item. Selecting this menu item should display a dialog with the application's name, version number, and author information.

13.5.3 Layout

First, we shall work on the task of adding two text labels to our interface: one at the top that is used to display the filename of the image currently displayed, and one at the bottom that is used for various status messages.

Creating these labels is easy—they are both simple **JLabel** instances. We store them in instance fields so that we can access them later to change their displayed text. The only question is how to arrange them on screen.

A first (naïve and incorrect) attempt could look like this:

```
Container contentPane = frame.getContentPane();
filenameLabel = new JLabel();
contentPane.add(filenameLabel);
imagePanel = new ImagePanel();
contentPane.add(imagePanel);
statusLabel = new JLabel("Version 1.0");
contentPane.add(statusLabel);
```

The idea here is simple: we get the frame's content pane and add, one after the other, all three components that we wish to display. The only problem is that we did not specify exactly how these three components should be arranged. We might want them to appear next to each other, or one below the other, or in any other possible arrangement. As we did not specify any layout, the container (the content pane) uses a default behavior. And this, it turns out, is not what we want.

Swing uses *layout managers* to arrange the layout of components in a GUI. Each container that holds components, such as the content pane, has an associated layout manager that takes care of arranging the components within that container.

Exercise 13.16 Continuing from your last version of the project, use the code fragment shown above to add the two labels. Test it. What do you observe?

Swing provides several different layout managers to support different layout preferences. The most important are: **FlowLayout**, **BorderLayout**, **GridLayout**, and **BoxLayout**. Each of those is represented by a Java class in the Swing library, and each lays out in different ways the components under its control.

Here follows a short description of each layout. The key differences between them are the ways in which they position components, and how the available space is distributed between the components. You can find the examples illustrated here in the *layouts* project.

A **FlowLayout** (Figure 13.5) arranges all components sequentially from left to right. It will leave each component at its preferred size and center them horizontally. If the horizontal space is not enough to fit all components, they wrap around to a second line. The **FlowLayout** can also be set to align components left or right. Because the components are not resized to fill the available space, there will be spare space around them if the window is resized.

A **BorderLayout** (Figure 13.6) places up to five components in an arranged pattern: one in the center and one each at the top, bottom, right, and left. Each of these positions may be empty, so it may hold fewer than five components. The five positions are named CENTER, NORTH, SOUTH, EAST, and WEST. There is no leftover space with a **BorderLayout** when the window is resized; it is all distributed (unevenly) between the components.

This layout may seem very specialized at first—one wonders how often this is needed. But in practice, this is a surprisingly useful layout that is used in many applications. In BlueJ,

Figure 13.5
FlowLayout

Figure 13.6
BorderLayout

for example, both the main window and the editor use a **BorderLayout** as the main layout manager.

When a **BorderLayout** is resized, the middle component is the one that gets stretched in both dimensions. The east and west components change in height but keep their width. The north and south components keep their height, and only the width changes.

As the name suggests, a **GridLayout** (Figure 13.7) is useful for laying out components in an evenly spaced grid. The numbers of rows and columns can be specified, and the **Grid-Layout** manager will always keep all components at the same size. This can be useful to force buttons, for example, to have the same width. The width of **JButton** instances is initially determined by the text on the button—each button is made just wide enough to

Figure 13.7
GridLayout

Figure 13.8
BoxLayout

display its text. Inserting buttons into a `GridLayout` will result in all buttons being resized to the width of the widest button. If an odd number of equal-size components cannot fill a 2D grid, there may be spare space in some configurations.

A `BoxLayout` lays out multiple components either vertically or horizontally. The components are not resized, and the layout will not wrap components when resized (Figure 13.8). By nesting multiple `BoxLayouts` inside each other, sophisticated two-dimensionally aligned layouts may be built.

Exercise 13.17 Using the *layouts* project from this chapter, experiment with the examples illustrated in this section. Add and remove components from the existing classes to get a proper feel for the key characteristics of the different layout styles. What happens if there is no CENTER component with `BorderLayout`, for instance?

13.5.4 Nested containers

All the layout strategies discussed above are fairly simple. The key to building good-looking and well-behaved interfaces lies in one last detail: layouts can be nested. Many of the Swing components are *containers*. Containers appear to the outside as a single component, but they can contain multiple other components. Each container has its own layout manager attached.

The most-used container is the class `JPanel`. A `JPanel` can be inserted as a component into the frame's content pane, and then more components can be laid out inside the `JPanel`. Figure 13.9, for example, shows an interface arrangement similar to that of the BlueJ main window. The content pane of this frame uses a `BorderLayout`, where the EAST position

Figure 13.9
Building an interface using nested containers

is unused. The NORTH area of this **BorderLayout** contains a **JPanel** with a horizontal **FlowLayout** that arranges its components (say toolbar buttons) in a row. The SOUTH area is similar: another **JPanel** with a **FlowLayout**.

The button group in the WEST area was first placed into a **JPanel** with a one-column **GridLayout** to give all buttons the same width. This **JPanel** was then placed into another **JPanel** with a **FlowLayout** so that the grid did not extend over the full height of the WEST area. The outer **JPanel** is then inserted into the WEST area of the frame.

Note how the container and the layout manager cooperate in the layout of the components. The container holds the components, but the layout manager decides their exact arrangement on screen. Every container has a layout manager. It will use a default layout manager if we do not explicitly set one. The default is different for different containers: the content pane of a **JFrame**, for example, has by default a **BorderLayout**, whereas **JPanel**s use a **FlowLayout** by default.

Exercise 13.18 Look at the GUI of the calculator project used in Chapter 9 (Figure 9.6). What kind of containers/layout managers do you think were used to create it? After answering in writing, open the *calculator-gui* project and check your answer by reading the code.

Exercise 13.19 What kind of layout managers might have been used to create the layout of BlueJ's editor window?

Exercise 13.20 In BlueJ, invoke the *Use Library Class* function from the *Tools* menu. Look at the dialog you see on screen. Which containers/layout managers might have been used to create it? Resize the dialog and observe the resize behavior to get additional information.

It is time to look again at some code for our **ImageViewer** application. Our goal is quite simple. We want to see three components above each other: a label at the top, the image in the middle, and another label at the bottom. Several layout managers can do this. Which one to choose becomes clearer when we think about resizing behavior. When we enlarge the window, we would like the labels to maintain their height and the image to receive all the extra space. This suggests a **BorderLayout**: the labels can be in the NORTH and SOUTH areas, and the image in the CENTER. Code 13.5 shows the source code to implement this.

Two details are worth noting. First, the **setLayout** method is used on the content pane to set the intended layout manager.[4] The layout manager itself is an object, so we create an instance of **BorderLayout** and pass it to the **setLayout** method.

Second, when we add a component to a container with a **BorderLayout**, we use a different **add** method that has a second parameter. The value for the second parameter is one of the public constants **NORTH**, **SOUTH**, **EAST**, **WEST**, and **CENTER**, which are defined in class **BorderLayout**.

Code 13.5
Using a **Border Layout** to arrange components

```
private void makeFrame()
{
    frame = new JFrame("ImageViewer");
    makeMenuBar(frame);

    ...

    Container contentPane = frame.getContentPane();

    contentPane.setLayout(new BorderLayout(6, 6));

    filenameLabel = new JLabel();
    contentPane.add(filenameLabel, BorderLayout.NORTH);

    imagePanel = new ImagePanel();
    contentPane.add(imagePanel, BorderLayout.CENTER);

    statusLabel = new JLabel("Version 1.0");
    contentPane.add(statusLabel, BorderLayout.SOUTH);

    ...
}
```

---

[4] Strictly speaking, the **setLayout** call is not needed here, as the default layout manager of the content pane is already a **BorderLayout**. We have included the call here for clarity and readability.

> **Exercise 13.21** Implement and test the code shown above in your version of the project.
>
> **Exercise 13.22** Experiment with other layout managers. Try in your project all of the layout managers mentioned above, and test whether they behave as expected.

13.5.5 Image filters

Two things remain to be done before our first image-viewer version is finished: adding some image filters, and adding a *Help* menu. Next, we shall do the filters.

The image filters are the first step toward image manipulation. Eventually, we want not only to be able to open and display images, but also to be able to manipulate them and save them back to disk.

Here, we start by adding three simple filters. A filter is a function that is applied to the whole image. (It could, of course, be modified to be applied to a part of an image, but we are not doing that just yet.)

The three filters are named *darker*, *lighter*, and *threshold*. *Darker* makes the whole image darker, and *lighter* makes it lighter. The threshold filter turns the image into a grayscale picture with only a few preset shades of gray. We have chosen a three-level threshold. This means we shall use three colors: black, white, and medium-gray. All pixels that are in the upper-third value range for brightness will be turned white, all that are in the lower third will be turned black, and the middle third will be gray.

To achieve this, we have to do two things:

- create menu items for each filter with an associated menu listener
- implement the actual filter operation

First the menus. There is nothing really new in this. It is just more of the same menu-creation code that we already wrote for our existing menu. We need to add the following parts:

- We create a new menu (class **JMenu**) named *Filter* and add it to the menu bar.
- We create three menu items (class **JMenuItem**) named *Darker*, *Lighter*, and *Threshold*, and add them to our filter menu.
- To each menu item, we add an action listener, using lambda expressions as we discussed for the other menu items. The action listeners should call the methods **makeDarker**, **makeLighter**, and **threshold**, respectively.

After we have added the menus and created the (initially empty) methods to handle the filter functions, we need to implement each filter.

13.5 ImageViewer 1.0: the first complete version

The simplest kinds of filters involve iterating over the image and making a change of some sort to the color of each pixel. A pattern for this process is shown in Code 13.6. More-complicated filters might use the values of neighboring pixels to adjust a pixel's value.

Exercise 13.23 Add the new menu and the menu items to your version of the *image-viewer0-4* project, as described here. In order to add the action listeners, you need to create the three methods `makeDarker`, `makeLighter`, and `threshold` as private methods in your `ImageViewer` class. They all have a `void` return type and take no parameters. These methods can initially have empty bodies, or they could simply print out that they have been called.

Code 13.6
Pattern for a simple filtering process

```
for(int y = 0; y < height; y++) {
    for(int x = 0; x < width; x++) {
        Color pixel = getPixel(x, y);
```
Alter the pixel's color value.
```
        setPixel(x, y, pixel);
    }
}
```

The filter function itself operates on the image, so following responsibility-driven design guidelines, it should be implemented in the `OFImage` class. On the other hand, handling the menu invocation also includes some GUI-related code (for instance, we have to check whether an image is open at all when we invoke the filter), and this belongs in the `ImageViewer` class.

As a result of this reasoning, we create two methods, one in `ImageViewer` and one in `OFImage`, to share the work (Code 13.7 and Code 13.8). We can see that the `makeDarker` method in `ImageViewer` contains the part of the task that is related to the GUI (checking that we have an image loaded, displaying a status message, repainting the frame), whereas the `darker` method in `OFImage` includes the actual work of making each pixel in the image a bit darker.

Code 13.7
The filter method in the `ImageViewer` class

```
public class ImageViewer
{
```
Fields, constructor, and all other methods omitted.
```
    /**
     * 'Darker' function: make the picture darker.
     */
```

Code 13.7 continued

The filter method in the `ImageViewer` class

```java
private void makeDarker()
{
    if(currentImage != null) {
        currentImage.darker();
        frame.repaint();
        showStatus("Applied: darker");
    }
    else {
        showStatus("No image loaded.");
    }
}
```

Code 13.8

Implementation of a filter in the `OFImage` class

```java
public class OFImage extends BufferedImage
{
    Fields, constructor, and all other methods omitted.

    /**
     * Make this image a bit darker.
     */
    public void darker()
    {
        int height = getHeight();
        int width = getWidth();
        for(int y = 0; y < height; y++) {
            for(int x = 0; x < width; x++) {
                setPixel(x, y, getPixel(x, y).darker());
            }
        }
    }
}
```

Exercise 13.24 What does the method call `frame.repaint()` do, which you can see in the `makeDarker` method?

Exercise 13.25 We can see a call to a method `showStatus`, which is clearly an internal method call. From the name, we can guess that this method should display a status message using the status label we created earlier. Implement this method in your version of the *imageviewer0-4* project. (*Hint*: Look at the `setText` method in the `JLabel` class.)

Exercise 13.26 What happens if the *Darker* menu item is selected when no image has been opened?

Exercise 13.27 Explain in detail how the `darker` method in `OFImage` works. (*Hint*: It contains another method call to a method also called `darker`. Which class does this second method belong to? Look it up.)

Exercise 13.28 Implement the *lighter* filter in `OFImage`.

Exercise 13.29 Implement the *threshold* filter. To get the brightness of a pixel, you can get its red, green, and blue values and add them up. The `Color` class defines static references to suitable black, white, and gray objects.

You can find a working implementation of everything described so far in the *imageviewer1-0* project. You should, however, attempt to do the exercises yourself first, before you look at the solution.

13.5.6 Dialogs

Our last task for this version is to add a *Help* menu that holds a menu item labeled *About ImageViewer . . .* When this item is selected, a dialog should pop up that displays some short information.

Now we have to implement the `showAbout` method so that it displays an "About" dialog.

Exercise 13.30 Again add a menu named *Help*. In it, add a menu item labeled *About ImageViewer . . .*

Exercise 13.31 Add a method stub (a method with an empty body) named `showAbout`, and add an event handler that calls `showAbout` to the *About ImageViewer . . .* menu item.

One of the main characteristics of a dialog is whether or not it is *modal*. A modal dialog blocks all interaction with other parts of the application until the dialog has been closed. It forces the user to deal with the dialog first. Non-modal dialogs allow interaction in other frames while the dialogs are visible.

Dialogs can be implemented in a similar way to our main `JFrame`. They often use the class `JDialog` to display the frame.

For modal dialogs with a standard structure, however, there are some convenience methods in class `JOptionPane` that make it very easy to show such dialogs. `JOptionPane` has, among other things, static methods to show three types of standard dialog. They are:

- *Message dialog:* This is a dialog that displays a message and has an *OK* button to close the dialog.

- *Confirm dialog:* This dialog usually asks a question and has buttons for the user to make a selection—for example, *Yes*, *No*, and *Cancel*.

- *Input dialog:* This dialog includes a prompt and a text field for the user to enter some text.

Our "About" box is a simple message dialog. Looking through the `JOptionPane` documentation, we find that there are static methods named `showMessageDialog` to do this.

> **Exercise 13.32** Find the documentation for **showMessageDialog**. How many methods with this name are there? What are the differences between them? Which one should we use for the "About" box? Why?
>
> **Exercise 13.33** Implement the **showAbout** method in your **ImageViewer** class, using a call to a **showMessageDialog** method.
>
> **Exercise 13.34** The **showInputDialog** methods of **JOptionPane** allow a user to be prompted for input via a dialog when required. On the other hand, the **JTextField** component allows a permanent text input area to be displayed within a GUI. Find the documentation for this class. What input causes an **ActionListener** associated with a **JTextField** to be notified? Can a user be prevented from editing the text in the field? Is it possible for a listener to be notified of arbitrary changes to the text in the field? (*Hint*: What use does a **JTextField** make of a **Document** object?)
>
> You can find an example of a **JTextField** in the *calculator* project in Chapter 9.

After studying the documentation, we can now implement our "About" box by making a call to the **showMessageDialog** method. The code is shown in Code 13.9. Note that we have introduced a string constant named **VERSION** to hold the current version number.

Code 13.9

Displaying a modal dialog

```
/**
 * Show the 'About...' dialog.
 */
private void showAbout()
{
    JOptionPane.showMessageDialog(frame,
                "ImageViewer\n" + VERSION,
                "About ImageViewer",
                JOptionPane.INFORMATION_MESSAGE);
}
```

This was the last task to be done to complete "version 1.0" of our image-viewer application. If you have done all the exercises, you should now have a version of the project that can open images, apply filters, display status messages, and display a dialog.

The *imageviewer1-0* project, included in the book projects, contains an implementation of all the functionality discussed thus far. You should carefully study this project and compare it with your own solutions.

In this project, we have also improved the **openFile** method to include better notification of errors. If the user chooses a file that is not a valid image file, we now show a proper error message. Now that we know about message dialogs, this is easy to do.

13.5.7 Summary of layout management

In this section, we have added some custom classes to deal with images, but more importantly for our GUI, we have looked at the layout of components. We have seen how containers and layout managers work together to achieve the exact arrangement we need on screen.

Learning to work with layout managers takes some experience and often some trial-and-error experimentation. Over time, however, you will get to know the layout managers well.

We have now covered the basics of all important areas of GUI programming. For the rest of the chapter, we can concentrate on fine-tuning and improving what we've got.

13.6 ImageViewer 2.0: improving program structure

Version 1.0 of our application has a useable GUI and can display images. It can also apply three basic filters.

The next obvious idea for an improvement of our application is to add some more interesting filters. Before we rush in and do it, however, let us think about what this involves.

With the current structure of filters, we have to do three things for each filter:

1. add a menu item
2. add a method to handle the menu activation in `ImageViewer`
3. add an implementation of the filter in `OFImage`

Numbers 1 and 3 are unavoidable—we need a menu item and a filter implementation. But number 2 looks suspicious. If we look at these methods in the `ImageViewer` class (Code 13.10 shows two of them as an example), this looks a lot like code duplication. These methods are essentially the same (except for some small details), and for each new filter we have to add another one of these methods.

As we know, code duplication is a sign of bad design and should be avoided. We deal with it by refactoring our code. We want to find a design that lets us add new filters without having to add a new dispatch method for the filter every time.

To achieve what we want, we need to avoid hard-coding every filter-method name (`lighter`, `threshold`, etc.) into our `ImageViewer` class. Instead, we shall use a collection of filters and then write a single filter-invocation method that finds and invokes the right filter. This will be similar in style to the introduction of an `act` method when decoupling the simulator from individual actor types in the *foxes-and-rabbits* project in Chapter 12.

In order to do this, filters must themselves become objects, rather than just method names. If we want to store them in a common collection, then all filters will need a common superclass, which we name `Filter` and give an `apply` method (Figure 13.10 shows the structure, Code 13.11 shows the source code).

Code 13.10

Two of the filter-handling methods from `ImageViewer`

```java
private void makeLighter()
{
    if(currentImage != null) {
        currentImage.lighter();
        frame.repaint();
        showStatus("Applied: lighter");
    }
    else {
        showStatus("No image loaded.");
    }
}

private void threshold()
{
    if(currentImage != null) {
        currentImage.threshold();
        frame.repaint();
        showStatus("Applied: threshold");
    }
    else {
        showStatus("No image loaded.");
    }
}
```

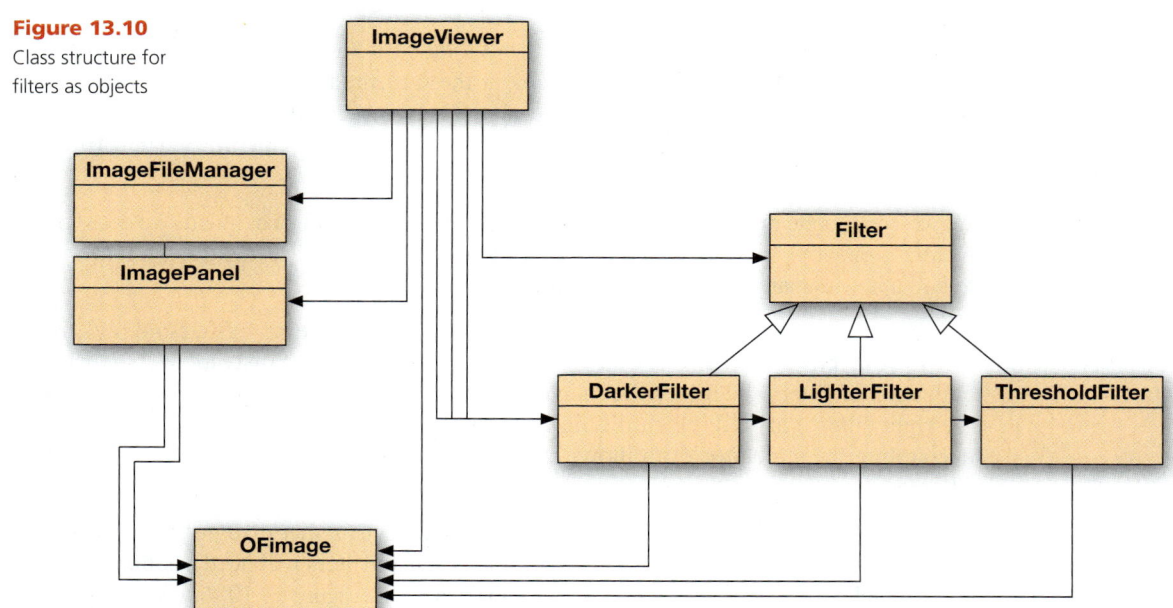

Figure 13.10

Class structure for filters as objects

Every filter will have an individual name, and its **apply** method will apply that particular sort of filter to an image. Note that this is an abstract class, as the **apply** method has to be abstract at this level, but the **getName** method can be fully implemented so it is not an interface.

Code 13.11

Abstract class **Filter**: Superclass for all filters

```java
public abstract class Filter
{
    private String name;

    /**
     * Create a new filter with a given name.
     * @param name The name of the filter.
     */
    public Filter(String name)
    {
        this.name = name;
    }

    /**
     * Return the name of this filter.
     * @return  The name of this filter.
     */
    public String getName()
    {
        return name;
    }

    /**
     * Apply this filter to an image.
     * @param  image  The image to be changed by this filter.
     */
    public abstract void apply(OFImage image);
}
```

Once we have written the superclass, it is not hard to implement specific filters as subclasses. All we need to do is provide an implementation for the **apply** method that manipulates an image (passed in as a parameter) using its **getPixel** and **setPixel** methods. Code 13.12 shows an example.

Code 13.12

Implementation of a specific filter class

```java
/**
 * An image filter to make the image a bit darker.
 *
 * @author Michael Kölling and David J. Barnes.
 * @version 1.0
 */
public class DarkerFilter extends Filter
{
    /**
     * Constructor for objects of class DarkerFilter.
     * @param name The name of the filter.
     */
```

Code 13.12 continued

Implementation of a specific filter class

```java
    public DarkerFilter(String name)
    {
        super(name);
    }

    /**
     * Apply this filter to an image.
     * @param  image  The image to be changed by this filter.
     */
    public void apply(OFImage image)
    {
        int height = image.getHeight();
        int width = image.getWidth();
        for(int y = 0; y < height; y++) {
            for(int x = 0; x < width; x++) {
                image.setPixel(x, y, image.getPixel(x, y).darker());
            }
        }
    }
}
```

As a side effect of this, the **OFImage** class becomes much simpler, as all of the filter methods can be removed from it. It now only defines the **setPixel** and **getPixel** methods.

Once we have defined our filters like this, we can create filter objects and store them in a collection (Code 13.13).

Code 13.13

Adding a collection of filters

```java
public class ImageViewer
{
    Other fields and comments omitted.
    private List<Filter> filters;

    /**
     * Create an ImageViewer show it on screen.
     */
    public ImageViewer()
    {
        filters = createFilters();
        ...
    }

    /**
     * Create and return a list with all the known filters.
     * @return The list of filters.
     */
```

13.6 ImageViewer 2.0: improving program structure

Code 13.13 continued

Adding a collection of filters

```java
    private List<Filter> createFilters()
    {
        List<Filter> filterList = new ArrayList<>();
        filterList.add(new DarkerFilter("Darker"));
        filterList.add(new LighterFilter("Lighter"));
        filterList.add(new ThresholdFilter("Threshold"));

        return filterList;
    }

    Other methods omitted.
}
```

Once we have this structure in place, we can make the last two necessary changes:

- We change the code that creates the filter menu items so that it iterates over the filter collection. For every filter, it creates a menu item and uses the filter's **getName** method to determine the item's label.
- Having done this, we can write a generic **applyFilter** method that receives a filter as a parameter and applies this filter to the current image.

The *imageviewer2-0* project includes a complete implementation of these changes.

Exercise 13.35 Open the *imageviewer2-0* project. Study the code for the new method to create and apply filters in class **ImageViewer**. Pay special attention to the **makeMenuBar** and **applyFilter** methods. Explain in detail how the creation of the filter menu items and their activation works. Draw an object diagram.

Exercise 13.36 What needs to be changed to add a new filter to your image viewer?

Exercise 13.37 *Challenge exercise* You might have observed that the **apply** methods of all of the **Filter** subclasses have a very similar structure: iterate over the whole image and change the value of each pixel independently of surrounding pixels. It should be possible to isolate this duplication in much the same way as we did in creating the **Filter** class.

Create a method in the **Filter** class that iterates over the image and applies a filter-specific transformation to each individual pixel. Replace the bodies of the **apply** methods in the three **Filter** subclasses with a call to this method, passing the image and something that can apply the appropriate transformation.

In this section, we have done pure refactoring. We have not changed the functionality of the application at all, but have worked exclusively at improving the implementation structure so that future changes become easier.

Now, after finishing the refactoring, we should test that all existing functionality still works as expected. In all development projects, we need phases like this. We do not always make perfect design decisions at the start, and applications grow and requirements change. Even though our main task in this chapter is to work with GUIs, we needed to step back and refactor our code before proceeding. This work will pay off in the long run by making all further changes easier.

Sometimes it is tempting to leave structures as they are, even though we recognize that they are not good. Putting up with a bit of code duplication may be easier in the short term than doing careful refactoring. One can get away with that for a short while, but for projects that are intended to survive for a longer time, this is bound to create problems. As a general rule: Take the time; keep your code clean!

Now that we have done this, we are ready to add some more filters.

Exercise 13.38 Add a *grayscale* filter to your project. The filter turns the image into a black-and-white image in shades of gray. You can make a pixel any shade of gray by giving all three color components (red, green, blue) the same value. The brightness of each pixel should remain unchanged.

Exercise 13.39 Add a *mirror* filter that flips the image horizontally. The pixel at the top left corner will move to the top right, and vice versa, producing the effect of viewing the image in a mirror.

Exercise 13.40 Add an *invert* filter that inverts each color. "Inverting" a color means replacing each color value x with $255 - x$.

Exercise 13.41 Add a *smooth* filter that "smoothes" the image. A smooth filter replaces every pixel value with the average of its neighboring pixels and itself (nine pixels in total). You have to be careful at the image's edges, where some neighbors do not exist. You also have to make sure to work with a temporary copy of the image while you process it, because the result is not correct if you work on a single image. (Why is this?) You can easily obtain a copy of the image by creating a new **OFImage** with the original as the parameter to its constructor.

Exercise 13.42 Add a *solarize* filter. Solarization is an effect one can create manually on photo negatives by re-exposing a developed negative. We can simulate this by replacing each color component of each pixel that has a value v of less than 128 with $255 - v$. The brighter components (value of 128 or more) we leave unchanged. (This is a very simple solarization algorithm—you can find more-sophisticated ones described in the literature.)

Exercise 13.43 Implement an *edge detection* filter. Do this by analyzing the nine pixels in a three-by-three square around each pixel (similar to the smooth filter), and then set the value of the middle pixel to the difference between the highest and the lowest value found. Do this for each color component (red, green, blue). This also looks good if you invert the image at the same time.

Exercise 13.44 Experiment with your filters on different pictures. Try applying multiple filters, one after another.

Once you have implemented some more filters of your own, you should change the version number of your project to "version 2.1."

13.7 ImageViewer 3.0: more interface components

Before we leave the image-viewer project behind us, we want to add a few last improvements, and in the process look at two more GUI components: buttons and borders.

13.7.1 Buttons

We now want to add functionality to the image viewer to change the size of the image. We do this by providing two functions: *larger*, which doubles the image size, and *smaller*, which halves the size. (To be exact, we double or halve both the width and the height, not the area.)

One way to do this is to implement filters for these tasks. But we decide against it. So far, filters never change the image size, and we want to leave it like that. Instead, we introduce a toolbar on the left side of our frame with two buttons in it labeled *Larger* and *Smaller* (Figure 13.11). This also gives us a chance to experiment a bit with buttons, containers, and layout managers.

So far, our frame uses a **BorderLayout**, where the **WEST** area is empty. We can use this area to add our toolbar buttons. There is one small problem, though. The **WEST** area of a **BorderLayout** can hold only one component, but we have two buttons.

The solution is simple. We add a **JPanel** to the frame's **WEST** area (as we know, a **JPanel** is a container), and then place the two buttons in the **JPanel**. Code 13.14 shows the code to do this.

Code 13.14
Adding a toolbar panel with two buttons

```
// Create the toolbar with the buttons
JPanel toolbar = new JPanel();

smallerButton = new JButton("Smaller");
toolbar.add(smallerButton);

largerButton = new JButton("Larger");
toolbar.add(largerButton);

contentPane.add(toolbar, BorderLayout.WEST);
```

Exercise 13.45 Add two buttons labeled *Larger* and *Smaller* to your latest version of the project, using code similar to Code 13.14. Test it. What do you observe?

Figure 13.11
Image viewer with toolbar buttons

When we try this out, we see that it works partially but does not look as expected. The reason is that a **JPanel** uses, by default, a **FlowLayout**, and a **FlowLayout** arranges its components horizontally. We would like them arranged vertically.

We can achieve this by using another layout manager. A **GridLayout** does what we want. When creating a **GridLayout**, constructor parameters determine how many rows and columns we wish to have. A value of zero has a special meaning here, standing for "as many as necessary."

Thus, we can create a single column **GridLayout** by using 0 as the number of rows and 1 as the number of columns. We can then use this **GridLayout** for our **JPanel** by using the panel's **setLayout** method immediately after creating it:

```
JPanel toolbar = new JPanel();
toolbar.setLayout(new GridLayout(0, 1));
```

Alternatively, the layout manager can also be specified as a constructor parameter of the container:

```
JPanel toolbar = new JPanel(new GridLayout(0, 1));
```

Exercise 13.46 Change your code so that your toolbar panel uses a **GridLayout**, as discussed above. Test. What do you observe?

13.7 ImageViewer 3.0: more interface components

If we try this out, we can see that we are getting closer, but we still do not have what we want. Our buttons now are much larger than we intended. The reason is that a container in a **BorderLayout** (our toolbar **JPanel** in this case) always covers its whole area (the **WEST** area in our frame). And a **GridLayout** always resizes its components to fill the whole container.

A **FlowLayout** does not do this; it is quite happy to leave some empty space around the components. Our solution is therefore to use both: the **GridLayout** to arrange the buttons in a column, and a **FlowLayout** around it to allow some space. We end up with a **GridLayout** panel inside a **FlowLayout** panel inside a **BorderLayout**. Code 13.15 shows this solution. Constructions like this are very common. You will often nest various containers inside other containers to create exactly the look you want.

Code 13.15

Using a nested **GridLayout** container inside a **FlowLayout** container

```java
// Create the toolbar with the buttons
JPanel toolbar = new JPanel();
toolbar.setLayout(new GridLayout(0, 1));

smallerButton = new JButton("Smaller");
toolbar.add(smallerButton);

largerButton = new JButton("Larger");
toolbar.add(largerButton);

// Add toolbar into panel with flow layout for spacing
JPanel flow = new JPanel();
flow.add(toolbar);

contentPane.add(flow, BorderLayout.WEST);
```

Our buttons now look quite close to what we were aiming for. Before adding the finishing polish, we can first focus on making the buttons work.

We need to add two methods for instance, **makeLarger** and **makeSmaller**, to do the actual work, and we need to add action listeners to the buttons that invoke these methods.

Exercise 13.47 In your project, add two method stubs named **makeLarger** and **makeSmaller**. Initially, put just a single **println** statement into these method bodies to see when they have been called. The methods can be private.

Exercise 13.48 Add lambda event handlers to the two buttons that invoke the two new methods. Adding event handlers to buttons is identical to adding them to menu items. You can essentially copy the code pattern from there. Test it. Make sure your **makeSmaller** and **makeLarger** methods get called by activating the buttons.

Exercise 13.49 Properly implement the `makeSmaller` and `makeLarger` methods. To do this, you have to create a new `OFImage` with a different size, copy the pixels from the current image across (while scaling it up or down), and then set the new image as the current image. At the end of your method, you should call the frame's `pack` method to rearrange the components with the changed size.

Exercise 13.50 All Swing components have a `setEnabled(boolean)` method that can enable and disable the component. Disabled components are usually displayed in light gray and do not react to input. Change your image viewer so that the two toolbar buttons are initially disabled. When an image is opened, they should be enabled, and when it is closed, they should be disabled again.

13.7.2 Borders

The last polish we want to add to our interface is some internal borders. Borders can be used to group components, or just to add some space between them. Every Swing component can have a border.

Some layout managers also accept constructor parameters that define their spacing, and the layout manager will then create the requested space between components.

The most used borders are `BevelBorder`, `CompoundBorder`, `EmptyBorder`, `EtchedBorder`, and `TitledBorder`. You should familiarize yourself with these.

We shall do three things to improve the look of our GUI:

- add some empty space around the outside of the frame
- add spacing between the components of the frame
- add a line around the image

The code to do this is shown in Code 13.16. The `setBorder` call on the content pane, with an `EmptyBorder` as a parameter, adds empty space around the outside of the frame. Note

Code 13.16

Adding spacing with gaps and borders

```
JPanel contentPane = (JPanel)frame.getContentPane();
contentPane.setBorder(new EmptyBorder(12, 12, 12, 12));

// Specify the layout manager with nice spacing
contentPane.setLayout(new BorderLayout(6, 6));

// Create the image pane in the center
imagePanel = new ImagePanel();
imagePanel.setBorder(new EtchedBorder());
contentPane.add(imagePanel, BorderLayout.CENTER);
```

that we now cast the **contentPane** to a **JPanel**, as the supertype **Container** does not have the **setBorder** method.[5]

Creating the **BorderLayout** with two **int** parameters adds spacing between the components that it lays out. And finally, setting an **EtchedBorder** for the **imagePanel** adds a line with an "etched" look around the image. (Borders are defined in the package **javax.swing.border**—we have to add an import statement for this package.)

All the improvements discussed in the section have been implemented in the next version of this application in the book projects: *imageviewer3-0*. In that version, we have also added a *Save As* function to the file menu so that images can be saved back to disk.

And we have added one more filter, called *Fish Eye*, to give you some more ideas about what you can do. Try it out. It works especially well on portraits.

13.8 Inner classes

Up to this point, we have implemented event-handling listeners using lambda notation. This has been possible because the listener interfaces have been functional interfaces—i.e., they have consisted of a single abstract method. However, this will not be the case with all listener interfaces. For instance, the **KeyListener**, **MouseListener** and **MouseMotionListener** interfaces in the **java.awt.event** package all consist of more than one abstract method, and so we cannot use lambda expressions to supply their implementations.

13.8.1 Named inner classes

The obvious approach, in such cases, is to define a separate class to implement the required interface, and then create an instance to act as the listening object. However, there are several drawbacks to this approach if we simply implement the interface as a normal class within a project, at the same level as all the other classes:

- There is usually a very tight *coupling* between a listener and the object managing the multiple components of the full GUI. The listener will often need to access and modify private elements of the GUI object's state. This degree of coupling cannot be avoided, but it would be more palatable if we could find a way to identify its existence more clearly among the multiple classes of a project.

- We have seen that a lambda expression has full access to even the private elements of the enclosing GUI class—this is how the very tight coupling arises. This would not be possible for an external class without the addition of accessor and mutator methods in the GUI class, likely provided solely for the listener's benefit. Furthermore, the methods' existence could invite unintended coupling to other classes.

- We often create just a single instance of a listener class, and a full-blown external class will often look like overkill for this sort of usage pattern.

---

[5] Using a cast in this way only works because the dynamic type of the content pane is already **JPanel**. The cast does not transform the content-pane object into a **JPanel**.

Fortunately, Java provides a construct that mitigates all of these problems. It is a construct that we have not discussed before: *inner classes*. Inner classes are classes that are declared textually inside another class:

```
class EnclosingClass
{
    ...
    class InnerClass
    {
        ...
    }
}
```

Instances of the inner class are attached to instances of the enclosing class; they can only exist together with an enclosing instance, and they exist conceptually *inside* the enclosing instance. It is immediately clear from this construct that the tight coupling between inner listener class and the enclosing GUI class is explicit. A further feature is that statements in methods of the inner class can see and access private fields and methods of the enclosing class—just as a lambda expression is able to do. The inner class is considered to be a part of the enclosing class just as are any of the enclosing class's methods. This deals effectively with the second problem we described above.

We can now use this construct to implement a **MouseListener**, say, within the **ImageViewer** class. The structure looks like this:

```
public class ImageViewer
{
    ...

    private class MouseHandler implements MouseListener
    {
        public void mouseClicked(MouseEvent event)
        {
            // perform click action
        }

        public void mouseEntered(MouseEvent event)
        {
            // perform entered action
        }

        ... remaining MouseListener methods omitted ...
    }
}
```

(As a style guide, we usually write inner classes at the end of the enclosing class—after the methods.) Note that we have given the inner class private visibility to reinforce the sense that it is performing a task that is highly specific to the **ImageViewer** class and should not be considered independent of it.

Once we have defined an inner class we can create instances of it in exactly the same way as for those of any other class:

```
// Detect mouse clicks on the image when the user
// wishes to edit it.
imagePanel.addMouseListener(new MouseHandler());
```

Notice a couple of typical usage characteristics of these listener inner classes:

- We do not bother storing the instances in variables—so, in effect, they are anonymous objects. Only the component to which they are attached has a reference to their specific listener object, so that they can call the listener's event-handling methods.

- We often only create just a single object from each of the inner classes, because each is highly specialized for a particular component within a specific GUI.

These characteristics will lead us to explore a further feature of Java in the next section.

Inner classes can generally be used in some cases to improve cohesion in larger projects. The *foxes-and-rabbits* project from Chapter 12, for example, has a class **SimulatorView** that includes an inner class **FieldView**. You might want to study this example to deepen your understanding.

13.8.2 Anonymous inner classes

The solution to implementing multi-method interfaces using inner classes is fairly good, but we want to take it one step further: we can use *anonymous inner classes*. To illustrate this feature we will develop another version of the image viewer project; one that allows simple editing of individual pixels. The idea is that the user can click anywhere on the image to change a pixel to a specific color. There are two aspects to this:

- Choosing the color to place on the image.
- Choosing which pixel to replace.

The color will be chosen via a **JColorChooser** dialog, which will appear when the user presses a mouse button with the *Shift* key held down, and the pixel to be replaced is chosen by pressing the mouse without the *Shift* key. Once a color has been chosen, pixels are replaced with that color until a new color is chosen. This is implemented as *imageviewer4-0*.

Clearly, the only mouse event we are interested in is a mouse click, but implementing the **MouseListener** requires that we implement five separate methods. This is a nuisance since four of the five method bodies will be empty, and we will often face similar issues when implementing other multi-method listener interfaces. Fortunately, the implementors of the Java API have recognized this problem and provided no-op implementations of these interfaces in the form of abstract **Adapter** classes; for instance, **MouseAdapter** and **MouseMotionAdapter**. What this means is that we can often create a subclass of an **Adapter** class, rather than implementing the full interface, and just override the one or two methods that we need for a particular task. So, for our example, we will create an inner class that is a subclass of **MouseAdapter**, and just override the **mousePressed** method.

We are now in a position to illustrate anonymous inner classes. The relevant code looks like this:

```
imagePanel = new ImagePanel();
imagePanel.addMouseListener(new MouseAdapter() {
    public void mousePressed(MouseEvent e)
    {
        ... take action on a mouse pressed event ...
    }
});
```

This code fragment looks quite mysterious when you encounter it for the first time, and you will probably have trouble interpreting it, even if you have understood everything we have discussed in this book so far. But don't worry—we shall investigate this slowly.

> **Concept**
>
> **Anonymous inner classes** are a useful construct for implementing event listeners that are not functional interfaces.

The idea for this construct is based on the observation that we only use each inner class exactly once to create a single, unnamed instance. For this situation, anonymous inner classes provide a syntactical shortcut: they let us define a class and create a single instance of this class, all in one step. The effect is identical to the inner-class version with the difference that we do not need to define separate named classes for the listeners and that the definition of the listener's methods is closer to the registration of the listener with the GUI component.

The scope coloring in BlueJ's editor gives us some hints that may help in understanding this structure (Figure 13.12). The green shading indicates a class, the yellowish color shows a method definition, and the white background identifies a method body. We can see that the body of the **makeFrame** method contains, very tightly packed, a (strange-looking) class definition, which has a single method definition with a short body.

When using an anonymous inner class, we create an inner class *without naming it* and immediately create a single instance of the class. In the mouse-listener code above, this is done with the code fragment

```
new MouseAdapter() {
    public void mousePressed(MouseEvent e) { ... }
}
```

An anonymous inner class is created by naming a supertype (often an abstract class or an interface—here **MouseAdapter**), followed by a block that contains an implementation for its abstract methods, or any methods we wish to override. This looks unusual, although there are some similarities to the syntax for lambda expressions.

In this example, we create a new subtype of **MouseAdapter** that overrides the **mousePressed** method. This new class does not receive a name. Instead, we precede it with the **new** keyword to create a single instance of this class. This single instance is a mouse-listener object (it is indirectly a subtype of **MouseListener**) and so it can be passed to a GUI component's **addMouseListener** method. Each subtype of **MouseListener** or **MouseAdapter** created in this way represents a unique anonymous class.

Just like lambdas and named inner classes, anonymous inner classes are able to access the fields and methods of their enclosing classes. In addition, because they are defined inside a method, they are able to access the local variables and parameters of that method.

13.8 Inner classes

Figure 13.12
Scope coloring with an anonymous inner class

```java
/**
 * Create the Swing frame and its content.
 */
private void makeFrame()
{
    frame = new JFrame("ImageViewer");
    JPanel contentPane = (JPanel)frame.getContentPane();
    contentPane.setBorder(new EmptyBorder(12, 12, 12, 12));

    makeMenuBar(frame);

    // Specify the layout manager with nice spacing
    contentPane.setLayout(new BorderLayout(6, 6));

    // Create the image pane in the center
    imagePanel = new ImagePanel();
    imagePanel.setBorder(new EtchedBorder());
    imagePanel.addMouseListener(new MouseAdapter() {
                public void mousePressed(MouseEvent e) { handleMousePressed(e); }
            });
    contentPane.add(imagePanel, BorderLayout.CENTER);

    // Create two labels at top and bottom for the file name and status message
```

It is worth emphasizing some observations about anonymous inner classes that are also shared with lambdas. This structure is nicely cohesive and extendable. If we need an additional menu item, we just add code to create the item and its listener, as well as the method that handles its function.

However, using anonymous inner classes can make code quite hard to read. It is strongly recommended to use them only for very short classes and for well-established code idioms. For instance, it is questionable whether a full implementation of the **MouseListener** interface would be appropriate as an anonymous inner class, in view of the amount of code required; a named inner class would probably be preferable in terms of cohesion. For us, implementing event listeners is the only example in this book where we use this construct.[6]

Exercise 13.51 Review the implementation of the pixel editor in *imageviewer4-0*. Consider whether the current mouse operations used to chose a color or choose a pixel are the most appropriate for a user. Change them if you feel that they are not.

Exercise 13.52 Add a menu to the project that allows a 'brush size' to be specified for the pixel editor. Use the brush size to edit multiple adjacent pixels on each mouse press.

Exercise 13.53 Override further methods of the **MouseAdapter** class to permit free-hand drawing on the image panel. Consider carefully whether to continue with the listener as an anonymous inner class, or whether to make it a named inner class.

---

[6] If you'd like to find out more about inner classes, have a look at these two sections of the online Java tutorial: `http://download.oracle.com/javase/tutorial/java/javaOO/nested.html` and `http://download.oracle.com/javase/tutorial/java/javaOO/innerclasses.html`.

13.9 Further extensions

Programming GUIs with Swing is a big subject area. Swing has many different types of components and many different containers and layout managers. And each of these has many attributes and methods.

Becoming familiar with the whole Swing library takes time, and is not something done in a few weeks. Usually, as we work on GUIs, we continue to read about details that we did not know before and become experts over time.

The example discussed in this chapter, even though it contains a lot of detail, is only a brief introduction to GUI programming. We have discussed most of the important concepts, but there is still a large amount of functionality to be discovered, most of which is beyond the scope of this book. There are various sources of information available to help you continue. You frequently have to look up the API documentation for the Swing classes; it is not possible to work without it. There are also many GUI/Swing tutorials available, both in print and on the web.

A very good starting point for this, as so often is the case, is the Java Tutorial, available publicly on Oracle's web site. It contains a section titled *Creating a GUI with JFC/Swing* (`http://download.oracle.com/javase/tutorial/uiswing/index.html`).

In this section, there are many interesting subsections. One of the most useful may be the section entitled *Using Swing Components* and in it the subsection *How To . . .* It contains these entries: *How to Use Buttons, Check Boxes, and Radio Buttons*; *How to Use Labels*; *How to Make Dialogs*; *How to Use Panels*; and so on.

Similarly, the top-level section *Laying Out Components within a Container* also has a *How To . . .* section that tells you about all available layout managers.

Exercise 13.54 Find the online Java Tutorial section *Creating a GUI with JFC/Swing* (the sections are called *trails* on the web site). Bookmark it.

Exercise 13.55 What do `CardLayout` and `GroupLayout` have to offer that is different from the layout managers we have discussed in this chapter?

Exercise 13.56 What is a *slider*? Find a description and summarize. Give a short example in Java code about creating and using a slider.

Exercise 13.57 What is a *tabbed pane*? Find a description and summarize. Give examples of what a tabbed pane might be used for.

Exercise 13.58 What is a *spinner*? Find a description and summarize.

Exercise 13.59 Find the demo application *ProgressBarDemo*. Run it on your computer. Describe what it does.

This is where we shall leave the discussion of the image-viewer example. It can, however, be extended in many directions by interested readers. Using the information from the online tutorial, you can add numerous interface components.

The following exercises give you some ideas, and obviously there are many more possibilities.

Exercise 13.60 Implement an *undo* function in your image viewer. This function reverses the last operation.

Exercise 13.61 Disable all menu items that cannot be used when no image is being displayed.

Exercise 13.62 Implement a *reload* function that discards all changes to the current image and reloads it from disk.

Exercise 13.63 The **JMenu** class is actually a subclass of **JMenuItem**. This means that nested menus can be created by placing one **JMenu** inside another. Add an *Adjust* menu to the menu bar. Nest within it a *Rotate* menu that allows the image to be rotated either 90 or 180 degrees, clockwise or counterclockwise. Implement this functionality. The *Adjust* menu could also contain menu items that invoke the existing *Larger* and *Smaller* functionality, for instance.

Exercise 13.64 The application always resizes its frame in order to ensure that the full image is always visible. Having a large frame is not always desirable. Read the documentation on the **JScrollPane** class. Instead of adding the **ImagePanel** directly to the content pane, place the panel in a **JScrollPane** and add the scroll pane to the content pane. Display a large image and experiment with resizing the window. What difference does having a scroll pane make? Does this allow you to display images that would otherwise be too large for the screen?

Exercise 13.65 Change your application so that it can open multiple images at the same time (but only one image is displayed at any time). Then add a pop-up menu (using class **JComboBox**) to select the image to display.

Exercise 13.66 As an alternative to using a **JComboBox** as in Exercise 13.65, use a tabbed pane (class **JTabbedPane**) to hold multiple open images.

Exercise 13.67 Implement a slide show function that lets you choose a directory and then displays each image in that directory for a specified length of time (say, 5 seconds).

Exercise 13.68 Once you have the slide show, add a slider (class **JSlider**) that lets you select an image in the slide show by moving the slider. While the slide show runs, the slider should move to indicate progress.

13.10 Another example: MusicPlayer

So far in this chapter, we have discussed one example of a GUI application in detail. We now want to introduce a second application to provide another example to learn from. This program introduces a few additional GUI components.

This second example is a music-player application. We shall not discuss it in any great amount of detail. It is intended as a basis for studying the source code largely on your own and as a source of code fragments for you to copy and modify. Here, in this chapter, we shall only point out a few selected aspects of the application that are worth focusing on.

> **Exercise 13.69** Open the *musicplayer* project. Create an instance of `MusicPlayerGUI`, and experiment with the application.

The *musicplayer* project provides a GUI interface to classes based on the *music-organizer* projects from Chapter 4. As there, the program finds and plays MP3 files stored in the *audio* folder inside the chapter folder (one level up from the project folder). If you have sound files of the right format of your own, you should be able to play them by dropping them into the *audio* folder.

The music player is implemented across three classes: `MusicPlayerGUI`, `MusicPlayer`, and `MusicFilePlayer`. Only the first is intended to be studied here. `MusicFilePlayer` can be used essentially as a library class; instances are created along with the name of the MP3 file to be played. Familiarize yourself with its interface, but you do not need to understand or modify its implementation. (You are welcome, of course, to study this class as well if you like, but it uses some concepts that we shall not discuss in this book.)

Following are some noteworthy observations about the *musicplayer* project.

Model/view separation

This application uses a better model/view separation than the previous example. This means that the application functionality (the model) is separated cleanly from the application's user interface (the GUI). Each of those two, the model and the view, may consist of multiple classes, but every class should be clearly in one or the other group to achieve a clear separation. In our example, the view consists of a single GUI class.

Separating the application's functionality from the interface is an example of good cohesion; it makes the program easier to understand, easier to maintain, and easier to adapt to different requirements (especially different user interfaces). It would, for example, be fairly easy to write a text-based interface for the music player, effectively replacing the `MusicPlayerGUI` class and leaving the `MusicPlayer` class unchanged.

Inheriting from JFrame

In this example, we are demonstrating the alternative popular version of creating frames that we mentioned at the start of the chapter. Our GUI class does not instantiate a `JFrame` object; instead, it extends the **JFrame** class. As a result, all the **JFrame** methods we need to call (such as **getContentPane**, **setJMenuBar**, **pack**, **setVisible**, and so on) can now be called as internal (inherited) methods.

There is no strong reason for preferring one style (using a **JFrame** instance) over the other (inheriting from **JFrame**). It is largely a matter of personal preference, but you should be aware that both styles are widely used.

Displaying static images

We often want want to display an image in a GUI. The easiest way to do this is to include in the interface a **JLabel** that has a graphic as its label (a **JLabel** can display either text or a graphic or both). The sound player includes an example of doing this. The relevant source code is

```
JLabel image = new JLabel(new ImageIcon("title.jpg"));
```

This statement will load an image file named "title.jpg" from the project directory, create an icon with that image, and then create a **JLabel** that displays the icon. (The term "icon" seems to suggest that we are dealing only with small images here, but the image can in fact be of any size.) This method works for JPEG, GIF, and PNG images.

Combo boxes

The sound player presents an example of using a **JComboBox**. A combo box is a set of values, one of which is selected at any time. The selected value is displayed, and the selection can be accessed through a pop-up menu. In the sound player, the combo box is used to select a particular ordering for the tracks—by artist, title, etc.

A **JComboBox** may also be editable, in which case the values are not all predefined but can be typed by a user. Ours is not.

Lists

The program also includes an example of a list (class **JList**) for the list of tracks. A list can hold an arbitrary number of values, and one or more can be selected. The list values in this example are strings, but other types are possible. A list does not automatically have a scrollbar.

Scrollbars

Another component demonstrated in this example is the use of scrollbars.

Scrollbars can be created by using a special container, an instance of class **JScrollPane**. GUI objects of any type can be placed into a scroll pane, and the scroll pane will, provide the necessary scrollbars if the held object is too big to be displayed in the available space.

In our example, we have placed our track list into a scroll pane. The scroll pane itself is then placed into its parent container. The scrollbars only become visible when necessary. You can try this by either adding more tracks until they do not fit into the available space, or by resizing the window to make it too small to display the current list.

Other elements demonstrated in this example are the use of a slider (which does not do much), and the use of color (in the list) for changing the look of an application. Each of the GUI's elements has many methods for modifying the component's look or behavior—you should look through the documentation for any component that interests you and experiment with modifying some properties of that component.

Exercise 13.70 Change the music player so that it displays a different image in its center. Find an image on the web to use, or make your own.

Exercise 13.71 Change the colors of the other components (foreground and background colors) to suit the new main image.

Exercise 13.72 Add a new component to display details of the current track when one is playing.

Exercise 13.73 Add a *reload* capability to the music player that rereads the files from the *audio* folder. Then you can drop a new file into the folder and load it without having to quit the player.

Exercise 13.74 Add an *Open* item to the file menu. When activated, it presents a file-selection dialog that lets the user choose a sound file to open. If the user chooses a directory, the player should open all sound files in that directory (as it does now with the *audio* directory).

Exercise 13.75 Modify the slider so that the start and end (and possibly other tick marks) are labeled with numbers. The start should be zero, and the end should be the length of the music file. The `MusicPlayer` class has a `getLength` method. Note that the slider is not currently functional.

Exercise 13.76 Modify the music player so that a double click on a list element in the track list starts playing that track.

Exercise 13.77 Improve the button look. All buttons that have no function at any point in time should be grayed out at that time, and should be enabled only when they can reasonably be used.

Exercise 13.78 The display of tracks is currently simply a `JList` of `String` objects. Investigate whether there are any Swing components available that would provide greater sophistication than this. For instance, can you find a way to provide a header line and align the artist, title, and other parts of the track information? Implement this in your version.

Exercise 13.79 *Challenge exercise* Have the position slider move as a track is being played.

13.11 Summary

In this chapter, we have supplied an introduction to GUI programming using the Swing and AWT libraries. We have discussed the three main conceptual areas: creating GUI components, layout, and event handling.

We have seen that building a GUI usually starts with creating a top-level frame, such as a **JFrame**. The frame is then filled with various components that provide information and functionality to the user. Among the components we have encountered are menus, menu items, buttons, labels, borders, and others.

Components are arranged on screen with the help of containers and layout managers. Containers hold collections of components, and each container has a layout manager that takes care of arranging the components within the container's screen area. Nesting containers, using combinations of different layout managers, is a common way to achieve the desired combination of component size and juxtaposition.

Interactive components (those that can react to user input) generate events when they are activated by a user. Other objects can become event listeners and be notified of such events by implementing standard interfaces. When the listener object is notified, it can take appropriate action to deal with the user event. Event listeners are often implemented using lambda notation.

We have introduced the concept of anonymous inner classes as an alternative modular, extendable technique for writing event listeners. These are particularly useful when a listener interface is not a functional interface (it has more than one abstract method) and cannot be implemented via a lambda expression.

And finally, we have given a pointer to an online reference and tutorial site that may be used to learn about details not covered in the chapter.

Terms introduced in this chapter:

> **GUI, AWT, Swing, component, layout, event, event handling, event listener, frame, menu bar, menu, menu item, content pane, modal dialog, anonymous inner class**

Exercise 13.80 Add a GUI to the *world-of-zuul* project from Chapter 8. Every room should have an associated image that is displayed when the player enters the room. There should be a non-editable text area to display text output. To enter commands, you can choose between different possibilities: you can leave the input text-based and use a text field (class **JTextField**) to type commands, or you can use buttons for command entry.

Exercise 13.81 Add sounds to the *word-of-zuul* game. You can associate individual sounds with rooms, items, or characters.

Exercise 13.82 Design and build a GUI for a text editor. Users should be able to enter text, edit, scroll, etc. Consider functions for formatting (font faces, style, and size) and a character/word-count function. You do not need to implement the *load* and *save* functions just yet—you might want to wait with that until you have read the next chapter.

CHAPTER 14

Handling Errors

> **Main concepts discussed in this chapter:**
>
> - defensive programming
> - exception throwing and handling
> - error reporting
> - basic file processing
>
> **Java constructs discussed in this chapter:**
>
> TreeMap, TreeSet, SortedMap, assert, exception, throw, throws, try, catch, File, FileReader, FileWriter, Path, Scanner, Stream

In Chapter 9, we saw that logical errors in programs are harder to spot than syntactical errors, because a compiler cannot give any help with logical errors. Logical errors arise for several reasons, which may overlap in some situations:

- The solution to a problem has been implemented incorrectly. For instance, a problem involving generating some statistics on data values might have been programmed to find the mean value rather than the median value (the "middle" value).

- An object might be asked to do something it is unable to. For instance, a collection object's `get` method might be called with an index value outside the valid range.

- An object might be used in ways that have not been anticipated by the class designer, leading to the object being left in an inconsistent or inappropriate state. This often happens when a class is reused in a setting that is different from its original one, perhaps through inheritance.

Although the sort of testing strategies discussed in Chapter 9 can help us identify and eliminate many logical errors before our programs are put to use, experience suggests that program failures will continue to occur. Furthermore, even the most thoroughly tested program may fail as a result of circumstances beyond the programmer's control. Consider the case of a web-browser asked to display a web page that does not exist, or a program that tries to write data to a disk that has no more space left. These problems are not the result of logical programming errors, but they could easily cause a program to fail if the possibility of their arising has not been taken into account.

In this chapter, we look at how to anticipate potential errors and how to respond to error situations as they arise during the execution of a program. In addition, we provide some suggestions on how to report errors when they occur. We also provide a brief introduction to how to perform textual input/output, as file processing is one of the situations where errors can easily arise.

14.1 The *address-book* project

We shall use the *address-book* family of projects to illustrate some of the principles of error reporting and error handling that arise in many applications. The projects represent an application that stores personal-contact details—name, address, and phone number—for an arbitrary number of people. Such a contacts list might be used on a mobile phone or in an e-mail program, for instance. The contact details are indexed in the address book by both name and phone number. The main classes we shall be discussing are **AddressBook** (Code 14.1) and **ContactDetails**. In addition, the **AddressBookDemo** class is provided as a convenient means of setting up an initial address book with some sample data.

Code 14.1

The **Address-Book** class

```java
import java.util.Iterator;
import java.util.LinkedList;
import java.util.List;
import java.util.Set;
import java.util.SortedMap;
import java.util.TreeMap;
import java.util.TreeSet;

/**
 * A class to maintain an arbitrary number of contact details.
 * Details are indexed by both name and phone number.
 *
 * @author David J. Barnes and Michael Kölling.
 * @version 2016.02.29
 */
public class AddressBook
{
    // Storage for an arbitrary number of details.
    private TreeMap<String, ContactDetails> book;
    private int numberOfEntries;

    /**
     * Perform any initialization for the address book.
     */
    public AddressBook()
    {
        book = new TreeMap<>();
        numberOfEntries = 0;
    }

    /**
     * Look up a name or phone number and return the
     * corresponding contact details.
     * @param key The name or number to be looked up.
     * @return The details corresponding to the key.
     */
    public ContactDetails getDetails(String key)
    {
        return book.get(key);
    }
```

Code 14.1 continued

The Address-Book class

```java
/**
 * Return whether or not the current key is in use.
 * @param key The name or number to be looked up.
 * @return true if the key is in use, false otherwise.
 */
public boolean keyInUse(String key)
{
    return book.containsKey(key);
}

/**
 * Add a new set of details to the address book.
 * @param details The details to associate with the person.
 */
public void addDetails(ContactDetails details)
{
    book.put(details.getName(), details);
    book.put(details.getPhone(), details);
    numberOfEntries++;
}

/**
 * Change the details previously stored under the given key.
 * @param oldKey One of the keys used to store the details.
 * @param details The replacement details.
 */
public void changeDetails(String oldKey, ContactDetails details)
{
    removeDetails(oldKey);
    addDetails(details);
}

/**
 * Search for all details stored under a key that starts with
 * the given prefix.
 * @param keyPrefix The key prefix to search on.
 * @return An array of those details that have been found.
 */
public ContactDetails[] search(String keyPrefix)
{
    // Build a list of the matches.
    List<ContactDetails> matches = new LinkedList<>();
    // Find keys that are equal-to or greater-than the prefix.
    SortedMap<String, ContactDetails> tail = book.tailMap(keyPrefix);
    Iterator<String> it = tail.keySet().iterator();
    // Stop when we find a mismatch.
    boolean endOfSearch = false;
    while(!endOfSearch && it.hasNext()) {
        String key = it.next();
        if(key.startsWith(keyPrefix)) {
            matches.add(book.get(key));
        }
        else {
            // As the list is sorted, there won't be any more.
            endOfSearch = true;
        }
    }
    ContactDetails[] results = new ContactDetails[matches.size()];
    matches.toArray(results);
    return results;
}
```

Code 14.1 continued

The Address-Book class

```java
/**
 * Return the number of entries currently in the
 * address book.
 * @return The number of entries.
 */
public int getNumberOfEntries()
{
    return numberOfEntries;
}

/**
 * Remove an entry with the given key from the address book.
 * @param key One of the keys of the entry to be removed.
 */
public void removeDetails(String key)
{
    ContactDetails details = book.get(key);
    book.remove(details.getName());
    book.remove(details.getPhone());
    numberOfEntries--;
}

/**
 * Return all the contact details, sorted according
 * to the sort order of the ContactDetails class.
 * @return A sorted list of the details.
 */
public String listDetails()
{
    // Because each entry is stored under two keys, it is
    // necessary to build a set of the ContactDetails. This
    // eliminates duplicates.
    StringBuilder allEntries = new StringBuilder();
    Set<ContactDetails> sortedDetails = new TreeSet<>(book.values());
    for(ContactDetails details : sortedDetails) {
        allEntries.append(details).append("\n\n");
    }
    return allEntries.toString();
}
}
```

New details can be stored in the address book via its **addDetails** method. This assumes that the details represent a new contact, and not a change of details for an existing one. To cover the latter case, the **changeDetails** method removes an old entry and replaces it with the revised details. The address book provides two ways to retrieve entries: the **getDetails** method takes a name or phone number as the key and returns the matching details; the **search** method returns an array of all those details that start with a given search string (for instance, the search string "**084**" would return all entries with phone numbers having that prefix).

There are two introductory versions of the *address-book* project for you to explore. Both provide access to the same version of **AddressBook**, as shown in Code 14.1. The *address-book-v1t* project provides a text-based user interface, similar in style to the interface of the *zuul* game discussed in Chapter 8. Commands are currently available to list the address book's contents, search it, and add a new entry. Probably more interesting as an interface, however, is the *address-book-v1g* version, which incorporates a simple GUI. Experiment with both versions to gain some experience with what the application can do.

Exercise 14.1 Open the *address-book-v1g* project and create an **AddressBookDemo** object. Call its **showInterface** method to display the GUI and interact with the sample address book.

Exercise 14.2 Repeat your experimentation with the text interface of the *address-book-v1t* project.

Exercise 14.3 Examine the implementation of the **AddressBook** class and assess whether you think it has been well-written or not. Do you have any specific criticisms of it?

Exercise 14.4 The **AddressBook** class uses quite a lot of classes from the `java.util` package; if you are not familiar with any of these, check the API documentation to fill in the gaps. Do you think the use of so many different utility classes is justified? Could a **HashMap** have been used in place of the **TreeMap**?

If you are not sure, try changing **TreeMap** to **HashMap** and see if **HashMap** offers all of the required functionality.

Exercise 14.5 Modify the **CommandWords** and **AddressBookTextInterface** classes of the *address-book-v1t* project to provide interactive access to the **getDetails** and **removeDetails** methods of **AddressBook**.

Exercise 14.6 The **AddressBook** class defines a field to record the number of entries. Do you think it would be more appropriate to calculate this value directly, from the number of unique entries in the **TreeMap**? For instance, can you think of any circumstances in which the following calculation would not produce the same value?

```
return book.size() / 2;
```

Exercise 14.7 How easy do you think it would be to add a **String** field for an email address to the **ContactDetails** class, and then to use this as a third key in the **AddressBook**? Don't actually try it, at this stage.

14.2 Defensive programming

14.2.1 Client–server interaction

An **AddressBook** is a typical server object, initiating no actions on its own behalf; all of its activities are driven by client requests. Programmers can adopt at least two possible views when designing and implementing a server class:

- They can assume that client objects will know what they are doing and will request services only in a sensible and well-defined way.

- They can assume that server objects will operate in an essentially problematic environment in which all possible steps must be taken to prevent client objects from using them incorrectly.

These views clearly represent opposite extremes. In practice, the most likely scenario usually lies somewhere in between. Most client interactions will be reasonable, with the occasional attempt to use the server incorrectly—either as the result of a logical programming error or of misconception on the part of the client programmer. A third possibility, of course, is an intentionally hostile client who is trying to break or find a weakness in the server.

These different views provide a useful base from which to discuss questions such as:

- How much checking should a server's methods perform on client requests?
- How should a server report errors to its clients?
- How can a client anticipate failure of a request to a server?
- How should a client deal with failure of a request?

If we examine the **AddressBook** class with these issues in mind, we shall see that the class has been written to trust completely that its clients will use it appropriately. Exercise 14.8 illustrates one of the ways in which this is the case, and how things can go wrong.

Exercise 14.8 Using the *address-book-v1g* project, create a new **AddressBook** object on the object bench. This will be completely empty of contact details. Now make a call to its **removeDetails** method with any string value for the key. What happens? Can you understand why this happens?

Exercise 14.9 For a programmer, the easiest response to an error situation arising is to allow the program to terminate (i.e., to "crash"). Can you think of any situations in which simply allowing a program to terminate could be very dangerous?

Exercise 14.10 Many commercially sold programs contain errors that are not handled properly in the software and cause them to crash. Is that unavoidable? Is it acceptable? Discuss this issue.

The problem with the `removeDetails` method is that it assumes that the key passed to it is a valid key for the address book. It uses the supposed key to retrieve the associated contact details:

```
ContactDetails details = book.get(key);
```

However, if the map does not have that particular key, then the `details` variable ends up containing `null`. That, of itself, is not an error; but the error arises from the following statement, where we assume that `details` refers to a valid object:

```
book.remove(details.getName());
```

It is an error to call a method on a variable containing `null`, and the result will be a runtime error. BlueJ reports this as a `NullPointerException` and highlights the statement from which it resulted. Later in this chapter, we shall be discussing exceptions in detail. For now, we can simply say that, if an error such as this were to occur in a running application, then the application would crash—i.e., terminate in an uncontrolled way—before it had completed its task.

There is clearly a problem here, but whose fault is it? Is it the fault of the client object for calling the method with a bad parameter value, or is it the fault of the server object for failing to handle this situation properly? The writer of the client class might argue that there is nothing in the method's documentation to say that the key must be valid. Conversely, the writer of the server class might argue that it is obviously wrong to try to remove details with an invalid key. Our concern in this chapter is not to resolve such disputes, but to try to prevent them from arising in the first place. We shall start by looking at error handling from the point of view of the server class.

Exercise 14.11 Save a copy, to work on, of one of the *address-book-v1* projects under another name. Make changes to the `removeDetails` method to avoid a `NullPointerException` arising if the key value does not have a corresponding entry in the address book. Use an if-statement. If the key is not valid, then the method should do nothing.

Exercise 14.12 Is it necessary to report the detection of an invalid key in a call to `removeDetails`? If so, how would you report it?

Exercise 14.13 Are there any other methods in the `AddressBook` class that are vulnerable to similar errors? If so, try to correct them in your copy of the project. Is it acceptable in all cases for the method simply to do nothing if its parameter values are inappropriate? Do the errors need reporting in some way? If so, how would you do it, and would it be the same way for each error?

14.2.2 Parameter checking

A server object is most vulnerable when its constructor and methods receive external values through their parameters. The values passed to a constructor are used to set up an object's initial state, while the values passed to a method will be used to influence the overall effect of the method call and may change the state of the object and a result the method returns. Therefore, it is vital that a server object knows whether it can trust parameter values to be valid, or whether it needs to check their validity for itself. The current situation in both the **ContactDetails** and **AddressBook** classes is that there is no checking at all on parameter values. As we have seen with the **removeDetails** method, this can lead to a fatal runtime error.

Preventing a **NullPointerException** in **removeDetails** is relatively easy, and Code 14.2 illustrates how this can be done. Note that, as well as improving the source code in the method, we have updated the method's comment, to document the fact that unknown keys are ignored.

Code 14.2

Guarding against an invalid key in **removeDetails**

```
/**
 * Remove the entry with the given key from the address book.
 * The key should be one that is currently in use.
 * @param key One of the keys of the entry to be removed.
 */
public void removeDetails(String key)
{
    if(keyInUse(key)) {
        ContactDetails details = book.get(key);
        book.remove(details.getName());
        book.remove(details.getPhone());
        numberOfEntries--;
    }
}
```

If we examine all the methods of **AddressBook**, we find that there are other places where we could make similar improvements:

- The **addDetails** method should check that its actual parameter is not **null**.
- The **changeDetails** method should check both that the old key is one that is in use and that the new details are not **null**.
- The **search** method should check that the key is not **null**.

These changes have all been implemented in the version of the application to be found in the *address-book-v2g* and *address-book-v2t* projects.

Exercise 14.14 Why do you think we have felt it unnecessary to make similar changes to the **getDetails** and **keyInUse** methods?

Exercise 14.15 In dealing with parameter errors, we have not printed any error messages. Do you think an **AddressBook** *should* print an error message whenever it receives a bad parameter value to one of its methods? Are there any situations where a printed error message would be inappropriate? For instance, do error messages printed to the terminal seem appropriate with the GUI version of the project?

Exercise 14.16 Are there any further checks you feel we should make on the parameters of other methods, to prevent an **AddressBook** object from functioning incorrectly?

14.3 Server error reporting

Having protected a server object from performing an illegal operation through bad parameter values, we could take the view that this is all that the server writer needs to do. However, ideally we should like to avoid such error situations from arising in the first place. Furthermore, it is often the case that incorrect parameter values are the result of some form of programming error in the client that supplied them. Therefore, rather than simply programming around the problem in the server and leaving it at that, it is good practice for the server to make some effort to indicate that a problem has arisen, either to the client itself or to a human user or programmer. In that way, there is a chance that an incorrectly written client will be fixed. But notice that those three "audiences" for the notification will often be completely different.

What is the best way for a server to report problems when they occur? There is no single answer to this question, and the most appropriate answer will often depend upon the context in which a particular server object is being used. In the following sections, we shall explore a range of options for error reporting by a server.

Exercise 14.17 How many different ways can you think of to indicate that a method has received incorrect parameter values or is otherwise unable to complete its task? Consider as many different sorts of applications as you can—for instance: those with a GUI; those with a textual interface and a human user; those with no sort of interactive user, such as software in a vehicle's engine-management system; or software in embedded systems such as a cash machine.

14.3.1 Notifying the user

The most obvious way in which an object might respond when it detects something wrong is to try to notify the application's user in some way. The main options are either to print an error message using **System.out** or **System.err** or to display an error message alert window.

The two main problems with both approaches are:

- They assume that the application is being used by a human user who will see the error message. There are many applications that run completely independently of a human user. An error message, or an error window, will go completely unnoticed. Indeed, the computer running the application might not have any visual-display device connected to it at all.

- Even where there is a human user to see the error message, it will be rare for that user to be in a position to do something about the problem. Imagine a user at an automatic teller machine being confronted with a `NullPointerException`! Only in those cases where the user's direct action has led to the problem—such as supplying invalid input to the application—is the user likely to be able take some appropriate corrective or avoiding action the next time.

Programs that print inappropriate error messages are more likely to annoy their users rather than achieve a useful outcome. Therefore, except in a very limited set of circumstances, notifying the user is not a general solution to the problem of error reporting.

> **Exercise 14.18** The Java API includes a sophisticated collection of error-logging classes in the `java.util.logging` package. The static `getLogger` method of the `Logger` class returns a `Logger` object. Investigate the features of the class for text-based diagnostic error logging. What is the significance of having different logging levels? How does the `info` method differ from the `warning` method? Can logging be turned off and then on again?

14.3.2 Notifying the client object

A radically different approach from those we have discussed so far is for the server object to feedback an indication to the client object when something has gone wrong. There are two main ways to do this:

- A server can use a non-`void` return type of a method to return a value that indicates either success or failure of the method call.

- A server can *throw an exception* if something goes wrong. This introduces a new feature of Java that is also found in some other programming languages. We shall describe this feature in detail in Section 14.4.

Both techniques have the benefit of encouraging the programmer of the *client* to take into account that a method call could fail. However, only the decision to throw an exception will actively prevent the client's programmer from ignoring the consequences of method failure.

The first approach is easy to introduce to a method that would otherwise have a `void` return type, such as `removeDetails`. If the `void` type is replaced by a `boolean` type, then the method can return `true` to indicate that the removal was successful, and `false` to indicate that it failed for some reason (Code 14.3).

Code 14.3

A **boolean** return type to indicate success or failure

```
/**
 * Remove the entry with the given key from the address book.
 * The key should be one that is currently in use.
 * @param key One of the keys of the entry to be removed.
 * @return true if the entry was successfully removed,
 *         false otherwise.
 */
```

Code 14.3 continued

A **boolean** return type to indicate success or failure

```java
public boolean removeDetails(String key)
{
    if(keyInUse(key)) {
        ContactDetails details = book.get(key);
        book.remove(details.getName());
        book.remove(details.getPhone());
        numberOfEntries--;
        return true;
    }
    else {
        return false;
    }
}
```

This allows a client to use an if-statement to guard statements that depend on the successful removal of an entry:

```java
if(contacts.removeDetails(". . .")) {
    // Entry successfully removed. Continue as normal.
    . . .
}
else {
    // The removal failed. Attempt a recovery, if possible.
    . . .
}
```

Where a server method already has a non-**void** return type—effectively preventing a **boolean** diagnostic value from being returned—there may still be a way to indicate that an error has occurred through the return type. This will be the case if a value from the return type's range is available to act as an error diagnostic value. For instance, the **getDetails** method returns a **ContactDetails** object corresponding to a given key, and the example below assumes that a particular key will locate a valid set of contact details:

```java
// Send David a text message.
ContactDetails details = contacts.getDetails("David");
String phone = details.getPhone();
. . .
```

One way for the **getDetails** method to indicate that the key is invalid or not in use is to have it return a **null** value instead of a **ContactDetails** object (Code 14.4).

Code 14.4

Returning an out-of-bounds error diagnostic value

```java
/**
 * Look up a name or phone number and return the
 * corresponding contact details.
 * @param key The name or number to be looked up.
 * @return The details corresponding to the key, or
 *         null if the key is not in use.
 */
```

Code 14.4 continued

Returning an out-of-bounds error diagnostic value

```
public ContactDetails getDetails(String key)
{
    if(keyInUse(key)) {
        return book.get(key);
    }
    else {
        return null;
    }
}
```

This would allow a client to examine the result of the call, then either continue with the normal flow of control or attempt to recover from the error:

```
ContactDetails details = contacts.getDetails("David");
if(details != null) {
    // Send a text message to David.
    String phone = details.getPhone();
    . . .
}
else {
    // Failed to find the entry. Attempt a recovery, if possible.
    . . .
}
```

It is common for methods that return object references to use the `null` value as an indication of failure or error. With methods that return primitive-type values, there will sometimes be an *out-of-bounds value* that can fulfill a similar role: for instance, the `indexOf` method of the `String` class returns a negative value to indicate that it has failed to find the character sought.

Exercise 14.19 Do you think the different interface styles of the *v2t* and *v2g* *address-book* projects mean that there should be a difference in the way errors are reported to users?

Exercise 14.20 Using a copy of the *address-book-v2t* project, make changes to the `AddressBook` class to provide failure information to a client when a method has received incorrect parameter values, or is otherwise unable to complete its task.

Exercise 14.21 Do you think that a call to the `search` method that finds no matches requires an error notification? Justify your answer.

Exercise 14.22 What combinations of parameter values would it be inappropriate to pass to the constructor of the `ContactDetails` class?

Exercise 14.23 Does a constructor have any means of indicating to a client that it cannot correctly set up the new object's state? What should a constructor do if it receives inappropriate parameter values?

Clearly, an out-of-bounds value cannot be used where all values from the return type already have valid meanings to the client. In such cases, it will usually be necessary to resort to the alternative technique of *throwing an exception* (see Section 14.4), which does, in fact, offer some significant advantages. To help you appreciate why this might be, it is worth considering two issues associated with the use of return values as failure or error indicators:

- Unfortunately, there is no way to require the client to check the return value for its diagnostic properties. As a consequence, a client could easily carry on as if nothing has happened, and could then end up terminating with a `NullPointerException`. Worse than that, it could even use the diagnostic return value as if it were a normal return value, creating a difficult-to-diagnose logical error!

- In some cases, we may be using the diagnostic value for two quite different purposes. This is the case in the revised `removeDetails` (Code 14.3) and `getDetails` (Code 14.4). One purpose is to tell the client whether its request was successful or not. The other is to indicate that there was something wrong with its request, such as passing bad parameter values.

In many cases, an *unsuccessful* request will not represent a logical programming error, whereas an *incorrect* request almost certainly does. We should expect quite different follow-up actions from a client in these different situations. Unfortunately, there is no general satisfactory way to resolve the conflict simply by using return values.

14.4 Exception-throwing principles

Throwing an exception is the most effective way a server object has of indicating that it is unable to fulfill a call on one of its methods. One of the major advantages this has over using a special return value is that it is (almost) impossible for a client to ignore the fact that an exception has been thrown and carry on regardless. Failure by the client to handle an exception will result in the application terminating immediately.[1] In addition, the exception mechanism is independent of the return value of a method, so it can be used for all methods, irrespective of the return type.

An important point to bear in mind throughout the following discussion is that, where exceptions are involved, the place where an error is discovered will be distinct from where recovery (if any) is attempted. Discovery will be in the server's method, and recovery will be in the client. If recovery were possible at the point of discovery, then there would be no point in throwing an exception.

14.4.1 Throwing an exception

Code 14.5 shows how an exception is thrown using a *throw statement*. Here, the `getDetails` method is throwing an exception to indicate that passing a `null` value for the key does not make sense because it is not a valid key.

---

[1] This is exactly what you will have experienced whenever your programs inadvertently died because of a `NullPointerException` or `IndexOutOfBoundsException`.

Code 14.5
Throwing an exception

```java
/**
 * Look up a name or phone number and return the corresponding
 * contact details.
 * @param key The name or number to be looked up.
 * @return The details corresponding to the key,
 *         or null if there are none matching.
 * @throws IllegalArgumentException if the key is invalid.
 */
public ContactDetails getDetails(String key)
{
    if(key == null){
        throw new IllegalArgumentException("null key in getDetails");
    }
    return book.get(key);
}
```

> **Concept**
>
> An **exception** is an object representing details of a program failure. An exception is thrown to indicate that a failure has occurred.

There are two stages to throwing an exception. First, an exception object is created using the **new** keyword (in this case, an **IllegalArgumentException** object); then the exception object is thrown using the **throw** keyword. These two stages are almost invariably combined in a single statement:

```
throw new ExceptionType("optional-diagnostic-string");
```

When an exception object is created, a diagnostic string may be passed to its constructor. This string is later available to the receiver of the exception via the exception object's **getMessage** and **toString** methods. The string is also shown to the user if the exception is not handled and leads to the termination of the program. The exception type we have used here, **IllegalArgumentException**, is defined in the **java.lang** package and is regularly used to indicate that an inappropriate actual parameter value has been passed to a method or constructor.

Code 14.5 also illustrates that the **javadoc** documentation for a method can be expanded to include details of any exceptions it throws, using the **@throws** tag.

14.4.2 Checked and unchecked exceptions

An exception object is always an instance of a class from a special inheritance hierarchy. We can create new exception types by creating subclasses in this hierarchy (Figure 14.1). Strictly speaking, exception classes are always subclasses of the **Throwable** class that is defined in the **java.lang** package. We shall follow the convention of defining and using exception classes that are subclasses of the **Exception** class, also defined in **java.lang**.[2] The **java.lang** package defines a number of commonly seen exception classes that you might already have run across inadvertently in developing programs, such as **NullPointerException**, **IndexOutOfBoundsException**, and **ClassCastException**.

Java divides exception classes into two categories: *checked exceptions* and *unchecked exceptions*. All subclasses of the Java standard class **RuntimeException** are unchecked exceptions; all other subclasses of **Exception** are checked exceptions.

---

[2] **Exception** is one of two direct subclasses of **Throwable**; the other is **Error**. Subclasses of **Error** are usually reserved for runtime-system errors rather than errors over which the programmer has control.

Figure 14.1
The exception class hierarchy

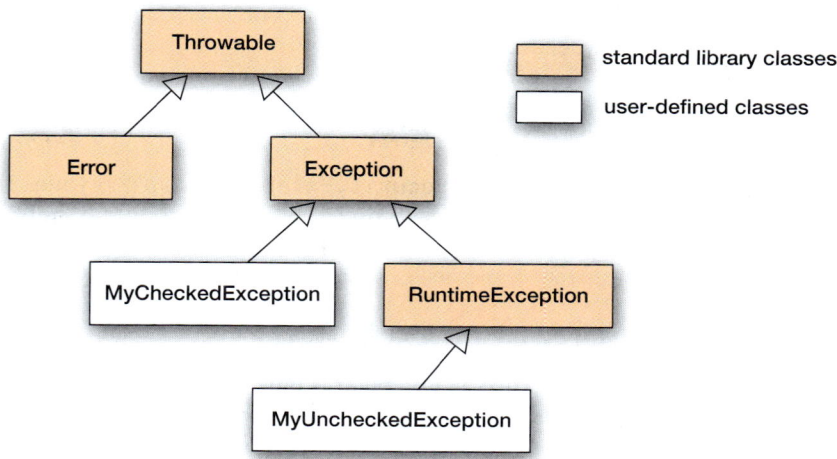

Slightly simplified, the difference is this: checked exceptions are intended for cases where the client should expect that an operation could fail (for example, if it tries to write to a disk, it should anticipate that the disk could be full). In such cases, the client will be forced to check whether the operation was successful. Unchecked exceptions are intended for cases that should never fail in normal operation—they usually indicate a program error. For instance, a programmer would never knowingly try to get an item from a position in a list that does not exist, so when they do, it elicits an unchecked exception.

Unfortunately, knowing which category of exception to throw in any particular circumstance is not an exact science, but we can offer the following general advice:

- One rule of thumb is to use unchecked exceptions for situations that should lead to program failure—typically because it is suspected that there is a logical error in the program that will prevent it from continuing any further. It follows that checked exceptions should be used where there may be a possibility of the client effecting a recovery. One problem with this policy is that it assumes that the server is aware enough of the context in which it is being used to be able to determine whether client recovery is likely or unlikely to be possible.

- Another rule of thumb is to use unchecked exceptions for situations that could reasonably be avoided. For instance, calling a method on a variable containing **null** is the result of a logical programming error that is completely avoidable, and the fact that **NullPointerException** is unchecked fits this model. It follows that checked exceptions should be used for failure situations that are beyond the control of the programmer, such as a disk becoming full when trying to write to a file or a network operation failing because a wireless network connection has dropped out.

The formal Java rules governing the use of exceptions are significantly different for unchecked and checked exceptions, and we shall outline the differences in detail in Sections 14.4.4 and 14.5.1, respectively. In simplified terms, the rules ensure that a client object calling a method that could throw a checked exception will contain code that anticipates the possibility of a problem arising and that attempts to handle the problem whenever it occurs.[3]

> **Exercise 14.24** List three exception types from the `java.io` package.
>
> **Exercise 14.25** Is `SecurityException` from the `java.lang` package a checked or an unchecked exception? What about `NoSuchMethodException`? Justify your answers.

14.4.3 The effect of an exception

What happens when an exception is thrown? There are really two effects to consider: the effect in the method where the problem is discovered, and the effect in the caller of the method.

When an exception is thrown, the execution of the throwing method finishes immediately; it does not continue to the end of the method body. A consequence of this is that a method with a non-**void** return type is not required to execute a return statement on a route that throws an exception. This is reasonable, because throwing an exception is an indication of the throwing method's inability to continue normal execution, which includes not being able to return a valid result. We can illustrate this principle with the following alternative version of the method body shown in Code 14.5:

```
if(key == null) {
    throw new IllegalArgumentException("null key in getDetails");
}
else {
    return book.get(key);
}
```

The absence of a return statement in the route that throws an exception is acceptable. Indeed, the compiler will indicate an error if any statements are written following a throw statement, because they could never be executed.

The effect of an exception on the point in the program that called the problem method is a little more complex. In particular, the full effect depends upon whether or not any code has been written to *catch* the exception. Consider the following contrived call to **getDetails**:

```
AddressDetails details = contacts.getDetails(null);
// The following statement will not be reached.
String phone = details.getPhone();
```

We *can* say that, in all cases, the execution of these statements will be left incomplete; the exception thrown by **getDetails** will interrupt the execution of the first statement, and no assignment will be made to the **details** variable. As a result, the second statement will not be executed either.

---

[3] In fact, it is still all too easy for the writer of the client to adhere to the rules in principle, but to fail to attempt a proper recovery from the problem, which rather subverts their purpose!

14.4.4 Using unchecked exceptions

> **Concept**
>
> An **unchecked exception** is a type of exception whose use will not require checks from the compiler.

Unchecked exceptions are the easiest to use from a programmer's point of view, because the compiler enforces few rules on their use. This is the meaning of *unchecked*: the compiler does not apply special checks, either on the method in which an unchecked exception is thrown or on the place from which the method is called. An exception class is unchecked if it is a subclass of the **RuntimeException** class, defined in the **java.lang** package. All of the examples we have used so far to illustrate exception throwing have involved unchecked exceptions. So there is little further to add here about how to throw an unchecked exception—simply use a throw statement.

If we also follow the convention that unchecked exceptions should be used in those situations where we expect the result to be program termination—i.e., the exception is not going to be caught—then there is also nothing further to be discussed about what the method's caller should do, because it will do nothing and let the program fail. However, if there is a need to catch an unchecked exception, then an exception handler *can* be written for it, exactly as for a checked exception. How to do this is described in Section 14.5.2.

We have already seen use of the unchecked **IllegalArgumentException**; this is thrown by a constructor or method to indicate that its parameter values are inappropriate. For instance, the **getDetails** method might also choose to throw this if the key string passed to it is a blank string (Code 14.6).

Code 14.6 Checking for an illegal parameter value

```java
/**
 * Look up a name or phone number and return the corresponding
 * contact details.
 * @param key The name or number to be looked up.
 * @throws IllegalArgumentException if the key is invalid.
 * @return The details corresponding to the key,
 *         or null if there are none matching.
 */
public ContactDetails getDetails(String key)
{
    if(key == null) {
        throw new IllegalArgumentException("null key in getDetails");
    }
    if(key.trim().length() == 0) {
        throw new IllegalArgumentException(
                        "Empty key passed to getDetails");
    }
    return book.get(key);
}
```

It is well worth having a method conduct a series of validity checks on its parameters before proceeding with the main purpose of the method. This makes it less likely that a method will get partway through its actions before having to throw an exception because of bad parameter values. A particular reason for avoiding this situation is that partial mutation of an object is likely to leave it in an inconsistent state for future use. If a method fails for any reason, the object on which it was called should ideally be left in the state it was before the operation was attempted.

The static `requireNonNull` method of the `java.util.Objects` class provides a convenient shorthand for testing an expression and throwing an exception if the expression is `null`. The following will throw a `NullPointerException`, with the associated string, if the value of `key` is `null`; otherwise it will do nothing:

```
Objects.requireNonNull(key, "null key passed to getDetails");
```

> **Exercise 14.26** Review all of the methods of the **AddressBook** class and decide whether there are any additional situations in which they should throw an `IllegalArgumentException`. Add the necessary checks and throw statements.
>
> **Exercise 14.27** If you have not already done so, add javadoc documentation to describe any exceptions thrown by methods in the **AddressBook** class.
>
> **Exercise 14.28** `UnsupportedOperationException` is an unchecked exception defined in the `java.lang` package. How might this be used in an implementation of the `java.util.Iterator` interface to prevent removal of items from a collection that is being iterated over? Try this out in the **LogfileReader** class of the *weblog-analyzer* project from Chapter 7.

14.4.5 Preventing object creation

An important use for exceptions is to prevent objects from being created if they cannot be placed in a valid initial state. This will usually be the result of inappropriate parameter values being passed to a constructor. We can illustrate this with the **ContactDetails** class. The constructor is currently fairly forgiving of the parameter values it receives: it does not reject `null` values but replaces them with empty strings. However, the address book needs at least a name or phone number from each entry to use as a unique index value, so an entry with both **name** and **phone** fields blank would be impossible to index. We can reflect this requirement by preventing construction of a **ContactDetails** object with no valid key details. The process of throwing an exception from a constructor is exactly the same as throwing one from a method. Code 14.7 shows the revised constructor that will prevent an entry from ever having both **name** and **phone** fields blank.

An exception thrown from a constructor has the same effect on the client as an exception thrown from a method. So the following attempt to create an invalid `ContactDetails` object will completely fail; it will *not* result in a `null` value being stored in the variable:

```
ContactDetails badDetails = new ContactDetails("", "", "");
```

Code 14.7

The constructor of the **Contact-Details** class

```java
/**
 * Set up the contact details. All details are trimmed to remove
 * trailing white space.
 * @param name The name.
 * @param phone The phone number.
 * @param address The address.
 * @throws IllegalStateException If both name and phone are blank.
 */
public ContactDetails(String name, String phone, String address)
{
    // Use blank strings if any of the arguments is null.
    if(name == null) {
        name = "";
    }
    if(phone == null) {
        phone = "";
    }
    if(address == null) {
        address = "";
    }

    this.name = name.trim();
    this.phone = phone.trim();
    this.address = address.trim();

    if(this.name.isEmpty() && this.phone.isEmpty()) {
        throw new IllegalStateException(
                    "Either the name or phone must not be blank.");
    }
}
```

14.5 Exception handling

The principles of exception throwing apply equally to unchecked and checked exceptions, but the rules of Java mean that exception handling is a requirement only with checked exceptions. A checked exception class is one that is a subclass of **Exception**, but not of **RuntimeException**. There are several more rules to follow when using checked exceptions, because the compiler enforces checks both in a method that throws a checked exception and in any caller of that method.

14.5.1 Checked exceptions: the throws clause

Concept

A **checked exception** is a type of exception whose use will require extra checks from the compiler. In particular, checked exceptions in Java require the use of throws clauses and try statements.

The first requirement of the compiler is that a method throwing a checked exception must declare that it does so in a *throws clause* added to the method's header. For instance, a method throwing a checked `IOException` from the `java.io` package might have the following header:[4]

```
public void saveToFile(String destinationFile)
    throws IOException
```

It is permitted to use a throws clause for unchecked exceptions, but the compiler does not require one. We recommend that a throws clause be used only to list the checked exceptions thrown by a method.

It is important to distinguish between a throws clause in the header of a method, and the `@throws` javadoc comment that precedes the method; the latter is completely optional for both types of exception. Nevertheless, we recommend that javadoc documentation be included for both checked and unchecked exceptions. In that way, as much information as possible will be available to someone wishing to use a method that throws an exception.

14.5.2 Anticipating exceptions: the try statement

The second requirement, when using checked exceptions, is that a caller of a method, that throws a checked exception must make provision for dealing with the exception. This usually means writing an *exception handler* in the form of a *try statement*. Most practical try statements have the general form shown in Code 14.8. This introduces two new Java keywords—**try** and **catch**—which mark a *try block* and a *catch block*, respectively.

Code 14.8
The try and catch blocks of an exception handler

```
try {
    Protect one or more statements here.
}
catch(Exception e) {
    Report and recover from the exception here.
}
```

Concept

Program code that protects statements in which an exception might be thrown is called an **exception handler**. It provides reporting and/or recovery code should one arise.

Suppose we have a method that saves the contents of an address book to a file. The user is requested in some way for the name of a file (perhaps via a GUI dialog window), and the address book's `saveToFile` method is then called to write out the list to the file. If we did not have to take exceptions into account, then this would be written as follows:

```
String filename = request-a-file-from-the-user;
addressbook.saveToFile(filename);
```

However, because the writing process could fail with an exception, the call to `saveToFile` must be placed within a try block to show that this has been taken into account. Code 14.9 illustrates how we would tend to write this, anticipating possible failure.

---

[4] Note that the keyword here is **throws** and not **throw**.

Code 14.9
An exception handler

```
String filename = null;
boolean successful;
try {
    filename = request-a-file-from-the-user;
    addressbook.saveToFile(filename);
    successful = true;
}
catch(IOException e) {
    System.out.println("Unable to save to " + filename);
    successful = false;
}
```

Any number of statements can be included in a try block, so we tend to place there not just the single statement that could fail, but all of the statements that are related to it in some way. The idea is that a try block represents a sequence of actions we wish to treat as a logical whole but recognize that they might fail at some point.[5] The catch block will then attempt to deal with the situation or report the problem if an exception arises from any statement within the associated try block. Note that, because both the try and catch blocks make use of the **filename** and **successful** variables, they have to be declared outside the try statement in this example, for reasons of scope.

In order to understand how an exception handler works, it is essential to appreciate that *an exception prevents the normal flow of control from being continued in the caller*. An exception interrupts the execution of the caller's statements, and hence any statements immediately following the problem statement will not be executed. The question then arises, "Where is execution resumed in the caller?" A try statement provides the answer: if an exception arises from a statement called in the try block, then execution is resumed in the corresponding catch block. So, if we consider the example in Code 14.9, the effect of an **IOException** being thrown from the call to **saveToFile** will be that control will transfer from the try block to the catch block, as shown in Code 14.10.

Code 14.10
Transfer of control in a try statement

1. Exception thrown from here
2. Control transfers to here

```
try {
    filename = request-a-file-from-the-user;
    addressbook.saveToFile(filename);
    successful = true;
}
catch(IOException e) {
    System.out.println("Unable to save to " + filename);
    successful = false;
}
```

---

[5] See Exercise 14.31 for an example of what can happen if a statement that might result in an exception is treated in isolation from the statements around it.

Statements in a try block are known as *protected statements*. If no exception arises during execution of protected statements, then the catch block will be skipped over when the end of the try block is reached. Execution will continue with whatever follows the complete try/catch statement.

A catch block names the type of exception it is designed to deal with in a pair of parentheses immediately following the **catch** word. As well as the exception type name, this also includes a variable name (traditionally, simply **e** or **ex**) that can be used to refer to the exception object that was thrown. Having a reference to this object can be useful in providing information that will support recovery from, or reporting of, the problem—e.g., accessing any diagnostic message placed in it by the throwing method. Once the catch block has been completed, control does *not* return to the statement that caused the exception.

Exercise 14.29 The *address-book-v3t* project includes some throwing of unchecked exceptions if parameter values are **null**. The project source code also includes the checked exception class **NoMatchingDetailsException**, which is currently unused. Modify the **removeDetails** method of **AddressBook** so that it throws this exception if its key parameter is not a key that is in use. Add an exception handler to the **remove** method of **AddressBookTextInterface** to catch and report occurrences of this exception.

Exercise 14.30 Make use of **NoMatchingDetailsException** in the **changeDetails** method of **AddressBook**. Enhance the user interface so that the details of an existing entry may be changed. Catch and report exceptions in **AddressBookTextInterface** that arise from use of a key that does not match any existing entry.

Exercise 14.31 Why is the following not a sensible way to use an exception handler? Will this code compile and run?

```
Person p = null;
try {
    // The lookup could fail.
    p = database.lookup(details);
}
catch(Exception e) {
}
System.out.println("The details belong to: " + p);
```

Note that in all the examples of try statements you have seen, the exception is not thrown *directly* by the statements in the try block, which is in the client object. Rather, the exception arises *indirectly*, passed back from a method in the server object, which is called from the statements within the try block. This is the usual pattern, and it would almost certainly be a programming error to enclose a throw statement directly within a try statement.

14.5.3 Throwing and catching multiple exceptions

Sometimes a method throws more than one type of exception in order to indicate different sorts of problems. Where these are checked exceptions, they must all be listed in the throws clause of the method, separated by commas. For instance:

```
public void process()
    throws EOFException, FileNotFoundException
```

An exception handler must cater for all checked exceptions thrown from its protected statements, so a try statement may contain multiple catch blocks, as shown in Code 14.11. Note that the same variable name can be used for the exception object in each case.

Code 14.11 Multiple catch blocks in a try statement

```
try {
    ...
    ref.process();
    ...
}
catch(EOFException e) {
    // Take action appropriate to an end-of-file exception.
    ...
}
catch(FileNotFoundException e) {
    // Take action appropriate to a file-not-found exception.
    ...
}
```

When an exception is thrown by a method call in a try block, the catch blocks are checked in the order in which they are written until a match is found for the exception type. So, if an **EOFException** is thrown, then control will transfer to the first catch block, and if a **FileNotFoundException** is thrown, then control will transfer to the second. Once the end of a single catch block is reached, execution continues following the last catch block.

Polymorphism can be used to avoid writing multiple catch blocks, if desired. However, this could be at the expense of being able to take type-specific recovery actions. In Code 14.12, the single catch block will handle *every* exception thrown by the protected statements. This is because the exception-matching process that looks for an appropriate catch block simply checks that the exception object is an instance of the type named in the block. As all exceptions are subtypes of the **Exception** class, the single block will catch everything, whether checked or unchecked. From the nature of the matching process, it follows that the order of catch blocks in a single try statement matters, and that a catch block for one exception type cannot follow a block for one of its supertypes (because the earlier supertype block will always match before the subtype block is checked). The compiler will report this as an error.

Code 14.12
Catching all exceptions in a single catch block

```
try {
    ...
    ref.process();
    ...
}
catch(Exception e) {
    // Take action appropriate to all exceptions.
    ...
}
```

A better way to handle multiple exceptions with the same recovery or reporting action is to list the exception types together, separated by the "|" symbol, in front of the exception variable name. See Code 14.13.

Code 14.13
Catching multiple exceptions

```
try {
    ...
    ref.process();
    ...
}
catch(EOFException | FileNotFoundException e) {
    // Take action appropriate to both exceptions.
    ...
}
```

Exercise 14.32 Enhance the try statements you wrote as solutions to Exercises 14.29 and 14.30 so that they handle checked and unchecked exceptions in different catch blocks.

Exercise 14.33 What is wrong with the following try statement?

```
Person p = null;
try {
    p = database.lookup(details);
    System.out.println("The details belong to: " + p);
}
catch(Exception e) {
    // Handle any checked exceptions . . .
    . . .
}
catch(RuntimeException e) {
    // Handle any unchecked exceptions . . .
    . . .
}
```

14.5.4 Propagating an exception

So far, we have suggested that an exception must be caught and handled at the earliest possible opportunity. That is, an exception thrown in a method **process** would have to be caught and handled in the method that called **process**. In fact, this is not strictly the case, as Java allows an exception to be *propagated* from the client method to the caller of the client method, and possibly beyond. A method propagates an exception simply by not including an exception handler to protect the statement that might throw it. However, for a checked exception, the compiler requires that the propagating method include a throws clause, even though it does not itself create and throw the exception. This means that you will sometimes see a method that has a throws clause, but with no throw statement in the method body. Propagation is common where the calling method is either unable to, or does not need to, undertake any recovery action itself, but this might be possible or necessary from within higher-level calls. It is also common in constructors, where a constructor's actions in setting up a new object fail and the constructor cannot recover from this.

If the exception being propagated is unchecked, then the throws clause is optional, and we prefer to omit it.

14.5.5 The finally clause

A try statement can include a third component that is optional. This is the *finally clause* (Code 14.14), and it is often omitted. The finally clause provides for statements that should be executed whether an exception arises in the protected statements or not. If control reaches the end of the try block, then the catch blocks are skipped and the finally clause is executed. Conversely, if an exception is thrown from the try block, the appropriate catch block is executed, and this is then followed by execution of the finally clause.

Code 14.14 A try statement with a finally clause

```
try {
    Protect one or more statements here.
}
catch(Exception e) {
    Report and recover from the exception here.
}
finally {
    Perform any actions here common to whether or not
    an exception is thrown.
}
```

At first sight, a finally clause would appear to be redundant. Doesn't the following example illustrate the same flow of control as Code 14.14?

```
try {
    Protect one or more statements here.
}
```

```
catch(Exception e) {
    Report and recover from the exception here.
}
Perform any actions here common to whether or not an exception is
thrown.
```

In fact, there are at least two cases where these two examples would have different effects:

- A finally clause is executed even if a return statement is executed in the try or catch blocks.
- If an exception is thrown in the try block but not caught, then the finally clause is still executed.

In the latter case, the uncaught exception could be an unchecked exception that does not require a catch block, for instance. However, it could also be a checked exception that is not handled by a catch block but propagated from the method, to be handled at a higher level in the call sequence. In such a case, the finally clause would still be executed.

It is also possible to omit the catch blocks in a try statement that has both a try block and a finally clause if the method is propagating all exceptions:

```
try {
    Protect one or more statements here.
}
finally {
    Perform any actions here common to whether or not
    an exception is thrown.
}
```

14.6 Defining new exception classes

Where the standard exception classes do not satisfactorily describe the nature of an error condition, new, more-descriptive exception classes can be defined using inheritance. New checked exception classes can be defined as subclasses of any existing checked exception class (such as **Exception**), and new unchecked exceptions would be subclasses of the **RuntimeException** hierarchy.

All existing exception classes support the inclusion of a diagnostic string passed to a constructor. However, one of the main reasons for defining new exception classes is to include further information within the exception object to support error diagnosis and recovery. For instance, some methods in the *address-book* application, such as **changeDetails**, take a **key** parameter that should match an existing entry. If no matching entry can be found, then this represents a programming error, as the methods cannot complete their task. In reporting the exception, it is helpful to include details of the key that caused the error. Code 14.15 shows a new checked exception class that is defined in the *address-book-v3t* project. It receives the key in its constructor and then makes it available through both the diagnostic string and a dedicated accessor method. If this exception were to be caught by an exception handler in the caller, the key would be available to the statements that attempt to recover from the error.

Code 14.15

An exception class with extra diagnostic information

```java
/**
 * Capture a key that failed to match an entry in the address book.
 *
 * @author David J. Barnes and Michael Kölling.
 * @version 2016.02.29
 */
public class NoMatchingDetailsException extends Exception
{
    // The key with no match.
    private String key;

    /**
     * Store the details in error.
     * @param key The key with no match.
     */
    public NoMatchingDetailsException(String key)
    {
        this.key = key;
    }

    /**
     * @return The key in error.
     */
    public String getKey()
    {
        return key;
    }

    /**
     * @return A diagnostic string containing the key in error.
     */
    public String toString()
    {
        return "No details matching: " + key + " were found.";
    }
}
```

The principle of including information that could support error recovery should be kept in mind particularly when defining new checked exception classes. Defining formal parameters in an exception's constructor will help to ensure that diagnostic information is available. In addition, where recovery is either not possible or not attempted, ensuring that the exception's `toString` method is overridden to include appropriate information will help in diagnosing the reason for the error.

Exercise 14.34 In the *address-book-v3t* project, define a new checked exception class: `DuplicateKeyException`. This should be thrown by the `addDetails` method if either of the non-blank key fields of its actual parameter is already currently in use. The exception class should store details of the offending key(s). Make any further changes to the user interface class that are necessary to catch and report the exception.

> **Exercise 14.35** Do you feel that `DuplicateKeyException` should be a checked or unchecked exception? Give reasons for your answer.

14.7 Using assertions

14.7.1 Internal consistency checks

When we design or implement a class, we often have an intuitive sense of things that should be true at a given point in the execution, but rarely state them formally. For instance, we would expect a `ContactDetails` object to always contain at least one non-blank field, or, when the `removeDetails` method is called with a particular key, we would expect that key to no longer be in use at the end of the method. Typically, these are conditions we wish to establish while developing a class, before it is released. In one sense, the sort of testing we discussed in Chapter 9 is an attempt to establish whether we have implemented an accurate representation of what a class or method should do. Characteristic of that style of testing is that the tests are *external* to the class being tested. If a class is changed, then we should take the time to run regression tests in order to establish that it still works as it should; it is easy to forget to do that. The practice of checking parameters, which we have introduced in this chapter, slightly shifts the emphasis from wholly external checking to a combination of external and internal checking. However, parameter checking is primarily intended to protect a server object from incorrect usage by a client. That still leaves the question of whether we can include some internal checks to ensure that the server object behaves as it should.

One way we could implement internal checking during development would be through the normal exception-throwing mechanism. In practice, we would have to use unchecked exceptions, because we could not expect regular client classes to include exception handlers for what are essentially internal server errors. We would then be faced with the issue of whether to remove these internal checks once the development process has been completed, in order to avoid the potentially high cost of runtime checks that are almost certainly bound to pass.

14.7.2 The assert statement

In order to deal with the need to perform efficient internal consistency checks, which can be turned on in development code but off in released code, an *assertion facility* is available in Java. The idea is similar to what we saw in Chapter 9 with JUnit testing, where we asserted the results we expected from method calls, and the JUnit framework tested whether or not those assertions were confirmed.

The *address-book-assert* project is a development version of the *address-book* projects that illustrates how assertions are used. Code 14.16 shows the `removeDetails` method, which now contains two forms of the *assert statement*.

14.7 Using assistants

Code 14.16
Using assertions for internal consistency checks

```java
/**
 * Remove the entry with the given key from the address book.
 * The key should be one that is currently in use.
 * @param key One of the keys of the entry to be removed.
 * @throws IllegalArgumentException If the key is null.
 */
public void removeDetails(String key)
{
    if(key == null) {
        throw new IllegalArgumentException(
                        "Null key passed to removeDetails.");
    }
    if(keyInUse(key)) {
        ContactDetails details = book.get(key);
        book.remove(details.getName());
        book.remove(details.getPhone());
        numberOfEntries--;
    }
    assert !keyInUse(key);
    assert consistentSize() : "Inconsistent book size in removeDetails";
}
```

> **Concept**
>
> An **assertion** is a statement of a fact that should be true in normal program execution. We can use assertions to state our assumptions explicitly and to detect programming errors more easily.

The `assert` keyword is followed by a boolean expression. The purpose of the statement is to assert something that should be true at this point in the method. For instance, the first assert statement in Code 14.16 asserts that `keyInUse` should return `false` at that point, either because the key wasn't in use in the first place or because it is no longer in use as the associated details have now been removed from the address book. This seemingly obvious assertion is more important than might at first appear; notice that the removal process does not actually involve use of the key with the address book.

Thus, an assert statement serves two purposes. It expresses explicitly what we assume to be true at a given point in the execution, and therefore increases readability both for the current developer and for a future maintenance programmer. Also, it actually performs the check at runtime so that we get notified if our assumption turns out to be incorrect. This can greatly help in finding errors early and easily.

If the boolean expression in an assert statement evaluates to `true`, then the assert statement has no further effect. If the statement evaluates to `false`, then an `AssertionError` will be thrown. This is a subclass of `Error` (see Figure 14.1) and is part of the hierarchy regarded as representing unrecoverable errors—hence, no handler should be provided in clients.

The second assert statement in Code 14.16 illustrates the alternative form of assert statement. The string following the colon symbol will be passed to the constructor of `AssertionError` to provide a diagnostic string. The second expression does not have to be an explicit string; any value-giving expression is acceptable, and will be turned into a `String` before being passed to the constructor.

The first assert statement shows that an assertion will often make use of an existing method within the class (e.g., `keyInUse`). The second example illustrates that it might be useful to provide a method specifically for the purpose of performing an assertion test (`consistentSize` in this example). This might be used if the check involves significant computation. Code 14.17 shows the `consistentSize` method, whose purpose is to ensure that the `numberOfEntries` field accurately represents the number of unique details in the address book.

Code 14.17

Checking for internal consistency in the address book

```java
/**
 * Check that the numberOfEntries field is consistent with
 * the number of entries actually stored in the address book.
 * @return true if the field is consistent, false otherwise.
 */
private boolean consistentSize()
{
    Collection<ContactDetails> allEntries = book.values();
    // Eliminate duplicates as we are using multiple keys.
    Set<ContactDetails> uniqueEntries = new HashSet<>(allEntries);
    int actualCount = uniqueEntries.size();
    return numberOfEntries == actualCount;
}
```

14.7.3 Guidelines for using assertions

Assertions are primarily intended to provide a way to perform consistency checks during the development and testing phases of a project. They are not intended to be used in released code. It is for this reason that a Java compiler will include assert statements in the compiled code only if requested to do so. It follows that assert statements should never be used to provide normal functionality. For instance, it would be wrong to combine assertions with removal of details, as follows, in the address book:

```java
// Error: don't use assert with normal processing!
assert book.remove(details.getName()) != null;
assert book.remove(details.getPhone()) != null;
```

Exercise 14.36 Open the *address-book-assert* project. Look through the **AddressBook** class and identify all of the assert statements to be sure that you understand what is being checked and why.

Exercise 14.37 The **AddressBookDemo** class contains several test methods that call methods of **AddressBook** that contain assert statements. Look through the source of **AddressBookDemo** to check that you understand the tests, and then try out each of the test methods. Are any assertion errors generated? If so, do you understand why?

Exercise 14.38 The `changeDetails` method of `AddressBook` currently has no assert statements. One assertion we could make about it is that the address book should contain the same number of entries at the end of the method as it did at the start. Add an assert statement (and any other statements you might need) to check this. Run the `testChange` method of `AddressBookDemo` after doing so. Do you think this method should also include the check for a consistent size?

Exercise 14.39 Suppose that we decide to allow the address book to be indexed by address as well as name and phone number. If we simply add the following statement to the `addDetails` method

```
book.put(details.getAddress(), details);
```

do you anticipate that any assertions will now fail? Try it. Make any further necessary changes to `AddressBook` to ensure that all of the assertions are now successful.

Exercise 14.40 `ContactDetails` are immutable objects—that is, they have no mutator methods. How important is this fact to the internal consistency of an `AddressBook`? Suppose the `ContactDetails` class had a `setPhone` method, for instance? Can you devise some tests to illustrate the problems this could cause?

14.7.4 Assertions and the BlueJ unit-testing framework

In Chapter 9, we introduced the support that BlueJ provides for the JUnit unit-testing framework. That support is based on the assertion facility we have been discussing in this section. Methods from the framework, such as `assertEquals`, are built around an assertion statement that contains a boolean expression made up from their parameters. If JUnit test classes are used to test classes containing their own assertion statements, then assertion errors from these statements will be reported in the test-results window along with test-class assertion failures. The *address-book-junit* project contains a test class to illustrate this combination. The `testAddDetailsError` method of `AddressBookTest` will trigger an assertion error, because `addDetails` should not be used to change existing details (see Exercise 14.34).

14.8 Error recovery and avoidance

So far, the main focus of this chapter has been on the problem of identifying errors in a server object and ensuring that any problem is reported back to the client if appropriate. There are two complementary issues that go with error reporting: error recovery and error avoidance.

14.8.1 Error recovery

The first requirement of successful error recovery is that clients take note of any error notifications that they receive. This may sound obvious, but it is not uncommon for a programmer to assume that a method call will not fail, and so not bother to check the return value. While ignoring errors is harder to do when exceptions are used, we have often seen the equivalent of the following approach to exception handling:

```java
AddressDetails details = null;
try {
    details = contacts.getDetails(. . .);
}
catch(Exception e) {
    System.out.println("Error: " + e);
}
String phone = details.getPhone();
```

The exception has been caught and reported, but no account has been taken of the fact that it is probably incorrect, just to carry on regardless.

Java's try statement is the key to supplying an error-recovery mechanism when an exception is thrown. Recovery from an error will usually involve taking some form of corrective action within the catch block, and then trying again. Repeated attempts can be made by placing the try statement in a loop. An example of this approach is shown in Code 14.18, which is an expanded version of Code 14.9. The efforts to compose an alternative filename could involve trying a list of possible folders, for instance, or prompting an interactive user for different names.

Code 14.18
An attempt at error recovery

```java
// Try to save the address book.
boolean successful = false;
int attempts = 0;
do {
    try {
        addressbook.saveToFile(filename);
        successful = true;
    }
    catch(IOException e) {
        System.out.println("Unable to save to " + filename);
        attempts++;
        if(attempts < MAX_ATTEMPTS) {
            filename = an alternative file name;
        }
    }
} while(!successful && attempts < MAX_ATTEMPTS);
if(!successful) {
    Report the problem and give up;
}
```

Although this example illustrates recovery for a specific situation, the principles it illustrates are more general:

- Anticipating an error, and recovering from it, will usually require a more complex flow of control than if an error cannot occur.
- The statements in the catch block are key to setting up the recovery attempt.
- Recovery will often involve having to try again.
- Successful recovery cannot be guaranteed.
- There should be some escape route from endlessly attempting hopeless recovery.

There won't always be a human user around to prompt for alternative input, so it might be the client object's responsibility to log the error, via something like a logging API, so that it will be noticed and can be investigated later.

14.8.2 Error avoidance

It should be clear that arriving at a situation where an exception is thrown will be, at worst, fatal to the execution of a program and, at best, messy to recover from in the client. It can be simpler to try to avoid the error in the first place, but this often requires collaboration between server and client.

Many of the cases where an **AddressBook** object is forced to throw an exception involve **null** parameter values passed to its methods. These represent logical programming errors in the client that could clearly be avoided by simple prior tests in the client. Null parameter values are usually the result of making invalid assumptions in the client. For instance, consider the following example:

```
String key = database.search(zipCode);
ContactDetails university = contacts.getDetails(key);
```

If the database search fails, then the key it returns may well be either blank or **null**. Passing that result directly to the **getDetails** method will produce a runtime exception. However, using a simple test of the search result, the exception can be avoided, and the real problem of a failed zip code search can be addressed instead:

```
String key = database.search(zipCode);
if(key != null && !key.isEmpty()) {
    ContactDetails university = contacts.getDetails(key);
    . . .
}
else {
    Deal with the zipcode error . . .
}
```

In this case, the client could establish for itself that it would be inappropriate to call the server's method. This is not always possible, and sometimes the client must enlist the help of the server.

Exercise 14.34 established the principle that the `addDetails` method should not accept a new set of details if one of the key values is already in use for another set. In order to avoid an inappropriate call, the client could make use of the address book's `keyInUse` method, as follows:

```
// Add what should be a new set of details to the address book.
if(contacts.keyInUse(details.getName()) {
    contacts.changeDetails(details.getName(), details);
}
else if(contacts.keyInUse(details.getPhone()) {
    contacts.changeDetails(details.getPhone(), details);
}
else {
    Add the details . . .
}
```

Using this approach, it is clearly possible to completely avoid a `DuplicateKeyException` being thrown from `addDetails`, which suggests that it could be downgraded from a checked to an unchecked exception.

This particular example illustrates some important general principles:

- If a server's validity-check and state-test methods are visible to a client, the client will often be able to avoid causing the server to throw an exception.

- If an exception can be avoided in this way, then the exception being thrown really represents a logical programming error in the client. This suggests use of an unchecked exception for such situations.

- Using unchecked exceptions means that the client does not have to use a try statement when it has already established that the exception will not be thrown. This is a significant gain, because having to write try statements for "cannot happen" situations is annoying for a programmer and makes it less likely that providing proper recovery for genuine error situations will be taken seriously.

The effects are not all positive, however. Here are some reasons why this approach is not always practical:

- Making a server class's validity-check and state-test methods publicly visible to its clients might represent a significant loss of encapsulation, and result in a higher degree of coupling between server and client than is desirable.

- It will probably not be safe for a server class to assume that its clients *will* make the necessary checks that avoid an exception. As a result, those checks will often be duplicated in both client and server. If the checks are computationally "expensive" to make, then duplication may be undesirable or prohibitive. However, our view would be that it is better to sacrifice efficiency for the sake of safer programming, where the choice is available.

14.9 File-based input/output

An important programming area in which error recovery cannot be ignored is input/output. This is because a programmer may have little direct control over the external environment in which their code is executed. For instance, a required data file may have been accidentally deleted or have become corrupted in some way, before the application is run; or an attempt to store results to the file system may be thwarted by lack of appropriate permissions or exceeding a file-system quota. There are many ways in which an input or output operation could fail at any stage. Furthermore, modern input/output has moved beyond a program simply accessing its local file store to a networked environment in which connectivity to the resources being accessed may be fragile and inconsistent—for example, when in a mobile environment.

The Java API has undergone a number of evolutions over the years, reflecting the increasing diversity of environments in which Java programs have come to be used. The core package for input/output-related classes has always been `java.io`. This package contains numerous classes to support input/output operations in a platform-independent manner. In particular, it defines the checked exception class **IOException** as a general indicator that something has gone wrong with an input/output operation, and almost any input/output operation must anticipate that one of these might be thrown. Instances of checked subclasses of **IOException** may be thrown at times to provide more detailed diagnostic information, such as `FileNotFoundException` and `EOFException`. In more recent versions of Java, a shift has taken place from a number of classes in the `java.io` package to those in the `java.nio` hierarchy, although without completely superseding everything in `java.io`.

A full description of the many different classes in the `java.io` and `java.nio` packages is beyond the scope of this book, but we shall provide some fundamental examples within the context of several of the projects we have already seen. This should give you enough background to experiment with input/output in your own projects. In particular, we shall illustrate the following common tasks:

- obtaining information about a file from the file system
- writing textual output to a file with the `FileWriter` class
- reading textual input from a file with the `FileReader` and `BufferedReader` classes
- anticipating **IOException** exceptions
- parsing input with the **Scanner** class

In addition, we look at reading and writing binary versions of objects as a brief introduction to Java's *serialization* feature.

For further reading on input/output in Java, we recommend Oracle's tutorial, which can be found online at:

`http://download.oracle.com/javase/tutorial/essential/io/index.html`

14.9.1 Readers, writers, and streams

Several of the classes of the `java.io` package fall into one of two main categories: those dealing with text files, and those dealing with binary files. We can think of text files as containing data in a form similar to Java's **char** type—typically simple, line-based, human-readable alphanumeric information. Web pages, written in HTML, are a particular example. Binary files are more varied: image files are one common example, as are executable programs such as word processors and media players. Java classes concerned with processing text files are known as *readers* and *writers*, whereas those concerned with binary files are known as *stream* handlers.[6] In the main, we shall focus on readers and writers.

14.9.2 The `File` class and `Path` interface

A file is much more than just a name and some contents. A file will be located in a particular *folder* or *directory* on a particular disk drive, for instance, and different operating systems have different conventions for which characters are used in file pathnames. The `File` class from `java.io` allows a program to enquire about details of an external file in a way that is independent of the particular file system on which the program is running. The name of the file is passed to the constructor of `File`. Creating a `File` object within a program does not create a file in the file system. Rather, it results in details about a file being stored in the `File` object if the external file exists.

The more modern `Path` interface and `Files` class (note the plural name) in `java.nio.file` fulfill a similar role to the legacy `File` class. Because `Path` is an interface rather than a class, a concrete instance of an implementing class is created via a static `get` method of the `Paths` class (plural again), which is also in the `java.nio.file` package. When working with legacy code, an equivalent `Path` object may be created from a `File` object via the `toPath` method of `File`.

We can sometimes avoid getting into situations that require an exception to be handled, by using the `Files` class and a `Path` object to check whether or not a file exists. The `Files` class has `exists` and `isReadable` methods, which make attempting to open a file less likely to fail if we use them first. However, because opening a file that we know exists *still* requires a potential exception to be handled, many programmers do not bother with checking first.

The `Files` class provides a large number of static methods for querying the attributes of a `Path` object.

> **Exercise 14.41** Read the API documentation for the `Files` class from the `java.nio.file` package. What sort of information is available on files/paths?
>
> **Exercise 14.42** What methods of the `Files` class tell you whether a `Path` represents an ordinary file or a directory (folder)?
>
> **Exercise 14.43** Is it possible to determine anything about *the contents* of a particular file using the `Files` class?

---

[6] It is important to note that the input-output `Stream` classes in the `java.io` package are different from the `Stream` classes in the `java.util.stream` package.

14.9.3 File output

There are three steps involved in storing data in a file:

1. The file is opened.
2. The data is written.
3. The file is closed.

The nature of file output means that any of these steps could fail, for a range of reasons, many completely beyond the application programmer's control. As a consequence, it will be necessary to anticipate exceptions being thrown at every stage.

In order to write a text file, it is usual to create a **FileWriter** object, whose constructor takes the name of the file to be written. The file name can be either in the form of a **String** or a **File** object. Creating a **FileWriter** has the effect of opening the external file and preparing it to receive some output. If the attempt to open the file fails for any reason, then the constructor will throw an **IOException**. Reasons for failure might be that file system permissions prevent a user from writing to certain files, or that the given file name does not match a valid location in the file system.

When a file has been opened successfully, then the writer's **write** methods can be used to store characters—often in the form of strings—into the file. Any attempt to write could fail, even if the file has been opened successfully. Such failures are rare, but still possible.

Once all output has been written, it is important for the file to be closed. This ensures that all the data really has been written to the external file system, and it often has the effect of freeing some internal or external resources. Once again, on rare occasions, the attempt to close the file could fail.

The basic pattern that emerges from the above discussion looks like this:

```
FileWriter writer = new FileWriter(" ... name of file ... ");
while(there is more text to write) {
    . . .
    writer.write(next piece of text);
    . . .
}
writer.close();
```

The main issue that arises is how to deal with any exceptions that are thrown during the three stages. An exception thrown when attempting to open a file is really the only one it is likely to be possible to do anything about, and only then if there is some way to generate an alternative name to try instead. As this will usually require the intervention of a human user of the application, the chances of dealing with it successfully are obviously application- and context-specific. If an attempt to write to the file fails, then it is unlikely that repeating the attempt will succeed. Similarly, failure to close a file is not usually worth a further attempt. The consequence is likely to be an incomplete file.

An example of this pattern can be seen in Code 14.19. The **LogfileCreator** class in the *weblog-analyzer* project includes a method to write a number of random log entries to a file whose name is passed as a parameter to the `createFile` method. This uses two different `write` methods: one to write a string, and one to write a character. After writing out the text of the entry as a string, we write a newline character so that each entry appears on a separate line.

Code 14.19

Writing to a text file

```java
/**
 * Create a file of random log entries.
 * @param filename The file to write.
 * @param numEntries How many entries.
 * @return true if successful, false otherwise.
 */
public boolean createFile(String filename, int numEntries)
{
    boolean success = false;
    try {
        FileWriter writer = new FileWriter(filename);
        LogEntry[] entries = new LogEntry[numEntries];
        for(int i = 0; i < numEntries; i++) {
            writer.write(entries[i].toString());
            writer.write('\n');
        }

        writer.close();
        success = true;
    }
    catch(IOException e) {
        System.err.println("There was a problem writing to " + filename);
    }
    return success;
}
```

14.9.4 The try-with-resource statement

It is important to close a file once it is finished, and there is a version of the try statement that simplifies the task of ensuring this happens. This form is called *try with resource* or *automatic resource management* (ARM). Code 14.20 shows its use with in the `Logfile-Creator` class in the *weblog-analyzer* project.

The resource object is created in a new parenthesized section immediately after the `try` word. In this case, the resource is associated with a file. Once the try statement is completed, the `close` method will be called automatically on the resource. This version of the try statement is only appropriate for objects of classes that implement the `AutoCloseable` interface, defined in the `java.lang` package. These will predominantly be classes associated with input/output.

Code 14.20

Writing to a text file using a try-with-resource statement

```java
/**
 * Create a file of random log entries.
 * @param filename The file to write.
 * @param numEntries How many entries.
 * @return true if successful, false otherwise.
 */
public boolean createFile(String filename, int numEntries)
{
    boolean success = false;
    try(FileWriter writer = new FileWriter(filename)) {
        Entry creation omitted.
        for(int i = 0; i < numEntries; i++) {
            writer.write(entries[i].toString());
            writer.write('\n');
        }
        success = true;
    }
    catch(IOException e) {
        System.err.println("There was a problem writing to " + filename);
    }
    return success;
}
```

Exercise 14.44 Modify the *world-of-zuul* project so that it writes a script of user input to a text file as a record of the game. There are several different ways that you might think of tackling this:

- You could modify the **Parser** class to store each line of input in a list and then write out the list at the end of the game. This will produce a solution that is closest to the basic pattern we have outlined in the discussion above.
- You could place all of the file handling in the **Parser** class so that, as each line is read, it is written out immediately in exactly the same form as it was read. File opening, writing, and closing will all be separated in time from one another (or would it make sense to open, write, and then close the file for every line that is written?).
- You could place the file handling in the **Game** class and implement a `toString` method in the **Command** class to return the **String** to be written for each command.

Consider each of these possible solutions in terms of responsibility-driven design and the handling of exceptions, along with the likely implications for playing the game if it proves impossible to write the script. How can you ensure that the script file is always closed when the end of the game is reached? This is important to ensure that all of the output is actually written to the external file system.

14.9.5 Text input

The complement to the output of text with a `FileWriter` is the input with a `FileReader`. As you might expect, a complementary set of three input steps is required: opening the file, reading from it, and closing it. Just as the natural units for writing text are characters and strings, the obvious units for reading text are characters and lines. However, although the `FileReader` class contains a method to read a single character,[7] it does not contain a method to read a line. The problem with reading lines from a file is that there is no predefined limit to the length of a line. This means that any method to return the next complete line from a file must be able to read an arbitrary number of characters. For this reason, we usually want to be working with the `BufferedReader` class, which does define a `readLine` method.

A `BufferedReader` is created via the static `newBufferedReader` method of the `Files` class. In addition to a `Path` parameter corresponding to the file to be opened, one complication is that a `Charset` parameter is also required. This is used to describe the character set to which the characters in the file belong. `Charset` can be found in the `java.nio.charset` package. There are a number of standard character sets, such as `US-ASCII` and `ISO-8859-1`, and more details can be found in the API documentation for `Charset`. The line-termination character is always removed from the `String` that `readLine` returns, and a `null` value is used to indicate the end of file.

This suggests the following basic pattern for reading the contents of a text file:

```
Charset charset = Charset.forName("US-ASCII");
Path path = Paths.get(filename);
BufferedReader reader =
    Files.newBufferedReader(path, charset);
String line = reader.readLine();
while(line != null) {
    do something with line
    line = reader.readLine();
}
reader.close();
```

Code 14.21 illustrates the practical use of a `BufferedReader` in the *tech-support* project from Chapter 6. This has been done so that we can read the system's default responses from a file, rather than hardwiring them into the code of the `Responder` class (project: *tech-support-io* in this chapter's folder).

As with output, the question arises as to what to do about any exceptions thrown during the whole process. In this example, we have printed an error message, then provided at least one response in case of a complete failure to read anything.

---

[7] In fact, its `read` method returns each character as an `int` value rather than as a `char`, because it uses an out-of-bounds value, -1, to indicate the end of the file. This is exactly the sort of technique we described in Section 14.3.2.

Code 14.21

Reading from a text file with a **BufferedReader**

```java
import java.io.*;
import java.nio.charset.Charset;
import java.nio.file.*;
import java.util.*;

public class Responder
{
    // Default responses to use if we don't recognize a word.
    private List<String> defaultResponses;
    // The name of the file containing the default responses.
    private static final String FILE_OF_DEFAULT_RESPONSES = "default.txt";

    Other fields and methods omitted.

    /**
     * Build up a list of default responses from which we can pick
     * if we don't know what else to say.
     */
    private void fillDefaultResponses()
    {
        Charset charset = Charset.forName("US-ASCII");
        Path path = Paths.get(FILE_OF_DEFAULT_RESPONSES);
        try (BufferedReader reader = Files.newBufferedReader(path, charset)) {
            String response = reader.readLine();
            while(response != null) {
                defaultResponses.add(response);
                response = reader.readLine();
            }
        }
        catch(FileNotFoundException e) {
            System.err.println("Unable to open " + FILE_OF_DEFAULT_RESPONSES);
        }
        catch(IOException e) {
            System.err.println("A problem was encountered reading " +
                            FILE_OF_DEFAULT_RESPONSES);
        }
        // Make sure we have at least one response.
        if(defaultResponses.size() == 0) {
            defaultResponses.add("Could you elaborate on that?");
        }
    }
}
```

There is an even simpler way of reading a complete file of text without having to use a **BufferedReader**. The **lines** method of the **Files** class takes a **Path** parameter and returns the contents of the file in the form of a **Stream<String>**. This can be processed as a stream, converted to a **String** array, or collected in an **ArrayList**, say, as required.

Exercise 14.45 The file `default.txt` in the project folder of the *tech-support-io* project contains the default responses read in by the `fillDefaultResponses` method. Using any text editor, change the content of this file so that it contains an empty line between any two responses. Then change your code to work correctly again in reading in the responses from this file.

Exercise 14.46 Change your code so that several lines of text found in the file not separated by an empty line are read as one single response. Change the `default.txt` file so that it contains some responses spanning multiple lines. Test.

Exercise 14.47 Modify the **Responder** class of the *tech-support-io* project so that it reads the associations between keywords and responses from a text file, rather than initializing `responseMap` with strings written into the source code in the `fillResponseMap` method. You can use the `fillDefaultResponses` method as a pattern, but you will need to make some changes to its logic, because there are two strings to be read for each entry rather than one—the keyword and the response. Try storing keywords and responses on alternating lines; keep the text of each response on a single line. You may assume that there will always be an even number of lines (i.e., no missing responses).

14.9.5 Scanner: parsing input

So far, we have treated input largely as unstructured lines of text, for which **BufferedReader** is the ideal class. However, many applications will then go on to decompose the individual lines into component pieces representing multi-typed data values. For instance, the comma-separated values (CSV) format is a commonly used way to store text files whose lines consist of multiple values, each of which is separated from its neighbors by a comma character.[8] In effect, such lines of text have an implicit structure. Identifying the underlying structure is known as *parsing*, while piecing the individual characters into separate data values is known as *scanning*.

The **Scanner** class, in the `java.util` package, is specifically designed to scan text and convert composite sequences of characters to typed values, such as integers (`nextInt`) and floating-point numbers (`nextDouble`). While a **Scanner** can be used to break up **String** objects, it is also often used to read and convert the contents of files directly instead of using **BufferedReader**. It has constructors that can take **String**, **File**, or **Path** arguments. Code 14.22 illustrates how a text file that is to be interpreted as containing integer data might be read in this way.

---

[8] In practice, any character can be used in place of a comma; for instance, a tab character is frequently used.

Code 14.22

Reading integer data with **Scanner**

```java
/**
 * Read integers from a file and return them as an array.
 * @param filename The file to be read.
 * @return The integers read.
 */
public int[] readInts(String filename)
{
    int[] data;
    try {
        List<Integer> values = new ArrayList<>();
        Scanner scanner = new Scanner(Paths.get(filename));
        while(scanner.hasNextInt()) {
            values.add(scanner.nextInt());
        }
        // Copy them to an array of the exact size.
        data = new int[values.size()];
        Iterator<Integer> it = values.iterator();
        int i = 0;
        while(it.hasNext()) {
            data[i] = it.next();
            i++;
        }
    }
    catch(IOException e) {
        System.out.println("Cannot find file: " + filename);
        data = new int[0];
    }
    return data;
}
```

Note that this method does not guarantee to read the whole file. The **Scanner**'s **hasNext-Int** method that controls the loop will return **false** if it encounters text in the file that does not appear to be part of an integer. At that point, the data gathering will be terminated. In fact, it is perfectly possible to mix calls to the different **next** methods when parsing a complete file, where the data it contains is to be interpreted as consisting of mixed types.

Another common use of **Scanner** is to read input from the "terminal" connected to a program. We have regularly used calls to the **print** and **println** methods of **System.out** to write text to the BlueJ terminal window. **System.out** is of type **java.io.PrintStream** and maps to what is often called the *standard output* destination. Similarly, there is a corresponding *standard input* source available as **System.in**, which is of type **java.io.InputStream**. An **Input-Stream** is not normally used directly when it is necessary to read user input from the terminal, because it delivers input one character at a time. Instead, **System.in** is usually passed to the constructor of a **Scanner**. The **InputReader** class in the *tech-support-complete* project of Chapter 6 uses this approach to read questions from the user:

```java
Scanner reader = new Scanner(System.in);
    . . . intervening code omitted . . .
String inputLine = reader.nextLine();
```

The `nextLine` method of `Scanner` returns the next complete line of input from standard input (without including the final newline character).

> **Exercise 14.48** Review the `InputReader` class of *tech-support-complete* to check that you understand how it uses the `Scanner` class.
>
> **Exercise 14.49** Read the API documentation for the `Scanner` class in the `java.util` package. What `next` methods does it have in addition to those we have discussed in this section?
>
> **Exercise 14.50** Review the `Parser` class of *zuul-better* to also see how it uses the `Scanner` class. It does so in two slightly different ways.
>
> **Exercise 14.51** Review the `LoglineTokenizer` class of *weblog-analyzer* to see how it uses a `Scanner` to extract the integer values from log lines.

14.9.7 Object serialization

Concept

Serialization allows whole objects, and object hierarchies, to be read and written in a single operation. Every object involved must be from a class that implements the **Serializable** interface.

In simple terms, serialization allows a whole object to be written to an external file in a single write operation and read back in at a later stage using a single read operation.[9] This works with both simple objects and multi-component objects such as collections. This is a significant feature that avoids having to read and write objects field by field. It is particularly useful in applications with persistent data, such as address books or media databases, because it allows all entries created in one session to be saved and then read back in at a later session. Of course, we have the choice to write out the contents of objects as text strings, but the process of reading the text back in again, converting the data to the correct types, and restoring *the exact state* of a complex set of objects is often difficult, if not impossible. Object serialization is a much more reliable process.

In order to be eligible to participate in serialization, a class must implement the `Serializable` interface that is defined in the `java.io` package. However, it is worth noting that this interface defines no methods. This means that the serialization process is managed automatically by the runtime system and requires little user-defined code to be written. In the *address-book-io* project, both `AddressBook` and `ContactDetails` implement this interface so that they can be saved to a file. The `AddressBookFileHandler` class defines the methods `saveToFile` and `readFromFile` to illustrate the serialization process. Code 14.23 contains the source of `saveToFile` to illustrate how little code is actually required to save the whole address book, in a single write statement. Note too that, because we are writing objects in binary form, a `Stream` object has been used rather than a `Writer`. The `AddressBookFileHandler` class also includes further examples of the basic reading and writing techniques used with text files. See, for instance, its `saveSearchResults` and `showSearchResults` methods.

---

[9] This is a simplification, because objects can also be written and read across a network, for instance, and not just within a file system.

Code 14.23
Serialization of a complete **Address Book** with all **Contact Details**

```java
public class AddressBookFileHandler
{

    Fields and methods omitted.

    /**
     * Save a binary version of the address book to the given file.
     * If the file name is not an absolute path, then it is assumed
     * to be relative to the current project folder.
     * @param destinationFile The file where the details are to be saved.
     * @throws IOException If the saving process fails for any reason.
     */
    public void saveToFile(String destinationFile)
        throws IOException
    {
        Path destination = Paths.get(destinationFile).toAbsolutePath();
        ObjectOutputStream os = new ObjectOutputStream(
                                    new FileOutputStream(
                                        destination.toString()));
        os.writeObject(book);
        os.close();
    }
}
```

Exercise 14.52 Modify the *network* project from Chapter 11 so that the data can be stored to a file. Use object serialization for this. Which classes do you have to declare to be serializable?

Exercise 14.53 What happens if you change the definition of a class by, say, adding an extra field, and then try to read back serialized objects created from the previous version of the class?

14.10 Summary

When two objects interact, there is always the chance that something could go wrong, for a variety of reasons. For instance:

- The programmer of a client might have misunderstood the state or the capabilities of a particular server object.

- A server object may be unable to fulfill a client's request because of a particular set of external circumstances.

- A client might have been programmed incorrectly, causing it to pass inappropriate parameter values to a server method.

If something does go wrong, a program is likely either to terminate prematurely (i.e., crash!) or to produce incorrect and undesirable effects. We can go a long way toward avoiding many of these problems by using exception throwing. This provides a clearly defined way for an object to report to a client that something has gone wrong. Exceptions prevent a client from simply ignoring the problem, and encourage programmers to try to find an alternative course of action as a workaround if something does go wrong.

When developing a class, assert statements can be used to provide internal consistency checking. These are typically omitted from production code.

Input/output is an area where exceptions are likely to occur. This is primarily because a programmer has little, if any, control over the environments in which their programs are run, but it also reflects the complexity and diversity of the environments in which programs are run.

The Java API supports input/output of both textual and binary data via readers, writers, and streams. More recent versions of Java introduced the `java.nio` packages, which supersede some of the older `java.io` classes.

Terms introduced in this chapter:

> **exception, unchecked exception, checked exception, exception handler, assertion, serialization**

> **Exercise 14.54** Add to the *address-book* project the ability to store multiple e-mail addresses in a `ContactDetails` object. All of these e-mail addresses should be valid keys. Use assertions and JUnit testing through all stages of this process to provide maximum confidence in the final version.

CHAPTER 15
Designing Applications

Main concepts discussed in this chapter:

- discovering classes
- CRC cards
- designing interfaces
- patterns

Java constructs discussed in this chapter:

(No new Java constructs are introduced in this chapter.)

In previous chapters of this book, we have described how to write good classes. We have discussed how to design them, how to make them maintainable and robust, and how to make them interact. All of this is important, but we have omitted one aspect of the task: finding the classes.

In all our previous examples, we assumed that we more or less know what the classes are that we should use to solve our problems. In a real software project, deciding what classes to use to implement a solution to a problem can be one of the most difficult tasks. In this chapter, we discuss this aspect of the development process.

These initial steps of developing a software system are generally referred to as *analysis and design*. We analyze the problem, and then we design a solution. The first step of design will be at a higher level than the class design discussed in Chapter 8. We will think about what classes we should create to solve our problem, and how exactly they should interact. Once we have a solution to this problem, then we can continue with the design of individual classes and start thinking about their implementation.

15.1 Analysis and design

Analysis and design of software systems is a large and complex problem area. Discussing it in detail is far outside the scope of this book. Many different methodologies have been described in the literature and are used in practice for this task. In this chapter, we aim only to give an introduction to the problems encountered in the process.

We will use a fairly simple method to address these tasks, which serves well for relatively small problems. To discover initial classes, we use the *verb/noun method*. Then we will use *CRC cards* to perform the initial application design.

15.1.1 The verb/noun method

> **Concept**
>
> **verb/noun**
> Classes in a system roughly correspond to nouns in the system's description. Methods correspond to verbs.

This method is all about identifying classes and objects, and the associations and interactions between them. The nouns in a human language describe "things," such as people, buildings, and so on. The verbs describe "actions," such as writing, eating, etc. From these natural-language concepts, we can see that, in a description of a programming problem, the nouns will often correspond to classes and objects, whereas the verbs will correspond to the things those objects do—that is, to methods. We do not need a very long description to be able to illustrate this technique. The description typically needs to be only a few paragraphs in length.

The example we will use to discuss this process is the design of a cinema booking system.

15.1.2 The cinema booking example

This time, we will not start by extending an existing project. We now assume that we are in a situation where it is our task to create a new application from scratch. The task is to create a system that can be used by a company operating cinemas to handle bookings of seats for movie screenings. People often call in advance to reserve seats. The application should, then, be able to find empty seats for a requested screening and reserve them for the customer.

We will assume that we have had several meetings with the cinema operators, during which they have described to us the functionality they expect from the system. (Understanding what the expected functionality is, describing it, and agreeing about it with a client is a significant problem in itself. This, however, is outside the scope of this book and can be studied in other courses and other books.)

Here is the description we wrote for our cinema booking system:

> *The cinema booking system should store seat bookings for multiple theaters. Each theater has seats arranged in rows. Customers can reserve seats and are given a row number and a seat number. They may request bookings of several adjoining seats.*
>
> *Each booking is for a particular show (that is, the screening of a given movie at a certain time). Shows are at an assigned date and time and are scheduled for a theater where they are screened. The system stores the customer's telephone number.*

Given a reasonably clear description such as this, we can make a first attempt at discovering classes and methods by identifying the nouns and verbs in the text.

15.1.3 Discovering classes

The first step in identifying the classes is to go through the description and mark all the nouns and verbs in the text. Doing this, we find the following nouns and verbs. (The nouns are shown in the order in which they appear in the text; verbs are shown attached to the nouns they refer to.)

15.1 Analysis and design

Nouns

cinema booking system

seat booking

theater

seat

row

customer

row number

seat number

show

movie

date

time

telephone number

Verbs

stores (seat bookings)

stores (telephone number)

has (seats)

reserves (seats)

is given (row number, seat number)

requests (seat booking)

is scheduled (in theater)

The nouns we identified here give us a first approximation for classes in our system. As a first cut, we can use one class for each noun. This is not an exact method; we might find later that we need a few additional classes or that some of our nouns are not needed. This, however, we will test a bit later. It is important not to exclude any nouns straight away; we do not yet have enough information to make an informed decision.

When we do this exercise with students, some students immediately leave out some nouns. For example, a student leaves out the noun *row* from the previous description. When questioned about this, students often say: "Well, that's just a number, so I just use an `int`. That doesn't need a class." It is really important at this stage not to do this. We really do not have enough information at this point to decide whether *row* should be an `int` or a class. We can make this decision only much later. For now, we just go through the paragraph mechanically, picking out *all* nouns. We make no judgments yet about which are "good ones" and which are not.

You might note that all of the nouns have been written in their singular form. It is typical that the names of classes are singular rather than plural. For instance, we would always choose to define a class as **Cinema** rather than **Cinemas**. This is because the multiplicity is achieved by creating multiple instances of a class.

Exercise 15.1 Review projects from earlier chapters in this book. Are there any cases of a class name being a plural name? If so, are those situations justified for a particular reason?

15.1.4 Using CRC cards

The next step in our design process is to work out interactions between our classes. In order to do this, we shall use a method called *CRC cards*.[1]

CRC stands for Class/Responsibilities/Collaborators. The idea is to take cardboard cards (normal index cards do a good job) and use one card for each class. It is important for this activity to do this using real, physical cards, not just a computer or a single sheet of paper. Each card is divided into three areas: one area at the top left, where the name of the class is written; one area below this, to note responsibilities of the class; and one area to the right for writing collaborators of this class (classes that this one uses). Figure 15.1 illustrates the layout of a CRC card.

Figure 15.1
A CRC card

Exercise 15.2 Make CRC cards for the classes in the cinema booking system. At this stage, you need only fill in the class names.

15.1.5 Scenarios

Concept

Scenarios (also known as "use cases") can be used to get an understanding of the interactions in a system.

Now we have a first approximation of the classes needed in our system, and a physical representation of them on CRC cards. In order to figure out necessary interactions between the classes in our system, we play through *scenarios*. A scenario is an example of an activity that the system has to carry out or support. Scenarios are also referred to as *use cases*. We do not use that term here because it is often used to denote a more formal way of describing scenarios.

Playing through scenarios is best done in a group. Each group member is assigned one class (or a small number of classes), and that person plays their role by saying out loud what the class is currently doing. While the scenario is played through, the person records on the CRC card everything that is found out about the class in action: what its responsibilities should be and which other classes it collaborates with.

---

[1] CRC cards were first described in a paper by Kent Beck and Ward Cunningham, titled *A Laboratory For Teaching Object-Oriented Thinking*. This paper is worth reading as information supplemental to this chapter. You can find it online at **http://c2.com/doc/oopsla89/paper.html** or by doing a web search for its title.

We start with a simple example scenario:

> A customer calls the cinema and wants to make a reservation for a seats tonight to watch the classic movie *The Shawshank Redemption*. The cinema employee starts using the booking system to find and reserve two seats.

Because the human user interacts with the booking system (represented by the `CinemaBookingSystem` class), this is where the scenario starts. Here is what might happen next:

- The user (the cinema employee) wants to find all showings of *The Shawshank Redemption* that are on tonight. So we can note on the `CinemaBookingSystem` CRC card, as a responsibility: *Can find shows by title and day*. We can also record class `Show` as a collaborator.

- We have to ask ourselves: How does the system find the show? Who does it ask? One solution might be that the `CinemaBookingSystem` stores a collection of shows. This gives us an additional class: the collection. (This might be implemented later by using an `ArrayList`, a `LinkedList`, a `HashSet`, or some other form of collection with additional methods appropriate to showings. We can make that decision later; for now, we just note this as a `ShowCollection`.) This is an example of how we might introduce additional classes during the playing of scenarios. It might happen every now and then that we have to add classes for implementation reasons that we initially overlooked. We add to the responsibilities of the `CinemaBookingSystem` card: *Stores collection of shows*. And we add `ShowCollection` to the collaborators.

Exercise 15.3 Make a CRC card for the newly identified `ShowCollection` class, and add it to your system.

- We assume that three shows come up: one at 5:30 p.m., one at 9:00 p.m., and one at 11:30 p.m. The employee informs the customer of the times, and the customer chooses the one at 9:00 p.m. So the employee wants to check the details of that show (whether it is sold out, which theater it runs at, etc.). Thus, in our system, the `CinemaBookingSystem` must be able to retrieve and display the show's details. Play this through. The person playing the booking system should ask the person playing the show to tell them the required details. Then we note on the card for `CinemaBookingSystem`: *Retrieves and displays show details*, and on the `Show` card you write: *Provides details about theater and number of free seats*.

- Assume that there are plenty of free seats. The customer chooses seats 13 and 14 in row 12. The employee makes that reservation. We note on the `CinemaBookingSystem` card: *Accepts seat reservations from user*.

- We now have to play through exactly how the seat reservation works. A seat reservation is clearly attached to a particular show, so the `CinemaBookingSystem` should probably tell the show about the reservation; it delegates the actual task of making the reservation to the `Show` object. We can note for the `Show` class: *Can reserve seats*. (You may have noticed that the notion of objects and classes is blurred when playing through CRC scenarios. In effect, the person representing a class is representing its instances too. This is intentional and not usually a problem.)

- Now it is the **Show** class's turn. It has received a request to reserve a seat. What exactly does it do? To be able to store seat reservations, it must have a representation of the seats in the theater. So we assume that each show has a link to a **Theater** object. (Note this on the card: *Stores theater*. This is also a collaborator.) The theater should probably know about the exact number and arrangement of seats it has. (We can also note in the back of our heads, or on a separate piece of paper, that each show must have its own instance of the **Theater** object, because several shows can be scheduled for the same **Theater** and reserving a seat in one does not reserve the same seat for another show. This is something to look out for when **Show** objects are created. We have to keep this in mind so that later, when we play through the scenario of *Scheduling a new show*, we remember to create a theater instance for each show.) The way a show deals with reserving a seat is probably by passing this reservation request on to the theater.

- Now the theater has accepted a request to make a reservation. (Note this on the card: *Accepts reservation request*.) How does it deal with it? The theater could have a collection of seats in it. Or it could have a collection of rows (each row being a separate object), and rows, in turn, hold seats. Which of these alternatives is better? Thinking ahead about other possible scenarios, we might decide to go with the idea of storing rows. If, for example, a customer requests four seats together in the same row, it might be easier to find four adjacent seats if we have them all arranged by rows. We note on the **Theater** card: *Stores rows*. **Row** is now a collaborator.

- We note on the **Row** class: *Stores collection of seats*. And then we note a new collaborator: **Seat**.

- Getting back to the **Theater** class, we have not yet worked out exactly how it should react to the seat reservation request. Let us assume it does two things: find the requested row and then make a reservation request with the seat number to the **Row** object.

- Next, we note on the **Row** card: *Accepts reservation request for seat*. It must then find the right **Seat** object (we can note that as a responsibility: *Can find seats by number*) and can make a reservation for that seat. It would do so by telling the **Seat** object that it is now reserved.

- We can now add to the **Seat** card: *Accepts reservations*. The seat itself can remember whether it has been reserved. We note on the **Seat** card: *Stores reservation status (free/reserved)*.

> **Exercise 15.4** Play this scenario through on your cards (with a group of people, if possible). Add any other information you feel was left out in this description.

Should the seat also store information about who has reserved it? It could store the name of the customer or the telephone number. Or maybe we should create a **Customer** object as soon as someone makes a reservation, and store the **Customer** object with the seat once the seat has been reserved? These are interesting questions, and we will try to work out the best solution by playing through more scenarios.

This was just the first, simple scenario. We need to play through many more scenarios to get a better understanding of how the system should work.

Playing through scenarios works best when a group of people sit around a table and move the cards around on it. Cards that cooperate closely can be placed close together to give an impression of the degree of coupling in the system.

Other scenarios to play through next would include the following:

- A customer requests five seats together. Work out exactly how five adjoining seats are found.
- A customer calls and says he forgot the seat numbers he was given for the reservation he made yesterday. Could you please look up the seat numbers again?
- A customer calls to cancel a reservation. He can give his name and the show, but has forgotten the seat numbers.
- A customer calls who already has a reservation. She wants to know whether she can reserve another seat next to the ones she already has.
- A show is canceled. The cinema wants to call all customers that have reserved a seat for that show.

These scenarios should give you a good understanding of the seat lookup and reservation part of the system. Then we need another group of scenarios: those dealing with setting up the theater, and scheduling shows. Here are some possible scenarios:

- The system has to be set up for a new cinema. The cinema has two theaters, each of a different size. Theater A has 26 rows with 18 seats each. Theater B has 32 rows. In this theater, the first six rows have 20 seats, the next 10 rows have 22 seats, and the other rows have 26 seats.
- A new movie is scheduled for screening. It will be screened for the next two weeks, three times each day (4:40 p.m., 6:30 p.m., and 8:30 p.m.). The shows have to be added to the system. All shows run in theater A.

Exercise 15.5 Play through these scenarios. Note on a separate piece of paper all the questions you have left unanswered. Make a record of all scenarios you have played through.

Exercise 15.6 What other scenarios can you think of? Write them down, and then play them out.

Playing through scenarios takes some patience and some practice. It is important to spend enough time doing this. Playing through the scenarios mentioned here could take several hours.

It is very common for beginners to take shortcuts and not question and record every detail about the execution of a scenario. This is dangerous! We will soon move on to developing this system in Java, and if details are left unanswered, it is very likely that *ad hoc* decisions will be made at implementation time that could later turn out to be poor choices.

It is also common for beginners to forget some scenarios. Forgetting to think through a part of the system before starting the class design and implementation can cause a large amount of work later, when an already partially implemented system would have to be changed.

Doing this activity well, carefully stepping through all necessary steps, and recording steps in sufficient detail takes some practice and a lot of discipline. This exercise is harder than it looks and more important than you realize.

> **Exercise 15.7** Make a class design for an airport-control-system simulation. Use CRC cards and scenarios. Here is a description of the system:
>
> The program is an airport simulation system. For our new airport, we need to know whether we can operate with two runways or whether we need three. The airport works as follows:
>
> There are multiple runways. Planes take off and land on runways. Air traffic controllers coordinate the traffic and give planes permission to take off or land. The controllers sometimes give permission right away, but sometimes they tell planes to wait. Planes must keep a certain distance from one another. The purpose of the program is to simulate the airport in operation.

15.2 Class design

Now it is time for the next big step: moving from CRC cards to Java classes. During the CRC card exercise, you should have gained a good understanding of how your application is structured and how your classes cooperate to solve the program's tasks. You may have come across cases where you had to introduce additional classes (this is often the case with classes that represent internal data structures), and you may have noticed that you have a card for a class that was never used. If the latter is the case, this card can now be removed.

Recognizing the classes for the implementation is now trivial. The cards show us the complete set of classes we need. Deciding on the interface of each class (that is, the set of public methods that a class should have) is a bit harder, but we have made an important step toward that as well. If the playing of the scenarios was done well, then the responsibilities noted for each class describe the class's public methods (and maybe some of the instance fields). The responsibilities of each class should be evaluated according to the class design principles discussed in Chapter 8: Responsibility-Driven Design, Coupling, and Cohesion.

15.2.1 Designing class interfaces

Before starting to code our application in Java, we can once more use the cards to make another step toward the final design by translating the informal descriptions into method calls and adding parameters.

To arrive at more formal descriptions, we can now play through the scenarios again, this time talking in terms of method calls, parameters, and return values. The logic and the structure of the application should not change any more, but we try to note complete information about method signatures and instance fields. We do this on a new set of cards.

Exercise 15.8 Make a new set of CRC cards for the classes you have identified. Play through the scenarios again. This time, note exact method names for each method you call from another class, and specify in detail (with type and name) all parameters that are passed and the methods' return values. The method signatures are written on the CRC card instead of the responsibilities. On the back of the card, note the instance fields that each class holds.

Once we have done the exercise described above, writing each class's interface is easy. We can translate directly from the cards into Java. Typically, all classes should be created and *method stubs* for all public methods should be written. A method stub is a placeholder for the method that has the correct signature and an empty method body.[2]

Many students find doing this in detail tedious. At the end of the project, however, you will hopefully come to appreciate the value of these activities. Many software development teams have realized after the fact that time saved at the design stage had to be spent many times over to fix mistakes or omissions that were not discovered early enough.

Inexperienced programmers often view the writing of the code as the "real programming." Doing the initial design is seen as, if not superfluous, at least annoying, and people cannot wait to get it over with so that the "real work" can start. This is a very misguided picture.

The initial design is one of the most important parts of the project. You should plan to spend at least as much time working on the design as on the implementation. Application design is not something that comes before the programming—it *is* (the most important part of) programming!

Mistakes in the code itself can later be fixed fairly easily. Mistakes in the overall design can, at best, be expensive to put right and, at worst, be fatal to the whole application. In unlucky cases, they can be almost unfixable (short of starting all over again).

---

[2] If you wish, you can include trivial return statements in the bodies of methods with non-**void** return types. Just return a **null** value for object-returning methods and a zero, or **false**, value for primitive types.

15.2.2 User interface design

One part that we have left out of the discussion so far is the design of the user interface.[3] At some stage, we have to decide in detail what users see on the screen and how they interact with our system.

In a well-designed application, this is quite independent of the underlying logic of the application, so it can be done independently of designing the class structure for the rest of the project. As we saw in the previous chapters, BlueJ gives us the means of interacting with our application before a final user interface is available, so we can choose to work on the internal structure first.

The user interface may be a GUI (graphical user interface) with menus and buttons, it can be text based, or we can decide to run the application using the BlueJ method-call mechanism. Maybe the system runs over a network, and the user interface is presented in a web browser on a different machine.

For now, we shall ignore the user-interface design and use BlueJ method invocation to work with our program.

15.3 Documentation

After identifying the classes and their interfaces, and before starting to implement the methods of a class, the interface should be documented. This involves writing a class comment and method comments for each class in the project. These should be described in sufficient detail to identify the overall purpose of each class and method.

Along with analysis and design, documentation is a further area that is often neglected by beginners. It is not easy for inexperienced programmers to see why documentation is so important. The reason is that inexperienced programmers usually work on projects that only have a handful of classes and are written in the span of a few weeks or months. A programmer can get away with bad documentation when working on these mini-projects.

However, even experienced programmers often wonder how it is possible to write the documentation before the implementation. This is because they fail to appreciate that good documentation focuses on high-level issues such as what a class or method does rather than on low-level issues such as exactly how it is done. This is usually symptomatic of viewing the implementation as being more important than the design.

If a software developer wants to progress to more interesting problems and starts to work professionally on real-life applications, it is not unusual to work with dozens of other people on an application over several years. The *ad hoc* solution of just "having the documentation in your head" does not work anymore.

---

[3] Note carefully the double meaning of the term *designing interfaces* here! Above, we were talking about the interfaces of single classes (a set of public methods); now, we talk about the *user interface*—what the user sees on screen to interact with the application. Both are very important issues, and unfortunately the term *interface* is used for both.

Exercise 15.9 Create a BlueJ project for the cinema booking system. Create the necessary classes. Create method stubs for all methods.

Exercise 15.10 Document all classes and methods. If you have worked in a group, assign responsibilities for classes to different group members. Use the `javadoc` format for comments, with appropriate `javadoc` tags to document the details.

15.4 Cooperation

> **Pair programming** Implementation of classes is traditionally done alone. Most programmers work on their own when writing the code, and other people are brought in only after the implementation is finished, to test or review the code.
>
> More recently, pair programming has been suggested as an alternative that is intended to produce better-quality code (code with better structure and fewer bugs). Pair programming is also one of the elements of a technique known as *Extreme Programming*. Do a web search for "pair programming" or "extreme programming" to find out more.

Software development is usually done in teams. A clean object-oriented approach provides strong support for teamwork, because it allows for the separation of the problem into loosely coupled components (classes) that can be implemented independently.

Although the initial design work was best done in a group, it is now time to split it up. If the definition of the class interfaces and the documentation was done well, it should be possible to implement the classes independently. Classes can now be assigned to programmers, who can work on them alone or in pairs.

In the remainder of this chapter, we shall not discuss the implementation phase of the cinema booking system in detail. That phase largely involves the sorts of task we have been doing throughout this book in previous chapters, and we hope that by now readers can determine for themselves how to continue from here.

15.5 Prototyping

Instead of designing and then building the complete application in one giant leap, *prototyping* can be used to investigate parts of a system.

A prototype is a version of the application where one part is simulated in order to experiment with other parts. You may, for example, implement a prototype to test a graphical user interface. In that case, the logic of the application may not be properly implemented. Instead, we would write simple implementations for those methods that simulate the task. For example, when calling a method to find a free seat in the cinema system, a method could always return *seat 3, row 15* instead of actually implementing the search. Prototyping allows us to

> **Concept**
>
> **Prototyping** is the construction of a partially working system in which some functions of the application are simulated. It serves to provide an understanding early in the development process of how the system will work.

quickly develop an executable (but not fully functional) system so that we can investigate parts of the application in practice.

Prototypes are also useful for single classes to aid a team development process. Often when different team members work on different classes, not all classes take the same amount of time to be completed. In some cases, a missing class can hold up continuation of development and testing of other classes. In those cases, it can be beneficial to write a class prototype. The prototype has implementations of all method stubs, but instead of containing full, final implementations, the prototype only simulates the functionality. Writing a prototype should be possible quickly, and development of client classes can then continue using the prototype until the class is implemented.

As we discuss in Section 15.6, one additional benefit of prototyping is that it can give the developers insights into issues and problems that were not considered at an earlier stage.

> **Exercise 15.11** Outline a prototype for your cinema-system example. Which of the classes should be implemented first, and which should remain in prototype stage?
>
> **Exercise 15.12** Implement your cinema-system prototype.

15.6 Software growth

Several models exist for how software should be built. One of the most commonly known is often referred to as the *waterfall model* (because activity progresses from one level to the next, like water in a cascading waterfall—there is no going back).

15.6.1 Waterfall model

In the waterfall model, several phases of software development are done in a fixed sequence:

- analysis of the problem
- design of the software
- implementation of the software components
- unit testing
- integration testing
- delivery of the system to the client

If any phase fails, we might have to step back to the previous phase to fix it (for example, if testing shows failure, we go back to implementation), but there is never a plan to revisit earlier phases.

This is probably the most traditional, conservative model of software development, and it has been in widespread use for a long time. However, numerous problems have been discovered with this model over the years. Two of the main flaws are that it assumes that developers understand the full extent of the system's functionality in detail from the start, and that the system does not change after delivery.

In practice, both assumptions are typically not true. It is quite common that the design of a system's functionality is not perfect at the start. This is often because the client, who knows the problem domain, does not know much about computing, and because the software engineers, who know how to program, have only limited knowledge of the problem domain.

15.6.2 Iterative development

One possibility to address the problems of the waterfall model is to use early prototyping and frequent client interaction in the development process. Prototypes of the systems are built that do not do much, but give an impression of what the system would look like and what it would do, and clients comment regularly on the design and functionality. This leads to a more circular process than the waterfall model. Here, the software development iterates several times through an *analysis/design/prototype -implementation–client-feedback* cycle.

Another approach is captured in the notion that good software is not designed, it is *grown*. The idea behind this is to design a small and clean system initially and get it into a working state in which it can be used by end users. Then additional features are gradually added (the software grows) in a controlled manner, and "finished" states (meaning states in which the software is completely usable and can be delivered to clients) are reached repeatedly and fairly frequently.

In reality, growing software is, of course, not a contradiction to designing software. Every growth step is carefully designed. What the software growth model does not try to do is design the complete software system right from the start. Even more, the notion of a complete software system does not exist at all!

The traditional waterfall model has as its goal the delivery of a complete system. The software growth model assumes that complete systems that are used indefinitely in an unchanged state do not exist. There are only two things that can happen to a software system: either it is continuously improved and adapted, or it will disappear.

This discussion is central to this book, because it strongly influences how we view the tasks and skills required of a programmer or software engineer. You might be able to tell that the authors of this book strongly favor the iterative development model over the waterfall model.[4]

As a consequence, certain tasks and skills become much more important than they would be in the waterfall model. Software maintenance, code reading (rather than just writing),

---

[4] An excellent book describing the problems of software development and some possible approaches to solutions is *The Mythical Man-Month* by Frederick P. Brooks Jr., Addison-Wesley. Even though the original edition is 40 years old, it makes for entertaining and very enlightening reading.

designing for extensibility, documentation, coding for understandability, and many other issues we have mentioned in this book take their importance from the fact that we know there will be others coming after us who have to adapt and extend our code.

Viewing a piece of software as a continuously growing, changing, adapting entity, rather than a static piece of text that is written and preserved like a novel, determines our views about how good code should be written. All the techniques we have discussed throughout this book work toward this.

> **Exercise 15.13** In which ways might the cinema booking system be adapted or extended in the future? Which changes are more likely than others? Write down a list of possible future changes.
>
> **Exercise 15.14** Are there any other organizations that might use booking systems similar to the one we have discussed? What significant differences exist between the systems?
>
> **Exercise 15.15** Do you think it would be possible to design a "generic" booking system that could be adapted or customized for use in a wide range of different organizations with booking needs? If you were to create such a system, at what point in the development process of the cinema system would you introduce changes? Or would you throw that one away and start again from scratch?

15.7 Using design patterns

In earlier chapters, we have discussed in detail some techniques for reusing some of our work and making our code more understandable to others. So far, a large part of these discussions has remained at the level of source code in single classes.

> **Concept**
>
> A **design pattern** is a description of a common computing problem and a description of a small set of classes and their interaction structure that help to solve that problem.

As we become more experienced and move on to design larger software systems, the implementation of single classes is not the most difficult problem any more. The structure of the overall system—the complex relationships between classes—becomes harder to design and to understand than the code of individual classes.

It is a logical step that we should try to achieve the same goals for class structures that we attempted for source code. We want to reuse good bits of work, and we want to enable others to understand what we have done.

At the level of class structures, both these goals can be served by using *design patterns*. A design pattern describes a common problem that occurs regularly in software development and then describes a general solution to that problem that can be used in many different contexts. For software design patterns, the solution is typically a description of a small set of classes and their interactions.

Design patterns help in our task in two ways. First, they document good solutions to problems so that these solutions can be reused later for similar problems. The reuse in this case is not at the level of source code, but at the level of class structures.

Second, design patterns have names and thus establish a vocabulary that helps software designers talk about their designs. When experienced designers discuss the structure of an application, one might say, "I think we should use a Singleton here." *Singleton* is the name of a widely known design pattern, so if both designers are familiar with the pattern, being able to talk about it at this level saves explanation of a lot of detail. Thus, the pattern language introduced by commonly known design patterns introduces another level of abstraction, one that allows us to cope with complexity in ever-more-complex systems.

Software design patterns were made popular by a book published in 1995 that describes a set of patterns, their applications, and benefits.[5] This book is still today one of the most important works about design patterns. Here, we do not attempt to give a complete overview of design patterns. Rather, we discuss a small number of patterns to give readers an impression of the benefits of using design patterns, and then we leave it up to the reader to continue the study of patterns in other literature.

15.7.1 Structure of a pattern

Descriptions of patterns are usually recorded using a template that contains some minimum information. A pattern description is not only information about a structure of some classes, but also includes a description of the problem(s) this pattern addresses and competing forces for or against use of the pattern.

A description of a pattern includes at least:

- a **name** that can be used to conveniently talk about the pattern
- a description of the **problem** that the pattern addresses (often split into sections such as *intent*, *motivation*, and *applicability*)
- a description of the **solution** (often listing *structure*, *participants*, and *collaborations*)
- the **consequences** of using the pattern, including results and trade-offs

In the following section, we shall briefly discuss some commonly used patterns.

15.7.2 Decorator

The *Decorator* pattern deals with the problem of adding functionality to an existing object. We assume that we want an object that responds to the same method calls (has the same interface) as the existing object, but has added or altered behavior. We may also want to add to the existing interface.

One way this could be done is by using inheritance. A subclass may override the implementation of methods and add additional methods. But using inheritance is a static solution: once created, objects cannot change their behavior.

A more dynamic solution is the use of a Decorator object. The Decorator is an object that encloses an existing object and can be used instead of the original (it usually implements

---

[5] *Design Patterns: Elements of Reusable Object-Oriented Software* by Erich Gamma, Richard Helm, Ralph Johnson, and John Vlissides, Addison-Wesley, 1995.

Figure 15.2

Structure of the decorator pattern

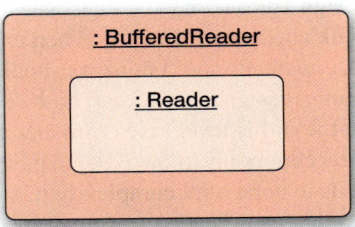

the same interface). Clients then communicate with the Decorator instead of with the original object directly (without a need to know about this substitution). The Decorator passes the method calls on to the enclosed object, but it may perform additional actions. We can find an example in the Java input/output library. There, a **BufferedReader** is used as a Decorator for a **Reader** (Figure 15.2). The **BufferedReader** implements the same interface and can be used instead of an unbuffered **Reader**, but it adds to the basic behavior of a **Reader**. In contrast to using inheritance, decorators can be added to existing objects.

15.7.3 Singleton

A common situation in many programs is to have an object of which there should be only a single instance. In our *world-of-zuul* game, for instance, we want only a single parser. If we write a software development environment, we might want only a single compiler or a single debugger.

The *Singleton* pattern ensures that only one instance will be created from a class, and it provides unified access to it. In Java, a Singleton can be defined by making the constructor private. This ensures that it cannot be called from outside the class, and thus client classes cannot create new instances. We can then write code in the Singleton class itself to create a single instance and provide access to it (Code 15.1 illustrates this for a **Parser** class).

Code 15.1

The Singleton pattern

```
public class Parser
{
    private static Parser instance = new Parser();

    public static Parser getInstance()
    {
        return instance;
    }

    private Parser()
    {
        ...
    }
}
```

In this pattern:

- The constructor is private so that instances can be created only by the class itself. This has to be in a static part of the class (initializations of static fields or static methods), because no instance will otherwise exist.
- A private static field is defined and initialized with the (sole) instance of the parser.
- A static `getInstance` method is defined, which provides access to the single instance.

Clients of the Singleton can now use that static method to gain access to the parser object:

```
Parser parser = Parser.getInstance();
```

In fact, Java offers an even easier way to obtain the fundamental features of a singleton—an enum with a single value (Code 15.2).

Code 15.2 A Singleton definition using a Java enum

```
public enum Parser
{
    INSTANCE;

    Parser-specific methods added here.

}
```

The singleton instance would then be accessed as `Parser.INSTANCE`. Since arbitrary additional functionality can be included in an enum definition in the same way as in a class, this approach, rather than a hand-crafted approach, is well worth considering in Java.

15.7.4 Factory method

The *Factory method* pattern provides an interface for creating objects, but lets subclasses decide which specific class of object is created. Typically, the client expects a superclass or an interface of the actual object's dynamic type, and the factory method provides specializations.

Iterators of collections are an example of this technique. If we have a variable of type `Collection`, we can ask it for an `Iterator` object (using the `iterator` method) and then work with that iterator (Code 15.3). The `iterator` method in this example is the Factory method.

Code 15.3 A use of the Factory method

```
public void process(Collection<Type> coll)
{
    Iterator<Type> it = coll.iterator();
    ...
}
```

From the client's point of view (in the code shown in Code 15.3), we are dealing with objects of type `Collection` and `Iterator`. In reality, the (dynamic) type of the collection may be `ArrayList`, in which case the `iterator` method returns an object of type `ArrayList-Iterator`. Or it may be a `HashSet`, and `iterator` returns a `HashSetIterator`. The Factory method is specialized in subclasses to return specialized instances to the "official" return type.

We can make good use of this pattern in our *foxes-and-rabbits* simulation from Chapter 12, to decouple the `Simulator` class from the specific animal classes. (Remember: In our version, `Simulator` was coupled to classes `Fox` and `Rabbit`, because it creates the initial instances.) Instead, we can introduce an interface `ActorFactory` and classes implementing this interface for each actor (for example, `FoxFactory` and `RabbitFactory`). The `Simulator` would simply store a collection of `ActorFactory` objects, and it would ask each of them to produce a number of actors. Each factory would, of course, produce a different kind of actor, but the `Simulator` talks to them via the `ActorFactory` interface.

15.7.5 Observer

In the discussions of several of the projects in this book, we have tried to separate the internal model of the application from the way it is presented on screen (the view). The *Observer* pattern provides one way of achieving this model/view separation.

More generally, the Observer pattern defines a one-to-many relationship so that when one object changes its state, many others can be notified. It achieves this with a very low degree of coupling between the observers and the observed object.

The Observer pattern not only supports a decoupled view on the model, but it also allows for multiple different views (either as alternatives or simultaneously). As an example, we can again use our *foxes-and-rabbits* simulation.

In the simulation, we presented the animal populations on screen in a two-dimensional animated grid. There are other possibilities. We might have preferred to show the population as a graph of population numbers along a timeline, or as an animated bar chart (Figure 15.3). We might even like to see all representations at the same time.

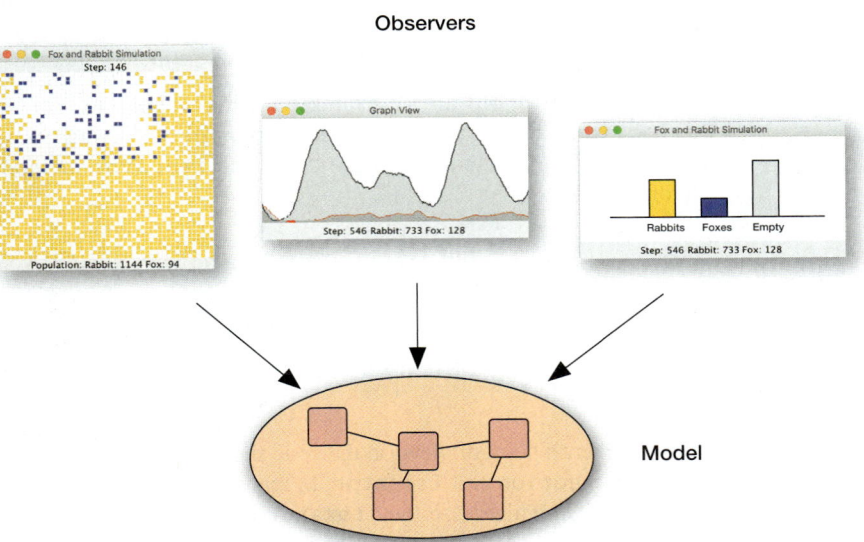

Figure 15.3
Multiple views of one subject

Figure 15.4
Structure of the Observer pattern

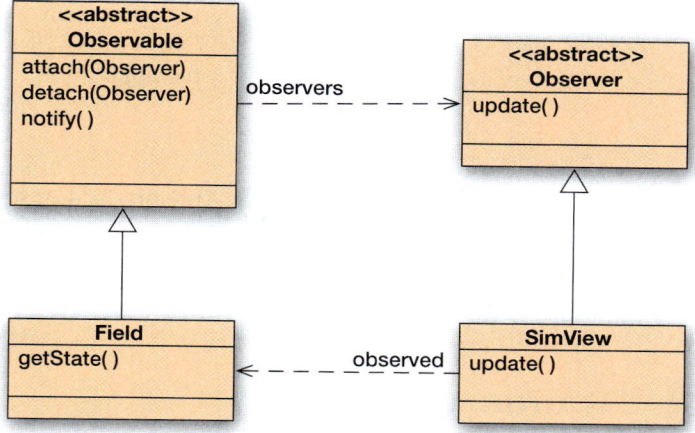

For the Observer pattern, we use two types: **Observable** and **Observer**.[6] The observable entity (the **Field** in our simulation) extends the **Observable** class, and the observer (**SimulatorView**) implements the **Observer** interface (Figure 15.4).

The **Observable** class provides methods for observers to attach themselves to the observed entity. It ensures that the observers' **update** method is called whenever the observed entity (the field) invokes its inherited **notify** method. The actual observers (the viewers) can then get a new, updated state from the field and redisplay.

The Observer pattern can also be used for problems other than a model/view separation. It can always be applied when the state of one or more objects depends on the state of another object.

15.7.6 Pattern summary

Discussing design patterns and their applications in detail is beyond the scope of this book. Here, we have presented only a brief idea of what design patterns are, and we have given an informal description of some of the more common patterns.

We hope, however, that this discussion serves to show where to go from here. Once we understand how to create good implementations of single classes with well-defined functionality, we can concentrate on deciding what kinds of classes we should have in our application and how they should cooperate. Good solutions are not always obvious, so design patterns describe structures that have proven useful over and over again for solving recurring classes of problems. They help us in creating good class structures.

The more experienced you get as a software developer, the more time you will spend thinking about higher-level structure rather than about implementation of single methods.

---

[6] In the Java **java.util** package, **Observer** is actually an interface with a single method, **update**.

Exercise 15.16 Three additional commonly used patterns are the *State* pattern, the *Strategy* pattern, and the *Visitor* pattern. Find descriptions of each of these, and identify at least one example application for each.

Exercise 15.17 Late in the development of a project, you find that two teams who have been working independently on two parts of an application have implemented incompatible classes. The interface of several classes implemented by one team is slightly different from the interface the other team is expecting to use. Explain how the *Adapter* pattern might help in this situation by avoiding the need to rewrite any of the existing classes.

15.8 Summary

In this chapter, we have moved up one step in terms of abstraction levels, away from thinking about the design of single classes (or cooperation between two classes) and toward the design of an application as a whole. Central to the design of an object-oriented software system is the decision about the classes to use for its implementation and the communication structures between these classes.

Some classes are fairly obvious and easy to discover. We have used as a starting point a method of identifying nouns and verbs in a textual description of the problem. After discovering the classes, we can use CRC cards and played-out scenarios to design the dependences and communication details between classes, and to flesh out details about each class's responsibilities. For less-experienced designers, it helps to play through scenarios in a group.

CRC cards can be used to refine the design down to the definition of method names and their parameters. Once this has been achieved, classes with method stubs can be coded in Java and the classes' interfaces can be documented.

Following an organized process such as this one serves several purposes. It ensures that potential problems with early design ideas are discovered before much time is invested in implementation. It also enables programmers to work on the implementation of several classes independently, without having to wait for the implementation of one class to be finished before implementation of another can begin.

Flexible, extensible class structures are not always easy to design. Design patterns are used to document generally good structures that have proven useful in the implementation of different classes of problems. Through the study of design patterns, a software engineer can learn a lot about good application structures and improve application design skills.

The larger a problem, the more important is a good application structure. The more experienced a software engineer becomes, the more time he or she will spend designing application structures rather than just writing code.

Terms introduced in this chapter:

> **analysis and design, verb/noun method, CRC card, scenario, use case, method stub, design pattern**

Exercise 15.18 Assume that you have a school management system for your school. In it, there is a class called **Database** (a fairly central class) that holds objects of type **Student**. Each student has an address that is held in an **Address** object (i.e., each **Student** object holds a reference to an **Address** object).

Now, from the **Database** class, you need to get access to a student's street, city, and zip code. The **Address** class has accessor methods for these. For the design of the **Student** class, you now have two choices:

Either you implement **getStreet**, **getCity**, and **getZipCode** methods in the **Student** class—which just pass the method call on to the **Address** object and hand the result back—or you implement a **getAddress** method in **Student** that returns the complete **Address** object to the **Database** and lets the **Database** object call the **Address** object's methods directly.

Which of these alternatives is better? Why? Make a class diagram for each situation and list arguments either way.

CHAPTER 16
A Case Study

> **Main concepts discussed in this chapter:**
>
> - whole-application development
>
> **Java constructs discussed in this chapter:**
>
> (No new Java constructs are introduced in this chapter.)

In this chapter, we draw together many of the object-oriented principles that we have introduced in this book by presenting an extended case study. We shall take the study from the initial discussion of a problem, through class discovery, design, and an iterative process of implementation and testing. Unlike previous chapters, it is not our intention here to introduce any major new topics. Rather, we are seeking to reinforce those topics that have been covered in the second half of the book, such as inheritance, abstraction techniques, error handling, and application design.

16.1 The case study

The case study we will be using is the development of a model for a taxi company. The company is considering whether to expand its operations into a new part of a city. It operates taxis and shuttles. Taxis drop their passengers at their target locations before taking on new passengers. Shuttles may collect several passengers from different locations on the same trip, taking them to similar locations (such as collecting several guests from different hotels and taking them to different terminals at the airport). Based on estimates of the number of potential customers in the new area, the company wishes to know whether an expansion would be profitable, and how many cabs it would need in the new location in order to operate effectively.

16.1.1 The problem description

The following paragraph presents an informal description of the taxi company's operating procedures, arrived at following several meetings with them.

The company operates both individual taxis and shuttles. The taxis are used to transport an individual (or small group) from one location to another. The shuttles are used to pick up individuals from different locations and transport them to their several destinations. When the company receives a call from an individual, hotel, entertainment venue, or tourist organization, it tries to schedule a vehicle to pick up the fare. If it has no free vehicles, it does not operate any form of queuing system. When a vehicle arrives at a pickup location, the driver notifies the company. Similarly, when a passenger is dropped off at their destination, the driver notifies the company.

As we suggested in Chapter 12, one of the common purposes of modeling is to help us learn something about the situation being modeled. It is useful to identify at an early stage what we wish to learn, because the resulting goals may well have an influence on the design we produce. For instance, if we are seeking to answer questions about the profitability of running taxis in this area, then we must ensure that we can obtain information from the model that will help us assess profitability. Two issues we ought to consider, therefore, are: how often potential customers are lost because no vehicle is available to collect them, and, at the opposite extreme, how much time taxis remain idle for lack of passengers. These influences are not found in the basic description of how the taxi company normally operates, but they do represent scenarios that will have to be played through when we draw up the design.

So we might add the following paragraph to the description:

The system stores details about passenger requests that cannot be satisfied. It also provides details of how much time vehicles spend in each of the following activities: carrying passengers, going to pickup locations, and being idle.

However, as we develop our model, we shall focus on just the original description of the company's operating procedures, and leave the additional features as exercises.

> **Exercise 16.1** Is there any additional data that you feel it would be useful to gather from the model? If so, add these requirements to the descriptions given above and use them in your own extensions to the project.

16.2 Analysis and design

As suggested in Chapter 15, we will start by seeking to identify the classes and interactions in the system's description, using the verb/noun method.

16.2.1 Discovering classes

The following (singular versions of) nouns are present in the description: company, taxi, shuttle, individual, location, destination, hotel, entertainment venue, tourist organization, vehicle, fare, pickup location, driver, and passenger.

The first point to note is that it would be a mistake to move straight from this list of nouns to a set of classes. Informal descriptions are rarely written in a way that suits that sort of direct mapping.

One refinement that is commonly needed in the list of nouns is to identify any *synonyms*: different words used for the same entity. For instance, "individual" and "fare" are both synonyms for "passenger."

A further refinement is to eliminate those entities that do not really need to be modeled in the system. For instance, the description identified various ways in which the taxi company might be contacted: by individuals, hotels, entertainment venues, and tourist organizations. Will it really be necessary to maintain these distinctions? The answer will depend upon the information we want from the model. We might wish to arrange discounts for hotels that provide large numbers of customers or send publicity material to entertainment venues that do not. If this level of detail is not required, then we can simplify the model by just "injecting" passengers into it according to some statistically reasonable pattern.

Exercise 16.2 Consider simplifying the number of nouns associated with the vehicles. Are "vehicle" and "taxi" synonyms in this context? Do we need to distinguish between "shuttle" and "taxi"? What about between the type of vehicle and "driver"? Justify your answers.

Exercise 16.3 Is it possible to eliminate any of the following as synonyms in this context: "location," "destination," and "pickup location"?

Exercise 16.4 Identify the nouns from any extensions you have added to the system, and make any necessary simplifications.

16.2.2 Using CRC cards

Figure 16.1 contains a summary of the noun and verb associations we are left with once some simplification has been performed on the original description. Each of the nouns should now be assigned to a CRC card, ready to have its responsibilities and collaborators identified.

Figure 16.1 Noun and verb associations in the taxi company

Nouns	Verbs
company	*operates taxis and shuttles*
	receives a call
	schedules a vehicle
taxi	*transports a passenger*
shuttle	*transports one or more passengers*
passenger	
location	
passenger-source	*calls the company*
vehicle	*picks up passenger*
	arrives at pickup location
	notifies company of arrival
	notifies company of drop-off

From that summary, it is clear that "taxi" and "shuttle" are distinct specializations of a more general vehicle class. The main distinction between a taxi and a shuttle is that a taxi is only ever concerned with picking up and transporting a single passenger or coherent group, but a shuttle deals with multiple *independent* passengers concurrently. The relationship between these two vehicles is suggestive of an inheritance hierarchy, where "taxi" and "shuttle" represent subtypes of vehicle.

> **Exercise 16.5** Create physical CRC cards for the nouns/classes identified in this section, in order to be able to work through the scenarios suggested by the project description.
>
> **Exercise 16.6** Do the same for any of your own extensions you wish to follow through in the next stage.

16.2.3 Scenarios

The taxi company does not actually represent a very complex application. We shall find that much of the total interaction in the system is explored by taking the fundamental scenario of trying to satisfy a passenger request to go from one location to another. In practice, this single scenario will be broken down into a number of steps that are followed in sequence, from the initial call to the final drop-off.

- We have decided that a passenger source creates all new passenger objects for the system. So a responsibility of **PassengerSource** is *Create a passenger*, and a collaborator is **Passenger**.

- The passenger source calls the taxi company to request a pickup for a passenger. We note **TaxiCompany** as a collaborator of **PassengerSource** and add *Request a pickup* as a responsibility. Correspondingly, we add to **TaxiCompany** a responsibility to *Receive a pickup request*. Associated with the request will be a passenger and a pickup location. So **TaxiCompany** has **Passenger** and **Location** as collaborators. When it calls the company with the request, the passenger source could pass the passenger and pickup location as separate objects. However, it is preferable to associate closely the pickup location with the passenger. So a collaborator of **Passenger** is **Location**, and a responsibility will be *Provide pickup location*.

- From where does the passenger's pickup location originate? The pickup location and destination could be decided when the **Passenger** is created. So add to **PassengerSource** the responsibility *Generate pickup and destination locations for a passenger*, with **Location** as a collaborator; and add to **Passenger** the responsibilities *Receive pickup and destination locations* and *Provide destination location*.

- On receipt of a request, the **TaxiCompany** has a responsibility to *Schedule a vehicle*. This suggests that a further responsibility is *Store a collection of vehicles*, with **Collection** and **Vehicle** as collaborators. Because the request might fail—there may be no vehicles free—a success or failure indication should be returned to the passenger source.

- There is no indication whether the company seeks to distinguish between taxis and shuttles when scheduling, so we do not need to take that aspect into account here.

However, a vehicle can be scheduled only if it is free. This means that a responsibility of **Vehicle** will be *Indicate whether free*.

- When a free vehicle has been identified, it must be directed to the pickup location. **TaxiCompany** has the responsibility *Direct vehicle to pickup*, with the corresponding responsibility in **Vehicle** being *Receive pickup location*. **Location** is added as a collaborator of **Vehicle**.

- On receipt of a pickup location, the behavior of taxis and shuttles may well differ. A taxi will have been free only if it was not already on its way to either a pickup or a destination location. So the responsibility of **Taxi** is *Go to pickup location*. In contrast, a shuttle has to deal with multiple passengers. When it receives a pickup location, it may have to choose between several possible alternative locations to head to next. So we add the responsibility to **Shuttle** to *Choose next target location*, with a **Collection** collaborator to maintain the set of possible target locations to choose from. The fact that a Vehicle moves between locations suggests that it has a responsibility to *Maintain a current location*.

- On arrival at a pickup location, a **Vehicle** must *Notify the company of pickup arrival*, with **TaxiCompany** as a collaborator; **TaxiCompany** must *Receive notification of pickup arrival*. In real life, a taxi meets its passenger for the first time when it arrives at the pickup location, so this is the natural point for the vehicle to receive its next passenger. In the model, it does so from the company, which received it originally from the passenger source. **TaxiCompany** responsibility: *Pass passenger to vehicle*; **Vehicle** responsibility: *Receive passenger*, with **Passenger** added as a collaborator to **Vehicle**.

- The vehicle now requests the passenger's intended destination. **Vehicle** responsibility: *Request destination location*; **Passenger** responsibility: *Provide destination location*. Once again, at this point the behavior of taxis and shuttles will differ. A **Taxi** will simply *Go to passenger destination*. A shuttle will *Add location to collection of target locations* and choose the next one.

- On arrival at a passenger's destination, a **Vehicle** has responsibilities to *Offload passenger* and *Notify the company of passenger arrival*. The **TaxiCompany** must *Receive notification of passenger arrival*.

The steps we have outlined represent the fundamental activity of the taxi company, repeated over and over as each new passenger requests the service. An important point to note, however, is that our computer model needs to be able to restart the sequence for each new passenger as soon as each fresh request is received, even if a previous request has not yet run to completion. In other words, within a single step of the program, one vehicle could still be heading to a pickup location while another could be arriving at a passenger's destination, and a new passenger might be requesting a pickup.

Exercise 16.7 Review the problem description and the scenario we have worked through. Are there any further scenarios that need to be addressed before we move on to class design? Have we adequately covered what happens, for instance, if there is no vehicle available when a request is received? Complete the scenario analysis if you feel there is more to be done.

> **Exercise 16.8** Do you feel that we have described the scenario at the correct level of detail? For instance, have we included too little or too much detail in the discussion of the differences between taxis and shuttles?
>
> **Exercise 16.9** Do you feel it is necessary to address *how* vehicles move between locations at this stage?
>
> **Exercise 16.10** Do you think that a need for further classes will emerge as the application is developed—classes that have no immediate reference in the problem description? If so, why is this the case?

16.3 Class design

In this section, we shall start to make the move from a high-level abstract design on paper to a concrete outline design within a BlueJ project.

16.3.1 Designing class interfaces

In Chapter 15, we suggested that the next step was to create a fresh set of CRC cards from the first, turning the responsibilities of each class into a set of method signatures. Without wishing to de-emphasize the importance of that step, we shall leave it for you to do and move directly to a BlueJ project outline containing stub classes and methods. This should provide a good feel for the complexity of the project and whether we have missed anything crucial in the steps taken so far.

It is worth pointing out that, at every stage of the project life cycle, we should expect to find errors or loose ends in what we have done in earlier stages. This does not necessarily imply that there are weaknesses in our techniques or abilities. It is more a reflection of the fact that project development is often a discovery process. It is only by exploring and trying things out that we gain a full understanding of what it is we are trying to achieve. So discovering omissions actually says something positive about the process we are using!

16.3.2 Collaborators

Having identified collaborations between classes, one issue that will often need to be addressed is how a particular object obtains references to its collaborators. There are usually three distinct ways in which this happens, and these often represent three different patterns of object interaction:

- A collaborator is received as an argument to a constructor. Such a collaborator will usually be stored in one of the new object's fields so that it is available through the new object's life. The collaborator may be shared in this way with several different objects. Example: A `PassengerSource` object receives the `TaxiCompany` object through its constructor.

- A collaborator is received as an argument to a method. Interaction with such a collaborator is usually transitory—just for the period of execution of the method—although the receiving object may choose to store the reference in one of its fields, for longer-term interaction. Example: `TaxiCompany` receives a `Passenger` collaborator through its method to handle a pickup request.

- The object constructs the collaborator for itself. The collaborator will be for the exclusive use of the constructing object, unless it is passed to another object in one of the previous two ways. If constructed in a method, the collaboration will usually be short term, for the duration of the block in which it is constructed. However, if the collaborator is stored in a field, then the collaboration is likely to last the full lifetime of the creating object. Example: `TaxiCompany` creates a collection to store its vehicles.

Exercise 16.11 As the next section discusses the *taxi-company-outline* project, pay particular attention to where objects are created and how collaborating objects get to know about each other. Try to identify at least one further example of each of the patterns we have described.

16.3.3 The outline implementation

The project *taxi-company-outline* contains an outline implementation of the classes, responsibilities, and collaborations that we have described as part of the design process. You are encouraged to browse through the source code and associate the concrete classes with the corresponding descriptions of Section 16.2.3. Code 16.1 shows an outline of the Vehicle class from the project.

Code 16.1
An outline of the **Vehicle** class

```
/**
 * Capture outline details of a vehicle.
 *
 * @author David J. Barnes and Michael Kölling
 * @version 2016.02.29
 */
public abstract class Vehicle
{
    private TaxiCompany company;
    // Where the vehicle is.
    private Location location;
    // Where the vehicle is headed.
    private Location targetLocation;

    /**
     * Constructor of class Vehicle
     * @param company The taxi company. Must not be null.
     * @param location The vehicle's starting point. Must not be null.
     * @throws NullPointerException If company or location is null.
     */
```

Code 16.1 continued

An outline of the **Vehicle** class

```java
public Vehicle(TaxiCompany company, Location location)
{
    if(company == null) {
        throw new NullPointerException("company");
    }
    if(location == null) {
        throw new NullPointerException("location");
    }
    this.company = company;
    this.location = location;
    targetLocation = null;
}

/**
 * Notify the company of our arrival at a pickup location.
 */
public void notifyPickupArrival()
{
    company.arrivedAtPickup(this);
}

/**
 * Notify the company of our arrival at a
 * passenger's destination.
 * @param passenger The passenger who has arrived.
 */
public void notifyPassengerArrival(Passenger passenger)
{
    company.arrivedAtDestination(this, passenger);
}

/**
 * Receive a pickup location.
 * How this is handled depends on the type of vehicle.
 * @param location The pickup location.
 */
public abstract void setPickupLocation(Location location);

/**
 * Receive a passenger.
 * How this is handled depends on the type of vehicle.
 * @param passenger The passenger being picked up.
 */
public abstract void pickup(Passenger passenger);

/**
 * Is the vehicle free?
 * @return Whether or not this vehicle is free.
 */
public abstract boolean isFree();

/**
 * Offload any passengers whose destination is the
 * current location.
 */
public abstract void offloadPassenger();

/**
 * Get the location.
 * @return Where this vehicle is currently located.
 */
```

Code 16.1 continued

An outline of the `Vehicle` class

```java
    public Location getLocation()
    {
        return location;
    }

    /**
     * Set the current location.
     * @param location Where it is. Must not be null.
     * @throws NullPointerException If location is null.
     */
    public void setLocation(Location location)
    {
        if(location != null) {
            this.location = location;
        }
        else {
            throw new NullPointerException();
        }
    }

    /**
     * Get the target location.
     * @return Where this vehicle is currently headed, or null
     *         if it is idle.
     */
    public Location getTargetLocation()
    {
        return targetLocation;
    }

    /**
     * Set the required target location.
     * @param location Where to go. Must not be null.
     * @throws NullPointerException If location is null.
     */
    public void setTargetLocation(Location location)
    {
        if(location != null) {
            targetLocation = location;
        }
        else {
            throw new NullPointerException();
        }
    }

    /**
     * Clear the target location.
     */
    public void clearTargetLocation()
    {
        targetLocation = null;
    }
}
```

The process of creating the outline project raised a number of issues. Here are some of them:

- You should expect to find some differences between the design and the implementation, owing to the different natures of design and implementation languages. For instance, discussion of the scenarios suggested that **PassengerSource** should have the responsibility

Generate pickup and destination locations for a passenger, and **Passenger** should have the responsibility *Receive pickup and destination locations*. Rather than mapping these responsibilities to individual method calls, the more natural implementation in Java is to write something like

```
new Passenger(new Location( . . . ), new Location( . . . ))
```

- We have ensured that our outline project is complete enough to compile successfully. That is not always necessary at this stage, but it does mean that undertaking incremental development at the next stage will be a little easier. However, it does have the corresponding disadvantage of making missing pieces of code potentially harder to spot, because the compiler will not point out the loose ends.

- The shared and distinct elements of the **Vehicle**, **Taxi**, and **Shuttle** classes only really begin to take shape as we move towards their implementation. For instance, the different ways in which taxis and shuttles respond to a pickup request is reflected in the fact that **Vehicle** defines **setPickupLocation** as an abstract method, which will have separate concrete implementations in the subclasses. On the other hand, even though taxis and shuttles have different ways of deciding where they are heading, they can share the concept of having a single target location. This has been implemented as a **targetLocation** field in the superclass.

- At two points in the scenario, a vehicle is expected to notify the company of its arrival at either a pickup point or a destination. There are at least two possible ways to organize this in the implementation. The direct way is for a vehicle to store a reference to its company. This would mean that there would be an explicit association between the two classes on the class diagram.

- An alternative is to use the *Observer* pattern introduced in Chapter 15, with **Vehicle** extending the **Observable** class and **TaxiCompany** implementing the **Observer** interface. Direct coupling between **Vehicle** and **TaxiCompany** is reduced, but implicit coupling is still involved, and the notification process is a little more complex to program.

- Up to this point, there has been no discussion about how many passengers a shuttle can carry. Presumably there could be different-sized shuttles. This aspect of the application has been deferred until a later resolution.

There is no absolute rule about exactly how far to go with the outline implementation in any particular application. The purpose of the outline implementation is not to create a fully working project, but to record the design of the outline structure of the application (which has been developed through the CRC card activities earlier). As you review the classes in the *taxi-company-outline* project, you may feel that we have gone too far in this case, or maybe even not far enough. On the positive side, by attempting to create a version that at least compiles, we certainly found that we were forced to think about the **Vehicle** inheritance hierarchy in some detail: in particular, which methods could be implemented in full in the superclass, and which were best left as abstract. On the negative side, there is always the risk of making implementation decisions too early: for instance, committing to particular sorts of data structures that might be better left until later or, as we did here, choosing to reject the *Observer* pattern in favor of the more direct approach.

Exercise 16.12 For each of the classes in the project, look at the class interface and write a list of JUnit tests that should be used to test the functionality of the class.

Exercise 16.13 The *taxi-company-outline* project defines a `Demo` class to create a pair of `PassengerSource` and `TaxiCompany` objects. Create a `Demo` object and try its `pickupTest` method. Why is the `TaxiCompany` object unable to grant a pickup request at this stage?

Exercise 16.14 Do you feel that we should have developed the source code further at this stage, to enable at least one pickup request to succeed? If so, how much further would you have taken the development?

16.3.4 Testing

Having made a start on implementation, we should not go too much further before we start to consider how we shall test the application. We do not want to make the mistake of devising tests only when the full implementation is complete. We can already put some tests in place that will gradually evolve as the implementation is evolved. Try the following exercises to get a feel for what is possible at this early stage.

Exercise 16.15 The *taxi-company-outline-testing* project includes some simple initial JUnit tests. Try them out. Add any further tests you feel are appropriate at this stage of the development, to form the basis of a set of tests to be used during future development. Does it matter if the tests we create fail at this stage?

Exercise 16.16 The `Location` class currently contains no fields or methods. How is further development of this class likely to affect existing test classes?

16.3.5 Some remaining issues

One of the major issues that we have not attempted to tackle yet is how to organize the sequencing of the various activities: passenger requests, vehicle movements, and so on. Another is that locations have not been given a detailed concrete form, so movement has no effect. As we further develop the application, resolutions of these issues and others will emerge.

16.4 Iterative development

We obviously still have quite a long way to go from the outline implementation developed in *taxi-company-outline* to the final version. However, rather than being overwhelmed by the magnitude of the overall task, we can make things more manageable by identifying some discrete steps to take toward the ultimate goal and undertaking a process of iterative development.

16.4.1 Development steps

Planning some development steps helps us to consider how we might break up a single large problem into several smaller problems. Individually, these smaller problems are likely to be both less complex and more manageable than the one big problem, but together they should combine to form the whole. As we seek to solve the smaller problems, we might find that we need to also break up some of them. In addition, we might find that some of our original assumptions were wrong or that our design is inadequate in some way. This process of discovery, when combined with an iterative development approach, means that we obtain valuable feedback on our design and on the decisions we make, at an early enough stage for us to be able to incorporate it back into a flexible and evolving process.

Considering what steps to break the overall problem into has the added advantage of helping to identify some of the ways in which the various parts of the application are interconnected. In a large project, this process helps us to identify the interfaces between components. Identifying steps also helps in planning the timing of the development process.

It is important that each step in an iterative development represent a clearly identifiable point in the evolution of the application toward the overall requirements. In particular, we need to be able to determine when each step has been completed. Completion should be marked by the passing of a set of tests and a review of the step's achievements, so as to be able to incorporate any lessons learned into the steps that follow.

Here is a possible series of development steps for the taxi company application:

- Enable a single passenger to be picked up and taken to her destination by a single taxi.
- Provide sufficient taxis to enable multiple independent passengers to be picked up and taken to their destinations concurrently.
- Enable a single passenger to be picked up and taken to his destination by a single shuttle.
- Ensure that details are recorded of passengers for whom there is no free vehicle.
- Enable a single shuttle to pick up multiple passengers and carry them concurrently to their destinations.
- Provide a GUI to display the activities of all active vehicles and passengers within the simulation.
- Ensure that taxis and shuttles are able to operate concurrently.
- Provide all remaining functionality, including full statistical data.

We will not discuss the implementation of all of these steps in detail, but we will complete the application to a point where you should be able to add the remaining functionality yourself.

Exercise 16.17 Critically assess the list of steps we have outlined, with the following questions in mind. Do you feel the order is appropriate? Is the level of complexity of each too high, too low, or just right? Are there any steps missing? Revise the list as you see fit, to suit your own view of the project.

Exercise 16.18 Are the completion criteria (tests on completion) for each stage sufficiently obvious? If so, document some tests for each.

16.4.2 A first stage

For the first stage, we want to be able to create a single passenger, have them picked up by a single taxi, and have them delivered to their destination. This means that we shall have to work on a number of different classes: `Location`, `Taxi`, and `TaxiCompany`, for certain, and possibly others. In addition, we shall have to arrange for simulated time to pass as the taxi moves within the city. This suggests that we might be able to reuse some of the ideas involving actors that we saw in Chapter 12.

The *taxi-company-stage-one* project contains an implementation of the requirements of this first stage. The classes have been developed to the point where a taxi picks up and delivers a passenger to their destination. The `run` method of the `Demo` class plays out this scenario. However, more important at this stage are really the test classes—`LocationTest`, `PassengerTest`, `PassengerSourceTest`, and `TaxiTest`—which we discuss in Section 16.4.3.

Rather than discuss this project in detail, we shall simply describe here some of the issues that arose from its development out of the previous outline version. You should supplement this discussion with a thorough reading of the source code.

The goals of the first stage were deliberately set to be quite modest, yet still relevant to the fundamental activity of the application—collecting and delivering passengers. There were good reasons for this. By setting a modest goal, the task seemed achievable within a reasonably short time. By setting a relevant goal, the task was clearly taking us closer toward completing the overall project. Such factors help to keep our motivation high.

We have borrowed the concept of actors from the *foxes-and-rabbits* project of Chapter 12. For this stage, only taxis needed to be actors, through their `Vehicle` superclass. At each step a taxi either moves toward a target location or remains idle (Code 16.2). Although we did not have to record any statistics at this stage, it was simple and convenient to have vehicles record a count of the number of steps for which they are idle. This anticipated part of the work of one of the later stages.

The need to model movement required the `Location` class to be implemented more fully than in the outline. On the face of it, this should be a relatively simple container for a two-dimensional position within a rectangular grid. However, in practice, it also needs to provide both a test for coincidence of two locations (`equals`), and a way for a vehicle to find out where to move to next, based on its current location and its destination (`nextLocation`). At this stage, no limits were put on the grid area (other than that coordinate values should be positive), but this raises the need in a later stage for something to record the boundaries of the area in which the company operates.

Code 16.2

The `Taxi` class as an actor

```java
/**
 * A taxi is able to carry a single passenger.
 *
 * @author David J. Barnes and Michael Kölling
 * @version 2016.02.29
 */
public class Taxi extends Vehicle
{
    private Passenger passenger;

    /**
     * Constructor for objects of class Taxi
     * @param company The taxi company. Must not be null.
     * @param location The vehicle's starting point. Must not be null.
     * @throws NullPointerException If company or location is null.
     */
    public Taxi(TaxiCompany company, Location location)
    {
        super(company, location);
    }

    /**
     * Carry out a taxi's actions.
     */
    public void act()
    {
        Location target = getTargetLocation();
        if(target != null) {
            // Find where to move to next.
            Location next = getLocation().nextLocation(target);
            setLocation(next);
            if(next.equals(target)) {
                if(passenger != null) {
                    notifyPassengerArrival(passenger);
                    offloadPassenger();
                }
                else {
                    notifyPickupArrival();
                }
            }
        }
        else {
            incrementIdleCount();
        }
    }

    /**
     * Is the taxi free?
     * @return Whether or not this taxi is free.
     */
    public boolean isFree()
    {
        return getTargetLocation() == null && passenger == null;
    }
```

Code 16.2 continued

The `Taxi` class as an actor

```java
    /**
     * Is the taxi free?
     * @return Whether or not this taxi is free.
     */
    public boolean isFree()
    {
        return getTargetLocation() == null && passenger == null;
    }

    /**
     * Receive a pickup location. This becomes the
     * target location.
     * @param location The pickup location.
     */
    public void setPickupLocation(Location location)
    {
        setTargetLocation(location);
    }

    /**
     * Receive a passenger.
     * Set their destination as the target location.
     * @param passenger The passenger.
     */
    public void pickup(Passenger passenger)
    {
        this.passenger = passenger;
        setTargetLocation(passenger.getDestination());
    }

    /**
     * Offload the passenger.
     */
    public void offloadPassenger()
    {
        passenger = null;
        clearTargetLocation();
    }

    /**
     * Return details of the taxi, such as where it is.
     * @return A string representation of the taxi.
     */
    public String toString()
    {
        return "Taxi at " + getLocation();
    }
}
```

One of the major issues that had to be addressed was how to manage the association between a passenger and a vehicle, between the request for a pickup and the point of the vehicle's arrival. Although we were required only to handle a single taxi and a single passenger, we tried to bear in mind that ultimately there could be multiple pickup requests outstanding at any one time. In Section 16.2.3, we decided that a vehicle should receive its passenger when it notifies the company that it has arrived at the pickup point. So, when a notification is received, the company needs to be able to work out which passenger has been assigned to that vehicle. The solution we chose was to have the company store a *vehicle:passenger* pairing in a map. When the vehicle notifies the company that it has arrived, the company passes the corresponding passenger to it. However, there are various reasons why this solution is not perfect, and we shall explore this issue further in the exercises below.

One error situation we addressed was that there might be no passenger found when a vehicle arrives at a pickup point. This would be the result of a programming error, so we defined the unchecked `MissingPassengerException` class.

As only a single passenger was required for this stage, development of the `PassengerSource` class was deferred to a later stage. Instead, passengers were created directly in the `Demo` and `Test` classes.

Exercise 16.19 If you have not already done so, take a thorough look through the implementation in the *taxi-company-stage-one* project. Ensure that you understand how movement of the taxi is effected through its `act` method.

Exercise 16.20 Do you feel that the `TaxiCompany` object should keep separate lists of those vehicles that are free and those that are not, to improve the efficiency of its scheduling? At what points would a vehicle move between the lists?

Exercise 16.21 The next planned stage of the implementation is to provide multiple taxis to carry multiple passengers concurrently. Review the `TaxiCompany` class with this goal in mind. Do you feel that it already supports this functionality? If not, what changes are required?

Exercise 16.22 Review the way in which *vehicle:passenger* associations are stored in the assignments' map in `TaxiCompany`. Can you see any weaknesses in this approach? Does it support more than one passenger being picked up from the same location? Could a vehicle ever need to have multiple associations recorded for it?

Exercise 16.23 If you see any problems with the current way in which *vehicle:passenger* associations are stored, would creating a unique identification for each association help—say a "booking number"? If so, would any of the existing method signatures in the `Vehicle` hierarchy need to be changed? Implement an improved version that supports the requirements of all existing scenarios.

16.4.3 Testing the first stage

As part of the implementation of the first stage, we have developed two test classes: `LocationTest` and `TaxiTest`. The first checks basic functionality of the `Location` class that is crucial to correct movement of vehicles. The second is designed to test that a passenger is picked up and delivered to her destination in the correct number of steps, and that the taxi becomes free again immediately afterwards. In order to develop the second set of tests, the **Location** class was enhanced with the **distance** method, to provide the number of steps required to move between two locations.[1]

In normal operation, the application runs silently, and without a GUI there is no visual way to monitor the progress of a taxi. One approach would be to add print statements to the core methods of classes such as **Taxi** and **TaxiCompany**. However, BlueJ does offer the alternative of setting a breakpoint within the **act** method of, say, the **Taxi** class. This would make it possible to "observe" the movement of a taxi by inspection.

Having reached a reasonable level of confidence in the current state of the implementation, we have simply left print statements in the notification methods of **TaxiCompany** to provide a minimum of user feedback.

As testimony to the value of developing tests alongside implementation, it is worth recording that the existing test classes enabled us to identify and correct two serious errors in our code.

Exercise 16.24 Review the tests implemented in the test classes of *taxi-company-stage-one*. Should it be possible to use these as regression tests during the next stages, or would they require substantial changes?

Exercise 16.25 Implement additional tests and further test classes that you feel are necessary to increase your level of confidence in the current implementation. Fix any errors you discover in the process of doing this.

16.4.4 A later stage of development

It is not our intention to discuss in full the completion of the development of the taxi company application, as there would be little for you to gain from that. Instead, we shall briefly present the application at a later stage, and we encourage you to complete the rest from there.

This more advanced stage can be found in the *taxi-company-later-stage* project. It handles multiple taxis and passengers, and a GUI provides a progressive view of the movements of both (Figure 16.2). Here is an outline of some of the major developments in this version from the previous one.

- A **Simulation** class now manages the actors, much as it did in the *foxes-and-rabbits project*. The actors are the vehicles, the passenger source, and a GUI provided by the **CityGUI** class. After each step, the simulation pauses for a brief period so that the GUI does not change too quickly.

- The need for something like the **City** class was identified during development of stage one. The **City** object defines the dimensions of the city's grid and holds a collection of all the items of interest that are in the city—the vehicles and the passengers.

---

[1] We anticipate that this will have an extended use later in the development of the application as it should enable the company to schedule vehicles on the basis of which is closest to the pickup point.

Figure 16.2

A visualization of the city

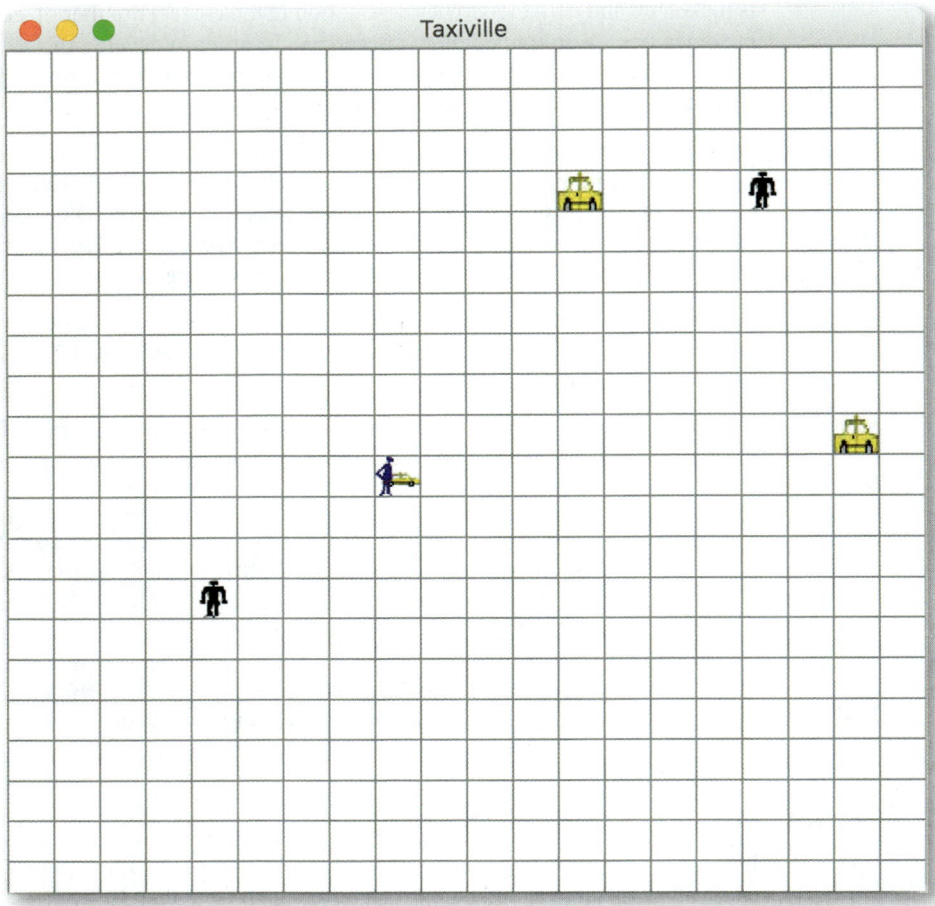

- Items in the city may optionally implement the **DrawableItem** interface, which allows the GUI to display them. Images of vehicles and people are provided in the **images** folder within the project folder for this purpose.

- The Taxi class implements the **DrawableItem** interface. It returns alternative images to the GUI, depending on whether it is occupied or empty. Image files exist in the **images** folder for a shuttle to do the same.

- The **PassengerSource** class has been refactored significantly from the previous version, to better fit its role as an actor. In addition, it maintains a count of missed pickups for statistical analysis.

- The **TaxiCompany** class is responsible for creating the taxis to be used in the simulation.

As you explore the source code of the *taxi-company-later-stage* project, you will find illustrations of many of the topics we have covered in the second half of this book: inheritance, polymorphism, abstract classes, interfaces, and error handling.

Exercise 16.26 Add assertion and exception-throwing consistency checks within each class, to guard against inappropriate use. For instance, ensure that a **Passenger** is never created with pickup and destination locations that are the same; ensure that a taxi is never requested to go to a pickup when it already has a target location; etc.

Exercise 16.27 Report on the statistical information that is being gathered by taxis and the passenger source; also on taxi idle time and missed pickups. Experiment with different numbers of taxis to see how the balance between these two sets of data varies.

Exercise 16.28 Adapt the vehicle classes so that records are kept of the amount of time spent traveling to pickup locations and passenger destinations. Can you see a possible conflict here for shuttles?

16.4.5 Further ideas for development

The version of the application provided in the *taxi-company-later-stage* project represents a significant point in the development toward full implementation. However, there is still a lot that can be added. For instance, we have hardly developed the **Shuttle** class at all, so there are plenty of challenges to be found in completing its implementation. The major difference between shuttles and taxis is that a shuttle has to be concerned with multiple passengers, whereas a taxi has to be concerned with only one. The fact that a shuttle is already carrying a passenger should not prevent it from being sent to pick up another. Similarly, if it is already on its way to a pickup, it could still accept a further pickup request. These issues raise questions about how a shuttle organizes its priorities. Could a passenger end up being driven back and forth while the shuttle responds to competing requests, the passenger never getting delivered? What does it mean for a shuttle not to be free? Does it mean that it is full of passengers, or that it has enough pickup requests to fill it? Suppose at least one of those pickups will reach their destination before the final pickup is reached: Does that mean it could accept more pickup requests than its capacity?!

Another area for further development is vehicle scheduling. The taxi company does not operate particularly intelligently at present. How should it decide which vehicle to send when there may be more than one available? No attempt is made to assign vehicles on the basis of their distance from a pickup location. The company could use the **distance** method of the **Location** class to work out which is the nearest free vehicle to a pickup. Would this make a significant difference to the average waiting time of passengers? How might data be gathered on how long passengers wait to be picked up? What about having idle taxis move to a central location, ready for their next pickup, in order to reduce potential waiting times? Does the size of the city have an impact on the effectiveness of this approach? For instance, in a large city, is it better to have idle taxis space themselves out from one another, rather than have all gather at the center?

Could the simulation be used to model competing taxi companies operating in the same area of the city? Multiple **TaxiCompany** objects could be created and the passenger source allocate passengers to them competitively on the basis of how quickly they could be picked up. Is this too fundamental a change to graft onto the existing application?

16.4.6 Reuse

Currently, our goal has been to simulate the operation of vehicles in order to assess the commercial viability of expanding a business into a new area of the city. You may have noticed that substantial parts of the application may actually be useful once the expansion is in operation.

Assuming that we develop a clever scheduling algorithm for our simulation to decide which vehicle should take which call, or that we have worked out a good scheme for deciding where to send the vehicles to wait while they are idle, we might decide to use the same algorithms when the company actually operates in the new area. The visual representation of each vehicle's location could also help.

In other words, there is potential to turn the simulation of the taxi company into a taxi management system used to help the real company in its operations. The structure of the application would change, of course: the program would not control and move the taxis, but rather record their positions, which it might receive from GPS (global positioning system) receivers in each vehicle. However, many of the classes developed for the simulation could be reused with little or no change. This illustrates the power of reuse that we gain from good class structure and class design.

16.5 Another example

There are many other projects that you could undertake along similar lines to the taxi company application. A popular alternative is the issue of how to schedule elevators in a large building. Coordination between elevators becomes particularly significant here. In addition, within an enclosed building, it may be possible to estimate numbers of people on each floor and hence to anticipate demand. There are also time-related behaviors to take account of: morning arrivals, evening departures, and local peaks of activity around lunchtimes.

Use the approach we have outlined in this chapter to implement a simulation of a building with one or more elevators.

16.6 Taking things further

We can only take you so far by presenting our own project ideas and showing you how we would develop them. You will find that you can go much further if you develop your own ideas for projects and implement them in your own way. Pick a topic that interests you, and work through the stages we have outlined: analyze the problem, work out some scenarios, sketch out a design, plan some implementation stages, and then make a start.

Designing and implementing programs is an exciting and creative activity. Like any worthwhile activity, it takes time and practice to become proficient at it. So do not become discouraged if your early efforts seem to take forever or are full of errors. That is normal, and you will gradually improve with experience. Do not be too ambitious to start with, and expect to have to rework your ideas as you go; that is all part of the natural learning process.

Most of all: Have fun!

APPENDIX A

Working with a BlueJ Project

A.1 Installing BlueJ

To work with BlueJ, you must download and install the BlueJ system. It is available for free download from `http://www.bluej.org/`. The download for Windows and Mac OS includes a copy of the JDK (the Java system)—this does not need to be installed separately. On Linux, the package dependencies will automatically install the right JDK version when you install BlueJ, if necessary.

A.2 Opening a project

You can download all of the example projects from the companion website for this book at `http://www.bluej.org/objects-first/`

Download the zip file and uncompress it to give you a folder called *projects*. After installing and starting BlueJ by double-clicking its icon, select *Open . . .* from the *Project* menu. Navigate to the projects folder and select a project. (You can have multiple projects open at the same time.) Each project folder contains a `bluej.project` file that, when associated with BlueJ, can be double-clicked to open a project directly.

More information about the use of BlueJ is included in the BlueJ Tutorial. The tutorial is accessible via the *BlueJ Tutorial* item in BlueJ's *Help* menu.

A.3 The BlueJ debugger

Information on using the BlueJ debugger may be found in Appendix F and in the BlueJ Tutorial. The tutorial is accessible via the *BlueJ Tutorial* item in BlueJ's *Help* menu.

A.4 Configuring BlueJ

Many of the settings of BlueJ can be configured to better suit your personal situation. Some configuration options are available through the *Preferences* dialog in the BlueJ system, but many more configuration options are accessible by editing the "BlueJ definitions file." The location of that file is *<bluej_home>/lib/bluej.defs*, where *<bluej_home>* is the folder where the BlueJ system is installed.[1]

---

[1] On Mac OS, the *bluej.defs* file is inside the application bundle. See the "Tips archive" for instructions how to find it.

Configuration details are explained in the "Tips archive" on the BlueJ web site. You can access it at

```
http://www.bluej.org/help/archive.html
```

Following are some of the most common things people like to configure. Many more configuration options can be found by reading the `bluej.defs` file.

A.5 Changing the interface language

You can change the interface language to one of several available languages. To do this, open the `bluej.defs` file and find the line that reads

```
bluej.language=english
```

Change it to one of the other available languages. For example:

```
bluej.language=spanish
```

Comments in the file list all available languages. They include at least Afrikaans, Catalan, Chinese, Czech, Danish, Dutch, English, French, German, Greek, Italian, Japanese, Korean, Portuguese, Russian, Slovak, Spanish, and Swedish.

A.6 Using local API documentation

You can use a local copy of the Java class library (API) documentation. That way, access to the documentation is faster and you can use the documentation without being online. To do this, download the Java documentation file from `http://www.oracle.com/technetwork/java/javase/downloads/` (a zip file) and unzip it at a location where you want to store the Java documentation. This will create a folder named *docs*.

Then open a web browser, and, using the *Open File . . . .* (or equivalent) function, open the file *docs/api/index.html*. Once the API view is correctly displayed in the browser, copy the URL (web address) from your browser's address field, open BlueJ, open the *Preferences* dialog, go to the *Miscellaneous* tab, and paste the copied URL into the field labeled *JDK documentation URL*. Using the *Java Class Libraries* item from the *Help* menu should now open your local copy.

A.7 Changing the new class templates

When you create a new class, the class's source is set to a default source text. This text is taken from a template and can be changed to suit your preferences. Templates are stored in the folders

```
<bluej_home>/lib/<language>/templates/ and
<bluej_home>/lib/<language>/templates/newclass/
```

where *<bluej_home>* is the BlueJ installation folder and *<language>* is your currently used language setting (for example, *english*).

Template files are pure text files and can be edited in any standard text editor.

APPENDIX B
Java Data Types

Java's type system is based on two distinct kinds of types: primitive types, and object types.

Primitive types are stored in variables directly, and they have value semantics (values are copied when assigned to another variable). Primitive types are not associated with classes and do not have methods.

In contrast, an object type is manipulated by storing a reference to the object (not the object itself). When assigned to a variable, only the reference is copied, not the object.

B.1 Primitive types

The following table lists all the primitive types of the Java language:

Type name	Description	Example literals		
Integer numbers				
byte	byte-sized integer (8 bit)	24	−2	
short	short integer (16 bit)	137	−119	
int	integer (32 bit)	5409	−2003	
long	long integer (64 bit)	423266353L	55L	
Real numbers				
float	single-precision floating point	43.889F		
double	double-precision floating point	45.63	2.4e5	
Other types				
char	a single character (16 bit)	'm'	'?'	'\u00F6'
boolean	a boolean value (true or false)	true	false	

Notes:

- A number without a decimal point is generally interpreted as an `int` but automatically converted to `byte`, `short`, or `long` types when assigned (if the value fits). You can declare a literal as `long` by putting an L after the number. (l, lowercase L, works as well but should be avoided because it can easily be mistaken for a one (1).)
- A number with a decimal point is of type `double`. You can specify a `float` literal by putting an F or f after the number.
- A character can be written as a single Unicode character in single quotes or as a four-digit Unicode value, preceded by "\u".
- The two boolean literals are `true` and `false`.

Because variables of the primitive types do not refer to objects, there are no methods associated with the primitive types. However, when used in a context requiring an object type, autoboxing might be used to convert a primitive value to a corresponding object. See Section B.4 for more details.

The following table details minimum and maximum values available in the numerical types.

Type name	Minimum	Maximum
byte	-128	127
short	-32768	32767
int	-2147483648	2147483647
long	-9223372036854775808	9223372036854775807
	Positive minimum	**Positive maximum**
float	1.4e-45	3.4028235e38
double	4.9e-324	1.7976931348623157e308

B.2 Casting of primitive types

Sometimes it is necessary to convert a value of one primitive type to a value of another primitive type—typically, a value from a type with a particular range of values to one with a smaller range. This is called *casting*. Casting almost always involves loss of information—for example, when converting from a floating-point type to an integer type. Casting is permitted in Java between the numeric types, but it is not possible to convert a `boolean` value to any other type with a cast, or vice versa.

The cast operator consists of the name of a primitive type written in parentheses in front of a variable or an expression. For instance,

```
int val = (int) mean;
```

If `mean` is a variable of type `double` containing the value 3.9, then the statement above would store the integer value 3 (conversion by truncation) in the variable `val`.

B.3 Object types

All types not listed in Section B.1, Primitive types, are object types. These include class and interface types from the Java library (such as `String`) and user-defined types.

A variable of an object type holds a reference (or "pointer") to an object. Assignments and parameter passing have reference semantics (i.e., the reference is copied, not the object). After assigning a variable to another one, both variables refer to the same object. The two variables are said to be aliases for the same object. This rule applies in simple assignment between variables, but also when passing an object as an actual parameter to a method. As a consequence, state changes to an object via a formal parameter will persist, after the method has completed, in the actual parameter.

Classes are the templates for objects, defining the fields and methods that each instance possesses.

Arrays behave like object types; they also have reference semantics. There is no class definition for arrays.

B.4 Wrapper classes

Every primitive type in Java has a corresponding wrapper class that represents the same type but is a real-object type. This makes it possible to use values from the primitive types where object types are required, through a process known as *autoboxing*. The following table lists the primitive types and their corresponding wrapper type from the `java.lang` package. Apart from `Integer` and `Character`, the wrapper class names are the same as the primitive-type names, but with an uppercase first letter.

Whenever a value of a primitive type is used in a context that requires an object type, the compiler uses autoboxing to automatically wrap the primitive-type value in an appropriate wrapper object. This means that primitive-type values can be added directly to a collection, for instance. The reverse operation—*unboxing*—is also performed automatically when a wrapper-type object is used in a context that requires a value of the corresponding primitive type.

Primitive type	Wrapper type
byte	Byte
short	Short
int	Integer
long	Long
float	Float
double	Double
char	Character
boolean	Boolean

B.5 Casting of object types

Because an object may belong to an inheritance hierarchy of types, it is sometimes necessary to convert an object reference of one type to a reference of a subtype lower down the inheritance hierarchy. This process is called *casting* (or *downcasting*). The cast operator consists of the name of a class or interface type written in parentheses in front of a variable or an expression. For instance,

    Car c = (Car) veh;

If the declared (i.e., static) type of variable `veh` is `Vehicle` and `Car` is a subclass of `Vehicle`, then this statement will compile. A separate check is made at runtime to ensure that the object referred to by `veh` really is a `Car` and not an instance of a different subtype.

It is important to appreciate that casting between object types is completely different from casting between primitive types (Section B.2, above). In particular, casting between object types involves *no change* of the object involved. It is purely a way of gaining access to type information that is already true of the object—that is, part of its full dynamic type.

APPENDIX C
Operators

C.1 Arithmetic expressions

Java has a considerable number of operators available for both arithmetic and logical expressions. Table C.1 shows everything that is classified as an operator, including things such as type casting and parameter passing. Most of the operators are either binary operators (taking a left and a right operand) or unary operators (taking a single operand). The main binary arithmetic operations are:

+ *addition*
− *subtraction*
* *multiplication*
/ *division*
% *modulus*, or *remainder after division*

The results of both division and modulus operations depend on whether their operands are integers or floating-point values. Between two integer values, division yields an integer result and discards any remainder, but between floating-point values, a floating-point value is the result:

5 / 3 gives a result of 1
5.0 / 3 gives a result of 1.6666666666666667

(Note that only one of the operands needs to be of a floating-point type to produce a floating-point result.)

When more than one operator appears in an expression, then *rules of precedence* have to be used to work out the order of application. In Table C.1, those operators having the highest precedence appear at the top, so we can see that multiplication, division, and modulus all take precedence over addition and subtraction, for instance. This means that both of the following examples give the result 100:

51 * 3 - 53
154 - 2 * 27

Binary operators with the same precedence level are evaluated from left to right, and unary operators with the same precedence level are evaluated right to left.

When it is necessary to alter the normal order of evaluation, parentheses can be used. So both of the following examples give the result 100:

(205 - 5) / 2
2 * (47 + 3)

Appendices

The main unary operators are `-`, `!`, `++`, `--`, `[]`, and `new`. You will notice that `++` and `--` appear in each of the top two rows in Table C.1. Those in the top row take a single operand on their left, while those in the second row take a single operand on their right.

Table C.1 Java operators, highest precedence at the top

`[]`	`.`	`++`	`--`	`(parameters)`	
`++`	`--`	`+`	`-`	`!`	`~`
`new`	`(cast)`				
`*`	`/`	`%`			
`+`	`-`				
`<<`	`>>`	`>>>`			
`<`	`>`	`>=`	`<=`	`instanceof`	
`==`	`!=`				
`&`					
`^`					
`|`					
`&&`					
`||`					
`?:`					
`=`	`+=`	`-=`	`*=`	`/=`	`%=`	`>>=`	`<<=`	`>>>=`	`&=`	`|=`	`^=`

C.2 Boolean expressions

In boolean expressions, operators are used to combine operands to produce a value of either `true` or `false`. Such expressions are usually found in the test expressions of if-else statements and loops.

The relational operators usually combine a pair of arithmetic operands, although the tests for equality and inequality are also used with object references. Java's relational operators are:

- `==` equal to   `!=` not equal to
- `<` less than   `<=` less than or equal to
- `>` greater than   `>=` greater than or equal to

The binary logical operators combine two boolean expressions to produce another boolean value. The operators are:

`&&` and
`||` or
`^` exclusive or

In addition,

`!` not

takes a single boolean expression and changes it from `true` to `false` and vice versa.

C.3 Short-circuit operators

Both && and || are slightly unusual in the way they are applied. If the left operand of && is false, then the value of the right operand is irrelevant and will not be evaluated. Similarly, if the left operand of || is true, then the right operand is not evaluated. Thus, they are known as short-circuit operators.

APPENDIX D

Java Control Structures

D.1 Control structures

Control structures affect the order in which statements are executed. There are two main categories: *selection statements* and *loops*.

A selection statement provides a decision point at which a choice is made to follow one route through the body of a method or constructor rather than another route. An *if-else statement* involves a decision between two different sets of statements, whereas a *switch statement* allows the selection of a single option from among several.

Loops offer the option to repeat statements, either a definite or an indefinite number of times. The former is typified by the *for-each loop* and *for loop*, while the latter is typified by the *while loop* and *do loop*.

In practice, exceptions to the above characterizations are quite common. For instance, an *if-else statement* can be used to select from among several alternative sets of statements if the *else* part contains a nested if-else statement, and a *for loop* can be used to loop an indefinite number of times.

D.2 Selection statements

D.2.1 if-else

The *if-else statement* has two main forms, both of which are controlled by the evaluation of a boolean expression:

```
if(expression) {
    statements
}
```

```
if(expression) {
    statements
}
else {
    statements
}
```

In the first form, the value of the boolean expression is used to decide whether or not to execute the statements. In the second form, the expression is used to choose between two alternative sets of statements, only one of which will be executed.

Examples:

```
if(field.size() == 0) {
    System.out.println("The field is empty.");
}

if(number < 0) {
    reportError();
}
else {
    processNumber(number);
}
```

It is very common to link if-else statements together by placing a second if-else in the else part of the first. This can be continued any number of times. It is a good idea to always include a final else part.

```
if(n < 0) {
    handleNegative();
}
else if(n == 0) {
    handleZero();
}
else {
    handlePositive();
}
```

D.2.2 switch

The *switch statement* switches on a single value to one of an arbitrary number of cases. Two possible patterns of use are:

```
switch(expression) {
    case value: statements;
                break;
    case value: statements;
                break;
    further cases possible
    default: statements;
             break;
}
```

```
switch(expression) {
    case value1:
    case value2:
    case value3:
        statements;
        break;
    case value4:
    case value5:
        statements;
        break;
    further cases possible
    default:
        statements;
        break;
}
```

Notes:

- A *switch statement* can have any number of `case` labels.
- The `break` instruction after every case is needed, otherwise the execution "falls through" into the next label's statements. The second form above makes use of this. In this case,

all three of the first values will execute the first *statements* section, whereas values four and five will execute the second *statements* section.
- The `default` case is optional. If no default is given, it may happen that no case is executed.
- The `break` instruction after the default (or the last case, if there is no default) is not needed but is considered good style.
- The expression used to switch on and the case labels may be strings.
- The expression and case labels may be of an enumerated type. The type name is omitted from the labels.

Examples:

```java
switch(day) {
    case 1: dayString = "Monday";
            break;
    case 2: dayString = "Tuesday";
            break;
    case 3: dayString = "Wednesday";
            break;
    case 4: dayString = "Thursday";
            break;
    case 5: dayString = "Friday";
            break;
    case 6: dayString = "Saturday";
            break;
    case 7: dayString = "Sunday";
            break;
    default: dayString = "invalid day";
            break;
}

switch(dow.toLowerCase()) {
    case "mon":
    case "tue":
    case "wed":
    case "thu":
    case "fri":
        goToWork();
        break;
    case "sat":
    case "sun":
        stayInBed();
        break;
}
```

D.3 Loops

Java has three loops: *while*, *do-while*, and *for*. The for loop has two forms. Both while and do-while are well suited for indefinite iteration. The *for-each loop* is intended for definite iteration over a collection, and the *for loop* falls somewhere between the two. Except for the *for-each* loop, repetition is controlled in each with a boolean expression.

D.3.1 While

The *while loop* executes a block of statements as long as a given expression evaluates to *true*. The expression is tested *before* execution of the loop body, so the body may be executed zero times (i.e., not at all). This capability is an important feature of the while loop.

```
while(expression) {
    statements
}
```

Examples:

```
System.out.print("Please enter a filename: ");
input = readInput();
while(input == null) {
    System.out.print("Please try again: ");
    input = readInput();
}


int index = 0;
boolean found = false;
while(!found && index < list.size()) {
    if(list.get(index).equals(item)) {
        found = true;
    }
    else {
        index++;
    }
}
```

D.3.2 do-while

The *do-while loop* executes a block of statements as long as a given expression evaluates to *true*. The expression is tested *after* execution of the loop body, so the body always executes at least once. This is an important difference from the *while loop*.

```
do {
    statements
} while(expression);
```

Example:

```
do {
    System.out.print("Please enter a filename: ");
    input = readInput();
} while(input == null);
```

D.3.3 for

The *for loop* has two different forms. The first form is also known as a *for-each loop* and is used exclusively to iterate over elements of a collection. The loop variable is assigned the value of successive elements of the collection on each iteration of the loop.

```
for(variable-declaration : collection) {
    statements
}
```

Example:

```
for(String note : list) {
    System.out.println(note);
}
```

No associated index value is made available for the elements of the collection. A *for-each loop* cannot be used if the collection is to be modified while it is being iterated over.

The second form of for loop executes as long as a *condition* evaluates to *true*. Before the loop starts, an *initialization statement* is executed exactly once. The *condition* is evaluated before every execution of the loop body (so the statements in the loop's body may execute zero times). An *increment statement* is executed after each execution of the loop body.

```
for(initialization; condition; increment) {
    statements
}
```

Example:

```
for(int i = 0; i < text.size(); i++) {
    System.out.println(text.get(i));
}
```

Both types of for loop are commonly used to execute the body of the loop a definite number of times—for instance, once for each element in a collection—although a *for loop* is actually closer in effect to a *while loop* than to a *for-each loop*.

D.4 Exceptions

Throwing and catching exceptions provides another pair of constructs to alter control flow. However, exceptions are primarily used to anticipate and handle error situations, rather than the normal flow of control.

```
try {
    statements
}
catch(exception-type name) {
    statements
}
finally {
    statements
}
```

Example:

```
try {
    FileWriter writer = new FileWriter("foo.txt");
    writer.write(text);
    writer.close();
}
catch(IOException e) {
    Debug.reportError("Writing text to file failed.");
    Debug.reportError("The exception is: " + e);
}
```

An exception statement may have any number of *catch clauses*. They are evaluated in order of appearance, and only the first matching clause is executed. (A clause matches if the dynamic type of the exception object being thrown is assignment-compatible with the declared exception type in the catch clause.) The *finally clause* is optional.

Java 7 introduced two mainstream additions to the try statement: multi-catch and try-with-resources, or automatic resource management (ARM).

Multiple exceptions may be handled in the same catch clause by writing the list of exception types separated by the "|" symbol.

Example:

```
try {
    ...
    var.doSomething();
    ...
}
catch(EOFException | FileNotFoundException e) {
    ...
}
```

Automatic resource management—also known as "try-with-resource"—recognizes that try statements are often used to protect statements that use resources that should be closed when their use is complete, both upon success and failure. The header of the try statement is amended to include the opening of the resource—often a file—and the resource will be closed automatically at the end of the try statement.

Example:

```
try (FileWriter writer = new FileWriter(filename)){
    ...
    Use the writer . . .
    ...
}
catch(IOException e) {
    ...
}
```

D.5 Assertions

Assertion statements are primarily used as a testing tool during program development rather than in production code. There are two forms of assert statement:

```
assert boolean-expression ;
assert boolean-expression : expression;
```

Examples:

```
assert getDetails(key) != null;
assert expected == actual:
       "Actual value: " + actual +
       "does not match expected value: " + expected;
```

If the assertion expression evaluates to *false*, then an `AssertionError` will be thrown.

A compiler option allows assertion statements to be rendered inactive in production code without having to remove them from the program source.

APPENDIX E

Running Java without BlueJ

Throughout this book, we have used BlueJ to develop and execute our Java applications. There is a good reason for this: BlueJ gives us tools to make some development tasks very easy. In particular, it lets us execute individual methods of classes and objects easily; this is very useful if we want to quickly test a segment of new code.

We separate the discussion of working without BlueJ into two categories: executing an application without BlueJ, and developing without BlueJ.

E.1 Executing without BlueJ

Usually, when applications are delivered to end users, they are executed differently than from within BlueJ. They then have one single starting point, which defines where execution begins when a user starts an application.

The exact mechanism used to start an application depends on the operating system. Usually, this is done by double-clicking an application icon, or by entering the name of the application on a command line. The operating system then needs to know which method of which class to invoke to execute the complete program.

In Java, this problem is solved using a convention. When a Java program is started, the name of the class is specified as a parameter of the start command, and the name of the method is `main`. The name "main" is arbitrarily chosen by the Java developers, but it is fixed—the method must have this name. (The choice of "main" for the name of the initial method actually goes back to the C language, from which Java inherits much of its syntax.)

Let us consider, for example, the following command, entered at a command line such as the Windows command prompt or a Unix terminal:

```
java Game
```

The `java` command starts the Java virtual machine. It is part of the Java Development Kit (JDK), which must be installed on your system. `Game` is the name of the class that we want to start.

The Java system will then look for a method in class `Game` with exactly the following signature:

```
public static void main(String[] args)
```

The method has to be `public` so that it can be invoked from the outside. It also has to be `static`, because no objects exist when we start off. Initially, we have only classes, so static methods are all we can call. This static method then typically creates the first object. The return type is `void`, as this method does not return a value.

The parameter is a `String` array. This allows users to pass in additional arguments. In our example, the value of the `args` parameter will be an array of length zero. The command line starting the program can, however, define arguments:

```
java Game 2 Fred
```

Every word after the class name in this command line will be read as a separate `String` and be passed into the main method as an element in the string array. In this case, the `args` array would contain two elements, which are the strings `"2"` and `"Fred"`. Command-line parameters are not very often used with Java.

The body of the main method can theoretically contain any statements you like. Good style, however, dictates that the length of the main method should be kept to a minimum. Specifically, it should not contain anything that is part of the application logic.

Typically, the main method should do exactly what you did interactively to start the same application in BlueJ. If, for instance, you created an object of class `Game` and invoked a method named `start` to start an application, you should add the following main method to the `Game` class:

```java
public static void main(String[] args)
{
    Game game = new Game();
    game.start();
}
```

Now, executing the main method will mimic your interactive invocation of the game.

Java projects are usually stored each in a separate directory. All classes for a project are placed inside this directory. When you execute the command to start Java and execute your application, make sure that the project directory is the active directory in your command terminal. This ensures that the classes will be found.

If the specified class cannot be found, the Java virtual machine will generate an error message similar to this one:

```
Could not find or load main class game
```

If you see a message like this, make sure that you have typed the class name correctly, and that the current directory actually contains this class. The class is stored in a file with the suffix `.class`. The code for class `Game`, for example, is stored in a file named `Game.class`.

If the class is found but does not contain a main method (or the main method does not have the right signature), you will see a message similar to this one:

```
Main method not found in class Game, please define the main method as:
public static void main(String[] args)
```

In that case, make sure that the class you want to execute has a correct main method.

E.2 Creating executable .jar files

Java projects are typically stored as a collection of files in a directory (or "folder"). We shall briefly discuss the different files below.

To distribute applications to others, it is often easier if the whole application is stored in a single file. Java's mechanism for doing this is the Java Archive (.jar) format. All of the files of an application can be bundled into a single file, and they can still be executed. (If you are familiar with the "zip" compression format, it might be interesting to know that the format is, in fact, the same. "Jar" files can be opened with zip programs and vice versa.)

To make a .jar file executable, it is necessary to specify the main class somewhere. (Remember: The executed method is always main, but we need to specify the class this method is in.) This is done by including a text file in the .jar file (the *manifest file*) with this information. Luckily, BlueJ takes care of this for you.

To create an executable .jar file in BlueJ, use the *Project—Create Jar File* function, and specify in the resulting dialog the class that contains the main method. (You must still write a main method exactly as discussed above.)

For details with this function, read the BlueJ tutorial, which you can get through the BlueJ menu *Help—Tutorial* or from the BlueJ web site.

Once the executable .jar file has been created, it can be executed by double-clicking it. The computer that executes this .jar file must have the JDK or JRE (Java Runtime Environment) installed and associated with .jar files.

E.3 Developing without BlueJ

If you want not only to execute but also develop your programs without BlueJ, you will need to edit and compile the classes. The source code of a class is stored in a file ending in .java. For example, class Game is stored in a file called Game.java. Source files can be edited with any text editor. There are many free or inexpensive text editors around. Some, such as *Notepad* or *WordPad*, are distributed with Windows, but if you really want to use the editor for more than a quick test, you will soon want to get a better one. Be careful with word processors, though. Word processors typically do not save text in plain text format, and the Java system will not be able to read it.

The source files can then be compiled from a command line with the Java compiler that is included with the JDK. It is called javac. To compile a source file named Game.java, use the command

```
javac Game.java
```

This command will compile the Game class and any other classes it depends on. It will create a file called Game.class. This file contains the code that can be executed by the Java virtual machine. To execute it, use the command

```
java Game
```

Note that this command does not include the .class suffix.

APPENDIX F
Using the Debugger

The BlueJ debugger provides a set of basic debugging features that are intentionally simplified yet genuinely useful, both for debugging programs and for gaining an understanding of the runtime behavior of programs.

The debugger window can be accessed by selecting the *Show Debugger* item from the *View* menu or by pressing the right mouse button over the work indicator and selecting *Show Debugger* from the pop-up menu. Figure F.1 shows the debugger window.

Figure F.1
The BlueJ debugger window

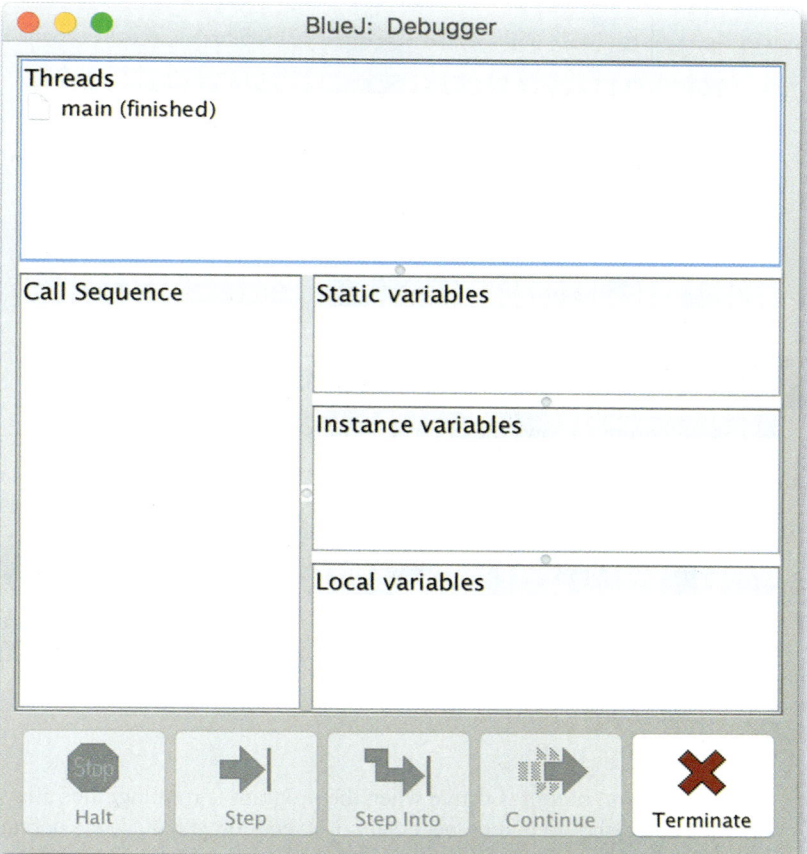

The debugger window contains five display areas and five control buttons. The areas and buttons become active only when a program reaches a breakpoint or halts for some other reason. The following sections describe how to set breakpoints, how to control program execution, and the purpose of each of the display areas.

F.1 Breakpoints

A breakpoint is a flag attached to a line of code (Figure F.2). When a breakpoint is reached during program execution, the debugger's displays and controls become active, allowing you to inspect the state of the program and control further execution.

Breakpoints are set via the editor window. Either press the left mouse button in the breakpoint area to the left of the source text, or place the cursor on the line of code where the breakpoint should be and select *Set/Clear Breakpoint* from the editor's *Tools* menu. Breakpoints can be removed by the reverse process. Breakpoints can be set only within classes that have been compiled.

Figure F.2
A breakpoint attached to a line of code

```
 * The '=' button was pressed.
 */
public void equals()
{
    // This should completes the building of a second operand,
    // so ensure that we really have a left operand, an operator
    // and a right operand.
    if(haveLeftOperand &&
            lastOperator != '?' &&
            buildingDisplayValue) {
        calculateResult();
        lastOperator = '?';
        buildingDisplayValue = false;
    }
    else {
        keySequenceError();
    }
}
```

F.2 The control buttons

Figure F.3 shows the control buttons that are active at a breakpoint.

Figure F.3
Active control buttons at a breakpoint

F.2.1 Halt

The *Halt* button is active when the program is running, thus allowing execution to be interrupted should that be necessary. If execution is halted, the debugger will show the state of the program as if a breakpoint had been reached.

F.2.2 Step

The *Step* button resumes execution at the current statement. Execution will pause again when the statement is completed. If the statement involves a method call, the complete method call is completed before the execution pauses again (unless the call leads to another explicit breakpoint).

F.2.3 Step Into

The *Step Into* button resumes execution at the current statement. If this statement is a method call, then execution will "step into" that method and be paused at the first statement inside it.

F.2.4 Continue

The *Continue* button resumes execution until the next breakpoint is reached, execution is interrupted via the *Halt* button, or the execution completes normally.

F.2.5 Terminate

The *Terminate* button aggressively finishes execution of the current program such that it cannot be resumed again. If it is simply desired to interrupt the execution in order to examine the current program state, then the *Halt* operation is preferred.

F.3 The variable displays

Figure F.4 shows all three variable display areas active at a breakpoint, in an example taken from the predator–prey simulation discussed in Chapter 12. Static variables are displayed in the upper area, instance variables in the middle area, and local variables in the lower area.

Figure F.4
Active-variable displays

```
Static variables
private Color EMPTY_COLOR = <object reference>
private Color UNKNOWN_COLOR = <object reference>
public int EXIT_ON_CLOSE = 3
```

```
Instance variables
private String STEP_PREFIX = "Step: "
private String POPULATION_PREFIX = "Population: "
private JLabel stepLabel = <object reference>
private JLabel population = <object reference>
private SimulatorView.FieldView fieldView = <object reference>
private Map<Class,Color> colors = <object reference>
private FieldStats stats = <object reference>
```

```
Local variables
int height = 80
int width = 120
Container contents = <object reference>
```

When a breakpoint is reached, execution will be halted at a statement of an arbitrary object within the current program. The *Static variables* area displays the values of the static variables defined in the class of that object. The *Instance variables* area displays the values of that particular object's instance variables. Both areas also include any variables inherited from superclasses.

The *Local variables* area displays the values of local variables and parameters of the currently executing method or constructor. Local variables will appear in this area only once they have been initialized, as it is only at that point that they come into existence within the virtual machine.

A variable in any of these areas that is an object reference may be inspected by double-clicking on it.

F.4 The Call Sequence display

Figure F.5 shows the *Call Sequence* display, containing a sequence six methods deep. Methods appear in the format `Class.method` in the sequence, irrespective of whether they are static methods or instance methods. Constructors appear as `Class.<init>` in the sequence.

The call sequence operates as a *stack*, with the method at the top of the sequence being the one where the flow of execution currently lies. The variable display areas reflect the details of the method or constructor currently highlighted in the call sequence. Selecting a different line of the sequence will update the contents of the other display areas.

Figure F.5
A call sequence

```
Call Sequence
Animal.setDead
Fox.findFood
Fox.act
Simulator.simulateOneStep
Simulator.simulate
Simulator.runLongSimulation
```

F.5 The Threads display

The *Threads display* area is beyond the scope of this book and will not be discussed further.

APPENDIX G

JUnit Unit-Testing Tools

In this appendix, we give a brief outline of the main features of BlueJ's support for JUnit-style unit testing. More details can be found in the testing tutorial that is available from the BlueJ web site.

G.1 Enabling unit-testing functionality

In order to enable the unit-testing functionality of BlueJ, it is necessary to ensure that the *Show unit testing tools* box is ticked under the *Tools–Preferences–Miscellaneous* menu. The main BlueJ window will then contain a number of extra buttons that are active when a project is open.

G.2 Creating a test class

A test class is created by right-clicking a class in the class diagram and choosing *Create Test Class*. The name of the test class is determined automatically by adding `Test` as a suffix to the name of the associated class. Alternatively, a test class may be created by selecting the *New Class . . .* button and choosing *Unit Test* for the class type. In this case, you have a free choice over its name.

Test classes are annotated with `<<unit test>>` in the class diagram, and they have a color distinct from ordinary classes.

G.3 Creating a test method

Test methods can be created interactively. A sequence of user interactions with the class diagram and object bench are recorded, then captured as a sequence of Java statements and declarations in a method of the test class. Start recording by selecting *Create Test Method* from the pop-up menu associated with a test class. You will be prompted for the name of the new method. Earlier versions of JUnit, up to version 3, required the method names to start with the prefix "test". This is not a requirement in current versions. The *recording* symbol to the left of the class diagram will then be colored red, and the *End* and *Cancel* buttons become available.

Once recording has started, any object creations or method calls will form part of the code of the method being created. Select *End* to complete the recording and capture the test, or select *Cancel* to discard the recording, leaving the test class unchanged.

Test methods have the annotation `@Test` in the source of the test class.

G.4 Test assertions

While recording a test method, any method calls that return a result will bring up a *Method Result* window. This offers the opportunity to make an assertion about the result value by ticking the *Assert that* box. A drop-down menu contains a set of possible assertions for the result value. If an assertion is made, this will be encoded as a method call in the test method which is intended to lead to an `AssertionError` if the test fails.

G.5 Running tests

Individual test methods can be run by selecting them from the pop-up menu associated with the test class. A successful test will be indicated by a message in the main window's status line. An unsuccessful test will cause the *Test Results* window to appear. Selecting *Test All* from the test class's pop-up menu runs all tests from a single test class. The *Test Results* window will detail the success or failure of each method.

G.6 Fixtures

The contents of the object bench may be captured as a *fixture* by selecting *Object Bench to Test Fixture* from the pop-up menu associated with the test class. The effect of creating a fixture is that a field definition for each object is added to the test class, and statements are added to its `setUp` method that re-create the exact state of the objects as they were on the bench. The objects are then removed from the bench.

The `setUp` method has the annotation `@Before` in the test class and the method is automatically executed before the run of any test method, so all objects in a fixture are available for all tests.

The objects of a fixture may be re-created on the object bench by selecting *Test Fixture to Object Bench* from the test class's menu.

A `tearDown` method, with the annotation `@After`, is called following each test method. This can be used to conduct any post-test housekeeping or clean-up operations, should they be needed.

APPENDIX H

Teamwork Tools

In this appendix, we briefly describe the tools available to support teamwork.

BlueJ includes teamwork support tools based on a source-code-repository model. In this model, a repository server is set up that is accessible over the Internet from the machines the users work on.

The server needs to be set up by an administrator. BlueJ supports both Subversion and CVS repositories.

H.1 Server setup

The setup of the repository server should normally be done by an experienced administrator. Detailed instructions can be found in the document, BlueJ Teamwork Repository Configuration, which is accessible via the *BlueJ Tutorial* item in BlueJ's *Help* menu.

H.2 Enabling teamwork functionality

The teamwork tools are initially hidden in BlueJ. To show the tools, open the *Preferences* dialog and, in the *Miscellaneous* tab, tick the *Show teamwork controls* box. The BlueJ interface then contains three extra buttons (*Update*, *Commit*, *Status*) and an additional submenu titled *Team* in the *Tools* menu.

H.3 Sharing a project

To create a shared project, one team member creates the project as a standard BlueJ project. The project can then be shared by using the *Share this Project* function from the *Team* menu. When this function is used, a copy of the project is placed into the central repository. The server name and access details need to be specified in a dialog; ask your administrator (the one who set up the repository) for the details to fill in here.

H.4 Using a shared project

Once a user has created a shared project in the repository, other team members can use this project. To do this, select *Checkout Project* from the *Team* menu. This will place a copy of the shared project from the central server into your local file system. You can then work on the local copy.

H.5 Update and commit

Every now and then, the various copies of the project that team members have on their local disks need to be synchronized. This is done via the central repository. Use the *Commit* function to copy your changes into the repository, and use the *Update* function to copy changes from the repository (which other team members have committed) into your own local copy. It is good practice to commit and update frequently so that the changes at any step do not become too substantial.

H.6 More information

More detailed information is available in the Team Work Tutorial, which is accessible via the *BlueJ Tutorial* item in BlueJ's *Help* menu.

APPENDIX I

Javadoc

Writing good documentation for class and interface definitions is an important complement to writing good-quality source code. Documentation allows you to communicate your intentions to human readers in the form of a natural-language, high-level overview, rather than forcing them to read relatively low-level source code. Of particular value is documentation for the `public` elements of a class or interface, so that programmers can make use of it without having to know the details of its implementation.

In all of the project examples in this book, we have used a particular commenting style that is recognized by the `javadoc` documentation tool, which is distributed as part of the JDK. This tool automates the generation of class documentation in the form of HTML pages in a consistent style. The Java API has been documented using this same tool, and its value is appreciated when using library classes.

In this appendix, we give a brief summary of the main elements of the documentation comments that you should get into the habit of using in your own source code.

I.1 Documentation comments

The elements of a class to be documented are the class definition as a whole, its fields, constructors, and methods. Most important from the viewpoint of a user of your class is to have documentation for the class and its public constructors and methods. We have tended not to provide javadoc-style commenting for fields, because we regard these as private implementation-level details, and not something to be relied upon by users.

Documentation comments are always opened with the character triplet "/**" and closed by the character pair "*/". Between these symbols, a comment can have a *main description* followed by a *tag section*, although both are optional.

I.1.1 The main description

The main description for a class should be a general description of the purpose of the class. Code I.1 shows part of a typical main description, taken from the `Game` class of the *world-of-zuul* project. Note how the description includes details of how to use this class to start the game.

Code I.1
The main description of a class comment

```
/**
 * This class is the main class of the "World of Zuul".
 * application.
 *
 * "World of Zuul" is a very simple, text-based adventure game.
 * Users can walk around some scenery. That's all. It should
 * really be extended to make it more interesting!
 * To play this game, create an instance of this class and call
 * the "play" method.
 */
```

The main description for a method should be kept fairly general, without going into a lot of detail about how the method is implemented. Indeed, the main description for a method will often only need to be a single sentence, such as

```
/**
 * Create a new passenger with distinct pickup and
 * destination locations.
 */
```

Particular thought should be given to the first sentence of the main description for a class, interface, or method, as it is used in a separate summary at the top of the generated documentation.

Javadoc also supports the use of HTML markup within these comments.

I.1.2 The tag section

Following the main description comes the *tag section*. Javadoc recognizes around 20 tags, of which we discuss only the most important here (Table I.1). Tags can be used in two forms: *block tags* and *in-line tags*. We shall only discuss block tags, as these are the most commonly used. Further details about in-line tags and the remaining available tags can be found in the *javadoc* section of the *Tools and Utilities* documentation that is part of the JDK.

Table .1
Common javadoc tags

Tag	Associated text
@author	author name(s)
@param	parameter name and description
@return	description of the return value
@see	cross-reference
@throws	exception type thrown and the circumstances
@version	version description

The @author and @version tags are regularly found in class and interface comments and cannot be used in constructor, method, or field comments. Both are followed by freetext, and there is no required format for either. Examples are

```
@author Hacker T. Largebrain
@version 2012.12.03
```

The `@param` and `@throws` tags are used with methods and constructors, whereas `@return` is just used with methods. Examples are

```
@param limit The maximum value allowed.
@return A random number in the range 1 to limit (inclusive).
@throws IllegalLimitException If limit is less than 1.
```

The `@see` tag has several different forms and may be used in any documentation comment. It provides a way to cross-reference a comment to another class, method, or other form of documentation. A *See Also* section is added to the item being commented. Here are some typical examples:

```
@see "The Java Language Specification, by Joy et al"
@see <a href="http://www.bluej.org/">The BlueJ web site</a>
@see #isAlive
@see java.util.ArrayList#add
```

The first simply embeds a text string with no hyperlink; the second embeds a hyperlink to the specified document; the third links to the documentation for the `isAlive` method in the same class; the fourth links to the documentation for the `add` method in the `ArrayList` class of the `java.util` package.

I.2 BlueJ support for javadoc

If a project has been commented using the `javadoc` style, then BlueJ provides support for generating the complete HTML documentation. In the main window, select the *Tools/Project Documentation* menu item, and the documentation will be generated (if necessary) and displayed within a browser window.

Within the BlueJ editor, the source-code view of a class can be switched to the documentation view by changing the *Source Code* option to *Documentation* at the right of the window (Figure I.1), or by using *Toggle Documentation View* from the editor's *Tools* menu. This provides a quick preview of the documentation, but will not contain references to documentation of superclasses or used classes.

Figure I.1
The *Source Code* and *Documentation* view option

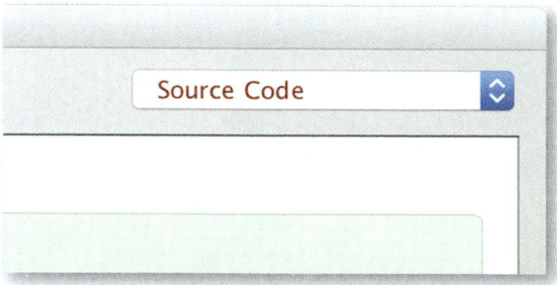

More details are available at:

```
http://www.oracle.com/technetwork/java/javase/documentation/
index-137868.html
```

APPENDIX J

Program Style Guide

J.1 Naming

J.1.1 Use meaningful names

Use descriptive names for all identifiers (names of classes, variables, and methods). Avoid ambiguity. Avoid abbreviations. Simple mutator methods should be named *setSomething*(. . .). Simple accessor methods should be named *getSomething*(. . .). Accessor methods with `boolean` return values are often called *isSomething*(. . .)—for example, `isEmpty()`.

J.1.2 Class names start with a capital letter

J.1.3 Class names are singular nouns

J.1.4 Method and variable names start with lowercase letters

All three—class, method, and variable names—use capital letters to begin each word after the first in order to increase readability of compound identifiers, e.g. `numberOfItems`.

J.1.5 Constants are written in UPPERCASE

Constants occasionally use underscores to indicate compound identifiers:

```
MAXIMUM_SIZE.
```

J.2 Layout

J.2.1 One level of indentation is four spaces

J.2.2 All statements within a block are indented one level

J.2.3 Braces for classes and methods are alone on one line

The braces for class and method blocks are on separate lines and are at the same indentation level. For example:

```
public int getAge()
{
    statements
}
```

J.2.4 For all other blocks, braces open at the end of a line

All other blocks open with braces at the end of the line that contains the keyword defining the block. The closing brace is on a separate line, aligned under the keyword that defines the block. For example:

```
while(condition) {
    statements
}

if(condition) {
    statements
}
else {
    statements
}
```

J.2.5 Always use braces in control structures

Braces are used in if statements and loops even if the body is only a single statement.

J.2.6 Use a space before the opening brace of a control structure's block

J.2.7 Use a space around operators

J.2.8 Use a blank line between methods (and constructors)

Use blank lines to separate logical blocks of code; this means at least between methods, but also between logical parts within a method.

J.3 Documentation

J.3.1 Every class has a class comment at the top

The class comment contains at least:

- a general description of the class
- the author's name(s)
- a version number

Every person who has contributed to the class has to be named as an author or has to be otherwise appropriately credited.

A version number can be a simple number, a date, or other format. The important thing is that a reader must be able to recognize whether two versions are different, and to determine which one is newer.

J.3.2 Every method has a method comment

J.3.3 Comments are Javadoc-readable

Class and method comments must be recognized by Javadoc. In other words, they should start with the comment symbol "/**".

J.3.4 Code comments (only) where necessary

Comments in the code should be included where the code is not obvious or is difficult to understand (and preference should be given to make the code obvious or easy to understand where possible) and where comments facilitate understanding of a method. Do not comment obvious statements—assume that your reader understands Java!

J.4 Language-use restrictions

J.4.1 Order of declarations: fields, constructors, methods

The elements of a class definition appear (if present) in the following order: package statement; import statements; class comment; class header; field definitions; constructors; methods; inner classes.

J.4.2 Fields may not be public (except for final fields)

J.4.3 Always use an access modifier

Specify all fields and methods as either private, public, or protected. Never use default (package private) access.

J.4.4 Import classes separately

Importing statements explicitly naming every class are preferred over importing whole packages. For example:

```
import java.util.ArrayList;
import java.util.HashSet;
```

is better than

```
import java.util.*;
```

J.4.5 Always include a constructor (even if the body is empty)

J.4.6 Always include a superclass constructor call

In constructors of subclasses, do not rely on automatic insertion of a superclass call. Include the super() call explicitly, even if it would work without it.

J.4.7 Initialize all fields in the constructor

Include assignments of default values. This makes it clear to a reader that the correct initialization of all fields has been considered.

J.5 Code idioms

J.5.1 Use iterators with collections

To iterate over a complete collection, use a for-each loop. When the collection must be changed during iteration, use an `Iterator` with a while loop or a for loop, not an integer index.

APPENDIX K

Important Library Classes

The Java platform includes a rich set of libraries that support a wide variety of programming tasks.

In this appendix, we briefly summarize details of some classes and interfaces from the most important packages of the Java API. A competent Java programmer should be familiar with most of these. This appendix is only a summary, and it should be read in conjunction with the full API documentation.

K.1 The `java.lang` package

Classes and interfaces in the `java.lang` package are fundamental to the Java language, as this package is automatically imported implicitly into any class definition.

Package `java.lang` —Summary of the most important classes	
interface `Comparable`	Implementation of this interface allows comparison and ordering of objects from the implementing class. Static utility methods such as `Arrays.sort` and `Collections.sort` can then provide efficient sorting in such cases, for instance.
interface `Runnable`	An interface that takes no parameters and returns no result and used as the type for lambdas with those characteristics.
class `Math`	`Math` is a class containing only static fields and methods. Values for the mathematical constants e and π are defined here, along with trigonometric functions and others such as `abs`, `min`, `max`, and `sqrt`.
class `Object`	All classes have `Object` as a superclass at the root of their class hierarchy. From it, all objects inherit default implementations for important methods such as `equals` and `toString`. Other significant methods defined by this class are `clone` and `hashCode`.
class `String`	Strings are an important feature of many applications, and they receive special treatment in Java. Key methods of the `String` class are `charAt`, `equals`, `indexOf`, `length`, `split`, and `substring`. Strings are immutable objects, so methods such as `trim` that appear to be mutators actually return a new `String` object representing the result of the operation.
class `StringBuilder`	The `StringBuilder` class offers an efficient alternative to `String` when it is required to build up a string from a number of components: e.g., via concatenation. Its key methods are `append`, `insert`, and `toString`.

K.2 The `java.util` package

The `java.util` package is a relatively incoherent collection of useful classes and interfaces.

Package `java.util` — Summary of the most important classes and interfaces	
interface `Collection`	This interface provides the core set of methods for most of the collection-based classes defined in the `java.util` package, such as `ArrayList`, `HashSet`, and `LinkedList`. It defines signatures for the `add`, `clear`, `iterator`, `remove`, and `size` methods.
interface `Iterator`	`Iterator` defines a simple and consistent interface for iterating over the contents of a collection. Its three core methods are `hasNext`, `next`, and `remove`.
interface `List`	`List` is an extension of the `Collection` interface and provides a means to impose a sequence on the selection. As such, many of its methods take an index parameter: for instance, `add`, `get`, `remove`, and `set`. Classes such as `ArrayList` and `LinkedList` implement `List`.
interface `Map`	The `Map` interface offers an alternative to list-based collections by supporting the idea of associating each object in a collection with a *key* value. Objects are added and retrieved via its `put` and `get` methods. Note that a `Map` does not return an `Iterator`, but its `keySet` method returns a `Set` of the keys, and its `values` method returns a `Collection` of the objects in the map.
interface `Set`	`Set` extends the `Collection` interface with the intention of mandating that a collection contain no duplicate elements. It is worth pointing out that `Set` has no implication to enforce this restriction. This means that `Set` is actually provided as a marker interface to enable collection implementers to indicate that their classes fulfill this particular restriction.
class `ArrayList`	`ArrayList` is an implementation of the `List` interface that uses an array to provide efficient direct access via integer indices to the objects it stores. If objects are added or removed from anywhere other than the last position in the list, then following items have to be moved to make space or close the gap. Key methods are `add`, `get`, `iterator`, `remove`, `removeIf`, `size`, and `stream`.
class `Collections`	`Collections` contains many useful static methods for manipulating collections. Key methods are `binarySearch`, `fill`, and `sort`.
class `HashMap`	`HashMap` is an implementation of the `Map` interface. Key methods are `get`, `put`, `remove`, and `size`. Iteration over a `HashMap` is usually a two-stage process: obtain the set of keys via its `keySet` method, and then iterate over the keys.
class `HashSet`	`HashSet` is a hash-based implementation of the `Set` interface. Key methods are `add`, `remove`, and `size`.
class `LinkedList`	`LinkedList` is an implementation of the `List` interface that uses an internal linked structure to store objects. Direct access to the ends of the list is efficient, but access to individual objects via an index is less efficient than with an `ArrayList`. On the other hand, adding objects or removing them from within the list requires no shifting of existing objects. Key methods are `add`, `getFirst`, `getLast`, `iterator`, `removeFirst`, `removeIf`, `removeLast`, `size`, and `stream`.
class `Random`	The `Random` class supports generation of pseudo-random values—typically, random numbers. The sequence of numbers generated is determined by a *seed value*, which may be passed to a constructor or set via a call to `setSeed`. Two `Random` objects starting from the same seed will return the same sequence of values to identical calls. Key methods are `nextBoolean`, `nextDouble`, `nextInt`, and `setSeed`.
class `Scanner`	The `Scanner` class provides a way to read and parse input. It is often used to read input from the keyboard. Key methods are `next` and `hasNext`.

K.3 The `java.io` and `java.nio.file` packages

The `java.io` and `java.nio.file` packages contain classes that support input and output and access to the file system. Many of the input/output classes in `java.io` are distinguished by whether they are *stream-based* (operating on binary data) or *readers* and *writers* (operating on characters). The `java.nio` package supplies several classes that support convenient access to the file system.

Package `java.io` — Summary of the most important classes and interfaces

interface `Serializable`	The `Serializable` interface is an empty interface requiring no code to be written in an implementing class. Classes implement this interface in order to be able to participate in the serialization process. `Serializable` objects may be written and read as a whole to and from sources of output and input. This makes storage and retrieval of persistent data a relatively simple process in Java. See the `ObjectInputStream` and `ObjectOutputStream` classes for further information.
class `BufferedReader`	`BufferedReader` is a class that provides buffered character-based access to a source of input. Buffered input is often more efficient than unbuffered, particularly if the source of input is in the external file system. Because it buffers input, it is able to offer a `readLine` method that is not available in most other input classes. Key methods are `close`, `read`, and `readLine`.
class `BufferedWriter`	`BufferedWriter` is a class that provides buffered character-based output. Buffered output is often more efficient than unbuffered, particularly if the destination of the output is in the external file system. Key methods are `close`, `flush`, and `write`.
class `File`	The `File` class provides an object representation for files and folders (directories) in an external file system. Methods exist to indicate whether a file is readable and/or writeable, and whether it is a file or a folder. A `File` object can be created for a nonexistent file, which may be a first step in creating a physical file on the file system. Key methods are `canRead`, `canWrite`, `createNewFile`, `createTempFile`, `getName`, `getParent`, `getPath`, `isDirectory`, `isFile`, and `listFiles`.
class `FileReader`	The `FileReader` class is used to open an external file ready for reading its contents as characters. A `FileReader` object is often passed to the constructor of another reader class (such as a `BufferedReader`) rather than being used directly. Key methods are `close` and `read`.
class `FileWriter`	The `FileWriter` class is used to open an external file ready for writing character-based data. Pairs of constructors determine whether an existing file will be appended to, or its existing contents discarded. A `FileWriter` object is often passed to the constructor of another Writer class (such as a `BufferedWriter`) rather than being used directly. Key methods are `close`, `flush`, and `write`.
class `IOException`	`IOException` is a checked exception class that is at the root of the exception hierarchy of most input/output exceptions.

Package `java.nio.file` —Summary of the most important classes and interfaces	
interface `Path`	The `Path` interface provides the key methods for accessing information about a file in the file system. `Path` is, in effect, a replacement for the older `File` class of the `java.io` package.
class `Paths`	The `Paths` class provides `get` methods to return concrete instances of the `Path` interface.
class `Files`	`Files` is a class that provides static methods to query attributes of files and directories (folders), as well as to manipulate the file system—e.g., creating directories and changing file permissions. It also includes methods for opening files, such as `newBufferedReader`.

K.4 The `java.util.function` package

The `java.util.function` package contains only interfaces. It supplies the commonly recurring types that are associated with lambdas and method references. Among these are consumer, supplier and predicate interfaces, as well as those for binary operators, for instance. All of the interfaces are important and we describe only a small selection here.

Package `java.util.function` —Summary of some of the typical interfaces	
interface `BiFunction`	The `BiFunction` interface takes two parameters and returns a result. The types of the parameters and result may be all different, so this is a generalization of the `BinaryOperator` interface.
interface `BinaryOperator`	The `BinaryOperator` interface takes two parameters of its parameterized type and returns a result of the same type. This is commonly used in *reduce* operations.
interface `Consumer`	The `Consumer` interface takes a single parameter of its parameterized type and has a `void` result.
interface `Predicate`	The `Predicate` interface takes a single parameter of its parameterized type and returns a `boolean` result. This is commonly used in *filter* operations.
interface `Supplier`	The `Supplier` interface takes no parameter and returns a result of its parameterized type.

K.5 The `java.net` package

The `java.net` package contains classes and interfaces supporting networked applications. Most of these are outside the scope of this book.

Package `java.net` —Summary of the most important classes	
class `URL`	The `URL` class represents a Uniform Resource Locator. In other words, it provides a way to describe the location of something on the Internet. In fact, it can also be used to describe the location of something on a local file system. We have included it here because classes from the `java.io` and `javax.swing` packages often use URL objects. Key methods are `getContent`, `getFile`, `getHost`, `getPath`, and `openStream`.

K.6 Other important packages

Other important packages are:

```
java.awt
java.awt.event
javax.swing
javax.swing.event
```

These are used extensively when writing graphical user interfaces (GUIs), and they contain many useful classes that a GUI programmer should become familiar with.

APPENDIX L

Concept Glossary

abstract class   An abstract class is a class that is not intended for creating instances. Its purpose is to serve as a superclass for other classes. Abstract classes may contain abstract methods.

abstract method   An abstract method definition consists of a method header without a method body. It is marked with the keyword `abstract`.

abstract subclass   For a subclass of an abstract class to become concrete, it must provide implementations for all inherited abstract methods. Otherwise, it will itself be abstract.

abstraction   Abstraction is the ability to ignore details of parts, to focus attention on a higher level of a problem.

access modifier   Access modifiers define the visibility of a field, constructor, or method. Public elements are accessible from inside the same class and from other classes; private elements are accessible only from within the same class.

accessor method   Accessor methods return information about the state of an object.

anonymous inner classes   Anonymous inner classes are a useful construct for implementing event listeners that are not functional interfaces.

array   An array is a special type of collection that can store a fixed number of elements.

assertion   An assertion is a statement of a fact that should be true in normal program execution. If the condition is false, we say that the assertion fails. We can use assertions to state our assumptions explicitly and to detect programming errors more easily.

assignment statement   Assignment statements store the value represented by the right-hand side of the statement in the variable named on the left.

autoboxing   Autoboxing is performed automatically when a primitive-type value is used in a context requiring a wrapper type.

boolean expression   Boolean expressions have only two possible values: true and false. They are commonly found controlling the choice between the two paths through a conditional statement.

checked exception   A checked exception is a type of exception whose use will require extra checks from the compiler. In particular, checked exceptions in Java require the use of throws clauses and try statements.

class   Objects are created from classes. The class describes the kind of object; the objects represent individual instances of the class. A class name can be used as the type for a variable. Variables that have a class as their type can store objects of that class.

class cohesion   A cohesive class represents one well-defined entity.

class diagram   The class diagram shows the classes of an application and the relationships between them. It gives information about the source code and presents the static view of a program.

class variable, static variable   Classes can have fields. These are known as class variables or static variables. Exactly one copy exists of a class variable at all times, independent of the number of created instances.

code duplication   Code duplication (having the same segment of code in an application more than once) is a sign of bad design. It should be avoided.

cohesion   The term cohesion describes how well a unit of code maps to a logical task or entity. In a highly cohesive system, each unit of code (method, class, or module) is responsible for a well-defined task or entity. Good class design exhibits a high degree of cohesion.

collection   A collection object can store an arbitrary number of other objects.

comment   Comments are inserted into the source code of a class to provide explanations to human readers. They have no effect on the functionality of the class.

components   A GUI is built by arranging components on screen. Components are represented by objects.

conditional statement   A conditional statement takes one of two possible actions based upon the result of a test.

constructor   Constructors allow each object to be set up properly when it is first created.

content pane, menu bar   Components are placed in a frame by adding them to the frame's menu bar, or content pane.

coupling   The term coupling describes the interconnectedness of classes. We strive for loose coupling in a system—that is, a system where each class is largely independent and communicates with other classes via a small, well-defined interface.

debugger   A debugger is a software tool that helps in examining how an application executes. It can be used to find bugs.

debugging   Debugging is the attempt to pinpoint and fix the source of an error.

design pattern   A design pattern is a description of a common computing problem and a description of a small set of classes and their interaction structure that helps to solve that problem.

documentation   The documentation of a class should be detailed enough for other programmers to use the class without the need to read the implementation.

dynamic type   The dynamic type of a variable *v* is the type of the object that is currently stored in *v*.

encapsulation   Proper encapsulation in classes reduces coupling and thus leads to a better design.

event handling   The term event handling refers to the task of reacting to user events, such as mouse-button clicks or keyboard input.

event listener   An object can listen to component events by implementing an event-listener interface.

exception An exception is an object representing details of a program failure. An exception is thrown to indicate that a failure has occurred.

exception handler Program code that protects statements in which an exception might be thrown is called an exception handler. It provides reporting and/or recovery code should one arise.

external method call Methods can call methods of other objects using dot notation. This is called an external method call.

field Fields store data for an object to use. Fields are also known as instance variables.

filter We can filter a stream to select only specific elements.

fixture A fixture is a set of objects in a defined state that serves as a basis for unit tests.

for loop An iterative control structure that is often used when an index variable is required to select consecutive elements from a collection, such as an ArrayList or an array.

functional style In the functional style of collection processing, we do not retrieve each element to operate on it. Instead, we pass a code segment to the collection to be applied to each element.

image format Images can be stored in different formats. The differences primarily affect file size and the quality of the image.

immutable An object is said to be immutable if its contents or state cannot be changed once it has been created. Strings are an example of immutable objects.

implementation The complete source code that defines a class is called the implementation of that class.

information hiding Information hiding is a principle that states that internal details of a class's implementation should be hidden from other classes. It ensures better modularization of an application.

inheritance hierarchy Classes that are linked through inheritance relationships form an inheritance hierarchy.

inheritance Inheritance allows us to define one class as an extension of another.

interface A Java `interface` is a specification of a type (in the form of a type name and a set of methods). It often does not provide an implementation for most of its methods.

interface The interface of a class describes what a class does and how it can be used without showing the implementation.

internal method call Methods can call other methods of the same class as part of their implementation. This is called an internal method call.

iterator An iterator is an object that provides functionality to iterate over all elements of a collection.

Java library The Java standard class library contains many classes that are very useful. It is important to know how to use the library.

lambda A lambda is a segment of code that can be stored and executed later.

layout Arranging the layout of components is achieved by using layout managers.

library documentation The Java class library documentation shows details about all classes in the library. Using this documentation is essential in order to make good use of library classes.

lifetime The lifetime of a variable describes how long the variable continues to exist before it is destroyed.

local variable A local variable is a variable declared and used within a single method. Its scope and lifetime are limited to that of the method.

localizing change One of the main goals of a good class design is that of localizing change: making changes to one class should have minimal effects on other classes.

loop A loop can be used to execute a block of statements repeatedly without having to write them multiple times.

map A map is a collection that stores key/value pairs as entries. Values can be looked up by providing the key.

map We can map a stream to a new stream, where each element of the original stream is replaced with a new element derived from the original.

menu bar, content pane Components are placed in a frame by adding them to the frame's menu bar or content pane.

method calling Objects can communicate by calling each other's methods.

method cohesion A cohesive method is responsible for one, and only one, well-defined task.

method polymorphism Method calls in Java are polymorphic. The same method call may at different times invoke different methods, depending on the dynamic type of the variable used to make that call.

method We can communicate with objects by invoking methods on them.

modularization Modularization is the process of dividing a whole into well-defined parts that can be built and examined separately and that interact in well-defined ways.

multiple inheritance A situation in which a class inherits from more than one superclass is called multiple inheritance.

multiple instances Many similar objects can be created from a single class.

mutator method Mutator methods change the state of an object.

negative testing Negative testing is the testing of cases that are expected to fail.

null The Java reserved word `null` is used to mean "no object" when an object variable is not currently referring to a particular object. A field that has not explicitly been initialized will contain the value `null` by default.

object All classes with no explicit superclass have `Object` as their superclass. Java objects model objects from a problem domain.

object creation Objects can create other objects, using the `new` operator. Some objects cannot be constructed unless extra information is provided.

object diagram The object diagram shows the objects and their relationships at one moment in time during the execution of an application. It gives information about objects at runtime and presents the dynamic view of a program.

object references   Variables of object types store references to objects.

overloading   A class may contain more than one constructor, or more than one method of the same name, as long as each has a distinctive set of parameter types.

overriding   A subclass can override a method implementation. To do this, the subclass declares a method with the same signature as the superclass, but with a different method body. The overriding method takes precedence for method calls on subclass objects.

parameter   Methods can have parameters to provide additional information for a task.

pipeline   A pipeline is the combination of two or more stream functions in a chain, where each function is applied in turns.

positive testing   Positive testing is the testing of cases that are expected to succeed.

primitive type   The primitive types in Java are the non-object types. Types such as `int`, `boolean`, `char`, `double`, and `long` are the most common primitive types. Primitive types have no methods.

println   The method `System.out.println` prints its parameter to the text terminal.

protected   Declaring a field or a method `protected` allows direct access to it from (direct or indirect) subclasses.

prototyping   Prototyping is the construction of a partially working system in which some functions of the application are simulated. It serves to provide an understanding early in the development process of how the system will work.

reduce   We can reduce a stream; reducing means to apply a function that takes a whole stream and delivers a single result.

refactoring   Refactoring is the activity of restructuring an existing design to maintain a good class design when the application is modified or extended.

responsibility-driven design   Responsibility-driven design is the process of designing classes by assigning well-defined responsibilities to each class. This process can be used to determine which class should implement which part of an application function.

result   Methods may return information about an object via a return value.

reuse   Inheritance allows us to reuse previously written classes in a new context.

scenarios   Scenarios (also known as "use cases") can be used to get an understanding of the interactions in a system.

scope   The scope of a variable defines the section of source code from which the variable can be accessed.

serialization   Serialization allows whole objects, and object hierarchies, to be read and written in a single operation. Every object involved must be from a class that implements the `Serializable` interface.

set   A set is a collection that stores each individual element at most once. It does not maintain any specific order.

signature   The method name and the parameter types of a method are called its signature. They provide the information needed to invoke that method.

source code The source code of a class determines the structure and behavior (the fields and methods) of each of the objects of that class.

state Objects have state. The state is represented by storing values in fields.

static type The static type of a variable v is the type as declared in the source code in the variable declaration statement.

static variable, class variable Classes can have fields. These are known as class variables or static variables. Exactly one copy exists of a class variable at all times, independent of the number of created instances.

streams Streams unify the processing of elements of a collection and other sets of data. A stream provides useful methods to manipulate these data sets.

subclass A subclass is a class that extends (inherits from) another class. It inherits all fields and methods from its superclass.

substitution Subtype objects may be used wherever objects of a supertype are expected. This is known as substitution.

subtype As an analog to the class hierarchy, types form a type hierarchy. The type defined by a subclass definition is a subtype of the type of its superclass.

superclass A superclass is a class that is extended by another class.

superclass constructor The constructor of a subclass must always invoke the constructor of its superclass as its first statement. If the source code does not include such a call, Java will attempt to insert a call automatically.

superclass method calls Calls to non-private instance methods from within a superclass are always evaluated in the wider context of the object's dynamic type.

switch statement A switch statement selects a sequence of statements for execution from multiple different options.

testing Testing is the activity of finding out whether a piece of code (a method, class, or program) produces the intended behavior.

toString Every object in Java has a `toString` method that can be used to return a string representation of itself. Typically, to make it useful, a class should override this method.

type Parameters have types. The type defines what kinds of values a parameter can take.

unchecked exception An unchecked exception is a type of exception whose use will not require checks from the compiler.

use cases Use cases (also known as "scenarios") can be used to get an understanding of the interactions in a system usually do something if we invoke a method.

variables and subtypes Variables may hold objects of their declared type or of any subtype of their declared type.

verb/noun Classes in a system roughly correspond to nouns in the system's description. Methods correspond to verbs.

walkthrough A walkthrough is an activity of working through a segment of code line by line while observing changes of state and other behavior of the application.

Index

A

abstract, 437
abstract class, 437–40
   `Filter`, 491
   interfaces, 447, 455–56
   library class, 451
abstract method, 435–37, 440–42, 446
abstract subclass, 438
Abstract Window Toolkit (AWT), 463
abstraction, 129, 417
   abstract class, 433–40
   abstract method, 435–37
   `ArrayList`, 137
   `Class`, 455
   collections, grouping objects, 130–31
   event-driven simulations, 456–57
   flexibility, 444
   foxes-and-rabbits project, 418–33
   interfaces, 445–52
   multiple inheritance, 442–45
   object interaction, 96–97
   `print`, 124
   simulations, 417–18
access modifiers, 232
access rights, 374–75
accessor method, 64–67, 70, 393
`act`, 436
`ActionEvent`, 470
`ActionListener`, 470, 473, 474, 488
`actionPerformed`, 472, 473, 474
`ActivityPost`, 371
`Actor`, 442–44
`Adapter`, 501
`add`, 135, 217, 466n, 483
`addActionListener`, 470, 471, 473
`addDetails`, 514, 518, 537, 544
`addMouseListener`, 502
`AddressBook`
   defensive programming, 516–19
   errors, 512–15, 543
   internal consistency, 540
   serialization, 555
`AdressBookFileHandler`, 554
`alive`, 434
analysis and design, 557–64, 580–84
and operator, 104, 154
`Animal`, 434–35, 437, 447
animal population, 178–82
`AnimalMonitor`, 180–81
annotation, 337, 342
anonymous function, 183
anonymous inner class, 501–3
anonymous object, 171
application design, 557–76
   analysis and design, 557–64
   class design, 564–66
   cooperation, 567
   design patterns, 570–76
   documentation, 566–67
   prototyping, 567–68
   waterfall model, 568–69
application testing, 325
`apply`, 489
`applyFilter`, 493

`applyPreviousOperator`, 346–47, 349
ARM *See* automatic resource management
array
    cellular automata, 264–72
    errors, 257
    expressions, 257
    fixed-size collection, 251–81
    index, 257
    initializer, 271
    log-file analyzer, 252–58
    `LogAnalyzer`, 254
    objects, 255–57
    streams, 279–80
    two-dimensional, 272–79
    variables, 254–55
`ArrayList`, 131–32, 134, 135, 137–38, 244–45, 247
    `add to`, 217
    auction project, 165–75
    collection hierarchy, 450
    collections, 161
    `elementData`, 330
    `getResponse`, 213
    inheritance, 387
    `iterator`, 159–62
    `LinkedList`, 173
    `listAllFiles`, 144
    `lots`, 170
    `Map`, 219
    network project, 362
    random numbers, 212
    `remove`, 138
    sets, 223
    source code, 200
    streams, 186–96
`ArrayList<String>`, 136
`ArrayListIterator`, 573
assert, 539
`assert`, 539
assert statement, 538–40
assertion, 338
    errors, 538–41

facility, 538
guidelines, 540–41
internal consistency checks, 538
unit testing, 541
`AssertionError`, 539
assignment, 62, 382–84
assignment statement, 62
association, 218–22
asynchronous simulation *See* event-driven simulations
`Auction`, 168–71
auction project
    anonymous objects, 171
    chaining method calls, 171–73
    collections, 173–75
    grouping objects, 165–75
Autoboxing, 227–29
`AutoCloseable`, 549
automatic resource management (ARM), 548
automaton, 265–66, 268
AWT *See* Abstract Window Toolkit

B

back command, 309
base types, 254
Beck, Kent, 332, 560n
better-ticket-machine project, 71
`BevelBorder`, 498
binary files, 545–46
Bloch, Joshua, 407
blocks, 63 *See also* catch blocks
boolean, 520–21
    `AssertionError`, 539
    condition, 149
    expression, 105
    conditional statements, 74
`boolean`, 62, 350
`BorderLayout`, 479–82
    components, 483
    containers, 497
    frames, 495

borders, 498–99
bouncing-balls project, 239, 241
boundaries
    random numbers, 213
    testing, 330
`BoxLayout`, 479, 481
brain project, 272–79
breakpoints, 120–22, 352
bricks project, 355
Brooks, Frederick P., 569n
`BufferedImage`, 476
`BufferedReader`, 550, 551, 552, 572
bugs, 117 *See also* debugger/debugging
`Button`, 463
buttons, 495–98

C

calculator-engine project, 340–54
call sequence, 352
`Canvas`, 32, 235–36
casting, 385–86
`catch`, 530
catch blocks, 530
    error recovery, 542
    polymorphism, 533
`cell`, 274–75
cellular automata, 264–72
chaining method calls, 171–73
`changeColor`, 36
`changeDetails`, 514, 518, 536
`char`, 227, 550n
`Charset`, 550
checked exceptions, 524–26, 530
`checkIndex`, 140
cinema booking project, 558–64
`Circle`, 32, 36
class, 31–32 *See also* abstract class; library class
    cohesion, 307–8
    collections, 177–97, 199–200
    define types, 98
    diagram, 99–100, 286, 419, 420
    generic, 134, 137–38
    implementation, 208–9, 453
        filters, 491–92
    inheritance, 371–73
    inner class
        anonymous, 501–3
        named, 499–501
    instance, 32
    interfaces, 208–9
        implementation, 446–47
    method, 39, 242–43 *See also* static method
    network project, 360–63
    reference class, 333
    scope, 79
    superclasses, 386
    taxi company project, 580–81
    testing, 589
    variables, 239–42
    verb/noun method, 558
    wrapper, 227–29
`Class`, 454, 455
`.class`, 455
class definition, 49–89
    accessor method, 64–67
    assignment statement, 62
    comments, 56
    conditional statements, 73–76
    constructors, 58–60
    exceptions, 536–38
    expressions, 87–89
    fields, 54–58, 79–81
    local variables, 77–79
    method calls, 85–86
    method, 63–64
    mutator method, 64–67
    parameters, 60–62, 79–81
    scope highlighting, 76–77
    ticket machine project, 49–53
class design, 283–321
    application design, 564–66
    code duplication, 288–91
    cohesion, 287–88, 306–10

class design (*continued*)
  coupling, 287–88, 294–98
  decoupling, 317–19
  enumerated types, 314–17
  execution, 244
  extensions, 291–93
  guidelines, 319–20
  implicit coupling, 302–5
  interfaces, 566
  localizing change, 301–2
  refactoring, 310–14
    language independence, 314–19
  responsibility-driven design, 298–301
  taxi company project, 584–89
  thinking ahead, 305–6
Class/Responsibilities/Collaborators (CRC), 560
  taxi company project, 581–82
`ClassCastException`, 385, 524
clause
  finally, 535–36
  implements, 447
  throws, 530
client–server interaction, 516–17
`ClockDisplay`
  GUI, 110n
  method calls, 112–16
  source code, 108–9
  `NumberDisplay`, 98, 100–102
  object diagram, 110
  object interaction, 108–10
  string concatenation, 105–7
`close`, 549
closures, 178
code, 39–40
  cohesion, 287–88
  compiler, 42
  completion, library class, 237–38
  duplication
    class design, 288–91
    inheritance, 379
    network project, 371
  indentation, 76
  inheritance, 457
  lambda, 182
Code Pad, 87–89
cohesion, 287–88, 306–10
  code duplication, 291
  loose, 294
  tight, 294
`Collection`, 573
collection
  abstraction, 130–31
  `ArrayList`, 161, 186, 187, 245, 451
  array, 251–81
  auction project, 173–75
  class, 199–200
  filters, 489, 492–93
  flexible-size, 129, 252
  functional programming, 177–97
  `get`, 162
  `HashMap`, 245
  `HashSet`, 245, 451
  hierarchy, 387
  `LinkedList`, 245, 451
  maps, 219
  numbering within, 138–41
  polymorphic, 244–46
  processing whole, 143–48
  search, 152–55
  selective processing, 146–47
  sets, 223
  streams, 246–47
  `TreeSet`, 245, 451
`Color`, 236
combo boxes, 507
comma-separated values (CSV), 552
`Command`, 286, 312
command strings, 472
`CommandWords`, 286, 304, 319
`CommentedPost`, 378
commenting style, 342–43
comments, 36, 56, 325

compiler, 42, 385–86, 526
complexity, 96
  debuggers, 117
components, 462
  `BorderLayout`, 483
  `ImageViewer`, 466–67, 495–99
compound assignment operator, 66n
`CompoundBorder`, 498
concatenation, strings, 69, 105–7
conditional operator, 267–68
conditional statements, 49, 73–75
confirm dialog, 487
constants, 241–42
constructor
  access modifiers, 232
  class definitions, 58–60
  exceptions, 524
  library class, 132
  local variables, 78
  `MailItem`, 119
  overloading, 112
  parameters, 60
  return type, 64, 70
  singleton pattern, 572–73
  superclass, 377
`ContactDetails`, 512, 521, 528–29
`Container`, 467, 499
containers, 481–84, 497
`contains`, 147
content equality, 405
content pane, frames, 467
coupling, 287, 294–98 *See also* decoupling
  implicit, 302–5
  localizing change, 301–2
  loose, 287
  responsibility-driven design, 298–301
  tight, 294
CRC *See* Class/Responsibilities/
    Collaborators
Crowther, Will, 284
CSV *See* comma-separated values
Cunningham, Ward, 560n

D

darker image, 484–87
data types, 35–36, 57
debugger/debugging, 324, 340–41, 352–53
  mail-system project, 117–24
  object interaction, 116–20
  single stepping, 122–23
  static variables, 121
  strategy choices, 354–55
  `toString`, 405
  turning information on off, 350–51
declaration, 63, 77, 254–55
decorator pattern, 572
decoupling, 317–19, 489
`default`, 448
default method, 448
defensive programming, 516–19
definite iteration, 155, 259
delegation, 136
design *See also* application design; class
        design; responsibility-driven design
  analysis and design, 557–64, 580–84
  user interface, 566
design patterns, 570–76
`details`, 517, 526
dialogs, 487–88
diamond notation, 134–35, 220
`display`, 361, 384, 391–93
  `MessagePost`, 398
  `NewsFeed`, 394–96
  `PhotoPost`, 398
  `Post`, 396, 398
  source code, 396–97
  superclass, 409
`displayString`, 110, 112
`displayValue`, 346
divide and conquer, 96
dividing strings, 223–25
documentation
  application design, 566–67
  library class, 200–201
    elements, 230–32

documentation (*continued*)
    reading, 206–11
    writing, 229–32
dot notation, 114
`Drawable`, 445
`DuplicateKeyException`, 537–38, 544
dynamic types, 393–96
dynamic view, 99

E

edge detection filters, 494
`elementData`, 330
`ElementType` element, 144
`else`, 74, 76
`EmptyBorder`, 498
encapsulation, 294–98
enhanced for loop *See* for-each loop
enumerated types, 314–37
`Environment`, 273, 275–76, 279
`EOFException`, 533, 545
`equals`, 387, 405–7
error, 511–56 *See also* exception
    `AddressBook`, 512–15
    array, 257
    assertions, 538–41
    avoidance, 543–44
    debugger, 117
    defensive programming, 516–19
    exception throwing, 523–29
    logical, 323
    `null`, 522
    out-of-bounds, 521–22
        `char`, 550n
    parameters, 517–19
    print statements, 349
    recovery, 541–44
        input/output, 544–55
    runtime, 517
    server-error reporting, 519–23
    strings, 209
    syntax, 323
`Error`, 524n
`EtchedBorder`, 498
`Event`, 457
event-driven simulations, 456–57
event handling, 462–63
    lambda expression, 473–74
    Swing, 470
event listeners, 470
`EventPost`, 377–78
`Exception`, 524n, 533
exception
    casting, 385–86
    checked, 524–26, 530
    class definition, 536–38
    `ClassCastException`, 385, 524
    constructors, 524
    `DuplicateKeyException`, 537–38, 544
    effects, 526–27
    `EOFException`, 533, 545
    `FileNotFoundException`, 533, 545
    finally clause, 535–36
    handler, 529–36
    hierarchy, 524–25
    `IllegalArgumentException`, 524
    `IndexOutOfBoundsException`, 138, 524
    `IOException`, 545, 547
    method, 525
    `NullPointerException`, 517, 518, 524
    propagation, 535
    `RuntimeException`, 524, 527, 536
    strings, 524
    try statement, 530–33
    unchecked, 524–26
exclusive boundaries, 213–14
expressions, 62, 85, 87–89, 257
`extends`, 372, 374
extensions, 291–93, 380, 504–5
external method calls, 113–15

F

factory method, 573–74
field, 55–58
    access modifiers, 232
    class definition, 54–58, 79–81
    class scope, 79
    constructor, 58–59
    final, 240, 446
    initialization, 59–60
    library class, 132
    local variables, 78, 79
    `MailItem`, 117–18
    mutable, 408
    objects, 38, 59–60
    print statements, 348
    private, 56, 234
    public, 234
    source code, 56
    `static`, 240, 446
    variables, 57, 79–80
`Field`, 420, 434, 575
`FieldStats`, 421, 444
`FieldView`, 501
`File`, 546
`FileNotFoundException`, 533, 545
`FileReader`, 550
files *See also* text files
    binary, 545–46
    log-file analyzer, 252–58
    output, 547–48
`FileWriter`, 547, 550
`fillResponses`, 215
`Filter`, 187–88, 191–92, 489–95
filters
    class, 491, 492
    collections, 489, 492–93
    image filters, 484–87
    `ImageViewer`, 489–95
final, 240, 446
finally clause, 535–36
`findFirst`, 155
fixed-size collections *See* array

fixtures, 338–39
`FlowLayout`, 479, 482, 496–97
for-each loop, 144–46, 149, 152, 258n, 405
    array, 260–61
    keywords, 259
for loop, 144, 252, 258–64, 258n
formal parameters, 80
`Fox`, 426–29
foxes-and-rabbits project
    abstraction techniques, 418–33
    decoupling, 489
    inner class, 501
    interfaces, 453
    observer pattern, 574–75
`Frame`, 463
`frame.pack`, 477
frames, 464–66, 467, 495
functional interface, 452
functional programming, collection, 177–97

G

`Game`, 286, 303
Game of Life, 272–79
Gamma, Erich, 332
general-purpose collection class, 134
`generateResponse`, 216, 222
generic class, 134, 137–38
`get`, 135, 162, 217, 219–20
`getActionCommand`, 472
`getClass`, 455
graphical user interface (GUI), 461–509
        See also `ImageViewer`
    anonymous inner class, 501–3
    AWT, 463
    combo boxes, 507
    components, 462
    event handling, 462–63, 470
    extensions, 504–5
    inner class, 499–503
    layout, 462
    lists, 507

Index

graphical user interface (*continued*)
   menu items, 469–70
   scrollbars, 507–8
   static images, 507
   Swing, 463
`GraphView`, 454
grayscale filters, 494
`GridLayout`, 480–81, 496–97
`GridView`, 453–54
grouping objects, 129–76
   auction project, 165–75
   collection abstraction, 130–31
   for-each loop, 144–46
   generic class, 137–38
   indefinite iteration, 148–56
   `Iterator`, 159–62
   library class, 131, 132–35
   `MusicOrganizer` project, 132–35
   numbering within collections, 138–41
   processing whole collection, 143–48
   `Track`, 156–59
GUI *See* graphical user interface

H

`hashCode`, 387, 405–7
`HashMap`, 219–21, 229, 244–45, 270, 299
`HashSet`, 223, 225, 244–45, 573
`HashSetIterator`, 573
`hasNext`, 162, 258
hierarchy
   collections, 387
   exceptions, 524–25
   inheritance, 373
Hopper, Grace Murray, 117
`Hunter`, 448

I

identity, 194
`if`, 74, 76
if statements, 114, 147
`IllegalArgumentException`, 524
image filters, 484–87

`ImageFileManager`, 475–76
`ImagePanel`, 475–76
`ImageViewer`
   alternative structure, 468
   anonymous inner class, 501–3
   borders, 498–99
   buttons, 495–98
   components, 466–67, 495–99
   containers, 481–84
   dialogs, 487–88
   event listeners, 470–73
   extensions, 504–5
   filters, 489–95
   first complete version, 475–89
   frames, 464–66
   GUI, 463–75
   image filters, 484–87
   improving program structure, 489–95
   layout, 478–81
immutable object, 209
implementation
   class, 208, 453
      interface, 446–47
   filter class, 491–92
   inheritance, 457
   method, 397
`implements` clause, 447
implicit coupling, 302–5
implicit numbering, 138
`import`, 225
import statements, 134, 217–18
inclusive boundaries, 213–14
`increment`, 103
`incrementAge`, 425, 440
indefinite iteration, 148–56
indentation, 76–77
`index`, 216
index access *versus* iterators, 160–61
index numbers, 138, 139
index variables, 140, 151–52
`indexOf`, 522
`IndexOutOfBoundsException`, 138, 524

infinite loops, 152
information hiding, 233–34
inheritance, 359–89, 374–77
    access rights, 374–75
    accessor method, 393
    advantages, 379–80
    class, 371–72
    code, 457
    code duplication, 379
    extensions, 380
    hierarchy, 373
    implementation, 457
    initialization, 375–77
    `instanceof`, 409–10
    `JFrame`, 506–7
    maintenance, 380
    method lookups, 398–401
    multiple interfaces, 442–45
    `Object`, 386–87
    object equality, 405–7
    object methods, 402–5
    overriding, 396–98, 410–13
    `private`, 374
    protected access, 407–9
    reuse, 377, 379
    subtypes, 380–86
    summary, 457
    `toString`, 402–5
    using, 371–73
    world-of-zuul game, 410
initialization, 58, 60, 78, 375–77
input dialog, 487
input/output error recovery, 544–55
`InputReader`, 202, 222
`insertMoney`, 64–65
inspectors, 329–31
instance, 32, 36, 499, 500
    method, 242–43
    variables, 55, 121 *See also* field
`instanceof`, 409–10, 435
`int`, 57, 62, 64
integer array, 254
integer expression, 256
interface, 234–39 *See also* graphical user interface; user interface
    abstract class, 447, 455–56
    abstract method, 446
    abstraction techniques, 445–52
    class, 208–9, 234–39
        design, 564–66
        implementation, 446–47
    decoupling, 317–19
    default method, 448
    foxes-and-rabbits project, 453
    functional, 452
    library class, 451
    multiple, 448–49
    types, 449–50
`interface`, 446
intermediate operations, 190
internal consistency checks, 538
internal method calls, 112–13
invert filters, 494
`IOException`, 545, 547
is-a relationship, 372
iteration, 140, 151–52, 268–70
    definite, 155, 259
    indefinite, 148–56
iterative control structures, 144
iterative development, 569–70, 589–98
`Iterator`, 159–62, 258, 261, 573
`iterator`, 159–60, 573
iterators, 160–61
`iwrap`, 227

J

`java.awt`, 466
`java.awt.event`, 466, 470, 499
`javadoc`, 231, 235, 524
`java.io`, 545, 546
`java.lang`, 218, 524, 527, 549
`java.nio`, 545
`java.util`, 244–46, 299, 552
`java.util.stream`, 246

javax.swing, 466
JButton, 463, 467, 480
JColorChooser, 501
JComboBox, 507
JComponent, 476
JDialog, 487
JFrame, 463, 468, 469, 482
   add, 466n
   inheritance, 506–7
   Swing, 464
JList, 507
JMenu, 463, 469, 484
JMenuBar, 469
JMenuItem, 469, 470, 473, 484
JOptionPane, 487
JPanel, 481–82, 495–96, 499n
JScrollPane, 507
JTextField, 488
JUnit, 332–35

K

key objects, 219
keyInUse, 540, 544
keywords, 54, 259
   access modifiers, 232

L

labels, 467
lambda, 178, 182–84
   benefit, 186
   expression, 452, 473–74
   forEach, 184–86
   processing, 182–83
   removeIf, 195–96
   syntax, 183–84
layout, 462, 478–81
layout managers, 478–79
length, 260
library class, 129
   abstract class, 451
   code completion, 237
   documentation, 200–201
   elements, 230–32
   reading, 206–11
   writing, 229–32
   grouping objects, 131, 132–35
   import statements, 134, 217–18
   interfaces, 451
   maps, 218–22
   method, 209–10
   MusicOrganizer project, 163–64
   packages, 217–18
   sets, 223
   standard, 200
   String, 205–6
lifetime, variables, 61
lighter image, 484–87
LinkedList, 173, 245, 246, 450, 451, 561, 638
List, 223, 246
list, 507
   ArrayList *see* ArrayList
   LinkedList, 173, 245, 246, 450, 451, 561, 638
listSize, 216
local variables
   class definitions, 77–79
   debugger, 121
   print statements, 348
localizing change, 301–2
Location, 420
log-file analyzer, 252–54, 257–58
LogAnalyzer, 253, 254, 262
LogEntry, 253, 258
LogfileCreator, 253, 547
LogfileReader, 253, 258
logic operators, 104
logical errors, 323
LoglineTokenizer, 253
LogReader, 253
long, 365
lookup table, 270–72
loop body, 149
loop statements, 144

loop variables, 145
loop, 140
   for, 144, 252, 258–64, 258n
   definite iteration, 155
   for-each, 144–46, 148, 152, 405
      array, 260–61
      keywords, 259
   infinite, 152
   removing elements, 161–62
   while, 149–51, 152, 205–6, 261
loose coupling, 287, 294
Lot, 167–68

M

Mac OS, 469n
machine code, 42
magic numbers, 403
mail-system project, 117–24
MailClient, 117, 118, 120, 124
MailItem, 117–18, 124
MailServer, 117, 124
main, 244
makeDarker, 484
makeFrame, 466, 477, 502
makeLarger, 497–98
makeLighter, 484
makeSmaller, 497–98
Map, 219, 246, 451
map, 188–89, 192–93
maps, 218–22
   associations, 218–22
   collections, 219
Menu, 463
menu bar
   frames, 467
   Mac OS, 469n
menu items
   ActionListener, 470
   GUI, 469–70
message dialog, 487
MessagePost, 360–62
   display, 398
   inheritance, 372
   source code, 363–65
   toString, 403
method, 43, 67, 70, 234, 446 *See also specific methods or method types*
   access modifiers, 232
   ArrayList, 135
   body, 63, 64, 67, 78, 80
   class definition, 63–64, 85–86
   class, 37
   cohesion, 306–8
   exceptions, 525
   header, 63, 80
   implementation, 397
   library class, 209–10
   limitations, 243
   lookups, 398–401
   overloading, 112
   overriding, 401–2
   parameters, 34, 60
   polymorphism, 402
   printing from, 67–69
   private, 234
   reference, 247
   return types, 70
   signature, 35
   space, 60
   statements, 500
   stubs, 565
   without BlueJ, 244
method calls, 33–34, 43
   chaining, 171–72
   class definition, 63–64
   debugger, 123
   mail-system project, 124
   object interaction, 112–16
   print statements, 348
   super, 401–2
   superclass, 441
mirror filters, 494
modal dialog, 487, 488
model-view-controller, 306

modularization, 96–97
modulo operator, 107
Moore neighborhood, 274
`MouseAdapter`, 501, 502
`MouseEvent`, 470
`MouseListener`, 500, 501–3
`MouseMotionAdapter`, 501
`mousePressed`, 501, 502
multiple constructors, 112
multiple exceptions, 533–34
multiple inheritance, 442–45, 448–49
multiple instances, 36–37
multiple interfaces, 448–49
`MusicOrganizer`, 140
    for-each loop, 144–46
    grouping objects, 131–64
    library class, 132–35
    numbering within collections, 138–41
    object diagram, 135–36
    playing music files, 141–43
    processing whole collection, 143–48
`MusicPlayer`, 141–43, 506–8
mutable fields, 408
mutator method, 64–67

N

name
    parameter, 35, 60
    variable, 62
need to know, 233
negative testing, 331
nested containers, 481–84
network project, 359–71
    adding other post types, 377–79
    class, 360–63
    code duplication, 371
    `display`, 391–93
    objects, 360–63
    source code, 363–70
`new`, 111, 112, 134, 135
`NewsFeed`, 363, 368–70, 380–81, 394–96, 404

`nextDouble`, 552
`nextInt`, 212, 552
`nextLine`, 554
not being allowed to know, 233
not operator, 205
`notify`, 575
`null`, 167, 517, 518, 522
`NullPointerException`, 167, 517, 518, 523, 523n, 524
`NumberDisplay`, 98, 100–103
`numberOfAccesses`, 262, 263
`numberOfEntries`, 540
numbers *See also* random numbers
    implicit numbering, 138
    index numbers, 138
    magic numbers, 403
    pseudo-random numbers, 212

O

object, 31–33, 38–39 *See also* grouping objects; wellbehaved objects
    bench, 33, 37, 120
    collections, 130
    creation, 50
        prevention, 528–29
    diagram, 99–100, 110, 118, 135–37
    equality, 405–7
    `equals`, 405–7
    fields, 38, 61
    `hashCode`, 405–7
    immutable, 209
    inspector, 37
    interaction, 40–41
    key objects, 219
    method, 33, 402–5
    mutator method, 64–67
    network project, 360–63
    `new`, 124
    parameters, 44–45
    reference, 99
    state, 37
    `toString`, 402–5

Index

types, 100
value, 219
variables, 100
`Object`, 386–87, 405–7, 455
object interaction, 40–41, 95–124, 129
   abstraction, 96–97
   debugger, 116–24
   method calls, 112–15
   modularization, 96–97
   multiple constructors, 112
   object types, 100
   object creating objects, 111–12
   primitive types, 100
object-oriented programming, 31, 97, 233, 359, 417
`Observable`, 575
`Observer`, 575
Observer pattern, 574–75
`OFImage`, 475–76, 485–86
`openFile`, 472, 477
operator
   compound assignment operator, 66n
   conditional, 267–68
   logic operators, 104
   modulo operator, 107
   not operator, 205
   and operator, 104, 154
   ternary, 267
out-of-bounds error, 521–22
   `char`, 550n
out-of-bounds value, 154, 522
overloading, 112
overriding
   `equals`, 405–7
   `hashCode`, 405–7
   inheritance, 396–98, 410–13
   method, 401–2
   `toString`, 402–5

P

`pack`, 467, 477
package level, 408
packages, 217–18
pair programming, 567
parameter, 34–35
   class definitions, 60–62, 79–81
   defensive programming, 516–19
   errors, 517–19
   name, 35
   names, 60
   objects, 44–45
   `println`, 75–76
   subtypes, 384
   types, 35
   value, 60, 348
   variables, 60
`Parser`, 286, 303, 305, 312, 572
parsing, 552–54
`Path`, 546
`PhotoPost`, 360–62, 372, 398
pipeline, 189–91
polymorphism, 244–46, 359, 384, 393
   catch block, 533
   method, 402
`PopulationGenerator`, 439
positive testing, 331
`Post`, 377–79, 396, 398
   constructors, 377
   for-each loop, 405
   inheritance, 372
   subclass, 374
   `toString`, 403
predator-prey simulations, 418–33
primitive types, 100
primitive values, 100
`print`, 124
print statements, 348–51
`printDebugging`, 351
`printHelp`, 304
printing, 67–69
`println`, 69, 75–76, 145, 183
`printLocationInfo`, 294
`printTicket`, 64–65

private, 56, 374
`private`, 183, 232–34, 407
propagation, 535
`protected`, 407
protected access, 407–9
protected statements, 532
prototyping, 567–68
pseudo-code, 74, 149, 159
pseudo-random numbers, 212
`public`, 183, 185, 232–34, 407, 446
public fields, 234
`put`, 219–20

R

`Rabbit`, 422–25
`Random`, 212–13
random numbers
    boundaries, 213
    generating random responses, 214–16
    limited range, 213–14
    TechSupport project, 211–22
`Randomizer`, 421
`RandomTester`, 213
`read`, 550n
readability, 309
`Reader`, 572
readers, 545–46
`reduce`, 193–95
refactoring, 310–14
    language independence, 314–19
reference class, 333
regression testing, 332
`remove`, 135, 138, 162
`removeFile`, 138, 141
reserved words *See* keywords
`reset`, 422
`Responder`, 202, 205, 214–16
responsibility-driven design, 156
    coupling, 298–301
    localizing change, 301–2
return statement, 64
return types, 64, 66, 70
return values, 43, 66–67, 67n
reuse
    cohesion, 309–10
    inheritance, 377, 379–80
    taxi company project, 598
`Room`, 286, 293, 299, 312
runtime, 99
runtime error, 517
`RuntimeException`, 524, 527, 536

S

`Scanner`, 552–54
scenarios, 560–64, 582–84
scope
    class scope, 79
    coloring, 503
    formal parameters, 80
    highlighting, 76–77
    local variables, 79–80
    variables, 60
scribble project, 234–39
scrollbars, 507–8
search, 152–55
selective drawing, 444–45
`Serializable`, 554
serialization, 545, 554–55
server-error reporting, 519–23
`Set`, 223, 246, 299, 451
`setBorder`, 498
`setColor`, 454, 455
`setJMenuBar`, 469
`setLayout`, 483
`setPixel`, 492
sets, 223
`showInputDialog`, 488
`showMessageDialog`, 488
`Sighting`, 179–80
signature, methods, 35
`simulateOneStep`, 431–33
`Simulator`, 419, 429–31, 454, 455
`SimulatorView`, 421, 454, 501
    class implementation, 453–54

Observer pattern, 575
single stepping, 122–23
Singleton pattern, 572
`size`, 135, 156, 216
smooth filters, 494
solarize filters, 494
source code, 41–42, 56
    debugger, 116
`split`, 224
stack, 352
`Stack`, 310
standard input, 553
standard library class, 200
standard output, 553
`startsWith`, 206
state
    debuggers, 352
    method, 43
    objects, 37
    walkthroughs, 346–48
statement
    assert, 538–40
    assignment, 62
    conditional, 49, 73–75
    if, 114, 147
    import, 134, 217–18
    loop, 145
    method, 500
    method body, 64, 67
    print, 348–51
    protected, 532
    return, 64
    throw, 523
    try, 549
        error recovery, 542–43
        exceptions, 530–33
        finally clause, 535
        resource, 548–49
        unchecked exceptions, 544
`static`, 239–40, 242–43, 446
static images, 507
static method, 546, 573
static types, 393–96, 405
static variables, 121
streams, 178, 186–96, 279–80
    `filter`, 187–88, 191–92
    `map`, 188–89, 192–33
    pipeline, 189–91
    `reduce`, 193–95
string
    checking equality, 211
    command strings, 472
    concatenation, 105–6
    dividing, 223–25
    exceptions, 524
    implementation, 211n
    limitations, 148
    literals, 68
    switch statements, 316n
`String`, 36, 62, 85
    concatenation, 69
    errors, 209
    `hashCode`, 407
    immutable object, 209
    `indexOf`, 522
    library class, 206–7
    method calls, 43
    `put`, 206, 210
    `Scanner`, 552–54
    `split`, 224
    `toString`, 319
    `trim`, 210
subclass, 372, 374, 393
    abstract, 438
    initialization, 376
    overriding, 397, 398
    subtype, 382
        superclass, 449
substitution, 382
`substring`, 85
subtype, 533
    assignment, 382–84
    casting, 385–86
    inheritance, 380–86

subtype (*continued*)
    parameters, 384
    subclass, 382
        superclass, 449
    superclass, 382
        subclass, 449
    variables, 382
`super`, 377, 401–2
superclass, 372, 409, 491
    casting, 385–86
    constructor, 377
    initialization, 376
    method calls, 441
    mutable fields, 408
    overriding, 397, 398
    subtypes, 382
        subclass, 449
`SupportSystem`, 202–3
Swing, 467
    event handling, 470
    GUI, 463
    layout managers, 478–79
switch statement, 316, 316n
synchronous simulation, 456
syntax errors, 323
`System.err`, 519
`System.out`, 68, 519
`System.out.print`, 404
`System.out.println`, 145, 192, 306, 404

T

taxi company project, 579–98
    analysis and design, 580–84
    class design, 584–89
    class testing, 589
    class, 580–81
    CRC, 581–82
    iterative development, 589–98
    reuse, 598
    scenarios, 582–84
TechSupport project, 201–6
    library class methods, 209–10

random numbers, 211–22
    `WordCounter`, 228–29
terminal operations, 190
ternary operator, 267
test class, 333
test harness, 332
testing, 324 *See also* unit testing
    automation, 332–39
    boundaries, 330
    class, 589
    negative, 331–32
    positive, 331–32
    recording, 335–38
text file, 548–49
    `FileReader`, 550–52
    `java.io`, 545
`this`, 119–20
threshold, 484
threshold image, 484–87
throw statement, 523
`Throwable`, 524n
throwing
    errors, 523–29
    file output, 547–48
    multiple exceptions, 533–34
    preventing object creation, 528–29
`@throws`, 524, 530
throws clause, 530
ticket machine project, 49–53
tight coupling, 294
time-based simulation, 456
time stamp, 365
title bar, 467
`TitleBorder`, 498
`toCollection`, 247
`toList`, 246
`toLowerCase`, 211
`toMap`, 246
toroidal arrangement, 277
`toSet`, 246
`toString`, 318
    inheritance, 402–5

Index

`String`, 319
`toUpperCase`, 209
`Track`, 156–59
`TrackReader`, 156
`TreeMap`, 245
`TreeSet`, 245
`Triangle`, 32
`trim`, 210
`try`, 530
try resource statement, 548–49
try statement, 549
   error recovery, 542
   exceptions, 530–33
   finally clause, 535–36
   unchecked exceptions, 544
two-dimensional array, 272–79
type *See also* subtype
   base types, 254
   data types, 35–36, 57
   dynamic types, 393–96
   enumerated types, 314–17
   interfaces, 449–50
   object types, 100
   parameters, 35
   primitive types, 100
   return types, 64, 66, 70
   static types, 393–96
   variables, 88

U
UML, 361n
unchecked exceptions, 524–26, 544
unit testing, 325–32
   assertions, 541
   inspectors, 329–31
use cases *See* scenarios
user interface, 566 *See also* graphical user interface

V
values
   CSV, 552
   expressions, 85
   objects, 219
   parameters, 348
   primitive, 100
   return values, 43, 66–67, 67n
variable, 167, 220 *See also specific variable types*
   dynamic types, 393–96
   fields, 57, 79–81
   formal parameters, 80
   lifetime, 61
   name, 60
   objects, 100
   parameters, 60–61
   polymorphism, 384–85
   primitive values, 100
   scope, 60
   static types, 393–96
   subtypes, 382
   types, 88
`Vehicle`, 585–87
verb/noun method, 558
verbal walkthroughs, 348
`void`, 520
   method, 43, 67, 70
   return values, 66–67, 67n

W
walkthroughs, 343–48
   breakpoints, 352
   state, 346–48
   verbal, 348
   well-behaved objects, 343–48
waterfall model, 568–69
well-behaved objects, 323–55
   commenting style, 342–43
   debugger/debugging, 324, 340–41, 352–53
      strategy choices, 354–55
   print statements, 348–51
   test automation, 332–39
   testing, 324

well-behaved objects (*continued*)
  unit testing, 325–32
  walkthroughs, 343–48
while loop, 149–51, 152, 205, 261
Wolfram, Stephen, 271
Wolfram code, 271
world-of-zuul game, 284–320
  code duplication, 288–91
  cohesion, 287, 306–8
  decoupling, 317–19
  enumerated types, 314–17
  extensions, 291–93
  implicit coupling, 302–5
  inheritance, 410
  localizing change, 301–2
  refactoring, 310–14
    language independence, 314–19
  responsibility-driven design, 298–301
wrapper class, 227–29
writers, 545–46
writing maintainability, 324